To: Norma &

With: All our Love

Gary-Ann & Amber & Buffy

Devotions for Morning and Evening

with
Mrs. Charles E. Cowman

Devotions for Morning and Evening

with
Mrs. Charles E. Cowman

THE COMPLETE DAILY DEVOTIONS OF

Streams in the Desert
—————— AND ——————
Springs in the Valley

COMPLETE IN ONE VOLUME

INSPIRATIONAL PRESS
NEW YORK

STREAMS IN THE DESERT

In 1925 the first edition of *Streams in the Desert* was released. In it were thoughts, quotations, spiritual inspiration which had helped to sustain Mrs. Charles E. Cowman during her years of missionary work in Japan and China—particularly the six years she nursed her husband while he was dying. After two years and three thousand books in print it was suggested to Mrs. Cowman that since all her friends had copies, there was probably no need to print any more.

From this humble beginning *Streams in the Desert* has become a daily devotional classic, a leader in its field for more than forty years. At various times it has appeared in more than a dozen languages, and at present is in four foreign language editions. Its ministry is worldwide, unhindered by national, political or geographic boundaries. From a royal palace in North Africa and a presidential mansion in Asia to wartime concentration camps . . . from primitive huts in remote corners of the world to elegantly furnished houses in cultural centers . . . to thousands of homes representing a cross section of the world today, *Streams in the Desert* continues to bring its spiritual refreshment, its word of encouragement and inspiration just suited for the moment's need.

For the readers of more than two million copies now in print, *Streams in the Desert* is more than a book—it is a living word of confidence and assurance, God's message for the day.

THE PUBLISHERS

SPRINGS IN THE VALLEY

꧁∞꧂

$\mathcal{T}$he first edition of *Springs in the Valley* was produced in 1939. Because of the tremendous success of its predecessor, *Streams in the Desert*, it was felt that another collection of thoughts, quotations, and spiritual inspiration from the pen and files of Mrs. Charles E. Cowman would be welcomed by the reading public. Thus was born *Springs in the Valley*.

The enthusiastic response accorded this devotional collection has more than justified the publishers' decision. *Springs in the Valley* has proved itself a worthy companion volume to the classic *Streams in the Desert*. The same spiritual insight and sensitivity to the deepest needs of people went into the selection of the devotional gems in this book. And the same kind of blessing and inspiration has been reported by those whose hearts have been warmed by this more recent collection.

It gives us great pleasure and deep satisfaction to issue this newest edition of *Springs in the Valley* with the prayer that it may continue its ministry of blessing and inspiration.

THE PUBLISHERS

A PERSONAL WORD . . .

‿⚮‿

*I*n the pathway of faith we come to learn that the Lord's thoughts are not our thoughts, nor His ways our ways. Both in the physical and spiritual realm, *great pressure means great power!* Although circumstances may bring us into the place of death, that need not spell disaster—for if we trust in the Lord and wait patiently, that simply provides the occasion for the display of His almighty power. "Remember his marvelous works that he hath done; his wonders and the judgments of his mouth" (Ps. 105:5).

MRS. CHARLES E. COWMAN

". . . In the wilderness shall waters break out, and streams in the desert" (Isa. 35:6).

He sendeth the springs into the valleys,
which run among the hills. (PS. 104:10)

Devotions for Morning and Evening

with
Mrs. Charles E. Cowman

January 1

〜〜〜

The land whither ye go to possess it is a land of hills and
valleys and drinketh water of the rain of heaven:
a land which the Lord thy God careth for: the eyes of the
Lord thy God are always upon it, from the beginning of the year even
unto the end of the year (DEUT. 11:11–12).

Today, dear friends, we stand upon the verge of the unknown. There lies before us the new year and we are going forth to possess it. Who can tell what we shall find? What new experiences, what changes shall come, what new needs shall arise? But here is the cheering, comforting, gladdening message from our heavenly Father, *"The Lord thy God careth for it." "His eyes are upon it away to the ending of the year."*

All our supply is to come from the Lord. Here are springs that shall never dry; here are fountains and streams that shall never be cut off. Here, anxious one, is the gracious pledge of the heavenly Father. If He be the source of our mercies they can never fail us. No heat, no drought can parch that river, "the streams whereof make glad the city of God."

The land is a land of *hills* and *valleys*. It is not all smooth nor all downhill. If life were all one dead level of dull sameness it would oppress us; we want the hills and the valleys. The hills collect the rain for a hundred fruitful valleys. Ah, so it is with us! It is the hill difficulty that drives us to the throne of grace and brings down the shower of blessing; the hills, the bleak hills of life that we wonder at and perhaps grumble at, bring down the showers. How many have perished in the wilderness, buried under its golden sands, who would have lived and thriven in the hill country; how many would have been killed by the frost, blighted with winds, swept desolate of tree and fruit but for the hill—stern, hard, rugged, so steep to climb. God's hills are a gracious protection for His people against their foes!

We cannot tell what loss and sorrow and trial are doing. Trust only. The Father comes near to take our hand and lead us on our way today. It shall be a good, a blessed new year!

He leads us on by paths we did not know;
Upward He leads us, though our steps be slow,
Though oft we faint and falter on the way,
Though storms and darkness oft obscure the day;
Yet when the clouds are gone,

We know He leads us on.
He leads us on through all the unquiet years;
Past all our dreamland hopes, and doubts and fears,
He guides our steps, through all the tangled maze
Of losses, sorrows, and o'er clouded days;
We know His will is done;
And still He leads us on.

N. L. ZINZENDORF

EVENING

For the LORD thy God bringeth thee into a good land,
a land of brooks of water, of fountains and depths that
spring out of valleys and hills; A land of wheat, and barley, and
vines, and fig trees, and pomegranates; a land of olive oil, and
honey; A land wherein thou shalt eat bread without scarceness,
thou shalt not lack any thing in it; a land whose stones are iron, and
out of whose hills thou mayest dig brass. When thou hast eaten and
art full, then thou shalt bless the LORD thy God for the
good land which he hath given thee. (DEUT. 8:7–10)

We are entering upon a new year—surely we cannot but believe, a new age. If we have rightly learned the lessons of the past, there lies before us a heritage of unspeakable blessing, which none of these vivid metaphors can too strongly describe; infinite sources of blessing, for the fountains and waterbrooks are but the figures of God's illimitable grace. For *with Him* is the fountain of life.

A Fountain Fed by Eternal Springs!

They tell us of boundless supply: "Bread without scarceness," the olive oil that speaks of the Holy Ghost, the honey that tells of the sweetness of His love, and the pomegranates that are the seed fruit which speak of a life that reproduces itself in the blessing of others.

They tell of the "nether springs" which flow from the depths of sorrow, in the hard places, in the desert places, in the lone places, in the common places which seem farthest from all that is sacred and Divine.

How delightful it is to have His gladness in the low places of sorrow, and to be able to *glory even in tribulation also.*

They tell us of pleasures that come out of the very heart of trial, treasures wrung from the grasp of the enemy.

How precious the springs that flow into the places of temptation, for there is nothing in life so trying as the touch of Satan's hand, and the breath of the destroyer. Oh, how sweet it is, *even there,* to find that the light is as deep as the shadow, and heaven is nearest when we are hard by the gates of hell, so that we can *count it all joy when we fall into diverse temptations,* and can say, "Blessed is the man that endureth temptation: for when he is tried, he shall receive the crown of life, which the Lord hath promised to them that love him."

How blessed to drink from the springs of health, and find our strength renewed day by day, and the life of God flowing into even our physical organs and functions!

"All my fresh springs are in thee!"

Beloved, God has for us these springs, and we need them every day. Let us drink of the living waters. Nay, let us receive them into our very hearts, so that we shall carry the fountain with us wherever we go.   A. B. SIMPSON

We shall never be "springs" until God comes to us. We shall never be fresh, or fruitful, or useful to others till God comes to us. If we do not have constant visitations of God, we shall soon cease to be "springs," and shall go back to the old dry and barren days.   HELENA GARRATT

Let us claim our inheritance in these coming days, and find the hardest places of life's experience God's greatest opportunities and faith's mightiest challenge.

Springs in the valley are very unusual;
but He will give us both the upper and the nether springs!

January 2
MORNING

And there was an enlarging, and a winding about
till upward to the side chambers: for the winding about
of the house went still upward round about the house:
therefore the breadth of the house was still upward and
so increased from the lowest chamber to the highest by the midst
(EZEK. 41:7).

Still upward be thine onward course:
For this I pray today;
Still upward as the years go by,
And seasons pass away.

Still upward in this coming year,
Thy path is all untried;
Still upward may'st thou journey on,
Close by thy Savior's side.

Still upward e'en though sorrow come,
And trials crush thine heart;
Still upward may they draw thy soul,
With Christ to walk apart.

Still upward till the day shall break,
And shadows all have flown;
Still upward till in Heaven you wake,
And stand before the throne.

We ought not to rest content in the mists of the valley when the summit of Tabor awaits us. How pure are the dews of the hills, how fresh is the mountain air, how rich the fare of the dwellers aloft, whose windows look into the New Jerusalem! Many saints are content to live like men in coal mines, who see not the sun. Tears mar their faces when they might anoint them with celestial oil. Satisfied I am that many a believer pines in a dungeon when he might walk on the palace roof, and view the goodly land and Lebanon. Rouse thee, O believer, from thy low condition! Cast away thy sloth, thy lethargy, thy coldness, or whatever interferes with thy chaste and pure love to Christ. Make Him the source, the center, and the circumference of all thy soul's range of delight. Rest no longer satisfied with thy dwarfish attainments. Aspire to a higher, a nobler, a fuller life. Upward to heaven! Nearer to God!   SPURGEON

I want to scale the utmost height,
And catch a gleam of glory bright;
But still I'll pray, till heaven I've found,
Lord, lead me on to higher ground!

Not many of us are living at our best. We linger in the lowlands because we are afraid to climb the mountains. The steepness and ruggedness dismay us, and so we stay in the misty valleys and do not learn the mystery of the hills. We do not know what we lose in our self-indulgence, what glory awaits us if only we had courage for the mountain climb, what blessing we should find if only we would move to the uplands of God.　　　　J. R. M.

Too low they build who build beneath the stars.

EVENING

Jesus himself drew near, and went with them. (LUKE 24:15)

A night in Spring . . . and two men walking the Emmaus road—saddened by their master's death—bowed down beneath their load, when suddenly *Another* overtakes them as they walk. A *Stranger* falls in step with them, and earnestly they talk—of what is in their hearts—moved by a warm soul-stirring glow—and when they reach Emmaus they are loath to let Him go; and so they bid Him stay awhile and share their simple board. And as He breaks the bread . . . *they know.* They know it is the Lord.

Oh, may He *overtake* us as the Path of Life we tread! Along our way of sorrow may His radiant Light be shed. . . . Oh, may He come to warm the heart and ease the heavy load—and walk with us as long ago He walked the Emmaus Road.

Take the road . . . the lonely road—courageous, unafraid; ready for the journey when the twilight shadows fade. . . . God whose Love is Omnipresent—will He fail us then?—or forget the covenant that He has made with men?　　　　**PATIENCE STRONG**

Jesus never sends a man ahead alone. He blazes a clear way through every thicket and woods, and then softly calls, "Follow me. Let's go on together, you and I." He has been everywhere that we are called to go. His feet have trodden down smooth a path through every experience that comes to us. He knows each road, and knows it well: the valley road of disappointment with its dark shadows; the steep path of temptation down through the rocky ravines and slippery gullies; the narrow path of pain, with the brambly thornbushes so close on each side, with their slash and sting; the dizzy road along the heights of victory; the old beaten road of commonplace daily routine. *Everyday paths He has trodden and glorified, and will walk anew with each of us. The only safe way to travel is with Him alongside and in control.*　　　　**S. D. GORDON**

Come, share the road with Me, My own,
Through good and evil weather;
Two better speed than one alone,
So let us go together.

Come, share the road with Me, My own,
You know I'll never fail you,
And doubts and fears of the unknown
Shall never more assail you.

Come, share the road with Me, My own,
I'll share your joys and sorrows.
And hand in hand we'll seek the throne
And God's great glad tomorrows.

Come, share the road with Me, My own,
And where the black clouds gather,
I'll share thy load with thee, My son,
And we'll press on together.

And as we go we'll share also
With all who travel on it.
For all who share the road with Me
Must share with all upon it.

So make we—all one company,
Love's golden cord our tether,
And, come what may, we'll climb the way
Together—aye, together!

ROADMATES, BY JOHN OXENHAM

After a long trying march over perilous Antarctic mountains and glaciers a South Pole explorer said to his leader, "I had a curious feeling on the march that there was another Person with us!"

Another Person! He is ever there to march side by side with those who trust Him!

Take His Hand and Walk with Him!

January 3

⤳⤳⤳

I will lead on softly, according as the cattle that goeth before me and the children be able to endure (GEN. 33:14).

What a beautiful picture of Jacob's thoughtfulness for the cattle and the children! He would not allow them to be overdriven even for one day. He would not lead on according to what a strong man like Esau could do and expected them to do, but only according to what they were able to endure. He knew exactly how far they could go in a day; and he made that his only consideration in arranging the marches. He had gone the same wilderness journey years before, and knew all about its roughness and heat and length, by personal experience. And so he said, "I will lead on softly (Gen. 33:14)." "For ye have not passed this way heretofore" (Josh. 3:4).

We have not passed this way heretofore, but the Lord Jesus has. It is all untrodden and unknown ground to us, but He knows it all by personal experience. The steep bits that take away our breath, the stony bits that make our feet ache so, the hot shadeless stretches that make us feel so exhausted, the rushing rivers that we have to pass through—Jesus has gone through it all before us. "He was wearied with his journey." Not some, but all the many waters went over Him, and yet did not quench His love. He was made a perfect leader by the things which He suffered. "He knoweth our frame; he *remembereth that we are dust.*" Think of that when you are tempted to question the gentleness of His leading. He is *remembering* all the time; and not one step will He make you take beyond what your foot is able to endure. Never mind if you think it will not be able for the step that seems to come next; either He will so strengthen it that it shall be able, or He will call a sudden halt, and you shall not have to take it at all.

FRANCES RIDLEY HAVERGAL

In "pastures green"? Not always; sometimes He
Who knowest best, in kindness leadeth me
In weary ways, where heavy shadows be.
So, whether on the hill-tops high and fair
I dwell, or in the sunless valleys, where
The shadows lie, what matter? He is there.

BARRY

EVENING

∽✺∾

*Do not be over-anxious . . . about tomorrow, for tomorrow
will bring its own cares. Enough for each day are its own troubles.*
(MATT. 6:34 WEYMOUTH)

There are two golden days in the week, upon which, and about
which, I never worry—two carefree days, kept sacredly free from fear
and apprehension.

One of these days is Yesterday; Yesterday, with its cares and frets, all its
pains and aches, all its faults, mistakes and blunders, has passed forever
beyond my recall. I cannot undo an act that I wrought, nor unsay a word
that I said. All that it holds of my life, of wrong, regret and sorrow, is in
the hands of the Mighty Love that can bring honey out of the rock and
sweetest waters out of the bitterest desert. Save for the beautiful memories—sweet and tender—that linger like the perfume of roses in the heart
of that day that is gone, I have nothing to do with Yesterday. It *was* mine!
It *is* God's!

And the other day that I do not worry about is Tomorrow; Tomorrow, with all its possible adversities, its burdens, its perils, its large
promise and poor performance, its failures and mistakes, is as far beyond
my mastery as its dead sister, Yesterday. It is a day of God's. Its sun will
rise in roseate splendor, or behind a mask of weeping clouds—*but it will
rise.*

Until then, the same Love and Patience that held Yesterday holds
Tomorrow. Save for the star of hope that gleams forever on the brow of
Tomorrow, shining with tender promise into the heart of Today, I have
no possession in that unborn day of grace. All else is in the safe keeping
of the Infinite Love that is higher than the stars, wider than the skies,
deeper than the seas. Tomorrow *is* God's day! It *will be* mine!

There is left for myself, then, but one day in the week—Today. *Any
man can fight the battles of Today! Any woman can carry the burdens of just
one day! Any man can resist the temptations of Today!* Oh, friends, *it is
when we willfully add the burdens of those two awful eternities—Yesterday
and Tomorrow—such burdens as only the Mighty God can sustain—that we
break down.* It isn't the experience of Today that drives men mad. It is the
remorse for something that happened Yesterday; the dread of what
Tomorrow may disclose.

These are God's days! Leave them with Him!

Therefore, I think and I do, and I journey *but one day* at a time! That
is the easy way. That is Man's Day. Dutifully I run my course and work

my appointed task on that Day of ours. God—the All-Mighty and All-Loving—takes care of Yesterday and Tomorrow.   BOB BURDETTE

—But, Lord, tomorrow!
Did I not die for thee?
Do I not live for thee?
Leave Me tomorrow!
CHRISTINA ROSSETTI

"Tomorrow is God's secret—but today is yours to live."

All the tomorrows of our lives have to pass Him before they can get to us.

I heard a voice at evening softly say,
"Bear not thy yesterday into tomorrow;
Nor load this week with last week's load of sorrow.
Lift all thy burdens as they come, nor try
To weight the present with the by and by.
One step, and then another, take thy way—
Live by the day."
JULIA HARRIS MAY

January 4

MORNING

❧

Jesus saith unto him, Go thy way; thy son liveth.
And the man believed the word that Jesus had spoken unto him, and
he went his way (JOHN 4:50).

When ye pray, believe (MARK 11:24).

When there is a matter that requires definite prayer, pray till you believe God, until with unfeigned lips you can thank Him for the answer. If the answer still tarries outwardly, do not pray for it in such a way that it is evident that you are not definitely believing for it. Such a prayer in place of being a help will be a hindrance; and when you are finished praying, you will find that your faith has weakened or has entirely gone. The urgency that you felt to offer this kind of prayer is clearly from self and Satan. It may not be wrong to mention the matter in question to the Lord again, if He is keeping you waiting, but be sure you do so in such a way that it implies faith. *Do not pray yourself out of faith.* You may tell Him that you are waiting and that you are still believing Him and therefore praise Him for the answer. There is nothing that so fully clinches faith as to be so sure of the answer that you can thank God for it. Prayers that pray us out of faith deny both God's promise in His Word and also His whisper "Yes," that He gave us in our hearts. Such prayers are but the expression of the unrest of one's heart, and unrest implies unbelief in reference to the answer to prayer. "For we which have believed do enter into rest" (Heb. 4:3). This prayer that prays ourselves out of faith frequently arises from centering our thoughts on the difficulty rather than on God's promise. Abraham "considered not his own body," "he staggered not at the promise of God" (Rom. 4:19–20). May we watch and pray that we enter not into temptation of praying ourselves out of faith.   C. H. P.

Faith is not a sense, nor sight, nor reason, but a taking God at His word.   EVANS

The beginning of anxiety is the end of faith, and the beginning of true faith is the end of anxiety.   GEORGE MUELLER

You will never learn faith in comfortable surroundings. God gives us the promises in a quiet hour; God seals our covenants with great and gracious words, then He steps back and waits to see how much we believe; then He lets the tempter come, and the test seems to contradict all that He has spoken. It is then that faith wins its crown. That is the time to look up through the storm, and among the trembling, frightened seamen cry, "I believe God that it shall be even as it was told me."

> *Believe and trust; through stars and suns,*
> *Through life and death, through soul and sense,*
> *His wise, paternal purpose runs;*
> *The darkness of His Providence*
> *Is starlit with Divine intents.*

*Whosoever drinketh of the water that I shall give him
shall never thirst.* (JOHN 4:14)

*M*y heart needs Thee, O Lord, my heart needs Thee! No part of my being needs Thee like my heart. All else within me can be filled by Thy gifts. My hunger can be satisfied by daily bread. My thirst can be allayed by earthly waters. My cold can be removed by household fires. My weariness can be relieved by outward rest. But no outward thing can make my heart pure. The calmest day will not calm my passions. The fairest scene will not beautify my soul. The richest music will not make harmony within. The breezes can cleanse the air, but no breeze can cleanse a spirit. This world has not provided for my heart. It has provided for my eye; it has provided for my ear; it has provided for my touch; it has provided for my taste; it has provided for my sense of beauty but it has not provided for my heart.

Lift up your eyes unto the hills! Make haste to Calvary, "Calvary's awful mountain-climb," and on the way there visit the slopes of Mount Olivet, where grow the trees of Gethsemane. Contemplate there the agony of the Lord, where He already tasted the tremendous cup which He drank to the dregs the next noontide on the Cross. *There* is the answer to your need.

Provide Thou for my heart, O Lord. It is the only unwinged bird in all creation. *Give it wings!* O Lord, *give it wings!* Earth has failed to give it wings; its very power of loving has often drawn it into the mire. Be Thou the strength of my heart. Be Thou its fortress in temptation, its shield in remorse, its covert in the storm, its star in the night, its voice in the solitude. Guide it in its gloom; help it in its heat; direct it in its doubt; calm it in its conflict; fan it in its faintness; prompt it in its perplexity; lead it through its labyrinth; raise it from its ruins.

I cannot rule this heart of mine; keep it under the shadow of Thine own wings.

GEORGE MATHESON

*None other Lamb! none other name!
None other hope in heaven, or earth, or sea!
None other hiding-place for sin and shame!
None beside Thee!*

*My faith burns low; my hope burns low;
Only my soul's deep need comes out in me
By the deep thunder of its want and woe,
Calls out to Thee.*

Lord, Thou art life though I be dead!
Love's Flame art Thou, however cold I be!
Nor heaven have I, nor place to lay my head,
Nor home, but Thee.
CHRISTINA ROSSETTI

"Come unto me . . . and I will give you rest."

January 5

MORNING

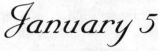

Lord, there is none beside thee to help (2 CHRON. 14:11 RV).

Remind God of His entire responsibility. "There is none beside thee to help." The odds against Asa were enormous. There were a million men in arms against him, besides three hundred chariots. It seemed impossible to hold his own against that vast multitude. There were no allies who would come to his help; his only hope, therefore, was in God. It may be that your difficulties have been allowed to come to so alarming a pitch that you may be compelled to renounce all creature aid, to which in lesser trials you have had recourse, and cast yourself back on your almighty Friend.

Put God between yourself and the foe. To Asa's faith, Jehovah seemed to stand between the might of Zerah and himself, as one who had no strength. Nor was he mistaken. We are told that the Ethiopians were destroyed before the Lord and *before His host,* as though celestial combatants flung themselves against the foe in Israel's behalf, and put the large host to rout, so that Israel had only to follow up and gather the spoil. Our God is Jehovah of hosts, who can summon unexpected reinforcements at any moment to aid His people. Believe that He is there between you and your difficulty, and what baffles you will flee before Him, as clouds before the gale. F. B. MEYER

When nothing whereon to lean remains,
When strongholds crumble to dust;
When nothing is sure but that God still reigns,
That is just the time to trust.

'Tis better to walk by faith than sight,
In this path of yours and mine;
And the pitch-black night, when there's no outer light
Is the time for faith to shine.

Abraham believed God, and said to sight, "Stand back!" and to the laws of nature, "Hold your peace!" and to a misgiving heart, "Silence, thou lying tempter!" He *believed* God.   JOSEPH PARKER

EVING

EVENING

And why take ye thought? (MATT. 6:28)

*W*hen a man is living on God's plan he has no need to worry himself about his trade, or about his house, or about anything that belongs to him.

Do not look at your own faith; look at God's faithfulness! Do not look around on circumstances; keep on looking at the resources of the Infinite God!

The only thing a man may be anxious about in this life is whether he is working on God's plan, doing God's work; and if that is so, all the care of everything else is back on God.

There are some things which we cannot definitely claim in prayer, because we do not know whether they are in God's mind for us. They may or may not be, but it is only by praying that we can tell. I am perfectly sure that in praying, there comes to men who dwell with God a kind of holy confidence; and when they get hold of a promise in God's Word, they look on that promise as granted.

Let us yield ourselves to God, that the living Godhead may flow through our poor, mean, frail human minds.

If the Lord careth for thee, be thyself at rest.

ARCHBISHOP LEIGHTON

When we see the lilies
Spinning in distress,
Taking thought to
Manufacture loveliness;
When we see the birds all
Building barns for store,
'Twill be time for us to worry—
Not before!

If the Pilot has come on board, why should the captain also pace the deck with weary foot?

January 6
MORNING

❧

When thou passest through the waters . . . they shall not overflow thee (ISA. 43:2).

God does not open paths for us in advance of our coming. He does not promise help before help is needed. He does not remove obstacles out of our way before we reach them. Yet when we are on the edge of our need, God's hand is stretched out.

Many people forget this, and are forever worrying about difficulties which they foresee in the future. They expect that God is going to make the way plain and open before them, miles and miles ahead; whereas He has promised to do it only step by step as they may need. You must get to the waters and into their floods before you can claim the promise. Many people dread death, and lament that they have not "dying grace." Of course, they will not have dying grace when they are in good health, in the midst of life's duties, with death far in advance. Why should they have it then? Grace for duty is what they need then, living grace; then dying grace when they come to die.　　　　　　　　　　J. R. M.

"When thou passest through the waters"
Deep the waves may be and cold
But Jehovah is our refuge,
And His promise is our hold;
For the Lord Himself hath said it,
He, the faithful God and true:
"When thou comest to the waters
Thou shalt not go down, BUT THROUGH"

Seas of sorrow, seas of trial,
Bitterest anguish, fiercest pain,
Rolling surges of temptation
Sweeping over heart and brain—
They shall never overflow us

For we know His word is true;
All His waves and all His billows
He will lead us safely THROUGH.

Threatening breakers of destruction,
Doubt's insidious undertow,
Shall not sink us, shall not drag us
Out to ocean depths of woe;
For His promise shall sustain us,
Praise the Lord, whose Word is true!
We shall not go down, or under,
For He saith, "Thou passest THROUGH."
ANNIE JOHNSON FLINT

EVENING

Have faith in God. (MARK 11:22)

*I*n the catacombs, we are told, explorers take a thread with them through all the dark passages and tortuous windings, and by this thread find their way back again to the light. There is such a thread running through all the dark corridors which we tread; and if we simply, practically trust in God we shall steer past every peril and land in the world of light. This is the counsel to remember in all the perplexities of our actual life.

There is an answer to every questioning "Why?" It is this: *Have faith in God.*

Have faith that *He knows all, sympathizes with all, can rectify what is amiss in all!* Have faith in the outworking of His beneficent purpose: that the ruin will become a magnificent pile; the desert will blossom into a garden. *Have faith in God.* Keep close to Him—His side, His will—and He will teach us the true thing, the right way. Have faith that God knows, and that we shall know by and by, why things are as they are.

We ask and are answered not,
And so we say, God has forgot,
Or else, there is no God.

The years
Roll back and through a mist of tears,
I see a child turn from her play,

And seek with eager feet, the way
That led her to her father's knee.

"If God is wise and kind," said she,
"Why did He let my roses die?"
A moment's pause, a smile, a sigh,
And then, "I do not know, my dear,
Some questions are not answered here."

"But is it wrong to ask?" "Not so,
My child; that we should seek to know
Proves right to know, beyond a doubt;
And someday we shall yet find out
Why roses die."

And then I wait,
Sure of my answer, soon or late;
Secure that love doth hold for me
The key to life's great mystery;
And oh, so glad to leave it there,
Tho' my dead roses were so fair.

AUTHOR UNKNOWN

January 7

MORNING

I have learned, in whatsoever state I am, therewith to be content
(PHIL. 4:11).

Paul, denied of every comfort, wrote the above words in his dungeon. A story is told of a king who went into his garden one morning, and found everything withered and dying. He asked the oak that stood near the gate what the trouble was. He found it was sick of life and determined to die because it was not tall and beautiful like the pine. The pine was all out of heart because it could not bear grapes, like the vine. The vine was going to throw its life away because it could not stand erect and have as fine a fruit as the peach tree. The geranium was fretting because it was not tall and fragrant like the lilac; and so on all through the garden. Coming to a heartsease, he found its bright face lifted as cheery as ever. "Well, heartsease, I'm glad, amidst all this discouragement, to find one brave little flower. You do not seem to be the least disheartened." "No, I am not of much account, but I thought that if you wanted an oak, or a pine, or a peach tree, or a lilac, you would have planted one; but as I knew you wanted a heartsease, I am determined to be the best little heartsease that I can."

Others may do a greater work,
But you have your part to do;
And no one in all God's heritage
Can do it so well as you.

They who are God's without reserve, are in every state content; for they will only what He wills, and desire to do for Him whatever He desires them to do; they strip themselves of everything, and in this nakedness find all things restored a hundredfold.

EVENING

Take you . . . twelve stones. . . . That this may be a sign among you
. . . when your children ask . . . in time to come . . .
What mean ye by these stones? Then ye shall answer . . .
the waters of Jordan were cut off: and these stones shall be for
a memorial . . . for ever. (JOSH. 4:3, 6–7)

*Y*ou will never get anywhere with God unless you take definite steps. God was very definite in His dealings with Abraham. *He brought him to a definite place, and Abraham marked the spot.*

When the children of Israel crossed over Jordan they marked the spot on the shore with twelve stones, and also placed twelve stones in the riverbed which were later covered with water—a hidden place.

God wants us, as Christians, *to take definite steps,* and to *mark* these steps. There are places in your heart over which the Jordan's waters roll—hidden places which no one sees, or of which no one knows the meaning; but He knows. When you have committed them unto Him that He might have His say, saying, "Search me, O God, and know my heart; try me, and know my thoughts; and see if there be any wicked way in me," *He knows and answers prayer.*

Is this a crisis hour in *your* life? If it is, settle it *now.*

We must never go back on our transactions with God.

It remains to be seen what God can do with a man irrevocably given to Him. It is because we are but partially His that His work in us and for us is incomplete.

If you have given yourself to God, you have just to *reckon* that He takes what you give. A time comes when you have to *cease praying and believe*. Some Christians say, "O Lord, come and fill me." They keep on praying, and He says, "Believe I have come; reckon that I am come; if you reckon, I will come."

A friend said, "If God tells me to reckon, *He pledges Himself to make the reckoning good.*" As we go on reckoning, we will go on realizing. No man makes a mistake who does what the Lord bids him do.

THOMAS COOK

Reckon some special time when you fully surrendered your life to the Lord. Build a pile of stones there to mark the spot, and then build another on the life side—the resurrection side! Do this today! Build a heap of stones to mark the time, and never fight the old battle again. We should not be dying and rising, and dying and rising again; we should build our memorial of stones once for all, and then *ever date from that time!*

January 8

MORNING

〜∞〜

I will cause the shower to come down in his season; there shall be showers of blessing (EZEK. 34:26).

What is thy *season* this morning? Is it a season of drought? Then that is the season for showers. Is it a season of great heaviness and black clouds? Then that is the season for showers. "As thy day so shall thy strength be." "I will give thee *showers* of blessing." The word is in the plural. All kinds of blessings God will send. All God's blessings go together, like links in a golden chain. If He gives converting grace, He will also give comforting grace. He will send "showers of blessings." Look up today, O parched plant, and open thy leaves and flowers for a heavenly watering.

SPURGEON

Let but thy heart become a valley low,
And God will rain on it till it will overflow.

Thou, O Lord, canst transform my thorn into a flower. And I want my thorn transformed into a flower. Job got the sunshine after the rain, but has the rain been all waste? Job wants to know, I want to know, if the shower had nothing to do with the shining. And Thou canst tell me—Thy cross can tell me. Thou hast crowned Thy sorrow. Be this my crown, O Lord. I only triumph in Thee when I have learned the radiance of the rain.

GEORGE MATHESON

The fruitful life seeks showers as well as sunshine.

The landscape, brown and sere beneath the sun,
Needs but the cloud to lift it into life;
The dews may damp the leaves of tree and flower,
But it requires the cloud-distilled shower
To bring rich verdure to the lifeless life.

Ah, how like this, the landscape of a life:
Dews of trial fall like incense, rich and sweet;
But bearing little in the crystal tray—
Like nymphs of night, dews lift at break of day
And transient impress leave, like lips that meet.

But clouds of trials, bearing burdens rare,
Leave in the soul, a moisture settled deep:
Life kindles by the magic law of God;
And where before the thirsty camel trod,
There richest beauties to life's landscape leap.

Then read thou in each cloud that comes to thee
The words of Paul, in letters large and clear:
So shall those clouds thy soul with blessing feed,
And with a constant trust as thou dost read,
All things together work for good. Fret not, nor fear!

EVENING

✺

He hath . . . made me a polished shaft. (ISA. 49:2)

Corner stones, polished after the similitude of a palace. (PS. 144:12)

Cut . . . to Shine!

"When in Amsterdam, Holland, last summer," says a traveler, "I was much interested in a visit we made to a place then famous for polishing diamonds. We saw the men engaged in the work. When a diamond is found it is rough and dark like a common pebble. It takes a long time to polish it, and it is very hard work. It is held by means of a piece of metal close to the surface of a large wheel, which is kept going round and round. Fine diamond dust is put on this wheel, nothing else being hard enough to polish the diamond. This work is kept up for months, and sometimes for several years, before it is finished. If the diamond is intended for a king, then greater time and trouble are spent on it."

What though the precious jewel may be torn and cut until its carats are reduced tenfold! When the cutting and polishing are completed, it will shine with a thousand flashes of reflected light—every carat will be multiplied an hundredfold in value by the process of reduction and threatened destruction!

Let us *wait His time*—let us *trust His love,* that "the trial of your faith . . . might be found unto praise and honor and glory at the appearing of Jesus Christ."

Rarest gems bear hardest grinding—
God's own workmanship are we.

January 9

MORNING

༺◦༻

For I reckon that the sufferings of this present time
are not worthy to be compared with the glory which shall
be revealed in us (ROM. 8:18).

I kept for nearly a year the flask-shaped cocoon of an emperor moth. It is very peculiar in its construction. A narrow opening is left in the neck of the flask, through which the perfect insect forces its way, so that a forsaken cocoon is as entire as one still tenanted, no rupture of the interlacing fibers having taken place. The great disproportion between the means of egress and the size of the imprisoned insect makes one wonder how the exit is ever accomplished at all—and it never is without great labor and difficulty. It is supposed that the pressure to which the moth's body is subjected in passing through such a narrow opening is a provision of nature for forcing the juices into the vessels of the wings, these being less developed at the period of emerging from the chrysalis than they are in other insects.

I happened to witness the first efforts of my prisoned moth to escape from its long confinement. During a whole forenoon, from time to time, I watched it patiently striving and struggling to get out. It never seemed able to get beyond a certain point, and at last my patience was exhausted. Very probably the confining fibers were drier and less elastic than if the cocoon had been left all winter on its native heather, as nature meant it to be. At all events I thought I was wiser and more compassionate than its Maker, and I resolved to give it a helping hand. With the point of my scissors I snipped the confining threads to make the exit just a very little easier, and lo! immediately, and with perfect ease, out crawled my moth dragging a huge swollen body and little shriveled wings. In vain I watched to see that marvelous process of expansion in which these silently and swiftly develop before one's eyes; and as I traced the exquisite spots and markings of diverse colors which were all there in miniature, I longed to see these assume their due proportions and the creature to appear in all its perfect beauty, as it is, in truth, one of the loveliest of its kind. But I looked in vain. My false tenderness had proved its ruin. It never was any-thing but a stunted abortion, crawling painfully through that brief life which it should have spent flying through the air on rainbow wings. I have thought of it often, often, when watching with pitiful eyes those who were struggling with sorrow, suffering, and distress; and I would fain cut short the discipline and give deliverance. Shortsighted man! How know I that one of these pangs or groans could be spared? The farsighted, perfect love that seeks the perfection of its object does not weakly shrink from present, transient suffering. Our Father's love is too true to be weak. Because He loves His children, He chastises them that they may be par-takers of His holiness. With this glorious end in view, He spares not for their crying. Made perfect through sufferings, as the Elder Brother was, the sons of God are trained up to obedience and brought to glory through much tribulation.   FROM A TRACT

EVENING

And Jacob was left alone; and there wrestled a man with him until the breaking of the day. . . . And he said . . . as a prince hast thou power with God . . . and hast prevailed. (GEN. 32:24, 28)

If you saw one of the intimates of the King on his knees, you would marvel at the sight. Look! He is in the Audience Chamber. He has a seat set for him among the peers. He is set down among the old nobility of the Empire. The King will not put on his signet ring to seal a command, till his friend has been heard. "Command Me," the King says to him. "Ask of Me," He says, "for the things of My sons: command the things to come concerning them!" And, as if that were not enough, that man-of-all-prayer is still on his knees. He is wrestling there. There is no enemy that I can see; yet he wrestles like a mighty man. What is he doing with such a struggle? Doing? Do you not know what he is doing? He is moving Heaven and earth. He is casting this mountain, and that, into the midst of the sea. He is casting down thrones. He is smiting old empires of time to pieces. Yes, he is wrestling indeed.   ALEXANDER WHYTE

Break through to God,
He fully understands
Thou art in His dear Hands,
To fulfill all His commands,
Break through to God!

Break through to God,
Be dauntless, faithful, strong,
E'en though the fight is long,
Raise to Him the victor's song,
Break through to God.

Break through to God,
Though thy heart may quail,
And the foe may rail,
Calvary's victory shall not fail,
Break through to God!

Looking back over the Welsh Revival about 1904, the Rev. Seth Joshua wrote: "The secret of the Lord was with many even before the blessing came. I know a man, who, for five years was carried out by the Spirit, and made to weep and pray along the banks of a Welsh river. At last the travail ceased, and calm expectation followed the soul pangs of this man about whom I now write. *He lived to see the answer to his heart-cries unto the Lord.* He was present in the services in which the first historical incidents took place."

Break through to God!

January 10
MORNING

❧

They were forbidden of the Holy Ghost to preach the word in Asia
(ACTS 16:6).

It is interesting to study the methods of His guidance as it was extended toward these early heralds of the cross. It consisted largely in prohibitions, when they attempted to take another course than the right. When they would turn to the left, to Asia, He stayed them. When they sought to turn to the right, to Bithynia, again He stayed them. In after years Paul would do some of the greatest work of his life in that very region; but just now the door was closed against him by the Holy Spirit. The time was not yet ripe for the attack on these apparently impregnable bastions of the kingdom of Satan. Apollos must come there for pioneer work. Paul and Barnabas are needed yet more urgently elsewhere, and must receive further training before undertaking this responsible task.

Beloved, whenever you are doubtful as to your course, submit your judgment absolutely to the Spirit of God, and ask Him to shut against you every door but the right one. Say,

"Blessed Spirit, I cast on Thee the entire responsibility of closing against my steps any and every course which is not of God. Let me hear Thy voice behind me whenever I turn to the right hand or the left."

In the meanwhile, continue along the path which you have been already treading. Abide in the calling in which you are called, unless you are clearly told to do something else. The Spirit of Jesus waits to be to you, O pilgrim, what He was to Paul. Only be careful to obey His least prohibition; and where after believing prayer, there are no apparent hindrances, go forward with enlarged heart. Do not be surprised if the answer comes in closed doors. But when doors are shut right and left, an open road is sure to lead to Troas. There Luke awaits, and visions will point the way, where vast opportunities stand open, and faithful friends are waiting.

FROM *PAUL, BY MEYER*

Is there some problem in your life to solve,
Some passage seeming full of mystery?
God knows, who brings the hidden things to light.
He keeps the key.

Is there some door closed by the Father's hand
Which widely opened you had hoped to see?
Trust God and wait—for when He shuts the door
He keeps the key.

Is there some earnest prayer unanswered yet,
Or answered NOT as you had thought 'twould be?
God will make clear His purpose by-and-by.
He keeps the key.

Have patience with your God, your patient God,
All wise, all knowing, no long tarrier He,
And of the door of all thy future life
He keeps the key.

Unfailing comfort, sweet and blessed rest,
To know of EVERY door He keeps the key.
That He at last when just HE sees 'tis best,
Will give it THEE.

ANONYMOUS

EVENING

Peter went up upon the housetop to pray. (ACTS 10:9)

He went up upon the housetop to pray, probably *for further light*. What was to be the next step in the fulfillment of his lifework? Was the cloud to move forward? Was some new development of the Divine pattern at hand which he must realize for himself? And for others?

While he prayed the heavens were opened, and God gave him a real vision of His will. Then when he was very much perplexed in himself at what the vision meant, the knocking at the gate, the voices of men that rose at noon-silence calling his name, together with the assurance of the Spirit that there was no need for fear or further hesitation—all indicated that the hour of Destiny had struck; that a new epoch was inaugurated; and that he was to lead the Church into the greatest revolution she had known since the Ascension of her Lord.

What a lesson for our perplexed and anxious hearts! We find it difficult to wait our Lord's leisure; like imprisoned birds we beat our breasts against the wires of the cage. Though we pray, we do not trust. We find it hard to obey the injunction of our Lord—to roll our care, our way, ourselves, onto God.

Give to the winds thy fears;
hope and be undismayed;
God hears thy sighs, and counts thy tears;
God shall lift up thy head.

Leave to His sovereign sway to choose
and to command;
With wonder filled, thou soon shall own
how wise, how strong His Hand!

Through waves and clouds and storms, He gently clears thy way.
Wait thou His time, so shall thy night
soon end in joyous day.

He everywhere hath sway, and all things serve
His might.
His every act pure blessing is
His path unsullied light.

January 11

MORNING

Comfort ye, comfort ye my people, saith your God (ISA. 40:1).

Store up comfort. This was the prophet's mission. The world is full of comfortless hearts, and ere thou are sufficient for this lofty ministry, thou must be trained. And thy training is costly in the extreme; for, to render it perfect, thou too must pass through the same afflictions as are wringing countless hearts of tears and blood. Thus thy own life becomes the hospital ward where thou art taught the divine art of comfort. Thou art wounded, that in the binding up of thy wounds by the Great Physician, thou mayest learn how to render first aid to the wounded everywhere. Dost thou wonder why thou art passing through some special sorrow? Wait till ten years are passed, and thou wilt find many others afflicted as thou art. Thou wilt tell them how thou hast suffered and hast been comforted; then as the tale is unfolded, and the anodynes applied which once thy God wrapped around thee, in the eager look and the gleam of hope that shall chase the shadow of despair across the soul, *thou shalt know why* thou wast afflicted, and bless God for the

discipline that stored thy life with such a fund of experience and helpfulness.   SELECTED

God does not comfort us to make us comfortable, but to make us
comforters.   DR. JOWETT

> *They tell me I must bruise*
> *The rose's leaf,*
> *Ere I can keep and use*
> *Its fragrance brief.*
>
> *They tell me I must break*
> *The skylark's heart,*
> *Ere her cage song will make*
> *The silence start.*
>
> *They tell me love must bleed,*
> *And friendship weep,*
> *Ere in my deepest need*
> *I touch that deep.*
>
> *Must it be always so*
> *With precious things?*
> *Must they be bruised and go*
> *With beaten wings?*
>
> *Ah, yes! by crushing days,*
> *By caging nights, by scar*
> *Of thorn and stony ways,*
> *These blessings are!*

EVENING

As dying, and, behold, we live. (2 COR. 6:9)

To one who asked him the secret of service, Mr. George Müller replied:
"There was a day when I died, utterly died to George Müller"—and, as
he spoke, he bent lower and lower until he almost touched the floor—"to
his opinions, preferences, tastes and will; died to the world, its approval or
censure; died to the approval or blame of even my brethren and friends.
Since then I have *studied to show myself approved only unto God.*"

> *We may not understand nor know*
> *Just how the giant oak trees throw*

Their spreading branches wide,
Nor how upon the mountainside
The dainty wildflowers grow.

We may not understand nor see
Into the depth and mystery
Of suffering and tears;
Yet, through the stress of patient years
The flowers of sympathy

Spring up and scatter everywhere
Their perfume on the fragrant air—
But lo! the seed must die,
If it would bloom and multiply
And ripened fruitage bear.
THOMAS KIMBER

Look at that splendid oak! Where was it born? In a grave. The acorn was put into the ground and in that grave it sprouted and sent up its shoots. And was it only one day that it stood in the grave? No, every day for a hundred years it has stood there, and in that place of death it has found its life. *"The creation of a thousand forests is in one acorn."*

How shall my leaves fly singing in the
wind unless my roots shall wither in the dark?
PERSIAN POET

January 12
MORNING

❧

Reckon it nothing but joy . . . whenever you find yourself
hedged in by the various trials, be assured that the
testing of your faith leads to power of endurance
(JAMES 1:2–3 WEYMOUTH).

God hedges in His own that He may preserve them, but oftentimes they only see the wrong side of the hedge, and so misunderstand His dealings. It was so with Job (Job 3:23). Ah, but Satan knew the value of that hedge! See his testimony in chapter 1:10. Through the leaves of every trial there are chinks of light to shine through. Thorns do not prick you unless you lean against them, and not one touches without His knowledge. The words that hurt you, the letter which gave you pain, the cruel wound of your dearest friend, shortness of money—are all known to Him, who sympathizes as none else can and watches to see, if, through all, you will dare to trust Him wholly.

The hawthorn hedge that keeps us from intruding,
Looks very fierce and bare
When stripped by winter, every branch protruding
Its thorns that would wound and tear.

But spring-time comes; and like the rod that budded,
Each twig breaks out in green;
And cushions soft of tender leaves are studded,
Where spines alone were seen.

The sorrows, that to us seem so perplexing,
Are mercies kindly sent
To guard our wayward souls from sadder vexing,
And greater ills prevent.

To save us from the pit, no screen of roses
Would serve for our defense,
The hindrance that completely interposes
Stings back like thorny fence.

At first when smarting from the shock, complaining
Of wounds that freely bleed,
God's hedges of severity us paining,
May seem severe indeed.

But afterwards, God's blessed spring-time cometh,
And bitter murmurs cease;
The sharp severity that pierced us bloometh,
And yields the fruits of peace.

Then let us sing, our guarded way thus wending
Life's hidden snares among,
Of mercy and of judgment sweetly blending;
Earth's sad, but lovely song.

Suffered the loss of all things . . . that I may win Christ. (PHIL. 3:8)

Every great life has had in it some great renunciation.

*A*braham began by letting go, and going out, and all the way it was just giving up; first his home, his father and his past; next his inheritance to Lot, his selfish nephew; and finally the very child of promise on the altar of Moriah; but he became the father of the faithful, whose inheritance was as the sands of the sea and the stars of the heavens.

Hear *David* saying, "Neither will I offer burnt offerings unto the LORD my God of that which doth cost me nothing" (2 Sam. 24:24). David paid the full price. And we read, "The throne of David shall be established before the LORD for ever" (1 Kings 2:45).

Hannah gave up her boy and he became the prophet of the restoration of ancient Israel.

Paul not only suffered the loss of all things, but counted them but refuse that he might win Christ. And Paul stood before the common people, and in the palaces of kings.

So it is always; *real sacrifice, unto complete surrender of self, brings to us the revelation of God in His fullness.* As we have already seen, it was only on condition of Jacob's releasing and the brothers' bringing the best they had, Benjamin, that they could even see Joseph's face again. And when Judah went farther than this, and offered himself to be Joseph's slave forever, then it was that Joseph could keep back nothing, but found himself compelled to reveal everything to those for whom his heart yearned. It is God's own way with us. God in Jesus Christ does not, and apparently cannot, make Himself fully known in His personality and love, until we have surrendered to Him unconditionally and forever not only all we have, but all we are. *Then God can refrain no longer, but lavishes upon us, in Christ, such a revealing of Himself that it cannot be told in words.*

But the supreme sacrifice!

God had to sacrifice Himself, in Christ, in order thus to reveal Himself to us; but His sacrifice alone will not suffice. Not until we in turn have sacrificed ourself to Him is the revelation possible and complete. But what a revelation it is! *What glory does God give us in the life that is Christ as our life!* How it changes everything for us thereafter *from famine to royal abundance!* **MESSAGES FOR THE MORNING WATCH**

I heard a voice so softly calling:
"Take up thy cross and follow me."
A tempest o'er my heart was falling,
A living cross this was to me.

His cross I took, which, cross no longer,
A hundredfold brings life to me;
My heart is filled with joy o'erflowing,
His love and life are light to me.
SELECTED

January 13

MORNING

∽≈∾

*In all these things we are more than conquerors through him
that loved us* (ROM. 8:37).

This is more than victory. This is a triumph so complete that we have not only escaped defeat and destruction, but we have destroyed our enemies and won a spoil so rich and valuable that we can thank God that the battle ever came. How can we be "more than conquerors"? We can get out of the conflict a spiritual discipline that will greatly strengthen our faith and establish our spiritual character. Temptation is necessary to settle and confirm us in the spiritual life. It is like the fire which burns in the colors of mineral painting, or like winds that cause the mighty cedars of the mountain to strike more deeply into the soil. Our spiritual conflicts are among our choicest blessings, and our great adversary is used to train us for his ultimate defeat. The ancient Phrygians had a legend that every time they conquered an enemy the victor absorbed the physical strength of his victim and added so much more to his own strength and valor. So temptation victoriously met doubles our spiritual strength and equipment. It is possible thus not only to defeat our enemy, but to capture him and make him fight in our ranks. The prophet Isaiah speaks of flying on the shoulders of the Philistines (Isa. 11:14). These Philistines were their deadly foes, but the figure suggested that they would be enabled not only to conquer the Philistines, but to use them to carry the victors on their shoulders for further triumphs. Just as the wise sailor can use a head wind to carry him forward by tacking and taking advantage of its impelling force; so it is possible for us in our spiritual life through the victorious grace of God to turn to account the things that seem most unfriendly and unfavorable, and to be able to say continually, "The things that were against me have happened to the furtherance of the gospel."

FROM LIFE MORE ABUNDANTLY

A noted scientist observing that "early voyagers fancied that the coral-building animals instinctively built up the great circles of the Atoll Islands to afford themselves protection in the inner parts," has disproved this fancy by showing that the insect builders can only live and thrive fronting the open ocean, and in a highly aerated foam of its resistless billows. So it has been commonly thought that protected ease is the most favorable condition of life, whereas all the noblest and strongest lives prove on the contrary that the endurance of hardship is the making of the men, and the factor that distinguishes between existence and vigorous vitality. Hardship makes character.

SELECTED

"Now thanks be unto God Who always leads us forth to triumph with the Anointed One, and Who diffuses by us the fragrance of the knowledge of Him in every place" (2 Cor. 2:14—literal translation).

EVENING

Ye shall have a song. (ISA. 30:29)

Someone writes of sitting one winter evening by an open wood fire, and listening to the singing of the green logs as the fire flamed about them. All manner of sounds came out of the wood as it burned, and the writer, with poetic fancy, suggests that they were imprisoned songs, long sleeping in silence in the wood, brought out now by the fire.

When the tree stood in the forest the birds came and sat on its boughs and sang their songs. The wind, too, breathed through the branches making a weird, strange music. One day a child sat on the moss by the tree's root and sang its happy gladness in a snatch of sweet melody. A penitent sat under the tree's shade and with trembling tones, amid falling leaves, sang the fifty-first Psalm. And all these notes of varied song sank into the tree as it stood there, and hid away in its trunk. There they slept until the tree was cut down and part of it became a backlog in the cheerful evening fire. Then the flames brought out the music.

This is but a poet's fancy as far as the tree and the songs of the backlog are concerned. But is there not here a little parable which may be likened to many a human life? Life has its varied notes and tones—some glad, some choked in tears. Years pass and the life gives out no music of praise, sings no songs to bless others. But, at length, grief comes, and in the flames the long-imprisoned music is set free and sings its praise to God and its notes of love to cheer and bless the world. Gathered in life's long summer and stored away in the heart, it is given out in the hours of suffering and pain.

Many a rejoicing Christian never learned to sing till the flames kindled upon him.   J. R. MILLER

Gather the driftwood that will light the winter fire!

January 14

MORNING

He putteth forth his own sheep (JOHN 10:4).

Oh, this is bitter work for Him and us—bitter for us to go, but equally bitter for Him to cause us pain; yet it must be done. It would not be conducive to our true welfare to stay always in one happy and comfortable lot. He therefore puts us forth. The fold is deserted, that the sheep may wander over the bracing mountain slope. The laborers must be thrust out into the harvest, else the golden grain would spoil.

Take heart! It could not be better to stay when He determines otherwise; and if the loving hand of our Lord puts us forth, it must be well. On, in His name, to green pastures and still waters and mountain heights! *He goeth before thee.* Whatever awaits us is encountered first by Him. Faith's eye can always discern His majestic presence in front; and when that cannot be seen, it is dangerous to move forward. Bind this comfort to your heart, that the Savior has tried for Himself all the experiences through which He asks you to pass; and He would not ask you to pass through them unless He was sure that they were not too difficult for your feet or too trying for your strength.

This is the blessed life—not anxious to see far in front, nor careful about the next step, not eager to choose the path, nor weighted with the heavy responsibilities of the future, but quietly following behind the Shepherd, *one step at a time.*

Dark is the sky! and veiled the unknown morrow!
Dark is life's way, for night is not yet o'er;
The longed-for glimpse I may not meanwhile borrow;
But, this I know, HE GOETH ON BEFORE.

Dangers are nigh! and fears my mind are shaking;
Heart seems to dread what life may hold in store;
But I am His—He knows the way I'm taking,
More blessed still—HE GOETH ON BEFORE.

Doubts cast their weird, unwelcome shadows o'er me,
Doubts that life's best—life's choicest things are o'er;
What but His Word can strengthen, can restore me,
And this blest fact; that still HE GOES BEFORE.

HE GOES BEFORE! Be this my consolation!
He goes before! On this my heart would dwell!
He goes before! This guarantees salvation!
HE GOES BEFORE! And therefore all is well.

J. DANSON SMITH

The Oriental shepherd was always *ahead* of his sheep. He was down *in front*. Any attack upon them had to take him into account. Now God is down in front. He is in the tomorrows. It is tomorrow that fills men with dread. *God is there already.* All the tomorrows of our life have to pass Him before they can get to us.

F. B. M.

God is in every tomorrow,
Therefore I live for today,
Certain of finding at sunrise,
Guidance and strength for the way;
Power for each moment of weakness,
Hope for each moment of pain,
Comfort for every sorrow,
Sunshine and joy after rain.

*For I determined not to know any thing among you,
save Jesus Christ, and him crucified.* (1 COR. 2:2)

*For other foundation can no man lay than that is laid, which is
Jesus Christ.* (1 COR. 3:11)

*In the Cross of Christ I glory,
Tow'ring o'er the wrecks of time—*

Martin Luther preached the doctrine of Atoning Blood to slumbering Europe, and Europe awoke from the dead.

Amid all his defenses of Divine Sovereignty, *Calvin* never ignored or belittled the Atonement.

Cowper sang of it among the water lilies of the Ouse.

Spurgeon thundered this glorious doctrine of Christ Crucified into the ears of peer and peasant with a voice like the sound of many waters.

John Bunyan made the Cross the starting-point to the Celestial City.

Moody's bells all chimed to the keynote of Calvary.

Napoleon, after conquering almost the whole of Europe, put his finger on the red spot on the map representing the British Isles, and said, "Were it not for that red spot, I'd conquer the world!"

So says Satan about the place called Calvary, where Jesus Christ shed His Blood.

*Beneath the Cross of Jesus
I fain would take my stand,
The shadow of a mighty rock
Within a weary land;
A home within the wilderness,
A rest upon the way,
From the burning of the noontide heat,
And the burden of the day.*

*Upon the Cross of Jesus
Mine eye at times can see
The very dying form of One
Who suffered there for me.
And from my smitten heart with tears,
These wonders I confess,*

The wonder of His glorious love,
And my own worthlessness.

I take, O Cross, thy shadow
For my abiding place;
I ask no other sunshine than
The sunshine of His face;
Content to let the world go by,
To know no gain nor loss,
My sinful self my only shame,
My glory all the Cross.

Every true preacher of the Gospel strings all his pearls on the Red Cord of the Atonement.
T. L. CUYLER

CALVARY COVERS IT ALL!

January 15

MORNING

❧

And the Lord appeared unto Isaac the same night (GEN. 26:24).

*A*ppeared the same night," the night on which he went to Beer-sheba. Do you think this revelation was an accident? Do you think the *time* of it was an accident? Do you think it could have happened on any other night as well as this? If so, you are grievously mistaken. Why did it come to Isaac in the night on which he reached Beer-sheba? Because that was the night on which he reached *rest*. In his old locality, he had been tormented. There had been a whole series of petty quarrels about the possession of paltry wells. There are no worries like *little* worries, particularly if there is an accumulation of them. Isaac felt this. Even after the strife was past, the place retained a disagreeable association. He determined to leave. He sought change of scene. He pitched his tent away from the place of former strife. That very night the revelation came. God spoke when there was no inward storm. He could not speak when the mind was fretted; His voice demands the silence of the soul. Only in the *hush* of the spirit could Isaac hear the garments of his God sweep by. His *still* night was his *starry* night.

My soul, hast thou pondered these words, "Be still, and know"? In the hour of perturbation, thou canst not hear the answer to thy prayers. How often has the answer seemed to come long after! The heart got no response in the moment of its crying—in its thunder, its earthquake, and its fire. But when the crying ceased, when the stillness fell, when thy hand desisted from knocking on the iron gate, when the interest of *other* lives broke the tragedy of thine own, then appeared the long-delayed reply. Thou must rest, O soul, if thou wouldst have thy heart's desire. Still the beating of thy pulse of personal care. Hide thy tempest of individual trouble behind the altar of a common tribulation and, that same night, the Lord shall appear to thee. The rainbow shall span the place of the subsiding flood, and in thy stillness thou shalt hear the everlasting music.

GEORGE MATHESON

Tread in solitude thy pathway,
Quiet heart and undismayed.
Thou shalt know things strange, mysterious,
Which to thee no voice has said.

While the crowd of petty hustlers
Grasps at vain and paltry things,
Thou wilt see a great world rising
Where soft mystic music rings.

Leave the dusty road to others,
Spotless keep thy soul and bright,
As the radiant ocean's surface
When the sun is taking flight.

FROM THE GERMAN OF V. SCHOFFEL—H. F.

EVENING

And he said unto me, It is done. (REV. 21:6)

*H*ow many persons are everlastingly *doing*, but how few ever *get through* with it! How few settle a thing and know that it is accomplished and can say, "It is done"!

The moment we really believe, we are conscious that there is power. We can touch God at such times, and the fire in our souls makes us sure that something is settled forever.

Faith must be a clear-cut taking hold of God; a grasping Him with fingers of iron, with an uncompromising commitment of all to God. In learning to float you must utterly abandon yourself to the water; you must believe that the water is able to hold you up. So you must take this step of commitment, and then look up to God with confidence and say, "It is done." Our part is *to commit;* God's part is *to work.* The very moment that we commit, that very moment He undertakes. We must believe that He has undertaken what we have committed. Faith must re-echo God's promise and dare to say, *"It is done."*

> *The thing is as good as done,*
> *since He has taken it in hand.*

Step out upon a bare promise right now, and "count the things that be not as though they were," and God will make your reckoning real. It will be done by actual experience.   **DAYS OF HEAVEN UPON EARTH**

My old professor, Lord Kelvin, once said in class a very striking thing. He said that there came a point in all his great discoveries when he had to take a leap into the dark. And nobody who is afraid of such a leap from the solid ground of what is demonstrated, will know the exhilaration of believing!

To commit ourselves unreservedly to Christ is just the biggest venture in the world! The wonderful thing is that when, with a certain daring, we take Lord Kelvin's "leap into the dark" we discover it is not dark at all, but life abundant, and liberty and peace.   **GEORGE H. MORRISON**

> *Believe that it is settled because God says so!*
> *"God said, and it happened"* (GEN. 1:2–7, FINNISH TRANS.).

January 16
MORNING

❦

And there arose a great storm (MARK 4:37).

Some of the storms of life come *suddenly:* a great sorrow, a bitter disappointment, a crushing defeat. Some come *slowly.* They appear upon the ragged edges of the horizon no larger than a man's hand, but, trouble that seems so insignificant spreads until it covers the sky and overwhelms us.

Yet it is in the storm that God equips us for service. When God wants an oak He plants it on the moor where the storms will shake it and the rains will beat down upon it, and it is in the midnight battle with elements that the oak wins its rugged fiber and becomes the king of the forest.

When God wants to make a man He puts him into some storm. The history of mankind is always rough and rugged. No man is made until he has been out into the surge of the storm and found the sublime fulfillment of the prayer: "O God, take me, break me, make me."

A Frenchman has painted a picture of universal genius. There stand orators, philosophers and martyrs, all who have achieved preeminence in any phase of life; the remarkable fact about the picture is this: Every man who is preeminent for his ability was first preeminent for suffering. In the foreground stands that figure of the man who was denied the promised land, Moses. Beside him is another, feeling his way—blind Homer. Milton is there, blind and heartbroken. Now comes the form of One who towers above them all. What is His characteristic? His face is marred more than any man's. The artist might have written under that great picture, "The Storm."

The beauties of nature come after the storm. The rugged beauty of the mountain is born in a storm, and the heroes of life are the storm-swept and battle-scarred.

You have been in the storms and swept by the blasts. Have they left you broken, weary, beaten in the valley, or have they lifted you to the sun-lit summits of a richer, deeper, more abiding manhood and womanhood? Have they left you with more sympathy with the storm-swept and the battle-scarred?   SELECTED

The wind that blows can never kill
The tree God plants;
It bloweth east, it bloweth west,
The tender leaves have little rest,
But any wind that blows is best.
The tree that God plants
Strikes deeper root, grows higher still,
Spreads greater boughs, for God's good will
Meets all its wants.

There is no storm hath power to blast
The tree God knows;
No thunderbolt, nor beating rain,
Nor lightning flash, nor hurricane;

When they are spent, it doth remain,
The tree God knows,
Through every tempest standeth fast,
And from its first day to its last
Still fairer grows.
SELECTED

EVENING

⤳⤵

Set a watch, O LORD, before my mouth;
keep the door of my lips.
(PS. 141:3)

Let me no wrong or idle word,
Unthinking say;
Set Thou a seal upon my lips—
Just for today.

Keep still! When trouble is brewing, keep still! When slander is getting on its legs, keep still! When your feelings are hurt, keep still till you recover from your excitement at any rate! Things look different through an unagitated eye.

In a commotion once I wrote a letter and sent it, and wished I had not. In my later years I had another commotion and wrote another long letter; my life had rubbed a little sense into me, and I kept that letter in my pocket until I could look it over without agitation, and without tears, and I was glad I did—less and less it seemed necessary to send it. I was not sure it would do any harm, but in my doubtfulness I learned reticence, and eventually it was destroyed.

Time works wonders! Wait till you can speak calmly and then perhaps you will not need to speak. Silence is the most powerful thing conceivable, sometimes. It is strength in its grandeur; it is like a regiment ordered to stand still in the mad fury of battle. To plunge in were twice as easy. *Nothing is lost by learning to keep still.*   HANNAH WHITALL SMITH

Lord, keep me still,
Though stormy winds may blow,
And waves my little bark may overflow,
Or even if in darkness I must go,
Yet keep me still, yet keep me still.

Lord, keep me still,
The waves are in Thy hand,
The roughest winds subside at Thy command.
Steer Thou my bark in safety to the land,
And keep me still, and keep me still.

Lord, keep me still,
And may I ever hear Thy still small voice
To comfort and to cheer;
So shall I know and feel Thee ever near.
And keep me still, and keep me still.

SELECTED

Silence is a great peacemaker.   HENRY WADSWORTH LONGFELLOW

January 17

MORNING

~∞~

*O Daniel, servant of the living God,
is thy God whom thou servest continually, able to deliver thee?*
(DAN. 6:20).

How many times we find this expression in the Scriptures, and yet it is just this very thing that we are so prone to lose sight of. We know it is written *"the living God";* but in our daily life there is scarcely anything we practically so much lose sight of as the fact that God is *the living God;* that He is now whatever He was three or four thousand years since; that He has the same sovereign power, the same saving love toward those who love and serve Him as ever He had and that He will do for them now what He did for others two, three, four thousand years ago, simply because He is the living God, the unchanging One. Oh, how therefore we should confide in Him, and in our darkest moments never lose sight of the fact that He *is* still and ever will be *the living God!*

Be assured, if you walk with Him and look to Him and expect help from Him, He will never fail you. An older brother who has known the Lord for forty-four years, who writes this, says to you for your encouragement that He has never failed him. In the greatest difficulties, in the heaviest trials, in the deepest poverty and necessities, He has never failed me; but because I was enabled by His grace to trust Him He has always appeared for my help. I delight in speaking well of His name.

GEORGE MUELLER

Luther was once found at a moment of peril and fear, when he had need to grasp unseen strength, sitting in an abstracted mood tracing on the table with his finger the words, "Vivit! Vivit!" ("He lives! He lives!"). It is our hope for ourselves, and for His truth, and for mankind. Men come and go; leaders, teachers, thinkers speak and work for a season, and then fall silent and impotent. He abides. They die, but He lives. They are lights kindled, and, therefore, sooner or later quenched; but He is the true light from which they draw all their brightness, and He shines forevermore.

ALEXANDER MACLAREN

"One day I came to know Dr. John Douglas Adam," writes C. G. Trumbull. "I learned from him that what he counted his greatest spiritual asset was his *unvarying consciousness of the actual presence of Jesus.* Nothing bore him up so, he said, as the realization that Jesus was *always* with him in actual presence; and that this was so independent of his own feelings, independent of his deserts, and independent of his own notions as to how Jesus would manifest His presence.

"Moreover, he said that Christ was the home of his thoughts. Whenever his mind was free from other matters it would turn to Christ; and he would talk aloud to Christ when he was alone—on the street, anywhere—as easily and naturally as to a human friend. So real to him was Jesus' *actual presence.*"

EVENING

∿

In the year that king Uzziah died I saw . . . the Lord. (ISA. 6:1)

We have to get our eyes off others before we can have the full vision of Jesus. Moses and Elias had to pass to make possible the vision of Jesus only. *In the year that King Uzziah died,* Isaiah says, *I saw the Lord.* His eyes and hopes had been upon the mighty and victorious earthly leader, and with his death all these hopes had sunk in despair. But *the stars come out when the lights of earth fade.* It was then Isaiah's true vision and life began.

It is not enough to see Jesus along with other things and persons. What we need is to have Him fill *all* our vision, *all* our sky, *all* our heart, *all* our plans, and *all* our future. What He wants from us is *"first love,"*

that is, the supreme place; and He cannot really be anything to us satis-
factorily until He is everything. He is able to fill every capacity of our
being and without displacing any rightful affection or occupation, yet so
blend with all, so control all, so become the very essence of all thought
and all delight that we can truly say, "For me to live is Christ," for "the
love of Christ constraineth me," shuts me up and in from everything else
as a pent-up torrent in its narrow course, to live not unto myself but
"unto him that loved me, and gave himself for me."

Holy Spirit, bring us our transfiguration, take us apart to our Mount
of vision, let Moses and Elias pass, and let us see no man save *Jesus only.*

ECHOES OF A NEW CREATION

Am I not enough, Mine own? Enough,
Mine own, for thee?
Hath the world its palace towers,
Garden glades of magic flowers,
Where thou wouldst be?
Fair things and false are there,
False things but fair,
All things thou findst at last
Only in Me.
Am I not enough, Mine own? I, forever
and alone? I, needing thee?

SUSO

January 18

MORNING

∽∾

Now thanks be unto God, which always causeth us to triumph in
Christ (2 COR. 2:14).

God gets His greatest victories out of apparent defeats. Very often the
enemy seems to triumph for a little, and God lets it be so; but then He
comes in and upsets all the work of the enemy, overthrows the apparent
victory, and as the Bible says, "turns the way of the wicked upside down."
Thus He gives a great deal larger victory than we would have known if He
had not allowed the enemy, seemingly, to triumph in the first place.

The story of the three Hebrew children being cast into the fiery furnace is a familiar one. Here was an apparent victory for the enemy. It *looked* as if the servants of the living God were going to have a terrible defeat. We have all been in places where it seemed as though we were defeated, and the enemy rejoiced. We can imagine what a complete defeat this looked to be. They fell down into the flames, and their enemies watched them to see them burn up in that awful fire, but were greatly astonished to see them walking around in the fire enjoying themselves. Nebuchadnezzar told them to "come forth out of the midst of the fire." Not even a hair was singed, nor was the smell of fire on their garments, "because there is no other god that can deliver after this sort."

This apparent defeat resulted in a marvelous victory.

Suppose that these three men had lost their faith and courage, and had complained, saying, *"Why* did not God keep us out of the furnace!" They would have been burned, and God would not have been glorified. If there is a great trial in your life today, do not own it as a *defeat*, but continue, by faith, to claim the victory through Him who is able to make you more than conqueror, and a glorious victory will soon be apparent. Let us learn that in all the hard places God brings us into, He is making opportunities for us to exercise such faith in Him as will bring about blessed results and greatly glorify His name.   *FROM* LIFE OF PRAISE

> *Defeat may serve as well as victory*
> *To shake the soul and let the glory out.*
> *When the great oak is straining in the wind,*
> *The boughs drink in new beauty, and the trunk*
> *Sends down a deeper root on the windward side.*
> *Only the soul that knows the mighty grief*
> *Can know the mighty rapture. Sorrows come*
> *To stretch out spaces in the heart for joy.*

EVENING

I came down from heaven, not to do mine own will, but the will of him that sent me. (JOHN 6:38)

When he was crossing the Irish Channel one dark starless night, says Dr. F. B. Meyer, he stood on the deck by the captain and asked him, "How do you know Holyhead Harbor on so dark a night as this?" He said, "You see those three lights? Those three must line up behind each other as one, and when we see them so united we know the exact position of the harbor's mouth."

When we want to know God's will there are three things which always concur: the inward impulse, the Word of God, and the trend of circumstances! God in the heart, impelling you forward; God in the Book, corroborating whatever He says in the heart; and God in circumstances, which are always indicative of His will. *Never start until these three things agree.*

Stand still at the crossroads ready to walk or run,
and you will not be kept waiting long.

When we're not quite certain if we turn to left or right—Isn't it a blessing when a *signpost* looms in sight! If there were no *signposts* we should wander miles astray—in the wrong direction if we didn't know the way.

God has set His *signposts* on Life's strange and winding road. When we're blindly stumbling with the burden of our load—He will lead our footsteps though the pathway twist and bend—In some form He guides us, through The Book, a song, a friend . . . In the dark uncertain hours, we need not be afraid—When we're at the crossroads, and decisions must be made . . . Though the track is unfamiliar, and the light is gray—Rest assured, there's bound to be a *signpost on the way.*   PATIENCE STRONG

Let us be silent unto Him, and believe that, even now, messengers are hastening along the road with the summons, or direction, or help which we need.

January 19
MORNING

❧

Men ought always to pray and not to faint (LUKE 18:1).

"Go to the ant." Tammerlane used to relate to his friends an anecdote of his early life. "I once," he said, "was forced to take shelter from my enemies in a ruined building, where I sat alone many hours. Desiring to divert my mind from my hopeless condition, I fixed my eyes on an ant that was carrying a grain of corn larger than itself up a high wall. I numbered the efforts it made to accomplish this object. The grain fell sixty-nine times to the ground; but the insect *persevered,* and the seventieth time it reached the top. This sight gave me courage at the moment, and I never forgot the lesson.   *FROM* THE KING'S BUSINESS

Prayer which takes the fact that past prayers have not been answered as a reason for languor, has already ceased to be the prayer of faith. To the prayer of faith the fact that prayers remain unanswered is only evidence that the moment of the answer is *so much nearer.* From first to last, the lessons and examples of our Lord all tell us that prayer which cannot persevere and urge its plea importunately, and renew, and renew itself again, and gather strength from every past petition, is not the prayer that will prevail.   WILLIAM ARTHUR

Rubenstein, the great musician, once said, "If I omit practice one day, I notice it; if two days, my friends notice it; if three days, the public notices it." It is the old doctrine, *"Practice makes perfect."* We must continue believing, continue praying, continue doing His will. Suppose along any line of art, one should cease practicing, we know what the result would be. If we would only use the same quality of common sense in our religion that we use in our everyday life, we should go on to perfection.

The motto of David Livingstone was in these words, "I determined never to stop until I had come to the end and achieved my purpose." By unfaltering persistence and faith in God he conquered.

EVENING

⮾

Can God? (PS. 78:19)

"Can God?" the subtle Tempter breathes within,
When all seems lost, excepting sure defeat,
"Can God roll back the raging seas of sin?"
"Can God?" the fainting heart doth quick repeat.

"God can!" in trumpet tones rings faith's glad cry,
And, David-like, it fears no giant foe,
For faith dwells on the Mount, serene, and high,
While unbelief's dark clouds roll far below.

"God can!" His Saints of old did ever give
Their fullest confirmation o'er and o'er,
And He who made the long-dead bones to live,
E'en now can bring the dead to life once more.

"God can!" Then let us fear not, but arise!
Our motto be this word that He doth give,
If we have faith, before our wondering eyes
A MIGHTY ARMY SHALL ARISE AND LIVE!

J. A. R.

"Can God?" Oh, fatal question! It shut Israel out of the Land of Promise. And we are in danger of making the same mistake. Can God find me a situation, or provide food for my children? Can God keep me from yielding to that besetting sin? Can God extricate me from this terrible snare in which I am entangled? We look at the difficulties, the surges that are rolling high, and we say, *"If* Thou canst do anything, help us!" They said, "Can God?" It hurt and wounded God deeply. Say no more, "Can God?" Rather say this, "God Can!" That will clear up many a problem. That will bring you through many a difficulty in your life.

There is no strength in unbelief.

Has the life of God's people reached the utmost limit of what God can do for them? *Surely not!* God has new places, and new developments, and new resources. *He can do new things, unheard-of things, hidden things! Let us enlarge our hearts and not limit Him.* "When thou didst terrible things which we looked not for, thou camest down, the mountains flowed down at thy presence" (Isa. 64:3).

We must desire and believe. We must ask and expect that God will do *unlooked-for things!* We must set our faith on a God of whom men do not know what He hath prepared for them that wait for Him. *The Wonder-doing God . . . must be the God of our confidence.*   ANDREW MURRAY

The Wonder-doing God can surpass all our expectation!

January 20

MORNING

Sorrow is better than laughter; for by the sadness of the countenance the heart is made better (ECCLES. 7:3).

When sorrow comes under the power of divine grace, it works out a manifold ministry in our lives. Sorrow reveals unknown depths in the soul, and unknown capabilities of experience and service. Gay, trifling people are always shallow, and never suspect the little meannesses in their nature. Sorrow is God's plowshare that turns up and subsoils the depths of the soul, that it may yield richer harvests. If we had never fallen, or were in a glorified state, then the strong torrents of divine joy would be the normal force to open up all our souls' capacities; but in a fallen world, sorrow, with despair taken out of it, is the chosen power to reveal ourselves to ourselves. Hence it is sorrow that makes us think deeply, long, and soberly.

Sorrow makes us go slower and more considerately, and introspect our motives and dispositions. It is sorrow that opens up within us the capacities of the heavenly life, and it is sorrow that makes us willing to launch our capacities on a boundless sea of service for God and our fellows.

We may suppose a class of indolent people living at the base of a great mountain range, who had never ventured to explore the valleys and canyons back in the mountains; and someday, when a great thunderstorm goes careening through the mountains, it turns the hidden glens into echoing trumpets, and reveals the inner recesses of the valley, like the convolutions of a monster shell, and then the dwellers at the foot of the hills are astonished at the labyrinths and unexplored recesses of a region so near by, and yet so little known. So it is with many souls who indolently live on the outer edge of their own natures until great thunderstorms of sorrow reveal hidden depths within that were never hitherto suspected.

God never uses anybody to a large degree, until after He breaks that one all to pieces. Joseph had more sorrow than all the other sons of Jacob, and it led him out into a ministry of bread for all nations. For this reason, the Holy Spirit said of him. "Joseph is a fruitful bough . . . by a well, whose branches run over the wall" (Gen. 49:22). It takes sorrow to widen the soul. FROM THE HEAVENLY LIFE

The dark brown mould's upturned
By the sharp-pointed plow;
And I've a lesson learned.

My life is but a field,
Stretched out beneath God's sky,
Some harvest rich to yield.

Where grows the golden grain?
Where faith? Where sympathy?
In a furrow cut by pain.
MALTBIE D. BABCOCK

Every person and every nation must take lessons in God's school of adversity. "We can say, 'Blessed is night, for it reveals to us the stars.' In the same way we can say, 'Blessed is sorrow, for it reveals God's comfort.' The floods washed away home and mill, all the poor man had in the world. But as he stood on the scene of his loss, after the water had subsided, brokenhearted and discouraged, he saw something shining in the bank which the waters had washed bare. 'It looks like gold,' he said. It was gold. The flood which had beggared him made him rich. So it is ofttimes in life."

H. C. TRUMBULL

EVENING

And he came and dwelt in a city called Nazareth. (MATT. 2:23)

Our Lord Jesus lived for thirty years amid the happenings of the little town of Nazareth. Little villages spell out their stories in small events. *And He, the young Prince of Glory, was in the carpenter's shop!* He moved amid humdrum tasks, petty cares, village gossip, trifling trade, *and He was faithful in that which was least.*

If these smaller things in life afford such riches of opportunity for the finest loyalty, all of our lives are wonderfully wealthy in possibility and promise. Even though our house is furnished with commonplaces it can be the home of the Lord all the days of our life.

J. H. JOWETT

> *When I am tempted to repine*
> *That such a lowly lot is mine,*
> *There comes to me a voice which saith,*
> *"Mine were the streets of Nazareth."*
>
> *So mean, so common and confined,*
> *And He the Monarch of mankind!*
> *Yet patiently He traveleth*
> *Those narrow streets of Nazareth.*
>
> *It may be I shall never rise*
> *To place or fame beneath the skies—*
> *But walk in straitened ways till death,*
> *Narrow as streets of Nazareth.*
>
> *But if through honor's arch I tread*
> *And there forget to bend my head,*
> *Ah! let me hear the voice which saith,*
> *"Mine were the streets of Nazareth."*

NETTIE ROOKER

There's sometimes a good hearty tree growin' out o' the bare rock, out o' some crack that just holds the roots, right on one o' them hills where you can't seem to see a wheelbarrowful o' good earth, but that tree'll keep a green top in the driest summer. You lay your ear down to the ground, and you'll hear a little stream runnin'. Every such tree has got its own livin' spring; there's folks made to match 'em.　　SARAH ORNE JEWETT

From the desire of being great, good Lord deliver us!

A MORAVIAN PRAYER

January 21

MORNING

᠆᠊ᢁ᠊᠆

None of these things move me (ACTS 20:24).

We read in the Book of Samuel that the moment that David was crowned at Hebron, "All the Philistines came up to seek David." And the moment we get anything from the Lord worth contending for, then the Devil comes to seek us.

When the enemy meets us at the threshold of any great work for God, let us accept it as "a token of salvation," and claim double blessing, victory, and power. Power is developed by resistance. The cannon carries twice as far because the exploding power has to find its way through resistance. The way electricity is produced in the powerhouse yonder is by the sharp friction of the revolving wheels. And so we shall find some day that even Satan has been one of God's agencies of blessing.

FROM DAYS OF HEAVEN UPON EARTH

A hero is not fed on sweets,
Daily his own heart he eats;
Chambers of the great are jails,
And head winds right for royal sails.

EMERSON

Tribulation is the way to triumph. The valleyway opens into the highway. Tribulation's imprint is on all great things. *Crowns are cast in crucibles.* Chains of character that wind about the feet of God are forged in earthly flames. No man is greatest victor till he has trodden the winepress of woe. With seams of anguish deep in His brow, the "Man of Sorrows" said, "In the world ye shall have tribulation"—but after this sob comes the psalm of promise, "Be of good cheer, I have overcome the world." The footprints are traceable everywhere. Bloodmarks stain the steps that lead to thrones. Scars are the price of scepters. Our crowns will be wrested from the giants we conquer. Grief has always been the lot of greatness. It is an open secret.

> *The mark of rank in nature*
> *Is capacity for pain;*
> *And the anguish of the singer*
> *Makes the sweetest of the strain.*

Tribulation has always marked the trail of the true reformer. It is the story of Paul, Luther, Savonarola, Knox, Wesley, and all the rest of the mighty army. They came through great tribulation to their place of power.

Every great book has been written with the author's blood. "These are they that have come out of great tribulation." Who was the peerless poet of the Greeks? Homer. But that illustrious singer was blind. Who wrote the fadeless dream of *Pilgrim's Progress*? A prince in royal purple upon a couch of ease? Nay! The trailing splendor of that vision gilded the dingy walls of old Bedford jail while John Bunyan, a princely prisoner, a glorious genius, made a faithful transcript of the scene.

> *Great is the facile conqueror;*
> *Yet haply, he, who, wounded sore,*
> *Breathless, all covered o'er with blood and sweat,*
> *Sinks fainting, but fighting evermore—*
> *Is greater yet.*
> SELECTED

EVENING

※

Remove not the ancient landmark, which thy fathers have set.
(PROV. 22:28)

Among the property owned jointly by two young brothers who were carpenters was the old tumbledown place of their birth. One of the brothers was soon to be married and the old house was to be torn down and a new one erected on its site. For years neither of the brothers had visited the cottage, as it had been leased.

As they entered now and started the work of demolishing the place, again and again floods of tender memories swept over them. By the time they reached the kitchen they were well-nigh overcome with their emotions. There was the place where the old kitchen table had stood—with the family Bible—where they had knelt every evening. They were recalling now with a pang how in later years they had felt a little superior to that time-honored custom carefully observed by their father.

Said one: "We're *better off* than he was, but we're not *better men.*"

The other agreed, saying, "I'm going back to the old church and the old ways, and in my new home I'm going to make room for worship as Dad did."

The strength of a nation lies in the homes of its people.

ABRAHAM LINCOLN

Says Dr. J. G. Paton: "No hurry for market, no rush for business, no arrival of friends or guests, no trouble or sorrow, no joy or excitement, ever prevented us from kneeling around the family altar while our high priest offered himself and his children to God." And on his father's life in his home was based Dr. Paton's decision to follow the Lord wholly. "He walked with God—why not I?"

"Stand ye in the . . . old paths, where is the good way" *(Jer. 6:16).*

January 22

MORNING

∿

Into a desert place apart (MATT. 14:13).

There is no music in a rest, but there is the making of music in it." In our whole life-melody the music is broken off here and there by "rests," and we foolishly think we have come to the end of the tune. God sends a time of forced leisure, sickness, disappointed plans, frustrated efforts, and makes a sudden pause in the choral hymn of our lives; and we lament that our voices must be silent, and our part missing in the music which ever goes up to the ear of the Creator. How does the musician read the "rest"? See him beat the time with unvarying count, and catch up the next note true and steady, as if no breaking place had come between.

Not without design does God write the music of our lives. Be it ours to learn the tune, and not be dismayed at the "rests." They are not to be slurred over, not to be omitted, not to destroy the melody, not to change the keynote. If we look up, God Himself will beat the time for us. With the eye on Him, we shall strike the next note full and clear. If we sadly say to ourselves, "There is no music in a 'rest,' " let us not forget "there is the making of music in it." The making of music is often a slow and painful process in this life. How patiently God works to teach us! How long He waits for us to learn the lesson!   RUSKIN

Called aside—
From the glad working of thy busy life,
From the world's ceaseless stir of care and strife,
Into the shade and stillness by thy Heavenly Guide
For a brief space thou hast been called aside.

Called aside—
Perhaps into a desert garden dim;
And yet not alone, when thou has been with Him,
And heard His voice in sweetest accents say:
"Child, wilt thou not with Me this still hour stay?"

Called aside—
In hidden paths with Christ thy Lord to tread,
Deeper to drink at the sweet Fountainhead,
Closer in fellowship with Him to roam,
Nearer, perchance, to feel thy Heavenly Home.

Called aside—
Oh, knowledge deeper grows with Him alone;
In secret oft His deeper love is shown,
And learnt in many an hour of dark distress
Some rare, sweet lesson of His tenderness.

Called aside—
We thank thee for the stillness and the shade;
We thank Thee for the hidden paths Thy love hath made,
And, so that we have wept and watched with Thee,
We thank Thee for our dark Gethsemane.

Called aside—
Oh, restful thought—He doeth all things well;
Oh, blessed sense, with Christ alone to dwell;
So in the shadow of Thy cross to hide,
We thank Thee, Lord, to have been called aside.

❧❧

And when they were come into the ship, the wind ceased.
(MATT. 14:32)

Faith can conquer every obstacle!

Some people insist upon holding Christ at a distance, waiting before going to Him until obstacles have been removed. *When economic skies are brighter; when doubts have been cleared; when the edge of sorrow has been dulled: then they will go to Jesus.*

Peter, knowing that the Master was near, in sublime faith asked to be permitted to go to Him across the surging waters. *Fear almost conquered him, but even then Jesus lifted him by the hand.*

There are always storms of difficulty and of assailing doubts. Unanswered questions and the problems of hideous wrongs are always battling against the good purposes of Christ. Do not let the storms keep *you* from the consoling presence of Christ. Build *a bridge out of the storms, and go to Him!*

SELECTED

"Get into the boat!" Thou didst whisper.
At first how I feared to obey;
I looked not at Thee, but the storm clouds,
The darkness, the waves, and the spray.

But then came the words, "Will you trust Him?
Will you claim and receive at His hand
All His definite fullness of blessing?
Launch out at thy Master's command!"

Thou art willing, my Lord, could I doubt Thee?
Hast Thou ever proved untrue?
Nay! out at Thy word I have ventured,
I have trusted. Thy part is to do.

LAURA A. BARTER-SNOW

When Jesus rises, the storm stops. The calm comes from the power of His Presence. As a strong quiet man steps in majestically among a crowd of noisy brawlers, his very appearance makes them ashamed and hushes their noise; so Jesus steps in among the elements, and they are still in a moment.

January 23

MORNING

∽≈∾

Why standest thou afar off, O Lord? (PS. 10:1).

Cod is "a very present help in trouble." But He permits trouble to pursue us, as though He were indifferent to its overwhelming pressure, that we may be brought to the end of ourselves, and led to discover the treasure of darkness, the unmeasurable gains of tribulation. We may be sure that He who permits the suffering is with us in it. It may be that we shall see Him only when the trial is passing; but we must dare to believe that He never leaves the crucible. Our eyes are holden; and we cannot behold Him whom our soul loveth. It is dark—the bandages blind us so that we cannot see the form of our High Priest; but He is there, deeply touched. Let us not rely on feeling, but on faith in His unswerving fidelity; and though we see Him not, let us talk to Him. Directly we begin to speak to Jesus, as being literally present, though His presence is veiled, there comes an answering voice which shows that He is in the shadow, keeping watch upon His own. Your Father is as near when you journey through the dark tunnel as when under the open heaven!

FROM **DAILY DEVOTIONAL COMMENTARY**

What though the path be all unknown?
What though the way be drear?
Its shades I traverse not alone
When steps of Thine are near.

EVENING

∽≈∾

I called him alone, and blessed him. (ISA. 51:2)

A celebrated Scottish nobleman and statesman once replied to a cor respondent that he was *"plowing his lonely furrow."* Whenever God has required someone to do a big thing for Him, He has sent him to a *lonely furrow.* He has called him to go alone.

You may have to become the loneliest person on earth, but if you do you will be able always to see around you the chariots of God, even twenty thousand, and thousands of thousands, and then you will forget your loneliness.

The soil is hard,
And the plow goes heavily.
The wind is fierce
And I toil on wearily—

But His hands made the yoke!
Ah wonder—that I should bear His yoke—
It is enough, if I may but plow the furrow,
For the Sower to sow the seed.

If you have taken hold of the plow, *hold on until the field is finished.* *"Let us not cave in" (fall out and leave a gap) (Gal. 6:9, Greek).*

Says Theodore L. Cuyler, "After long and painful perplexities about accepting a certain attractive call, I opened the Book and read: *'Why gaddest thou about so much to change thy way?'* " (Jer. 2:36).

"Your present field may be limited, but you are not limited by your field. Great men have sprung from the furrows. Great men have plowed and harrowed, and leaving these things have written their names deep in history. There are heights undreamed of, ecstasies unthought of for the one who follows on. So follow on in the valley, *looking for hills.* One day you will look back with surprise, and then turning go forward with fresh courage."

You were made to MOUNT and not to crawl!

"One lonely soul on fire with the love of God may set the whole universe ablaze" *(see Acts 2:41; Rev. 5:11).*

January 24

MORNING

∽৩৩৩৵

But the dove found no rest for the sole of her foot, and she returned unto him. . . . And the dove came in to him in the evening; and, lo, in her mouth was an olive leaf (GEN. 8:9–11).

God knows just when to withhold from us any visible sign of encouragement, and when to grant us such a sign. How good it is that we may trust Him anyway! When all visible evidences that He is remembering us are withheld, that is best; He wants us to realize that His Word,

His promise of remembrance, is more substantial and dependable than any evidence of our senses. When He sends the visible evidence, that is well also; we appreciate it all the more after we have trusted Him without it. Those who are readiest to trust God without other evidence than His Word always receive the greatest number of visible evidences of His love.

C. G. TRUMBULL

Believing Him; if storm-clouds gather darkly 'round,
And even if the heaven seem brass, without a sound?
He hears each prayer and even notes the sparrow's fall.

And praising Him; when sorrow, grief, and pain are near,
And even when we lose the thing that seems most dear?
Our loss is gain. Praise Him; in Him we have our All.

Our hand in His; e'en though the path seems long and drear
We scarcely see a step ahead, and almost fear?
He guides aright. He has it thus to keep us near.

And satisfied; when every path is blocked and bare,
And worldly things are gone and dead which were so fair?
Believe and rest and trust in Him, He comes to stay.

Delays are not refusals; many a prayer is registered, and underneath it the words: "My time is not yet come." God has a set time as well as a set purpose, and He who orders the bounds of our habitation orders also the time of our deliverance. **SELECTED**

EVENING

There is nothing. (1 KINGS 18:43)

Elijah was a man who hoped perfectly; hoped against hope until the abundant answer came. He continued, in the very face of darkness and perplexity, *to expect*, because the very God of hope lived *in* him and expected *through* him. And he was not ashamed, for it came to pass the seventh time his servant said, "Behold, there ariseth a little cloud out of the sea, about the size of a man's hand," and in a little while the heaven was black with clouds and there was a great rain!

Can *you* count God faithful when only *the still small voice* speaks? When there is neither wind, earthquake, nor fire? Can you start *when you see the cloud no bigger than a man's hand*? Can you say: " 'There is nothing,' *but I wait on Thee.* My mind is peculiarly in the dark regarding the way I am to take, *but Thou knowest. Unto Thee do I look up!"*

"There is nothing"—though the raindrops needed sorely and so long
Have been promised by Jehovah, by the Father true and strong.
And the sky is blue and cloudless, and the earth is parched and dry,
Yet no showers are forthcoming from the reservoir on high.

"There is nothing"—but the prophet knows and trusts his Master's word;
He is not a senseless idol, but the mighty, powerful God.
He has seen His wondrous working, he believes Him faithful still;
So he humbly waits in patience for Jehovah's perfect will.

"There is nothing"—oh, how often doth the enemy declare,
Nothing for your constant wrestlings; nothing for your cries and tears.
And the faithless heart says
"Nothing," though deceived she ne'er has been,
For the little cloud so longed for, at the seventh time is seen.

"There is nothing"—but there shall be: God is still the Great "I AM."
He is NOW Almighty, faithful, and forevermore the same;
And the tears, and cries, and wrestlings, have been recorded on high;
Not forgotten, nor neglected, to be answered by and by.

JAMES BOOBBYER

"Get thee up, eat and drink; for there is a sound of abundance of rain!"

January 25

MORNING

~⚬~

Thy rod and thy staff they comfort me (PS. 23:4).

*A*t my father's house in the country there is a little closet in the chimney corner where are kept the canes and walkingsticks of several generations of our family. In my visits to the old house, when my father and I are going out for a walk, we often go to the cane closet and pick out our sticks to suit the fancy of the occasion. In this I have frequently been reminded that the Word of God is a staff.

During the war, when the season of discouragement and impending danger was upon us, the verse, "He shall not be afraid of evil tidings; his heart is fixed, trusting in the Lord," was a staff to walk with on many dark days.

When death took away our child and left us almost heartbroken, I found another staff in the promise that "weeping may endure for the night, but joy cometh in the morning."

When in impaired health, I was exiled for a year, not knowing whether I should be permitted to return to my home and work again, I took with me this staff which never failed, "He knoweth the thoughts that he thinketh toward me, thoughts of peace and not of evil."

In times of special danger or doubt, when human judgment has seemed to be set at naught, I have found it easy to go forward with this staff, "In quietness and confidence shall be your strength." And in emergencies, when there has seemed to be no adequate time for deliberation or for action, I have never found that this staff has failed me, "He that believeth shall not make haste."

BENJAMIN VAUGHAN ABBOTT, IN THE OUTLOOK

"I had never known," said Martin Luther's wife, "what such and such things meant, in such and such psalms, such complaints and workings of spirit; I had never understood the practice of Christian duties, had not God brought me under some affliction." It is very true that God's rod is as the schoolmaster's pointer to the child, pointing out the letter, that he may the better take notice of it; thus He pointeth out to us many good lessons which we should never otherwise have learned.   **SELECTED**

God always sends His staff with His rod.

"Thy shoes shall be iron and brass; and as thy days, so shall thy strength be" (Deut. 33:25).

Each of us may be sure that if God sends us on stony paths He will provide us with strong shoes, and He will not send us out on any journey for which He does not equip us well.   **MACLAREN**

EVENING

Produce your cause, saith the LORD; bring forth your strong reasons, saith the King of Jacob. (ISA. 41:21)

Over in Canada there lived an Irish saint called "Holy Ann." She lived to be one hundred years old. When she was a young girl, she was working in a family for very small wages under a very cruel master and mistress. They made her carry water for a mile up a steep hill. At one time there had been a well dug there; it had gone dry, but it stood there year after year. One night she was very tired, and she fell on her knees and cried to God; and while on her knees she read these words: "I will open . . . fountains in the midst of the valleys: I will make . . . the dry land springs of water." "Produce your cause, saith the LORD; bring forth your strong reasons." These words struck Holy Ann, and she produced her cause before the Lord. She told Him how badly they needed the water and how hard it was for her to carry the water up the steep hill; then she lay down and fell asleep. She had pleaded her cause and brought forth her strong reasons. The next morning early she was seen to take a bucket and start for the well. Someone asked her where she was going, and she replied, "I am going to draw water from the well." "Why, it is dry," was the answer. But that did not stop Holy Ann. She knew whom she had believed, and on she went; and, lo and behold, there in the well was eighty-three feet of pure, cold water, and she told me that the well never did run dry! That is the way the Lord can fulfill His promises. "Produce your cause . . . bring forth your strong reasons," and see Him work in your behalf.

How little we use this method of holy argument in prayer; and yet there are many examples of it in Scripture: Abraham, Jacob, Moses, Elijah, Daniel—all used arguments in prayer, and claimed the Divine interposition on the ground of the pleas which they presented.

January 26
MORNING

❧

I have begun to give; . . . begin to possess (DEUT. 2:31).

A great deal is said in the Bible about waiting for God. The lesson cannot be too strongly enforced. We easily grow impatient of God's delays. Much of our trouble in life comes out of our restless, sometimes reckless, haste. We cannot *wait* for the fruit to ripen, but insist on plucking it while it is green. We cannot *wait* for the answers to our prayers, although the things we ask for may require long years in their preparation for us. We are exhorted to walk with God; but ofttimes God walks very slowly. But there is another phase of the lesson. God *often waits for us.*

We fail many times to receive the blessing He has ready for us, because we do not go forward with Him. While we miss much good through not waiting for God, we also miss much through *over-waiting*. There are times when our strength is to sit still, but there are also times when we are to go forward with a firm step.

There are many divine promises which are conditioned upon the beginning of some action on our part. When we begin to obey, God will begin to bless us. Great things were promised to Abraham, but not one of them could have been obtained by waiting in Chaldea. He must leave home, friends, and country, and go out into unknown paths and press on in unfaltering obedience in order to receive the promises. The ten lepers were told to show themselves to the priest, and *"as they went they were cleansed."* If they had waited to *see the cleansing* come in their flesh before they would start, they would never have seen it. God was waiting to cleanse them; and the moment their faith began to work, the blessing came.

When the Israelites were shut in by a pursuing army at the Red Sea, they were commanded to "Go forward." Their duty was no longer one of waiting, but of rising up from bended knees and going forward in the way of heroic faith. They were commanded to show their faith at another time by beginning their march over the Jordan while the river ran to its widest banks. The key to unlock the gate into the land of promise they held in their own hands, and the gate would not turn on its hinges until they had approached it and unlocked it. That key was faith. We are set to fight certain battles. We say we can never be victorious; that we never can conquer these enemies; but, as we enter the conflict, *One* comes and fights by our side, and through Him we are more than conquerors. If we had waited, trembling and fearing, for our Helper to come before we would join the battle, we should have waited in vain. This would have been the *over-waiting* of unbelief. God is waiting to pour richest blessings upon you. Press forward with bold confidence and take what is yours. "I have begun to give, begin to possess."   J. R. MILLER

EVENING

I being in the way, the LORD led me. (GEN. 24:27)

"The way" means God's way, the pathway prepared for us; not our way; not any kind of way (Prov. 14:12); not man's way; but the direct way of duty and command. In such a way the Lord will be sure to lead and guide us. The Lord answered the servant's prayer *exactly* as he prayed, step by step.

"God never gives guidance for two steps at a time. I must take one step, and then I receive light for the next."

> *As thou dost travel down the corridor of Time*
> *Thou wilt find many doors of usefulness;*
> *To gain some there are many weary steps to climb,*
> *And then they will not yield! but onward press,*
> *For there before thee, in the distance just beyond*
> *Lies one which yet will open; enter there,*
> *And thou shalt find all realized thy visions fair*
> *Of fields more vast than thou hast yet conceived.*
> *Press on, faint not; though briars strew thy way,*
> *The greatest things are yet to be achieved;*
> *And he who falters not will win the day.*
> *No man can shut the door which God sets wide,*
> *He bids thee enter there—thy work awaits inside.*
>
> **FAIRELIE THORNTON**

> *Keep to your post and watch His signals!*
> *Implicitly rely on the methods of His guidance.*

January 27

MORNING

Stablish, strengthen, settle you (1 PETER 5:10).

In taking Christ in any new relationship, we must first have sufficient intellectual light to satisfy our mind that we are entitled to stand in this relationship. The shadow of a question here will wreck our confidence. Then, having seen this, we must make the venture, the committal, the choice, and take the place just as definitely as the tree is planted in the soil, or the bride gives herself away at the marriage altar. It must be once and for all, without reserve, without recall.

Then there is a season of establishing, settling, and testing, during which we must "stay put" until the new relationship gets so fixed as to become a permanent habit. It is just the same as when the surgeon sets the broken arm. He puts it in splints to keep it from vibration. So God has His spiritual splints that He wants to put upon His children and keep them quiet and unmoved until they pass the first stage of faith. It is not always easy work for us, "but the God of all grace, who hath called us unto his eternal glory by Jesus Christ, after that ye have suffered awhile, stablish, strengthen, settle you."

A. B. SIMPSON

There is a natural law in sin and sickness; and if we just let ourselves go and sink into the trend of circumstances, we shall go down and sink under the power of the tempter. But there is another law of spiritual life and of physical life in Christ Jesus to which we can rise, and through which we can counterpoise and overcome the other law that bears us down.

But to do this requires real spiritual energy and fixed purpose and a settled posture and habit of faith. It is just the same as when we use the power in our factory. We must turn on the belt and keep it on. The power is there, but we must keep the connection; and while we do so, the higher power will work and all the machinery will be in operation.

There is a spiritual law of choosing, believing, abiding, and holding steady in our walk with God, which is essential to the working of the Holy Ghost either in our sanctification or healing.

FROM DAYS OF HEAVEN UPON EARTH

EVENING

And a light shined in the prison: and he [the angel] smote Peter on the side . . . saying, Arise up quickly. (ACTS 12:7)

If we fear the Lord, we may look for timely interpositions when our case is at its worst. Angels are not kept from us by storms, nor hindered by darkness. Seraphs think it no humiliation to visit the poorest of the heavenly family. If angels' visits are few and far between at ordinary times, they shall be frequent in our nights of tempest and tossing. Dear reader, is this an hour of distress with you? Then ask for peculiar help. Jesus is the Angel of the Covenant, and if His presence be now earnestly sought it will not be denied. What that presence brings is heart cheer.

CHARLES H. SPURGEON

And a light shined in my cell,
And there was not any wall,

And there was no dark at all,
Only THOU, Emmanuel.

Light of love shined in my cell,
Turned to gold the iron bars,
Opened windows to the stars,
Peace stood there as sentinel.

Dearest Lord, how can it be
That Thou art so kind to me?
Love is shining in my cell,
Jesus, my Emmanuel.

A. W. C.

January 28

MORNING

I am jealous over you with God's own jealousy
(2 COR. 11:2 WEYMOUTH).

How an old harper dotes on his harp! How he fondles and caresses it, as a child resting on his bosom! His life is bound up in it. But, see him tuning it. He grasps it firmly, strikes a chord with a sharp, quick blow; and while it quivers as if in pain, he leans over intently to catch the first note that rises. The note, as he feared, is false and harsh. He strains the chord with the torturing thumbscrew; and though it seems ready to snap with the tension, he strikes it again, bending down to listen softly as before, till at length you see a smile on his face as the first true tone trembles upward.

So it may be that God is dealing with you. Loving you better than any harper loves his harp, He finds you a mass of jarring discords. He wrings your heartstrings with some torturing anguish; He bends over you tenderly, striking and listening; and, hearing only a harsh murmur, strikes you again, while His heart bleeds for you, anxiously waiting for that strain—"Not my will, but thine be done"—which is melody sweet to His ear as angels' songs. Nor will He cease to strike until your chastened soul shall blend with all the pure and infinite harmonies of His own being.

SELECTED

Oh, the sweetness that dwells in a harp of many strings,
While each, all vocal with love in a tuneful harmony rings!
But, oh, the wail and discord, when one and another is rent,
Tensionless, broken and lost, from the cherished instrument.

For rapture of love is linked with the pain or fear of loss,
And the hand that takes the crown, must ache with many a cross;
Yet he who hath never a conflict, hath never a victor's palm,
And only the toilers know the sweetness of rest and calm.

Only between the storms can the Alpine traveller know
Transcendent glory of clearness, marvels of gleam and glow;
Had he the brightness unbroken of cloudless summer days,
This had been dimmed by the dust and the veil of brooding haze.

Who would dare the choice, neither or both to know,
The finest quiver of joy or the agony thrill of woe!
Never the exquisite pain, then never the exquisite bliss,
For the heart that is dull to that can never be strung to this.

EVENING

Go forth, and stand upon the mount before the LORD.
(1 KINGS 19:11)

A rebuke is often a blessing in disguise. Elijah needed this form of address in order to arouse him to an understanding of his causeless fear. Such a one as he has no right to be fitful and repining. If he will *go forth and stand upon the mount before the Lord,* instead of hiding away in a cave, he will find new inspiration in a new vision of His power! When we are living on earth's low levels we fail to catch the inspiring visions of God which are the true support of the prophetic life. We must come out into the sunshine and make the ascent of the mountain if we would discern those evidences of God's power which are always available for the re-creation of faith and courage.

The golden-crested wren is one of the tiniest of birds; it is said to weigh only the fifth part of an ounce; and yet, on frailest pinions, it braves hurricanes and crosses northern seas.

It often seems in nature as though Omnipotence works but through frailest organisms; certainly the Omnipotence of grace is seen to the greatest advantage in the trembling but resolute saint.

On the American prairies the butterflies start westward in their migrations and make steady progress though the wind is against them and the sea in front. The delicate butterflies rebuke me.

> *Step out on the waves*
> *That would crush you!*
> *Step out in the storm*
> *That would hush you!*
> *And you will find,*
> *As you touch the crest*
> *You feared so much,*
> *And walk on its breast,*
> *There was One walking there,*
> *The whole night through,*
> *Walking, watching,*
> *Waiting—FOR YOU!*

January 29
MORNING

God is in the midst of her; she shall not be moved:
God shall help her, and that right early (PS. 46:5).

Shall not be moved"—what an inspiring declaration! Can it be possible that we, who are so easily moved by the things of earth, can arrive at a place where nothing can upset us or disturb our calm? Yes, it is possible; and the Apostle Paul knew it. When he was on his way to Jerusalem where he foresaw that "bonds and afflictions" awaited him, he could say triumphantly, "But none of these things move me." Everything in Paul's life and experience that could be shaken had been shaken, and he no longer counted his life, or any of life's possessions, dear to him. And we, if we will but let God have His way with us, may come to the same place, so that neither the fret and tear of little things of life, nor the great and heavy trials, can have power to move us from the peace that passeth understanding, which is declared to be the portion of those who have learned to rest only on God.

"Him that overcometh will I make a pillar in the temple of my God; and he shall go no more out." To be as immovable as a pillar in the house of our God, is an end for which one would gladly endure all the shakings that may be necessary to bring us there!   HANNAH WHITALL SMITH

When God is in the midst of a kingdom or city He makes it as firm as Mount Zion, that cannot be removed. When He is in the midst of a soul, though calamities throng about it on all hands, and roar like the billows of the sea, yet there is a constant calm within, such a peace as the world can neither give nor take away. What is it but want of lodging God in the soul, and that in His stead the world is in men's hearts, that make them shake like leaves at every blast of danger?   ARCHBISHOP LEIGHTON

"They that trust in the Lord shall be as Mount Zion, which cannot be removed, but abideth forever." There is a quaint old Scottish version that puts iron into our blood:

> *Who sticketh to God in stable trust*
> *As Zion's mount he stands full just,*
> *Which moveth no whit, nor yet doth reel,*
> *But standeth forever as stiff as steel!*

EVENING

I will make all my mountains a way. (ISA. 49:11)

Do not try to tunnel under them, nor to squeeze through them, nor to run away from them, but to *claim them.*

Tighten your loins with the promises of God!

These mountains of difficulty are His stepping-stones; walk on them with holy joy.

Keep the strong staff of faith well in hand, and *trust God in the dark.*

We are safer with Him in the dark than without Him in the sunshine. *At the end of the gloomy passage beams the heavenly light!* When we reach heaven we may discover that the richest and most profitable experiences that we had in this world were those gained in the very roads from which we shrank back in dread.

It was because Job was on God's main line that he found so many tunnels.

The great thing to remember is that *God's darknesses are not His goals.* His tunnels must be traveled *to get somewhere else.* Therefore, be patient, my soul! The darkness is not thy bourne; the tunnel is not thy abiding home!

The traveler who would pass from the wintry slopes of Switzerland into the summer beauty of the plains of Italy, *must be prepared to tunnel the Alps.*

*Often darkness fills the pathway of the
pilgrim's onward track,
And we shrink from going forward—trembling,
feel like going back:
But the Lord, who plans so wisely, leads us on
both day and night,
Till at last, in silent wonder, we rejoice in
Wisdom's light.*

*Though the tunnel may be tedious through the
narrow, darkened way,
Yet it amply serves its purpose—soon it brings
the light of day:
And the way so greatly dreaded, as we
backward take a glance,
Shows the skill of careful planning: never the
result of chance!*

*Is your present path a tunnel, does the darkness
bring you fear?
To the upright, oh, remember, He doth cause
a light to cheer.
Press on bravely, resting calmly, though a way
you dimly see,
Till, at length, so safely guided, you emerge
triumphantly.*

*Trust the Engineer Eternal, surely all His works
are right,
Though we cannot always trace them, faith will
turn at last to sight:
Then no more the deepening shadows of the
dark and dismal way,
There forever in clear sunlight, we'll enjoy
"the perfect day."*
SELECTED

The tunnel is never on a siding—it is planned to lead somewhere!

January 30
MORNING

I will be as the dew unto Israel (HOS. 14:5).

The dew is a source of freshness. It is nature's provision for renewing the face of the earth. It falls at night, and without it the vegetation would die. It is this great value of the dew which is so often recognized in the Scriptures. It is used as the symbol of spiritual refreshing. Just as nature is bathed in dew, so the Lord renews His people. In Titus 3:5 the same thought of spiritual refreshing is connected with the ministry of the Holy Ghost—"renewing the Holy Ghost."

Many Christian workers do not recognize the importance of the heavenly dew in their lives, and as a result they lack freshness and vigor. Their spirits are drooping for lack of dew.

Beloved fellow-worker, you recognize the folly of a laboring man attempting to do his day's work without eating. Do you recognize the folly of a servant of God attempting to minister without eating of the heavenly manna? Nor will it suffice to have spiritual nourishment occasionally. Every day you must receive the renewing of the Holy Ghost. You know when your whole being is pulsating with the vigor and freshness of divine life and when you feel jaded and worn. Quietness and absorption bring the dew. At night when the leaf and blade are still, the vegetable pores are open to receive the refreshing and invigorating bath; so spiritual dew comes from quiet lingering in the Master's presence. Get still before Him. Haste will prevent your receiving the dew. Wait before God until you feel saturated with His presence; then go forth to your next duty with the conscious freshness and vigor of Christ.   **DR. PARDINGTON**

Dew will never gather while there is either heat or wind. The temperature must fall, and the wind cease, and the air come to a point of coolness and rest—absolute rest, so to speak—before it can yield up its invisible particles of moisture to bedew either herb or flower. So the grace of God does not come forth to rest the soul of man until the *still point* is fairly and fully reached.

Drop Thy still dews of quietness,
Till all our strivings cease:
Take from our souls the strain and stress;
And let our ordered lives confess
The beauty of Thy peace.

Breathe through the pulses of desire
Thy coolness and Thy balm;
Let sense be dumb, its beats expire:
Speak through the earthquake, wind and fire,
O still small voice of calm!

EVENING

~⁂~

Get thee out of thy country . . . unto a land that I will show thee.
(GEN. 12:1)

*I*t was one of the great moments of history when this primitive caravan set out for Haran. As we dimly picture them setting forth in the pale dawn of history, we seem to see the laden camels, pacing slowly, towering above the slow-footed sheep; we hear the drovers' cries and bleating of the flocks, broken by the wail of parting women.

With those who stay behind we strain wistful eyes across the broad flood of old Euphrates, till in the wilderness beyond, the caravan is lost in a faint dust-haze—a stain and no more on the southern horizon.

Who does not feel that the grandeur of that moment centers in *the loyalty of one human soul to one word of God?*

"There's no sense in going further—it's the edge of cultivation."
So they said and I believed it—broke my land and sowed my crop—
Built my barns and strung my fences in the little border station—
Tucked away below the foothills where the trails run out and stop.

Till a voice, as bad as conscience, rang interminable changes
On one everlasting whisper, day and night repeated so:
"Something hidden. Go and find it. Go and look behind the Ranges—
Something lost behind the Ranges, lost and waiting for you. Go!"
Anybody might have found it, but—His whisper came to me!

KIPLING

There remaineth yet very much land to be possessed! Like the western prairies, there is no limit; it extends beyond the power of the human mind. "Eye hath not seen, nor ear heard, neither have entered into the heart of man, the things which God hath prepared for them that love him" (1 Cor. 2:9).

The Holy Ghost is looking for simple-hearted believers *who will claim for Jesus Christ the great stretches of unoccupied places of darkness.*

Who will strike the Trail?

January 31
MORNING

∽∾

He giveth quietness (JOB 34:29).

Quietness amid the dash of the storm. We sail the lake with Him still; and as we reach its middle waters, far from land, under midnight skies, suddenly a great storm sweeps down. Earth and hell seem arrayed against us, and each billow threatens to overwhelm. Then He arises from His sleep, and rebukes the winds and the waves; His hand waves benediction and repose over the rage of the tempestuous elements. His voice is heard above the scream of the wind in the cordage and the conflict of the billows, "Peace, be still!" Can you not hear it? And there is instantly a great calm. "He giveth quietness." *Quietness amid the loss of inward consolations.* He sometimes withdraws these, because we make too much of them. We are tempted to look at our joy, our ecstasies, our transports, or our visions, with too great complacency. Then love for love's sake, withdraws them. But, by His grace, He leads us to distinguish between them and Himself. He draws nigh, and whispers the assurance of His presence. Thus an infinite calm comes to keep our heart and mind. "He giveth quietness."

"He giveth quietness." O Elder Brother,
Whose homeless feet have pressed our path of pain,
Whose hands have borne the burden of our sorrow,
That in our losses we might find our gain.

Of all Thy gifts and infinite consolings,
I ask but this: in every troubled hour
To hear Thy voice through all the tumults stealing,
And rest serene beneath its tranquil power.

Cares cannot fret me if my soul be dwelling
In the still air of faith's untroubled day;

Grief cannot shake me if I walk beside thee,
My hand in Thine along the darkening way.

Content to know there comes a radiant morning
When from all shadows I shall find release;
Serene to wait the rapture of its dawning—
Who can make trouble when Thou sendest peace?

EVING

EVENING

For he shall be as a tree planted by the waters. (JER. 17:8)

Trees that brave storms are not propagated in hothouses!
The staunchest tree is not found in the shelter of the forest, but out in the open where the winds from every quarter beat upon it, and bend and twist it until it becomes a giant in stature.

It requires storms to produce the rooting.

Out on the meadow it stands to shelter the herds and flocks. The earth about the tree hardens. The rains do little good for the water runs off.

But the terrific storm strikes. It twists, turns, wrenches, and at times all but tears it out of its place. If the tree could speak it might bitterly complain. Should nature listen and cease the storm process?

The storm almost bends the tree double. It is wrath now. What can such seeming cruelty mean? Is that love? But *wait!*

About the tree the soil is all loosened. Great cracks are opened up away down into the ground. Deep wounds they might appear to the inexperienced. The rain now comes in with its gentle ministry. The WOUNDS fill up. The moisture reaches away down deep even to the utmost root. The sun again shines. New and vigorous life bursts forth. The roots go deeper and deeper. The branches shoot forth. Now and again one hears something snap and crack like a pistol: it is getting too big for its clothes! It is growing into a giant! *It is rooting!*

This is the tree from which the mechanic wants his tools made—the tree which the wagon-maker seeks.

When you see a spiritual giant, think of the road over which he has traveled—not the sunny lane where wildflowers ever bloom, but a steep, rocky, narrow pathway where the blasts of hell will almost blow you off your feet, where the sharp rocks cut the feet, where the projecting thorns scratch the brow, and the venomous serpents hiss on every side.

The Lord provides deep roots
when there are to be wide-spreading branches.

God of the gallant trees
Give to us fortitude:
Give as Thou givest to these,
Valorous hardihood.
We are the trees of Thy planting, O God,
We are the trees of Thy wood.

Now let the life-sap run
Clean through our every vein,
Perfect what Thou hast begun,
God of the sun and rain.
Thou who dost measure the weight of wind,
Fit us for stress and strain!

A. W. C.

Blessed be storms!

February 1
MORNING

～∞～

This thing is from me (1 KINGS 12:24).

Life's disappointments are veiled love's appointments.

REV. C. A. FOX

My child, I have a message for you today; let me whisper it in your ear, that it may gild with glory any storm clouds which may arise, and smooth the rough places upon which you may have to tread. It is short, only five words, but let them sink into your inmost soul; use them as a pillow upon which to rest your weary head. *This thing is from ME.*

Have you ever thought of it, that all tht concerns you concerns Me too? For, "he that toucheth you, toucheth the apple of mine eye" (Zech. 2:8). You are very precious in My sight (Isa. 43:4). Therefore, it is My special delight to educate you.

I would have you learn when temptations assail you, and the "enemy comes in like a flood," that this thing is from Me, that your weakness needs My might, and your safety lies in letting Me fight for you.

Are you in difficult circumstances, surrounded by people who do not understand you, who never consult your taste, who put you in the background? This thing is from Me. I am the God of circumstances. Thou camest not to thy place by accident, it is the very place God meant for thee.

Have you not asked to be made humble? See then, I have placed you in the very school where this lesson is taught; your surroundings and companions are only working out My will.

Are you in money difficulties? Is it hard to make both ends meet? This thing is from Me, for I am your purse-bearer and would have you draw from and depend upon Me. My supplies are limitless (Phil. 4:19). I would have you prove my promises. Let it not be said of you, "In this thing ye did not believe the Lord your God" (Deut. 1:32).

Are you passing through a night of sorrow? This thing is from Me. I am the Man of Sorrows and acquainted with grief. I have let earthly comforters fail you, that by turning to Me you may obtain everlasting consolation (2 Thess. 2:16–17). Have you longed to do some great work for Me and instead have been laid aside on a bed of pain and weakness? This thing is from Me. I could not get your attention in your busy days and I want to teach you some of My deepest lessons. "They also serve who only stand and wait." Some of My greatest workers are those shut out from active service, that they may learn to wield the weapon of all-prayer.

This day I place in your hand this pot of holy oil. Make use of it free, My child. Let every circumstance that arises, every word that pains you, every interruption that would make you impatient, every revelation of your weakness be anointed with it. The sting will go as you learn to see Me in all things.

LAURA A. BARTER SNOW

"This is from Me," the Saviour said,
As bending low He kissed my brow,
"For One who loves you thus has led.
Just rest in Me, be patient now,
Your Father knows you have need of this,
Tho', why perchance you cannot see—
Grieve not for things you've seemed to miss.
The thing I send is best for thee."

Then, looking through my tears, I plead,
"Dear Lord, forgive, I did not know,
'Twill not be hard since Thou dost tread,

Each path before me here below.
And for my good this thing must be,
His grace sufficient for each test.
So still I'll sing, 'Whatever be
God's way for me is always best.' "

EVENING

Jesus knowing that the Father had given all things into his hands,
and that he was come from God, and went to God;
He riseth from supper, and laid aside his garments; and took a towel,
and girded himself. After that he poureth water into a basin,
and began to wash the disciples' feet, and to wipe them with the
towel wherewith he was girded.
(JOHN 13:3–5)

Not to sit on a lifted throne, nor to rule superbly alone; not to be ranked on the left or right in the kingdom's glory, the kingdom's might; not to be great and first of all, not to hold others in humble thrall; not to lord it over the world, a scepter high and a flag unfurled; not with authority, not with pride, vain dominion, mastery wide—nothing to wish for, nothing to do—not, in short, to be ministered to! Ah, but to minister! Lowly to sup with the servant's bread and the servant's cup; down where the waters of sorrow flow; full-baptized in the stream of woe; out where the people of sorrow are, walking brotherly, walking far; known to bitterness, known to sin, to the poor and wretched comrade and kin; so to be helper, the last and the least serf in the kingdom, slave at the feast; so to obey, and so to defer, and so, my Savior, to minister. Yes, for never am I alone: this is Thy glory and this is Thy throne. Infinite Servant, well may I be bondman and vassal and toiler—with Thee.   AMOS R. WELLS

I would be simply used,
Spending myself in humble task or great,
Priest at the altar, keeper of the gate,
So be my Lord requireth just that thing
Which at the needful moment I may bring.
O joy of serviceableness Divine!

Of merging will and work, dear Lord, in Thine,
Of knowing that results, however small,
Fitly into Thy stream of purpose fall.

I would be simply used!
ANONYMOUS

I want to be a humble soul
Commended in the sky.
JOHN SHOBER KIMBER

February 2

MORNING

~~~

In the shadow of his hand hath he hid me, and made me a polished
shaft: in his quiver hath he hid me (ISA. 49:2).

"In the shadow." We must all go there sometimes. The glare of the
daylight is too brilliant; our eyes become injured, and unable to discern the delicate shades of color, or appreciate neutral tints—the shadowed chamber of sickness, the shadowed house of mourning, the shadowed life from which the sunlight has gone.

But fear not! It is the shadow of God's hand. He is leading thee. There
are lessons that can be learned only there.

The photograph of His face can only be fixed in the dark chamber. But
do not suppose that He has cast thee aside. Thou art still in His quiver;
He has not flung thee away as a worthless thing.

He is only keeping thee close till the moment comes when He can
send thee most swiftly and surely on some errand in which He will be glorified. Oh, shadowed, solitary ones, remember how closely the quiver is
bound to the warrior, within easy reach of the hand, and guarded jeal-
ously. *FROM* CHRIST IN ISAIAH, *BY MEYER*

In some spheres the shadow condition is the condition of greatest
growth. The beautiful Indian corn never grows more rapidly than in the
shadow of a warm summer night. The sun curls the leaves in the sultry
noon light, but they quickly unfold, if a cloud slips over the sky. There
is a service in the shadow that is not in the shine. The world of stellar beauty
is never seen at its best till the shadows of night slip over the sky. There
are beauties that bloom in the shade that will not bloom in the sun. There
is much greenery in lands of fog and clouds and shadow. The florist has

"evening glories" now, as well as "morning glories." The "evening glory" will not shine in the noon's splendor, but comes to its best as the shadows of evening deepen.

If all of life were sunshine,
Our faces would be fain
To feel once more upon them
The cooling splash of rain.
HENRY VAN DYKE

EVENING

That it may bring forth more fruit. (JOHN 15:2)

Two years ago I set out a rosebush in the corner of my garden. It was to bear yellow roses. And it was to bear them profusely. Yet, during these two years, it has not produced a blossom!

I asked the florist from whom I bought the bush why it was so barren of flowers. I had cultivated it carefully; had watered it often; had made the soil around it as rich as possible. And it had grown well.

"That's just why," said the florist. "That kind of rose needs the poorest soil in the garden. Sandy soil would be best, and never a bit of fertilizer. Take away the rich soil and put gravelly earth in its place. Cut the bush back severely. Then it will bloom."

I did—and the bush blossomed forth in the most gorgeous yellow known to nature. Then I moralized: that yellow rose is just like many lives. Hardships develop beauty in the soul; the soul thrives on troubles; trials bring out all the best in them; ease and comfort and applause only leave them barren.
PASTOR JOYCE

The bark by tempest vainly tossed
May founder in the calm;
And he who braved the polar frost
Faint by the isles of balm.
WHITTIER

The finest of flowers bloom in the sandiest of deserts as well as in the hothouses. God is the same Gardener.

February 3

MORNING

∽

And immediately the spirit driveth him into the wilderness
(MARK 1:12).

It seemed a strange proof of divine favor. "Immediately." Immediately after what? After the opened heavens and the dovelike peace and voice of the Father's blessing, "Thou art my beloved Son, in whom I am well pleased." It is no abnormal experience. Thou, too, hast passed through it, O my soul. Are not the times of thy deepest depression just the moments that follow thy loftiest flight? Yesterday thou wert soaring far in the firmament, and singing in the radiance of the morn; today thy wings are folded and thy song silent. At noon thou wert basking in the sunshine of a Father's smile; at eve thou art saying in the wilderness, "My way is hid from the Lord."

Nay, but, my soul, the very suddenness of the change is a proof that it is not revolutionary.

Hast thou weighed the comfort of that word "Immediately"? Why does it come so soon after the blessing? Just to show that it is the sequel to the blessing. God shines on thee to make thee fit for life's desert-places—for its Gethsemanes, for its Calvaries. He lifts thee up that He may give thee strength to go farther down; He illuminates thee that He may send thee into the night, that He may make thee a help to the helpless.

Not at all times art thou worthy of the wilderness; thou art only worthy of the wilderness after the splendors of Jordan. Nothing but the Son's vision can fit thee for the Spirit's burden; only the glory of the baptism can support the hunger of the desert.　　**GEORGE MATHESON**

After benediction comes battle.

The time of testing that marks and mightily enriches a soul's spiritual career is no ordinary one, but a period when all hell seems let loose, a period when we realize our souls are brought into a net, when we know that God is permitting us to be in the Devil's hand. But it is a period which always ends in certain triumph for those who have committed the keeping of their souls to Him, a period of marvelous "nevertheless afterward" of abundant usefulness, the sixty-fold that surely follows.

APHRA WHITE

EVENING

❧

And the chief priests accused him of many things.
And Pilate again asked him, saying, Answerest thou nothing? behold
how many things they accuse thee of. But Jesus no more answered
anything; insomuch that Pilate marvelled.
(MARK 15:3–5 ASV)

*T*he apostle writes years afterwards of this wonderful silence of the
God-man:

"Who, when he was reviled, reviled not again;
when he suffered, he threatened not" (1 PETER 2:23).

His silence was Divine. No mere human could thus remain dumb, and
innocent and guiltless allow Himself to be "led as a lamb to the slaughter," to be as a sheep dumb in the hand of the shearers. This silence before
Pilate, and then the silence on the Cross in the midst of untold agony—
silence, broken only seven times, with brief words of wondrous meaning—this silence of Jesus was the climax to a life of God-like silence in circumstances when men must speak; a life of silent waiting until He was
thirty years of age ere He entered on public ministry, and made His lamb-
like way to the Cross; a life of silence over glory unspeakable with His
Father, and suffering untold at the hands of men; of tender silence over
blessing to others, and over Judas' traitor path.

This is the pattern for all who would *follow His steps;* the pattern for
the one who would walk as He walked, by His walking again in them.
And how can it be? Only by seeing the *calling* and accepting it (1 Peter
1:15). And by taking His Cross as *our* Cross, "we having died" *in* Him
and *with* Him can thus live unto God, and then the silence of Jesus can
be known in truth, and we shall be:

SILENT in our lowly service among others, not seeking to be seen of men.
SILENT over the glory of the hours on the Mount, lest others think of us above
    that which is written.
SILENT over the depths of the Calvary pathway that led us unto God.
SILENT over the human instruments permitted of God to hand us over to the
    judgment hall, and the forsaking of our nearest and our dearest.
SILENT whilst we stoop to serve the very ones who have betrayed us.
SILENT over the deep things of God revealed in the secret places of the Most
    High, *impossible to utter* to those who have not yet been *baptized* with
    that baptism without which they will be *straightened* in spiritual percep-
    tion *until it be accomplished.*

SILENT over questions only to be answered by God, the Holy Ghost, when *that day* dawns for the questioning heart, and silences all doubt by the glorious revelation of Him who is the answer to all our needs.

SILENT when forced by others to some position where apparent rivalry with another much-used servant of God seems imminent, only to be hushed by utter self-effacement, and our silent withdrawal without explanation, *irrespective of our rights.*

SILENT—yea, silent in the judgment hall of our co-religionists, when criticized and falsely accused of many things.

TRACT

Live Thou this life in me.

February 4

MORNING

I will cause thee to ride upon the high places of the earth
(ISA. 58:14).

Those who fly through the air in airships tell us that one of the first rules they learn is to turn their ship toward the wind, and fly against it. The wind lifts the ship up to higher heights. Where did they learn that? They learned it from the birds. If a bird is flying for pleasure, it goes with the wind. But if the bird meets danger, it turns right around and faces the wind, in order that it may rise higher; and it flies away toward the very sun.

Sufferings are God's winds, His contrary winds, sometimes His strong winds. They are God's hurricanes, but they take human life and lift it to higher levels and toward God's heavens.

You have seen in the summertime a day when the atmosphere was so oppressive that you could hardly breathe? But a cloud appeared on the western horizon and that cloud grew larger and threw out rich blessing for the world. The storm rose, lightning flashed and thunder pealed. The storm covered the world, and the atmosphere was cleansed; new life was in the air, and the world was changed.

Human life is worked out according to exactly the same principle. When the storm breaks, the atmosphere is changed, clarified, filled with new life; and a part of heaven is brought down to earth. SELECTED

Obstacles ought to set us singing. The wind finds voice, not when rushing across the open sea, but when hindered by the outstretched arms of the pine trees, or broken by the fine strings of an aeolian harp. Then it has songs of power and beauty. Set your freed soul sweeping across the obstacles of life, through grim forests of pain, against even the tiny hindrances and frets that love uses, and it, too, will find its singing voice.

SELECTED

Be like a bird that, halting in its flight,
Rests on a bough too slight.
And feeling it give way beneath him sings,
Knowing he hath wings.

EVENING

We had the sentence of death in ourselves,
that we should not trust in ourselves. (2 COR. 1:9)

These are weighty words for all Christ's servants; but we must be His servants *in reality,* in order to enter into their deep significance. If we are content to live a life of indolence and ease, a life of self-seeking and self-pleasing, it is impossible for us to understand such words, or indeed to enter into any of those intense exercises of soul through which Christ's true-hearted servants and faithful witnesses, in all ages, have been called to pass.

We find, invariably, that all those who have been most used of God in public have gone through deep waters in secret. Paul could say to the Corinthians, *"Death worketh in us, but life in you."* Death working in the poor earthen vessel; but streams of life, heavenly grace, and spiritual power flowing into those to whom he ministered.

How the professing church has departed from the Divine reality of ministry! Where are the Pauls, the Gideons, and the Joshuas? Where are the deep heart-searchings and profound soul exercises which have characterized Christ's servants in other days? Flippant, worldly, shallow, empty, self-sufficient and self-indulgent are we! *Need we wonder at the small results?*

How can we expect to see life working in others, when we know so little about death working in us?

May the eternal Spirit stir us all up! May He work in us a more powerful sense of what it is to be *true-hearted, single-eyed, devoted servants of the Lord Jesus Christ!*

From prayer that asks that I may be
Sheltered from winds that beat on Thee,
From fearing when I should aspire,
From faltering when I should climb higher,
From silken self, O Captain, free
Thy soldier who would follow Thee.

From subtle love of softening things,
From easy choices, weakenings,
(Not thus are spirits fortified,
Not this way went the Crucified)
From all that dims Thy Calvary
O Lamb of God, deliver me.

Give me the love that leads the way,
The faith that nothing can dismay,
The hope no disappointments tire,
The passion that will burn like fire;
Let me not sink to be a clod:
Make me Thy fuel, Flame of God.

AMY WILSON CARMICHAEL

Write the death sentence upon self, that the power of resurrection life in
Christ may shine forth!

February 5

MORNING

❧❧

Ye shall not go out with haste (ISA. 52:12).

I do not believe that we have begun to understand the marvelous power there is in stillness. We are in such a hurry—we must be doing—so that we are in danger of not giving God a chance to work. You may depend upon it; God never says to us, "Stand still," or "Sit still," or "Be still," unless *He* is going to do something.

This is our trouble in regard to our Christian life; *we* want to do something to be Christians when we need to let *Him* work in us. Do you know how still you have to be when your likeness is being taken?

Now God has one eternal purpose concerning us, and that is that we should be like His Son; and in order that this may be so, we must be passive. We hear so much about activity, maybe we need to know what it is to be quiet. *FROM* CRUMBS

Sit still, my daughter! Just sit calmly still!
Nor deem these days—these waiting days—as ill!
The One who loves thee best, who plans thy way,
Hath not forgotten thy great need today!
And, if He waits, 'tis sure He waits to prove
To thee, His tender child, His heart's deep love.

Sit still, my daughter! Just sit calmly still!
Thou longest much to know thy dear Lord's will!
While anxious thoughts would almost steal their way
Corrodingly within, because of His delay—
Persuade thyself in simple faith to rest
That He, who knows and loves, will do the best.

Sit still, my daughter! Just sit calmly still!
Nor move one step, not even one, until
His way hath opened. Then, ah then, how sweet!
How glad thy heart, and then how swift thy feet
Thy inner being then, ah then, how strong!
And waiting days not counted then too long.

Sit still, my daughter! Just sit calmly still!
What higher service could'st thou for Him fill?
'Tis hard! ah yes! But choicest things must cost!
For lack of losing all how much is lost!
'Tis hard, 'tis true! But then—He giveth grace
To count the hardest spot the sweetest place.

J. DANSON SMITH

EVENING

Hezekiah went up unto the house of the LORD, and spread it before the LORD. (ISA. 37:14)

Does it not often happen that you are in great difficulty how to act in some particular case? Your course is not plain; your way is not open: each side seems equally balanced, and you cannot tell which to choose.

Your wishes, perhaps, point one way; your fears, another. You are afraid lest you should decide wrongly; lest you should take what, in the end, may prove hurtful to you.

It is very trying to be brought into this painful conflict. And it adds to our distress if we are forced to go forward at once, and take one course or the other. Shall I tell you how you may be sure to find unspeakable relief?

Go and lay your matter before the Lord, as Hezekiah did with the king of Assyria's letter. Do not, however, deceive yourself, as many do, and seek counsel of God, *having determined to act according to your own will, and not according to His.* But, simply and honestly, ask that He would guide you. Commit your case to your Father in heaven; surrender yourself as a little child to be led as He pleases. This is the way to be guided aright, and to realize the blessing of having a heavenly Counselor.

A. OXENDEN

"Confide all your works to the Lord, and He will arrange for all your plans" (PROV. 16:3 FENTON'S TRANS.).

Surrendered—led alone by Thee,
And wait Thy guidance still.

February 6

MORNING

He turned the sea into dry land; they went through the flood on foot: there did we rejoice in him (PS. 66:6).

It is a striking assertion, "through *the floods*" (the place where we might have expected nothing but trembling and terror, anguish and dismay), "there," says the psalmist, "did we rejoice in him!"

How many there are who can endorse this as their experience: that "there," in their very seasons of distress and sadness, they have been enabled, as they never did before, to triumph and rejoice.

How near their God in covenant is brought! How brightly shine His promises! In the day of our prosperity we cannot see the brilliancy of these. Like the sun at noon, hiding out the stars from sight, they are indiscernible; but when night overtakes, the deep, dark night of sorrow, out come these clustering stars—blessed constellations of Bible hope and promise of consolation.

Like Jacob at Jabbok, it is when our earthly sun goes down that the Divine Angel comes forth, and we wrestle with Him and prevail.

It was at night, "in the evening," Aaron lit the sanctuary lamps. It is in the night of trouble the brightest lamps of the believer are often kindled.

It was in his loneliness and exile John had the glorious vision of his Redeemer. There is many a Patmos still in the world, whose brightest remembrances are those of God's presence and upholding grace and love in solitude and sadness.

How many pilgrims, still passing through these Red Seas and Jordans of earthly affliction, will be enable in the retrospect of eternity to say— full of the memories of God's great goodness—"We went through the flood on foot, *there*—there, in these dark experiences, with the surging waves on every side, deep calling to deep, Jordan, as when Israel crossed it, in 'the time of the overflowing' (flood), yet, *'there did* we rejoice in Him!' "

DR. MACDUFF

"And I will give her her vineyards from thence, and the valley of Achor for a door of hope: and she shall sing THERE" (HOS. 2:15).

EVENING

❧

If thou canst believe, all things are possible to him that believeth.
(MARK 9:23)

Prayer takes the people to the Bank of Faith, and obtains the golden blessing. Mind how you pray! Pray! Make real business of it! Never let it be a dead formality! People pray a long time, but do not get what they are supposed to ask for, *because they do not plead the promise in a truthful businesslike way.* If you were to go into a bank and stand an hour talking to the clerk, and then come out again without your cash, what would be the good of it?

CHARLES H. SPURGEON

Have you ever given God the chance to answer the Prayer of Faith? Do not let us lose our last chance of believing by waiting till the dawn has broken into day!

LILIAS TROTTER

If radio's slim finger can pluck a melody
From night, and toss it over a continent or sea;

If the petaled white notes of a violin
Are blown across a mountain or a city's din;
If songs, like crimson roses, are culled from thin blue air—
Why should mortals wonder if God hears prayer?
ETHEL ROMIG FULLER

When all things can be accomplished by prayer, why not yield to the test?
Why not pray on? And through?

February 7

MORNING

Why are thos cast down, O my soul? (PS 43:5).

Is there ever any ground to be cast down? There are two reasons, but only two. If we are as yet unconverted, we have ground to be cast down; or if we have been converted and live in sin, then we are rightly cast down.

But except for these two things there is no ground to be cast down, for all else may be brought before God in prayer with supplication and thanksgiving. And regarding all our necessities, all our difficulties, all our trials, we may exercise faith in the power of God, and in the love of God.

"Hope thou in God." Oh, remember this: There is never a time when we may not hope in God. Whatever our necessities, however, great our difficulties, and though to all appearance help is impossible, yet our business is to hope in God, and it will be found that it is not in vain. In the Lord's own time help will come.

Oh, the hundreds, yea, the thousands of times that I have found it thus within the past seventy years and four months!

When it seemed impossible that help could come, help did come; for God has His own resources. He is not confined. In ten thousand different ways, and at ten thousand different times God may help us.

Our business is to spread our cases before the Lord, in childlike simplicity to pour out all our heart before God, saying "I do not deserve that Thou shouldst hear me and answer my requests, but for the sake of my precious Lord Jesus; for His sake answer my prayer, and give me grace quietly to wait till it please Thee to answer my prayer. For I believe Thou wilt do it in Thine own time and way."

"For I shall yet prasise him." More prayer, more exercise of faith, more patient waiting, and the result will be blessing, abundant blessing. Thus I have found it many hundreds of times, and therefore I continually say to myself, *"Hope thou in God."*   GEORGE MUELLER

EVENING

～⁓

Before they call, I will answer; and while they are yet speaking, I will hear. (ISA. 65:24)

*I*n one of his great Gospel campaigns in Chicago, Moody asked his helpers to join him in prayer for $6,000 and to ask that it *might be sent at once.* They prayed long and earnestly, and before they rose from their knees a telegram was brought in. It was in some such words as these:

Your friends at Northfield had a feeling that you needed money for your work in Chicago. We have taken up a collection and there are $6,000 in the baskets.

"God had prepared the people" (2 CHRON. 29:36).

In connection with the work of the West London Mission, the Rev. Hugh Price Hughes and his colleagues once found themselves in pressing need of £1,000, and to get quiet they met at midnight to pray for it. After some time of pleading, one of the number burst into praise, being assured that the prayer had been heard and would be answered. Mr. Hughes did not share this absolute confidence. He believed with trembling.

When the day came for announcing the sum received, it was found that £990 had come in within a very short time and in very extraordinary ways—but there was the deficiency of £10. When Mr. Hughes went home he found a letter which he now remembered had been there in the morning, but through pressure he had left it unopened. It contained a check for £10!

I'll trust Thy grace—'tis infinite;
And knows no bound, nor end.

After Dan Crawford had passed to his eternal rest, it was written of him: "He lived (and his work was supported) by strong faith in the unlimited riches of God, and in the power of prayer. He felt, too, *that those riches and that power were available for all Africa, though he knew that not all had the same faith."*

He had a strong sense of unity of God's work. A certain missionary in

Africa, held up in some work for God, wrote to Dan Crawford asking for £100, and excused himself by saying, "You are rich." When he saw that the same weekly mail that had brought the request had brought also contributions amounting to about the sum mentioned, Dan Crawford sent the whole week's income to his correspondent with this reply: "Rich? Yes, I am rich—rich in faith for you all."

"And God is able to give you an overflowing measure of all good gifts, that all your wants of every kind may be supplied at all times, and you may give of your abundance to every good work."

He might have doled His blossoms out quite grudgingly,
God might have used His sunset gold so sparingly,
He might have put but one wee star in all the sky—
But since He gave so lavishly, why should not I?
A. C. H.

February 8
MORNING

❧

Lo, I am with you all the appointed days
(MATT. 28:20, VARIORUM VERSION).

Do not look forward to the changes and chances of this life in fear. Rather look at them with full hope that, as they arise, God, whose you are, will deliver you out of them. He has kept you hitherto; do you but hold fast to His dear hand, and He will lead you safely through all things; and when you cannot stand, He will bear you in His arms.

Do not look forward to what may happen tomorrow. The same everlasting Father who cares for you today will take care of you tomorrow, and every day. Either He will shield you from suffering, or He will give you unfailing strength to bear it. Be at peace, then, put aside all anxious thoughts and imaginations. FRANCES DE SALES

The Lord is my shepherd.

Not was, not may be, nor will be. "The Lord is my shepherd," is on Sunday, is on Monday, and is through every day of the week; is in January, is in December, and every month of the year; is at home, and is in China; is in peace, and is in war; in abundance, and in penury.

J. HUDSON TAYLOR

HE will silently plan for thee,
Object thou of omniscient care;
God Himself undertakes to be
Thy Pilot through each subtle snare.

He WILL silently plan for thee,
So certainly, He cannot fail!
Rest on the faithfulness of God,
In Him thou surely shalt prevail.

He will SILENTLY plan for thee
Some wonderful surprise of love.
Eye hath not seen, nor ear hath heard,
But it is kept for thee above.

He will silently PLAN for thee,
His purposes shall all unfold;
The tangled skein shall shine at last,
A masterpiece of skill untold.

He will silently plan FOR THEE,
Happy child of a Father's care,
As thou no other claimed His love,
But thou alone to Him wert dear.

E. MARY GRIMES

Whatever our faith says God is, He will be.

EVING

EVENING

And there came thither [to Lystra] certain Jews . . . who persuaded the people, and, having stoned Paul, drew him out of the city supposing he had been dead. . . . The next day he departed . . . to Derbe. And when they had preached the gospel to that city . . . they returned again to Lystra. (ACTS 14:19–21)

The cruel stones unerring fell upon him—
Until they deemed his bleeding form was dead;

His worth and work they knew not, and they cared not;
Enough, they madly hated what he said.

God touched him! and he rose, with new life given;
Nor in his bosom burned resentful pain;
And, by and by, when need and call both guided,
He to the stoning-place RETURNED AGAIN.

Perchance thou, too, hast tasted cruel stoning—
And might'st be glad if call came ne'er again
To turn to scenes where surely there awaits thee
The cruel, cutting stones which make life vain.

Yet, if "back to the stones" the Finger pointeth,
Then thou shalt know there is no better way;
And there, just there, shall matchless grace await thee,
And God Himself shall be thy strength and stay.
                    J. DANSON SMITH

The most sublime moments lie very close to the most painful situations.
Are we familiar with the road that leads back to the stones?

February 9

MORNING

∽∾

He answered her not a word (MATT. 15:23).

He will rest in his love (ZEPH. 3:17).

*I*t may be a child of God is reading these words who has had some great crushing sorrow, some bitter disappointment, some heartbreaking blow from a totally unexpected quarter. You are longing for your Master's voice bidding you, "Be of good cheer," but only silence and a sense of mystery and misery meet you—"He answered her not a word."

God's tender heart must often ache listening to all the sad, complaining cries which arise from our weak, impatient hearts, because we do not see that for our own sakes He answers not at all or otherwise than seems best to our tear-blinded, shortsighted eyes.

The silences of Jesus are as eloquent as His speech and may be a sign, not of His disapproval, but of His approval and of a deep purpose of blessing for you.

"Why art thou cast down, O . . . soul?" Thou shalt yet praise Him, yes, even for His silence. Listen to an old and beautiful story of how one Christian dreamed that she saw three others at prayer. As they knelt the Master drew near to them.

As He approached the first of the three, He bent over her in tenderness and grace, with smiles full of radiant love and spoke to her in accents of purest, sweetest music.

Leaving her, He came to the next, but only placed His hand upon her bowed head, and gave her one look of loving approval.

The third woman He passed almost abruptly without stopping for a word or glance. The woman in her dream said to herself, "How greatly He must love the first one, to the second He gave His approval, but none of the special demonstrations of love He gave the first; and the third must have grieved Him deeply, for He gave her no word at all and not even a passing look.

"I wonder what she has done, and why He made so much difference between them?" As she tried to account for the action of her Lord, He Himself stood by her and said: "O woman! how wrongly hast thou interpreted Me. The first kneeling woman needs all the weight of My tenderness and care to keep her feet in My narrow way. She needs My love, thought, and help every moment of the day. Without it she would fail and fall.

"The second has stronger faith and deeper love, and I can trust her to trust Me however things may go and whatever people do.

"The third, whom I seemed not to notice, and even to neglect has faith and love of the finest quality, and her I am training by quick and drastic processes for the highest and holiest service.

"She knows Me so intimately, and trusts Me so utterly, that she is independent of words or looks or any outward intimation of My approval. She is not dismayed nor discouraged by any circumstances through which I arrange that she shall pass; she trusts Me when sense and reason and every finer instinct of the natural heart would rebel—because she knows that I am working in her for eternity, and that what I do, though she knows not the explanation now, she will understand hereafter.

"I am silent in My love because I love beyond the power of words to express, or of human hearts to understand, and also for your sakes that you may learn to love and trust Me in Spirit-taught, spontaneous response to My love, without the spur of anything outward to call it forth."

He "will do marvels" if you will learn the mystery of His silence, and praise Him, for every time He withdraws His gifts that you may better know and love the Giver.

SELECTED

EVENING

God led them not through the way of the . . .
Philistines, although that was near. (EX. 13:17)

Why not? Because the people needed disciplining and molding as a Nation. They would have been destroyed by way of Philistia, but by the way of the wilderness they were trained slowly for the great task at their journey's end. God, who chose the route, also chose the leader. God, who disciplined the people, also disciplined the man who led them.

History and experience seem to point to the fact that God's line for us is not usually a straight line, but a winding zigzag path.

The roundabout way may be the nearest!

JOSEPH PARKER

Over the Apennines there is a wonderful railroad—one passes through forty-three tunnels in less than seventy miles—magnificent outlooks, but every few minutes, a tunnel! The road has been built to carry the traveler to his destination by the shortest way; anyone getting off at the first station simply because he did not like tunnels, and striking into the mountains to find another path, would be almost sure of being lost and starving to death.

Can we not believe the same thing of God's way? His way lies through tunnels—long ones often, but it is the best and safest road. And it is not all tunnels; in the region of the high rocks there are most glorious prospects! Places so full of beauty, and commanding such outlooks of love and mercy, as ought to reconcile us to the intervals of darkness.

Be not afraid of the *winding way* if God turns you into it.

Travel the road He points out to you!

God brings men to His consummations *only by His own road.*

We climbed the height by the zigzag path
And wondered why—until
We understood it was made zigzag
To break the force of the hill.

A road straight up would prove too steep
For the traveler's feet to tread;
The thought was kind in its wise design
Of a zigzag path instead.

It is often so in our daily life;
We fail to understand
That the twisting way our feet must tread
By love alone was planned.

Then murmur not at the winding way,
It is our Father's will
To lead us Home by the zigzag path,
To break the force of the hill.
ANONYMOUS

Simply following God is the true philosophy of life.

February 10

MORNING

Dearly beloved, avenge not yourselves (ROM. 12:19).

There are seasons when to be *still* demands immeasurably higher strength than to act. Composure is often the highest result of power. To the vilest and most deadly charges Jesus responded with deep, unbroken silence, such as excited the wonder of the judge and the spectators. To the grossest insults, the most violent ill-treatment and mockery that might well bring indignation into the feeblest heart, He responded with voiceless, complacent calmness. Those who are unjustly accused, and causelessly ill-treated know what tremendous strength is necessary to keep silence to God.

Men may misjudge thy aim,
Think they have cause to blame,
Say, thou art wrong;
Keep on thy quiet way,
Christ is the Judge, not they,
Fear not, be strong.

Saint Paul said, "None of these things move me."

He did not say, none of these things *hurt* me. It is one thing to be hurt, and quite another to be moved. Saint Paul had a very tender heart. We do not read of any apostle who cried as Saint Paul did. It takes a strong man to cry. Jesus wept, and He was the manliest Man that ever lived. So it does not say, none of these things hurt me. But the apostle had determined not to move from what he believed was right. He did not count as we are apt to count; he did not care for ease; he did not care for this mortal life. He cared for only one thing, and that was to be loyal to Christ, to have His smile. To Saint Paul, more than to any other man, His work was wages, His smile was heaven.   MARGARET BOTTOME

EVENING

The angel of the LORD encampeth round about them that fear him, and delivereth them. (PS. 34:7)

A wonderful story is told by a Moravian missionary in connection with angelic protection.

An American missionary and his wife bravely went to their station, where, twenty years before, two missionaries had been killed and eaten by the natives. They said as they took up their work it seemed as if often they were surrounded not only by the hostile natives, but by the very powers of darkness. These latter were so real, that night after night they were forced to get up and strengthen their hearts by reading the Word of God. Again, they would pray.

One day a man came and said, "I would like to see your watchmen close at hand."

The missionary replied: "I have no watchmen; I have only a cook and a little herd boy. What watchmen do you mean?"

The man asked permission to look through the missionaries' home. Every corner of the house was carefully searched, and the man came out of the house greatly disappointed.

Then the missionary asked the man to tell him about the watchmen to whom he referred. Here is the man's answer.

"When you and your wife came here we determined to kill you as we did the missionaries twenty years ago. Night after night we came to carry out our intentions, but *there always stood around your house a double row of watchmen with glittering weapons, and we dared not come near.* At last we hired a professional assassin, who said he feared neither God nor devil. Last night he came close to your house—we followed at a distance—brandishing his spear. *There stood the shining watchmen,* and the killer fled in terror. So we have given up our purpose to kill you, but tell me, *who are the watchmen?"*

The missionary opened the Word of God and read: *"The angel of the* LORD *encampeth round about them that fear him, and delivereth them."*

"The beloved of the LORD *shall dwell in safety by him"*
(DEUT. 33:12).

"The LORD *hid them"* (JER. 36:26).

February 11
MORNING

As soon as the soles of the feet of the priests . . . shall rest in the waters . . . the waters . . . shall be cut off (JOSH. 3:13).

The people were not to wait in their camps until the way was opened, they were to walk by faith. They were to break camp, pack up their goods, form in line to march, and move down to the very banks before the river would be opened.

If they had come down to the edge of the river and then had stopped for the stream to divide before they stepped into it, they would have waited in vain. They must take one step into the water before the river would be cut off.

We must learn to take God at His Word, and go straight on in duty, although we see no way in which we can go forward. The reason we are so often balked by difficulties is that we expect to see them removed before we try to pass through them.

If we would move straight on in faith, the path would be opened for us. We stand still, waiting for the obstacle to be removed, when we ought to go forward as if there were no obstacles.

FROM EVENING THOUGHTS

What a lesson of perseverance Columbus gave to the world in the face of tremendous difficulties!

Behind him lay the gray Azores,
Behind the gates of Hercules;
Before him not the ghost of shores,
Before him only shoreless seas,
The good Mate said: "Now we must pray,
For lo! the very stars are gone.
Brave Admiral, speak, what shall I say?"
"Why, say, 'Sail on! sail on! and on!' "

"My men grow mutinous day by day;
My men grow ghastly wan and weak!"
The stout Mate thought of home; a spray
Of salt wave washed his swarthy cheek.
"What shall I say, brave Admiral, say,
If we sight naught but seas at dawn?"
"Why, you shall say at break of day,
'Sail on! sail on! sail on! and on!' "

They sailed. They sailed. Then spake the Mate:
"This mad sea shows its teeth tonight.
He curls his lip, he lies in wait,
With lifted teeth, as if to bite!
Brave Admiral, say but one good word;
What shall we do when hope is gone?"
The words leapt like a leaping sword:
"Sail on! sail on! sail on! and on!"

Then, pale and worn, he kept his deck
And peered through darkness. Ah! that night
Of all dark nights! And then a speck—
A light! A light! A light! A light!
It grew, a starlit flag unfurled!
It grew to be Time's burst of dawn.
He gained a world; he gave that world
Its grandest lesson: "On! sail on!"

JOAQUIN MILLER

Faith that goes forward triumphs.

~∾~

He mounts me upon high places, that I may conquer by song.
(HAB. 3:19, TRANS.)

𝒥n "Marble Faun," Miriam, the brokenhearted singer, puts into a burst of song the pent-up grief of her soul. This was better, surely, than if she had let forth a wild shriek of pain.

It is nobler to sing a victorious song in time of trial than to lie crushed in grief. Songs bless the world more than wails. It is better for our own heart, too, to put our sorrows and pains into songs. *"We shall conquer by song."*

"Our minister is a skylark Christian," boasted one of his people. Fine bird! It sings morning, noon, and evening; sings as it springs from the flowery sod; sings when the ground is white with snow. What a song, too!—a shower of melody and infinite sweetness—*with no undertone of pain.*

If we could only realize the full truth and blessedness of our faith we should continually go up and down singing, until one fine day we would go up singing—up, up, beyond the sun—and come down no more, lost in the eternal light!

Help me to make of all my sorrows music for the world!

> *Turn your troubles into treasure,*
> *Turn your sorrows into song;*
> *Then all men will know the measure,*
> *In which you to Christ belong.*
> *When they see your bright behavior*
> *Under provocation great,*
> *They may ask what mighty Savior*
> *Can impart that happy state.*
>
> *Paul and Silas in the prison,*
> *With their feet fast in the stocks,*
> *Praised their glorious Lord, arisen,*
> *Till the earthquake rent the rocks.*
> *There was none to join their singing,*
> *So the earthquake roared "Amen!"*
> *And glad chains fell down a-ringing,*
> *As their voices rang again!*
>
> *Oh, then sing with us His praises*
> *When there seems least cause to praise;*

Faith the sweetest anthem raises
When the darkness hides God's ways;
He brings forth His "new creation"
Only there where ends "the old."
Let us praise Him for salvation,
When all feels most dead and cold.

My soul, keep up thy singing,
Turn thy sorrows into song.
ARTHUR S. BOOTH-CLIBBORN

Let every sigh be changed into a Hallelujah!
OTTO STOCKMAYER

"None might enter into the king's gate clothed with sackcloth."

February 12

MORNING

Your heavenly Father knoweth (MATT. 6:32).

A visitor at a school for the deaf and dumb was writing questions on the blackboard for the children. By and by he wrote this sentence: "Why has God made me hear and speak, and made you deaf and dumb?"

The awful sentence fell upon the little ones like a fierce blow in the face. They sat palsied before that dreadful "Why?" And then a little girl arose.

Her lip was trembling. Her eyes were swimming with tears. Straight to the board she walked, and, picking up the crayon, wrote with firm hand these precious words: *"Even so, Father, for so it seemed good in thy sight!"* What a reply! It reaches up and lays hold of an eternal truth upon which the maturest believer as well as the youngest child of God may alike securely rest—the truth that God is your Father.

Do you mean that? Do you really and fully believe that? When you do, then your dove of faith will no longer wander in weary unrest, but will settle down forever in its eternal resting place of peace. "Your Father!"

I can still believe that a day comes for all of use, however far off it may be, when we shall understand; when these tragedies that now blacken and darken the very air of heaven for us, will sink into their places in a scheme so august, so magnificent, so joyful, that we shall laugh for wonder and delight.   ARTHUR CHRISTOPHER BACON

> *No chance hath brought this ill to me;*
> *'Tis God's own hand, so let it be,*
> *He seeth what I cannot see.*
> *There is a need-be for each pain,*
> *And He one day will make it plain*
> *That earthly loss is heavenly gain.*
> *Like as a piece of tapestry*
> *Viewed from the back appears to be*
> *Naught but threads tangled hopelessly;*
> *But in the front a picture fair*
> *Rewards the worker for his care,*
> *Proving his skill and patience rare.*
> *Thou art the Workman, I the frame.*
> *Lord, for the glory of Thy Name,*
> *Perfect Thine image on the same.*
>   **SELECTED**

EVENING

For thou art my lamp, O LORD: and the LORD will lighten my darkness. (2 SAM. 22:29).

There are times when a Christian needs to lie still, when our only safety is doing nothing. The voice of our Savior-God is heard beside many a Red-Sea difficulty—"*Stand still,* and *see* the salvation of the LORD." It is a hard thing to "stand still" in the presence of opposing forces. Jehovah is the *Living God.* Cloud and storm are beneath His feet and His throne remains unmoved.

"Am I in the dark?" asks Charles H. Spurgeon. "Then Thou, O Lord, 'will lighten my darkness.' Before long things will change. Affairs may grow worse and more dreary, and cloud upon cloud may be piled upon cloud; but if it grows so dark that I cannot see my own hand, I shall see the Hand of the Lord."

When I cannot find a light within me, or among my friends, or in the whole world, the Lord who said, "Let there be light" and there was light, can say the same thing again. He will speak me into sunshine yet. The day is already breaking. This sweet text shines like a morning star: "For thou art my lamp, O LORD: and the LORD will lighten my darkness."

Clouds pass; stars remain!

My lamp is shattered, I'm deprived of light; my lamp is shattered, and so dark the night. My lamp is shattered,
yet to my glad sight—a star shines on.
My lamp is shattered, but a star shines bright, and by its glowing I can wend aright. My lamp is shattered, but I still can fight—
for a star shines on.
My lamp is shattered, sad indeed my plight. My lamp is shattered,
yet I'll reach the height—for a star shines on!
WILHELMINA STITCH

February 13

MORNING

❧

The hill country shall be thine (JOSH. 17:18 RV).

There is always room higher up. When the valleys are full of Canaanites, whose iron chariots withstand your progress, get up into the hills, occupy the upper spaces. If you can no longer work for God, pray for those who can. If you cannot move earth by your speech, you may move heaven. If the development of life on the lower slopes is impossible, through limitations of service, the necessity of maintaining others, and suchlike restrictions, let it break out toward the unseen, the eternal, the divine.

Faith can fell forests. Even if the tribes had realized what treasures lay above them, they would hardly have dared to suppose it possible to rid the hills of their dense forest growth. But as God indicated their task, He reminded them that they had power enough. The visions of things that seem impossible are presented to us, like these forest-covered steeps, not to mock us, but to incite us to spiritual exploits which would be impossible unless God had stored within us the great strength of His own indwelling.

Difficulty is sent to reveal to us what God can do in answer to the faith that prays and works. Are you straitened in the valleys? Get away to the hills, live there; get honey out of the rock, and wealth out of the terraced slopes now hidden by forest.

FROM DAILY DEVOTIONAL COMMENTARY

Got any rivers they say are uncrossable,
Got any mountains they say "can't tunnel through"?
We specialize in the wholly impossible,
Doing the things they say you can't do.
SONG OF THE PANAMA BUILDERS

EVENING

And the kine took the straight way . . . and went along the highway,
lowing as they went, and turned not aside to the right hand
or to the left. (1 SAM. 6:12)

There was another yoke upon those kine that day than the yoke of wood fashioned by the hands of Philistines: they were constrained of God. It was that that made them patient and willing to walk together; that, too, made them choose the new road. Born and stalled in Ekron, familiar with the field and the manger, they herded off to Beth-shemesh, along the road they had never been before.

Why did they do it? *It was God.*

And as surely it is God when men choose the new way and walk along the road to the heavenly kingdom. They are *apprehended of Christ,* and not only *born* of the Spirit, but *borne* of the Spirit. *Men moved of God have a new instinct.*

Nature would have sent those kine back to their calves; but something has been known to make a man forsake father and mother, renounce life or a love dearer than life, for the Kingdom of God. And

Whoso hath felt the Spirit of the Highest
Cannot confound Him, or doubt Him, or deny.

It means pain. Christ's martyrs, living or dying, though they rejoice to follow in His steps, are not insensible.

The kine went, *lowing as they went.* That was part of the proof; they had not forgotten their calves although they had forsaken them. Every low of the kine was a witness for God; and God who asks His people to sacrifice for His sake does not chide us because we feel it.

The reward of sacrifice is a call to sacrifice still more complete. The Lord never pays spiritual service in earthly currency. The impulse that carried the kine to the destined country led them to pause beside the stone that became an altar. The happy reapers of Beth-shemesh welcomed the Ark, *but the kine who under God's hand had brought it to them were not feasted and garlanded.*

"They clave the wood of the cart, and offered the kine a burnt offering unto the LORD." So the service was followed by sacrifice, and the story is in the Book to make us glad when, our active life a thing of the past, we can still render ourselves unto God in a great renunciation.

GOD'S HIGHWAY

Measure all by the Cross!

February 14
MORNING

And again I say, Rejoice (PHIL. 4:4).

It is a good thing to rejoice in the Lord. Perhaps you have tried this, and the first time seemed to fail. Never mind, keep right on and when you cannot *feel* any joy, when there is no spring, and no seeming comfort and encouragement, still rejoice, and *count it all joy.* Even when you fall into diverse temptations, reckon it joy and delight and God will make your reckoning good. Do you suppose your Father will let you carry the banner of His victory and His gladness on to the front of the battle, and then coolly stand back and see you captured or beaten back by the enemy? NEVER! The Holy Spirit will sustain you in your bold advance, and fill your heart with gladness and praise, and you will find your heart all exhilarated and refreshed by the fullness within. Lord teach me to rejoice in Thee, and to "rejoice evermore." SELECTED

The weakest saint may Satan rout,
Who meets him with a praiseful shout.

"Be filled with the Spirit, . . . singing and making melody in your heart to the Lord" (EPH. 5:18–19).

Here the apostle urges the use of singing as one of the inspiring helps in the spiritual life. He counsels his readers not to seek their stimulus through the body, but through the spirit; not by the quickening of the flesh, but by the exaltation of the soul.

Sometimes a light surprises
The Christian while he sings.

Let us sing even when we do not feel like it, for thus we may give wings to leaden feet and turn weariness into strength.
J. H. JOWETT

"At midnight Paul and Silas prayed, and sang praises unto God: and the prisoners heard them" (ACTS 16:25).

Oh, Paul, thou wondrous example to the flock, who could thus glory, bearing in the body as thou didst "the marks of the Lord Jesus"! Marks from the stoning almost to the death, from thrice beating with rods, from those hundred and ninety-five stripes laid on thee by the Jews, and from stripes received in that Philippian jail, which had they not drawn blood would not have called for washing! Surely the grace which enabled thee to sing praises under such suffering is all-sufficient grace.   **J. ROACH**

Oh, let us rejoice in the Lord, evermore,
When darts of the tempter are flying,
For Satan still dreads, as he oft did of yore,
Our singing much more than our sighing.

EVENING
∽◇∾

He maketh me to lie down in green pastures. (PS. 23:2)

There are times when a Christian needs to lie still, like the earth under the spring rain, letting the lesson of experience and the memories of the Word of God sink down to the very roots of his life and fill the deep reservoirs of his soul.

Those are not always lost days when his hands are not busy, any more than rainy days in summer are lost because they keep the farmer indoors. The Great Shepherd makes his servant to *lie down* there.

There are times when men say they are too busy to stop; when they think they are doing God service by going on. Now and then God makes such a one to lie down. He has been driving through the pastures so fast that he has not known their greenness, nor apprehended their sweet savor; and God does not mean that he shall lose all that, and so *He makes him lie down.*

Many a man has had to thank God for some such enforced season of rest, in which he first learned the sweetness of meditation on the Word, and of lying still in God's hands and waiting God's pleasure.

The soul cannot be hurried!

God is not in a hurry, dear!
The work He chose for you
Can wait, if He is giving you another
task to do,
Or, if He call you from your work
to quietness and rest,
Be sure that in the silence
you may do His bidding best.

You cannot be a joy to Him,
if thus with frown and fret
You turn at each new call of His,
to find new lessons set.
The old familiar tasks were dear,
and ordered by His hand;
But come and tread another way:
it is as He has planned.

And yesterday He led you there;
and now He wants you here;
And what shall be tomorrow's work,
tomorrow shall make clear.
So patiently and faithfully let each
day's course be run;
God is not in a hurry, dear,
His work will all be done.
EDITH HICKMAN DIVALL

There must be a Selah!

February 15

❦

Fret not thyself (PS. 37:1).

Do not get into a perilous heat about things. If ever heat were justi-fied, it was surely justified in the circumstances outlined in the psalm. Evildoers were moving about clothed in purple and fine linen, and faring sumptuously every day. "Workers of iniquity" were climbing into the supreme places of power, and were tyrannizing their less fortunate brethren. Sinful men and women were stalking through the land in the pride of life and basking in the light and comfort of great prosperity, and good men were becoming heated and fretful.

"Fret not thyself." Do not get unduly heated! Keep cool! Even in a good cause, fretfulness is not a wise helpmeet. Fretting only heats the bear-ings; it does not generate the steam. It is no help to a train for the axles to get hot; their heat is only a hindrance. When the axles get heated, it is because of unnecessary friction; dry surfaces are grinding together, which ought to be kept in smooth cooperation by a delicate cushion of oil.

And is it not a suggestive fact that this word "fret" is closely akin to the word "friction," and is an indication of absence of the anointing oil of the grace of God?

In fretfulness, a little bit of grit gets into the bearings—some slight dis-appointment, some ingratitude, some discourtesy—and the smooth working of the life is checked. Friction begets heat; and with the heat, most dangerous conditions are created.

Do not let thy bearing get hot. Let the oil of the Lord keep thee cool, lest by reason of an unholy heat thou be reckoned among the evildoers.

FROM THE SILVER LINING

Dear restless heart, be still; don't fret and worry so;
God has a thousand ways His love and help to show;
Just trust, and trust, and trust, until His will you know.

Dear restless heart, be still, for peace is God's own smile,
His love can every wrong and sorrow reconcile;
Just love, and love, and love, and calmly wait awhile.

Dear restless heart, be brave; don't moan and sorrow so,
He hath a meaning kind in chilly winds that blow;
Just hope, and hope, and hope, until you braver grow.

Dear restless heart, repose upon His breast this hour,
His grace is strength and life, His love is bloom and flower;
Just rest, and rest, and rest, within His tender power.

Dear restless heart, be still! Don't struggle to be free;
God's life is in your life, from Him you may not flee;
Just pray, and pray, and pray, till you have faith to see.
EDITH WILLIS LINN

EVENING

But the fruit of the Spirit is . . . gentleness. (GAL. 5:22)

One day at an auction a man bought a vase of cheap earthenware for a few pennies. He put into the vase a rich perfume—the attar of roses. For a long time the vase held this perfume, and when it was empty it had been so soaked through with the sweet perfume that the fragrance lingered. One day the vase fell and was broken to pieces, but every fragment still smelled of the attar of roses.

We are all common clay—plain earthenware, but if the love of Christ is kept in our hearts it will sweeten all our life, and we shall become as loving as He. That is the way the beloved disciple learned the lesson and grew into such lovingness. He leaned on Christ's breast, and Christ's gentleness filled all his life.

As John upon his dear Lord's breast,
So would I lean, so would I rest;
An empty shell in depths of sea,
So would I sink, be filled with Thee.

Like singing bird in high blue air,
So would I soar, and sing Thee there.
Nor rain, nor stormy wind can be,
When all the air is full of Thee.

And so, though daily duties crowd,
And dust of earth be like a cloud,
Through noise of words, O Lord, my Rest,
Thy John would lean upon Thy breast.
ROSE FROM BRIER

Save me from growing hard!

February 16

❧

Though I have afflicted thee, I will afflict thee no more
(NAH. 1:12).

There is a limit to affliction. God sends it, and removes it. Do you sigh and say, "When will the end be?" Let us quietly wait and patiently endure the will of the Lord till He cometh. Our Father takes away the rod when His design in using it is fully served.

If the affliction is sent for testing us, that our graces may glorify God, it will end when the Lord has made us bear witness to His praise.

We would not wish the affliction to depart until God has gotten out of us all the honor which we can possibly yield Him. There may be today "a great calm." Who knows how soon those raging billows will give place to a sea of glass, and the sea birds sit on the gentle waves?

After long tribulation, the flail is hung up, and the wheat rests in the garner. We may, before many hours are past, be just as happy as now we are sorrowful.

It is not hard for the Lord to turn night into day. He that sends the clouds can as easily clear the skies. Let us be of good cheer. It is better farther on. *Let us sing Hallelujah by anticipation.*   C. H. SPURGEON

The great Husbandman is not always threshing. Trial is only for a season. The showers soon pass. Weeping may tarry only for the few hours of the short summer night; it must be gone at daybreak. Our light affliction is but for a moment. Trial is for a purpose, "If needs be."

The very fact of trial proves that there is something in us very precious to our Lord; else He would not spend so much pains and time on us. Christ would not test us if He did not see the precious ore of faith mingled in the rocky matrix of our nature; and it is to bring this out into purity and beauty that He forces us through the fiery ordeal.

Be patient, O sufferer! The result will more than compensate for all our trials, when we see how they wrought out the far more exceeding and eternal weight of glory. To have one word of God's commendation; to be honored before the holy angels; to be glorified in Christ, so as to be better able to flash His glory on Himself—ah! that will more than repay for all.   *FROM* TRIED BY FIRE

As the weights of the clock, or the ballast in the vessel, are necessary for their right ordering, so is trouble in the soul-fire. The sweetest scents are only obtained by tremendous pressure; the fairest flowers grow amid alpine snow-solitudes; the fairest gems have suffered longest from the lapidary's wheel; the noblest statues have borne most blows of the chisel. All, however, are under law. Nothing happens that has not been *appointed* with consummate care and foresight.

FROM DAILY DEVOTIONAL COMMENTARY

EVENING

And we know that all things work together for good to them that love God, to them who are the called according to his purpose.
(ROM. 8:28)

*H*e was weaving.

"That is a strange-looking carpet you are making!" said the visitor.

"Just stoop down and look underneath," was the reply.

The man stooped. *The plan was on the other side,* and in that moment a light broke upon his mind.

The Great Weaver is busy with His plan. Do not be impatient; suffice to know that you are part of the plan and that *He never errs.* Wait for the light of the later years, and the peep at the other side. *Hope on!*

> *White and black, and hodden-gray,*
> *Weavers of webs are we;*
> *To every weaver one golden strand*
> *Is given in trust by the Master-Hand;*
> *Weavers of webs are we.*
>
> *And that we weave, we know not,*
> *Weavers of webs are we.*
> *The thread we see, but the pattern is known*
> *To the Master-Weaver alone, alone;*
> *Weavers of webs are we.*
> JOHN OXENHAM

Of many of the beautiful carpets made in India it may be said that the weaving is done to music. The designs are handed down from one generation to another, and the instructions for their making are in script that looks not unlike a sheet of music. Indeed, it is more than an accidental resemblance, for each carpet has a sort of tune of its own. The thousands of threads are stretched on a great wooden frame, and behind it on a long bench sit the workers. The master in charge reads the instructions for each stitch in a strange chanting tone, each color having its own particular note.

The story makes us think of our own life web. We are all weavers and day by day we work in the threads—now dark, now bright—that are to go into the finished pattern. But blessed are they who feel sure that there is a pattern; who hear and trust the directing Voice, and so weave the changing threads to music.   W. J. HART

Fallen threads I will not search for—I will weave.

GEORGE MACDONALD

February 17

MORNING

The land which I do give to them, even to the children of Israel
(JOSH. 1:2).

God here speaks in the immediate present. It is not something He is going to do, but something He does do, this moment. So faith ever speaks. So God ever gives. So He is meeting you today, in the present moment. This is the test of faith. So long as you are waiting for a thing, hoping for it, looking for it, you are not believing. It may be hope, it may be earnest desire, but it is not faith; for "faith is the substance of things hoped for, the evidence of things not seen." The command in regard to believing prayer is the present tense. "When ye pray, believe that ye receive the things that ye desire, and ye shall have them." Have we come to that moment? Have we met God in His everlasting NOW?

FROM JOSHUA, *BY SIMPSON*

True faith counts on God, and believes before it sees. Naturally, we want some evidence that our petition is granted before we believe; but when we walk by faith we need no other evidence than God's Word. He has spoken, and according to our faith it shall be done unto us. We shall see because we have believed, and this faith sustains us in the most trying places, when everything around us seems to contradict God's Word.

The psalmist says, "I had fainted, unless I had believed to see the goodness of the Lord in the land of the living" (Ps. 27:13). He did not see as yet the Lord's answer to his prayers, but he believed to see and this kept him from fainting.

If we have the faith that believes to see, it will keep us from growing discouraged. We shall "laugh at impossibilities," we shall watch with delight to see how God is going to open up a path through the Red Sea when there is no human way out of our difficulty. It is just in such places of severe testing that our faith grows and strengthens.

Have you been waiting upon God, dear troubled one, during long nights and weary days, and have feared that you were forgotten? Nay, lift up your head, and begin to praise Him even now for the deliverance which is on its way to you.   *FROM* LIFE OF PRAISE

EVENING

My presence shall go with thee, and I will give thee rest. (EX. 33:14)

What is rest?

To step out of self-life into Christ-life; to lie still, and let Him lift you out of it; to fold your hands close, and hide your face on the hem of His garment; to let Him lay His cooling, soothing, healing hands upon your soul, and draw all the hurry and fever from its veins; to realize that you are not a mighty messenger, an important worker of His, full of care and responsibility, but only a little child, with a Father's gentle bidding to heed and fulfill; to lay your busy plans and ambitions confidently in His hands, as a child brings its broken toys at its mother's call; to serve Him by waiting; to praise Him by saying, "Holy, Holy, Holy"; to cease to hurry, so you may not lose sight of His face; to learn to follow Him, and not to run ahead of orders! to cease to live in self and for self, and to live in Him and for Him; to love His honor more than your own; to be a clear medium for His life-tide to shine and glow through. This is consecration, this is rest.

Thou sweet, beloved will of God,
My anchor ground, my fortress hill,
My spirit's silent, fair abode,
In Thee I hide me and am still.

Thy beautiful sweet will, my God,
Holds fast in its sublime embrace

My captive will, a gladsome bird,
Prison'd in such a realm of grace.

Upon God's will I lay me down,
As child upon its mother's breast,
No silken couch, nor softest bed,
Could ever give me such deep rest.

TERSTEEGEN

February 18

MORNING

Have faith that whatever you ask for in prayer is already granted you, and you will find that it will be (MARK 11:24).

When my little son was about ten years of age, his grandmother promised him a stamp album for Christmas. Christmas came, but no stamp album, and no word from Grandmother. The matter, however, was not mentioned; but when his playmates came to see his Christmas presents, I was astonished, after he had named over this and that as gifts received, to hear him add,

"And a stamp album from Grandmother."

I had heard it several times, when I called him to me, and said, "But, Georgie, you did not get an album from your grandmother. Why do you say so?"

There was a wondering look on his face, as if he thought it strange that I should ask such a question, and he replied, "Well, Mamma, Grandma said, so it is the same as." I could not say a word to check his faith.

A month went by, and nothing was heard about the album. Finally, one day, I said, to test his faith, and really wondering in my heart why the album had not been sent,

"Well, Georgie, I think Grandma has forgotten her promise."

"Oh, no Mamma," he quickly and firmly said, "she hasn't."

I watched the dear, trusting face, which, for a while, looked very sober, as if debating the possibilities I had suggested. Finally a bright light passed over it, and he said,

"Mamma, do you think it would do any good if I should write to her *thanking* her for the album?"

"I do not know," I said, "but you might try it."

A rich spiritual truth began to dawn upon me. In a few minutes a letter was prepared and committed to the mail, and he went off whistling his confidence in his grandma. In just a short time a letter came, saying:

"My dear Georgie: I have not forgotten my promise to you, of an album. I tried to get such a book as you desired, but could not get the sort you wanted; so I sent on to New York. It did not get there till after Christmas, and it was still not right, so I sent for another, and as it has not come as yet, I send you three dollars to get one in Chicago. Your loving grandma."

As he read the letter, his face was the face of a victor. "Now, Mamma, didn't I tell you?" came from the depths of a heart that never doubted, that, "against hope, believed in hope" that the stamp album would come. While he was trusting, Grandma was working, and in due season faith became sight.

It is so human to want sight when we step out on the promises of God, but our Savior said to Thomas, and to the long roll of doubters who have ever since followed him: "Blessed are they who have not seen, and yet have believed."   MRS. ROUNDS

EVENING

I will go before thee and unwind the snarls. (ISA. 45:2, FREE TRANS.)

Have I no power to deliver? (ISA. 50:2)

*I*f any of you, beloved, seem to be in a knot of difficulty of which you cannot get the thread, look to Him who is perfect wisdom, and *let the tangle go out of your hands into His; turn the matter over to Him.* What is impossible with you is perfectly possible with Him who is Almighty!

A little child at mother's knee
Plies woolen strands and needles bright.
Small, eager hands strive earnestly
To fasten every stitch aright.

But soon perplexing knots appear
Which vex and hinder progress' flow;

Impatient fingers pull and tear,
While ever worse the tangles grow.

How surely then in wiser hands
The roughest places are made plain!
How easy now the task's demands,
How wonderful the lesson's gain!

Thus, God, we bring our snarls to Thee;
Though human sense and stubborn will
Oft clamor loud for mastery,
We hear alone Thy "Peace, be still."
EDITH SHAW BROWN

How tangled some of our problems do become as the days pass and no way appears by which the matter may be straightened out! Perhaps we have been keeping the problems too much in our own hands. No wonder, then, we cannot find the beginning or the end of the line, or how to loosen the knotted strand in just the right places. A young man writing to his father about a personal problem says: "Once again, just yesterday, I have put this whole matter in the Lord's hands, and asked Him to guide me about it all. I often think of how I'd get my fishing line all tangled up. The more I pulled the worse it got. Finally I'd hand the whole thing over to you, and you'd smooth it all out. So I generally do that with my problems now; and I'm trying to learn not to pull at the line much, before I give it to Him." Have you been pulling at the line in that problem that troubles you today? Just hand it over to your heavenly Father, and see how swiftly and lovingly He will untangle the crisscross and knotty impossibility that has troubled you so! SUNDAY SCHOOL TIMES

With thoughtless and
Impatient hands
We tangle up
The plans
The Lord hath wrought.

And when we cry
In pain, He saith,
"Be quiet, dear,
While I untie the knot."

February 19

〜

And every branch that beareth fruit he purgeth it, that it may bring forth more fruit (JOHN 15:2).

A child of God was dazed by the variety of afflictions which seemed to make her their target. Walking past a vineyard in the rich autumnal glow she noticed the untrimmed appearance and the luxuriant wealth of leaves on the vines, that the ground was given over to a tangle of weeds and grass, and that the whole place looked utterly uncared for; and as she pondered, the heavenly Gardener whispered so precious a message that she would fain pass it on:

"My dear child, are you wondering at the sequence of trials in your life? Behold that vineyard and learn of it. The gardener ceases to prune, to trim, to harrow, or to pluck the ripe fruit only when he expects nothing more than the vine during that season. It is left to itself, because the season of fruit is past and further effort for the present would yield no profit. Comparative uselessness is the condition of freedom from suffering. Do you then wish me to cease pruning your life? Shall I leave you alone?" And the comforted heart cried, "No!"   HOMERA HOMER-DIXON

It is the branch that bears the fruit,
That feels the knife,
To prune it for a larger growth,
A fuller life.

Though every budding twig be lopped,
And every grace
Of swaying tendril, springing leaf,
Be lost a space.

O thou whose life of joy seems reft,
Of beauty shorn;
Whose aspirations lie in dust,
All bruised and torn,

Rejoice, tho' each desire, each dream,
Each hope of thine
Shall fall and fade; it is the hand
Of Love Divine

That holds the knife, that cuts and breaks
With tenderest touch,
That thou, whose life has borne some fruit
May'st now bear much.
ANNIE JOHNSON FLINT

EVELING

He healeth the broken in heart, and bindeth up their wounds.
He telleth the number of the stars; he calleth them all by their names.
(PS. 147:3–4)

A beautiful picture has just been painted by one of the greatest of the European artists: *The Consoler*. It is a picture of a bedroom in an English cottage. On the bed sits a beautiful little babe, perhaps a year in age, having in his hand a toy soldier that he is holding very lovingly to his body. He is unconscious of anything about him. Back of him on the wall is the picture of a young man in soldier's dress—the baby's father. On her knees, her head in her hands, is the young widow robed in deepest black, sobbing her heart out. One of the saddest pictures the world shall ever know—a baby to forget and never know his father; a young widow to go down through life with burdened, broken heart. But leaning over her, with the light of heaven on His beautiful face, is One who lays His hand lovingly on her shoulder. We do not wonder the great artist has called the picture *The Consoler*.

With His healing hand on a broken heart,
And the other on a star,
Our wonderful God views the miles apart,
And they seem not very far.

Oh, it makes us cry—then laugh—then sing,
Tho' 'tis all beyond our ken;
He bindeth up wounds on that poor crushed thing,
And He makes it whole again.

Was there something shone from that healed new heart
Made the Psalmist think of stars—
That bright as the sun or the lightning's dart,
Sped away past earthly bars?

In a low place sobbing by death's lone cart,
Then a flight on whirlwind's cars;
One verse is about a poor broken heart,
And the next among the stars.

There is hope and help for our sighs and tears,
For the wound that stings and smarts;
Our God is at home with the rolling spheres,
And at home with broken hearts.
MAMIE PAYNE FERGUSON

"Let God cover thy wounds," said Augustine, "do not thou. For if thou wish to cover them being ashamed, the Physician will not come. Let Him cover; for by the covering of the Physician the wound is healed; by the covering of the wounded man the wound is concealed. And from whom? From Him who knoweth all things."

The Great Lover comes close behind the storm,
And whispers softly to the broken mountaintops,
And fills their wounds with clean fresh odors.

The Great Lover knows the pain of blasted trees
And binds up tenderly their broken arms;
The Great Lover has gone through many storms.
MATTHEW BILLER

February 20
MORNING
❧

Nothing shall be impossible unto you (MATT. 17:20).

It is possible, for those who really are willing to reckon on the power of the Lord for keeping and victory, to lead a life in which His promises are taken as they stand and are found to be true.

It is possible to cast all our care upon Him daily and to enjoy deep peace in doing it.

It is possible to have the thoughts and imaginations of our hearts purified, in the deepest meaning of the word.

It is possible to see the will of God in everything, and to receive it, not with sighing, but with singing.

It is possible by taking complete refuge in divine power to become strong through and through; and, where previously our greatest weakness lay, to find that things which formerly upset all our resolves to be patient, or pure, or humble, furnish today an opportunity—through Him who loved us, and works in us as an agreement with His will and a blessed sense of His presence and His power—to make sin powerless over us.

These things are DIVINE POSSIBILITIES, and because they are His work, the true experience of them will always cause us to bow lower at His feet and to learn to thirst and long for more.

We cannot possibly be satisfied with anything less—each day, each hour, each moment, in Christ, through the power of the Holy Spirit—than to WALK WITH GOD.   H. C. G. MOULE

We may have as much of God as we will. Christ puts the key of the treasure chamber into our hand, and bids us take all that we want. If a man is admitted into the bullion vault of a bank, and told to help himself, and comes out with one cent, whose fault is it that he is poor? Whose fault is it that Christian people generally have such scanty portions of the free riches of God?   MCLAREN

EVENING

These were the potters, and those that dwelt among plants and hedges: there they dwelt with the king for his work. (1 CHRON. 4:23)

> *Is your place a small place?*
> *Tend it with care!—*
> *He set you there.*
>
> *Is your place a large place?*
> *Guard it with care!*
> *He set you there.*
>
> *Whate'er your place, it is*
> *Not yours alone, but His.*
> *He set you there.*
> JOHN OXENHAM

With infinite care and forethought God has chosen the best place in which you can do your best work for the world. You may be lonely, but you have no more right to complain than the lamp has, which has been placed in a niche to illumine a dark landing or a flight of dangerous stone steps. The master of the house may have put you in a very small corner and on a very humble stand; but it is enough if it be His blessed will. Someday He will pass by, and you shall light His steps as He goes forth to seek and save that which is lost; or you shall kindle some great light that shall shine like a beacon over the storm-swept ocean. Thus the obscure Andrew was the means of igniting his brother Peter, when he brought him to Jesus. — SELECTED

When the Master of all the workmen called me into the field,
I went for Him light and happy, the tools of His service to wield;
Expectant of high position, as suited my lofty taste—
When Lo! He set me weeding and watering down in the waste.

Such puttering down in the hedges! A task so thankless and small!
Yet I stifled my vain discomfort and wrought for the Lord of all,
Till, meeker grown, as nightly I sank to my hard-won rest
I cared but to hear in my dreaming, "This one has done his best."

The years have leveled distinctions, there is no more "great" nor "small";
Only faithful service counts with the Lord of all;
And I know that, tilled with patience, the dreariest waste of clod
Shall yield the perfect ideal planned in the heart of God.
— SELECTED

Are YOU willing to be a "stopper of chinks" (EZEK. 27:9)?

February 21

MORNING

⤙⤚

Rest in the Lord, and wait patiently for him (PS. 37:7).

Have you prayed and prayed and waited and waited, and still there is no manifestation?

Are you tired of seeing nothing move? Are you just at the point of giving it all up? Perhaps you have not waited in the right way? This would take you out of the right place—the place where He can meet you.

"With patience wait" (Rom. 8:25). Patience takes away *worry*. He said He would come, and His promise is equal to His presence. Patience takes away your *weeping*. Why feel sad and despondent? He knows your need better than you do, and His purpose in waiting is to bring more glory out of it all. Patience takes away self-*works*. The work He desires is that you "believe" (John 6:29), and when you believe, you may then know that all is well. Patience takes away all *want*. Your desire for the thing you wish is perhaps stronger than your desire for the will of God to be fulfilled in its arrival.

Patience takes away all *weakening*. Instead of having the delaying time, a time of letting go, know that God is getting a larger supply ready and must get you ready too. Patience takes away all *wobbling*. "Make me stand upon my standing" (Dan. 8:18, margin). God's foundations are steady; and when His patience is within, we are steady while we wait. Patience gives *worship*. A praiseful patience sometimes "longsuffering with joyfulness" (Col. 1:11) is the best part of it all. "Let [all these phases of] patience have her perfect work" (James 1:4), while you wait, and you will find great enrichment.

C. H. P.

> *Hold steady when the fires burn,*
> *When inner lessons come to learn,*
> *And from this path there seems no turn—*
> *"Let patience have her perfect work."*
>
> L. S. P.

EVENING

～◌～

The things which happened unto me have fallen out rather unto the furtherance of the gospel. (PHIL. 1:12)

We cannot expect to learn much of the life of trust without passing through hard places. When they come let us not say as Jacob did, "All these things are against me" (Gen. 42:36).

Let us rather climb our Hills of Difficulty and say, *"These are faith's opportunities!"*

> *I would not lose the hard things from my life,*
> *The rocks o'er which I stumbled long ago,*

The griefs and fears, the failures and mistakes,
That tried and tested faith and patience so.

I need them now: they make the deep-laid wall,
The firm foundation-stones on which I raise—
To mount therein from stair to higher stair—
The lofty towers of my House of Praise.

Soft was the roadside turf to weary feet,
And cool the meadows where I fain had trod,
And sweet beneath the trees to lie at rest
And breathe the incense of the flower-starred sod;

But not on these might I securely build;
Nor sand nor sod withstand the earthquake shock;
I need the rough hard boulders of the hills,
To set my house on everlasting rock.
ANNIE JOHNSON FLINT

Crises reveal character: when we are put to the test we reveal exactly the hidden resources of our character.

February 22
MORNING
~~

If thou canst believe, all things are possible to him that believeth
(MARK 9:23).

Seldom have we heard a better definition of faith than was given once in one of our meetings, by a dear old colored woman, as she answered the question of a young man *how to take the Lord for needed help.*

In her characteristic way, pointing her finger toward him, she said with great emphasis: "You've just got to believe that He's done it and it's done." The great danger with most of us is that, after we ask Him to do it, we do not believe that it is done, but we keep on helping Him, and getting others to help Him; and waiting to see how He is going to do it.

Faith adds its "Amen" to God's "Yea," and then takes its hands off, and leaves God to finish His work. Its language is, "Commit thy way unto the Lord, trust also in him; and he worketh."

FROM DAYS OF HEAVEN UPON EARTH

I simply take Him at His word,
I praise Him that my prayer is heard,
And claim my answer from the Lord;
I take, He undertakes.

An active faith can give thanks for a promise,
though it be not as yet performed; knowing that God's bonds are
as good as ready money.
MATTHEW HENRY

Passive faith accepts the word as true—
But never moves.
Active faith begins with work to do,
And thereby proves.

Passive faith says, "I believe it! every word of God is true.
Well I know He hath not spoken what He cannot, will not, do.
He hath bidden me, 'Go forward!' but a closed-up way I see,
When the waters are divided, soon in Canaan's land I'll be.
Lo! I hear His voice commanding, 'Rise and walk: take up thy bed';
And, 'Stretch forth thy withered member!' which for so long has been dead.
When I am a little stronger, then, I know I'll surely stand:
When there comes a thrill of healing, I will use with ease my other hand.
Yes, I know that 'God is able' and full willing all to do:
I believe that every promise, sometime, will to me come true."

Active faith says, "I believe it! and the promise now I take,
Knowing well, as I receive it, God, each promise, real will make.
So I step into the waters, finding there an open way;
Onward press, the land possessing; nothing can my progress stay.
Yea, I rise at His commanding, walk straightway, and joyfully:
This, my hand so sadly shrivelled, as I reach, restored shall be.
What beyond His faithful promise, would I wish or do I need?
Looking not for 'signs or wonders,' I'll no contradiction heed.
Well I know that 'God is able,' and full willing all to do:
I believe that every promise, at this moment can come true."

Passive faith but praises in the light,
When sun doth shine.
Active faith will praise in darkest night—
Which faith is thine?
SELECTED

≈ 120 ≈

❧❧

Faint not. (2 COR. 4:16)

One day a naturalist, out in his garden, observed a most unusually large and beautiful butterfly, fluttering as though in great distress; it seemed to be caught as though it could not release itself. The naturalist, thinking to release the precious thing, took hold of the wings and set it free. It flew but a few feet and fell to the ground dead.

He picked up the poor thing, took it into his laboratory and put it under a magnifying glass to discover the cause of its death. There he found the lifeblood flowing from the tiny arteries of its wings. Nature had fastened it to its chrysalis and was allowing it to flutter and flutter so that its wings might grow strong. It was the muscle-developing process that nature was giving the dear thing so that it might have an unusual range among the flowers and gardens. *If it had only fluttered long enough the butterfly would have come forth ready for the wide range; but release ended the beautiful dream.*

So with God's children: *how the Father wishes for them wide ranges in experience and truth. He permits us to be fastened to some form of struggle. We would tear ourselves free.* We cry out in our distress and sometimes think Him cruel that He does not release us. He permits us to flutter and flutter on. Struggle seems to be His program sometimes.

Prayer alone will hod us steady while in the struggles; so we keep sweet and learn, oh, such wonderful lessons.

> *God laid upon my back a grievous load,*
> *A heavy cross to bear along the road.*
>
> *I staggered on, and lo! one weary day,*
> *An angry lion sprang across my way.*
>
> *I prayed to God, and swift at His command*
> *The cross became a weapon in my hand.*
>
> *It slew my raging enemy, and then*
> *Became a cross upon my back again.*
>
> *I reached a desert. O'er the burning track*
> *I persevered, the cross upon my back.*
>
> *No shade was there, and in the cruel sun*
> *I sank at last, and thought my days were done.*
>
> *But lo! the Lord works many a blest surprise—*
> *The cross became a tree before my eyes!*

I slept; I woke, to feel the strength of ten.
I found the cross upon my back again.

And thus through all my days from then to this,
The cross, my burden, has become my bliss.

Nor ever shall I lay the burden down,
For God someday will make the cross a crown!
AMOS R. WELLS

You are bound to a cross. I entreat you not to struggle. The more loving-
ly the cross is carried by the soul, the lighter it becomes!

February 23
MORNING

∽◦∾

And there came a lion (1 SAM. 17:34).

*I*t is a source of inspiration and strength to come in touch with the youthful David, trusting God. Through faith in God he conquered a lion and a bear, and afterward overthrew the mighty Goliath. When that lion came to despoil that flock, it came as a wonderous *opportunity* to David. if he had failed or faltered he would have missed God's opportunity for him and probably would never have come to be God's chosen king of Israel. *"And there came a lion."*

One would not think that a lion was a special blessing from God; one would think that only an occasion of alarm. The lion was *God's opportunity in disguise.* Every difficulty that presents itself to us, if we receive it in the right way, is God's opportunity. Every temptation that comes is God's opportunity.

When the "lion" comes, recognize it as God's opportunity no matter how rough the exterior. The very tabernacle of God was covered with badgers' skins and goats' hair; one would not think there would be any glory there. The Shekinah of God was manifest under that kind of covering. May God open our eyes to see Him, whether in temptations, trials, dangers, or misfortunes.   C. H. P.

⤶⤷

Hope thou in God: for I shall yet praise him. (PS. 42:5)

During a truce in the Civil War in America, when the hostile armies sat sullenly facing each other with a field between them, a little brown bird rose suddenly from the long grass and darted skyward. There, a mere speck in the blue, it poured forth its liquid music of which the lark alone has the secret. And steely eyes melted to tears, and hard hearts grew pitiful and tender. There was a God who cared. There was hope for men.

Hope is like the lark on the battlefield. It will not sing in a gilded cage. It cannot soar in an atmosphere of religious luxury. But brave souls, exposing themselves fearlessly for God and their fellow men on the battlefield of life, hear its song and are made strong and glad.

E. HERMAN

Persons who held on in hope, with seemingly little for which to hope, were known to say:

Then was our mouth filled with laughter . . .
We were like them that dream.

The tide may turn, the wind may change. New eras have been heard of before now!

In "hope against hope," I wait, Lord,
Faced by some fast-barred gate, Lord,
Hope never says "Too late," Lord,
Therefore in Thee I hope!

Hope though the night be long, Lord,
Hope of a glowing dawn, Lord,
Morning must break in song, Lord,
For we are "saved by hope."
HYMNS OF CONSECRATION AND FAITH

"Hope thou in God!"

February 24

〜◆〜

John did no miracle: but all things that
John spake of this man were true (JOHN 10:41).

You may be very discontented with yourself. You are no genius, have no brilliant gifts, and are inconspicuous for any special faculty. Mediocrity is the law of your existence. Your days are remarkable for nothing but sameness and insipidity. Yet you may live a great life.

John did no miracle, but Jesus said that among those born of women there had not appeared a greater than he.

John's main business was to bear witness to the Light, and this may be yours and mine. John was content to be only a voice, if men would think of Christ.

Be willing to be only a voice, heard but not seen; a mirror whose surface is lost to view, because it reflects the dazzling glory of the sun; a breeze that springs up just before daylight, and says, "The dawn! the dawn!" and then dies away.

Do the commonest and smallest things as beneath His eye. If you must live with uncongenial people, set to the conquest by love. If you have made a great mistake in your life, do not let it becloud all of it; but, locking the secret in your breast, compel it to yield strength and sweetness.

We are doing more good than we know, sowing seed, starting streamlets, giving men true thoughts of Christ, to which they will refer one day as the first things that started them thinking of Him; and, of my part, I shall be satisfied if no great mausoleum is raised over my grave, but that simple souls shall gather there when I am gone, and say,

"He was a good man; he wrought no miracles, but he spake words about Christ, which led me to know Him for myself."

GEORGE MATHESON

Thy Hidden Ones (PS. 83:3)

Thick green leaves from the soft brown earth,
Happy springtime hath called them forth;
First faint promise of summer bloom
Breathes from the fragrant, sweet perfume,
Under the leaves.

Lift them! what marvelous beauty lies
Hidden beneath, from our thoughtless eyes!
Mayflowers, rosy or purest white,
Lift their cups to the sudden light,
Under the leaves.

Are there no lives whose holy deeds—
Seen by no eye save His who reads
Motive and action—in silence grow
Into rare beauty, and bud and blow
Under the leaves?

Fair white flowers of faith and trust,
Springing from spirits bruised and crushed;
Blossoms of love, rose-tinted and bright,
Touched and painted with Heaven's own light
Under the leaves.

Full fresh clusters of duty borne,
Fairest of all in that shadow grown;
Wondrous the fragrance that sweet and rare
Come from the flower-cups hidden there
Under the leaves.

Though unseen by our vision dim,
Bud and blossom are known to Him;
Wait we content for His heavenly ray—
Wait till our Master Himself one day
Lifteth the leaves.

God calls many of His most valued workers from the
unknown multitude (LUKE 14:23).

EVENING

After he had seen the vision, immediately we endeavored to go into Macedonia, assuredly gathering that the Lord had called us for to preach the gospel unto them. (ACTS 16:10)

There is a simplicity about God in working out His plans, yet a resourcefulness equal to any difficulty, an unswerving faithfulness to His trusting child, and an unforgetting steadiness in holding to His purpose. Through a fellow-prisoner, then a dream, He lifts Joseph from a prison to a premiership. And the length of stay in the prison prevents dizziness in the premier.

It's safe to trust God's methods, and to go by His clock.

THE BENT KNEE TIME, BY S. D. GORDON

The path was veiled! The Master's will was hidden,
And further progress for the time was stayed;
But in good time he would again be bidden
And, waiting meantime, he was unafraid.

Then came that night when, maybe, softly sleeping,
The vision came—the clarion call to move;
And once again, with all in God's good keeping,
He could step forth, God's faithfulness to prove.

No human voice conveyed the word of leading;
No human hand was sent, his way to guide;
No human heart full knew his depth of needing,
Or could assist him to his steps decide.

And so, without to other minds appealing,
"Assuredly" he "gathered" now God's will,
Yet—to his inner soul there came revealing—
He started forth, God's purpose to fulfill.

Perhaps, O soul, thou waitest for His leading,
Thy longing heart His further will would'st know;
Rest thou in God: His ear hath heard thy pleading,
The "further steps" He yet to thee will show.

Keep looking Himwards—He alone can lead thee;
Nor count from choicest friends thy way to glean;
He knoweth best where He Himself doth need thee,
And He can lead thee on by means unseen.

"Assuredly" thy longing heart shall "gather"
The guidance thou dost long for; therefore wait;
Fret not thyself! Ah, no! But learn this rather—
God's guidance never comes to us too late.

J. DANSON SMITH

February 25

MORNING

❧❧

*Every place that the sole of your foot shall tread upon,
that have I given unto you* (JOSH. 1:3).

*B*eside the literal ground, unoccupied for Christ, there is the
unclaimed, untrodden territory of *divine promises.* What did God
say to Joshua? *"Every place* that the sole of your foot shall tread upon,
that *have I given* unto you." And then He draws the outlines of the
land of promise—all theirs on one condition: *that they shall march
through the length and breadth of it,* and measure it off with their own
feet.

They never did that to more than one-third of the property, and con-
sequently they never *had* more than one-third; they had just what they
measured off, and no more.

In 2 Peter, we read of the "land of promise" that is opened up to us,
and it is God's will that we should, as it were, measure off that territory
by the feet of obedient faith and believing obedience, thus claiming and
appropriating it for our own.

How many of us have ever taken possesion of the promises of God in
the name of Christ?

Here is a magnificent territory for faith to lay hold on and march
through the length and breadth of, and faith has never done it yet.

Let us enter into all our inheritance. Let us lift up our eyes to the
north and to the south, to the east and to the west, and hear Him say,
"All the land that thou seest will I give to thee."   A. T. PIERSON

Wherever Judah should set his foot that should be his; wherever
Benjamin should set his foot, that should be his. Each should get his
inheritance by setting his foot upon it. Now, think you not, when either
had set his foot upon a given territory, he did not instantly and instinctively feel, "This is mine"?

An old colored man, who had a marvelous experience in grace, was
asked: "Daniel, why is it that you have so much peace and joy in religion?" "O Massa!" he replied, "I just fall flat on the exceeding great and
precious promises, and I have all that is in them. Glory! Glory!" He who
falls flat on the promises feels that all the riches embraced in them are
his.   *FROM* FAITH PAPERS

The Marquis of Salisbury was criticized for his Colonial policies and replied: "Gentlemen, get larger maps."

EVENING

∽∾

Jesus taketh Peter, James, and John his brother,
and bringeth them up into an high mountain apart,
And was transfigured before them.... Then ... Peter ... said unto
Jesus, Lord, it is good for us to be here. (MATT. 17:1-2, 4)

*I*t is good to be the possessor of some mountaintop experience. *Not to know life on the heights is to suffer an impoverishing incompleteness.*

Those times when the Lord's presence is marvelously manifest to you—the moments of self-revelation—*do not despise them.* But beware of *not acting upon what you see in your moments on the mount with God!*

Horizons broaden when we stand on the heights. There is always, we find, the danger that we will make of life too much of a dead-level existence; a monotonous tread of beaten paths; a matter of absorbing, spiritless, deadening routine.

Do not drop your life into the passing current, to be steadily going you scarcely know *where,* or *why.*

Christian life, writes one, *is not all a valley of humiliation. It has its heights of vision.*

Abraham saw in the glorious depths of the starry firmament visions that no telescope could ever have revealed! Jacob's stony pillow led up to the ladder of vision!

Joseph's early dreams kept him in the hours of discouragement and despair that followed!

Moses, who spent one-third of his life in the desert, we find crying out: "I beseech thee, show me thy glory!"

Job's vision showed him God and lifted him out of himself!

The mariner does not expect to see the sun and stars every day, but when he does, he takes his observations and sails by their light for many days to come.

God gives days of special illumination that we may be able to call to memory in the days of shadow, and say: "Therefore will I remember thee from the land of Jordan, and of the Hermonites, from the hill Mizar."

In the life of Paul, we find a few of these blessed interludes—when the Lord gave to him words of promise to remember in his days of trial that followed.

If these special experiences came too often they would lose their flavor!
He walks in glory on the hills,
And longs for men to join Him there.

February 26

MORNING

❦

My grace is sufficient for thee (2 COR. 12:9).

The other evening I was riding home after a heavy day's work. I felt very wearied, and sore depressed, when swiftly, and suddenly as a lightning flash, that text came to me, "My grace is sufficient for thee." I reached home and looked it up in the original, and at last it came to me in this way, *"MY grace is sufficient for thee";* and I said, "I should think it is, Lord," and burst out laughing. I never fully understood what the holy laughter of Abraham was until then. It seemed to make unbelief so absurd. It was as though some little fish, being very thirsty, was troubled about drinking the river dry, and Father Thames said, "Drink away, little fish, my stream is sufficient for thee." Or, it seemed after the seven years of plenty, a mouse feared it might die of famine; and Joseph might say, "Cheer up, little mouse, my granaries are sufficient for thee." Again, I imagined a man away up yonder, in a lofty mountain, saying to himself, "I breathe so many cubic feet of air every year, I fear I shall exhaust the oxygen in the atmosphere," but the earth might say, "Breathe away, O man, and fill the lungs ever, my atmosphere is sufficient for thee." Oh, brethren, be great believers! Little faith will bring your souls to heaven, but great faith will bring heaven to your souls.　　C. H. SPURGEON

His grace is great enough to meet the great things—
The crashing waves that overwhelm the soul,
The roaring winds that leave us stunned and breathless,
The sudden storms beyond our life's control.

His grace is great enough to meet the small things—
The little pin-prick troubles that annoy,
The insect worries, buzzing and persistent,
The squeaking wheels that grate upon our joy.
ANNIE JOHNSON FLINT

There is always a large balance to our credit in the bank of heaven waiting for our exercise of faith in drawing it. Draw heavily upon His resources.

EVENING

There came a woman having an alabaster box of ointment of spikenard very precious; and she brake the box, and poured it on his head. (MARK 14:3)

And the house was filled with the odour of the ointment. (JOHN 12:3)

Mary wanted it to be known that this act of hers was done *for Him exclusively.* Just for HIM, without thought of self, or anything else. Martha was serving, but it was *not exclusively for Him.* It might be in His honor, but it was done for others also. Simon might entertain, but others were included in the entertainment also. What Mary did was for HIM ALONE. "When *Jesus understood it,* he said unto them, Why trouble ye the woman?"

JESUS UNDERSTOOD!

Jesus said to Peter: "Lovest thou Me?" Peter replied: "Thou knowest that I love Thee." Jesus said to him: "Feed my sheep FOR ME. . . . Feed my lambs FOR ME" (John 21:15–17, Syriac version).

"Take this child away, and nurse it FOR ME, and I will give thee thy wages" (Ex. 2:9).

> Under an Eastern sky
> Amid a rabble cry
> A Man went forth to die
> For me—for me.
>
> Thorn-crowned His blessed Head,
> Bloodstained His every tread,
> To Calvary He was led
> For me—for me.
>
> Pierced were His Hands, His Feet,
> Three hours o'er Him did beat
> Fierce rays of noonday heat,
> For me—for me.

Since Thou wast made all mine,
Lord, make me wholly Thine.
Grant strength and grace Divine
For me—for me.

Thy will to do, Oh, lead
In thought and word and deed
My heart, e'en though it bleed,
To Thee—to Thee.

SELECTED

FOR ME!

"For Him! For Him!" the man cries as he planes his boards, sells his goods, adds his figures, or writes his letters. "For Him! For Him!" sings the woman as she plies her needle, makes her bed, cooks her food, or dusts her house.

All day long the hand is outstretched to touch the invisible Christ, and at night the work done is brought to Him for His benediction.

February 27

MORNING

And Jacob was left alone; and there wrestled a man with him until the breaking of the day (GEN. 32:24).

Left alone! What different sensations those words conjure up to each of us. To some they spell loneliness and desolation, to others rest and quiet. To be left alone *without* God, would be too awful for words, but to be left alone *with* Him is a foretaste of heaven! If His followers spent more time alone with Him, we should have spiritual giants again.

The Master set us an example. Note how often He went to be alone with God; and He had a mighty purpose behind the command, "When thou prayest, enter into thy closet and when thou hast shut thy door, pray."

The greatest miracles of Elijah and Elisha took place when they were alone with God. It was alone with God that Jacob became a prince; and just there that we, too, may become princes—"men [aye, and women too!] wondered at" (Zech. 3:8). Joshua was alone when the Lord came to him. (Josh. 1:1). Gideon and Jephthah were by themselves when commissioned to save Israel (Judg. 6:11 and 11:29). Moses was by himself at the wilderness bush (Exod. 3:1–5). Cornelius was praying by himself when the angel came to him (Acts 10:2). No one was with Peter on the housetop, when he was instructed to go to the Gentiles (Acts 10:9). John the Baptist was alone in the wilderness (Luke 1:80), and John the Beloved alone in Patmos, when nearest to God (Rev. 1:9).

Covet to get alone with God. If we neglect it, we not only rob ourselves, but others too, of blessing, since when we are blessed we are able to pass on blessing to others. It may mean less outside work; it must mean more depth and power, and the consequence, too, will be "they saw no man save Jesus only."

To be alone with God in prayer cannot be overemphasized.

> *If chosen men had never been alone,*
> *In deepest silence open-doored to God,*
> *No greatness would ever have been dreamed or done.*

EVINING

A vessel unto honour, sanctified, and meet for the master's use, and prepared unto every good work. (2 TIM. 2:21)

> *Here, O my Father, is Thy making stuff!*
>
> *Set Thy wheel going; let it whir and play.*
> *The chips in me, the stones, the straws, the sand,*
> *Cast them out with fine separating hand,*
> *And make a vessel of Thy yielding clay.*

Martin Wells Knapp was once undergoing a severe trial, and in his secret devotions he asked God to remove his trial. As he waited before the Lord the vision of a rough piece of marble rose before him with a sculptor grinding and chiseling. Watching the dust and chips fill the air, he noticed a beautiful image begin to appear in the marble. The Lord spoke to him and said, "Son, you are that block of marble. I have an image in My mind, and I desire to produce it in your character, and will do so if you will stand the grinding; but I will stop now if you so desire." Mr. Knapp broke down and said, *"Lord, continue the chiseling and grinding."*

When God wants to drill a man,
And thrill a man,
And skill a man,
When God wants to mold a man
To play the noblest part;
When He yearns with all His heart
To create so great and bold a man
That all the world shall be amazed,
Watch His methods, watch His ways!
How He ruthlessly perfects
Whom He royally elects!
How He hammers him and hurts him,
And with mighty blows converts him
Into trial shapes of clay which
Only God understands;
While his tortured heart is crying
And he lifts beseeching hands!
How He bends but never breaks
When his good He undertakes;
How He uses whom He chooses,
And with every purpose fuses him;
But every act induces him
To try His splendor out—
God knows what He's about.

SELECTED

Life is a quarry, out of which we are to mold and chisel and complete a character.   **GOETHE**

February 28

MORNING

৵৽

Let us offer the sacrifice of praise to God continually (HEB. 13:15).

A city missionary, stumbling through the dirt of a dark entry, heard a voice say, "Who's there, Honey?" Striking a match, he caught a vision of earthly want and suffering, of saintly trust and peace, "cut in ebony"—calm, appealing eyes set amid the wrinkles of a pinched, black face that lay on a tattered bed. It was a bitter night in February, and she had no fire, no fuel, no light. She had had no supper, no dinner, no breakfast. She seemed to have nothing at all but rheumatism and faith in God. One could not well be more completely exiled from all pleasantness of circumstances, yet the favorite song of this old creature ran:

Nobody knows de trouble I see,
Nobody knows but Jesus;
Nobody knows de trouble I see—
Sing Glory Hallelu!

Sometimes I'm up, sometimes I'm down,
Sometimes I'm level on the groun'
Sometimes the glory shines aroun'—
Sing Glory Hallelu!

And so it went on: "Nobody knows de work I does, Nobody knows de griefs I has," the constant refrain being the *"Glory Hallelu!"* until the last verse rose:

Nobody knows de joys I has,
Nobody knows but Jesus!

"Troubled on every side, yet not distressed; perplexed, but not in despair; persecuted, but not forsaken; cast down, but not destroyed." It takes great Bible words to tell the cheer of the old negro auntie.

Remember Luther on his sickbed. Between his groans he managed to preach on this wise: "These pains and trouble here are like the type which the printers set; as they look now, we have to read them backwards, and they seem to have no sense or meaning in them; but up yonder, when the Lord God prints us off in the life to come, we shall find they make brave reading." Only we do not need to wait till then. Remember Paul walking the hurricane deck amid a boiling sea, bidding the frightened crew "Be of good cheer," Luther, the old negro auntie—all of them human sunflowers.   WM. C. GARNETT

EVENING

❧❧

Up . . . is not the LORD *gone out before thee?* (JUDG. 4:14)

God has guided the heroes and saints of all ages to do things which the common sense of the community has regarded as ridiculous and mad. Have *you* ever taken any risks for Christ?   CHARLES E. COWMAN

"Have not I sent thee?" (JUDG. 6:14).

God knows, and you know, what He has sent you to do. God sent Moses to Egypt to bring three millions of bondmen out of the house of bondage into the Promised Land. Did he fail? It looked at first as if he were going to. But *did* he? God sent Elijah to stand before Ahab, and it was a bold thing for him to say that there should be neither dew nor rain: but did he not lock up the heavens for three years and six months? Did he fail?

And you cannot find any place in Scripture where a man was ever sent by God to do a work in which he ever failed.   **D. L. MOODY**

> *Had Moses failed to go, had God*
> *Granted his prayer, there would have been*
> *For him no leadership to win;*
> *No pillared fire; no magic rod;*
> *No wonders in the land of Zin;*
> *No smiting of the sea; no tears*
> *Ecstatic, shed on Sinai's steep;*
> *No Nebo with a God to keep*
> *His burial; only forty years*
> *Of desert, watching with his sheep.*
>
> **J. R. MILLER**

Our might is His Almightiness.

February 29

MORNING

Launch out into the deep (LUKE 5:4).

How deep He does not say. The depth into which we launch will depend upon how perfectly we have given up the shore, and the greatness of our need, and the apprehension of our possibilities. The fish were to be found in the deep, not in the shallow water.

So with us; our needs are to be met in the deep things of God. We are to launch out into the deep of God's Word, which the Spirit can open up to us in such crystal fathomless meaning that the same words we have accepted in times past will have an ocean meaning in them, which renders their first meaning to us very shallow.

Into the deep of the atonement, until Christ's precious blood is so illuminated by the Spirit that it becomes an omnipotent balm, and food and medicine for the soul and body.

Into the deep of the Father's will, until we apprehend it in its infinite minuteness and goodness, and its far-sweeping provision and care for us.

Into the deep of the Holy Spirit, until He becomes a bright, dazzling, sweet, fathomless summer sea, in which we bathe and bask and breathe, and lose ourselves and our sorrows in the calmness and peace of His everlasting presence.

Into the deep of the Holy Spirit, until He becomes a bright, marvelous answer to prayer, the most careful and tender guidance, the most thoughtful anticipation of our needs, the most accurate and supernatural shaping of our events.

Into the deep of God's purposes and coming kingdom, until the Lord's coming and His millennial reign are opened up to us; and beyond these the bright entrancing ages on ages unfold themselves, until the mental eye is dazed with light, and the heart flutters with inexpressible anticipations of its joy with Jesus and the glory to be revealed.

Into all these things, Jesus bids us launch. He made us and He made the deep, and to its fathomless depths He has fitted our longings and capabilities.   FROM SOUL FOOD

> *Its streams the whole creation reach,*
> *So plenteous is the store;*
> *Enough for all, enough for each;*
> *Enough forevermore.*

The deep waters of the Holy Spirit are always accessible, because they are always *proceeding*. Will you not this day claim afresh to be immersed and drenched in these waters of life? The waters in Ezekiel's vision first of all oozed from under the doors of the temple. Then the man with the measuring line measured and found the waters to the ankles. Still further measurement, and they were waters to the knees. Once again they were measured and the waters to the loins. Then they became waters to swim in—a river that could not be passed over (read Ezek. 47). How far have we advanced into this river of life? The Holy Spirit would have a complete self-effacement. Not merely ankle-deep, knee-deep, loin-deep, but self-deep. We ourselves hidden out of sight and bathed in this life-giving stream. Let go the shorelines and launch out into the deep. Never forget, the Man with the measuring line is with us today.   J. G. M.

March 1

‿◠◡◠‿

Consider the work of God: for who can make that straight, which he hath made crooked? (ECCLES. 7:13).

Often God seems to place His children in positions of profound difficulty, leading them into a wedge from which there is no escape; contriving a situation which no human judgment would have permitted, had it been previously consulted. The very cloud conducts them thither. You may be thus involved at this very hour.

It does seem perplexing and very serious to that degree, but it is perfectly right. The issue will more than justify Him who has brought you hither. It is a platform for the display of His almighty grace and power.

He will not only deliver you; but in doing so, He will give you a lesson that you will never forget, and to which, in many a psalm and song, in after days, you will revert. You will never be able to thank God enough for having done just as He has. SELECTED

We may wait till He explains,
Because we know that Jesus reigns.

It puzzles me; but, Lord, Thou understandest,
And wilt one day explain this crooked thing.
Meanwhile, I know that it has worked out Thy best—
Its very crookedness taught me to cling.

Thou has fenced up my ways, made my paths crooked,
To keep my wand'ring eyes fixed on Thee,
To make me what I was not, humble, patient;
To draw my heart from earthly love to Thee.

So I will thank and praise Thee for this puzzle,
And trust where I cannot understand.
Rejoicing Thou dost hold me worth such testing,
I cling the closer to Thy guiding hand.

F. E. M. I.

Pass through the host . . . armed. (JOSH. 1:11, 14)

Pass through, pass through, nor sit among
The hosts encamped around.
The glorious Victor paved the way,
Put all His armor on you may.
With shield of faith held well in view,
Thy song ere long—"He brought me through!"
E. N. P.

*A*fter a step of faith most persons are looking for sunny skies and unruffled seas, and when they meet a storm or tempest they are filled with astonishment and perplexity. *But this is just what we must expect if we have received anything of the Lord.* The best token of His presence is the adversary's defiance, and the more real our blessing the more certainly it will be challenged. It is a good thing to go out looking for the worst, then if it comes we are not surprised; while if our path be smooth and the way unopposed it is all the more delightful because it comes as a glad surprise.

But let us quite understand what we mean by *temptation*. You, especially, who have stepped out with the assurance that you have died to self and sin, may be greatly amazed to find yourself assailed with a tempest of thoughts and feelings that seem to come wholly from within, and you will be impelled to say, "Why, I thought I was dead, but I seem to be alive!" This, beloved, is the time to remember that in temptation the instigation is not your sin but only the voice of the evil one. A. B. SIMPSON

Why does the battle thicken so—
The darts rain fast upon my breast,
While missiles hurled with cruel force
Ring loud against my burnished crest?
Above the din I seem to hear
My Captain's voice in accents clear,
"Because your shield is down!"

Why does the enemy advance
And hem us 'round on every hand
While we, the army of the Lord,
Can scarce his arrogance withstand?

Above the shouts I seem to hear
My Captain's voice in accents clear,
"Because your shields are down!"

Ah! Now it's brighter—now I see
The enemy is taking flight,
And lo, the banner of the Cross
Streams red against the morning light;
But as they flee I seem to hear
My Captain call in accents clear,
"Let not your shields go down!"

THOMAS KIMBER

Failure in our faith is fatal. Faith is our spiritual shield
protecting us from the darts of the devil. Lay this shield aside
even for a moment, and disaster follows. Any departure
from the living God is the result of unbelief.

March 2

MORNING

~~~~

Be ready in the morning, and come up . . . present thyself there to me
in the top of the mount. And no man shall come up with thee
(EXOD. 34:2–3).

The morning watch is essential. You must not face the day until you have faced God, nor look into the face of others until you have looked into His.

You cannot expect to be victorious, if the day begins only in your own strength. Face the work of every day with the influence of a few thoughtful, quiet moments with your heart and God. Do not meet other people, even those of your own home, until you have first met the great Guest and honored Companion of your life—Jesus Christ.

Meet Him alone. Meet Him regularly. Meet Him with His open Book of counsel before you; and face the regular and the irregular duties of each day with the influence of His personality definitely controlling your every act.

Begin the day with God!
He is thy Sun and Day!
His is the radiance of thy dawn;
To Him address thy day.

Sing a new song at morn!
Join the glad woods and hills:
Join the fresh winds and seas and plains,
Join the bright flowers and rills.

Sing thy first song to God!
Not to thy fellow men;
Not to the creatures of His hand,
But to the glorious One.

Take thy first walk with God!
Let Him go forth with thee;
By stream, or sea, or mountain path,
Seek still His company.

Thy first transaction be
With God Himself above;
So shall thy business prosper well,
All the day be love.

HORATIUS BONAR

The men who have done the most for God in this world have been early upon their knees.

Matthew Henry used to be in his study at four, and remain there till eight; then, after breakfast and family prayer, he used to be there again till noon; after dinner, he resumed his book or pen till four, and spent the rest of the day in visiting friends.

Doddridge himself alludes to his "Family Expositor" as an example of the difference of rising between five and seven, which, in forty years, is nearly equivalent to ten years more of life.

Dr. Adam Clark's "Commentary" was chiefly prepared very early in the morning.

Barnes's popular and useful "Commentary" has been also the fruit of "early morning hours."

Simeon's "Sketches" were chiefly worked out between four and eight.

༄༅

And apart to his disciples he explained all.
(MARK 4:34, ENGLISHMAN'S GREEK N.T.)

God may not explain to you a thousand things which puzzle your reason in His dealings with you, but if you always see yourself to be His love-slave, He will awaken in you a jealous love, and bestow upon you many blessings which come only to those who are in the inner circle.

I can still believe that a day comes for all of us, however far off it may be, when we shall understand; when these tragedies that now blacken and darken the very air of heaven for us will sink into their places in a scheme so august, so magnificent, so joyful, that we shall laugh for wonder and delight.

ARTHUR CHRISTOPHER BENSON

Will not the end explain
The crossed endeavor, earnest purpose foiled,
The strange bewilderment of good work spoiled,
The clinging weariness, the inward strain?
Will not the end explain?

Meanwhile He comforteth
Them that are losing patience. 'Tis His way:
But none can write the words they heard Him say,
For men to read; only they know He saith
Sweet words and comforteth.

Not that He doth explain
The mystery that baffleth; but a sense
Husheth the quiet heart, that far, far hence
Lieth a field set thick with golden grain
Wetted in seedling days by many a rain.
The end—it will explain.

GOLD CORD

March 3

∿

And the spirit cried, and rent him sore, and came out of him
(MARK 9:26).

Evil never surrenders its hold without a sore fight. We never pass into any spiritual inheritance through the delightful exercises of a picnic, but always through the grim contentions of the battlefield. It is so in the secret realm of the soul. Every faculty which wins its spiritual freedom does so at the price of blood. Apollyon is not put to flight by a courteous request; he straddles across the full breadth of the way, and our progress has to be registered in blood and tears. This we must remember or we shall add to all the other burdens of life the gall of misinterpretation. We are not "born again" into soft and protected nurseries, but in the open country where we suck strength from the very terror of the tempest. "We must through much tribulation enter into the kingdom of God."

DR. J. H. JOWETT

Faith of our Fathers! living still,
In spite of dungeon, fire and sword:
O how our hearts beat high with joy
Whene'er we hear that glorious word.
Faith of our Fathers! Holy Faith!
We will be true to Thee till death!
Our fathers, chained in prisons dark,
Were still in heart of conscience free;
How sweet would be their children's fate,
If they, like them, could die for Thee!

∿

Where there is no vision, the people perish. (PROV. 29:18)

We must see something before we make our ventures! Faith must first have visions: faith sees a light, if you will, an imaginary light, and leaps! Faith is always born of vision and hope! We must have the gleam of the thing hoped for shining across the waste before we can have an energetic and energizing faith.

Are we not safe in saying that the majority of people have no fine hopes, are devoid of *the vision splendid,* and therefore, have no spiritual audacity in spiritual adventure and enterprise? Our hopes are petty and peddling, and they don't give birth to crusades. There are no shining towers and minarets on our horizon, no new Jerusalem, and therefore we do not set out in chivalrous explorations.

We need a transformation in "the things hoped for." We need to be *renewed in mind,* and renewed in mind *daily.* We need to have the far-off towering summits of vast and noble possibilities enthroned in our imaginations. Our gray and uninviting horizons must glow with the unfading colors of immortal hopes. SELECTED

> So few men venture out beyond the blazed trail,
> 'Tis he who has the courage to go past this sign
> That cannot in his mission fail.
> He will have left at least some mark behind
> To guide some other brave exploring mind.

No man is of any use until he has dared everything.

ROBERT LOUIS STEVENSON

March 4

MORNING

∽⧉∾

*Followers of them who through faith and patience
inherit the promises* (HEB. 6:12).

They (heroes of faith) are calling to us from the heights that they have won, and telling us that what man once did man can do again. Not only do they remind us of the necessity of faith, but also of that patience by which faith has its perfect work. Let us fear to take ourselves out of the hands of our heavenly Guide or to miss a single lesson of His loving discipline by discouragement or doubt.

"There is only one thing," said a village blacksmith, "that I fear, and that is to be thrown on the scrap heap.

"When I am tempering a piece of steel, I first heat it, hammer it, and then suddenly plunge it into the bucket of cold water. I very soon find whether it will take temper or go to pieces in the process. When I discover after one or two tests that it is not going to allow itself to be tempered, I throw it on the scrap heap and sell it for a cent a pound when the junkman comes around.

"So I find the Lord tests me, too, by fire and water and heavy blows of His heavy hammer, and if I am willing to stand the test, or am not going to prove a fit subject for His tempering process, I am afraid He may throw me on the scrap heap."

When the fire is hottest, hold still, for there will be a blessed "afterward"; and with Job we may be able to say, "When he hath tried me I shall come forth as gold."   SELECTED

Sainthood springs out of suffering. It takes eleven tons of pressure on a piano to tune it. God will tune you to harmonize with heaven's keynote if you can stand the strain.

> *Things that hurt and things that mar*
> *Shape the man for perfect praise;*
> *Shock and strain and ruin are*
> *Friendlier than the smiling days.*

EVENING

∽∾

God shall hear. (PS. 55:19)

I was standing at a bank counter in Liverpool waiting for a clerk to come. I picked up a pen and began to print on a blotter in large letters two words which had gripped me like a vise: "PRAY THROUGH." I kept talking to a friend and printing until I had the desk blotter filled from top to bottom with a column. I transacted my business and went away. The next day my friend came to see me, and said he had a striking story to tell.

A businessman came into the bank soon after we had gone. He had grown discouraged with business troubles. He started to transact some business with the same clerk, over that blotter, when his eye caught the long column of "PRAY THROUGH." He asked who wrote those words and when he was told exclaimed, "That is the very message I needed. *I will pray through.* I have tried in my own strength to worry through, and have merely mentioned my troubles to God; now I am going to pray the situation through until I get light."   CHARLES M. ALEXANDER

> *Don't stop praying, but have more trust;*
> *Don't stop praying! for pray we must;*

Faith will banish a mount of care;
Don't stop praying! God answers prayer.
C. M. A.

All I have seen teaches me to trust the Creator for what I have not seen!

March 5

MORNING

∾∾

We are made partakers of Christ, if we hold the beginning of our
confidence steadfast unto the end (HEB. 3:14).

It is the last step that wins; and there is no place in the pilgrim's progress where so many dangers lurk as the region that lies hard by the portals of the Celestial City. It was there that Doubting Castle stood. It was there that the enchanted ground lured the tired traveler to fatal slumber. It is when heaven's heights are full in view that hell's gate is most persistent and full of deadly peril. "Let us not be weary in well-doing, for in due season we shall reap, *if we faint not.*" "So run, that ye may obtain."

In the bitter waves of woe
Beaten and tossed about
By the sullen winds that blow
From the desolate shores of doubt,
Where the anchors that faith has cast
Are dragging in the gale,
I am quietly holding fast
To the things that cannot fail.

And fierce through the fiends may fight,
And long though the angels hide,
I know that truth and right
Have the universe on their side;
And that somewhere beyond the stars
Is a love that is better than fate.
When the night unlocks her bars.
I shall see Him—and I will wait.
WASHINGTON GLADDEN

The problem of getting great things from God
is being able to hold on for the last half hour.
SELECTED

EVENING

❦

So the children of Joseph, Manasseh and Ephraim,
took their inheritance. (JOSH. 16:4)

A dying judge said to his pastor, "Do you know enough about law to understand what is meant by joint tenancy?"

"No," was the reply; "I know nothing about law; I know a little about grace, and that satisfies me."

"Well," he said, "if you and I were joint tenants on a farm, I could not say to you, 'That is your field of corn, and this is mine; that is your blade of grass, and this is mine,' but we would share alike in everything on the place. I have just been lying here and thinking with unspeakable joy that Christ Jesus has nothing apart from me; that everything He has is mine, and that we will share alike through all eternity."

God wants you to have all that He has—His Son, His life, His love, His Spirit, His glory. "All things are yours; and ye are Christ's; and Christ is God's." "Son, thou art ever with me, and all that I have is thine" (Luke 15:31). What a privilege! What a life for a child of God! Only unbelief can blind us to the Father's love. Only with a false humility the children of the King set limitations about their lives that He never appointed. The full table is set for us, and we eat so sparingly, forgetful of the voice that cries, "Eat, O friends: drink, yea, drink abundantly, O beloved!"

"The resources of the Christian life," says Dr. Robert F. Horton, "are just Jesus Christ." He is our regal provision for the way. He is the way. Let us draw upon these Divine resources. Whom should He bless, even on earth, if not His own?

Supply yourself from Him!

God is to be adored, but He is also to be *used*. Merely to worship Him in the awe of His greatness and holiness is not to please Him fully. He wants us to draw upon Him as an asset of our practical life, and as a priceless possession. We live in Him; but He also lives in us to bring to our soul the power of His own infinite life. *To possess* HIM *is to possess all things and to have power to attain our noblest purposes.*

He is always at our service. Use Him, then; for He is there and waits for you to use Him. *All the unclaimed wealth of the forty thousand checks in the bankbook of the Bible is ours!* And "He satisfieth [satiates] the longing soul" (Ps. 107:9). *God is our God to be used for things we need Him for.*

> *My need and Thy great fullness meet,*
> *And I have all in Thee.*

God has a separate inheritance for each one. Do not fail to enter upon *yours.*

"The right of inheritance is thine" (JER. 32:8).

March 6

MORNING

We trusted (LUKE 24:21).

I have always felt so sorry that in that walk to Emmaus the disciples had not said to Jesus, "We *still* trust"; instead of *"We trusted."* That is so sad—something that is all over.

If they had only said, "Everything is against our hope; it looks as if our trust was vain, but we do not give up; we believe we shall see Him again." But no they walked by His side declaring their lost faith, and He had to say to them, "O fools, and slow of heart to believe!"

Are we not in the same danger of having these words said to us? We can afford to lose anything and everything if we do not lose our faith in the God of truth and love.

Let us never put our faith, as these disciples did, in a past tense—*"We trusted."* But let us ever say, *"I am trusting."*   **FROM CRUMBS**

> *The soft, sweet summer was warm and glowing,*
> *Bright were the blossoms on every bough:*
> *I trusted Him when the roses were blooming;*
> *I trust Him now. . . .*
>
> *Small were my faith should it weakly falter*
> *Now that the roses have ceased to blow;*
> *Frail were the trust that now should alter,*
> *Doubting His love when storm clouds grow.*

THE SONG OF A BIRD IN A WINTER STORM

For me and thee. (MATT. 17:27)

Peter had been a fisherman. Jesus had said, "Follow me," and Peter had given up his fishing business to follow. We read that *straightway* he forsook his nets, and followed. That must have been a tremendous experience for Peter—giving up his means of livelihood, upkeep of his home, not to mention the money for those taxes. Peter, the Fisherman, left *all* to follow Christ. The Lord knew that he had given up his means of livelihood to answer His call, and from the very thing that Peter had given up for His sake—*fish*—the Lord met His servant's need when the time for paying the taxes came around. *No servant of Christ will ever be the loser.*

So our dear Lord is always thinking in advance of *our* needs, and He loves to save us from embarrassment and anticipate our anxieties and cares by laying up His loving acts and providing before the emergency comes. "For me and thee," He had said, bracketing those words together in a wondrous, sacred intimacy. He puts Himself first in the embarrassing need, and bears the heavy end of the burden for His distressed and suffering child. He makes our cares, *His* cares; our sorrows, *His* sorrows; our shame, *His* shame.

> *The tax was due—the Master's and disciple's,*
> *And to the sea the Master strangely sent:*
> *A fish would yield the needful piece of silver!*
> *Strange bank, indeed, from which to pay that rent.*
>
> *"One piece of silver!" Not two equal portions!*
> *One piece of silver—one, and shining bright;*
> *"That use for Me and thee," thus spoke the Master,*
> *"That claims on Me and thee we thus unite."*
>
> *Blest, happy bond! May I thus sweetly know Him!*
> *Am I His servant? Hath He use of me?*
> *Then, O my soul, why shouldst thou own law's limit,*
> *If they dear Lord doth find delight in thee?*
>
> *If thou art His—joint-heir in all His riches,*
> *Then, O my soul, a simpler spirit grow;*
> *"How shall He not, with Him, why, give us all things,"*
> *All that we need, to do His work below!*
>
> J. DANSON SMITH

March 7

We were troubled on every side (2 COR. 7:5).

Why should God have to lead us thus, and allow the pressure to be so hard and constant? Well, in the first place, it shows His all-sufficient strength and grace much better than if we were exempt from pressure and trial. "The treasure is in earthen vessels, that the excellency of the power may be of God, and not of us."

It makes us more conscious of our dependence upon Him. God is constantly trying to teach us our dependence, and to hold us absolutely in His hand and hanging upon His care.

This was the place where Jesus Himself stood and where He wants us to stand, not with self-constituted strength, but with a hand ever leaning upon His, and a trust that dare not take one step alone. It teaches us trust.

There is no way of learning faith except by trial. It is God's school of faith, and it is far better for us to learn to trust God than to enjoy life.

The lesson of faith once learned, is an everlasting acquisition and an eternal fortune made; and without trust even riches will leave us poor.

FROM DAYS OF HEAVEN UPON EARTH

Why must I weep when others sing?
"To test the deeps of suffering."
Why must I work while others rest?
"To spend my strength at God's request."
Why must I lose while others gain?
"To understand defeat's sharp pain."
Why must this lot of life be mine
When that which fairer seems is thine?
"Because God knows what plans for me
Shall blossom in eternity."

They came and saw where he dwelt, and abode with him that day.
(JOHN 1:39)

I wonder what it was that lured your feet to follow Him upon His homeward way. Was it mere eagerness to see the street, and house in which He sojourned, and to stay at closer quarters with Him for one day?

. . . Or, did you feel a strange attractive Power, which lured you from your boat beside the bay; when, heeding not the passing of the hour, and caring not what other folk might say, you made your home with Him for that brief day?

. . . Perhaps you felt a holy discontent, after the hours spent in that presence fair? Certain it is you thenceforth were intent on fishing men; for, from His side you went, and straightway brought your brother to Him there!

. . . Oh, Andrew! you could never be the same, after the contact of that wondrous day. You ne'er again could play with passion's flame, or harbor pride or hate, or grasp for fame, or give to avarice a place to stay.

. . . Rather, I think, you might be heard to say, "Something about Him burned my pride away, and cooled my hate and changed it for Love's way . . . *After the healing contact of that stay, I must bring Simon to have one such day!*"

. . . And, ever after, as men passed your way, they would be conscious of some strange, new spell; some unexplained, mysterious miracle. Then, in an awe-filled whisper they would say, *"Andrew is greatly altered since that day!"*

. . . Oh! Wondrous Sojourner on life's dark way. Savior! Who understands what sinners say, *Grant me to come beneath Thy magic sway, lest, rough-edged, loveless, sin-stained, I should stay, lacking the impress of just such a day!*
                                        ELEANOR VELLACOTT WOOD

Stradivari of Cremona is said to have marked every one of the priceless violins which he made, with the name of Jesus, and so well-known did this become that his work is still called *"Stradivarius del Gesu."*

If our lives might become equally well known because of that sacred mark by which He said that *all men shall know,* there would be more people who, like the blind beggar, would come to Him that they might receive their sight, and who, too, would *worship Him.*

March 8

༺৯৩

Do as thou hast said . . . that thy name may be magnified forever
(1 CHRON. 17:23–24).

This is a most blessed phase of true prayer. Many a time we ask for things which are not absolutely promised. We are not sure therefore until we have persevered for some time whether our petitions are in the line of God's purpose or no. There are other occasions, and in the life of David this was one, when we are fully persuaded that what we ask is according to God's will. We feel led to take up and plead some promise from the page of Scripture, under the special impression that it contains a message for us. At such times, in confident faith, we say, "Do as Thou hast said." There is hardly any position more utterly beautiful, strong, or safe, than to put the finger upon some promise of the divine word, and claim it. There need be no anguish, or struggle, or wrestling; we simply present the check and ask for cash, produce the promise, and claim its fulfillment; nor can there be any doubt as to the issue. It would give much interest to prayer, if we were more definite. It is far better to claim a few things specifically than a score vaguely. F. B. MEYER

Every promise of Scripture is a writing of God, which may be pleaded before Him with this reasonable request: *"Do as Thou hast said."* The Creator will not cheat His creature who depends upon His truth; and far more, the heavenly Father will not break His word to His own child.

"Remember the word unto thy servant, on which thou hast caused me to hope," is most prevalent pleading. It is a double argument: it is Thy *Word.* Wilt Thou not keep it? Why hast Thou spoken of it, if Thou wilt not make it good. Thou hast caused me to hope in it, wilt Thou disappoint the hope which Thou has Thyself begotten in me? C. H. SPURGEON

"Being absolutely certain that whatever promise he is bound by, he is able also to make good" (ROM. 4:21 WEYMOUTH).

It is the everlasting faithfulness of God that makes a Bible promise "exceeding great and precious." Human promises are often worthless. Many a broken promise has left a broken heart. But since the world was made, God has never broken a single promise made to one of His trusting children.

Oh, it is sad for a poor Christian to stand at the door of the promise, in the dark night of affliction, afraid to draw the latch, whereas he should then come boldly for shelter as a child into his father's house. GURNAL

Every promise is built upon four pillars: God's justice and holiness, which will not suffer Him to deceive; His grace or goodness, which will not suffer Him to forget; His truth, which will not suffer Him to change, which makes Him able to accomplish. SELECTED

EVENING

God having provided some better thing for us. (HEB. 11:40)

Our heavenly Father never takes any earthly thing from His children, unless He means to give them *something better instead.*

GEORGE MÜLLER

> *An easy thing, O Power Divine,*
> *To thank Thee for these gifts of Thine!*
> *For summer's sunshine, winter's snow,*
> *For hearts that kindle, thoughts that glow;*
> *But when shall I attain to this:*
> *To thank Thee for the things I miss?*
>
> *For all young fancy's early gleams,*
> *The dreamed-of joys that still are dreams,*
> *Hope unfulfilled, and pleasures known*
> *Through others' fortunes, not my own,*
> *And blessings seen that are not given,*
> *And ne'er will be—this side of heaven.*
>
> *Had I, too, shared the joys I see,*
> *Would there have been a heaven for me?*
> *Could I have felt Thy presence near*
> *Had I possessed what I held dear?*
> *My deepest fortune, highest bliss,*
> *Have grown, perchance, from things I miss.*
>
> *Sometimes there comes an hour of calm;*
> *Grief turns to blessing, pain to balm;*
> *A Power that works above my will*
> *Still leads me onward, upward still;*
> *And then my heart attains to this:*
> *To thank Thee for the things I miss.*

THOMAS WENTWORTH HIGGINSON

Instead of the dry land, springs of water!
Instead of heaviness, the garment of praise!
Instead of the thorn, the fir tree!
Instead of the brier, the myrtle tree!
Instead of ashes, beauty!
ISAIAH 41:18; 55:13; 61:3

March 9

MORNING

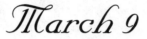

Look from the top (SONG OF SOL. 4:8).

Crushing weights give the Christian wings. It seems like a contradiction in terms, but it is a blessed truth. David out of some bitter experience cried: "Oh, that I had wings like a dove! for then would I fly away, and be at rest" (Ps. 55:6). But before he finished this meditation he seems to have realized that his wish for wings was a realizable one. For he says, "Cast thy burden upon the Lord, and he shall sustain thee."

The word "burden" is translated in the Bible margin, "what he (Jehovah) hath given thee." The saints' burdens are God-given; they lead him to "wait upon Jehovah," and when that is done, in the magic of trust, the "burden" is metamorphosed into a pair of wings, and the weighted one "mounts up with wings as eagles." **FROM SUNDAY SCHOOL TIMES**

One day when walking down the street,
On business bent, while thinking hard
About the "hundred cares" which seemed
Like thunder clouds about to break
In torrents, Self-pity said to me:
"You poor, poor thing, you have too much
To do. Your life is far too hard.
This heavy load will crush you soon."
A swift response of sympathy
Welled up within. The burning sun
Seemed more intense. The dust and noise

Of puffing motors flying past
With rasping blast of blowing horn
Incensed still more the whining nerves,
The fabled last back-breaking straw
To weary, troubled, fretting mind.

"Ah, yes, 'twill break and crush my life;
I cannot bear this constant strain
Of endless, aggravating cares;
They are too great for such as I."
So thus my heart condoled itself,
"Enjoying misery," when lo!
A "still small voice" distinctly said,
"'Twas sent to lift you—not to crush."
I saw at once my great mistake.
My place was not beneath the load
But on the top! God meant it not
That I should carry it. He sent
It here to carry me. Full well
He knew my incapacity
Before the plan was made. He saw
A child of His in need of grace
And power to serve; a puny twig
Requiring sun and rain to grow;
An undeveloped chrysalis;
A weak soul lacking faith in God.
He could not help but see all this
And more. And then, with tender thought
He placed it where it had to grow—
Or die. To lie and cringe beneath
One's load means death, but life and power
Await all those who dare to rise above.
Our burdens are our wings; on them
We soar to higher realms of grace;
Without them we must roam for aye
On plains of undeveloped faith,
(For faith grows but by exercise
In circumstance impossible).

Oh, paradox of Heaven. The load
We think will crush was sent to lift us
Up to God! Then, soul of mine,

Climb up! for naught can e'er be crushed
Save what is underneath the weight.
How may we climb! By what ascent
Shall we surmount the carping cares
Of life! Within His word is found
The key which opens His secret stairs;
Alone with Christ, secluded there,
We mount our loads, and rest in Him.

MISS MARY BUTTERFIELD

EVENING

Now Jacob's well was there. Jesus therefore, being wearied with his journey, sat thus on the well: and it was about the sixth hour.
(JOHN 4:6)

I have known thy continued enduring, and thy being patient, and thy unwearied painstaking for My Name's sake.
(REV. 2:2–3, TAMIL)

Our Lord took His apostles aside when they were fatigued, and said, "Let us rest awhile." He never drove His overtired faculties. When tired, "He sat by the well." He used to go and rest in the home of Martha and Mary after the fatigue of working in Jerusalem. The Scripture shows it was His custom. He tells us all—you, and me, and all—to let tomorrow take care of itself, and merely to meet the evil of the present day.

As Elijah slept under a juniper tree, an angel touched him and said, "Arise and eat." God had sent His wearied servant to sleep. In his over-wrought condition sleep was his greatest need, and it is precisely under such conditions that sleep is often wooed in vain. Are we ever astonished at the miracle of sleep? Remember you have to do with the same God who ministered to Elijah, and

Though thy way be long and dreary,
Eagle strength He'll still renew.

Real foresight consists in reserving our own forces. If we labor with anxiety about the future, we destroy that strength which will enable us to meet the future. If we take more in hand now than we can well do, we break up and the work is broken up with us.

Bakers of bread for others to eat must be very careful to husband their strength. They are not much seen, but much felt; unknown multitudes would feel their loss and their failing means others famishing.

We need to take lessons of Sir William Cecil, once Lord Mayor of London. Upon throwing off his gown at night he would say to it, "Lay there, Lord Treasurer!" and forget all the cares of State until he resumed his official garb in the morning. **THE GOLDEN MILESTONE**

"Be still, and know!"

The Hebrew word signifies more than quietness and meditation before God; it means to let the tension go out of our life, just as the great cable holds in place the great steamer until the vessel reaches its channel and can go with its own steam. **JOHN TIMOTHY STONE**

March 10

MORNING

∽≈∾

The just shall live by faith (HEB. 10:38).

Seemings and feelings are often substituted for faith. Pleasurable emotions and deep satisfying experiences are part of the Christian life, but they are not all of it. Trials, conflicts, battles and testings lie along the way, and are not to be counted as misfortunes, but rather as part of our necessary discipline.

In all these varying experiences we are to reckon on Christ as dwelling in the heart, regardless of our feelings if we are walking obediently before Him. Here is where many get into trouble; they try to walk by feeling rather than faith.

One of the saints tells us that it seemed as though God had withdrawn Himself from her. His mercy *seemed* clean gone. For six weeks her desolation lasted, and then the heavenly Lover seemed to say:

"Catherine, thou hast looked for Me without in the world of sense, but all the while I have been within waiting for thee; meet Me in the inner chamber of thy spirit, *for I am there.*"

Distinguish between the fact of God's presence, and the *emotion* of the fact. It is a happy thing when the soul seems desolate and deserted, if our faith can say, "I see Thee not. I feel Thee not, but Thou art certainly and graciously here, where I am as I am." Say it again and again: "Thou are here: though the bush does not seem to burn with fire, it *does* burn. I will take the shoes from off my feet, for the place on which I stand is holy ground." LONDON CHRISTIAN

Believe God's Word and power more than you believe your own feelings and experiences. Your Rock is Christ, and it is not the Rock which ebbs and flows, but your sea. SAMUEL RUTHERFORD

Keep your eye steadily fixed on the infinite grandeur of Christ's finished work and righteousness. Look to Jesus and believe, look to Jesus and live! Nay, more; as you look to him, hoist your sails and buffet manfully the sea of life. Do not remain in the haven of distrust, or sleeping on your shadows in inactive repose, or suffering your frames and feelings to pitch and toss on one another like vessels idly moored in a harbor. The religious life is not a brooding over emotions, grazing the keel of faith in the shallows, of dragging the anchor of hope through the oozy tide mud as if afraid of encountering the healthy breeze. Away! With your canvas spread to the gale, trusting in Him, who rules the raging of the waters. The safety of the tinted bird is to be on the wing. If its haunt be near the ground—if it fly low—it exposes itself to the fowler's net or snare. If we remain groveling on the low ground of feeling and emotion, we shall find ourselves entangled in a thousand meshes of doubt and despondency, temptation and unbelief. "But surely in vain the net is spread in the sight of THAT WHICH HATH A WING" (marginal reading Prov. 1:17). Hope thou in God. J. R. MACDUFF

When I cannot enjoy the faith of assurance,
I live by the faith of adherence.
MATTHEW HENRY

EVENING

〰

Faultless . . . with exceeding joy! (JUDE 24)

When a young girl, an intense passion for music was awakened within my soul. Father brought great joy into my life by presenting me with a beautiful organ. It would thrill me to the very fiber of my being, as the days slipped by, to be able to draw forth such wonderful harmony from my beloved instrument.

I used to sit at the organ in the early morning hours, just as the birds began to awaken, and through the open windows listen to their sweet little bird notes as they mingled with the melody of the organ, like a paean of praise to our Creator!

Then, one morning, quite suddenly, and at a time when I was preparing with girlish enthusiasm for my first concert appearance, one of the notes became faulty. How the discordant sound grated upon my sensitive ear. Father, sensing my grief, said: "Never mind, daughter, I will have the tuner come." Long hours the tuner worked on that faulty note before it again rang out all sweet and true with the others. And the concert was a success, *because the tuner was successful!*

Good Tuner, why
This ruthless, slow examination?
Why, on that one poor note,
Expend such careful concentration?
Just pass it by.
How I will let my soul respond to thee!
And see

But, no! Again, and yet again,
With skilled determination,
Rang out that meaningless reiteration.
While, ever and anon, through the great aisle's dim space,
Echoed the reverent chord; the loud harmonious phrase,

Till day began to wane.
And still, more patiently, the Tuner wrought
With that one faulty note; until, with zest,
All sweet and true, it answered like the rest.
Then, as the haloed glories of the sunset flamed
and gleamed,
Swift through the storied windows long shafts of crimson streamed:
And we poor whispering wayfarers heard, round about and o'er us,
The throbbing, thundering triumphs of the Hallelujah Chorus!

THE TOWER IN THE CATHEDRAL, BY FAY INCHFAWN

March 11

Now after the death of Moses, the servant of the Lord, it came to pass that the Lord spake unto Joshua, the son of Nun, Moses' minister, saying, Moses my servant is dead; now, therefore arise, go over this Jordan, thou and all this people (JOSH. 1:1–2).

Sorrow came to you yesterday, and emptied your home. Your first impulse now is to give up, and sit down in despair amid the wrecks of your hopes. But you dare not do it. You are in the line of battle, and the crisis is at hand. To falter a moment would be to imperil some holy interest. Other lives would be harmed by your pausing, holy interests would suffer, should your hands be folded. You must not linger even to indulge your grief.

A distinguished general related this pathetic incident of his own experience in time of war. The general's son was a lieutenant of battery. An assault was in progress. The father was leading his division in a charge; as he pressed on in the field, suddenly his eye was caught by the sight of a dead battery-officer lying just before him. One glance showed him it was his own son. His fatherly impulse was to stop beside the loved form and give vent to his grief, but the duty of the moment demanded that he should press on in the charge; so, quickly snatching one hot kiss from the dead lips, he hastened away, leading his command in the assault.

Weeping inconsolably beside a grave can never give back love's banished treasure, nor can any blessing come out of such sadness. Sorrow makes deep scars; it writes its record ineffaceably on the heart which suffers. We really never get over our great griefs; we are never altogether the same after we have passed through them as we were before. Yet there is a humanizing and fertilizing influence in sorrow which has been rightly accepted and cheerfully borne. Indeed, they are poor who have never suffered, and have none of sorrow's marks upon them. The joy set before us should shine upon our griefs as the sun shines through the clouds, glorifying them. God has so ordered, that in pressing on in duty we shall find the truest, richest comfort for ourselves. Sitting down to brood over our sorrows, the darkness deepens about us and creeps into our heart, and our strength changes to weakness. But, if we turn away from the gloom, and take up the tasks and duties to which God calls us, the light will come again, and we shall grow stronger.   J. R. MILLER

Thou knowest that through our tears
Of hasty, selfish weeping
Comes surer sin, and for our petty fears
Of loss thou hast in keeping
A greater gain than all of which we dreamed;
Thou knowest that in grasping
The bright possessions which so precious seemed
We lose them; but if, clasping
Thy faithful hand, we tread with steadfast feet
The path of thy appointing,
There waits for us a treasury of sweet
Delight, royal anointing
With oil of gladness and of strength.

HELEN HUNT JACKSON

EVENING

And thou shalt be like a watered garden, and like a spring of water, whose waters fail not. (ISA. 58:11)

Holiness appeared to me to be of a sweet, pleasant . . . calm nature. It seemed to me . . . that it made the soul like a field or garden of God, with all manner of pleasant flowers—all pleasant, delightful and undisturbed; enjoying a sweet calm, and the gently vivifying beams of the sun.

The soul of a true Christian appeared like such a little white flower as we see in the spring of the year—low and humble on the ground—opening its bosom to receive the pleasant beams of the sun's glory—rejoicing, as it were, in a calm rapture—diffusing around a sweet fragrancy.

Once I rode out into the woods for my health. Having alighted from my horse in a retired place as my manner commonly had been, to walk for Divine contemplation and prayer, I had a view—that was for me extraordinary—of the glory of the Son of God. As near as I can judge, this continued about an hour; and kept me the greater part of the time in a flood of tears and weeping aloud. I felt an ardency of soul to be—what I know not otherwise how to express—*emptied and annihilated; to love Him with a holy and pure love; to serve and follow Him; to be perfectly sanctified, and made pure with a Divine and heavenly purity.*   JONATHAN EDWARDS

I never thought it could be thus, month after month to know
The river of Thy peace without one ripple in its flow;
Without one quiver in the trust, one flicker in the glow.

March 12

MORNING

The Lord brought an east wind upon the land all that day, and all that night; and when it was morning, the east wind brought the locusts. . . . Then Pharaoh called for Moses and Aaron in haste. . . . And the Lord turned a mighty strong west wind, which took away the locusts, and cast them into the Red sea; there remained not one locust in all the coasts of Egypt (EXOD. 10:13, 16, 19).

See how in the olden times, when the Lord fought for Israel against the cruel Pharaoh, the *stormy winds* wrought out their deliverance; and yet again, in that grandest display of power—the last blow that God struck at the proud defiance of Egypt. A strange, almost cruel thing it must have seemed to Israel to be hemmed in by such a host of dangers—in front the wild sea defying them, on either hand the rocky heights cutting off all hope of escape, the night of hurricane gathering over them. It was as if that first deliverance had come only to hand them over to more certain death. Completing the terror there rang out the cry: *"The Egyptians are upon us!"*

When it seemed they were trapped for the foe, then came the glorious triumph. Forth swept the *stormy wind* and beat back the waves, and the hosts of Israel marched forward, down into the path of the great deep—a way arched over with God's protecting love.

On either hand were the crystal walls glowing in the light of the glory of the Lord; and high above them swept the thunder of the storm. So on through all that night; and when, at dawn the next day, the last of Israel's host set foot upon the other shore, the work of the *stormy wind* was done.

Then sang Israel unto the Lord the song of the *"stormy wind fulfilling his word."*

"The enemy said, I will pursue, I will overtake, I will divide the spoil. . . . Thou didst blow with thy wind, the sea covered them: they sank as lead in the mighty waters."

One day, by God's great mercy, we, too, shall stand upon the sea of glass, having the harps of God. Then we shall sing the song of Moses, the servant of God, and the song of the Lamb: "Just and true are thy ways, thou King of saints." We shall know then how the *stormy winds* have wrought out our deliverance.

Now you see only the mystery of this great sorrow; then you shall see how the threatening enemy was swept away in the wild night of fear and grief.

Now you look only at the loss; then you shall see how it struck at the evil that had begun to rivet its fetters upon you.

Now you shrink from the howling winds and muttering thunders; then you shall see how they beat back the waters of destruction, and opened up your way to the goodly land of promise.

MARK GUY PEARSE

Though winds are wild,
And the gale unleashed,
My trusting heart still sings:
I know that they mean
No harm to me,
He rideth on their wings.

EVENING

⤳

If we suffer, we shall also reign with him. (2 TIM. 2:12)

There is only one place where we can receive *no answer but peace* to our question "Why?" All torturing questions find answer beneath those old gray olive trees. An hour at the foot of the Cross steadies the soul as nothing else can. Love that loves like that can be trusted with this question.

"O Christ Beloved, Thy Calvary stills all questions."

For Calvary interprets human life;
No path of pain but there we meet our Lord;
And all the strain, the terror and the strife
Die down like waves before His peaceful word,
And nowhere but beside the awful Cross,
And where the olives grow along the hill,
Can we accept the unexplained, the loss,
The crushing agony, and hold us still.

ROSE FROM BRIER

Every Gethsemane has beside it the serene, sweet heights of the Mount of Olives, and from its summit the resurrection into the heaven of heavens.

We have missed human history if we have not seen that out of the shadows of suffering have sprung the great literatures, the great paintings, the great philosophies, the great civilizations. All of them have blossomed into the light out of the shadows of suffering.

"Where a great thought is born," said one who knew by bitter experience, "there is always Gethsemane."

> The mark of rank in nature is capacity for pain,
> And the anguish of the singer makes the sweetness of the strain.

In Scotland there is a battlefield on which the Scots and their Saxon foes met in deadly conflict. A monument marks the spot; and here and there, tradition tells us, a little blue flower grows. It is called the *Flower of Culloden*. The baptism of blood, tradition avers, brought the flower into fertilization.

The choicest flowers are always "Culloden flowers." They spring only from the soil on which lifeblood of a brave heart has been spilt.

CHARLES KINGSLEY

March 13

MORNING

∽∾

Just and true are thy ways, thou King of saints (REV. 15:3).

The following incident is related by Mrs. Charles Spurgeon, who was a great sufferer for more than a quarter of a century:

"At the close of a dark and gloomy day, I lay resting on my couch as the deeper night drew on; and though all was bright within my cozy room, some of the external darkness seemed to have entered into my soul and obscured its spiritual vision. Vainly I tried to see the hand which I knew held mine, and guided my fog-enveloped feet along a steep and slippery path of suffering. In sorrow of heart I asked,

" 'Why does my Lord thus deal with His child? Why does He so often send sharp and bitter pain to visit me? Why does He permit lingering weakness to hinder the sweet service I long to render to His poor servants?'

"These fretful questions were quickly answered, and through a strange language; no interpreter was needed save the conscious whisper of my heart.

"For a while silence reigned in the little room, broken only by the crackling of the oak log burning in the fireplace. Suddenly I heard a sweet, soft sound, a little, clear, musical note, like the tender trill of a robin beneath my window.

" 'What can it be? Surely no bird can be singing out there at this time of the year and night.'

"Again came the faint, plaintive notes, so sweet, so melodious, yet mysterious enough to provoke our wonder. My friend exclaimed,

" 'It comes from the log on the fire!' The fire was letting loose the imprisoned music from the old oak's inmost heart!

"Perchance he had garnered up this song in the days when all was well with him, when birds twittered merrily on his branches, and the soft sunlight flecked his tender leaves with gold. But he had grown old since then, and hardened; ring after ring of knotty growth had sealed up the long-forgotten melody, until the fierce tongues of the flames came to consume his callousness, and the vehement heart of the fire wrung from him at once a song and a sacrifice. 'Ah,' thought I, 'when the fire of affliction draws songs of praise from us, then indeed we are purified, and our God is glorified!'

"Perhaps some of us are like this old oak log, cold, hard, insensible; we should give forth no melodious sounds, were it not for the fire which kindles around us, and releases notes of trust in Him, and cheerful compliance with His will.

"As I mused the fire burned, and my soul found sweet comfort in the parable so strangely set forth before me.

"Singing in the fire! Yes, God helping us, if that is the only way to get harmony out of these hard apathetic hearts, let the furnace be heated seven times hotter than before."

That your love may abound yet more and more. (PHIL. 1:9)

Tradition says that when they carried Saint John for the last time into the church, he lifted up his feeble hands to the listening congregation, and said,

"Little children, love one another."

The words are echoing yet throughout the world.

More precious and important even than faith is heavenly love. Without it faith must ultimately wither. Many of God's most powerful workers after a time lose their power *because they lose the spirit of love.* This is the crowning grace of Christian character. *It has a thousand shades, and it is in the finer touches that its glory consists.* Every new experience of life is but a school to learn some lesson of love. Let us not try to expel our teachers. *Let us welcome them* and so learn the lesson, that they may soon pass on and leave us to make new advances.

If mountains can be removed by faith is there less power in love?

The immense arms from either side of the *Forth Bridge* had been completed; slowly and steadily they had been built out; all that was now needed at the center of the mighty arch was the final riveting.

The day fixed was cold and chilly, and cold contracts metals. In spite of fires set under the iron to expand it the inch or two required, the union could not be completed and the day's program was a failure.

But the next day the sun rose bright; under its genial warmth the iron expanded, the holes came opposite each other, and the riveters had nothing to do but drive the binding bolts home.

"Love unbinds others by its bonds."

Love through me, Love of God,
There is no love in me,
O Fire of love, light thou the love,
That burns perpetually.

Flow through me, Peace of God,
Calm river, flow until
No wind can blow, no current stir
A ripple of self-will.

Shine through me, Joy of God,
Make me like Thy clear air

Which Thou dost pour Thy colors thro'
As though it were not there.

O blessed Love of God,
That all may taste and see
How good Thou art, once more I pray:
Love through me, even me.

A. W. C.

"Love never faileth!"

March 14

MORNING

❧

Moses drew near unto the thick darkness where God was
(EXOD. 20:21).

God has still His hidden secrets, hidden from the wise and prudent. Do not fear them; be content to accept things that you cannot understand; wait patiently. Presently He will reveal to you the treasures of darkness, the riches of the glory of the mystery. Mystery is only the veil of God's face.

Do not be afraid to enter the cloud that is settling down on your life. God is in it. The other side is radiant with His glory. "Think it not strange concerning the fiery trial which is to try you, as though some strange thing happened unto you; but rejoice, inasmuch as ye are partakers of Christ's sufferings." When you seem loneliest and most forsaken, God is nigh. He is in the dark cloud. Plunge into the blackness of its darkness without flinching; under the shrouding curtain of His pavilion you will find God awaiting you. **SELECTED**

Hast thou a cloud?
Something that is dark and full of dread;
A messenger of tempest overhead?
A something that is darkening the sky;
A something growing darker bye and bye;
A something that thou fear'st will burst at last;
A cloud that doth a deep, long shadow cast,
God cometh in that cloud.

Hast thou a cloud?
It is Jehovah's triumph car: in this
He rideth to thee, o'er the wide abyss
It is the robe in which He wraps His form;
For He doth gird Him with the flashing storm.
It is the veil in which He hides the light
Of His fair face, too dazzling for thy sight.
God cometh in that cloud.

Hast thou a cloud?
A trial that is terrible to thee?
A black temptation threatening to see?
A loss of some dear one long thine own?
A mist, a veiling, bringing the unknown?
A mystery that unsubstantial seems:
A cloud between thee and the sun's bright beams?
God cometh in that cloud.

Hast thou a cloud?
A sickness—weak old age—distress and death?
These clouds will scatter at thy last faint breath.
Fear not the clouds that hover o'er they barque,
Making the harbour's entrance dire and dark;
The cloud of death, though misty, chill and cold,
Will yet grow radiant with a fringe of gold.
GOD cometh in that cloud.

As Dr. C. stood on a high peak of the Rocky Mountains watching a storm raging below him, an eagle came up through the clouds and soared away toward the sun, and the water upon him glistened in the sunlight like diamonds. Had it not been for the storm he might have remained in the valley. The sorrows of life cause us to rise toward God.

EVENING

❧

Behold, he cometh! (REV. 1:7)

The exclamation is a striking one. The Greek word "behold" means "See; look!" It is used to quickly call attention to some striking spectacle which suddenly breaks upon the gaze—as though one should say of some great sight appearing in the heavens before all eyes, "Behold the meteor!" Suddenly in mid-heaven, without a second's warning, is staged by God the most stupendous sight upon which human eyes have ever gazed—the outflashing, dazzling, awful splendor of the personal coming of the Lord Jesus Christ in His glory.

The earth beholds and thrills with the first ecstatic moment of her deliverance from the bondage of corruption into the glorious liberty of the sons of God.

The angels behold and cry, "The kingdoms of this world are become the kingdoms of our Lord, and of his Christ" (Rev. 11:15).

The kings and princes of the world behold and cry to the rocks and hills to fall upon them and hide them from His presence.

The Antichrist beholds and falls palsied and helpless before the breath of His mouth and the glory of His coming.

The nations of the earth behold and wail because of Him.

BEHOLD!

Let *us* study the picture as the Scripture word-paints it. For not since the skies were stretched by the omnipotent hand of God in the ages that are past, has their blue canopy been the setting for such a scene as now floods them with its glory.　　　　　　　　　　JAMES H. MCCONKEY

"Midnight is past," sings the sailor on the Southern Ocean; "midnight is past; the Cross begins to bend."

"It is high time to awake out of sleep." "Our Lord will come."

The Morning Cometh!
A shout!
A trumpet note!
A Glorious Presence in the azure sky!
A gasp,
A thrill of joy,
And we are with Him in the twinkling of an eye!

A glance,
An upward look,
Caught up to be with Christ forevermore!
The dead alive!
The living glorified!
Fulfilled are all His promises that came before!

His face!
His joy supreme
Our souls find rapture only at His feet!

Blameless!
Without a spot!
We enter into heaven's joy complete!

Strike harps,
Oh, sound His praise . . .
We know Him as we never knew before!
God's love!
God's matchless grace!
'Twill take eternity to tell while we adore!
ANNE CATHERINE WHITE

"His going forth is certain as the dawn" (HOS. 6:3, ARABIC).

March 15

MORNING

Fear not, thou worm Jacob. . . . I will make thee a new sharp threshing instrument having teeth (ISA. 41:14, 15).

Could any two things be in greater contrast than a worm and an instrument with teeth? The worm is delicate, bruised by a stone, crushed beneath the passing wheel; an instrument with teeth can break and not be broken; it can grave its mark upon the rock. And the mighty God can convert the one into the other. He can take a man or a nation, who has all the impotence of the worm, and by the invigoration of His own Spirit, He can endow with strength by which a noble mark is left upon the history of the time.

And so the "worm" may take heart. The mighty God can make us stronger than our circumstances. He can bend them all to our good. In God's strength we can make them all pay tribute to our souls. We can even take hold of a black disappointment, break it open, and extract some jewel of grace. When God gives us will like iron, we can drive through difficulties as the iron share cuts through the toughest soil. "I will make thee," and shall He not do it?   DR. JOWETT

Christ is building His kingdom with earth's broken things. Men want only the strong, the successful, the victorious, the unbroken, in building their kingdoms; but God is the God of the unsuccessful, of those who have failed. Heaven is filling with earth's broken lives, and there is no bruised reed that Christ cannot take and restore to glorious blessedness and beauty. He can take the life crushed by pain or sorrow and make it into a harp whose music shall be all praise. He can lift earth's saddest failure up to heaven's glory.   J. R. MILLER

> *Follow Me, and I will make you . . .*
> *Make you speak My words with power,*
> *Make you channels of My mercy,*
> *Make you helpful every hour.*
>
> *Follow Me, and I will make you . . .*
> *Make you what you cannot be—*
> *Make you loving, trustful, godly,*
> *Make you even like to Me.*
>   L. S. P.

EVENING

Married to another, even to him. (ROM. 7:4)

The most joyous moment in the life of the bride ought to be the moment when she loses her own name and self-dependence at the marriage altar, taking her husband's name instead of her own, and merging her life in his. And the most blissful moment of our life ought to be that in which we, by renouncing our right to self-ownership, become the bride of Another, the Lord Jesus Christ.

In marriage the wealth of the husband is, of course, placed at the disposal of the wife. Many will recall the story of the Earl of Burleigh, which Tennyson has immortalized. Under the guise of a landscape painter, the Earl won the heart of a simple village maiden. Imagining they were going to the cottage of which he had spoken, in which they were to spend their happy wedded life, they passed one beautiful dwelling after another, until . . .

> *. . . a gateway she discerns*
> *With armorial bearings stately,*
> *And beneath the gate she turns,*
> *Sees a mansion more majestic*
> *Than all those she saw before:*

Many a gallant gay domestic
Bows before him at the door.
And they speak in gentle murmur,
When they answer to his call,
While he treads with footstep firmer,
Leading on from hall to hall.
And while now she wonders blindly,
Nor the meaning can divine,
Proudly turns he round and kindly,
"All of this is mine and thine."

So by the union of hearts and lives the simple village maiden became the Lady of Burleigh, and *all* her husband's wealth was *hers*.

Who shall tell of the wealth which they inherit who are truly united to Jesus?

"The exceeding riches of his grace" (EPH. 2:7).

"The unsearchable riches of Christ" (EPH. 3:8).

Oh, sacred union with the Perfect Mind,
Transcendent bliss, which Thou alone canst give;
How blest are they this Pearl of Price who find,
And, dead to earth, have learnt in Thee to live.

Thus in Thine arms of love, O God, I lie,
Lost, and forever lost to all but Thee.
My happy soul, since it hath learnt to die,
Hath found new life in Thine Infinity.

Go then, and learn this lesson of the Cross,
And tread the way the saints and prophets trod:
Who, counting life and self and all things loss,
Have found in inward death the life of God.

Give up your identity!

March 16

❦

For our profit (HEB. 12:10).

*I*n one of Ralph Conner's books he tells a story of Gwen. Gwen was a wild, willful lassie and one who had always been accustomed to having her own way. Then one day she met with a terrible accident which crippled her for life. She became very rebellious and in the murmuring state she was visited by the sky pilot, as the missionary among the mountaineers was termed.

He told her the parable of the canyon. "At first there were no canyons, but only the broad, open prairie. One day the Master of the prairie, walking over his great lawns, where were only grasses, asked the prairie, 'Where are your flowers?' and the prairie said, 'Master, I have no seeds.'

"Then he spoke to the birds, and they carried seeds of every kind of flower and strewed them far and wide, and soon the prairie bloomed with crocuses and roses and buffalo beans and the yellow crowfoot and the wild sunflowers and the red lilies all summer long. Then the Master came and was well pleased; but he missed the flowers he loved best of all, and he said to the prairie: 'Where are the clematis and the columbine, the sweet violets and wildflowers, and all the ferns and flowering shrubs?'

"And again he spoke to the birds, and again they carried all the seeds and scattered them far and wide. But, again, when the Master came he could not find the flowers he loved best of all, and he said:

" 'Where are those my sweetest flowers?' and the prairie cried sorrowfully:

" 'Oh, Master, I cannot keep the flowers, for the winds sweep fiercely, and the sun beats upon my breast, and they wither up and fly away.'

"Then the Master spoke to the lightning, and with one swift blow the lightning cleft the prairie to the heart. And the prairie rocked and groaned in agony, and for many a day moaned bitterly over the black, jagged, gaping wound.

"But the river poured its waters through the cleft, and carried down deep black mold, and once more the birds carried seeds and strewed them in the canyon. And after a long time the rough rocks were decked out with soft mosses and trailing vine, and all the nooks were hung with clematis and columbine, and great elms lifted their huge tops high up into the sunlight, and down about their feet clustered the low cedars and balsams, and everywhere the violets and windflower and maidenhair grew and bloomed, till the canyon became the Master's favorite place for rest and peace and joy."

Then the sky pilot read to her: "The fruit—I'll read 'flowers'—of the Spirit are love, joy, peace, longsuffering, gentleness—and some of these grow only in the canyon."

"Which are the canyon flowers?" asked Gwen softly, and the pilot answered: "Gentleness, meekness, longsuffering; but though the others, love, joy, peace, bloom in the open, yet never with so rich a bloom and so sweet a perfume as in the canyon."

For a long time Gwen lay quite still, and then said wistfully, while her lips trembled: "There are no flowers in my canyon but only ragged rocks."

"Some day they will bloom, Gwen dear; the Master will find them, and we, too, shall see them."

Beloved, when *you* come to your canyon, remember!

EVENING

And, lo, it was the latter growth after the king's mowings.
(AMOS 7:1)

Our Lord is so intent on the life harvest of the saints, that He Himself often mows our fields for us, and takes away the things that seem to us *good*, in order to give us *the best*.

Our great King Himself is far more concerned for the worker than for the work.

When your heart fails you God sends His sunshine and the rain, and your hopes that were laid low sprout again, new growths appear—fertilized, perhaps, by your tears; perhaps by your heart's blood. Not only is the latter growth given after the king's mowing, but *because* of it. Like a grass lawn, the saints' lives become better the more they are beaten and rolled and mown. Do not think, then, that some strange thing has befallen you when you are tempted or tried. *It is by these things men live.*

There are, it may be, lives where the first growth is the worthiest, but I have seen few, and these—though beautiful—have not been strong.

The second crop of roses is the best, and *the greatest saints are those who have felt the scythe.* But *if the King is He who mows, then welcome the mowing that brings Him into the life.*

Better a bare field *with Christ* than the best harvest *without Him!*

Where He comes, Heaven's verdure springs; where He treads, earth's
virtues grow.   GOD'S HIGHWAY

They took them all away—my toys—
Not one was left;
They set me here, shorn, stripped of humblest joys,
Anguished, bereft.

I wondered why. The years have flown;
Unto my hand
Cling weaker, sadder ones who walk alone—
I understand.
ANONYMOUS

March 17

MORNING

Be thou there till I bring thee word (MATT. 2:13).

I'll stay where You've put me; I will, dear Lord,
Though I wanted so badly to go;
I was eager to march with the "rank and file,"
Yes, I wanted to lead them, You know.
I planned to keep step to the music loud,
To cheer when the banner unfurled,
To stand in the midst of the fight straight and proud,
But I'll stay where You've put me.

I'll stay where You've put me; I'll work, dear Lord,
Though the field be narrow and small,
And the ground be fallow, and the stones lie thick,
And there seems to be no life at all.
The field is thine own, only give me the seed,
I'll sow it with never a fear;
I'll till the dry soil while I wait for the rain,
And rejoice when the green blades appear;
I'll work where You've put me.

I'll stay where You've put me; I will, dear Lord;
I'll bear the day's burden and heat,
Always trusting Thee fully; when even has come
I'll lay heavy sheaves at Thy feet.
And then, when my earth work is ended and done,
In the light of eternity's glow,
Life's record all closed, I surely shall find
It was better to stay than to go;
I'll stay where You've put me.

"Oh, restless heart, that beat against your prison bars of circumstances, yearning for a wider sphere of usefulness, leave God to order all your days. Patience and trust, in the dullness of the routine of life, will be the best preparation for a courageous bearing of the tug and strain of the larger opportunity which God may sometime send you."

EVENING

Doth the plowman plow all day to sow? (ISA. 28:24)

*I*s not the plowing merely a preparation for the seed-sowing to follow, and after that for the wheat which is to feed many? *When the plowshare goes through human hearts, surely it is for something!* Someday we shall see when the ripe ears of corn appear, that the plowshare had to come for a season. We thought it would kill us! And no plowshare goes through the earth but some life *is* destroyed, *but only that something better than that life may come.*

Be still, poor heart! God is effectual in working. "Let him do what seemeth him good."

God will not let my field lie fallow.
The plowshare is sharp, the feet of the oxen are heavy.
They hurt.
But I cannot stay God from His plowing.
He will not let my field lie fallow.
KARLE WILSON BAKER

I have seen a farmer drive his plowshare through the velvet greensward, and it looked like a harsh and cruel process; but the farmer's eye foresaw the springing blades of wheat, and knew that within a few months that torn soil would laugh with a golden harvest.

Deep soul-plowing brings rich fruits of the Spirit. There are bitter mercies as well as sweet mercies; *but they are all mercies,* whether given in honey or given in wormwood.   T. L. CUYLER

The iron plowshare goes over the field of the heart until the nighttime . . . down the deep furrows the angels come and sow.

March 18

MORNING

He answered nothing (MARK 15:3).

There is no spectacle in all the Bible so sublime as the silent Savior answering not a word to the men who were maligning Him, and whom He could have laid prostrate at His feet by one look of divine power, or one word of fiery rebuke. But He let them say and do their worst, and He stood in THE POWER OF STILLNESS—God's holy silent Lamb.

There is a stillness that lets God work for us, and holds our peace; the stillness that ceases from its contriving and its self-vindication, and its expedients of wisdom and forethought, and lets God provide and answer the cruel blow, in His own unfailing, faithful love.

How often we lose God's interposition by taking up our own cause, and striking for our defense. God give to us this silent power, this conquered spirit! And after the heat and strife of earth are over, men will remember us as we remember the morning dew, the gentle light and sunshine, the evening breeze, the Lamb of Calvary, and the gentle, holy heavenly Dove.   A. B. SIMPSON

The day when Jesus stood alone
And felt the hearts of men like stone,
And knew He came but to atone—
That day "He held His peace."

They witnessed falsely to His word,
They bound Him with a cruel cord,
And mockingly proclaimed Him Lord;
"But Jesus held His peace."

They spat upon Him in the face,
They dragged Him on from place to place,
They heaped upon Him all disgrace;
"But Jesus held His peace."

My friend, have you for far much less,
With rage, which you called righteousness,
Resented slights with great distress?
Your Saviour "held His peace."

L. S. P.

I remember once hearing Bishop Whipple, of Minnesota, so well known as "The Apostle of the Indians," utter these beautiful words: "For thirty years I have tried to see the face of Christ in those with whom I differed." When this spirit actuates us we shall be preserved at once from a narrow bigotry and an easygoing tolerance, from passionate vindictiveness and everything that would mar or injure our testimony for Him who came not to destroy men's lives, but to save them.

W. H. GRIFFITH THOMAS

EVELING

EVENING

I have chosen you. (JOHN 15:16)

Myron Niesley, California tenor, is called the highest-paid radio singer because he receives £5 for singing *one note*—the final and top one of a theme song, which others in the chorus cannot hit so perfectly.

God has just one person to come at the right moment; a place which no one can fill but that person and at that time!

Toil-worn I stood and said,
"O Lord, my feet have bled,
My hands are sore,
I weep, my efforts vainly poor.
With fainting heart I pray of Thee,
Give some brave other, work designed for me."

But my Lord answer made,
"O child of Mine,
I have looked through space and searched through time,
There is none can do the work called thine."

Soul-sick I knelt and cried,
"Let me forever hide
My little soul
From sight of Him who made me whole,
My one small spirit in the vast,
Vast throngs of like mean myriads, present, past!"

But my Lord answer made,
"O child of Mine,
I have looked through space and searched through time,
But I find no soul is like to thine!"
FRANCES BENT DILLINGHAM

Ask God if you are in His place for you.

Our life is but a little holding lent
To do a mighty labor. We are one
With heaven and the stars when it is spent
To do God's will.

It is possible for us to cross God's plan for our lives.

March 19

MORNING

*Beloved, do not be surprised at the ordeal that has come to test you
. . . you are sharing what Christ suffered; so rejoice in it*
(1 PETER 4:12).

Many a waiting hour was needful to enrich the harp of David, and many a waiting hour in the wilderness will gather for us a psalm of "thanksgiving, and the voice of melody," to cheer the hearts of fainting ones here below, and to make glad our Father's house on high.

What was the preparation of the son of Jesse for the songs like unto which none others have ever sounded on this earth?

The outrage of the wicked, which brought forth cries for God's help; then, the faint hope in God's goodness blossomed into a song of rejoicing for His mighty deliverances and manifold mercies. Every sorrow was another string to his harp; every deliverance another theme for praise.

One thrill of anguish spared, one blessing unmarked or unprized, one difficulty or danger evaded, how great would have been our loss in that thrilling psalmody in which God's people today find the expression of their grief or praise!

To wait for God, and to suffer His will, is to know Him in the fellowship of His sufferings, and to be conformed to the likeness of His Son. So now, if the vessel is to be enlarged for spiritual understanding, be not affrighted at the wider sphere of suffering that awaits you. The divine capacity of sympathy will have a more extended sphere, for the breathing of the Holy Ghost in the new creation never made a stoic, but left the heart's affection tender and true. ANNA SHIPTON

"He tested me ere He entrusted me"
(1 TIM. 1:12, WAY'S TRANSLATION).

EVENING

෴

From henceforth let no man trouble me: for I bear in my body the marks of the Lord Jesus. (GAL. 6:17)

*D*o we carry any wound marks? Have we sought the protected areas while others met clash on clash the onset of the evil one? Has compromise robbed us of our war trophies? *Shall we not have done with such?* Someday we shall see Him face to face; shall see the nailprints in His hands. Shall we stand ashamed in His presence because we wear no scars of battle? DAILY COMMUNION

Hast thou no scar?
No hidden scar on foot, or side, or hand?
I hear thee sung as mighty in the land,
I hear them hail thy bright ascendant star,
Hast thou no scar?

Hast thou no wound?
Yet I was wounded by the archers, spent,
Leaned me against a tree to die; and rent
By ravening wolves that compassed me, I swooned;
Hast thou no wound?

No wound? No scar?
Yet, as the Master shall the servant be,

And pierced are the feet that follow Me;
But thine are whole; can he have followed far
Who hath no wound nor scar?
                    A. W. C.

Our path does not lie all the way through Beulah.

Garibaldi, the great Italian reformer of a past generation, in a fiery speech urged some thousands of Italy's young men to fight for the freedom of their homeland. One timid young fellow approached him, asking, "If I fight, Sir, what will be my reward?" Swift as a lightning flash came the uncompromising answer: "Wounds, scars, bruises, and perhaps death. But remember that through your bruises Italy will be free."

Are you not willing to endure scars in order to liberate souls?

The roughest road goes straight to the hilltop!

March 20

MORNING

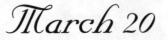

As sorrowful, yet always rejoicing (2 COR. 6:10).

$\mathcal{T}$he stoic scorns to shed a tear; the Christian is not forbidden to weep. The soul may be dumb with excessive grief, as the shearer's scissors pass over the quivering flesh; or, when the heart is on the point of breaking beneath the meeting surges of trial, the sufferer may seek relief by crying out with a loud voice. *But there is something even better.*

They say that springs of sweet fresh water well up amid the brine of salt seas; that the fairest alpine flowers bloom in the wildest and most rugged mountain passes; that the noblest psalms were the outcome of the profoundest agony of soul.

Be it so. And thus amid manifold trials, souls which love God will find reasons for bounding, leaping joy. Though deep call to deep, yet the Lord's song will be heard in silver cadence through the night. And *it is possible in the darkest hour* that ever swept a human life to bless the God and Father of our Lord Jesus Christ. Have you learned this lesson yet? Not simply to endure God's will, nor only to choose it; but to rejoice in it with joy unspeakable and full of glory.   *FROM* TRIED AS BY FIRE

I will be still, my bruised heart faintly murmured,
As o'er me rolled a crushing load of woe;
Then cry, the call, e'en the low moan was stifled;
I pressed my lips; I barred the tear drop's flow.

I will be still, although I cannot see it,
The love that bares a soul and fans pain's fire;
That takes away the last sweet drop of solace,
Breaks the lone harp string, hides Thy precious lyre.

But God is love, so I will bide me, bide me—
We'll doubt not, Soul, we will be very still;
We'll wait till after while, when He shall lift us—
Yes, after while, when it shall be His will.

And I did listen to my heart's brave promise;
And I did quiver, struggling to be still;
And I did lift my tearless eyes to Heaven,
Repeating ever, "Yea, Christ, have Thy will."

But soon my heart upspake from 'neath our burden,
Reproved my tight-drawn lips, my visage sad:
"We can do more than this, O Soul," it whispered.
"We can be more than still, we can be glad!"

And now my heart and I are sweetly singing—
Singing without the sound of tuneful strings;
Drinking abundant waters in the desert;
Crushed, and yet soaring as on eagle's wings.

S. P. W.

EVENING

❧

Bread corn is bruised. (ISA. 28:28)

*B*e content; ye are the wheat growing in our Lord's field; and, *if* wheat, ye must go under our Lord's threshing instrument on His barn floor, and through His sieve; and through His will be bruised, as was the Prince of your salvation (Isa. 53:10); that ye may be found good bread in your Lord's house.   SAMUEL RUTHERFORD

When the wheat is carried home
And the threshing time has come,

Close the door.
When the flail is lifted high,
Like the chaff I would not fly;
At His feet, oh, let me lie,
On the floor!

All the cares that o'er me steal,
All the sorrows that I feel
Like a dart,
When my enemies prevail,
When my strength begins to fail—
'Tis the beating of the flail,
On my heart!

It becomes me to be still,
Though I cannot all His will
Understand.
I would be the purest wheat
Lying humbly at His feet,
Kissing oft the rod that beats,
In His hand!

By and by I shall be stored
In the garner of my Lord
Like a prize;
Thanking Him for every blow
That in sorrow laid me low,
But in beating made me grow
For the skies!

VOICE OF TRIUMPH

"Look at God's method of producing corn, and see something of His method of producing saints."

March 21

૭⌇ૐ

According to your faith be it unto you (MATT. 9:29).

"P raying through" might be defined as *praying one's way into full faith,* emerging while yet praying into the assurance that one has been accepted and heard, so that one becomes actually aware of receiving, by firmest anticipation and in advance of the event, the thing for which he asks.

Let us remember that no earthly circumstances can hinder the fulfillment of His Word if we look steadfastly at the immutability of that Word and not at the uncertainty of this ever-changing world. God would have us believe His Word without other confirmation, *and then* He is ready to give us "according to our faith."

> *When once His Word is past,*
> *When He hath said, "I will," (Heb. 13:5)*
> *The thing shall come at last;*
> *God keeps His promise still (2 Cor. 1:20).*

The prayer of the Pentecostal age was like a cheque to be paid in coin over the counter. SIR R. ANDERSON

"And God said . . . and it was so" (Gen. 1:9).

૭⌇ૐ

To the uttermost. (HEB. 7:25)

J ohn B. Gough, the world's greatest temperance lecturer, was given a text by his godly mother, which indeed became like buried treasure, for it lay hidden within his heart for seven long years of dissipation. It was

> *He is able to save them to the uttermost*
> *that come unto God by him.*

His sins rose mountain-high before him; they seemed indelible; the past could not be undone! But he met Jesus Christ and found that His Blood availed for even him. "I have suffered," he cried, "and come out of the fire scorched and scathed with the marks upon my person, and with the memory of it burnt right into my soul." He likened his life to a snow-drift that had been badly stained; no power on earth could restore its former whiteness and purity. "The scars remain! The scars remain!" he used to say with bitter self-reproaches.

Giant Yesterday pointed to the black, black past derisively; held it a threat over the poor penitent's bowed and contrite head; told in tones that sounded like thunderclaps that there was no escape.

> *Wounds of the soul, though healed, will ache;*
> *The reddening scars remain*
> *And make confession.*
> *Lost innocence returns no more,*
> *We are not what we were*
> *Before transgression!*

Jesus is able to save to the uttermost. Says a writer, "God paints in many colors, but He never paints so gorgeously as when He paints in white." The crimson of the sunset; the azure of the ocean; the green of the valleys; the scarlet of the poppies; the silver of the dewdrops; the gold of the gorse: these are exquisite—so perfectly beautiful, indeed, that we cannot imagine an attractive heaven without them. But in the soul of John B. Gough we feel that the Divine art is at its very best.

Forty-four years have passed away since he had that grim struggle with sin. Gough is again in America, addressing a vast audience of young men in Philadelphia.

"Young men," he cries, perhaps with a bitter memory of those seven indelible years. "Young men, keep your record clean!" He pauses—a longer pause than usual, and the audience wonders. But he regains his voice.

"Young men," he repeats, more feebly this time, "keep your record clean!" Another pause—longer than the previous one. But again he finds the power of speech.

"Young men," he cries the third time, but in a thin, wavering voice. "Young men, keep your record clean!"

He falls heavily on the platform. Devout men carry him to his burial, and make lamentation over him. His race is finished; his voyage completed; his battle won. The promise has been literally and triumphantly fulfilled. The grace that saved him has kept him *to the very last inch, of the very last yard, of the very last mile; to the very last minute, of the very last hour, of the very last day! For* "He is able to save them *to the uttermost* that come unto God by him"!   SELECTED

March 22

❧

And when forty years were expired, there appeared to him in the wilderness of Mount Sinai an angel of the Lord in a flame of fire in a bush . . . saying . . . I have seen the affliction of my people which is in Egypt, and I have heard their groaning, and am come down to deliver them. And now come, I will send thee into Egypt (ACTS 7:30, 32, 34).

That was a long wait in preparation for a great mission. When God delays, He is not inactive. He is getting ready His instruments, He is ripening our powers; and at the appointed moment we shall arise equal to our task. Even Jesus of Nazareth was thirty years in privacy, growing in wisdom before He began His work. DR. JOWETT

God is never in a hurry but spends years with those He expects to greatly use. He never thinks the days of preparation too long or too dull.

The hardest ingredient in suffering is often *time*. A short, sharp pang is easily borne, but when a sorrow drags its weary way through long, monotonous years, and day after day returns with the same dull routine of hopeless agony, the heart loses its strength, and without the grace of God, is sure to sink into the very sullenness of despair. Joseph's was a long trial, and God often has to burn His lessons into the depths of our being by the fires of protracted pain. "He shall sit as a refiner and purifier of silver," but He knows how long, and like a true goldsmith. He stops the fires the moment He sees His image in the glowing metal. We may not see now the outcome of the beautiful plan which God is hiding in the shadow of His hand; it yet may be long concealed; but faith may be sure that He is sitting on the throne, calmly waiting the hour when, with adoring rapture, we shall say, "All things have worked together for good." Like Joseph, let us be more careful to learn all the lessons in the school of sorrow than we are anxious for the hour of deliverance. There is a "need-be" for every lesson, and when we are ready, our deliverance will surely come, and we shall find that we could not have stood in our place of higher service without the very things that were taught us in the ordeal. God is educating us for the future, for higher service and nobler blessings; and if we have the qualities that fit us for a throne, nothing can keep us from it when God's time has come. Don't steal tomorrow out of

God's hands. Give God time to speak to you and reveal His will. He is never too late; learn to wait.   SELECTED

He never comes too late; He knoweth what is best;
Vex not thyself in vain; until He cometh—REST.

Do not run impetuously before the Lord; learn to wait His time: the minute hand as well as the hour hand must point the exact moment for action.

EVANING

And told him, saying, Joseph is yet alive, and he is governor over all the land of Egypt. . . . It is enough; Joseph my son is yet alive: I will go and see him before I die. (GEN. 45:26, 28)

There are *heartbreaks of joy in God's plan for His children.* We can no more imagine the good things He has waiting ahead for us, both in this life and in the life to come, than Jacob could have imagined his lost boy alive and ruling Egypt. *That is the sort of miracle-surprise awaiting me daily in the tingling, vibrant, throbbing life of Jesus Christ who is my life, when I let Him fulfill His will and lavish Himself and His gifts and surprises upon me;* when I let Him become all that there is of me. *What a here and hereafter He gives me,* when I can say, "To me to live is Christ, and to die is gain"!   **MESSAGES FOR THE MORNING WATCH**

I have a heritage of joy
That yet I must not see;
The Hand that bled to make it mine
Is keeping it for me.
My heart is resting on His truth
Who hath made all things mine,
Who draws my captive will to Him
And makes it one with Thine!
A. L. WARING

"Thou surprisest him" (Ps. 21:3, Kay's trans.).

March 23

∾

Out of the spoils won in battles did they dedicate to maintain the house of the Lord (1 CHRON. 26:27).

Physical force is stored in the bowels of the earth, in the coal mines, which came from the fiery heat that burned up great forests in ancient ages; and so spiritual force is stored in the depths of our being, through the very pain which we cannot understand.

Someday we shall find that the spoils we have won from our trials were just preparing us to become true "Great Hearts" in the *Pilgrim's Progress,* and to lead our fellow pilgrims triumphantly through trial to the city of the King.

But let us never forget that the source of helping other people must be victorious suffering. The whining, murmuring pang never does anybody any good.

Paul did not carry a cemetery with him, but a chorus of victorious praise; and the harder the trial, the more he trusted and rejoiced, shouting from the very altar of sacrifice. He said, "Yea, and if I be offered upon the service and sacrifice of your faith, I joy and rejoice with you all." Lord, help me this day to draw strength from all that comes to me!

FROM DAYS OF HEAVEN UPON EARTH

He placed me in a little cage,
Away from gardens fair;
But I must sing the sweetest songs
Because He placed me there.
Not beat my wings against the cage
If it's my Maker's will,
But raise my voice to heaven's gate
And sing the louder still!

༄༅

God is our refuge and strength, a very present help in trouble.
(PS. 46:1)

Constrained at the darkest hour to confess humbly that without God's help I was helpless, I vowed a vow in the forest solitude that I would confess His aid before men. A silence as of death was around me; it was midnight and I was weakened by illness, prostrated with fatigue and worn with anxiety for my white and black companions, whose fate was a mystery. In this physical and mental distress I besought God to give me back my people. Nine hours later we were exulting with rapturous joy. In full view of all was the crimson flag with the crescent and beneath its waving folds was the long-lost rear column. **HENRY M. STANLEY**

My horse was very lame, and my head did ache exceedingly. Now what occurred I here avow as truth—though let each man account for it as he will.

Suddenly I thought, "Cannot God heal man or beast as He will?"

Immediately my weariness and headache ceased, and my horse was no longer lame! **JOHN WESLEY**

March 24

MORNING

༄༅

And Jacob said, O God of my father Abraham,
and God of my father Isaac, the Lord which saidst unto me,
Return unto thy country, and to thy kindred, and I will deal well
with thee: Deliver me, I pray thee (GEN. 32:9, 11).

There are many healthy symptoms in that prayer. In some respects it may serve as a mold into which our own spirits may pour themselves, when melted in the fiery furnace of sorrow.

He began by quoting God's promise: "Thou saidst." He did so twice (9 and 12). Ah, he has got God in his power then! God puts Himself within our reach in His promises; and when we can say to Him, "Thou saidst," He cannot say nay. He must do as He has said. If Herod was so particular for his oath's sake, what will not our God be? Be sure in prayer, to get your feet well on a promise; it will give you purchase enough to force open the gates of heaven, and to take it by force.

FROM PRACTICAL PORTIONS FOR THE PRAYER-LIFE

Jesus desires that we shall be definite in our requests, and that we shall ask for some special thing. "What will ye that I shall do unto you?" is the question that He asks of every one who in affliction and trial comes to Him. Make your requests with definite earnestness if you would have definite answers. Aimlessness in prayer accounts for so many seemingly unanswered prayers. Be definite in your petition. Fill out your check for something definite, and it will be cashed at the bank of heaven when presented in Jesus' name. *Dare to be definite with God.*   SELECTED

Miss Havergal has said: "Every year, I might almost say every day, that I live, I seem to see more clearly how all the rest and gladness and power of our Christian life hinges on one thing; and that is, taking God at His word, believing that He really means exactly what He says, and accepting the very words in which He reveals His goodness and grace, without substituting others or altering the precise modes and tenses which He has seen fit to use."

Bring Christ's Word—Christ's promise, and Christ's sacrifice—His blood, with thee, and not one of heaven's blessing can be denied thee.

ADAM CLARKE

EVENING

Peace I leave with you, my peace I give unto you. . . . Let not your heart be troubled, neither let it be afraid. (JOHN 14:27)

The late Bishop Moule has told how once, during the war, at the close of an entertainment given for men going out to the front, a young officer arose at his Colonel's request to express the thanks of the men. He did so in genial words of charm and humor. Then suddenly, as if in afterthought, and in a different tone, he added: "We are soon crossing to France and to the trenches, and very possibly of course to death. Will any of our friends here tell us how to die?" There was a long, strained silence. Then the answer came. One of the singers made her way quietly forward to the front of the stage and began to sing the great *Aria from Elijah*, "O Rest in the Lord." There were few dry eyes when the song was concluded.

Here, above all else, is what each one of us needs in the battle of life: *a heart that has come to rest in God; a will fully surrendered.* That is the great secret. *That, alone, will bring us through with honor.*

JAMES STEWART

When the soldiers of Napoleon were weak and discouraged on the Alpine ascent, we are told that their leader ordered: "Sound the French *Gloria*"; and the music gave the men new heart, and triumphantly they pressed forward. Beloved, whatever your cross, look up to your loving Master and sound the *Gloria!*

And when the fight is fierce, the warfare long,
Steals on the air the distant triumph song,
And hearts are brave again, and hands are strong,
Alleluia!

The music of the Gospel leads us Home!

March 25

MORNING

But without faith it is impossible to please him: for he that cometh to God must believe that he is, and that he is a rewarder of them that diligently seek him (HEB. 11:6).

The faith for desperate days.

The Bible is full of such days. Its record is made up of them, its songs are inspired by them, its prophecy is concerned with them, and its revelation has come through them.

The desperate days are the stepping-stones in the path of light. They seem to have been God's opportunity and man's school of wisdom.

There is a story of an Old Testament love feast in Psalm 107, and in every story of deliverance the point of desperation gave God His chance. The "wit's end" of desperation was the beginning of God's power. Recall the promise of seed as the stars of heaven, and as the sands of the sea, to a couple as good as dead. Read again the story of the Red Sea and its deliverance, and of Jordan with its ark standing midstream. Study once more the prayers of Asa, Jehoshaphat, and Hezekiah, when they were sore pressed and knew not what to do. Go over the history of Nehemiah,

Daniel, Hosea, and Habakkuk. Stand with awe in the darkness of Gethsemane, and linger by the grave in Joseph's garden through those terrible days. Call the witnesses of the early church, and ask the apostles the story of their desperate days.

Desperation is better than despair.

Faith did not make our desperate days. Its work is to sustain and solve them. The only alternative to a desperate faith is despair, and faith holds on and prevails.

There is no more heroic example of desperate faith than that of the three Hebrew children. The situation was desperate, but they answered bravely, "Our God whom we serve is able to deliver us from the burning, fiery furnace; and he will deliver us out of thine hand, O king. But if not, be it known unto thee, O king, that we will not serve thy gods, nor worship the golden image which thou hast set up." I like that, "but if not!"

I have only space to mention Gethsemane. Ponder deeply its "Nevertheless." "If it is possible . . . nevertheless!" Deep darkness had settled upon the soul of our Lord. Trust meant anguish unto blood and darkness to the descent of hell—Nevertheless! Nevertheless!!

Now get your hymn book and sing your favorite hymn of desperate faith.

REV. S. CHADWICK

When obstacles and trials seem
Like prison walls to be,
I do the little I can do
And leave the rest to Thee.

And when there seems no chance, no change,
From grief can set me free,
Hope finds its strength in helplessness,
And calmly waits for Thee.

EVENING

Fill up that which is behind of the afflictions of Christ. (COL. 1:24)

The suggestion is this: *all ministry for the Master must be possessed of the sacrificial spirit of the Master.* If Paul is to help in the redemption of Rome, he must himself incarnate the death of Calvary. If he is to be a minister of Life, he must "die daily." The spirit of Calvary is to be reincarnate in Ephesus, in Athens, in Rome . . . the sacrificial succession is to be maintained through the ages, and *we are to "fill up that which is behind of the sufferings of Christ."*

Here, then, is a principle: *the gospel of a broken heart demands the ministry of bleeding hearts. As soon as we cease to bleed we cease to bless. When our sympathy loses its pangs we can no longer be the servants of the Passion.* I do not know how any Christian service is to be fruitful if the servant is not primarily baptized in the spirit of a suffering compassion. *We can never heal the needs we do not feel. Tearless hearts can never be the heralds of the Passion. We must bleed if we would be the ministers of the saving blood.* We must, by our own suffering sympathies, "fill up that which is behind of the sufferings of Christ."

Are we in the succession?   J. H. JOWETT

Ignatius said, when facing the lions in the arena, *"I am a grain of God. Let me be ground between the teeth of lions if I may thus become bread to feed God's people."* Were such martyred lives wasted? Thrown away? Is any life wasted that becomes seed-corn to produce bread for the world?

The way to make *nothing* of our lives is to be very careful of them. The way to make our lives an *eternal success* is to do with them just what Christ did with His.

Watch the opportunities to *"fill up that which remains behind of the afflictions of Christ."* How many of us can show Him wounds that worship *Him?*   SEED THOUGHT CALENDAR

March 26

MORNING

∾⧜∽

Look from the place where thou art, northward, and southward, and eastward, and westward: for all the land which thou seest, to thee will I give it (GEN. 13:14–15).

No instinct can be put in you by the Holy Ghost but He purposes to fulfill. Let your faith then rise and soar away and claim all the land you can discover.   S. A. KEEN

All you can apprehend in the vision of faith is your own. Look as far as you can, for it is all yours. All that you long to be as a Christian, all that you long to do for God, are within the possibilities of faith. Then come, still closer, and with your Bible before you, and your soul open to all the influences of the Spirit, let your whole being receive the baptism of His presence; and as He opens your understanding to see all His fullness, believe He has it all for you. Accept for yourself all the promises of His Word, all the desires He awakens within you, all the possibilities of what you may be as a follower of Jesus. All the land you see is given to you.

The actual provisions of His grace come from the inner vision. He who puts the instinct in the bosom of yonder bird to cross the continent in search of summer sunshine in the southern clime is too good to deceive it, and just as surely as He has put the instinct in its breast, so has He also put the balmy breezes and the vernal sunshine yonder to meet it when it arrives.

He who breathes into our hearts the heavenly hope, will not deceive or fail us when we press forward to its realization. SELECTED

"And found as he had said unto them" (LUKE 22:13).

EVENING

Get thee hence . . . and hide thyself. (1 KINGS 17:3)

This is not a very gratifying endorsement of Elijah. Doubtless the man's heart swelled with eagerness to start a great reformation; his mind expanded with dreams of world-empire. To flee now, when the audacious approach to the king has been made, is to contradict all accepted methods of operation. Nothing now but solitude? But God knows His plans and Elijah, his servant. There is wholesome truth here. To trust where we cannot trace is to give our God the full sovereignty that He longs for. The most formidable barrier in His dealings with His children is their self-will. *"Let him do what seemeth him good"* (1 Sam. 3:18) *is not resignation, but triumphant faith, if we trust.*

And so by the brook Cherith the lonely man abides. It is lost time in the judgment of the flesh-depending critics; here is a thread in the fabric of society capable of great accomplishment, doing nothing. But they who argue so fail to see what God is to do. If we weigh things in the scales of human reasoning we shall always deal with economics and expediency; but no time is lost if God can have His way. *The real truth is, that He is to come into the life of His servant to better qualify him for a more vital revelation of Himself;* for with God *"the worker is more than the work."*

There may be many dear saints of God who doubt their saintship because their activities have been taken from them. Circumstances have closed in upon them; doors have been shut in their faces; funds for the prosecution of their work have ceased. It may be that, physically exhausted, they lie on their beds wondering why He can consent to so unreasonable a situation. Be assured of one thing: *Elijah is not to remain in obscurity and inactivity for all time.* Our error lies in mentally fixing our future according to present conditions. Let us arouse ourselves from this deadly coma. There is always the *afterward* of His gracious promising.

KENNETH MACKENZIE

"He knows, and loves, and cares!"

"Immediately I conferred not with flesh and blood," says Paul, and he went away into a desert place.

A desert place . . . and rest!

March 27

MORNING

❧❧

I do not count the sufferings of our present life worthy of mention when compared with the glory that is to be revealed and bestowed upon us
(ROM. 8:18, 20TH-CENTURY TRANSLATION).

A remarkable incident occurred recently at a wedding in England. A young man of large wealth and high social position, who had been blinded by an accident when he was ten years old, and who won university honors in spite of his blindness, had won a beautiful bride, though he had never looked upon her face. A little while before his marriage he submitted to a course of treatment by experts, and the climax came on the day of his wedding.

The day came, and the presents, and guests. There were present cabinet ministers and generals and bishops and learned men and women. The bridegroom, dressed for the wedding, his eyes still shrouded in linen, drove to the church with his father, and the famous oculist met them in the vestry.

The bride entered the church on the arm of her white-haired father. So moved was she that she could hardly speak. Was her lover at last to see her face that others admired, but which he knew only through his delicate fingertips?

As she neared the altar, while the soft strains of the wedding march floated through the church, her eyes fell on a strange group.

The father stood there with his son. Before the latter was the great oculist in the act of cutting away the last bandage. The bridegroom took a step forward, with the spasmodic uncertainty of one who cannot believe that he is awake. A beam of rose-colored light from a pane in the chancel window fell across his face, but he did not seem to see it.

Did he see anything? Yes! Recovering in an instant his steadiness of mien, and with a dignity and joy never before seen in his face, he went forward to meet his bride. They looked into each other's eyes, and one would have thought that his eyes would never wander from her face.

"At last!" she said. "At last" he echoed solemnly, bowing his head. That was a scene of great dramatic power, and no doubt of great joy, and is but a mere suggestion of what will actually take place in heaven when the Christian who has been walking through this world of trial and sorrow, shall see HIM face-to-face.   SELECTED

> *Just a-wearying for you,*
> *Jesus, Lord, beloved and true;*
> *Wishing for you, wondering when*
> *You'll be coming back again,*
> *Under all I say and do,*
> *Just a-wearying for you.*
>
> *Some glad day, all watching past,*
> *You will come for me at last;*
> *Then I'll see you, hear your voice,*
> *Be with you, with you rejoice;*
> *How the sweet hope thrills me through,*
> *Sets me a-wearying for you.*

EVENING

❧

Bringing into captivity every thought. (2 COR. 10:5)

They compassed me about like bees," the Psalmist says. Every second we get a sting from some fiery shaft, some imagination, some memory, some foreboding, some fear, some care, and God lets us get them in order that they may be destroyed and we so armed against them that they can never hurt us anymore. The only way to be armed against them is to refuse them and the source from which they come.

There is a world of truth here that most Christians have entirely overlooked. They give their spirit and heart to the Lord and they keep their head to themselves. Our intellect must be sanctified by being slain and replaced by *the mind of Christ*.

The only remedy for bad thoughts is to stop thinking all our own thoughts, to be spiritually decapitated, and to be delivered from the natural mind as well as the natural heart. God will, therefore, put us to school in the difficult task of stopping thinking. We will not only try to think right, but *we will stop our thoughts* and *wait for Him to give us His mind*.

This may seem to you like annihilation; but you will come to it if you are going to enter into the deepest, sweetest, strongest life, until *you shall be afraid to think at all until God first thinks in you*.

Have you given your thoughts to God? Have you learned the meaning of that cry of David, "I hate thoughts, but thy law do I love"?

A. B. SIMPSON

Each sin has its door of entrance.
Keep—that—door—closed!
Bolt it tight!
Just outside, the wild beast crouches
In the night.
Pin the bolt with a prayer,
God will fix it there.
BEES IN AMBER, BY JOHN OXENHAM

"Carelessness with thoughts is as dangerous as toying with explosives!"

Bolt that door!

March 28

MORNING

❧

And it shall come to pass, as soon as the soles of the feet of the priests
that bear the ark of the Lord, the Lord of all the earth,
shall rest in the waters of Jordan, that the waters of Jordan shall be
cut off from the waters that come down from above;
and they shall stand upon an heap (JOSH. 3:13).

Brave Levites! Who can help admiring them, to carry the ark right into the stream; for the waters were not divided till their feet dipped in the water (v. 15). God had not promised aught else. God honors faith.

"Obstinate faith," that the PROMISE sees and "looks to that alone." You can fancy how the people would watch these holy men march on, and some of the bystanders would be saying, "You would not catch me running that risk! Why, man, the ark will be carried away!" Not so; "the priests stood firm on dry ground." We must not overlook the fact that faith on our part helps God to carry out His plans. "Come up to the help of the Lord."

The ark had staves for the shoulders. Even the ark did not move itself; it was carried. When God is the architect, men are the masons and laborers. Faith assists God. It can stop the mouth of the lions and quench the violence of fire. It yet honors God, and God honors it. Oh, for this faith that will go on, leaving God to fulfill His promise when He sees fit! Fellow Levites, let us shoulder our load, and do not let us look as if we were carrying God's coffin. It is the ark of the living God! Sing as you march toward the flood!   THOMAS CHAMPNESS

One of the special marks of the Holy Ghost in the apostolic church was the spirit of boldness. One of the most essential qualities of the faith that is to attempt great things for God, and expect great things from God, is holy audacity. Where we are dealing with a supernatural Being, and taking from Him things that are humanly impossible, it is easier to take much than little; it is easier to stand in a place of audacious trust than in a place of cautious, timid clinging to the shore.

Like wise seamen in the life of faith, let us launch out into the deep, and find that all things are possible with God, and all things are possible unto him that believeth.

Let us, today, attempt great things for God; take His faith and believe for them and His strength to accomplish them.

FROM DAYS OF HEAVEN UPON EARTH

EVENING

He made it again another vessel,
as seemed good to the potter to make it. (JER. 18:4)

God wants to make the very best He can of each of His children. He puts us on His wheel, and subjects us to the discipline which He deems most likely to secure our greatest blessedness and usefulness. But alas! How often He finds a marred vessel left on His hands when He desired and sought perfect beauty and strength! This is through no failure on His part; but because some bubble of vanity or grit of self-will has hindered Him.

When this has been the case, He does not cast us utterly away; but puts us afresh on the wheel and "makes us again." If He cannot do what He desired at first, He will still make the best of us; and the weakness of God is stronger than men. *Yield yourselves afresh to God.* Confess that you have marred His work. Humbly ask that He should make you again, as He made Jacob again, and Peter, and John, and Mark.

There is simply no limit to the progress and development of the soul which is able to meet God with a never-faltering "Yes." *Be very prompt to obey all that He may impress upon you as being His holy will. Let the lifelike clay in the potter's hands, be plastic to the Maker's touch!*

DAILY DEVOTIONAL COMMENTARY

The potter worked at his task
With patience, love and skill.
A vessel, marred and broken,
He altered again to his will.
It was blackened, bent and old
But with traces of beauty left,
So he worked, this mender of pottery,
To restore the charm bereft,
Till at last it stood transformed
And he viewed it with tender eyes,
The work of his hands and love,
This potter, patient and wise.

I know a Mender of broken hearts,
And of lives that are all undone;
He takes them all, as they come to Him
And He loves them, every one.
With patience, love and skill
That surpasses the knowledge of men,
This Master Potter gathers the lost
And restores to His image again.
O Lover of folk with broken lives,
O wonderful Potter Divine,
I bring my soul for Thy healing touch;
In me, let Thy beauty shine.

There is no type of failure that He has not taken hold of and remade.

March 29

Consider the lilies . . . how they grow (MATT. 6:28).

"I need oil," said an ancient monk; so he planted an olive sapling. "Lord," he prayed, "it needs rain that its tender roots may drink and swell. Send gentle showers." And the Lord sent gentle showers. "Lord," prayed the monk, "my tree needs sun. Send sun, I pray Thee." And the sun shone, gilding the dripping clouds. "Now frost, my Lord, to brace its tissues," cried the monk. And behold, the little tree stood sparkling with frost, but at evening it died.

Then the monk sought the cell of a brother monk, and told his strange experience. "I, too, planted a little tree," he said, "and see! it thrives well. But I entrust my tree to its God. He who made it knows better what it needs than a man like me. I laid no condition. I fixed not ways or means. 'Lord, send what it needs,' I prayed, 'storm or sunshine, wind, rain, or frost. Thou hast made it and Thou dost know.' "

> *Yes, leave it with Him,*
> *The lilies all do,*
> *And they grow—*
> *They grow in the rain,*
> *And they grow in the dew—*
> *Yes, they grow:*
> *They grow in the darkness, all hid in the night—*
> *They grow in the sunshine, revealed by the light—*
> *Still they grow.*
>
> *Yes, leave it with Him,*
> *'Tis more dear to His heart,*
> *You will know,*
> *Than the lilies that bloom,*
> *Or the flowers that start*
> *'Neath the snow:*
> *Whatever you need, if you seek it in prayer,*
> *You can leave it with Him—for you are His care.*
> *You, you know.*
> SELECTED

༄

He is faithful that promised. (HEB. 10:23)

Oftentimes it is difficult to see how certain promises of God are to be realized. *We have nothing to do with that whatever!* God keeps our hands off His promises quite as surely as He keeps them off His stars. If He will not let us intermeddle with His planets, He will not ask us to have anything to do with the outworking and realization of His promises. He asks that their fulfillment be left to Him; and afterwards He will challenge our own life as the witness and answer, and confirmation of all that is gracious and all that is sure in the outworking of His words of promise.

JOSEPH PARKER

The One who rolls the stars along
Speaks all the promises.

Trust the untraceable ways of God and remember that "these are parts of his ways."

In Thy strong arms I lay me down,
So shall the work be done;
For who can work so wondrously,
As the Almighty One!

March 30

MORNING

༄

Behold, all ye that kindle a fire, that compass yourselves
about with sparks: walk in the light of your fire,
and in the sparks that ye have kindled. This shall ye have of mine
hand; ye shall lie down in sorrow (ISA. 50:11).

What a solemn warning to those who walk in darkness and yet who try to help themselves out into the light. They are represented as kindling a fire, and compassing themselves with sparks. What does this mean?

Why, it means that when we are in darkness the temptation is to find a way without trusting in the Lord and relying upon Him. Instead of letting Him help us out, we try to help ourselves out. We seek the light of nature, and get the advice of our friends. We try the conclusions of our reason, and might almost be tempted to accept a way of deliverance which would not be of God at all.

All these are fires of our own kindling; rushlights that will surely lead us onto the shoals. And God will let us walk in the light of those sparks, but the end will be sorrow.

Beloved, do not try to get out of a dark place, except in God's time and in God's way. The time of trouble is meant to teach you lessons that you sorely need.

Premature deliverance may frustrate God's work of grace in your life. Just commit the whole situation to Him. Be willing to abide in darkness so long as you have His presence. Remember that it is better to walk in the dark with God than to walk alone in the light.

FROM THE STILL SMALL VOICE

Cease meddling with God's plans and will. You touch anything of His, and you mar the work. You may move the hands of a clock to suit you, but you do not change the time; so you may hurry the unfolding of God's will, but you harm and do not help the work. You can open a rosebud but you spoil the flower. Leave all to Him. Hands down. Thy will, not mine.

STEPHEN MERRITT

His Way

God bade me go when I would stay
('Twas cool within the wood);
I did not know the reason why.
I heard a boulder crashing by
Across the path where I stood.

He bade me stay when I would go;
"Thy will be done," I said.
They found one day at early dawn,
Across the way I would have gone,
A serpent with a mangled head.

No more I ask the reason why,
Although I may not see
The path ahead, His way I go;
For though I know not, He doth know,
And He will choose safe paths for me.

FROM THE SUNDAY SCHOOL TIMES

EVENING

〜〜

And she went up, and laid him on the bed of the man of God,
and shut the door upon him, and went out.
(2 KINGS 4:21)

The Shunammite woman had lost her only son who had been given to her as the special gift of God. She held him dead in her arms. What could she do? She had a consecrated room where she entertained the prophet of God, and this room meant to her the very presence of God. She took up her precious burden *and she went up* there. How blessed it is to be able *to go up to the secret place of the Most High,* and *to bring our troubles under the shadow of the Almighty!* This is the place of refuge where the weary, helpless and heartbroken find relief.

"And she . . . laid him on the bed of the man of God." This is a beautiful picture of committal—laying our trouble, our business, our whole way over on God.

"Commit . . . trust . . . and He worketh" (PS. 37:5).

This poor bereaved mother was laying her burden on the Lord and leaving it there. That is one of the most difficult things to do: to *leave* our burdens with the Lord after we have placed them there.

"And shut the door . . . and went out." The temptation is *not* to shut the door. We still see our trouble; we still handle it; we go over it again and again; we think our presence is needed, while His presence is more than sufficient. It takes faith to *"shut the door"* and go out. It takes real confidence for us to let the matter that is troubling us pass entirely *out of our* hands *into God's* hands. *In no other way can God fully work.*

The corn of wheat *must be hidden from the eyes of man if it is to bring forth fruit!* This Shunammite woman committed her dead son entirely to God and went out, shutting the door. No wonder that she could then say when questioned regarding her son, *"It is well."* There is no safer place in all the universe in which to leave our loved ones than in the hands of God. *No wonder that she received her dead son back to life!*

We certainly believe that there is many a son and daughter given as a special gift of God and now dead in trespasses and sins, *who, if fully committed to God in definite faith, would certainly be restored and saved.*

We certainly believe, also, that in every burden, trial, or care, *which we thus fully leave with God, and for which we fully trust Him, He will work above all we ask or think.*
C. H. P.

〜 202 〜

When thou hast shut thy door,
Shut out from thee its anxious care
With all its sharp temptations sore,
For He is there.

When thou hast shut thy door,
Shut out from thee its pain and grief,
Bereavements—pressures to the core;
He gives relief.

When thou hast shut thy door,
And left all there behind that wall
Of God's own care, forevermore—
He takes it all.

When thou hast shut thy door,
Shut out thyself—He only in,
Nothing for thee but to adore—
He works within.

L. S. P.

March 31

MORNING

The wind was contrary (MATT. 14:24).

Rude and blustering the winds of March often are. Do they not typify the tempestuous seasons of my life? But, indeed, I ought to be glad that I make acquaintance with these seasons. Better it is that the rains descend and the floods come than that I should stay perpetually in the Lotus Land where it seems always afternoon, or in that deep meadowed Valley of Avilion where never wind blows loudly. Storms of temptation appear cruel, but do they not give intense earnestness to prayer? Do they not compel me to seize the promises with a tighter hand grip? Do they not leave me with a character refined?

Storms of bereavement are keen; but, then, they are one of the Father's ways of driving me to Himself, that in the secret of His presence His voice may speak to my heart, soft and low. There is a glory of the

Master which can be seen only when the wind is contrary and the ship tossed with waves.

"Jesus Christ is no security *against* storms, but He is perfect security *in* storms. He has never promised you an easy passage, only a safe landing."

> *Oh, set your sail to the heavenly gale,*
> *And then, no matter what winds prevail,*
> *No reef can wreck you, no calm delay;*
> *No mist shall hinder, no storm shall stay;*
> *Though far you wander and long you roam*
> *Through salt sea sprays and o'er white sea foam,*
> *No wind that can blow but shall speed you Home.*
> ANNIE JOHNSON FLINT

EVENING

The Spirit itself maketh intercession for us. (ROM. 8:26)

The highest ideal of prayer is to have the Holy Spirit pray through us. He is in us *to inspire our desires and longings, to quicken our minds and hearts,* and *giving us prayers, to pray them through us.* A great deal has been said about "praying through"; and when it means to pray until we believe God it is a most helpful and scriptural suggestion. However, if we approach this subject of prayer from the Divine standpoint, it may be truly said that all effectual prayer is only that which the Holy Spirit *prays through us.*

In His *praying through us* He quickens and uses our individual powers of will, intellect, and affection. His action is just as natural as if it had all originated with and was carried on by ourselves, but He is the *pray-er* for we have yielded ourselves to Him by an act of the will in definite faith for His working.

Although His praying is as natural as our own would be, yet when He is the *pray-er,* there is often the consciousness of a depth and power unutterable. These are God's infinitely loving desires striving to find expression through finite and human channels. Beside, there will be the leading out in prayer for objects and persons that otherwise would have been neglected, and *such spirit of prayer will come upon us just as there is need, and may sometimes even seem to be at the most unlikely time and place.*

How limitless are the possibilities of prayer when we have such a mighty, loving Helper! *How certain we may be of the answer when He breathes the prayer through us!* What wonderful fellowship this kind of prayer gives!

We can only realize His ideal for our prayer-life by abiding in Him and trusting Him moment by moment *to pray through us with His own mighty intercessions.*   C. H. P.

Can it be that some souls are still in sins "retained" because you and I have shrunk from the travail of intercession?

April 1

MORNING

〰️

Though he slay me, yet will I trust in him (JOB 13:15).

For I know whom I have believed (2 TIM. 1:12).

> I will not doubt, though all my ships at sea
> Come drifting home with broken masts and sails;
> I will believe the Hand which never fails,
> From seeming evil worketh good for me.
> And though I weep because those sails are tattered,
> Still will I cry, while my best hopes lie shattered:
> "I trust in Thee."
>
> "I will not doubt, though all my prayers return
> Unanswered from the still, white realm above;
> I will believe it is an all-wise love
> Which has refused these things for which I yearn;
> And though at times I cannot keep from grieving,
> Yet the pure ardor of my fixed believing
> Undimmed shall burn.
>
> I will not doubt, though sorrows fall like rain,
> And troubles swarm like bees about a hive.
> I will believe the heights for which I strive
> Are only reached by anguish and by pain;
> And though I groan and writhe beneath my crosses.
> I yet shall see through my severest losses
> The greater gain.

I will not doubt. Well anchored in this faith,
Like some staunch ship, my soul braves every gale;
So strong its courage that it will not quail
To breast the mighty unknown sea of death.
Oh, may I cry, though body parts with spirit,
"I do not doubt," so listening worlds may hear it,
With my last breath.

"In fierce storms," said an old seaman, "we must do one thing; there is only one way: we must put the ship in a certain position and keep her there."

This, Christian, is what you must do. Sometimes, like Paul, you can see neither sun nor stars, and no small tempest lies on you; and then you can do but one thing; there is only one way.

Reason cannot help you; past experiences give you no light. Even prayer fetches no consolation. Only a single course is left. You must put your soul in one position and keep it there.

You must stay upon the Lord; and come what may—winds, waves, cross-seas, thunder, lightning, frowning rocks, roaring breakers—no matter what, you must lash yourself to the helm, and hold fast your confidence in God's faithfulness, His covenant engagement, His everlasting love in Christ Jesus. RICHARD FULLER

EVENING

❧

His heart is fixed, trusting. (PS. 112:7)

*B*efore my window is a beautiful branch of a tree now in full spring dress. Only a few weeks ago that same branch was loaded with ice—it seemed as if it must break! I remember one hour: it seemed it could not keep up. I expected to see it give way; but it did not break. Today it is beautiful!

There are many in this sad world who are as my bare branch was—loaded with ice. Their sorrows seem like hailstorms, and how to keep up, how to hold on, seems to be the one vital question. If one such should read about my branch, let me say to that one, "Don't break; cling for your life to the one truth, *that God has not forgotten you!* He holds the winds in His fists; and the waves that now seem as though they would swallow you up, in the hollow of His hands." You may look up and say,

Thou hast a charge no waves can wash away;
And let the storm that does Thy work
Deal with me as it may.

And so, by simple faith in God's goodness and love you hold on, and when in the future—like the branch near my window—it shall be all spring with you, you will remember your sorrows as waters that have passed away. "Hold on! It is not always winter; spring is coming. The birds are yet to sing on the very branch loaded with ice. *Only, don't break!*"

My branch did not have a will of its own, but we have wills, and God can energize them. We must use our wills and say, "Though He slay me, yet will I trust in Him," and *He never slays but to make alive.*

Thus trusting, though you may bend to the blast, *you will not break; you will hold on; you will see your Spring!*

And I know not any trouble, for I have the tempest's King
To change my winter's fury to the gladness of His spring.

Blessed is the man who, when the tempest has spent its fury, recognizes his Father's Voice in the undertone.

April 2

MORNING

❧

They looked . . . and behold, the glory of the Lord appeared in the cloud (EXOD. 16:10).

Get into the habit of looking for the silver lining of the cloud and when you have found it, continue to look at it, rather than at the leaden gray in the middle.

Do not yield to discouragement no matter how sorely pressed or beset you may be. A discouraged soul is helpless. He can neither resist the wiles of the enemy himself, while in this state, nor can he prevail in prayer for others.

Flee from every symptom of this deadly foe as you would flee from a viper. And be not slow in turning your back on it, unless you want to bite the dust in bitter defeat.

Search out God's promises and say aloud of each one: "This promise is *mine.*" If you still experience a feeling of doubt and discouragement, pour out your heart to God and ask Him to rebuke the adversary who is so mercilessly nagging you.

The very instant you wholeheartedly turn away from every symptom of distrust and discouragement, the blessed Holy Spirit will quicken your faith and inbreathe divine strength into your soul.

At first you may not be conscious of this, still as you resolutely and uncompromisingly *"snub"* every tendency toward doubt and depression that assails you, you will soon be made aware that the powers of darkness are falling back.

Oh, if our eyes could only behold the solid phalanx of strength, of power, that is ever behind every turning away from the hosts of darkness, God-ward, what scant heed would be given to the effort of the wily foe to distress, depress, discourage us!

All the marvelous attributes of the Godhead are on the side of the weakest believer, who in the name of Christ, and in simple, childlike trust, yields himself to God and turns to Him for help and guidance.

SELECTED

On a day in the autumn, I saw a prairie eagle mortally wounded by a rifle shot. His eyes still gleamed like a circle of light. Then he slowly turned his head, and gave one more searching and longing look at the sky. He had often swept those starry spaces with his wonderful wings. The beautiful sky was the home of his heart. It was the eagle's domain. A thousand times he had exploited there his splendid strength. In those far-away heights he had played with the lightnings, and raced with the winds, and now, so far away from home, the eagle lay dying, done to the death, because for once he forgot and flew too low. The soul is that eagle. This is not its home. It must not lose the skyward look. We must keep faith, we must keep hope, we must keep courage, we must keep Christ. We would better creep away from the battlefield at once if we are not going to be brave. There is no time for the soul to stampede. Keep the skyward look, my soul; keep the skyward look!

> *Keep looking up—*
> *The waves that roar around thy feet,*
> *Jehovah-Jireh will defeat*
> *When looking up.*

> *Keep looking up—*
> *Though darkness seems to wrap thy soul;*
> *The Light of Light shall fill thy soul*
> *When looking up.*

Keep looking up—
When worn, distracted with the fight;
Your Captain gives you conquering might
When you look up.

We can never see the sun rise by looking into the west.
JAPANESE PROVERB

EVENING

❦

Be still, and know that I am God. (PS. 46:10)

There is immense power in stillness. A great saint once said, "All things come to him who knows how to trust and be silent." The words are pregnant with meaning. A knowledge of this fact would immensely change our ways of working. Instead of restless struggles, we would "sit down" inwardly before the Lord, and would let the Divine forces of His Spirit work out in silence the ends to which we aspire. You may not see or feel the operations of this silent force, but be assured it is always working mightily, and will work for you, if you only get your spirit still enough to be carried along by the currents of its power.   HANNAH WHITALL SMITH

There is a stillness in the Christian's life:
An inner stillness only known to him
Who has so gladly laid at Jesus' feet
His all, and now He reigns alone within,
Master of every motion, wish, and plan.
In stillness crowned, He rules supreme as King,
And in that inner chamber of the heart
Has made a little sanctuary within.

There is a stillness in the Christian's life:
The corn of wheat must fall into the ground
And die, then if it die, out of that death
Life, fullest life, will blessedly abound.
It is a mystery no words can tell,
But known to those who in this stillness rest;
Something Divinely incomprehensible:
That for my nothingness, I get God's best!

Leave it all quietly with Him: failures, fears, foes, future!

April 3

❧❧

Glorify ye the Lord in the fires (ISA. 24:15).

Mark the little word *"in"*! We are to honor Him in the trial—in that which is an affliction indeed and though there have been cases where God did not let His saints feel the fire, yet, ordinarily, fire hurts.

But just here we are to glorify Him by our perfect faith in His goodness and love that has permitted all this to come upon us.

And more than that, we are to believe that out of this is coming something more for His praise than could have come but for this fiery trial.

We can only go through some fires with a large faith; little faith will fail. We must have the victory in the furnace.   MARGARET BOTTOME

A man has as much religion as he can show in times of trouble. The men who were cast into the fiery furnace came out as they went in—except their *bonds*.

How often in some furnace of affliction God strikes *them* off! Their bodies were unhurt—their skin not even blistered. Their hair was unsinged, their garments not scorched, and even the smell of fire had not passed upon them. And that is the way Christians should come out of furnace trials—liberated from their bonds, but untouched by the flames.

"Triumphing over them in it" (COL. 2:15).

That is the real triumph—triumphing over sickness, *in it;* triumphing over death, *dying;* triumphing over adverse circumstances, *in them.* Oh, believe me, there is a power that can make us victors in the strife. There are heights to be reached where we can look down and over the way we have come, and sing our song of triumph on this side of heaven. We can make others regard us as rich, while we are poor, and make many rich in our poverty. Our triumph is to be *in it.* Christ's triumph was *in* His humiliation. Possibly our triumph, also, is to be made manifest in what seems to others humiliation.   MARGARET BOTTOME

Is there not something captivating in the sight of a man or a woman burdened with many tribulations and yet carrying a heart as sound as a bell? Is there not something contagiously valorous in the vision of one who is greatly tempted, but is more than conqueror? Is it not heartening to see some pilgrim who is broken in body, but who retains the splendor

of an unbroken patience? What a witness all this offers to the enduement of His grace!
J. H. JOWETT

When each earthly prop gives under,
And life seems a restless sea,
Are you then a God-kept wonder,
Satisfied and calm and free?

EVENING

Say unto the peoples: the Lord reigneth from the tree.
(PS. 96:10, LATIN)

Home of our hearts, lest we forget
What our redemption meant to Thee,
Let our most reverent thought be set
Upon Thy Calvary.
A. W. C.

When Christ hung on the Cross of Calvary He was, apparently, the biggest failure the world had ever seen; for no other man had even dared to make such astounding claims as He, yet there He hung; nailed to the cross of shame, exposed to the view of a coarse, mocking crowd; cut off in early manhood; betrayed by one of His own personal friends; deserted by all of the other apostles—one of whom, after loud professions of devotion had denied Him with oaths and curses. It seemed as if that most wonderful and touching of all intercessory prayers (recorded in John 17) had never reached the Father's ear; and as if the words "Father, the hour is come; glorify thy Son" were impossible of fulfillment.

Not one soul, even of those who loved the Savior best, understood Him and His lifework; therefore not one friend could really sympathize with the God-man, who, on His human side, so hungered for sympathy.

If you and I are truly following in the Master's footsteps, we too must be willing to risk apparent failure in the eyes of the world; and, harder still, must often be content to be misunderstood by our fellow-Christians. It is only when we have learned the faith and obedience which leave all consequences with God, that we can know the power and deep joy contained in these words, that once sounded so terrible—"I am crucified with Christ."
E. A. G.

JESUS, THOU LIVING BREAD,
Ground in the mills of death,
Let me by Thee be fed;
Thy servant hungereth.

JESUS, THOU CHOICEST VINE,
Nailed to the Cross of woe,
Now let Thy life Divine
Into my being flow.

Strength for the coming day
Thy Body doth impart,
Thy Blood doth cleanse away
The sins that stain my heart.

Let not my heart be cold,
Nor doubt when faith doth prove
That in my hand I hold
Thy Sacrament of love.

JESUS, be not a guest
That tarrieth but a day;
Come to my longing breast,
Come, and forever stay.

R. F. PECHEY

He reigneth! He reigneth, but let us never forget that it is from the throne on Golgotha!

April 4

MORNING

Elisha prayed, and said, Lord, I pray thee, open his eyes, that he may see (2 KINGS 6:17).

This is the prayer we need to pray for ourselves and for one another, "Lord, open our eyes that we may see"; for the world all around us, as well as around the prophet, is full of God's horses and chariots, waiting to carry us to places of glorious victory. And when our eyes are thus opened, we shall see in all events of life, whether great or small, whether joyful or sad, a "chariot" for our souls.

Everything that comes to us becomes a chariot the moment we treat it as such; and, on the other hand, even the smallest trial may be a juggernaut car to crush us into misery or despair if we consider it.

It lies with each of us to choose which they shall be. It all depends, not upon what these events are, but upon how we take them. If we lie down under them, and let them roll over us and crush us, they become juggernaut cars, but if we climb up into them, as into a car of victory, and make them carry us triumphantly onward and upward, they become the chariots of God. HANNAH WHITALL SMITH

The Lord cannot do much with a crushed soul, hence the adversary's attempt to push the Lord's people into despair and hopelessness over the condition of themselves, or of the church. It has often been said that a dispirited army goes forth to battle with the certainty of being beaten. We heard a missionary say recently that she had been invalided home purely because her spirit had fainted, with the consequence that her body sunk also. We need to understand more of these attacks of the enemy upon our spirits and how to resist them. If the enemy can dislodge us from our position, then he seeks to "wear us out" (Dan. 7:25) by a prolonged siege, so that at last we, out of sheer weakness, let go the cry of victory.

EVENING

Repair the breaches. (2 KINGS 12:5)

A God-fearing Armenian Christian was sending some merchandise to a distant city. There were no railroads in that part of the country, and as it was a valuable lot of goods the merchant himself accompanied the caravan.

Such caravans usually camp at night, and this is an opportune time for the highwaymen, who make their living by attacking caravans, to steal unnoticed upon the campers. At the chosen time, under cover of the night, the Kurds drew near. All was strangely silent. There seemed to be no guards. But as they pressed closer, imagine their astonishment to find *high walls where walls had never stood before.* The next night they found the same impassable walls. On the third night they found the same walls, but there were breaches in them through which the robbers entered.

The captain of the marauding band was so terrified by the mystery that he woke up the Armenian, asking what it meant. He told how his band had followed intent on robbing them; how they had found the high walls around the caravan on the first and second nights; but on this night they had been able to enter through breaches. "If you will tell us the secret of all this, we will not molest you," said the captain.

The merchant himself was puzzled. "My friends," he said, "I have done nothing to have walls raised about us. All I do is pray every evening, committing myself and those with me to God. I fully trust in Him to keep me from all evil; but tonight, being very tired and sleepy, I made a rather halfhearted prayer. That must be why you were allowed to break through."

The Kurds were overcome by this testimony. Then and there they accepted the Lord Jesus Christ as their Savior. *But the Armenian never forgot the breach in the wall of prayer.*

Have you broken your tryst with God?

April 5
MORNING

Thou shalt shut the door upon thee and upon thy sons (2 KINGS 4:4).

They were to be alone with God, for they were not dealing with the laws of nature, nor human government, nor the church, nor the priesthood, nor even with the great prophet of God, but they must needs be isolated from all creatures, from all leaning circumstance, from all props of human reason, and swung off, as it were, into the vast blue interstellar space, hanging on God alone, in touch with the fountain of miracles.

Here is a part in the program of God's dealings, a secret chamber of isolation in prayer and faith which every soul must enter that is very fruitful.

There are times and places where God will form a mysterious wall around us, and cut away all props, and all the ordinary ways of doing things, and shut us up to something divine, which is utterly new and unexpected, something that old circumstances do not fit into, where we do not know just what will happen, where God is cutting the cloth of our lives on a new pattern, where He makes us look to Himself.

Most religious people live in a sort of treadmill life, where they can calculate almost everything that will happen, but the souls that God leads out into immediate and special dealings, He shuts in where all they know is that God has hold of them, and is dealing with them, and their expectation is from Him alone.

Like this widow, we must be detached from *outward* things and *attached inwardly to the Lord alone* in order to see His wonders.

FROM SOUL FOOD

In the sorest trials God often makes the sweetest discoveries of Himself.

FROM GEMS

God sometimes shuts the door and shuts us in,
That He may speak, perchance through grief or pain,
And softly, heart to heart, above the din,
May tell some precious thought to us again.

EVENING

And he bearing his cross went forth into . . . Golgotha. (JOHN 19:17)

When the two single beams were lifted from the Lord's bleeding shoulders and laid on those of the sturdy Cyrenian, Simon became what none ever had been, or ever would be, in all the history of the Lord's Passion—he became for a brief space *the substitute of Jesus!* Simon came into Jerusalem that morning, from the village home where he had been a guest, unconscious of the tragedy enacted there during the night, and was soon caught in the throng accompanying Jesus to Calvary. Through the dense excited mass of life this heavily-built countryman forced his insistent body till he came to the edge of the procession. From this vantage point he could peer in and get sight of Jesus—could catch the weariness of His face. Was it the merest accident that Simon was taken into the heart of the tragedy? The guard looked round and saw Simon—his prominence and bulk—perhaps an unconscious sympathy growing on his face—and before Simon knew what had happened he had been dragged out from among the people and the cross was on his shoulders, and *he was walking beside Jesus to Calvary.*

O good fortune of the Cyrenian to have a stout body—to be born a countryman—to carry a kindly heart! It had won him an honor *denied to kings and conquerors.*

And none so favored as this Cyrenian, for *they journeyed together* within an iron wall—no man could interrupt or annoy—neither priest nor people; they were so close together *that the cross seemed to be on them both.* That Jesus spoke to Simon as He did to few in all His ministry, there can be little doubt, since no one could render Jesus the slightest service without being instantly repaid, and this man had succored Him in His dire extremity. What Jesus said to *His substitute* Simon never told. But one thing is certain: in the heart of the tragedy on the way to Calvary, *Simon met Jesus.* And with what kindness Jesus must have spoken to *His cross-bearer* as they went forward together under one cross—one common disgrace! *Alone with the Redeemer* one gathers precious treasure!

For a short while *this man carried the load of wood.* In return, *Jesus carried his sin, and that of his children after him;* for by the time this Gospel was given unto the world Simon was known as the head of a distinguished Christian house—a man honored in his sons, Alexander and Rufus.

Nothing save . . . a few drops of blood on the ground remained of the great tragedy as Simon journeyed homeward that evening; but, in the meantime, *Jesus had accomplished the deliverance of the world*—and *Simon, the Cyrenian, had carried the Lord's cross!* What a privilege!

Taken from the throng to carry another's cross—Via Dolorosa with Jesus!

JOHN WATSON

April 6

MORNING

❦

I will stand upon my watch, and set me upon the tower, and will watch to see what he will say unto me (HAB. 2:1).

There is no waiting on God for help, and there is no help from God, without watchful expectation on our part. If we ever fail to receive strength and defense from Him, it is because we are not on the outlook for it. Many a proffered succor from heaven goes past us, because we are not standing on our watchtower to catch the far-off indications of its approach, and to fling open the gates of our heart for its entrance. He whose expectation does not lead him to be on the alert for its coming will get but little. Watch for God in the events of your life.

The old homely proverb says: "They that watch for providence will never want a providence to watch for," and you may turn it the other way and say, "They that do not watch for providences will never have a providence to watch for." Unless you put out your water jars when it rains you will catch no water.

We want to be more businesslike and use common sense with God in pleading promises. If you were to go to one of the banks, and see a man go in and out and lay a piece of paper on the table, and take it up again and nothing more—if he did that several times a day, I think there would soon be orders to keep the man out.

Those men who come to the bank in earnest present their checks, they wait until they receive their gold, and then they go; but not without having transacted real business.

They do not put the paper down, speak about the excellent signature, and discuss the excellent document; but they want their money for it, and they are not content without it. These are the people who are always welcome at the bank, and not triflers. Alas, a great many people play at praying. They do not expect God to give them an answer, and thus they are mere triflers. Our heavenly Father would have us do real business with Him in our praying.   C. H. SPURGEON

Thine expectation shall not be cut off.

EVENING

∽∾

In all these things we are more than conquerors. (ROM. 8:37)

This is one of the greatest chapters in the Bible. If doubt overtakes you, read it. If your sorrows have been too consuming, this chapter has a message for you. If you are weak, it will give you strength. If you are discouraged, hope will be restored by its inescapable logic. Read it often; become familiar with its truths, its reasoning process, its conclusion. Believe it. Live it. *Here is not only promised victory, but more than victory!*

How can we be "more than conquerors"? The American Indians believed that every foe tomahawked sent fresh strength into the warrior's arm. Temptation victoriously met increases our spiritual strength and equipment. It is possible not only to defeat the enemy but to capture him and make him fight in our ranks. God wants all His children *to turn the storm clouds into chariots.*

The ministry of thorns has often been a greater ministry to man than the ministry of thrones. Appropriate this truth.

Face the forces of darkness today Fearlessly!

I dare not be defeated
Since Christ, my conquering King,
Has called me to the battle
Which He did surely win.
Come, Lord, and give me courage,
Thy conquering Spirit give,
Make me an overcomer,
In power within me live.

I dare not be defeated,
Just at the set of sun,
When Jesus waits to whisper,
"Well done, beloved, well done!"
Come, Lord, bend from the Glory,
On me Thy Spirit cast,
Make me an overcomer,
A victor to the last.

THE VERSES OF A PILGRIM

April 7

MORNING

≈

Their strength is to sit still (ISA. 30:7).

In order really to know God, *inward stillness* is absolutely necessary. I remember when I first learned this. A time of great emergency had risen in my life, when every part of my being seemed to throb with anxiety, and when the necessity for immediate and vigorous action seemed overpowering; and yet circumstances were such that I could do nothing, and the person who could, would not stir.

For a little while it seemed as if I must fly to pieces with the inward turmoil, when suddenly the still small voice whispered in the depths of my soul, "Be still, and know that I am God." The word was with power, and I hearkened. I composed my body to perfect stillness, and I constrained my troubled spirit into quietness, and looked up and waited; and then I did "know" that it was God, God even in the very emergency and in my helplessness to meet it; and I rested in Him. It was an experience that I would not have missed for worlds; and I may add also, that out of this stillness seemed to arise a power to deal with the emergency, that very soon brought it to a successful issue. I learned then effectually that my "strength was to sit still."   HANNAH WHITALL SMITH

There is a perfect passivity which is not indolence. It is a living stillness born of trust. Quiet tension is not trust. It is simply *compressed anxiety*.

Not in the tumult of the rending storm,
Not in the earthquake or devouring flame;
But in the hush that could all fear transform,
The still, small whisper to the prophet came.

O Soul, keep silence on the mount of God,
Though cares and needs throb around thee like a sea;
From supplications and desires unshod,
Be still, and hear what God shall say to thee.

All fellowship hath interludes of rest,
New strength maturing in each poise of power;
The sweetest Alleluias of the blest
Are silent, for the space of half an hour.

O rest, in utter quietude of soul,
Abandon words, leave prayer and praise awhile;
Let thy whole being, hushed in His control,
Learn the full meaning of His voice and smile.

Not as an athlete wrestling for a crown,
Not taking Heaven by violence of will;
But with thy Father as a child sit down,
And know the bliss that follows His "Be Still!"
MARY ROWLES JARVIS

EVENING

The LORD is my shepherd. (PS. 23:1).

Who is it that is your Shepherd? The Lord! Oh, my friends, what a wonderful announcement! The Lord God of heaven and earth, and Almighty Creator of all things; He who holds the universe in His Hand as though it were a very little thing. He is your Shepherd, and has charged Himself with the care and keeping of you, as a shepherd is charged with the care and keeping of his sheep. If your hearts could really take in this thought you would never have a fear or a care again; for with such a Shepherd how could it be possible for you ever to want any good thing?

HANNAH WHITALL SMITH

Come, my sheep, shadows deep fall over land and sea,
Fast the day fades away;
Come and rest with me. Come, and in my fold abide—
Dangers lurk on every side—till at last night is past;
In my fold abide.

Come, my sheep, I will keep watch the long night through.
Safe from harm and alarm,
I will shelter you. Through the night my lambs shall rest
Safe upon the Shepherd's breast, folded there free from care
Through the night shall rest.

Come, my sheep, calmly sleep sheltered in the fold,
Weary one homeward come—
Winds are blowing cold. Rest until the dawn shall break,
Then with joy my flocks shall wake; pastures new wait for you
When the dawn shall break.

DOROTHY B. POLSUE

The Shepherd is responsible for the sheep; not the sheep for the Shepherd. The worst of it is, that we sometimes think we are both the Shepherd and the sheep, and that we have both to guide and follow. Happy are we when we realize that He is responsible; that He goes before, and goodness and mercy follow.

April 8

Therefore I take pleasure in infirmities, in reproaches,
in necessities, in persecutions, in distresses for Christ's sake:
for when I am weak, then am I strong (2 COR. 12:10).

The literal translation of this verse gives a startling emphasis to it, and makes it speak for itself with a force that we have probably never realized. Here it is: "Therefore I take pleasure in being without strength, in insults, in being pinched, in being chased about, in being cooped up in a corner for Christ's sake; for when I am without strength, then am I *dynamite.*"

Here is the secret of divine all-sufficiency, to come to the end of everything in ourselves and in our circumstances. When we reach this place, we will stop asking for sympathy because of our hard situation or bad treatment, for we will recognize these things as the very conditions of our blessing, and we will turn from them to God and find in them a claim upon Him. **A. B. SIMPSON**

George Matheson, the well-known blind preacher of Scotland, who recently went to be with the Lord, said: "My God, I have never thanked Thee for my thorn. I have thanked Thee a thousand times for my roses, but not once for my thorn. I have been looking forward to a world where I shall get compensation for my cross; but I have never thought of my cross as itself a present glory.

"Teach me the glory of my cross; teach me the value of my thorn. Show me that I have climbed to Thee by the path of pain. Show me that my tears have made my rainbows."

Alas for him who never sees
The stars shine through the cypress trees.

He was oppressed, and he was afflicted. (ISA. 53:7)

Christ was *chosen out of the people,* that He might know our wants, and sympathize with us. I believe some of the rich have no notion whatever of what the distress of the poor is. They have no idea of what it is to labor for their daily bread. They have a very faint conception of what a rise in the price of bread means; they do not *know* anything about it. And when we put men in power who never were of the people, they do not understand the art of governing us. But our great and glorious Jesus Christ is one *chosen out of the people;* and therefore He knows our wants.

Jesus suffered *temptation and pain* before us; our *sicknesses* He bore; *weariness*—He has endured it, for weary He sat by the well; *poverty*—He knows it, for sometimes He had no bread to eat save that bread of which the world knows nothing; *to be houseless*—He knew that, too, for the foxes had holes and the birds of the air had nests, but He had nowhere to lay His head.

My fellow-Christian, there is no place where thou canst go, where Christ has not been before thee—sinful places alone excepted. *He hath been before thee;* He hath smoothed the way; He hath entered the grave, that He might make the tomb the royal bedchamber of the ransomed race, the closet where they lay aside the garments of labor to put on the vestments of eternal rest.

In all places whithersoever we go, the Angel of the covenant has been our forerunner. Each burden we have to carry has once been laid on the shoulders of Immanuel.

> *His way was much rougher and darker than mine;*
> *Did Christ my Lord suffer and shall I repine?*

Dear fellow-traveler, take courage! Christ has consecrated the road.

CHARLES H. SPURGEON

> *And is Thy spotless life on earth to end*
> *Ere Thy young manhood has but scarce begun?*
> *Will not Thy Father heaven's guardians send?*
> *Thou art His Son.*
>
> *Is there no other way to save mankind*
> *Without Thine agony and utter loss?*
> *Is there no road which Heavenly Love may find*
> *Beside the Cross?*
>
> *There is no path His weary feet may know*
> *But that which leads Him to the shameful tree;*
> *That Great Forgiving Love will even go*
> *To Calvary.*

NO OTHER ROAD, BY E. LILLIAN LOWTHER

April 9

All these things are against me (GEN. 42:36).

All things work together for good to them that love God
(ROM. 8:28).

any people are wanting power. Now how is power produced? The other day we passed the great works where the trolley engines are supplied with electricity. We heard the hum and roar of the countless wheels, and we asked our friend,

"How do they make the power?"

"Why," he said, "just by the revolution of those wheels and the friction they produce. The rubbing creates the electric current."

And so, when God wants to bring more power into your life, He brings more pressure. He is generating spiritual force by hard rubbing. Some do not like it and try to run away from the pressure, instead of getting the power and using it to rise above the painful causes.

Opposition is essential to a true equilibrium of forces. The centripetal and centrifugal forces acting in opposition to each other keep our planet in her orbit. The one propelling, and the other repelling, so act and react, that instead of sweeping off into space in a pathway of desolation, she pursues her even orbit around her solar center.

So God guides our lives. It is not enough to have an impelling force— we need just as much a repelling force, and so He holds us back by the testing ordeals of life, by the pressure of temptation and trial, by the things that seem against us, but really are furthering our way and establishing our goings.

Let us thank Him for both, let us take the weights as well as the wings, and thus divinely impelled, let us press on with faith and patience in our high and heavenly calling.   A. B. SIMPSON

> *In a factory building there are wheels and gearings,*
> *There are cranks and pulleys, beltings tight or slack—*
> *Some are whirling swiftly, some are turning slowly,*
> *Some are thrusting forward, some are pulling back;*
> *Some are smooth and silent, some are rough and noisy,*
> *Pounding, rattling, clanking, moving with a jerk;*

In a wild confusion in a seeming chaos,
Lifting, pushing, driving—but they do their work.
From the mightiest lever to the tiniest pinion,
All things move together for the purpose planned;
And behind the working is a mind controlling,
And a force directing, and a guiding hand.

So all things are working for the Lord's beloved;
Some things might be hurtful if alone they stood;
Some might seem to hinder; some might draw us backward;
But they work together, and they work for good,
All the thwarted longings, all the stern denials,
All the contradictions, hard to understand.
And the force that holds them, speeds them and retards them,
Stops and starts and guides them—is our Father's hand.

ANNIE JOHNSON FLINT

EVENING

❧

By reason of breakings they purify themselves. (JOB 41:25)

Do you know the lovely fact about the opal: that, in the first place, it is made of desert dust, sand and silica, and owes its beauty and preciousness to a defect? It is a stone with a broken heart. It is full of minute fissures, which admit air, and the air refracts the light. Hence, its lovely hues and that sweet "lamp of fire" that ever burns at its heart; for *the breath of the Lord is in it.*

You are only conscious of the cracks and desert sand, but so He makes *His precious opals.*

We must be broken in ourselves before we can give back the lovely hues of His light, and the lamp of the Temple can burn in us and never go out.

ELLICE HOPKINS

Then hush! oh, hush! for the Father knows what thou knowest not,
The need and the thorn and the shadow linked with the fairest lot;
Knows the wisest exemption from many an unseen snare,
Knows what will keep thee nearest, knows what thou could'st not bear.

Hush! oh, hush! for the Father portioneth as He will,
To all His beloved children, and shall they not be still?
Is not His will the wisest, is not His choice the best?
And in perfect acquiescence is there not perfect rest?

Hush! oh, hush! for the Father, whose ways are true and just,
Knoweth and careth and loveth, and waits for thy perfect trust;
The cup He is slowly filling shall soon be full to the brim,
And infinite compensations forever be found in Him.
FRANCES RIDLEY HAVERGAL

April 10

MORNING

Show me wherefore thou contendest with me (JOB 10:2).

Perhaps, O tried soul, the Lord is doing this to develop thy graces. There are some of thy graces which would never have been *discovered* if it were not for the trials. Dost thou not know that thy faith never looks so grand in summer weather as it does in winter? Love is too oft like a glowworm, showing but little light except it be in the midst of surrounding darkness. Hope itself is like a star—not to be seen in the sunshine of prosperity, and only to be discovered in the night of adversity. Afflictions are often the black folds in which God doth set the jewels of His children's graces, to make them shine the better.

It was but a little while ago that, on thy knees, thou wast saying, "Lord, I fear I have no faith: let me know that I have faith."

Was not this really, though perhaps unconsciously, praying for trials?—for how canst thou know that thou hast faith until thy faith is exercised? Depend upon it. God often sends us trials that our graces may be discovered, and that we may be certified of their existence. Besides, it is not merely discovery; *real growth in grace* is the result of sanctified trials.

God trains His soldiers, not in tents of ease and luxury, but by turning them out and using them to forced marches and hard service. He makes them ford through streams, and swim through rivers and climb mountains, and walk many a weary mile with heavy knapsacks on their backs. Well, Christian, may not this account for the troubles through which you are passing? Is not this the reason why He is contending with you?   C. H. SPURGEON

To be left unmolested by Satan is no evidence of blessing.

Be filled with the Spirit. (EPH. 5:18)

General Gordon regretted that no one had told him when he was a young man that there was a Holy Spirit which he could possess and which could possess him. The knowledge would have saved him weakness, and sorrow, and loss. But when the later loneliness came, Gordon knew the inner strengthening of the Spirit. A power not his own came to his help. He was "strengthened with all might."

This is the apostle's sense of the magnitude of the Spirit. There is nothing we can need at any time of pressure, whether of duty or of danger, of temptation or of anxiety, but the Divine Ally will make Himself the resource of the soul to meet and endure the strain.

The apostle urges *that the utmost room should be made for the Spirit; that a man possess the Divine gift in its utmost measure.* He seems to suggest that there are degrees of possession; there are measurements we make, limitations we impose, and in his eager way he urges *that we make the utmost room for the Spirit's fullness.* Do not go in for small measures; do not restrict your allowance. The gift of the Spirit is not on a rationing basis. Do not confine yourself to mean and petty degrees of the Spirit. "Be filled with the Spirit." There is no surfeit here, nor need there be any restriction.   **THE LIFE OF A CHRISTIAN, BY JOHN MACBETH**

There are deep things of God. Push out from shore,
Hast thou found much? Give thanks and look for more.
Dost fear the generous Giver to offend?
Then know His store of bounty hath no end.
He doth not need to be implored or teased;
The more we take the better He is pleased.

Beside the common inheritance of the land, there are some special possessions.   **A. B. SIMPSON**

"Have ye received the Holy Ghost since ye believed?"

April 11

MORNING

≪≫

What I tell you in darkness, that speak ye in light (MATT. 10:27).

Our Lord is constantly taking us into the dark, that He may tell us things. Into the dark of the shadowed home, where bereavement has drawn the blinds; into the dark of the lonely, desolate life, where some infirmity closes us in from the light and stir of life; into the dark of some crushing sorrow and disappointment.

Then He tells us His secrets, great and wonderful, eternal and infinite; He causes the eye which has become dazzled by the glare of the earth to behold the heavenly constellations; and the ear to detect the undertones of His voice, which is often drowned amid the tumult of earth's strident cries.

But such revelations always imply a corresponding responsibility—"that *speak ye* in the light—that *proclaim* upon the housetops."

We are not meant to always linger in the dark, or stay in the closet; presently we shall be summoned to take our place in the rush and storm of life; and when that moment comes, we are to speak and proclaim what we have learned.

This gives new meaning to suffering, the saddest element in which is often its apparent aimlessness. "How useless I am!" "What am I doing for the betterment of men?" "Wherefore this waste of the precious spikenard of my soul?"

Such are the desperate laments of the sufferer. But God has a purpose in it all. He has withdrawn His child to the higher altitudes of fellowship, that he may hear God speaking face-to-face, and bear the message to his fellows at the mountain foot.

Were the forty days wasted that Moses spent on the mount or the period spent at Horeb by Elijah, or the years spent in Arabia by Paul?

There is no shortcut to the life of faith, which is the all-vital condition of a holy and victorious life. We must have periods of lonely meditation and fellowship with God. That our souls should have their mountains of fellowship, their valley of quiet rest beneath the shadow of the great rock, their nights beneath the stars, when darkness has veiled the material and silenced the stir of human life, and has opened the view of the infinite and eternal, is as indispensable as that our bodies should have food.

Thus alone can the sense of God's presence become the fixed possession of the soul, enabling it to say repeatedly, with the psalmist, "Thou art near, O God."

F. B. MEYER

Some hearts, like evening primroses, open more beautifully in the shadows of life.

EVENING

Instead of the thorn shall come up the fir tree,
and instead of the brier shall come up the myrtle tree:
and it shall be to the LORD for a name, for an everlasting sign
that shall not be cut off. (ISA. 55:13)

At the Jerusalem Conference on Good Friday we were out on the Mount of Olives, and our hearts were deeply and strangely moved as we thought about *His* going out of the city yonder, up the hillside, to die. I said to myself, "I would like to follow in His train, and catch the same passion and the same vision." As the meeting was closing I thought, "I will take something by which to remember this hour." I leaned over to pluck a flower, one of the flowers that bloom in lovely profusion across the hillsides of Palestine. As I was about to pick my wildflower, an inner voice said, "No, not the wildflower; here is the thornbush yonder; take a piece of that." It was the thornbush from which the crown of thorns was taken, and crushed upon the brow of Jesus. I protested, "The thornbush is not beautiful, it is ugly; I would rather have the flower," and I again leaned over to pick my flower. The voice was more imperious this time, and said, "No, not the flower, but the thornbush; there is something in the thornbush you do not see now; take it!"

Rather reluctantly I turned away from the wildflower and plucked a piece from the thornbush and put it in the folds of my Bible. No, deeper; I put it within the folds of my heart and wore it there.

Weeks went by—months. One day I chanced to look at my thornbush I had worn within my heart, and to my amazement I found it was all abloom! The Rose of Sharon was there in lovely profusion. There was something else in the thornbush I had not seen.

"From thy brier, dear heart, shall blow a rose for others."

To some people there comes this cross, the *absence* of the Cross. There is always the shadow of the Cross. Suppose God took it away, what then?

And shall there be no cross for me
In all this life of mine?

Shall mine be all a flowery path
And all the thorns be Thine?

April 12

MORNING

And Jesus being full of the Holy Ghost returned from Jordan,
and was led by the Spirit into the wilderness,
being forty days tempted of the devil (LUKE 4:1–2).

Jesus was full of the Holy Ghost, and yet He was tempted. Temptation often comes upon a man with its strongest power when he is nearest to God. As someone has said, "The Devil aims high." He got one apostle to say he did not even know Christ.

Very few men have such conflicts with the Devil as Martin Luther had. Why? Because Martin Luther was going to shake the very kingdom of hell. Oh, what conflicts John Bunyan had!

If a man has much of the Spirit of God, he will have great conflicts with the tempter. God permits temptation because it does for us what the storms do for the oaks—it roots us; and what the fire does for the paintings on the porcelain—it makes them permanent.

You never know that you have a grip on Christ, or that He has a grip on you, as well as when the Devil is using all his force to attract you from Him; then you feel the pull of Christ's right hand.   SELECTED

Extraordinary afflictions are not always the punishment of extraordinary sins, but sometimes the trial of extraordinary graces. God hath many sharp-cutting instruments, and rough files for the polishing of His jewels; and those He especially loves, and means to make the most resplendent, He hath oftenest His tools upon.   ARCHBISHOP LEIGHTON

I bear my willing witness that I owe more to the fire, and the hammer, and the file, than to anything else in my Lord's workshop. I sometimes question whether I have ever learned anything except through the rod. When my schoolroom is darkened, I see most.   C. H. SPURGEON

~~~

If thou hadst been here. (JOHN 11:21)

*I*f only my circumstances and my environment were altered . . .
"If only So-and-So were not trying to live with . . .

"If only I had the opportunities, the advantages, that other people
have . . .

"*If* only that insurmountable difficulty, that sorrow, that trouble,
could be moved out of my life; then how different things would be! and
how different I should be."

Ah, dear friend, you are not the only one who has had such thoughts.
No less a person than Paul the Apostle besought the Lord three times that
the thorn in the flesh might depart from him; *and yet, it was allowed to
remain.*

A certain gentleman had a garden which might have been very beautiful had it not been disfigured by an immense boulder which reached far
under the soil. He tried to blast it out with dynamite, but in the attempt
only shattered the windows of the house. Being very self-willed he used
without success one harsh method after another to get rid of the disfigurement until finally he died of worry and blighted hopes.

The heir, a man who *not only had common sense but used it,* soon per-
ceived the hopelessness of striving to budge the boulder and therefore set
to work to convert it into a rockery, which he covered with frescoes, flowers, ferns, and vines. It soon came about that the visitors to the garden
commented on its unsurpassed beauty, and the owner could never quite
decide which gave him the greater happiness—the harmonious aspect of
his garden, or the success in adapting himself to the thing that was too
deep to move.

So the unsightly boulder which could not be removed, proved to be
the most valuable asset in that garden *when dealt with by one who knew
how to turn its very defects to account.*   SELECTED

God often plants His flowers among rough rocks!

April 13

ᕦᕤ

And the hand of the Lord was there upon me;
and he said unto me, Arise, go forth into the plain,
and I will there talk with thee (EZEK. 3:22).

*D*id you ever hear of anyone being much used for Christ who did not have some *special* waiting time, some complete *upset* of all his or her plans first; from Saint Paul's being sent off into the desert of Arabia for three years, when he must have been boiling over with the glad tidings, down to the present day?

You were looking forward to telling about trusting Jesus in Syria; now He says, "I want you to *show* what it is to trust Me, without waiting for Syria."

My own case is far less severe, but the same in principle, that when I thought the door was flung open for me to go with a bound into literary work, it is opposed, and doctor steps in and says, simply, "Never! She must choose between writing and living; she can't do both."

That was in 1860. Then I came out of the shell with *Ministry of Song* in 1869, and saw the evident wisdom of being kept waiting nine years in the shade. God's love being unchangeable, He is just as loving when we do not see or feel His love. Also His love and His sovereignty are co-equal and universal; so He withholds the enjoyment and conscious progress because He knows best what will really ripen and further His work in us.

MEMORIALS OF FRANCES RIDLEY HAVERGAL

I laid it down in silence,
This work of mine,
And took what had been sent me—
A resting time.
The Master's voice had called me
To rest apart;
"Apart with Jesus only,"
Echoed my heart.

I took the rest and stillness
From His own Hand,
And felt this present illness
Was what He planned.

How often we choose labor,
When He says "Rest"—
Our ways are blind and crooked;
His way is best.

The work Himself has given,
He will complete.
There may be other errands
For tired feet;
There may be other duties
For tired hands,
The present, is obedience
To His commands.

There is a blessed resting
In lying still,
In letting His hand mould us,
Just as He will.
His work must be completed.
His lesson set;
He is the higher Workman:
Do not forget!

It is not only "working."
We must be trained;
And Jesus "learnt" obedience,
Through suffering gained.
For us, His yoke is easy,
His burden light.
His discipline most needful,
And all is right.

We are but under-workmen;
They never choose
If this tool or if that one
Their hands shall use.
In working or in waiting
May we fulfill
Not ours at all, but only
The Master's will!

SELECTED

God provides resting places as well as working places. Rest, then, and
be thankful when He brings you, wearied to a wayside well.

❦

He is risen. (MARK 16:6)

Arise! for He is risen today;
And shine, for He is glorified!
Put on thy beautiful array,
And keep perpetual Eastertide.

A little lad was gazing intently at the picture in the art store window: the store was displaying a notable picture of the crucifixion. A gentleman approached, stopped, and looked. The boy, seeing his interest, said: "That's Jesus." The man made no reply, and the lad continued: "Them's Roman soldiers." And, after a moment: "They killed Him."

"Where did you learn that?" asked the man.

"In the Mission Sunday school," was the reply.

The man turned and walked thoughtfully away. He had not gone far when he heard a youthful voice calling: "Say, Mister," and quickly the little street lad caught up with him. "Say, Mister," he repeated, "I wanted to tell you that He rose again."

That message, which was nearly forgotten by the boy, is the message which has been coming down through the ages. It is the Easter message—the story of the eternal triumph of life over death; the promise and pledge of man's immortality.

The grave to Him was not a terminus!

This is the day of glad tidings! Go quickly, and tell the message! "He is risen!" Hallelujah! Christ is risen! Hades could not hold Him! Corruption could not devour Him! "I am He that liveth and was dead; and, behold, I am alive forevermore, Amen; and have the keys of death and Hades." Blessed be God! Jesus lives to die no more! Go quickly, and tell everywhere the glad news!

And I think the Shining Ones marvel much
As they gaze from the world above,
To see how slowly we spread the news
Of that Sacrifice of love.

There is, to my mind, a natural sequence in one of the accounts of that first Easter morning, as beautiful as it is suggestive. It is the story of the women who hastened to the sepulcher, and it says: *"They came unto the sepulcher at the rising of the sun."*

April 14

MORNING

∽◦◦◦∽

For the Lord himself shall descend from heaven with a shout,
with the voice of the archangel, and with the trump of God:
and the dead in Christ shall rise first: then we which are alive
and remain shall be caught up together with them in the clouds,
to meet the Lord in the air: and so shall we ever be with the Lord
(1 THESS. 4:16, 17).

It was "very early in the morning" while "it was yet dark," that Jesus rose from the dead. Not the sun, but only the morning star shone upon His opening tomb. The shadows had not fled, the citizens of Jerusalem had not awaked. It was still night—the hour of sleep and darkness, when He arose. Nor did His rising break the slumbers of the city. So shall it be "very early in the morning while it is yet dark," and when nought but the morning star is shining, that Christ's body, the church, shall arise. Like Him, His saints shall awake when the children of the night and darkness are still sleeping their sleep of death. In their arising they disturb no one. The world hears not the voice that summons them. As Jesus laid them quietly to rest, each in his own still tomb, like children in the arms of their mother, so, as quietly, as gently, shall He awake them when the hour arrives. To them come the quickening words, "Awake and sing, ye that dwell in dust" (Isa. 26:19). Into their tomb the earliest ray of glory finds its way. They drink in the first gleams of morning, while as yet the eastern clouds give but the faintest signs of the uprising. Its genial fragrance, its soothing stillness, its bracing freshness, its sweet loneliness, its quiet purity, all so solemn and yet so full of hope, these are theirs.

Oh, the contrast between these things and the dark night through which they have passed! Oh, the contrast between these things and the grave from which they have sprung! And as they shake off the encumbering turf, flinging mortality aside and rising, in glorified bodies, to meet their Lord in the air they are lighted and guided upward, along the untrodden pathway, by the beams of that Star of the morning, which, like the Star of Bethlehem, conducts them to the presence of the King. "Weeping may endure for a night, but joy cometh in the morning."

HORATIUS BONAR

While the hosts cry Hosanna, from heaven descending,
With glorified saints and the angels attending,
With grace on His brow, like a halo of glory,
Will Jesus receive His own.
Even so, come quickly.

A soldier said, "When I die do not sound taps over my grave, but reveille, the morning call, the summons to rise."

EVENING

Be strong in the grace that is in Christ Jesus. . . . Endure hardness, as a good soldier of Jesus Christ. (2 TIM. 2:1, 3)

The post of honor in war is so called because it is attended by difficulties and dangers to which but few are equal; yet generals usually allot these hard services to their favorites and friends, who on their part eagerly take them as tokens of favor and marks of confidence.

Should we not, therefore, account it an honor and a privilege when the Captain of our salvation assigns us a difficult post, since He can and does inspire His soldiers, which no earthly commander can, with wisdom, courage, and strength suitable to their situation?

Listen to Ignatius shouting as the lion's teeth tear his flesh, "Now I begin to be a Christian!"

The Christian's badge of honor here, has ever been the Cross.

No church or movement can survive unless it is ready to be crucified.

BISHOP OF WINCHESTER

If I did not see that the Lord kept watch over the ship, I should long since have abandoned the helm. But I see Him! through the storm, strengthening the tackling, handling the yards, spreading the sails—aye more, commanding the very winds! Should *I* not be a coward if I abandoned *my* post? Let Him govern, let Him carry us forward, let Him hasten or delay, *we will fear nothing!*

MARTIN LUTHER

For us, swords drawn, up to the gate of heaven:
Oh, may no coward spirit seek to leaven

The warrior code, the calling that is ours!
Forbid that we should sheathe our sword in flowers!

Captain beloved, battle wounds were Thine,
Let me not wonder if some hurt be mine.
Rather, O Lord, let my deep wonder be
That I may share a battle wound with Thee.
GOLD CORD

April 15

MORNING

❧

I trust in thy word (PS. 119:42).

Just in proportion in which we believe that God will do just what He has said, is our faith strong or weak. Faith has nothing to do with feelings, or with impressions, with improbabilities, or with outward appearances. If we desire to couple them with faith, then we are no longer resting on the Word of God because faith needs nothing of the kind. *Faith rests on the naked Word of God*. When we take Him at His Word the heart is at peace.

God delights to exercise faith, first for blessing in our own souls, then for blessing in the church at large, and also for those without. But this exercise we shrink from instead of welcoming. When trials come, we should say: "My heavenly Father puts this cup of trial into my hands, that I may have something sweet afterwards."

Trials are the food of faith. Oh, let us leave ourselves in the hands of our heavenly Father! It is the joy of His heart to do good to all His children.

But trials and difficulties are not the only means by which faith is exercised and thereby increased. *There is the reading of the Scriptures, that we may by them acquaint ourselves with God as He has revealed Himself in His Word.*

Are you able to say, from the acquaintance you have made with God, that He is a lovely Being? If not, let me affectionately entreat you to ask God to bring you to this, that you may admire His gentleness and kindness, that you may be able to say how good He is, and what a delight it is to the heart of God to do good to His children.

Now the nearer we come to this in our inmost souls, the more ready we are to leave ourselves in His hands, satisfied with all His dealings with us. And when trial comes, we shall say:

"I will wait and see what good God will do to me by it, assured He will do it." Thus we shall bear an honorable testimony before the world, and thus we shall strengthen the hands of others.   GEORGE MUELLER

EVENING

〜∞〜

Although the fig tree shall not blossom, neither shall fruit be in the vines; the labor of the olive shall fail, and the fields shall yield no meat; the flock shall be cut off from the fold, and there shall be no herd in the stalls: Yet I will rejoice in the LORD, I will joy in the God of my salvation. (HAB. 3:17–18)

*H*ow irrational it seems! We, with whom God hath dealt bountifully, can understand praising Him, but we should have the greatest respect for a man, who under these circumstances would not repine. To bring it closer home than the time of Habakkuk, translate all this into current experience. Instead of flocks and herds, use profits; instead of figs and olives, read credit balances; for husbandry and its terms, use business and its terms; for flocks and stalls, substitute bank balances and securities; for Chaldean invasion, the economic blizzard which is sweeping through the world—and then see where you stand!

Although there shall be no balances and securities, and all dividends shall be passed, and though I be reduced to utter penury, yet will I rejoice in the Lord!

You say that is impossible! Of course, apart from some supernatural aid he could not have done it, nor can we. Habakkuk learned that life cannot be a solo affair: it is a duet. If life were a solo, it would mean a tragic breakdown when the high notes must be reached, or the low ones melodiously sounded. A duet means harmony—*human life linked on to Divine purpose and power.* Habakkuk's experience shows that *you have lost nothing if you have not lost God.*   J. STUART HOLDEN

Pilgrim, look up!

The road is dusty; the journey is long. Look up! *Look up in the early morning* when the sun comes peeping over the horizon, out of the shadows of the night. Look up *in the noontide* when the resting-spot is still afar in the distance. Look up *when you see the evening star.*

Look up! There shines the City!

April 16

〜

By faith Abraham, when he was called to go out into a place which he should after receive for an inheritance, obeyed (HEB. 11:8).

Whither he went, he knew not; it was enough for him to know that he went with God. He leant not so much upon the promises as upon the Promiser. He looked not on the difficulties of his lot, but on the King, eternal, immortal, invisible, the only wise God, who had deigned to appoint his course, and would certainly vindicate Himself. O glorious faith! This is thy work, these are thy possibilities; contentment to sail with sealed orders, because of unwavering confidence in the wisdom of the Lord High Admiral; willinghood to rise up, leave all, and follow Christ, because of the glad assurance that earth's best cannot bear comparison with heaven's least.

F. B. M.

It is by no means enough to set out cheerfully with your God on any venture of faith. Tear into smallest pieces any itinerary for the journey which your imagination may have drawn up.

Nothing will fall out as you expect.

Your guide will keep to no beaten path. He will lead you by a way such as you never dreamed your eyes would look upon. He knows no fear, and He expects you to fear nothing while He is with you.

> *The day had gone; alone and weak*
> *I groped my way within a bleak*
> *And sunless land.*
> *The path that led into the light*
> *I could not find! In that dark night*
> *God took my hand.*
>
> *He led me that I might not stray,*
> *And brought me by a new, safe way*
> *I had not known.*
> *By waters still, through pastures green*
> *I followed Him—the path was clean*
> *Of briar and stone.*
>
> *The heavy darkness lost its strength,*
> *My waiting eyes beheld at length*

The streaking dawn.
On, safely on, through sunrise glow
I walked, my hand in His, and lo,
The night had gone.
ANNIE PORTER JOHNSON

EVENING

Speak unto the children of Israel, that they go forward. (EX. 14:15)

*L*et us move on and step out boldly, though it be into the night where one can scarcely see the way. The path will open as we press on, like the trail through the forest, or the Alpine pass which discloses but a few rods of its length. There are things God gives us to do without any light or illumination at all except His own command, but *those who know the way to God can find it in the dark.* ALEXANDER MACLAREN

The God of Israel, the Savior, is sometimes a God that hideth Himself, but never a God that absenteth Himself; sometimes in the dark, but never at a distance. MATTHEW HENRY

There was a rift tonight;
I saw a gray cloud break and let the light
Shine through—a ray of hope to all the earth;
Long had I waited here; I found it hard to say,
"The clouds will drift apart, the darkness melt away
Before the radiance of the night's new birth."

That promised glow to guide a wayward one;
At last, after long hours of doubt and fear,
Came light again and life, and sweet security,
As though a hidden ray from God's eternity
Peeped out, that I might look and see it there.

So, if I can but wait,
I know that God will send it, soon or late—
This break within my life's gray cloud; His gift
To me, one star of perfect love to shine and show
That they who walk by faith are told the way to go,
And after storm will come the blessed rift.
RUTH M. GIBBS

April 17

MORNING

〜〜

The hand of the Lord hath wrought this (JOB 12:9).

Several years ago there was found in an African mine the most magnificent diamond in the world's history. It was presented to the king of England to blaze in his crown of state. The king sent it to Amsterdam to be cut. It was put into the hands of an expert lapidary. And what do you suppose he did with it?

He took the gem of priceless value, and cut a notch in it. Then he struck it a hard blow with his instrument, and lo! the superb jewel lay in his hand cleft in twain. What recklessness! what wastefulness! what criminal carelessness!

Not so. For days and weeks that blow had been studied and planned. Drawings and models had been made of the gem. Its quality, its defects, its lines of cleavage had all been studied with minutest care. The man to whom it was committed was one of the most skillful lapidaries in the world.

Do you say that blow was a mistake? Nay. It was the climax of the lapidary's skill. When he struck that blow, he did the one thing which would bring that gem to its most perfect shapeliness, radiance, and jewelled splendor. That blow which seemed to ruin the superb precious stone was, in fact, its perfect redemption. For, from those two halves were wrought the two magnificent gems which the skilled eye of the lapidary saw hidden in the rough, uncut stone as it came from the mine.

So, sometimes, God lets a stinging blow fall upon your life. The blood spurts. The nerves wince. The soul cries out in agony. The blow seems to you an appalling mistake. But it is not, for you are the most priceless jewel in the world to God. And He is the most skilled lapidary in the universe.

Someday you are to blaze in the diadem of the King. As you lie in His hand now He knows just how to deal with you. Not a blow will be permitted to fall upon your shrinking soul but that the love of God permits it, and works out from its depths, blessing and spiritual enrichment unseen, and unthought of by you.   J. H. MCC.

In one of George MacDonald's books occurs this fragment of conversation: "I wonder why God made me," said Mrs. Faber bitterly. "I'm sure I don't know what was the use of making me!"

"Perhaps not much yet," said Dorothy, "but then He hasn't done with you yet. He is making you now, and you are quarreling with the process."

If men would but believe that they are in process of creation, and consent to be made—let the Maker handle them as the potter the clay, yielding themselves in resplendent motion and submissive, hopeful action with the turning of His wheel—they would ere long find themselves able to welcome every pressure of that hand on them, even when it was felt in pain; and sometimes not only to believe but to recognize the divine end in view, the bringing of a son unto glory.

Not a single shaft can hit,
Till the God of love sees fit.

EVENING

✦

Blessed is that servant, whom his lord when he cometh
shall find so doing. (MATT. 24:46)

A story is related, which has to do with the Second Coming of our blessed Lord; and the general dissemination of this precious truth. At last it reached the black people in the South as they worked in the cotton fields. Said one of the old black brethren, *"What's de use of us pickin' cotton if de Lawd is comin' back?"* And scores of others agreed. The cotton pickers stopped their work and the cotton wasted in the fields. Everybody was busy attending conferences and camp meetings, singing the praises of God, and looking for His return.

The following winter was one of great need and privation, because their crops had been so woefully neglected.

Then one of their number, an evangelist, began preaching on this text: *"Blessed is that servant, whom his lord when he cometh shall find so doing."*

Before long the black people were once again tilling their ground, and picking cotton in the rows. It remained for Bertrand Shadwell to give us the following poem which suggests their change in attitude:

There's a King and Captain high,
Who'll be coming by and by;
And He'll find me hoeing cotton when He comes.
You can hear His legions charging in the thunder of the sky;
And He'll find me hoeing cotton when He comes.
When He comes!

When He comes!
All the dead shall rise, in answer to His drums.
Oh, the fires of His encampment star the firmament on high;
And the heavens shall roll asunder, when He comes.
There's a Man they thrust aside,
Who was tortured till He died;
And He'll find me hoeing cotton when He comes.
He was spat upon and mocked at;
He was scourged and crucified;
And He'll find me hoeing cotton when He comes.
When He comes!
When He comes!
He'll be loved by saints and angels when He comes;
They'll be calling out "Hosanna!" to the Man that men denied;
And I'll kneel among the cotton—
When He comes!
"Occupy till I come."

April 18

MORNING

⸎

And he shall bring it to pass (PS. 37:5).

I once thought that after I prayed that it was my duty to do every thing that I could do to bring the answer to pass. He taught me a better way, and showed that my self-effort always hindered His working, and that when I prayed and definitely believed Him for anything, He wanted me to wait in the spirit of praise, and only do what He bade me. It seems so unsafe to just sit still, and do nothing but trust the Lord; and the temptation to take the battle into our own hands is often tremendous.

We all know how impossible it is to rescue a drowning man who tries to help his rescuer, and it is equally impossible for the Lord to fight our battles for us when we insist upon trying to fight them ourselves. It is not that He will not, but He cannot. Our interference hinders His working.

C. H. P.

Spiritual forces cannot work while earthly forces are active.

It takes God time to answer prayer. We often fail to give God a chance in that respect. It takes time for God to paint a rose. It takes time for God to grow an oak. It takes time for God to make bread from wheat fields. He takes the earth. He pulverizes. He softens. He enriches. He wets with showers and dews. He warms with life. He gives the blade, the stock, the amber grain, and then at last the bread for the hungry.

All this takes time. Therefore we sow, and till, and wait, and trust, until all God's purpose has been wrought out. We give God a chance in this matter of time. We need to learn this same lesson in our prayer life. It takes God time to answer prayer.   J. H. M.

EVENING

And he brought him forth abroad, and said, Look now toward heaven, and tell the stars, if thou be able to number them: and he said unto him, So shall thy seed be. (GEN. 15:5)

We are profoundly impressed with the unlimited resources of the God of the Bible. He never does anything small. When He makes an ocean He makes it so deep that no man can fathom it. When He makes a mountain He makes it so large that no one can measure or weigh it. When He makes flowers, He scatters multiplied millions of them where there is no one to admire them but Himself. When He makes grace, He makes it without sides or bottom and leaves the top off. Instead of giving salvation with a medicine dropper, He pours it forth like a river.

When God sets out to do a thing for us, *He does it with a prodigality of love-prompted abundance that fairly staggers one who reckons things by the coldly calculating standards of earth.*

Whatever blessing is in our cup it is sure to *run over.* With Him the calf is always the *fatted calf;* the robe is always the *best robe;* the joy is *unspeakable;* the peace *passeth understanding;* the grace is *so abundant that the recipient has all-sufficiency for all things, and abounds to every good work.*

There is no grudging in God's benevolence; He does not measure out His goodness as the apothecary counts his drops and measures his drams, slowly and exactly, drop by drop. God's way is always characterized by multitudinous and overflowing bounty, like that in nature which is so profuse in beauty and life that every drop of the ocean, every square inch of the forest glade, every molecule of water, teems with marvels and defies the research and investigation of man. Well may we cry with the apostle,

"I have all, and abound."

April 19

MORNING

⥈⥊

Stand still, and see the salvation of the Lord (EXOD. 14:13).

These words contain God's command to the believer when he is reduced to great straits and brought into extraordinary difficulties. He cannot retreat; he cannot go forward; he is shut upon the right hand and on the left. What is he now to do?

The Master's word to him is "stand still." It will be well for him if, at such times, he listens only to his Master's word, for other and evil advisers come with their suggestions. *Despair* whispers, "Lie down and die; give it all up." But God would have us put on a cheerful courage, and even in our worst times, rejoice in His love and faithfulness.

Cowardice says, "Retreat; go back to the worldling's way of action; you cannot play the Christian's part; it is too difficult. Relinquish your principles."

But, however much Satan may urge this course upon you, you cannot follow it, if you are a child of God. His divine fiat has bid thee go from strength to strength, and so thou shalt, and neither death nor hell shall turn thee from thy course. What if for a while thou art called to stand still; yet this is but to renew thy strength for some greater advance in due time.

Precipitancy cries, "Do something; stir yourself; to stand still and wait is sheer idleness." We *must* be doing something at once—*we* must do it, so we think—instead of looking to the Lord, who will not only do something, but will do everything.

Presumption boasts, "If the sea be before you, march into it, and expect a miracle." But faith listens neither to presumption, nor to despair, not to cowardice, nor to precipitancy, but it hears God say, "Stand still," and immovable as a rock it stands.

"Stand still"—keep the posture of an upright man, ready for action, expecting further orders, cheerfully and patiently awaiting the directing voice; and it will not be long ere God shall say to you, as distinctly as Moses said it to the people of Israel, "Go forward." SPURGEON

Be quiet! why this anxious heed
About thy tangled ways?
God knows them all. He giveth speed
And He allows delays.
'Tis good for thee to walk by faith

And not by sight.
Take it on trust a little while.
Soon shalt thou read the mystery aright
In the full sunshine of His smile.

In times of uncertainty, wait. Always, if you have any doubt, *wait*. Do not force yourself to any action. If you have a restraint in your spirit, wait until all is clear, and do not go against it.

EVENING

❧

When thou prayest, enter into thy closet. (MATT. 6:6)

The apostolic men, the saintly men, the heroic servants of God, the strong soldiers of Jesus Christ, have everywhere and always *prayed without ceasing.*

If Francis of Assisi knew how to do battle among men, it was because he loved to "fly away as a bird to its nest in the mountains." John Welsh spent eight hours out of the twenty-four in communion with God; therefore he was equipped and armed and dared to suffer! David Brainerd rode through the endless American woods praying, and so fulfilled his ministry in a short time. John Wesley came out from his seclusion to change the face of England. Andrew Bonar did not once miss his mercy seat, and his fellowship with heaven made him the winsome Christian that he was. John Fletcher sometimes prayed all night. Adoniram Judson won Burma for Christ through unwearied prayer. Such was *the habit of those who wrought nobly for God.*

If we would attempt great things for God, and achieve something before we die, we must pray at every moment and in every place.

God commits Himself into the hands of those who truly pray.

Alone, dear Lord, in solitude serene,
Thy servant Moses was constrained to go,
Into the silent desert with the sheep;
The silvery stars his lovely vigil know.

And Paul, the fiery warrior, zealous, bold,
In desert places, 'neath Arabian skies,
Learned God's own lessons, harkened to His voice,
Grew calm, resourceful, humble, meek and wise.

Alone, dear Lord, I fear to be alone;
My heart demands the blest companionship

Of those that love Thee; friendship's nectar sweet,
With those beloved, I evermore would sip.

But in the desert, Moses, David, Paul,
Were not alone, afar from love or care:
They companied with heav'nly visitors,
They knew no loneliness, for Thou wert there.
ALICE E. SHERWOOD

The first-century Christians were said to be *power conscious*. We are *problem* conscious. What did *they* believe about prayer? What do *we*?

April 20
MORNING
∽≈∾

Not by might, nor by power, but by my spirit, saith the Lord of hosts
(ZECH. 4:6).

ℳy way led up a hill, and right at the foot I saw a boy on a bicycle. He was pedaling uphill against the wind, and evidently found it a tremendously hard work. Just as he was working most strenuously and doing his best painfully, there came a trolley car going in the same direction—up the hill.

It was not going too fast for the boy to get behind it, and with one hand to lay hold at the bar at the back. Then you know what happened. He went up the hill like a bird. Then it flashed upon me:

"Why, I am like that boy on the bicycle in my weariness and weakness. I am pedaling uphill against all kinds of opposition, and am almost worn out with the task. But here at hand is a great available power, the strength of the Lord Jesus.

"I have only to get in touch with Him and to maintain communication with Him, though it may be only one little finger of faith, and that will be enough to make His power mine for the doing of this bit of service that just now seems too much for me." And I was helped to dismiss my weariness and to realize this truth.

FROM **THE LIFE OF FULLER PURPOSE**

Abandoned

Utterly abandoned to the Holy Ghost!
Seeking all His fulness at whatever cost;
Cutting all the shore-lines, launching in the deep
Of His mighty power—strong to save and keep.

Utterly abandoned to the Holy Ghost!
Oh! the sinking, sinking, until self is lost!
Until the emptied vessel lies broken at His feet;
Waiting till His filling shall make the work complete.

Utterly abandoned to the will of God;
Seeking for not other path than my Master trod;
Leaving ease and pleasure, making Him my choice,
Waiting for His guidance, listening for His voice.

Utterly abandoned! no will of my own;
For time and for eternity, His, and His alone;
All my plans and purposes lost in His sweet will,
Having nothing, yet in Him all things possessing still.

Utterly abandoned! 'tis so sweet to be
Captive in His bonds of love, yet so wondrous free;
Free from sin's entanglements, free from doubt and fear,
Free from every worry, burden, grief or care.

Utterly abandoned! oh, the rest is sweet,
As I tarry, waiting, at His blessed feet;
Waiting for the coming of the Guest divine,
Who my inmost being shall perfectly refine.

Lo! He comes and fills me, Holy Spirit sweet!
I, in Him, am satisfied! I, in Him, complete!
And the light within my soul shall nevermore grow dim
While I keep my covenant—abandoned unto Him!

AUTHOR UNKNOWN

*But himself went a day's journey into the wilderness, and came and
sat down under a juniper tree: and he requested for himself that he
might die; and said, It is enough. . . . And, behold,
the* LORD *passed by, and a great . . . wind . . . ; but the* LORD *was
not in the wind: . . . an earthquake; but the* LORD *was not in the
earthquake: . . . a fire; but the* LORD *was not in the fire: and after
the fire a still small voice. . . . And the* LORD *said unto him,
Go, return on thy way . . . and . . . anoint Hazael to be king
over Syria.* (1 KINGS 19:4, 11–12, 15)

When a man loses heart he loses everything. To keep one's heart in
the midst of life's stream, and to maintain an undiscourageable front
in the face of its difficulties is not an achievement that springs from anything that a laboratory can demonstrate, or that logic can affirm. *It is an
achievement of faith.*

If you lose your sky, you will soon lose your earth.

From under the juniper tree Elijah is called into an audience with the
King of Kings. While listening to his own defeated wail, the accents of the
still small Voice fall upon his weary ear. God refused him his unworthy
request; rested him from his service; reminded him that he was still
needed; and returned him to his work. He thought his work was done
and that life had left him in the shadows. God says: "No, I am commis-
sioning you to go forth and anoint kings and prophets, and climax the
service of other days."

*Not till His hour strikes is our day done; as long as we live we serve the
King!*

The tempter is always ready to take advantage of a time of weariness
and reaction. *He loves to fish in troubled waters.*

Juniper trees make poor sanctuaries.

*It is good to have things settled by faith, before they are unsettled by feel-
ing.*

April 21

〜∞〜

And being absolutely certain that whatever promise
He is bound by, He is able to make good (ROM. 4:21).

We are told that Abraham could look at his own body and consider it as good as death without being discouraged, because he was not looking at himself but at the almighty One.

He did not *stagger* at the promise, but stood straight up unbending beneath his mighty load of blessing. Instead of growing weak he waxed strong in the faith and grew more robust; the more difficulties became apparent, glorifying God through His very sufficiency and being "fully persuaded" (as the Greek expresses it) "that he who had promised was," not merely able, but—as it literally means "abundantly able"—munificently able, able with an infinite surplus of resources, infinitely able "to perform."

He is the God of boundless resources. The only limit is in us. Our asking, our thinking, our praying are too small; our expectations are too limited. He is trying to lift us up to a higher conception, and lure us on to a mightier expectation and appropriation. Oh, shall we put Him in derision? There is no limit to what we may ask and expect of our glorious El-Shaddai; and there is but one measure here given for His blessing, and that is "according to the power that worketh in us."   A. B. SIMPSON

"Climb to the treasure house of blessing on the ladder made of divine promises. By a promise as by a key open the door to the riches of God's grace and favor."

EVENING

〜∞〜

God hath chosen the weak things of the world to confound
the things which are mighty. (1 COR. 1:27)

We must not be fainthearted because we are consciously poor instruments. The main question is *the mastery of Him who uses the instruments.*

Once Paganini, standing before a vast audience, broke string after string of his violin. Men had come to hear his greatest sonata, "Napoleon." They hissed as he seemed to destroy all hope for continuing his performance. Then the artist held up his violin: "One string—and Paganini," and on that one string he made the first complete manifestation of his greatness!

It would be a poor violin, indeed, out of which Paganini could not bring music; a poor pencil with which Raphael could not create a masterpiece; and *the power of the Spirit behind the least gifted one can work to glorious issues.*

It is said that Gainsborough, the artist, longed also to be a musician. He bought musical instruments of many kinds and tried to play them. He once heard a great violinist bringing ravishing music from his instrument. Gainsborough was charmed and thrown into transports of admiration. He bought the violin on which the master played so marvelously. He thought that if he had the wonderful instrument that he could play, too. But he soon learned that the music was not in the violin, but was in the master who played it.

Are you discouraged because there is so little strength, no ability you can call your own? Are you dejected because you have no resources? Think, then, what this may mean: *one hour, one talent—and God!* Let me put myself wholly at God's service, whatever I may be; *greatness is not required,* but *meetness for the Master's use.*

Only let Him have a free hand!

> *They called him a genius,*
> *The Fiddler;*
> *But he said, "I am only*
> *The strings*
> *Of God's instrument, He*
> *Playing on it.*
> *It is not I, but the fiddle*
> *That sings."*
> **GOD'S FIDDLER**

April 22

MORNING

He knoweth the way that I take (JOB 23:10).

Believer! What a glorious assurance! This way of thine—this, it may be, a crooked, mysterious, tangled way—this way of trial and tears. "He knoweth it." The furnace seven times heated—He lighted it. There is an almighty Guide knowing and directing our footsteps, whether it be to the bitter Marah pool, or to the joy and refreshment of Elim.

That way, dark to the Egyptians, has its pillar of cloud and fire for His own Israel. The furnace is hot; but not only can we trust the hand that kindles it, but we have the assurance that the fires are lighted not to consume, but to refine; and that when the refining process is completed (no sooner—no later) He brings His people forth as gold.

When they think Him least near, He is often nearest. *"When my* spirit was overwhelmed, *then* thou knewest my path."

Do we know of One brighter than the brightest radiance of the visible sun, visiting our chamber with the first waking beam of the morning; an eye of infinite tenderness and compassion following us throughout the day, knowing the way that we take?

The world, in its cold vocabulary in the hour of adversity, speaks of *"Providence"*—"the will of *Providence"*—"the strokes of *Providence."* *Providence!!* What is that?

Why dethrone a living, directing God from the sovereignty of His own earth? Why substitute an inanimate, deathlike abstraction, in place of an acting, controlling, personal Jehovah?

How it would take the sting from many a goading trial, to see what Job saw (in his hour of aggravated woe, when every earthly hope lay prostrate at his feet)—no hand but the divine. He saw that hand behind the gleaming swords of the Sabeans—he saw it behind the lightning flash—he saw it giving wings to the careening tempest—he saw it in the awful silence of his rifled home.

"The Lord gave, and *the Lord* hath taken away; blessed be the name of *the Lord!"*

Thus, seeing God in everything, his faith reached its climax when this once powerful prince of the desert, seated on his bed of ashes, could say, "Though he slay me, yet will I trust him."   MACDUFF

〜

By faith Moses . . . choosing rather to suffer. (HEB. 11:24–25)

*B*y faith Moses . . . refused." Faith rests on promise; to faith the promise is *equivalent to fulfillment;* and if only we have the one, we may dare to count on the other as already ours. It matters comparatively little that the thing promised is not given; it is sure and certain because God has pledged His word for it, and in anticipation we may enter on its enjoyment. Had Moses simply acted on what he saw, he would never have left Pharaoh's palace. But his faith told him of things hidden from his contemporaries; and these led him to act in a way which to them was perfectly incomprehensible.

One blow struck when the time is fulfilled is worth a thousand struck in premature eagerness. It is not for thee, O my soul, to know the times and seasons which the Father hath put in His own power; wait thou only upon God; let thy expectation be from Him.

It was a rude surprise when he essayed to adjust a difference between two Hebrews to find himself repulsed from them by the challenge, "Who made thee a prince and a judge over us?" *"For he supposed his brethren would have understood how that God by his hand would deliver them"* (Acts 7:25). Evidently, then, God's time had not arrived; nor could it come until the heat of his spirit had slowly evaporated in the desert air, and he had learned the hardest of all lessons, that *"by strength shall no man prevail."*

Faith is only possible when we are on God's plan and stand on God's promise. It is useless to pray for increased faith until we have fulfilled the conditions of faith. It is useless to waste time in regrets and tears over the failures which are due to our unbelief. *"Wherefore liest thou thus upon thy face?"* Faith is as natural to right conditions of soul, as a flower is to a plant.

Ascertain your place in God's plan, and get on to it. Feed on God's promises. When each of these conditions is realized, faith comes of itself; and there is absolutely nothing which is impossible. The believing soul will then be as the metal track along which God travels to men in love, grace, and truth.

Oh, for grace to wait and watch with God!　　　　　F. B. MEYER

Faith is not a magic drug, a spiritual anesthetic: it is the victory that overcometh the world by doing battle with it.　　　　　E. HERMAN

April 23
MORNING

〜✦〜

Though I walk in the midst of trouble, thou wilt revive me
(PS. 138:7).

The Hebrew rendering of the above is "go on in the center of trouble." What descriptive words! We *have* called on God in the day of trouble; we have pleaded His promise of deliverance but no deliverance has been given; the enemy has continued oppressing until we were in the very thick of the fight, in the center of trouble. Why then trouble the Master any further?

When Martha said, "Lord if thou hadst been here my brother had not died," our Lord met her lack of hope with His further promise, "Thy brother shall rise again." And when we walk "in the center of trouble" and are tempted to think like Martha that the time of deliverance is past, He meets us too with a promise from His Word. "Though I walk in the midst of trouble, *thou wilt revive me.*"

Though His answer has so long delayed, though we may still continue to "go on" in the midst of trouble, *"the center of trouble" is the place where He revives, not the place where He fails us.*

When in the hopeless place, the continued hopeless place, is the very time when He will stretch forth His hand against the wrath of our enemies and perfect that which concerneth us, the very time when He will make the attack to cease and fail and come to an end. What occasion is there then for fainting?

APHRA WHITE

The Eye of the Storm

Fear not that the whirlwind shall carry thee hence,
Nor wait for its onslaught in breathless suspense,
Nor shrink from the whips of the terrible hail,
But pass through the edge to the heart of the tale,
For there is a shelter, sunlighted and warm,
And Faith sees her God through the eye of the storm.

The passionate tempest with rush and wild roar
And threatenings of evil may beat on the shore,
The waves may be mountains, the fields battle plains,
And the earth be immersed in a deluge of rains,

〜 253 〜

Yet, the soul, stayed on God, may sing bravely its psalm,
For the heart of the storm is the center of calm.

Let hope be not quenched in the blackness of night,
Though the cyclone awhile may have blotted the light,
For behind the great darkness the stars ever shine,
And the light of God's heavens, His love shall make thine,
Let no gloom dim thine eyes, but uplift them on high
To the face of thy God and the blue of His sky.

The storm is thy shelter from danger and sin,
And God Himself takes thee for safety within;
The tempest with Him passeth into deep calm,
And the roar of the winds is the sound of a psalm.
Be glad and serene when the tempest clouds form;
God smiles on His child in the eye of the storm.

EVENING

Faith which worketh by love. (GAL. 5:6)

Faith without works is dead. (JAMES 2:26)

God never gave us faith to play with. It is a sword, but it was not made for presentation on a gala day, nor to be worn on state occasions only, nor to be exhibited upon a parade ground. It is a sword that was meant to cut and wound and slay; and he who has it girt about him may expect that between here and heaven, he shall know what battle means. *Faith is a sound seagoing vessel, and not meant to lie in dock and perish of dry rot.* To whom God has given faith, it is as though one gave a lantern to his friend because he expected it to be dark on his way home. *The very gift of faith is a hint to you that you will want it; that at certain points and places you will especially require it; and that, at all points and in every place you will really need it.*

Faith must begin to use its resources!

Use the faith God has already given you. You have faith, or you could not be a Christian. Use your little faith and it will increase by use. Plant a few grains of it, and you will find it will grow and multiply. George Müller said that when he began his ministry it was as hard to believe for a pound as it was forty years later to believe for one thousand pounds.

He was like the Thessalonians to whom Paul wrote, "Your faith groweth exceedingly."

Do not be satisfied with prayer and desire, but DO!

April 24

MORNING

❧

Faith is . . . the evidence of things not seen (HEB. 11:1).

True faith drops its letter in the post office box, and lets it go. Distrust holds on to a corner of it, and wonders that the answer never comes. I have some letters in my desk that have been written for weeks, but there was some slight uncertainty about the address or the contents, so they are yet unmailed. They have not done either me or anybody else any good yet. They will never accomplish anything until I let them go out of my hands and trust them to the postman and the mail.

This the way with true faith. It hands its case over to God, and then He works. That a fine verse in the Thirty-seventh Psalm: "Commit thy way unto the Lord, trust also in him, and he shall bring it to pass." But He never worketh till we commit. Faith is a receiving or still better, a taking of God's proffered gifts. We may believe, and come, and commit, and rest; but we will not fully realize all our blessings until we begin to receive and come into the attitude of abiding and taking.

FROM DAYS OF HEAVEN UPON EARTH

Dr. Payson, when a young man, wrote as follows, to an aged mother, burdened with intense anxiety on account of the condition of her son: "You give yourself too much trouble about him. After you have prayed for him, as you have done, and committed him to God, should you not cease to feel anxious respecting him? The command, 'Be careful for nothing,' is unlimited; and so is the expression, 'Casting *all* your care on him.' If we cast our burdens upon another, can they continue to press upon us? If we bring them away with us from the throne of grace, it is evident we do not leave them there. With respect to myself, I have made this one test of my prayers: if after committing anything to God, I can, like Hannah, come away and have my mind no more sad, my heart no more pained or anxious, I look upon it as one proof that I have prayed in faith; but, if I bring away my burden, I conclude that faith was not in exercise."

EVENING

⤡⤢

Lord, teach us to pray. (LUKE 11:1)

Pray ye. (MATT. 9:38)

Dr. John Timothy Stone tells of a visit which he paid to the old church of Robert Murray McCheyne. The aged sexton showed him around. Taking Dr. Stone into the study he pointed to a chair and said, "Sit there; that is where the master used to sit." Then he said, "Now put your elbows on the table." This was done. "Now bow your head upon your hands." Dr. Stone did so. "Now let the tears flow; that is the way the master used to do."

The visitor was then taken up into the pulpit, and the old sexton said, "Stand there behind the pulpit." Dr. Stone obeyed. "Now," said the sexton, "lean your elbows on the pulpit and put your face in your hands." This having been done, he said, "Now let the tears flow; that is the way the master used to do."

Then the old man added a testimony which gripped the heart of his hearer. With tearful eyes and trembling voice he said, *"He called down the power of God upon Scotland, and it is with us still."*

SUNDAY SCHOOL TIMES

Oh that *we* had a passion to save others! It was a compact between that holy Indian missionary known as "Praying Hyde," and God—that each day He should have at least four souls.

And Brainerd tells us that one Sunday night he offered himself to be used by God and for Him. "It was raining and the roads were muddy; but this desire grew so strong, that I kneeled down by the side of the road, and told God all about it. While I was praying, I told Him that my hands should work for Him, my tongue speak for Him, if He would only use me as His instrument—when suddenly the darkness of the night lit up, and I knew that God had heard and answered my prayer; and I felt that I was accepted into the inner circle of God's loved ones."

April 25

❦

And there was Mary Magdalene and the other Mary,
sitting over against the sepulchre (MATT. 27:61).

*H*ow strangely stupid is grief. It neither learns nor knows nor wishes to learn or know. When the sorrowing sisters sat over against the door of God's sepulchre, did they see the two thousand years that have passed triumphing away? Did they see anything but this: "Our Christ is gone!"

Your Christ and my Christ came from their loss. Myriad mourning hearts have had resurrection in the midst of their grief; and yet the sorrowing watchers looked at the seed-form of this result and saw nothing. What they regarded as the end of life was the very preparation for coronation; for Christ was silent that He might live again in tenfold power.

They saw it not. They mourned, they wept, and went away, and came again, driven by their hearts to the sepulchre. Still it was a sepulchre, unprophetic, voiceless, lusterless.

So with us. Every man sits over against the sepulchre in his garden, in the first instance, and says, "This woe is irremediable. I see no benefit in it. I will take no comfort in it." And yet, right in our deepest and worst mishaps, often, our Christ is lying, waiting for resurrection.

Where our death seems to be, there our Savior is. Where the end of hope is, there is the brightest beginning of fruition. Where the darkness is thickest, there the bright beaming light that never is set is about to emerge. When the whole experience is consummated, then we find that a garden is not disfigured by a sepulchre. Our joys are made better if there be sorrow in the midst of them. And our sorrows are made bright by the joys that God has planted around about them. The flowers may not be pleasing to us, they may not be such as we are fond of plucking, but they are heart flowers, love, hope, faith, joy, peace—these are flowers which are planted around every grave that is sunk in the Christian heart.

'Twas by a path of sorrows drear
Christ entered into rest;
And shall I look for roses here,
Or think that earth is blessed?
Heaven's whitest lilies blow
From earth's sharp crown of woe:

Who here his cross can meekly bear,
Shall wear the kingly purple there.

EVENING

❧

Go unto him at midnight. (LUKE 11:5)

Summoned to the couch of a dying little girl, the mighty Master had time to tarry by the way until a poor helpless woman was healed by a touch of His garment. Meanwhile that little life had ebbed away, and human unbelief hastened to turn back the visit which was now too late. "Trouble not the Master; she is dead." It was then that His strong and mighty love rose to its glorious height of power and victory. *"Be not afraid,"* is His calm reply; *"Only believe and she shall be made whole."*

"Too late," says Martha. "Four days buried." But He only answers, *"Said I not unto thee, that, if thou wouldst believe, thou shouldest see the glory of God?"*

"Go unto Him at midnight!" Let us go when all other doors are barred and even the heavens seem brass, for the gates of prayer are open evermore; and it is only when the sun is gone down and our pillow is but a stone of the wilderness, that we behold the ladder that reaches unto heaven with our Infinite God above it, and the angels of His providence ascending and descending for our help and deliverance. He is a friend in extremity. He is able for the hardest occasions. He is seated on His throne for the very purpose of giving help in time of need.

No matter if the case is wholly hopeless, and your situation one where you have nothing, and the hour is dark as midnight, *"Go unto Him."* Go unto Him at midnight. *He* loves the hour of extremity. It is His chosen time of Almighty interposition.

"There's a budding morrow in midnight," so fold your griefs away, and wait for the bud to open, a fragrant and fair new day. Wait for the bud to open, cease to worry and grope, "there's a budding morrow in midnight," its name is *The Dawn of Hope.* **A NEW TRAIL**

"God will help us when the sun comes up" *(Ps. 46:5, Spanish).*

April 26

∽∽

I even reckon all things as pure loss because of the priceless privilege of knowing Christ Jesus my Lord (PHIL. 38:8 WEYMOUTH).

Shining is always costly. Light comes only at the cost of that which produces it. An unlit candle does no shining. Burning must come before shining. We cannot be of great use to others without cost to ourselves. Burning suggests suffering. We shrink from pain.

We are apt to feel that we are doing the greatest good in the world when we are strong, and able for active duty, and when the heart and hands are full of kindly service.

When we are called aside and can only suffer; when we are sick; when we are consumed with pain; when all our activities have been dropped, we feel that we are no longer of use, that we are not doing anything.

But, if we are patient and submissive, it is almost certain that we are a greater blessing to the world in our time of suffering and pain than we were in the days when we thought we were doing the most of our work. We are burning now, and shining because we are burning.

FROM EVENING THOUGHTS

"The glory of tomorrow is rooted in the drudgery of today."
Many want the glory without the cross, the shining without the burning, but crucifixion comes before coronation.

> *Have you heard the tale of the aloe plant,*
> *Away in the sunny clime?*
> *By humble growth of a hundred years*
> *It reaches its blooming time;*
> *And then a wondrous bud at its crown*
> *Breaks into a thousand flowers;*
> *This floral queen, in its blooming seen,*
> *Is the pride of the tropical bowers,*
> *But the plant to the flower is sacrifice,*
> *For it blooms but once, and it dies.*
>
> *Have you further heard of the aloe plant,*
> *That grows in the sunny clime;*
> *How every one of its thousand flowers,*
> *As they drop in the blooming time,*

Is an infant plant that fastens its roots
In the place where it falls on the ground,
And as fast as they drop from the dying stem,
Grow lively and lovely around?
By dying, it liveth a thousand-fold
In the young that spring from the death of the old.

Have you heard the tale of the pelican,
The Arabs' Gimel el Bahr,
That lives in the African solitudes,
Where the birds that live lonely are?
Have you heard how it loves its tender young,
And cares and toils for their good,
It brings them water from mountains far,
And fishes the seas for their food.
In famine it feeds them—what love can devise!
The blood of its bosom—and, feeding them, dies.

Have you heard this tale—the best of them all—
The tale of the Holy and True,
He dies, but His life, in untold souls
Lives on in the world anew;
His seed prevails, and is filling the earth,
As the stars fill the sky up above.
He taught us to yield up the love of life,
For the sake of the life of love.
His death is our life, His loss is our gain;
The joy for the tear, the peace for the pain.

SELECTED

EVENING

*I plead with you therefore, brethren, by the compassions of God,
to present all your faculties to him as a living and holy sacrifice
acceptable to him. This with you will be an act of
reasonable worship.* (ROM. 12:1 WEYMOUTH)

Someone has said very pertinently, "There was no rudder to Noah's
ark." It was hardly necessary. He had obeyed God and now was shut
in, with God only to steer his ark; for he was on God's errand. The man

who could endure what he endured for more than a century, while preaching the Word amidst a hostile people, did not have any fears as to where he was going. The fulfillment of the prophecy regarding the deluge must have confirmed a faith already strong.

It is a delightful experience when we really believe that God is steering our little bark over life's tempestuous sea. *Only supreme and absolute abandonment to the will of God will give perfect rest of soul.* It is this that enlarges the soul. Fenelon says: "If there be anything that is capable of setting the soul in a large place it is *absolute abandonment to God.* It diffuses in the soul a peace that flows like a river and the righteousness which is as the waves of the sea" (Isa. 48:18). If there be anything that can render the soul calm, dissipate its scruples and dispel its fears, sweeten its sufferings by the anointing of love, impart strength to all its actions, and spread abroad the joy of the Holy Ghost in its countenance and words, it is this simple and childlike repose in the arms of God.

God could give to Abraham, because he had made such a wide opening into his life. God can give only into an open hand. This hand was opened wide. This door swung clear back. God had a free swing and He used it. He *could,* and He did. He always does. Let this be our rule: "Give all He asks; then take all He gives." And the cup will be spilling joyously over the brim.

S. D. GORDON

"Beware of every hesitation to abandon to God!"

April 27

MORNING

∾

*I am he that liveth, and was dead; and, behold,
I am alive for evermore* (REV. 1:18).

Flowers! Easter lilies! speak to me this morning the same dear old lesson of immortality which you have been speaking to so many sorrowing souls.

Wise old Book! let me read again in your pages of firm assurance that to die is gain.

Poets! recite to me your verses which repeat in every line the gospel of eternal life.

Singers! break forth once more into songs of joy; let me hear again the well-known resurrection psalms.

Tree and blossom and bird and sea and sky and wind whisper it, sound it afresh, warble it, echo it, let it throb and pulsate through every atom and particle; let the air be filled with it.

Let it be told nd retold and still retold until hope rises to conviction, and conviction to certitude of knowledge; until we, like Paul, even though going to our death, go with triumphant mien, with assured faith, and with serene and shining face.

> O sad-faced mourners, who each day are wending
> Through churchyard paths of cypress and of yew,
> Leave for today the low graves you are tending,
> And lift your eyes to God's eternal blue!
>
> It is no time for bitterness or sadness;
> Twine Easter lilies, not pale asphodels;
> Let your souls thrill to the caress of gladness,
> And answer the sweet chime of Easter bells.
>
> If Christ were still within the grave's low prison,
> A captive of the enemy we dread;
> If from that moldering cell He had not risen,
> Who then could chide the gloomy tears you shed?
>
> If Christ were dead there would be need to sorrow,
> But He has risen and vanquished death for aye;
> Hush, then you sighs, if only till the morrow,
> At Easter give your grief a holiday.
>
> **MAY RILEY SMITH**

A well-known minister was in his study writing an Easter sermon when the thought gripped him that his Lord was *living*. He jumped up excitedly and paced the floor repeating to himself, "Why Christ is alive, His ashes are warm, He is not the great 'I was,' He is the great 'I am.'" He is not only a fact, but a *living* fact. Glorious truth of Easter Day!

We believe that out of every grave there blooms an Easter lily, an in every tomb there sits an angel. We believe in a risen Lord. Turn not your faces to the past that we may worship only at His grave, but above and within that we may worship the Christ that lives. And because He lives, we shall live also.

ABBOTT

Is any thing too hard for the LORD? (GEN. 18:14)

GOD *wants us to ask Him for the impossible!* God can do things that man cannot do. He would not be God if this were not so. That is why He has graciously made prayer a law of life. *"If ye shall ask . . . I will do."* This inviting promise from the Lord means that He will do for us what we cannot do for ourselves; He will do for others what we cannot do for them—*if we but ask Him.* How little do we avail ourselves of this immense privilege!

Someone spoke this searching word at Edinburgh in 1910: *"We have lost the eternal youthfulness of Christianity, and have aged into calculating manhood. We seldom pray in earnest for the extraordinary, the limitless, the glorious. We seldom pray with any confidence, for any good to the realization of which we cannot imagine a way. And yet, we suppose ourselves to believe in an Infinite Father."*

The natural man calculates results. Calculations have no place in our relation with God.

That matter which has been so burdening us just now, and with which we can see no way of dealing, *how are we praying about it? In anxiety, or with thanksgiving?*

Worrying prayer defeats its own answer; rejoicing prayer gets through. "In nothing be anxious; but in everything by prayer and supplication with thanksgiving let your requests be made known unto God." Then will come the answer *"exceeding abundantly above all that we ask or think."*

The more we are cut off from human help, the greater claim we can make on Divine help. The more impossible a thing is to human or mortal power, the more at peace can we be when we look to Him for deliverance.

"Only those who see the invisible can do the impossible!"

God will answer when to thee,
Not a possibility
Of deliverance seems near;
It is then He will appear.

God will answer when you pray;
Yeah, though mountains block thy way,
At His word, a way will be
E'en through mountains, made for thee.

God who still divides the sea,
Willingly will work for thee;
God, before whom mountains fall,
Promises to hear thy call.

M. E. B.

April 28

MORNING

And when the children of Israel cried unto the Lord,
the Lord raised up a deliverer . . . who delivered them, even
Othniel . . . Caleb's younger brother. And the Spirit of the
Lord came upon him (JUDG. 3:9–10).

God is preparing His heroes; and when opportunity comes, He can fit them into their place in a moment, and the world will wonder where they came from.

Let the Holy Ghost prepare you, dear friend, by the discipline of life; and when the last finishing touch has been given to the marble, it will be easy for God to put it on the pedestal, and fit it into its niche.

There is a day coming when, like Othniel, we, too, shall judge the nations, and rule and reign with Christ on the millennial earth. But ere that glorious day can be we must let God prepare us, as He did Othniel at Kirjath-sepher, amid the trials of our present life, and the little victories, the significance of which, perhaps, we little dream. At least, let us be sure of this, and if the Holy Ghost has an Othniel ready, the Lord of heaven and earth has a throne prepared for him. **A. B. SIMPSON**

Human strength and human greatness
Spring not from life's sunny side,
Heroes must be more than driftwood
Floating on a waveless tide.

"Every highway of human life dips in the dale now and then. Every man must go through the tunnel of tribulation before he can travel on the elevated road of triumph."

EVENING

⁂

Here have we no continuing city, but we seek one to come.
(HEB. 13:14)

℧r. Rothschild was the wealthiest man in the world, but he lived and died in an unfinished mansion. He had power to frighten a nation by calling for gold. Yet, one of the cornices of his house was purposely unfinished, to bear testimony that he was a pilgrim in the land. He was an orthodox Jew, and the house of every Jew, according to the Talmud, must be left unfinished. The finishing cornice says: "Beautiful as this is, it is not my home; I am looking for a city."

Beloved, does the unfinished cornice appear in your life? Do you know that you are a stranger as were our fathers?

> *One place have I in heaven above—*
> *The glory of His throne;*
> *On this dark earth, whence He is gone,*
> *I have one place alone;*
> *And if His rest in heaven I know,*
> *I joy to find His path below.*
>
> *One lowly path across the waste,*
> *The lowly path of shame;*
> *I would adore Thy wondrous grace*
> *That I should tread the same.*
> *The Stranger and the Alien, Thou—*
> *And I the stranger, alien, now.*
>
> G. T. S.

We bless Thee, that life is a pilgrimage; that the earth is not our rest; that every day brings us nearer our home in the city of God, and that Thou art willing to be our Companion in every step of the desert march!

Am I a pilgrim or a tramp?
"Build thee more stately mansions, O my soul!"

April 29

Elias was a man subject to like passions as we are (JAMES 5:17).

Thank God for that! He got under a juniper tree, as you and I have often done; he complained and murmured, as we have often done; was unbelieving, as we have often been. But that was not the case when he really got into touch with God. Though "a man subject to like passions as we are," "he prayed praying." It is sublime in the original—not "earnestly," but "he prayed in prayer." He kept on praying. What is the lesson here? You must *keep praying*.

Come up on the top of Carmel, and see that remarkable parable of faith and sight. It was not the descent of the fire that now was necessary, but the descent of the flood; and the man that can command the fire can command the flood by the same means and methods. We are told that he bowed himself to the ground with his face between his knees; that is, shutting out all sights and sounds. He was putting himself in a position where, beneath his mantle, he could neither see nor hear what was going forward.

He said to his servant, "Go and take an observation." He went and came back, and said—how sublimely brief! one word—"Nothing!"

What do we do under such circumstances?

We say, "It is just as I expected!" and we give up praying. Did Elijah? No, he said, "Go again." His servant again came back and said, "Nothing!" "Go again." "Nothing!"

By and by he came back, and said, "There is a little cloud like a man's hand." A man's hand had been raised in supplication, and presently down came the rain; and Ahab had not time to get back to the gate of Samaria with all his fast steeds. This is a parable of faith and sight—faith shutting itself up with God; sight taking observations and seeing nothing; faith going right on, and "praying in prayer," with utterly hopeless reports from sight.

Do you know how to pray that way, how to pray prevailingly? Let sight give as discouraging reports as it may, but pay no attention to these. The living God is still in the heavens and even to delay is part of His goodness.   ARTHUR T. PIERSON

Each of three boys gave a definition of faith which is an illustration of the tenacity of faith. The first boy said, "It is taking hold of Christ"; the second, "Keeping hold"; and the third, "Not letting go."

❧❧

God is ever true to His promises. (1 COR. 1:9 WEYMOUTH)

God puts Himself within our reach in His promises; and when we can say to Him, "Thou saidst," He cannot say nay—He must do as He has said. In prayer, be sure to *get your feet on a promise;* it will give you purchase enough to force open the gates of heaven to take it by force! When once you can lay hold of a promise, you have a leverage with God which enables you to count upon the fulfillment of your petition. God cannot go back from His plighted word.　　　　　　　　**F. B. MEYER**

"God could no more disappoint faith than
He could deny Himself."

A friend gives me a check which reads: "Pay to the order of C. H. Spurgeon the sum of ten pounds." His name is good and his bank is good, but I get nothing from his kindness until I put my own name on the back of the check. It is a very simple act but the signature cannot be dispensed with. There are many nobler names than mine, but none of these can be used instead of my own. If I wrote the Queen's name it would not avail me . . . I must affix my own name.

Even so, each one must personally accept, adopt, and endorse the promise of God by his own individual faith, or he will derive no benefit from it. If you were to write Miltonic lines in honor of the bank, or exceed Tennyson in verses in praise of the generous benefactor, it would avail nothing. The simple, self-written name is demanded, and nothing will be accepted instead of it. We must *believe the promise,* each one for himself, and declare that we know it to be true, or it will bring us no blessing.　　　　　　　　**CHARLES H. SPURGEON**

"God is always greater than His promises; He does not only fulfill His promises, He over-fulfills them" *(see Eph. 3:20).*

Upon Thy Word I rest
Each pilgrim day;
This golden staff is best
For all the way.
What Jesus Christ hath spoken
Cannot be broken!

Upon Thy Word I rest
So strong, so sure!

So full of comfort blest,
So sweet, so pure!
The charter of salvation,
Faith's broad foundation.

Upon Thy Word I stand,
That cannot die;
Christ seals it in my hand,
He cannot lie!
Thy Word that faileth never,
Abideth ever.

FRANCES RIDLEY HAVERGAL

April 30

MORNING

And the ill-favored and lean-fleshed kine did eat up the
seven well favored and fat kine . . . and the seven thin ears devoured
the seven rank and full ears (GEN. 41:4, 7).

There is a warning for us in that dream, just as it stands; It is possible for the best years of our life, the best experiences, the best victories won, the best service rendered, to be swallowed up by times of failure, defeat, dishonor, uselessness in the kingdom. Some men's lives of rare promise and rare achievement have ended so. It is awful to think of, but it is true. *Yet it is never necessary.*

S. D. Gordon has said that the only assurance of safety against this tragedy is "fresh touch with God," daily, hourly. The blessed, fruitful, victorious experiences of yesterday are not only of no value to me today, but they will actually be eaten up or reversed by today's failures, *unless* they serve as incentives to still better, richer experiences today.

"Fresh touch with God," by abiding in Christ, alone will keep the lean kine and the ill-favored grain out of my life.

FROM MESSAGES FOR THE MORNING WATCH

John . . . was in the isle that is called Patmos, for the word of God.
(REV. 1:9)

Can we not imagine how eagerly John would lay himself out for a life in incessant service for His Divine Master and Lord? No task would seem too great, no toil too arduous, if only His Lord might be glorified; and we can well imagine how all his plans, ambitions, desires would center round the extension of the kingdom of Jesus Christ. Then, suddenly —Patmos! What now became of all his hopes and longings, his plans and projects? Surely he buried them all as he set foot on Patmos. They died when he first heard his sentence; they were interred with no prospect of a resurrection. Patmos was, for the beloved disciple

The Island of Buried Hopes!

But John soon discovered that Patmos had its compensations. True, he could no longer entertain the hope of carrying out all his plans, yet he learned in Patmos that truer and nobler service would yet be his than any he had ever contemplated. To him came the assurance that not only has the Lord *loved us, and washed us from our sins in His own blood,* but *He hath set us apart as both kings and priests, and nothing can ever terminate that royal priesthood.* John had caught sight of a far greater honor and holier service awaiting him in the land that lies beyond.

It might have been thought that John in his dreary exile was terribly isolated. Someone has said *not isolated, but insulated,* and there is a world of difference between the two. True, the island was small and his confines narrow, but that was only the outer circumstance of his life, his daily environment.

Nothing to see! Alone! Ah, but John found it not so! The overwhelming glory of the sight of his risen Lord robbed him of his strength until he felt the gracious gentle pressure of the pierced Hand resting upon him. Again and again he tells us that he heard a Voice speaking to him, Whilst these things were so he could never feel that there was nothing to see! He could never feel alone! And the Spirit so insulated John *that God's messages might pass through him to the entire world!*

Most of us are well acquainted with this experience. We may not have had to suffer at the hands of any earthly potentate, but there must be comparatively few who have not, at some time, had to bury their fondest hopes, their most eager desires. Oh, weary troubled heart, if God has led *you to the Island of Buried Hopes,* it is that He may show you yet more wonderful things. He has not failed you, nor forgotten you, but has led you into the darkened room because, in His own time and way, *He would reveal to you the unsuspected glory of His grace and power.*

Is our life lonely? Monotonous? We need opened eyes. Standing near us all the time is the same wonderful Lord who stood by John in Patmos. *Oh, the joy, even of Patmos, when it is filled with the presence of Jesus!*

Patmos HAS its compensations!

But if we would share in them, and Patmos is to be a blessing to us, we must fulfill certain conditions. Here is the secret that transforms all disappointments, suffering, monotony, loneliness—*love to Christ,* that impels us to learn of Him day by day, to lean upon Him in constant communion, to look upon Him as the all-sufficient Savior.

To those who fulfill these conditions there is no Patmos that is not irradiated by a glory that is not of earth. SELECTED

Our Father makes no mistakes!

May 1
MORNING
God that cannot lie promised (TITUS 1:2).

Faith is not working up by willpower a sort of certainty that something is coming to pass, but it is seeing as an actual fact that God has said that this thing shall come to pass, and that it is true, and then rejoicing to know that it is true, and just resting because God has said it.

Faith turns the promise into a prophecy. While it is merely a promise it is contingent upon our cooperation. But when faith claims it, it becomes a prophecy, and we go forth feeling that it is something that must be done because God cannot lie.

FROM DAYS OF HEAVEN UPON EARTH

I hear men praying everywhere for more faith, but when I listen to them carefully, and get at the real heart of their prayer, very often it is not more faith at all that they are wanting, but a change from faith to sight.

Faith says not, "I see that it is good for me, so God must have sent it," but, "God sent it, and so it must be good for me."

Faith, walking in the dark with God, only prays Him to clasp its hand more closely. **PHILLIPS BROOKS**

The Shepherd does not ask of thee
Faith in thy faith, but only faith in Him;
And this He meant in saying, "Come to me."
In light or darkness seek to do His will,
And leave the work of faith to Jesus still.

EVENING

❧

Minding himself to go afoot. (ACTS 20:13)

*W*hy did Paul prefer to go *afoot?* And how may we account for his desire to go *alone?*

There are times in every man's life when he wants no comrade on the road with him. A precious part of our Creed is "I believe in the communion of saints," but, after all, it is not in such communion that we have the closest fellowship with God in Christ. It is *in secret* that we learn the secret of the Lord.

It was in the eerie solitude of Beth-el, and in the gray dawn by the ford Jabbok that Jacob was granted visions of God.

It was when he was alone in the silent desert that Moses was shown the burning bush, and received the Divine commission.

It was when Joshua walked unattended under the stars by the wall of Jericho that the Captain of the Lord's hosts stood before him.

It was when Isaiah was alone in the Temple that a live coal touched his lips.

It was when Mary was alone that the angel brought to her the message of the Lord.

It was when Elisha was plowing his lonely furrow that the prophet's mantle fell upon his shoulders.

Noah built and voyaged alone. His neighbors laughed at his strangeness and perished.

Abraham wandered and worshiped alone; Sodomites smiled at the simple shepherd, followed the fashion, and fed the flames.

Daniel dined and prayed alone.

Jesus lived and died alone.

Ah, it is good to be "minded . . . to go afoot" sometimes; when even our nearest and dearest go by another road. *For when we are alone we have a better chance of One joining us, and making our hearts burn while He talks with us by the way.*

I love the lonely creative hours with God.   MADAME GUYON

When storms of life are round me beating,
When rough the path that I have trod,
Within my closet doors retreating,
I love to be alone with God.

What tho' the clouds have gathered o'er me
What tho' I've passed beneath the rod?
God's perfect will there lies before me,
When I am thus alone with God.

Alone with God, the world forbidden,
Alone with Him, O blest retreat!
Alone with God and in Him hidden,
To hold with Him communion sweet.
HYMNAL

May 2
MORNING

The Lord hath prepared his throne in the heavens;
and his kingdom ruleth over all (PS. 103:19).

Some time since, in the early spring, I was going out at my door when round the corner came a blast of east wind—defiant and pitiless, fierce and withering—sending a cloud of dust before it.

I was just asking the latchkey from the door as I said, Half impatiently, *"I wish the wind would—"* I was going to say *change;* but the word was checked, and the sentence was never finished.

As I went on my way, the incident became a parable to me. There came an angel holding out a key, and he said:

"My Master sends thee His love, and bids me give you this."

"What is it?" I asked wondering. *"The key of the winds,"* said the angel, and disappeared.

Now indeed should I be happy. I hurried away up into the heights whence the winds came, and stood amongst the caves. "I will have done with the east wind at any rate—and that shall plague us no more," I cried; and calling in that friendless wind, I closed the door, and heard the echoes ringing in the hollow places. I turned the key triumphantly. "There," I said, "now we have done with that."

"What shall I choose in its place?" I asked myself, looking about me. "The south wind is pleasant"; and I thought of the lambs, and the young life on every hand, and the flowers that had begun to deck the hedgerows. But as I set the key within the door, it began to burn my hand.

"What am I doing?" I cried; "who knows what mischief I may bring about? How do I know what the fields want! Ten thousand things of ill may come of this foolish wish of mine."

Bewildered and ashamed, I looked up and prayed that the Lord would send His angel yet again to take the key; and for my part I promised that I would never want to have it anymore.

But lo, the Lord Himself stood by me. He reached His hand to take the key; and as I laid it down, I saw that it rested against the sacred wound-print.

It hurt me indeed that I could ever have murmured against anything wrought by Him who bear such sacred tokens of His love. Then He took the key and hung it on His girdle.

"Dost Thou keep the key of the winds?" I asked.

"I do, my child," He answered graciously.

And lo, I looked again and there hung all the keys of my life. He saw my look of amazement, and asked, *"Didst thou not know, my child, that my kingdom ruleth over all?"*

"Over all, my Lord?" I answered; "then it is not safe for me to murmur at anything?" Then did He lay His hand upon me tenderly. "My child," He said, "thy only safety is, in everything, to love and trust and praise."

MARK GUY PEARSE

EVENING

⮞⮜

They looked unto him and were radiant. (PS. 34:5, AMERICAN REV.)

How lovely are the faces of
The men who talk with God—
Lit with an inner sureness of
The path their feet have trod;
How gentle is the manner of
A man who walks with Him!
No strength can overcome him, and

No cloud his courage dim.
Keen are the hands and feet—ah yes—
Of those who wait His will,
And clear as crystal mirrors, are
The hearts His love can fill.

Some lives are drear from doubt and fear
While others merely plod;
But lovely faces mark the men
Who walk and talk with God.

MARKED FOR HIS OWN, BY PAULINE PROSSER-THOMPSON

I presume everybody has known saints whose lives were just radiant. Joy beamed out of their eyes; joy bubbled over their lips; joy seemed to fairly run from their fingertips. You could not come in contact with them without having a new light come into your own life. They were like electric batteries charged with joy.

If you look into the eyes of such radiantly happy persons—not those people who are sometimes on the mountaintop, and sometimes in the valley, but people who are always radiantly happy—you will find that every one is a man or a woman who spends a great deal of time in prayer with God alone. *God is the source of all joy, and if we come into contact with Him, His infinite joy comes into our lives.*

Would *you* like to be a radiant Christian? You may be. Spend time in prayer. You cannot be a radiant Christian in any other way. Why is it that prayer in the Name of Christ makes one radiantly happy? It is because prayer makes God real. *The gladdest thing upon earth is to have a real God!* I would rather give up anything I have in the world, or anything I ever may have, than give up my faith in God. You cannot have vital faith in God if you give all your time to the world and to secular affairs, to reading the newspapers and to reading literature, no matter how good it is. *Unless you take time for fellowship with God, you cannot have a real God. If you do take time for prayer you will have a real, living God, and if you have a living God you will have a radiant life.* R. A. TORREY

Of all the lights you carry in your face,
Joy will reach the farthest out to sea.

H. W. BEECHER

It was said by Chesterfield, the heartless dandy, upon his return from visiting Fenelon, the Archbishop of Cambrai: "If I had stayed another day in his presence, *I am afraid I would have had to become a Christian; his spirit was so pure, so attractive and beautiful.*"

May 3
MORNING

And it shall come to pass that whosoever shall call on the name of the Lord shall be delivered (JOEL 2:32).

Why do not I call on His name? Why do I run to this neighbor and that when God is so near and will hear my faintest call? Why do I sit down and devise schemes and invent plans? Why not at once roll myself and my burden upon the Lord?

Straightforward is the best runner—why do not I run at once to the living God? In vain shall I look for deliverance anywhere else; but with God I shall find it; for here I have His royal *shall* to make it sure.

I need not ask whether I may call on Him or not, for that word "Whosoever" is a very wide and comprehensive one. Whosoever means me, for it means anybody and everybody who calls upon God. I will therefore follow the leading of the text, and at once call upon the glorious Lord who has made so large a promise.

My case is urgent, and I do not see how I am to be delivered; but this is no business of mine. He who makes the promise will find ways and means of keeping it. It is mine to obey His commands; it is not mine to direct His counsels. I am His servant, not His solicitor. I call upon Him, and He will deliver.

C. H. SPURGEON

EVENING

No man, having put his hand to the plow, and looking back, is fit for the kingdom of God. (LUKE 9:62)

Keep me from turning back!
Deep indeed is the world's debt to people who would not quit!

Suppose Columbus had not sailed! Suppose Anne Sullivan, discouraged, had lost hope for Helen Keller! Suppose Louis Pasteur, searching for a cure for rabies, had not said to his weary helpers: "Keep on! The important thing is not to leave the subject!"

Many a race is lost at the last lap! Many a ship is washed on the reefs outside the final port! Many a battle is lost on the last charge!

What hope have *we* of completing the course upon which we have embarked? What hope? Ah! *He is able to keep.* "He is able to save them *to the uttermost* that come unto God by him."

God cannot help us until we stop running away. We must be willing to stand somewhere and trust Him. He has reinforcements to send, but there must be somebody there to meet them when they come, and *fear takes flight as well as fright.* "Fear not" is the first step.

> *Keep me from turning back*
> *My hand is on the plow, my faltering hand:*
> *But all in front of me is untilled land,*
> *The wilderness and solitary place,*
> *The lonely desert with its interspace.*
> *What harvest have I but this paltry grain,*
> *These dwindling husks, a handful of dry corn,*
> *These poor lean stalks? My courage is outworn.*
> *Keep me from turning back.*
> *The handles of my plow with tears are wet,*
> *The shares with rust are spoiled, and yet, and yet,*
> *My God! My God! Keep me from turning back.*
> AUTHOR UNKNOWN

May 4

MORNING

∽◦∾

He maketh sore, and bindeth up: he woundeth and his hands make whole (JOB 5:18).

The Ministry of a Great Sorrow

As we pass beneath the hills which have been shaken by the earthquake and torn by convulsion, we find that periods of perfect repose succeed those of destruction. The pools of calm water lie clear beneath their fallen rocks, the water lilies gleam, and the reeds whisper among the shadows; the village rises again over the forgotten graves, and its church tower, white through the storm twilight, proclaims a renewed appeal to His protection "in whose hand are all the corners of the earth, and the strength of the hills is his also."
RUSKIN

God ploughed one day with an earthquake,
And drove His furrows deep!
The huddling plains upstarted,
The hills were all aleap!

But that is the mountains' secret,
Age-hidden in their breast;
"God's peace is everlasting,"
Are the dream-words of their rest.

He made them the haunts of beauty,
The home elect of His grace;
He spreadeth His mornings upon them,
His sunsets light their face.

His winds bring messages to them—
Wild storm-news from the main;
They sing it down the valleys
In the love-song of the rain.

They are nurseries for young rivers,
Nests for His flying cloud,
Homesteads for new-born races,
Masterful, free, and proud.

The people of tired cities
Come up to their shrines and pray;
God freshens again within them,
As He passes by all day.

And lo, I have caught their secret!
The beauty deeper than all!
This faith—that life's hard moments,
When the jarring sorrows befall,

Are but God ploughing His mountains;
And those mountains yet shall be
The source of His grace and freshness,
And His peace everlasting to me.

WILLIAM C. GANNETT

But the God of all grace, who hath called us unto his eternal glory by Christ Jesus, AFTER THAT YE HAVE SUFFERED A WHILE, makes you perfect. (1 PETER 5:10, EMPHASIS ADDED)

What a singular wish! The singular thing about it is the blot in the middle—*after ye have suffered a while.* What would you think of receiving this wish from a friend?

Yet this is what Peter desired for those to whom he wrote: all the gifts and graces of the Christ-life in perfection, but not until after they had "suffered a while." Peter wrote out of the bitter experience of his own past: *he* had come into his kingdom too soon; he had obtained his crown before he could support its cares. His faith had been drenched in the brine; his love had been cooled in the judgment hall as he sat by the fire and cried, "I know not the man."

In essence he is saying, "I do not want you to find the keys too soon." He does not want them to be innocent only; pure because there is no temptation; loyal because there is no danger.

There is a peace, which is not the peace of the Son of God. Be not *that* our peace, O God!

We cannot know Thy stillness until it is broken. There is no music in the silence until we have heard the roar of battle! We cannot see Thy beauty until it is shaded. **LEAVES FOR QUIET HOURS**

"After the shadows, the sunlight will come."

May 5
MORNING

When they began to sing and praise, the Lord set ambushments . . . and they were smitten (2 CHRON. 20:22).

Oh, that we could reason less about our troubles, and sing and praise more! There are thousands of things that we wear as shackles which we might use as instruments with music in them, if we only knew how.

Those men that ponder, and meditate, and weigh the affairs of life, and study the mysterious developments of God's providence, and wonder why they should be burdened and thwarted and hampered—how different and how much more joyful would be their lives, if, instead of forever indulging in self-revolving and inward thinking, they would take their experiences, day by day, and lift them up, and praise God for them.

We can sing our cares away easier than we can reason them away. Sing in the morning. The birds are the earliest to sing, and birds are more without care than anything else that I know of.

Sing at evening. Singing is the last thing that robins do. When they have done their daily work; when they have flown their last flight, and picked up their last morsel of food, then on a topmost twig, they sing one song of praise.

Oh, that we might sing morning and evening, and let song touch song all the way through.   SELECTED

Don't let the song go out of your life
Though it chance sometimes to flow
In a minor strain; it will blend again
With the major tone you know.

What though shadows rise to obscure live's skies,
And hide for a time the sun,
The sooner they'll lift and reveal the rift,
If you let the melody run.

Don't let the song go out of your life;
Though the voice may have lost its trill,
Though the tremulous note may die in your throat,
Let it sing in your spirit still.

Don't let the song go out of your life;
Let it ring in the soul while here;
And when you go hence, 'twill follow you thence,
And live on in another sphere.

EVENING

When he saw the wagons . . . the spirit of Jacob . . . revived.
(GEN. 45:27)

A very simple sight: just some farm wagons laden with corn—food for the starving household. It was these wagons turning into the courtyard that raised the fast-falling hopes of Jacob to expectancy. They remind me of other wagons laden and sent by another One greater than Joseph, even our Lord Jesus Christ. These wagons of His are a great stimulus to our faith. They come unseen to us in our hours of darkness—when our hopes are dashed to the ground. Yes, *when we are in the awful grips of spiritual starvation, how blessed ar these wagons as they are seen approaching!*

Lift up your eyes! Look out for them! When they come they will not be empty! You will be fed and nourished with the choicest of His stores. *"Blessed be the Lord, who daily loadeth us with benefits."*

"All these things are against me!" Yet those things,
Those very things, were God's machinery
For working out your heart's imaginings,
For turning hope to blessed certainty.
Oh, man who walked by sight,
You should have known the darkest hour of night
Is just before the earliest streak of gray.
Your wagons, all the time, were on their way!

Faith? yes, but with a flaw.
Here was a man who trusted when he saw!
And yet,
The Holy One has set
His name beside two men of saintly will,
And calls Himself the "God of Jacob" still!
That you and I,
Lacking in faith, maybe, or gentleness
May yet stretch out weak hands of hopelessness,
And find the GOD OF JACOB very nigh.

Oh, sorrowful soul! Trust just a little longer.
Who knows, but o'er your bare, brown hill
The wagons may be coming nearer still?
Give faith a chance. For soon, how soon it may
Give place to sight; and then
Never again
Will you have opportunity to show
That you can trust, albeit you cannot know.

FAY INCHFAWN

The secret of the Lord is with them that fear him (PS. 25:14).

There are secrets of providence which God's dear children may learn. His dealings with them often seem, to the outward eye, dark and terrible. Faith looks deeper and says, "This is God's secret. You look only on the outside; I can look deeper and see the hidden meaning."

Sometimes diamonds are done up in rough packages, so that their value cannot be seen. When the tabernacle was built in the wilderness there was nothing rich in its outward covering and rough badger skin gave no hint of the valuable things which it contained.

God may send you, dear friends, some costly packages. Do not worry if they are done up in rough wrappings. You may be sure there are treasures of love, and kindness, and wisdom hidden within. If we take what He sends, *and trust Him* for the goodness in it, even in the dark, we shall learn the meaning of the secrets of providence. A. B. SIMPSON

> *Not until each loom is silent,*
> *And the shuttles cease to fly,*
> *Will God unroll the pattern*
> *And explain the reason why*
> *The dark threads are as needful*
> *In the Weaver's skillful hand,*
> *As the threads of gold and silver*
> *For the pattern which he planned.*

He that is mastered by Christ is the master of every circumstance. Does the circumstance press hard against you? Do not push it away. It is the Potter's hand. Your mastery will come, not by arresting its progress, but by enduring its discipline, for it is not only shaping you into a vessel of beauty and honor, but it is making your resources available.

EVENING

❦

He answered . . . never a word. (MATT. 27:14)

Not railing for railing; not a word. How much is lost by a word! Be still! Keep quiet! If they smite you on one cheek turn the other also. Never retort! Hush—not a word! *Never mind your reputation or your character; they are in His hands; you mar them by trying to retain them.*

Do not strive. Open not your mouth. Silence! A word will grieve, disturb the gentle dove. Hush—not a word!

Are you misunderstood? Never mind! Will it hurt your influence and weaken your power for good? *Leave it to Him*—His to take care and take charge.

Are you wronged and your good name tarnished? All right! Be it yours to be meek and lowly; simple and gentle—not a word! *Let Him keep you in perfect peace; stay your mind on Him; trust in Him.*

Not a word of argument, debate, or controversy. Mind your own business. Be still!

Never judge, condemn, arraign, censure. Not a word! Never a disparaging remark of another. *As you would others should do to you, so do you.*

Pause! Be still! Selah! Not a word, emphatically; not even a look that will mar the sweet serenity of the soul. Get still! Know God! *Keep silence before Him!* Stillness is better than noise.

Not a word of murmuring or complaining in supplication; not a word of nagging or persuading. Let language be simple, gentle, quiet; you utter not a word, but give Him opportunity to speak. *Hearken to hear His voice.*

This is the way to honor and to know Him. Not a word—not the least word! Listen to obey. Words make trouble. *Be still! This is the voice of the Spirit.*

Restlessness, fret, worry, makes the place of His abiding unpleasant. *He is to keep in perfect peace;* take it not out of his hands.

I rode with a dear brother in the cars, and poured my weighty burdens in his ears. I took his earnest advice to my heart. His counsel was not the mind of the Spirit, and when I returned to my seat in the car the Spirit gently said to me: "So you went to him! Could you not trust me?" I confessed, was forgiven, restored. And I determined never again to take my case out of His hands.

"Ye are my witnesses." Witness in love. Not a word! And, like the dew of the morning, or the sweet breeze of eventide, you will be quietly blessed, and you will be so glad that you uttered—*never a word!* STEPHEN MERRITT

Let me no wrong or idle word
Unthinking say;
Set Thou a seal upon my lips,
Just for today.

May 7
MORNING
❦

*He spake a parable unto them . . . that men ought always to pray,
and not to faint* (LUKE 18:1).

No temptation in the life of intercession is more common than this of failure to *persevere*. We begin to pray for a certain thing; we put up our petitions for a day, a week, a month; and then, receiving as yet no definite answer, straightway we faint, and cease altogether from prayer concerning it.

This is a deadly fault. It is simply the snare of many beginnings with no completions. It is ruinous in all spheres of life.

The man who forms the habit of beginning without finishing has simply formed the habit of failure. The man who begins to pray about a thing and does not pray it through to a successful issue of answer has formed the same habit in prayer.

To faint is to fail; then defeat begets disheartenment, and unfaith in the reality of prayer, which is fatal to all success.

But someone says, "How long shall we pray? Do we not come to a place where we may cease from our petitions and rest the matter in God's hands?"

There is but one answer. *Pray until the thing you pray for has actually been granted, or until you have the assurance in your heart that it will be.*

Only at one of these two places dare we stay our importunity, for prayer is not only a calling upon God, but also a conflict with Satan. And inasmuch as God is using our intercession as a mighty factor of victory in that conflict, He alone, and not we, must decide when we dare cease from our petitioning. So we dare not stay our prayer until the answer itself *has* come, or until we receive the assurance that it *will* come.

In the first case we stop because we see. In the other, we stop because we believe, and the faith of our hearts is just as sure as the sight of our eyes; for it is faith *from*, yes, the faith *of* God, within us.

More and more, as we live the prayer life, shall we come to experience and recognize this God-given assurance, and know when to rest quietly in it, or when to continue our petitioning until we receive it.

FROM THE PRACTICE OF PRAYER

Tarry at the promise till God meets you there. He always returns by way of His promises.

SELECTED

EVENING

And he went down with them . . . and was subject unto them.
(LUKE 2:51)

An extraordinary exhibition of submissiveness! And "the disciple is not above his master."

Think of it! Thirty years at home with His brothers and sisters who did not believe in Him! We fix on the three years which were extraordinary, and forget altogether the thirty years of absolute submissiveness.

If God is putting you through a spell of submission, and you seem to be losing your individuality and everything else, *it is because Jesus is making you one with Him.*

Let Dr. A. J. Gossip, the great gifted Scottish preacher, tell us how once on a day in France, the bonniest of experiences befell him.

He had been for weeks amid the appalling desolation and sickening sights of the war front. Then they had gone back to rest where there were budding hedgerows, a shimmer of green on living trees, grass and flowers—glorious flowers in the first splendor of spring. It seemed Heaven! Then came the order to return to Passchendaele and the battlefront.

"It reached us," says Dr. Gossip, "On a perfect afternoon of sunshine; and with a heart grown hot and hard I turned down a little land with a brown burn wimpling beside it and a lush meadow—all brave sheets of purple and golden flowers—on either side. The earth was very beautiful, and life seemed very sweet, and it was hard to go back into the old purgatory and face death again. And, with that, through the gap in the hedge there came a shepherd laddie tending his flock of some two dozen sheep. He was not driving them in our rough way, with two barking dogs: he went first, and they were following him; if one loitered he called it by name and it came running to him. So they moved on down the lane, up a little hill, up to the brow and over it, and so out of my life. I stood there staring after them, hearing as if the words were spoken aloud, to me first, and to me only:

"And when he putteth forth his own sheep, he goeth before them."

> Peter, outworn,
> And menaced by the sword,
> Shook off the dust of Rome;
> And, as he fled,
> Met one, with eager face,
> Hastening cityward,
> And, top his vast amaze,
> It was the Lord.
>
> "Lord, whither goest Thou?"
> He cried, importunate;
> And Christ replied,
> "Peter, I suffer loss,
> I go to take thy place,
> To bear thy cross."
>
> Then Peter bowed his head,
> Discomforted;
> Then, at the Master's feet,
> Found grace complete,
> And courage, and new faith,
> And turned, with Him
> To death.

JOHN OXENHAM

May 8

MORNING

Walking in the midst of the fire (DAN. 3:25).

The fire did not arrest their motion; they walked in the midst of it. It was one of the streets through which they moved to their destiny. The comfort of Christ's revelation is not that it teaches their emancipation *from* sorrow, but emancipation *through* sorrow.

O my God, teach me, when the shadows have gathered, that I am only in a tunnel. It is enough for me to know that it will be all right some day.

They tell me that I shall stand upon the peaks of Olivet, the heights of resurrection glory. But I want more, O my Father; I want Calvary to lead up to it. I want to know that the shadows of this world are the shades of an avenue—the avenue to the house of my Father. Tell me I am only forced to climb because Thy house is on the hill! I shall receive *no* hurt from sorrow if I shall *walk* in the midst of the fire.

GEORGE MATHESON

"The road is too rough," I said;
"It is uphill all the way;
No flowers, but thorns instead;
And the skies over head are grey."
But One took my hand at the entrance dim,
And sweet is the road that I walk with Him.

"The cross is too great," I cried—
"More than the back can bear,
So rough and heavy and wide,
And nobody by to care."
And One stooped softly and touched my hand:
"I know. I care. And I understand."

Then why do we fret and sigh;
Cross-bearers all we go:
But the road ends by-and-by
In the dearest place we know,
And every step in the journey we
May take in the Lord's own company.

EVENING

Under utterly hopeless circumstances he hopefull believed.
(ROM. 4:18 WEYMOUTH)

When God is going to do something *wonderful*, He begins with a difficulty. If it is going to be something *very wonderful*, He begins with an impossibility.

CHARLES INWOOD

O God of the impossible!
Since all things are to Thee
But soil in which Omnipotence
Can work almightily,

Each trial may to us become
The means that will display
How o'er what seems impossible
Our God hath perfect sway!

The very storms that beat upon
Our little bark so frail,
But manifest Thy power to quell
All forces that assail.

The things that are to us too hard,
The foes that are too strong,
Are just the very ones that may
Awake a triumph song.

O God of the impossible,
When we no hope can see,
Grant us the faith that still believes
ALL possible to Thee!

J. H. S.

May 9

MORNING

❧

Abraham stood yet before the Lord (GEN. 18:22).

The friend of God can plead with Him for others. Perhaps Abraham's height of faith and friendship seems beyond our little possibilities. Do not be discouraged, Abraham grew; so may we. He went step by step, not by great leaps.

The man whose faith has been deeply tested and who has come off victorious, is the man to whom supreme tests must come.

The finest jewels are most carefully cut and polished; the hottest fires try the most precious metal. Abraham would never have been called the father of the faithful if he had not been proved to the uttermost. Read Genesis, twenty-second chapter:

"Take thy son, thine only son, whom thou lovest." See him going with a chastened, wistful, yet humbly obedient heart up Moriah's height, with the idol of his heart beside him about to be sacrificed at the command of God whom he had faithfully loved and served!

What a rebuke to our questionings of God's dealings with us! Away with all doubting explanations of this stupendous scene! It was an object lesson for the ages. Angels were looking.

Shall this man's faith stand forever for the strength and help of all God's people? Shall it be known through him that unfaltering faith will always prove the faithfulness of God?

Yes; and when faith has borne victoriously its uttermost test, the angel of the Lord—who? The Lord Jesus, Jehovah, he in whom "all the promises of God are yea and amen"—spoke to him, saying, "now I know that thou fearest God." Thou hast trusted me to the uttermost. I will also trust thee; thou shalt ever be My friend, and I will bless thee, and make thee a blessing.

It is always so, and always will be. *"They that are of faith are blessed with faithful Abraham."*   SELECTED

It is no small thing to be on terms of friendship with God.

EVENING

∽✤∾

Come unto me, all ye that labor and are heavy laden, and I will give you rest. (MATT. 11:28)

I wonder why the easiest thing in the Christian life is the most diffi-cult? I wonder why I work by a guttering candle when there is an electric light switch within easy reach of my hand? The answer, of course, is that I don't. I am not so foolish—except in one direction, and that is Godward. In our spiritual life many of us seem to be content struggling along with all the poor primitive resources of a weak, human nature, while all the infinite power of the Godhead is at our disposal. There is no con-dition of human nature, no circumstance of human life, that is not com-pletely provided for in the all-embracing love of our Father God; yet the vast majority of His children struggle along life's road, bearing burdens that He is eager to carry, and has urged them to entrust to Him. I won-der why?

It should be an easy thing, an alluring thing,
a thrilling thing to talk to God,

to hold converse with Christ. Yet, strange to relate, prayer is the most neglected of all the Christian ministries. The most perfunctory, abbreviated and ofttimes omitted exercise of many a Christian's life is the prayer-time. I wonder why?

Perhaps the difficulty lies in its very ease, its utter simplicity. Just to kneel at your bedside, and with the old abandon of childhood and the same unquestioning faith, leave all burdens and cares and needs with the Father! How childlike, but how difficult! How hard to relax; to spare an hour or even half that time out of our busy, rushing, worried lives, and go quietly to our room, shut the door and be still in His presence! How hard to divest ourselves of our sophistication, of our self-consciousness and self-centeredness, and ever-present feeling that I have to face and meet and shoulder all these cares and responsibilities! How hard just to be a child again, and with a great, happy sigh, settle down carefree at His feet, perfectly assured that He careth; that the government is upon His shoulder.
A. STUART M'NAIRN

May 10

MORNING

❧

I had fainted unless . . . (PS. 27:13).

FAINT NOT!

How great is the temptation at this point! How the soul sinks, the heart grows sick, and the faith staggers under the keen trials and testings which come into our lives in times of special bereavement and suffering.

"I cannot bear up any longer, I am fainting under this providence. What shall I do? God tells me not to faint. But what can one do when he is fainting?"

What do you do when you are about to faint physically? You cannot *do* anything. You *cease* from your own doings. In your faintness, you fall upon the shoulder of some strong loved one. You lean hard. You rest. You lie still and trust.

It is so when we are tempted to faint under affliction. God's message to us is not, "Be strong and of good courage," for He knows our strength and courage have fled away. But it is that sweet word, "Be still, and know that I am God."

Hudson Taylor was so feeble in the closing months of his life that he wrote a dear friend: "I am so weak I cannot write; I cannot read my Bible; I cannot even pray. I can only lie still in God's arms like a little child, and trust."

This wondrous man of God with all his spiritual power came to a place of physical suffering and weakness where he could only lie still and trust.

And that is all God asks of you, His dear child, when you grow faint in the fierce fires of affliction. Do not try *to be strong*. Just be *still* and *know that He is God,* and will sustain you, and bring you through.

God keeps His choicest cordials for our deepest faintings.

"Stay firm and let thine heart take courage"
(PS. 27:14, AFTER OSTERWALD).

Stay firm, He has not failed thee
In all the past,
And will He go and leave thee
To sink at last?
Nay, He said He will hide thee
Beneath His wing;
And sweetly there in safety
Thou mayest sing.
SELECTED

EVENING

Yield . . . ye your members as instruments . . . unto God.
(ROM. 6:13)

God can do nothing with us if *we do not yield*. We recall a day of sightseeing in the palace of Genoa. We entered a room seemingly empty; bare walls, floors, and tables greeted us. Presently the guide led us across the room to the wall at the farther side. There we espied a niche in the wall. It was covered with a glass case. Behind the case was a magnificent violin, in perfect preservation—Paganini's favorite violin; the rich old Cremona upon which he loved most of all to display his marvelous skill. We gazed intently upon the superb instrument, with its warm rich tints, sinuous curves, and perfect model. And then we tried to imagine the wondrous strains the touch of the great master would bring forth if he were there in that quiet palace chamber . . . Nay, but this could not be! He could not possibly do so! For *it was locked up against him!* It gave the master no chance.

It is not how much do you have, but how *much of yours does God have.*

Present your members as instruments to God. To present means "to place near the hand of one." *Yielded, reachable, usable*—this gives God a chance.

Make it a real transaction!
God-yielded wills find the God-planned life.
JAMES H. MCCONKEY

I owned a little boat a while ago
And sailed a Morning Sea without a fear,
And whither any breeze might fairly blow
I'd steer the little craft afar or near.

Mine was the boat, and mine the air,
And mine the sea; not mine, a care.

My boat became my place of nightly toil.
I sailed at sunset to the fishing ground.
At morn the boat was freighted with the spoil
That my all-conquering work and skill had found.

Mine was the boat, and mine the net,
And mine the skill, and power to get.

One day there passed along the silent shore,
While I my net was casting in the sea,
A man, who spoke as never man before;
I followed Him—new life begun in me.

Mine was the boat, but His the voice,
And His the call; yet mine, the choice.

Ah, 'twas a fearful night out on the lake,
And all my skill availed not at the helm,
Till Him asleep I waken, crying "Take,
Take Thou command, lest waters overwhelm!"

His was the boat, and His the Sea,
And His the Peace o'er all and me.

Once from His boat He taught the curious throng,
Then bade me let down nets out in the Sea;
I murmured, but obeyed, nor was it long
Before the catch amazed and humbled me.

His was the boat, and His the skill,
And His the catch—and His, my will.
JOSEPH ADDISON RICHARDS

Give God a chance!

May 11
MORNING

We went through fire and through water:
But thou broughtest us out into a wealthy place (PS. 66:12).

*P*aradoxical though it be, only that man is at rest who attains it through conflict. This peace, born of conflict, is not like the deadly hush preceding the tempest, but the serene and pure-aired quiet that follows it.

It is not generally the prosperous one, who has never sorrowed, who is strong and at rest. His quality has never been tried, and he knows not how he can stand even a gentle shock. He is not the safest sailor who never saw a tempest; he will do for fair-weather service, but when the storm is rising, place at the important post the man who has fought out a gale, who has tested the ship, who knows her hulk sound, her rigging strong, and her anchor-flukes able to grasp and hold by the ribs of the world.

When first affliction comes upon us, how everything gives way! Our clinging, tendril hopes are snapped, and our heart lies prostrate like a vine that the storm has torn from its trellis; but when the first shock is past, and we are able to look up, and say, "It is the Lord," faith lifts the shattered hopes once more, and binds them fast to the feet of God. Thus the end is confidence, safety, and peace.   SELECTED

The adverse winds blew against my life;
My little ship with grief was tossed;
My plans were gone—heart full of strife,
And all my hope seemed to be lost—

"Then He arose"—one word of peace.
"There was a calm"—a sweet release.

A temptest great of doubt and fear
Possessed my mind; no light was there
To guide, or make my vision clear.
Dark night! 'twas more than I could bear—
"Then He arose," I saw His face—
"There was a calm" filled with His grace.

My heart was sinking 'neath the wave
Of deepening test and raging grief;
All seemed as lost, and none could save,
And nothing could bring me relief—
"Then He arose"—and spoke one word,
"There was a calm!" IT IS THE LORD.

L.S.P.

EVENING

∾

God's tilled land. (1 COR. 3:9 RSV MARGIN)

God's farm. (TRANS.)

The plowing and harrowing are painful processes. And surely the Divine Plowman is at work in the world as never before. He plows *by His Spirit, by His Word, and by His providences.* Though painful be the processes of cultivation, they are essential.

Could the earth speak, it would say, "I felt the hard plow today; I knew what was coming; when the plow-point first struck me I was full of pain and distress and I could have cried out for very agony for the point was sharp and driven through me with great energy; but now, I think, *this means the blade, the ear, the full corn in the ear, the golden harvest and harvest-home.*"

When the plow of God's providence first cuts up a man's life, what wonder if the man should exclaim a little; yea, if he should give way to one hour's grief! But the man may come to himself, ere eventide, and say, "Plow on, Lord! I want my life to be *plowed all over,* that it may be sown all over, and *that in every corner there may be the golden grain or the beautiful flowers.* Pity me that I exclaimed when I first felt the plowshare.

Thou knowest my frame; Thou rememberest that I am dust. But now I recollect; I put things together; I see Thy meaning; *so drive on, Thou Plowman of Eternity!"*

He does not use the plow and harrow without intention. Where God plows, He intends to sow. *His plowing is a proof He is* FOR *and not against you.*

"For, behold, I am for you, and I will turn unto you, and ye shall be tilled and sown" (EZEK. 36:9).

Let us never forget that the Husbandman is never so near the land as when He is plowing it, the very time when we are tempted to think He hath forsaken us.

His plowing is a proof that He thinks you of value, and worth chastening; for He does not waste His plowing on the barren sand. He will not plow continually, but only for a time, and for a definite purpose. Soon He will close that process. "Doth the plowman plow continually to sow? Doth he continually open and break the clods of His ground?" (Isa. 28:24 rsv). Verily, No! Soon, aye soon, we shall, through these painful processes and by His gentle showers of grace become His fruitful land.

"The desolate land shall be tilled. . . . And they shall say, This land that was desolate is become like the garden of Eden" (Ezek. 36:34–35), and thus we shall be a praise unto Him.

> *Come ill, come well, the cross, the crown,*
> *The rainbow or the thunder—*
> *I fling my soul and body down*
> *For God to plow them under.*
> **A PRINCE OF THE CAPTIVITY, BY JOHN BUCHAN**

May 12
MORNING

All things are possible to him that believeth (MARK 9:23).

The "all things" do not always come simply for the asking, for the reason that God is ever seeking to teach us the way of faith, and in our training in the faith-life there must be room for the trial of faith, the discipline of faith, the patience of faith, the courage of faith, the discipline of faith, the patience of faith, the courage of faith, and often many stages are passed before we really realize what is the end of faith, namely, the victory of faith.

Real moral fiber is developed through discipline of faith. You have made your request of God, but the answer does not come. What are you to do?

Keep on believing God's Word; never be moved away from it by what you see or feel, and thus as you stand steady, enlarged power and experience is being developed. The fact of looking at the apparent contradiction as to God's Word and being unmoved from your position of faith make you stronger on every other line.

Often God delays purposely, and the delay is just as much an answer to your prayer as is the fulfillment when it comes.

In the lives of all the great Bible characters, God worked thus. Abraham, Moses, and Elijah were not great in the beginning, but were made great through the discipline of their faith, and only thus were they fitted for the positions to which God had called them.

For example, in the case of Joseph whom the Lord was training for the throne of Egypt, we read in the Psalms:

"The word of the Lord tried him." It was not the prison life with its hard beds or poor food that tried him, but it was the word God had spoken into his heart in the early years concerning elevation and honor which were greater than his brethren were to receive; it was this which was ever before him, when every step in his career made it seem more and more impossible of fulfillment, until he was there imprisoned, and all in innocency, while others who were perhaps justly incarcerated, were released, and he was left to languish alone.

These were hours that tried his soul, but hours of spiritual growth and development, that, "when his word came" (the word of release), found him fitted for the delicate task of dealing with his wayward brethren, with a love and patience only surpassed by God Himself.

No amount of persecution tries like such experiences as these. When God has spoken of His purpose to do, and yet the days go on and He does not do it, that is truly hard; but it is a discipline of faith that will bring us into a knowledge of God which would otherwise be impossible.

~∞~

As an eagle stirreth up her nest. (DEUT. 32:11)

God, like the eagle, stirs our nest. Yesterday it was the place for us; today there is a new plan. He wrecks the nest, although He knows it is dear to us; perhaps, because it *is* dear to us. He loves us too well not to spoil our meager contentment. Let not our minds, therefore, dwell on second causes. It is His doing! Do not let us blame the thorn that pierces us.

Though the destruction of the next may seem wanton, and almost certainly come at an hour when I do not expect it; though the things happen that I least anticipate—let me guard my heart and be not forgetful of God's care, lest I miss the meaning of the wreckage of my hopes. He has *something better for me.*

God will not spoil our nest, and leave us without a nest, *if a nest is best for us.* His seeming cruelty is love; therefore, *let us always sit light with the things of time.*

The eaglet says, *"Teach me to fly!"* The saints often sit idly *wishing that they were like to their Lord.* Neither is likely to recognize that the prayer is heard *when the nest is toppled over!*

The breaking up of a nest an act of God's benevolence? What a startling thought!

Yet, here is an old writer who makes it a subject of praise; blesses God for it; declares it to be the first step of my education! I can understand praising Him for His gifts to body and soul; but I lose my breath in surprise when I am asked to make the first stanza of my hymn the adoration of His mercy in loosing the ties of home!

Nay, my soul, it is to *strengthen these ties* that my Father breaks up the nest; not to get rid of home, but to teach thee to fly! Travel with thy Teacher and thou shalt learn that

The Home is wider than any nest!

He would have thee learn of the many mansions of which thy nest is only one. He would tell thee of a brotherhood in Christ, which includes, yet transcends, thy household fires. He would tell thee of the family altar, which makes thee brother to the outcast, sister to the friendless—in kinship to all.

Thy Father hath given thee wings in the breaking of thy ties!
The storm that shook thy next taught thee to fly!

LEAVES FOR QUIET HOURS

God spreads broad wings;
And by His lifting, holy grace,
We find a wider, fairer place,
The freedom of untrammeled space;
Where clearer vision shows us things
The nest-view never brings.

The wing-life is characterized by comprehensiveness. High soaring gives wide seeing!

J. H. JOWETT

May 13
MORNING

We know not what we should pray for as we ought (ROM. 8:26).

Much that perplexes us in our Christian experience is but the answer to our prayers. We pray for patience, and our Father sends those who tax us to the utmost; for *"tribulation worketh patience."*

We pray for submission, and God sends sufferings; for *"we learn obedience by the things we suffer."*

We pray for unselfishness, and God gives us opportunities to sacrifice ourselves by thinking on the things of others, and by laying down our lives for the brethren.

We pray for strength and humility, and some messenger of Satan torments us until we lie in the dust crying for its removal.

We pray, "Lord, increase our faith," and money takes wings; or the children are alarmingly ill; or a servant comes who is careless, extravagant, untidy or slow, or some hitherto unknown trial calls for an increase of faith along a line where we have not needed to exercise much faith before.

We pray for the Lamb-life, and are given a portion of lowly service, or we are injured and must seek no redress; for "he was led as a lamb to the slaughter and . . . opened not his mouth."

We pray for gentleness, and there comes a perfect storm of temptation to harshness and irritability. We pray for quietness, and every nerve is strung to the utmost tension, so that looking to Him we may learn that when He giveth quietness, no one can make trouble.

We pray for love, and God sends peculiar suffering and puts us with apparently unlovely people, and lets them say things which rasp the nerves and lacerate the heart; for love suffereth long and is kind, love is not impolite, love is not provoked. LOVE BEARETH ALL THINGS, believeth, hopeth and endureth, love never faileth. We pray for likeness to Jesus, and the answer is, "I have chosen thee in the furnace of affliction." "Can thine heart endure, or can thine hands be strone?" "Are ye able?"

The way to peace and victory is to accept every circumstance, every trial, straight from the hand of a loving Father; and to live up in the heavenly places, above the clouds, in the very presence of the throne, and to look down from the glory upon our environment as lovingly and divinely appointed. SELECTED

I prayed for strength, and then I lost awhile
All sense of nearness, human and divine;
The love I leaned on failed and pierced my heart,
The hands I clung to loosed themselves from mine;
But while I swayed, weak, trembling, and alone,
The everlasting arms upheld my own.

I prayed for light; the sun went down in clouds,
The moon was darkened by a misty doubt,
The stars of heaven were dimmed by earthly fears,
And all my little candle flames burned out;
But while I sat in shadow, wrapped in night,
The face of Christ made all the darkness bright.

I prayed for peace, and dreamed of restful ease,
A slumber drugged from pain, a hushed repose;
Above my head the skies were black with storm,
And fiercer grew the onslaught of my foes;
But while the battle raged, and wild winds blew,
I heard His voice and perfect peace I knew.

I thank Thee, Lord, Thou wert too wise to heed
My feeble prayers, and answer as I sought,
Since these rich gifts Thy bounty has bestowed
Have brought me more than all I asked or thought;
Giver of good, so answer each request
With Thine own giving, better than my best.
ANNIE JOHNSON FLINT

EVENING

A little past the top of the hill. (2 SAM. 16:1)

*I*t was a hard climb up that hill for a man with a burdened heart; he was tired and done. Then came God's provision for him through Ziba.

Are you a little past the top of the hill? Feeling tired and almost done? Take heart! God has something ready at the precise moment! God's help will meet you!

Just a little farther on—and all who honor Me, with joy shall prove My promise true; they too shall honored be. Full well I know thy heart's desire, the heights to which thou dost aspire; thy love which burns with holy fire— and all to honor Me.

Just a little farther on—the "Victor's song will then be sung by all who honor Me." Thou hast done well, yet still press on—and greater words I'll trust to thee, and grander glories thou shalt see; thus thou shalt fully honored be—a little farther on!

SEE JOHN 12:26; PS. 91:15

Just over the hill, by the climbing way,
Is a place where all good travelers stay—
Just over the hill and up along.

At the side of the road is a garden-gate,
Which is always open, early and late—
Just over the hill and up along.

And inside the gate is a House of Rest,
Where the Host will give you His very best—
Just over the hill and up along.

JOHN OXENHAM

God never permits any of His children to come up a steep hill along life's pathway without having provided at the foot of the hill a cooling spring from which the traveler may drink in refreshment and strength ere he begins to climb.

He climbs beside you; lean upon Him!

God has no road without its springs!

May 14

MORNING

❧

In the selfsame day, as God had said unto him (GEN. 17:23).

*I*nstant obedience is the only kind of obedience there is; *delayed* obedience is disobedience. Every time God calls us to any duty, He is offering to make a covenant with us; doing the duty is our part, and He will do His part in special blessing.

The only way we can obey is to obey *"in the selfsame day,"* as Abraham did. To be sure, we often postpone a duty and then later on do it as fully as we can. It is better to do this than not to do it at all. But it is then, at best, only a crippled, disfigured, halfway sort of duty-doing; and a *postponed duty never can bring the full blessing that God intended, and that it would have brought if done at the earliest possible moment.*

It is a pity to rob ourselves, along with robbing God and others, by procrastination. *"In the selfsame day"* is the Genesis way of saying, "Do it now." **FROM MESSAGES FOR THE MORNING WATCH**

Luther says that a "true believer will crucify the question, 'Why?' He will obey without questioning." I will not be one of those who, except they see signs and wonders, will in no wise believe. I will obey without questioning.

> *Ours not to make reply,*
> *Ours not to reason why,*
> *Ours but to do and die.*

Obedience is the fruit of faith; patience, the bloom on the fruit.

CHRISTINA ROSSETTI

EVENING

❧

Study to be quiet. (1 THESS. 4:11)

*B*eloved! this is our spirit's deepest need. It is thus that we can learn to know God. It is thus that we receive spiritual refreshment and nutriment. It is thus that we are nourished and fed. It is thus that we receive the Living Bread. It is thus that our very bodies are healed, and our spirits drink in the life of our risen Lord, and we go forth to life's conflicts and duties like the flower that has drunk in, through the shades of the night, the cool and crystal drops of dew. But the dew never falls on a stormy night, so the dews of His Grace never come to the restless soul.

We cannot go through life strong and fresh on constant express trains with ten minutes for lunch: we must have quiet hours, secret places of the Most High, times of waiting upon the Lord, when we renew our strength and learn to mount up on wings as eagles, and then come back to run and not be weary, and to walk and not faint.

The best thing about this stillness is, that it gives God a chance to work. "He that is entered into His rest hath ceased from his own works, even as God did from His"; and when we cease from our thoughts, God's thoughts come into us; when we get still from our restless activity, "God worketh in us, both to will and to do of His good pleasure," and we have but to work it out.

Beloved! let us take His stillness!
A. B. SIMPSON

Jesus, Deliverer, come Thou to me;
Soothe Thou my voyaging,
Over life's sea!

May 15
MORNING

❧

Men see not the bright light which is in the clouds (JOB 37:21).

The world owes much of its beauty to cloudland. The unchanging blue of the Italian sky hardly compensates for the changefulness and glory of the clouds. Earth would become a wilderness apart from their ministry. There are clouds in human life, shadowing, refreshing, and sometimes draping it in blackness of night; but there is never a cloud without its bright light. "I do set my bow in the cloud!"

If we could see the clouds from the other side where they lie in billowy glory, bathed in the light they intercept, like heaped ranges of Alps, we should be amazed at their splendid magnificence.

We look at their underside; but who shall describe the bright light that bathes their summits and searches their valleys and is reflected from every pinnacle of their expanse? Is not every drop drinking in health-giving qualities, which it will carry to earth?

O child of God! If you could see your sorrows and troubles from the other side; if instead of looking up at them from earth, you would look down on them from the heavenly places where you sit with Christ; if you knew how they are reflecting in prismatic beauty before the gaze of heaven, the bright light of Christ's face, you would be content that they should cast their deep shadows over the mountain slopes of existence. Only remember that clouds are always moving and passing before God's cleansing wind.   SELECTED

I cannot know why suddenly the storm
Should rage so fiercely round me in its wrath;
But this I know—God watches all my path,
And I can trust.

I may not draw aside the mystic veil
That hides the unknown future from my sight,
Nor know if for me waits the dark or light;
But I can trust.

I have no power to look across the tide,
To see while here the land beyond the river;
But this I know—I shall be God's forever;
So I can trust.

EVENING

∽∾

This he said to prove him: for he himself knew what he would do.
(JOHN 6:6)

At this very hour you may have to come face to face with a most tremendous need, and Christ stands beside you looking at it and questioning you about it. He says, in effect, "How are you going to meet it?"

He is scrutinizing you . . . watching you with a gentle tender sympathy. How many of us have failed in the test! We have taken out our pencil and our paper and commenced to figure out the two hundred pennyworth of bread; or we have run off hither and thither to strong and wealthy friends to extricate us; or we have sat down in utter despondency; or we have murmured against Him for bringing us into such a position.

Should we not have turned a sunny face to Christ saying: *Thou hast a plan! Thine is the responsibility, and Thou must tell me what to do. I have come so far in the path of obedience to Thy Guiding Spirit: and now, what art Thou going to do?*

They understood not how that God by his hand would deliver them (Acts 7:25). *It is so today.*

> Leave the HOW with Jesus,
> Secret things He knows;
> Infinite in wisdom,
> Time will all disclose.

> Leave the HOW with Jesus,
> He will comfort bring;
> Thro' the storm He'll hide thee
> Underneath His wing.

"God does not explain to us His technique."

"My times are in thy hand." If you quote this verse to the native of Congo, he will translate it in the gorgeous words: *"All my life's whys and whens and wheres and wherefores are in God's Hand!"*   DAN CRAWFORD

We want to know more than the silent God deems it good to tell; to understand the "why" which He bids us wait to ask; to *see* the path which He has spread on purpose in the dark. The Infinite Father does not stand by us to be catechized and to explain Himself to our vain minds; He is here for our trust.

May 16
MORNING

Fear not, Daniel: for from the first day that thou didst set thine heart to understand, and to chasten thyself before thy God, thy words were heard, and I am come for thy words. But the prince of the kingdom of Persia withstood me one and twenty days (DAN. 10:12–13).

We have wonderful teaching here on prayer, and we are shown the direct hindrance from Satan.

Daniel had fasted and prayed twenty-one days, and had a very hard time in prayer. As far as we read the narrative, it was not because Daniel was not a good man, nor because his prayer was not right; but it was because of a special attack of Satan.

The Lord started a messenger to tell Daniel that his prayer was answered the moment Daniel began to pray; but an evil angel met the good angel and wrestled with him, hindering him. There was a conflict in the heavens; and Daniel seemed to go through an agony on earth the same as that which was going on in the heavens.

"We wrestle not against flesh and blood, but against principalities, against powers . . . against wicked spirits in high places (Eph. 6:12, margin).

Satan delayed the answer three full weeks. Daniel nearly succumbed, and Satan would have been glad to kill him; but God will not suffer anything to come above that we "are able to bear."

Many a Christian's prayer is hindered by Satan; but you need not fear when your prayers and faith pile up; for after a while they will be like a flood, and will not only sweep the answer through, but will also bring some new accompanying blessing.　　　　　*FROM* A SERMON

Hell does its worst with the saints. The rarest souls have been tested with high pressures and temperatures, but heaven will not desert them.

W. L. WATKINSON

EVENING

∽∾

*At even my wife died; and I did in the morning as
I was commanded.* (EZEK. 24:18)

*A*t even my wife died." The light of the home went out. Darkness brooded over the face of every familiar thing. The trusted companion who had shared all the changes of the ever-changing way was taken from my side. The light of our fellowship was suddenly extinguished as by some mysterious hand stretched forth from the unseen. I lost "the desire of mine eyes." I was alone. "At even my wife died; and . . . in the morning . . ." Aye, what about the next morning, when the light broke almost obtrusively upon a world which had changed into a cemetery containing only one grave? *"In the morning I did as I was commanded."*

The command had been laid upon him in the days before his bereavement. Life in his home had been a source of inspiring fellowship. In the evening-time, after the discharge of the burdensome tasks of the day, he had turned to his home as weary dust-choked pilgrims turn to a bath; and immersed in the sweet sanctities of weeded life he had found such retoration of soul as fitted him for the renewed labor of the morrow. But "at even my wife died." The home was no longer a refreshing bath, but part of the dusty road; no longer an oasis, but a repetition of the wilderness.

How now shall it be concerning the prophet's command? "At even my wife died; and in the morning" the commandment? How does the old duty appear in the gloom of the prophet's bereavement? Duty still, clamant and clamorous now in the shadows as it was loud and importunate in the light. What shall the prophet do? Take up the old burden, and faithfully trudge the old road. Go out in his loneliness, and go on with the old tasks. But why? You will find the secret of it all in the last clause of the chapter:

> *"Thou shalt be a sign unto them;*
> *and they shall know that I am the LORD."*

A brokenhearted prophet patiently and persistently pursuing an old duty, and by his manner of doing it compelling people to believe in the Lord! That is the secret motive of the heavy discipline.

The great God wants our conspicuous crises to be occasions of conspicuous testimony; our seasons of darkness to be opportunities for the unveiling of the Divine. *He wants duty to shine more resplendently because of the environing shadows.* He wants tribulation only to furbish and burnish our signs. He wants tribulation only to furbish and burnish our signs. He wants us to manifest the sweet grace of continuance amid all the sudden and saddening upheavals of our intensely varied life. This was the prophet's triumph. He made his calamity a witness to the eternal. He made his very loneliness minister to his God. He made his very bereavement intensify his calling. He took up the old task, and in taking it up he glorified it. "At even my wife died; and in the morning I did as I was commanded."

The evening sorrow will come to all of us: what shall we be found doing in the morning? We shall have to dig graves; have burials; how shall it be with us when the funeral is over?   J. H. JOWETT

Make a pulpit of every circumstance.

May 17

≈∽

And when forty years were expired, there appeared to him in the
wilderness . . . an angel of the Lord . . . saying, . . .
now come, I will send thee into Egypt (ACTS 7:30–34).

Often the Lord calls us aside from our work for a season, and bids us be still and learn ere we go forth again to minister. There is no time lost in such waiting hours.

Fleeing from his enemies, the ancient knight found that his horse needed to be reshod. Prudence seemed to urge him on without delay, but higher wisdom taught him to halt a few minutes at the blacksmith's forge by the way, to have the shoe replaced; and although he heard the feet of his pursuers galloping hard behind, yet he waited those minutes until his charger was refitted for his flight. And then, leaping into his saddle just as they appeared a hundred yards away, he dashed away from them with the fleetness of the wind, and knew that his halting had hastened his escape.

So often God bids us tarry ere we go, and fully recover ourselves for the next stage of the journey and work.

FROM DAYS OF HEAVEN UPON EARTH

Waiting! Yes, patiently waiting!
Till next steps made plain shall be;
To hear, with the inner hearing,
The Voice that will call for me.

Waiting! Yes, hopefully waiting!
With hope that need not grow dim;
The Master is pledged to guide me,
And my eyes are unto Him.

Waiting! Expectantly waiting!
Perhaps it may be today
The Master will quickly open
The gate to my future way.

Waiting! Yes, waiting! still waiting!
I know, though I've waited long,
That, while He withholds His purpose,
His waiting cannot be wrong.

Waiting! yes, waiting!
The Master will not be late:
He knoweth that I am waiting
For Him to unlatch the gate.

EVENING

～∞～

To sojourn in the land are we come; for thy servants have no
pasture for their flocks; for the famine is sore in the land of Canaan.
. . . The land of Egypt is before thee; in the best of the land make thy
father andbrethren to dwell. (GEN. 47:4, 6)

Did you ever come to a time of the most awful famine—spiritual famine—in your life, when there was no pasture upon which to feed? At such a time Christ Himself takes the matter for us to the throne of God. He tells God we are His own brothers. And what is the answer? "The kingdom of heaven is before thee; *in the best of the kingdom make thy brethren to dwell.*" Do you realize what it means *to have Jesus Christ intercede for you*—the Christ whom you repudiated by your own sin? Pharoah knew not these men; but he knew Joseph, and nothing was too good for Joseph and every relative of Joseph.

We are "joint-heirs with Christ." Because of Christ, God flings wide open the whole kingdom, and simply asks *that we take its best.* Out of famine—into the best that the kingdom affords! Not only that, but rulers of the King's own property! Oh, Lord Jesus, forgive my unfaith! Open my sin-bound, self-centered eyes to the wonders of Thy love. Teach me how to receive more. *The best of the kingdom:* that means *Thee.* I take Thee, Lord, as my feast of Eternal Life.

MESSAGES FOR THE MORNING WATCH

I am not the brood of the dust and sod,
Nor a shuttled thread in the loom of fate;
But the child Divine of the living God,
With eternity for my life's estate.
I am not a sport of a cosmic night,
Nor a thing of chance that has grown to man;
But a deathless soul on my upward flight,
And my Father's heir in His wondrous plan.

ALVA ROMANES

We are His only heirs.

May 18
MORNING

〜〜

I was crushed . . . so much so that I despaired even of life,
but that was to make me rely not on myself, but on the God
who raises the dead (2 COR. 1:8–9).

Pressed out of measure and pressed to all length;
Pressed so intensely it seems, beyond strength;
Pressed in the body and pressed in the soul,
Pressed in the mind till the dark surges roll.
Pressure by foes, and a pressure from friends.
Pressure on pressure, till life nearly ends.

Pressed into knowing no helper but God;
Pressed into loving the staff and the rod.
Pressed into liberty where nothing clings;
Pressed into faith for impossible things.
Pressed into living a life in the Lord,
Pressed into living a Christ-life outpoured.

The pressure of hard places makes us value life. Every time our life is given back to us from such a trial, it is like a new beginning, and we learn better how much it is worth, and make more of it for God and man. The pressure helps us to understand the trials of others, and fits us to help and sympathize with them.

There is a shallow, superficial nature, that gets hold of a theory or a promise lightly, and talks very glibly about the distrust of those who shrink from every trial; but the man or woman who has suffered much never does this, but is very tender and gentle, and knows what suffering really means. This is what Paul meant when he said, "Death worketh in you."

Trials and hard places are needed to press us forward, even as the furnace fires in the hold of that mighty ship give force that moves the piston, drives the engine, and propels that great vessel across the sea in the face of the winds and waves.

A. B. SIMPSON

◈

They need not depart. (MATT. 14:16)

What a task lay before the Lord on that day! There were five thousand men, besides women and children. To feed such a crowd at a moment's notice might well-nigh seem impossible. Well might the disciples say, "Send the multitude away, that they may go into the villages, and buy themselves victuals." Well might they look startled when the reply came back. "They need not depart; give ye them to eat." Their hearts must have sunk within them as their eyes again and again scanned that surging crowd.

The prospect of feeding that multitude did not alarm the Lord. He asked Philip, indeed, "Whence shall *we* buy bread, that these may eat?" but we learn immediately that He said this "to prove him." The Lord Jesus is perfectly confident that He can meet our needs and He would have us confident, too; for He is the One who for thousands of years has met the needs of those who put their trust in Him. As the God of providence He keeps the barrel of meal from wasting, and the cruse of oil from failing. He draws from one the testimony: "I have been young, and now am old; yet have I not seen the righteous forsaken, nor his seed begging bread." And from another, "There hath not failed one word of all his good promise."   SELECTED

> *Say not, my soul, "From whence*
> *Can God relieve my care?"*
> *Remember that Omnipotence*
> *Hath servants everywhere.*
>
> *His help is always sure,*
> *His methods seldom guessed;*
> *Delay will make our pleasure pure:*
> *Surprise will give it zest.*
>
> *His wisdom is sublime,*
> *His heart profoundly kind;*
> *God never is before His time,*
> *And never is behind.*
>
> *Hast thou assumed a load*
> *Which none will bear with thee?*
> *And art thou bearing it for God,*
> *And shall He fail to see?*

Be comforted at heart,
Thou art not left alone;
Now thou the Lord's companion art—
Soon thou shalt share His throne.

J. J. LYNCH

Jesus fed the multitude in a desert place.

May 19

MORNING

And it came to pass, before he had done speaking . . .
*and he said, Blessed be Jehovah . . . who hath not forsaken his loving
kindness and his truth* (GEN. 24:15, 27).

Every right prayer is answered before the prayer itself is finished—
before we have "done speaking." This is because God has pledged His
Word to us that whatsoever we ask in Christ's name (that is, in oneness
with Christ and His will) and in faith, shall be done.

As God's Word cannot fail, whenever we meet those simple conditions
in prayer, the answer to our prayer has been granted and completed in
heaven *as we pray,* even though its showing forth on earth may not occur
until long afterward.

So it is well to close every prayer with *praise* to God for the answer that
He has already granted; He who never forsakes His loving kindness and
His truth. (See Dan. 9:20–27 and 10:12.)

FROM MESSAGES FOR THE MORNING WATCH

When we believe for a blessing, we must take the attitude of faith; and
begin to act and pray as if we had the blessing. We must treat God as if
He had given us our request. We must lean our weight over upon Him
for the thing that we have claimed, and just take it for granted that He
gives it, and is going to continue to give it. This is the attitude of trust.

When the wife is married, she at once falls into a new attitude, and acts
in accordance with the fact; and so when we take Christ as our Savior, as
our Sanctifier, as our Healer, or as our Deliverer, He expects us to fall into
the attitude of recognizing Him in the capacity that we have claimed, and
expect Him to be to us all that we have trusted Him for. **SELECTED**

The thing I ask when God doth bid me pray,
Begins in that same act to come my way.

EVENING

⤳⤳

God, even our own God, shall bless us. (PS. 67:6)

When ye pray, say . . . Father. (LUKE 11:2)

*I*t is strange how little use we have of the spiritual blessings which God gives us, but it is stranger still *how little use we make of God Himself.* Though He is "our own God," we apply ourselves but little to Him. How seldom do we ask counsel at the hands of the Lord! How often do we go about our business without seeking His guidance! In our troubles how constantly do we strive to bear our burdens ourselves, instead of casting them upon the Lord that He may sustain us! This is not because we *may* not, for the Lord seems to say, "I am thine, soul; come and make use of Me as thou wilt; thou mayst come freely to My store, and the oftener the more welcome." It is our own fault if we do not make free with the riches of our own God.

Then, since thou hast such a Friend, and He invites thee, draw from Him daily. *Never want whilst thou hast a God to go to; never fear or faint whilst thou hast God to help thee; go to thy treasure and take whatever thou needest—there is all that thou canst want.*

Learn the Divine skill of making God all things to thee. He can supply thee with all; or, better still, He can be to thee instead of all. Let me urge thee, then, to make use of thy God. Make use of Him in prayer; go to Him often, because *He is thy God.* Oh, wilt thou fail to use so great a privilege? Fly to Him; tell Him all thy wants. Use Him constantly by faith at all times. If some dark providence has beclouded thee, use thy God as a "sun"; if some strong enemy has beset thee, find in Jehovah a "shield"; *for He is a sun and a shield to His people.* If thou hast lost thy way in the mazes of life, use Him as a "guide"; *for He will direct thee.* Whatever thou art, and wherever thou art, remember God is just *what thou wantest,* and just *where thou wantest* and that He *can do all thou wantest!*

CHARLES H. SPURGEON

The life of faith is the life that uses the Lord.   H. C. G. MOULE

☙ 311 ☙

O little heart of mine! Shall pain
Or sorrow make thee moan,
When all this God is all for thee—
A Father all thine own?

May 20

MORNING

❧∾

*Shall I refuse to drink the cup of sorrow which the Father
has given me to drink?* (JOHN 18:11 WEYMOUTH).

God takes a thousand times more pains with us than the artist with
his picture, by many touches of sorrow, and by many colors of circumstance, to bring us into the form which is the highest and noblest in
His sight, if only we receive His gifts of myrrh in the right spirit.

But when the cup is put away, and these feelings are stifled or un-
heeded, a greater injury is done to the soul than can ever be amended.
For no heart can conceive in what surpassing love God giveth us this
myrrh; yet this which we ought to receive to our souls' good we suffer to
pass by us in our sleepy indifference, and nothing comes of it.

Then we come and complain: "Alas, Lord! I am so dry, and it is so
dark within me!" I tell thee, dear child, open thy heart to the pain, and it
will do thee more good than if thou wert full of feeling and devoutness.

TAULER

The cry of man's anguish went up to God,
"Lord take away pain:
The shadow that darkens the world Thou hast made,
The close-coiling chain
That strangles the heart, the burden that weighs
On the wings that would soar,
Lord, take away pain from the world Thou hast made,
That it love Thee the more."
Then answered the Lord to the cry of His world:
"Shall I take away pain,
And with it the power of the soul to endure,

Made strong by the strain?
Shall I take away pity, that knits heart to heart
And sacrifice high?
Will ye lose all your heroes that lift from the fire
White brows to the sky?
Shall I take away love that redeems with a price
And smiles at its loss?
Can ye spare from your lives that would climb unto Me
The Christ on His cross?"

EVISODE

EVENING

And being in an agony he prayed . . . Father, if thou be willing,
remove this cup from me: nevertheless, not my will, but thine,
be done. And there appeared an angel unto him from heaven,
strengthening him. (LUKE 22:42–44)

There is a story of a woman who had had many sorrows: parents, husband, children, wealth, all were gone. In her great grief she prayed for death, but death did not come. She would not take up any of her wonted work for Christ. One night she had a dream: she thought she had gone to heaven. She saw her husband and ran to him with eager joy, expecting a glad welcome. But, strange to say, no answering joy shone on his face—only surprise and displeasure. "How did you come here?" he asked. "They did not say that you were to be sent for today; I did not expect you for a long time yet." With a bitter cry she turned from him to seek her parents. But instead of the tender love for which her heart was longing she met from them only the same amazement and the same surprised questions. "I'll go to my Savior," she cried. "He will welcome me if no one else does." When she saw Christ, there was infinite love in His look, but His words throbbed with sorrow as He said: "Child, child, who is doing your work down there?" At last she understood; she had no right yet to be in heaven; her work was not finished; she had fled away from her duty.

This is one of the dangers of sorrow: *that in our grief for those who are gone we lose our interest in those who are living, and slacken our zeal in the work which is allotted to us.* However great our bereavements we may not drop our tasks until the Master calls us away.   J. R. MILLER

Finish thy work, the time is short;
The sun is in the west,

The night is coming down; till then
Think not of rest.

Rest? Finish thy work, then rest;
Till then, rest never.
The rest prepared for thee by God
Is rest forever.

Finish thy work, then sit thee down
On some celestial hill,
And of heaven's everlasting bliss
Take thou thy fill.

Finish thy work, then go in peace,
Life's battle fought and won;
Hear from the throne the Master's voice,
"Well done! Well done!"

Finish Thy work, then take the harp,
Give praise to God above;
Sing a new song of mighty joy
And endless love!

Take not your rest too soon, else you will never enter into *your real rest*. It is not here on this plank amid the billows, but yonder on that shore. **GEORGE BOWEN**

Nothing ever happens but once in this world. What I do now I do once and forever. It is over, it is gone with a still eternity of solemn meaning.

May 21
MORNING
~∞~

I call to remembrance my song in the night (PS. 77:6).

I have read somewhere of a little bird that will never sing the melody his master wishes while his cage is full of light. He learns a snatch of this, a bar of that, but never an entire song of its own until the cage is covered and the morning beams shut out.

A good many people never learn to sing until the darkling shadows fall. The fabled nightingale carols with his breast against a thorn. It was in the night that the song of the angels was heard. It was at midnight that the cry came, "Behold, the bridegroom cometh; go ye out to meet him."

Indeed it is extremely doubtful if a soul can really know the love of God in its richness and in its comforting, satisfying completeness until the skies are black and lowering.

Light comes out of darkness, morning out of the womb of the night.

James Creelman, in one of his letters, describes his trip through the Balkan states in search of Natalie, the exiled queen of Serbia.

"In that memorable journey," he says, "I learned for the first time that the world's supply of attar of roses comes from the Balkan Mountains. And the thing that interested me most," he goes on, "is that the roses must be gathered in the darkest hours. The pickers start out at one o'clock and finish picking them at two.

"At first it seemed to me a relic of superstition; but I investigated the picturesque mystery, and learned that actual scientific tests had proven that fully forty percent of the fragrance of roses disappeared in the light of day."

And in human life and human culture that is not a playful, fanciful conceit; it is a real veritable fact. MALCOLM J. MCLEOD

EVENING

Make this valley full of ditches. (2 KINGS 3:16)

*D*o we say, "Lord, I want my life to be a channel through which Thy power may flow"? Then let the spade of His Word go down into the depths of your heart, that the hidden things may be revealed. Blessing must be prepared for. You can hinder it, and shirk it; you can shut your ears to His voice; or you can get alone with the Lord Jesus and let Him have His way. *God has a glorious work to do in every yielded life;* He has a glorious fullness to bestow. But there is also a work for *us* to do; there must be a digging down into the depths of our heart; we must resolve to get rid of all the rubbish, and to prepare for the living water.

H. EARNSHAW SMITH

Lord, spare nothing in me that would hinder the flowing of the rivers of water of life. Carry Thy cross to every root and corner of my most secret being.

Do you recall the bit of teaching brought out in connection with the river of the Sanctuary? *Waters to the ankles—waters to the knees—waters to the loins.* Afterward the prophet measured it again, and it was a *river! Waters to swim in!*

"Beware of paddling in the ocean of God's truth, when you should be out swimming!"

Go deeper into me, Lord Jesus;
Yes, deeper every day,
Till Thou hast conquered me, Lord Jesus;
Go deeper all the way.

Go deeper into me, Lord Jesus;
Search all the secret springs
Of thought and action, words and feelings,
Of great and little things.

Go deeper into me, Lord Jesus,
Cleanse all the hidden part,
Where pride, or touchiness, or temper,
May lurk within my heart.

Go deeper into me, Lord Jesus,
Till Thou canst really rise,
Out of the depths of this my being,
Through Thy great Sacrifice.

As Thou dost rise in me, Lord Jesus,
The life shall be Thine own,
Till o'er my humbled broken spirit
Thou reignest on Thy throne.

E. E. B. ROGERS

"We get no deeper into Christ than we allow Him to get into us."

May 22

MORNING

He worketh (PS. 37:5).

The translation that we find in Young of "Commit thy way unto the Lord; trust also in him; and he shall bring it to pass," reads: *"Roll upon Jehovah thy way; trust upon him: and he worketh."*

It calls our attention to the *immediate action of God when we truly commit, or roll out of our hands into His, the burden of whatever kind it may be; a way of sorrow, of difficulty, of physical need, or of anxiety for the conversion of some dear one.*

"He worketh." When? *Now.* We are so in danger of postponing our expectation of His *acceptance of the trust,* and His undertaking to accomplish what we ask Him to do, instead of saying *as we commit, "He worketh."* "He worketh" *even now;* and praise Him that it is so.

The very expectancy enables the Holy Spirit to do the very thing we have *rolled upon Him.* It is out of *our* reach. We are not *trying* to do it anymore. *"He worketh!"*

Let us take the comfort out of it and not put our hands on it again. Oh, what a relief it brings! *He is* really working on the difficulty.

But someone may say, "I see no results." Never mind. *"He worketh,"* if you have *rolled it over* and are looking to Jesus to do it. Faith may be tested, but *"He worketh";* the *Word is sure!*   V. H. F.

"I will cry unto God most high; unto God that performeth all things for me" (Ps. 57:2).

The beautiful old translation says, "He shall perform the cause which I have in hand." Does not that make it very real to us today? Just the very thing that "I have in hand"—my own particular bit of work today, this cause that I cannot manage, this thing that I undertook in miscalculation of my own powers—*this* is what I may ask Him to do "for me," and rest assured that He will perform it. "The wise and their works are in the hands of God."   HAVERGAL

The Lord will go through with His covenant engagements. Whatever He takes in hand He will accomplish; hence past mercies are guarantees for the future and admirable reasons for continuing to cry unto Him.

C. H. SPURGEON

EVENING

He giveth quietness. (JOB 34:29)

The calm sea says more to the thoughtful soul than the same sea in a storm and tumult. But we need the understanding of eternal things, and the sentiment of the Infinite to be able to feel this.

Napoleon, with his arms crossed over his breast, is more expressive than the furious Hercules beating the air with his athletic fists.

People of passionate temperament never understand this.

AMIEL'S JOURNEY

The lovely things are quiet things
Soft falling snow,
And feathers dropped from flying wings
Make no sound as they go.

A petal loosened from a rose,
Quietly seeks the ground,
And love, if lovely, when it goes,
Goes without sound.

The silent seasons of life are imperative. The winter is the mother of spring; the night is the fountain of the physical forces of the day; the silent soil is the womb where vegetable life is born. The greatest things in our spiritual life come out of our waiting hours, when all activity is suspended and the soul learns to be "silent unto God" while He shapes and molds us for future activities and fruitful years.

The greatest forces in nature are quiet ones. The law of gravitation is silent, yet invincible. So, back of all our activities and actions the law of faith is the mightiest force of the spiritual world, and mightiest when quietest and least demonstrative. When the soul is anchored to the will of God and His exceeding great and precious promises, with the calm unwavering confidence that His power and love are behind us and can never fail us until all His will for us is accomplished, *our life must be victorious.*

In the center of the whirlpool, while the waters rush around, There's a space of perfect stillness, though with turmoil it is bound: All is calm, and all is quiet, scarcely e'en a sense of sound. So with us—despite the conflict—when in Christ His Peace is found. There is no other real peace; how comparatively few know the secret. *God's noiseless workers own His calm control.*

NORA C. USHER

We need not be noisy if we are sure.

MARY E. SHANNON

At their wit's end, then they cry unto the Lord in their trouble, and he bringeth them out (PS. 107:27–28).

Are you standing at "Wit's End Corner,"
Christian, with troubled brow?
Are you thinking of what is before you,
And all you are bearing now?
Does all the world seem against you,
And you in the battle alone?
Remember—at "Wit's End Corner"
Is just where God's power is shown.

Are you standing at "Wit's End Corner,"
Blinded with wearying pain,
Feeling you cannot endure it,
You cannot bear the strain,
Bruised through the constant suffering,
Dizzy, and dazed, and numb?
Remember—at "Wit's End Corner"
Is where Jesus loves to come.

Are you standing at "Wit's End Corner"?
Your work before you spread,
All lying begun, unfinished,
And pressing on heart and head,
Longing for strength to do it,
Stretching out trembling hands?
Remember—at "Wit's End Corner"
The Burden-bearer stands.

Are you standing at "Wit's End Corner"?
Then you're just in the very spot
To learn the wondrous resources
Of Him who faileth not:
No doubt to a brighter pathway
Your footsteps will soon be moved,

But only at "Wit's End Corner"
Is the "God who is able" proved.
ANTOINETTE WILSON

Do not get discouraged; it may be the last key in the bunch that opens the door. STANSIFER

EVENING

⤬

*Though it tarry, wait for it; because it will surely come,
it will not tarry.* (HAB. 2:3)

Some things have their cycle in an hour and some in a century; but His plans shall complete their cycle whether long or short. The tender annual which blossoms for a season and dies, and the Columbian aloe which develops in a century, each is true to its normal principle. Many of us desire to pluck our fruit in June rather than wait until October, and so, of course, it is sour and immature; but God's purposes ripen slowly and fully, and faith waits while He tarries, knowing He will surely come and will not tarry too long.

It is perfect rest to fully learn and wholly trust this glorious promise. We may know without a question that His purposes shall be accomplished when we have fully committed our ways to Him, and are walking in watchful obedience to His every prompting. This faith will give a calm and tranquil poise to the spirit and save us from the restless fret of trying to do too much ourselves.

Wait, and every wrong will righten;
Wait, and every cloud will brighten,
If you will only wait.
A. B. SIMPSON

How much depends upon knowing when the time is exactly ripe! Not to interfere before the crisis arrives; not to let the opportunity pass when the crisis has arrived. This power of discernment, of patience, of promptitude, is a gift of superlative value.

Who knows the psychological moment like the Keeper of Israel? He does not interfere too soon; He allows the enemy rope enough to hang himself; He waits until His people know their weakness and peril, and are shut up to Him. He does not interpose too late; at the critical juncture He smites the pride of His people.

We see in nature how precisely God works by the clock; certainly He is not less exact in the times and seasons of human life. We often speak of "the hour and the man"; let us remember "the hour and the God."

May 24

MORAL

MORNING

᠅

For Sarah conceived and bare Abraham a son in his old age, at the set time of which God had spoken to him (GEN. 21:2).

"The counsel of the Lord standeth for ever, the thoughts of His heart to all generations" (Ps. 33:11). But we must be prepared to wait God's time. God has His *set times*. It is not for us to know them; indeed, we cannot know them; we must wait for them.

If God had told Abraham in Haran that he must wait for thirty years until he pressed the promised child to his bosom, his heart would have failed him. So, in gracious love, the length of the weary years was hidden, and only as they were nearly spent, and there were only a few more months to wait, God told him that "according to the time of life, Sarah shall have a son" (Gen. 18:14).

The *set time* came at last; and then the laughter that filled the patriarch's home made the aged pair forget the long and weary vigil.

Take heart, waiting one, thou waitest for One who cannot disappoint thee; and who will not be five minutes behind the appointed moment: ere long "your sorrow shall be turned into joy."

Ah, happy soul, when God makes thee laugh! Then sorrow and crying shall flee away forever, as darkness before the dawn.   SELECTED

It is not for us who are passengers, to meddle with the chart and with the compass. Let that all-skilled Pilot alone with His own work.   HALL

"Some things cannot be done in a day. God does not make a sunset glory in a moment, but for days may be massing the mist out of which He builds His palaces beautiful in the west."

> *Some glorious morn—but when? Ah, who shall say?*
> *The steepest mountain will become a plain,*
> *And the parched land be satisfied with rain.*
> *The gates of brass all broken; iron bars,*

Transfigured, form a ladder to the stars.
Rough places plain, and crooked ways all straight,
For him who with a patient heart can wait.
These things shall be on God's appointed day:
It may not be tomorrow—yet it may.

EVENING

⤬

And they departed into a desert place by ship privately.
(MARK 6:32)

If you have a desert place in your heart to which you must some times go, you should depart to it in a ship *privately. No man should make a thoroughfare of his desert.* Keep your grief for the private ship. Never go into company with an abstracted mind; that is to display your desert.

You have sometimes refrained from God's table of communion because your thoughts were away. You did well. Man's table of communion has the same need. If you are bidden to a feast when you are troubled in your mind, try first whether you can carry your burden privately away. If you can, then leave the desert behind you; *"anoint thine head, and wash thy face; that thou appear not unto men to fast."* But if you cannot, if there is no ship that can take away your burden in secret, then *come not yet* to the feast. Journey not while the cloud is resting over the tabernacle. Tarry under the cloud. Watch one hour in the garden. Bury thy sorrow in the silence. Let thy heart be reconciled to the Father, and then come to the world and offer thy gift.

Hide your thorn in the rose. Bury your sigh in the song. Keep your cross, if you will, but keep it hidden away under a wreath of flowers. Keep a singing heart!

O Thou that hast hid Thy thorn beneath a rose, steer the ship in which I conceal my burden! Thou hast gone down to the feast of Cana from the fast in the wilderness; where hast Thou hid the print of the nails? In love. Steer me to that burying ground! Let the ship on its way to my desert touch for an hour at the desert of my brother! Let me feel the fellowship of grief, the community of sorrow, the kindredness of pain! Let me hear the voices from other wildernesses, the sighs from other souls, the groans from other graves! And, when I come to my own landing-place and put down my hand to lift up my burden, I shall meet a wondrous surprise. *It will be there, but it will be there half-sized.* Its heaviness will be gone, its impossibility will have vanished. I shall lift it easily; I shall carry it lightly;

I shall bury it swiftly. I shall be ready for Cana in an hour, ready for Calvary in a few minutes. I shall go back to enter into the struggle of the multitude; and the multitude will say, *"There is no desert with him!"*

> *Give others the sunshine,*
> *Tell Jesus the rest.*
> **LEAVES FOR QUIET HOURS**

> *Lie down and sleep,*
> *Leave it with God to keep*
> *This sorrow which is part*
> *Now of thy heart.*
> *When thou dost wake*
> *If still 'tis thine to take,*
> *Utter no wild complaint,*
> *Work waits thy hand.*
> *If thou shouldst faint*
> *God understands.*

May 25
MORNING

I endure all things for the sake of God's own people;
so that they also may obtain salvation . . . and with it eternal glory
(2 TIM. 2:10 WEYMOUTH).

If Job could have known as he sat there in the ashes, bruising his heart on this problem of providence—that in the trouble that had come upon him he was doing what one man may do to work out the problem for the world, he might again have taken courage. No man lives to himself. Job's life is but your life and mine written in larger text. . . . So, then, though we may not know what trials wait on any of us, we can believe that, as the days in which Job wrestled with his dark maladies are the only days that make him worth remembrance, and but for which his name had never been written in the Book of Life, so the days through which we struggle, finding no way, but never losing the light, will be the most significant we are called to live.

ROBERT COLLYER

Who does not know that our most sorrowful days have been amongst our best? When the face is wreathed in smiles and we trip lightly over meadows bespangled with spring flowers, the heart is often running to waste.

The soul which is always blithe and gay misses the deepest life. It has its reward, and it is satisfied to its measure, though that measure is a very scanty one. But the heart is dwarfed; and the nature, which is capable of the highest heights, the deepest depths, is undeveloped; and life presently burns down to its socket without having known the resonance of the deepest chords of joy.

"Blessed are they that mourn." Stars shine brightest in the long dark night of winter. The gentians show their fairest bloom amid almost inaccessible heights of snow and ice.

God's promises seem to wait for the pressure of pain to trample out their richest juice as in a winepress. Only those who have sorrowed know how tender is the "Man of Sorrows." SELECTED

Thou hast but little sunshine, but thy long glooms are wisely appointed thee; for perhaps a stretch of summer weather would have made thee as a parched land and barren wilderness. Thy Lord knows best, and He has the clouds and the sun at His disposal. SELECTED

"It is a gray day." "Yes, but dinna ye see the patch of blue?"
SCOTCH SHOEMAKER

EVENING

Take root downward, and bear fruit upward. (ISA. 37:31)

Why is it that the mountain hemlocks can attain such stateliness in spite of fierce winter gales and crushing snows? If you look at one of them closely you will see that it has foliage almost as delicate as a fir, its dark needles being as dainty as fairy feathers. Yet if you try to break a twig or a bough you will learn that therein lies the strength and the tenacious power of the hemlock. It will bend and yield but it will not break. Winds may whip and toss it this way and that, but they cannot break it—nor can elements, however fierce, pull its roots out of the ground. For months it may have its graceful form held down by a mighty weight of snow, but when the warm breath of summer winds and the melting influence of summer's sun relieve it of its burden it straightens up as proud and as noble as it was before.

Beautiful, wonderful hemlock of the mountains—what a lesson you bring to us! Though we may be storm-tossed and bent by the winds of sorrow, we need not be crushed and broken *if our souls are anchored to the Rock of Ages.*

Lord, make me strong! Let my soul rooted be
Afar from vales of rest,
Flung close to heaven upon a great Rock's breast,
Unsheltered and alone, but strong in Thee.

What though the lashing tempests leave their scars?
Has not the Rock been bruised?
Mine, with the strength of ages deep infused,
To face the storms, and triumph with the stars!

Lord, plant my spirit high upon the crest
Of Thine eternal strength!
Then, though life's breaking struggles come at length,
Their storms shall only bend me to Thy breast.
DOROTHY CLARK WILSON

May 26

MORNING

Spring up, O well; sing ye unto it (NUM. 21:17).

This was a strange song and a strange well. They had been traveling over the desert's barren sands, no water was in sight and they were famishing with thirst. Then God spake to Moses and said:

"Gather the people together, and I will give them water," and this is how it came.

They gathered in circles on the sands. They took their staves and dug deep down into the burning earth and as they dug, they sang,

"Spring up, O well, sing ye unto it," and lo, there came a gurgling sound, a rush of water and a flowing stream which filled the well and ran along the ground.

When they dug this well in the desert, they touched the stream that was running beneath, and reached the flowing tides that had long been out of sight.

How beautiful the picture given, telling us of the river of blessing that flows all through our lives, and we have only to reach by *faith* and *praise* to find our wants supplied in the most barren desert.

How did they reach the waters of this well? It was by *praise*. They sang upon the sand their song of faith, while with their staff of promise they dug the well.

Our *praise* will still open fountains in the desert, when murmuring will only bring us judgment, and even prayer may fail to reach the fountains of blessing.

There is nothing that pleases the Lord so much as *praise*. There is no test of faith so true as the grace of thanksgiving. *Are you praising God enough?* Are you thanking Him for your actual blessings that are more than can be numbered, and are you daring to praise Him even for those trials which are but blessings in disguise? Have you learned to praise Him in advance for the things that have not yet come?   SELECTED

> *Thou waitest for deliverance!*
> *O soul, thou waitest long!*
> *Believe that now deliverance*
> *Doth wait for thee in song!*
>
> *Sigh not until deliverance*
> *Thy fettered feet doth free:*
> *With songs of glad deliverance*
> *God now doth compass thee.*

EVENING

I am the resurrection, and the life. (JOHN 11:25)

*B*ishop Foster was one of the leading bishops of the Methodist Church in his day, and was a very godly man. After an earnest search for thirty years he found what is here related in the hope that it may be a help to some other hearts who sought light as he did.

"I have perused all of the books written on the immortality of the soul, bought them at great prices, studied them with great earnestness. I have spent thirty years at it, hoping someday I might be able to present the argument with more force and make its impression stronger upon the mind and heart of the world.

"But when death came to my home and struck down my darlings, when I went and looked into their graves, I saw nothing but utter darkness. With an anguish I cannot express I went out into the deep woods, and looked up into the great vault above, and beat upon my breast and cried to my Father until my heart was crushed and broken. In speechless silence I lay with my face upon the earth to see if I could not hear Him; but I found that it was dark and silent; not a ray, not a voice.

"I went and sat down by the philosophers, but now I found they gave me nothing but husks. I read their arguments which once had cheered me, but now they broke my heart. There was nothing in them, not even enough for me to found a conjecture upon. I was desolate with an utter desolation. I wrung my hands in an agony I cannot describe.

"Nor did I find relief until I heard a Voice coming through the gloom. Out of the darkness and silence, with heavenly music and sweetness in it, it said:

> *I am Jesus, the resurrection and the*
> *life; and thy dead shall live again.*

"And with that single idea that I could rest my hope and my faith upon, He has revealed that great doctrine; He has established the truth which ever eluded mankind till He came down out of heaven telling the story of the Fatherhood of God and the immortality of His own spiritual children."

> *I know not how that Bethlehem's Babe*
> *Could in the Godhead be:*
> *I only know the Manger Child*
> *Has brought God's life to me.*

> *I know not how that Calvary's Cross*
> *A world from sin could free:*
> *I only know its matchless love*
> *Has brought God's love to me.*

> *I know not how that Joseph's tomb*
> *Could solve death's mystery:*
> *I only know a living Christ,*
> *Our immortality.*
>
> MAJOR HARRY W. FARRINGTON

May 27

Bring them hither to me (MATT. 14:18).

*A*re you encompassed with needs at this very moment, and almost overwhelmed with difficulties, trials, and emergencies? These are all divinely provided vessels for the Holy Spirit to fill, and if you but rightly understood their meaning, they would become opportunities for receiving new blessings and deliverances which you can get in no other way.

Bring these vessels to God. Hold them steadily before Him in faith and prayer. Keep still, and stop your own restless working until He begins to work. Do nothing that He does not Himself command you to do. Give Him a chance to work, and He will surely do so; and the very trials that threatened to overcome you with discouragement and disaster, will become God's opportunity for the revelation of His grace and glory in your life, as you have never known Him before. "Bring them *[all needs]* to me."

A. B. SIMPSON

"My God shall supply all your need according to his riches in glory by Christ Jesus" (Phil. 4:19).

What a source—"God!" What a supply—"His riches in glory!" What a channel—"Christ Jesus!" It is your sweet privilege to place *all your need* over against *His riches,* and lose sight of the former in the presence of the latter. His exhaustless treasury is thrown open to you, in all the love of His heart; go and draw upon it, in the artless simplicity of faith, and you will never have occasion to look to a creature-stream, or lean on a creature-prop.

C. H. M.

MY CUP RUNNETH OVER

There is always something over,
When we trust our gracious Lord;
Every cup He fills o'erfloweth,
His great rivers all are broad.

Nothing narrow, nothing stinted,
Ever issues from His store;
To His own He gives full measure,
Running over, evermore.

There is always something over,
When we, from the Father's hand,
Take our portion with thanksgiving,
Praising for the path He planned.

Satisfaction, full and deepening,
Fills the soul, and lights the eye,
When the heart has trusted Jesus
All its need to satisfy.

There is always something over,
When we tell of all His love;
Unplumbed depths still lie beneath us,
Unscaled heights rise far above:

Human lips can never utter
All His wondrous tenderness,
We can only praise and wonder,
And His name forever bless.
MARGARET E. BARBER

"How can He but, in giving Him, lavish on us all things" (Rom. 8:32).

EVIL EVENING

EVENING

I rejoice at thy word, as one that findeth great spoil. (PS. 119:162)

It has pleased the Lord to teach me a truth, the benefit of which I have not lost for more than fourteen years. The point is this: I saw more clearly than ever that the first great and primary business to which I ought to attend every day was *to have my soul happy in the Lord.*

The first thing to be concerned about was not how much I might serve the Lord; but how I might get my soul in a happy state, and how my inner man might be nourished. For I might seek to set the truth before the unconverted, I might seek to benefit believers, I might seek to relieve the distressed, I might in other ways seek to behave myself as it becomes a child of God in this world; and yet, not being happy in the Lord and not being strengthened in my inner man day by day, all this might not be attended to in the right spirit. Before this time my practice had been, at least for ten years previously, as an habitual thing to give myself to prayer after having dressed myself in the morning. Now I saw that the most important thing I had to do was *to give myself to the reading of the Word of God, and to meditate on it,* that thus my heart might be comforted, encouraged, warmed, reproved, instructed; and that thus, by means of the Word of God, whilst meditating on it, my heart might be brought into experimental communion with the Lord.

I began therefore to meditate on the New Testament from the beginning, early in the morning. The first thing I did, after having asked in a few words the Lord's blessing upon His precious Word, was to begin to meditate on the Word of God, searching as it were every verse to get a blessing out of it, not for the sake of the public ministry of the Word, not for the sake of preaching upon what I had meditated upon, but *for obtaining food for my own soul.*

The result I have found to be almost invariably this, that after a few minutes my soul has been led to confession, or to thanksgiving, or to intercession, or to supplication; so that, though I did not as it were give myself to prayer, but to meditation, yet it turned almost immediately more or less into prayer. When thus I have been for a while making confession or intercession or supplication, or have given thanks, I go on to the next words or verse, turning all as I go on into prayer for myself or others as the Word may lead to it, but still continually keeping before me that *food for my own soul is the object of my meditation.*

Formerly I often spent a quarter of an hour, or half an hour, or even an hour on my knees, before being conscious of having derived comfort, encouragement, humbling of soul, etcetera and often, after having suffered much from wandering of mind for the first ten minutes, or a quarter of an hour, or even half an hour, I only then began to really pray. I scarcely ever suffer now in this way; for my heart being nourished by the truth, being brought into experimental fellowship with God, I speak to my Father and to my Friend (vile though I am and unworthy) about the things that He has brought before me in His precious Word. It often now astonishes me that I did not sooner see this point.

> *Take the golden key, He calleth thee.*
> *Enter into the holy place.*
> GEORGE MÜLLER'S SECRET

Do you know this secret?

May 28

MORNING

~∽~

I will not let thee go, except thou bless me . . .
and he blessed him there (GEN. 32:26, 29).

*J*acob got the victory and the blessing not by wrestling, *but by cling-*
ing. His limb was out of joint and he could struggle no longer, but
he would not let go. Unable to wrestle, he wound his arms around the
neck of his mysterious antagonist and hung all his helpless weight upon
him, until at last he conquered.

We will not get victory in prayer until we too cease our struggling, giving up our own will, and throw our arms about our Father's neck in clinging faith.

What can puny human strength take by force out of the hand of
omnipotence? Can we wrest blessing by force from God? It is never the
violence of willfulness that prevails with God. It is the might of clinging
faith, that gets the blessing and the victories. It is not when we press and
urge our own will, but when humility and trust unite in saying, "Not my
will, but Thine." We are strong with God only in the degree that self is
conquered and is dead. Not by wrestling, but by clinging can we get the
blessing.   J. R. MILLER

An incident from the prayer life of Charles H. Usher (illustrating
"soul-cling" as a hindrance to prevailing prayer): "My little boy was very
ill. The doctors held out little hope of his recovery. I had used all the
knowledge of prayer which I possessed on his behalf, but he got worse
and worse. This went on for several weeks.

"One day I stood watching him as he lay in his cot, and I saw that he
could not live long unless he had a turn for the better. I said to God, 'O
God, I have given much time in prayer for my boy and he gets no better; I
must now leave him to Thee, and I will give myself to prayer for others. If it
is Thy will to take him, I choose Thy will—I surrender him entirely to Thee.'

"I called in my dear wife, and told her what I had done. She shed some
tears, but handed him over to God. Two days afterward a man of God
came to see us. He had been very interested in our boy Frank, and had
been much in prayer for him.

"He said, 'God has given me faith to believe that he will recover—have
you faith?'

"I said, 'I have surrendered him to God, but I will go again to God regarding him.' I did; and in prayer I discovered that I had faith for his recovery. From that time he began to get better. It was the *'soul-cling'* in my prayers which had hindered God answering; and if I had continued to cling and had been unwilling to surrender him, I doubt if my boy would be with me today.

"Child of God! If you want God to answer your prayers, you must be prepared to follow the footsteps of 'our father Abraham,' even to the Mount of Sacrifice." (*See* Rom. 4:12.)

EVENING

In a great trial of affliction, the abundance of their joy and their deep poverty abounded unto the riches of their liberality. (2 COR. 8:2)

Joy is not gush; Joy is not jolliness. Joy is simply perfect acquiescence in God's will, because the soul delights itself in God Himself. "I delight to do thy will," said Jesus, though the cup was the Cross, in such agony as no man knew. *It cost Him blood.* Oh, take the Fatherhood of God in the blessed Son the Savior, and by the Holy Ghost; rejoice in the will of God, and nothing else. Bow down your heads and your hearts before God, and let the will, the blessed will of God, be done.

PREBENDARY WEBB-PEPLOE

"Joy and deep poverty!" Truly strange blending.
Fullness and emptiness! Contrasting themes.
Spiritual richness and temporal leanness!
None but the Spirit could wed such extremes.

"Joy and deep poverty!" Servant of Jesus,
Doth it perplex that thy portion is this?
Doth it offend that reward for thy faithfulness
Seemeth to lie much in things thou must miss?

"Joy and deep poverty!" Pause thee, and ponder!
Joy for thy spirit—the world cannot give;
If therewith leanness—extreme limitation—
Mayhap 'tis by e'en such need thou shalt LIVE!

J. DANSON SMITH

One of the happiest men who ever lived—
Saint Francis de Assisi—was one of the poorest.

May 29

MORNING

჻

I have called you friends (JOHN 15:15).

*Y*ears ago there was an old German professor whose beautiful life was a marvel to his students. Some of them resolved to know the secret of it; so one of their number hid in the study where the old professor spent his evenings.

It was late when the teacher came in. He was very tired, but he sat down and spent an hour with his Bible. Then he bowed his head in secret prayer; and finally closing the Book of books, he said.

"Well, Lord Jesus, we're on the same old terms."

To *know Him* is life's highest attainment; and at all costs, every Christian should strive to be "on the same old terms with Him."

The reality of Jesus comes as a result of secret prayer, and a personal study of the Bible that is devotional and sympathetic. Christ becomes more real to the one who persists in the cultivation of His presence.

> *Speak thou to Him for He heareth,*
> *And spirit with spirit will meet!*
> *Nearer is He than breathing,*
> *Nearer than hands and feet.*
> MALTBIE D. BABCOCK

EVENING

჻

And there stood no man with him,
while Joseph made himself known. (GEN. 45:1)

In the secret places of the stairs, let me see thy countenance,
let me hear thy voice; for sweet is thy voice. (SONG 2:14)

*T*here are feelings and experiences too tender and too sacred for the public gaze. Joseph could not reveal himself to his brethren in the face of the Egyptian Court. The stranger could not be allowed to intermeddle with the demonstration of his love.

It is so with Christ's revelation of Himself to the human soul. Not in the busy marketplace, not in the social circle, not even in the crowded sanctuary do we come into the closest touch with the heart of our Elder Brother and our Friend. In the hour of silent communion, when the door is shut; when the world is excluded; in the hush of breathless and holy silence there comes to us the fullest apocalypse of the Divine affection. It is then that we see with clearest vision the glory of the face of Christ, and hear most distinctly the melody of the Divine voice as it tells to us the story of His love.

No public feast with Him can compensate for the loss of the private interview.

Make time to be alone with God. He has visions to reveal to us that are not for the eye of the worldling. *Alone with God*—to know the depth and sweetness of our relationship to Him!

> *Precious, gentle, holy Jesus!*
> *Blessed Bridegroom of my heart,*
> *In Thy secret inner chamber*
> *Thou wilt whisper what Thou art.*

A calm hour with God is worth a whole lifetime with man.

ROBERT MURRAY MCCHEYNE

May 30

MORNING

❧

And no man could learn that song but the hundred and forty and four thousand, which were redeemed from the earth (REV. 14:3).

There are songs which can only be learned in the valley. No art can teach them; no rules of voice can make them perfectly sung. Their music is in the heart. They are songs of memory, of personal experience. They bring out their burden from the shadow of the past; they mount on the wings of yesterday.

Saint John says that even in heaven there will be a song that can only be fully sung by the sons of earth—the strain of redemption. Doubtless it is a song of triumph, a hymn of victory to the Christ who made us free. But the sense of triumph must come from the memory of the chain.

No angel, no archangel can sing it so sweetly as I can. To sing it as I sing it, they must pass through my exile, and this they cannot do. None can learn it but the children of the cross.

And so, my soul, thou art receiving a music lesson from thy Father. Thou art being educated for the choir invisible. There are parts of the symphony that none can take but thee.

There are chords too minor for the angels. There may be heights in the symphony which are beyond the scale—heights which angels alone can reach; but there are depths which belong to *thee*, and can only be touched by thee.

Thy Father is training thee for the part the angels cannot sing; and the school is sorrow. I have heard many say that He sends sorrow to *prove* thee; nay, He sends sorrow to *educate* thee, to train thee for the choir invisible.

In the night He is preparing thy song. In the valley He is tuning thy voice. In the cloud He is deepening thy chords. In the rain He is sweetening thy melody. In the cold He is molding thy expression. In the transition from hope to fear He is perfecting thy lights.

Despise not thy school of sorrow, O my soul; it will give thee a unique part in the universal song.　　　　　　　　GEORGE MATHESON

> *Is the midnight closing round you?*
> *Are the shadows dark and long?*
> *Ask Him to come close beside you,*
> *And He'll give you a new, sweet song.*
> *He'll give it and sing it with you;*
> *And when weakness lets it down,*
> *He'll take up the broken cadence,*
> *And blend it with His own.*
>
> *And many a rapturous minstrel*
> *Among those sons of light,*
> *Will say of His sweetest music*
> *"I learned it in the night."*
> *And many a rolling anthem,*
> *That fills the Father's home,*
> *Sobbed out its first rehearsal,*
> *In the shade of a darkened room.*

EVENING

I have finished my course. (2 TIM. 4:7)

There is a course prepared for each believer from the moment of his new birth, providing for the fullest maturity of the new life within him, and the highest which God can make of his life in the use of every faculty for His service. To discover that *course* and fulfill it is the one duty of every soul. Others cannot judge what that course is; God alone knows it. And God can just as certainly make known and guide the believer into that course today, as He did with Jeremiah and other prophets, Paul and Timothy and other apostles.   J. P. L.

> *Why do I drift on a storm-tossed sea,*
> *With neither compass, nor star, nor chart,*
> *When, as I drift, God's own plan for me*
> *Waits at the door of my slow-trusting heart?*
>
> *Down from the heavens it drops like a scroll,*
> *Each day a bit will the Master unroll,*
> *Each day a mite of the veil will He lift.*
> *Why do I falter? Why wander, and drift?*
>
> *Drifting, while God's at the helm to steer;*
> *Groping, when God lays the course so clear;*
> *Swerving, though straight into port I might sail;*
> *Wrecking, when heaven lies just within hail.*
>
> *Help me, O God, in the plan to believe;*
> *Help me my fragment each day to receive.*
> *Oh, that my will may with Thine have no strife!*
> *God-yielded wills find the God-planned life.*
>   JAMES H. MCCONKEY

Allow God to carry out His plans for you without anxiety or interference.

May 31
MORNING

Like a shock of corn fully ripe (JOB 5:26).

A gentleman writing about the breaking up of old ships recently said that it is not the age alone which improves the quality of the fiber in the wood of an old vessel, but the straining and wrenching of the vessel by the sea, the chemical action of the bilge water, and of many kinds of cargoes.

Some planks and veneers made from an oak beam which had been part of a ship eighty years old were exhibited a few years ago at a fashionable furniture store on Broadway, New York, and attracted general notice for the exquisite coloring and beautiful grain.

Equally striking were some beams of mahogany taken from a bark which sailed the seas sixty years ago. The years and the traffic had contracted the pores and deepened the color, until it looked as superb in its chromatic intensity as an antique Chinese vase. It was made into a cabinet, and has today a place of honor in the drawing room of a wealthy New York family.

So there is a vast difference between the quality of old people who have lived flabby, self-indulgent, useless lives, and the fiber of those who have sailed all seas and carried all cargoes as the servants of God and the helpers of their fellowmen.

Not only the wrenching and straining of life, but also something of the sweetness of the cargoes carried get into the very pores of fiber of character. LOUIS ALBERT BANKS

When the sun goes below the horizon he is not set; the heavens glow for a full hour after his departure. And when a great and good man sets, the sky of this world is luminous long after he is out of sight. Such a man cannot die out of this world. When he goes he leaves behind him much of himself. Being dead, he speaks. BEECHER

When Victor Hugo was past eighty years of age he gave expression to his religious faith in these sublime sentences: "I feel in myself the future life. I am like a forest which has been more than once cut down. The new shoots are livelier than ever. I am rising toward the sky. The sunshine is on my head. The earth gives me its generous sap, but heaven lights me with its unknown worlds.

"You say the soul is nothing but the resultant of the bodily powers. Why, then, is my soul more luminous when my bodily powers begin to fail? Winter is on my head, but eternal spring is in my heart. I breathe at this hour the fragrance of the lilacs, the violets, and the roses as at twenty years. The nearer I approach the end the plainer I hear around me the immortal symphonies of the worlds which invite me. It is marvelous, yet simple."

❦

*There came a woman having an alabaster box of ointment of
spikenard very precious; and she brake the box,
and poured it on his head.* (MARK 14:3)

The very nature of God is extravagance. How many sunrises and sunsets does God make?

> *Gloriously wasteful, O my Lord, art Thou!*
> *Sunset faints after sunset into the night . . .*

How many flowers and birds, how many ineffable beauties all over the world, lavish desert blossoms that only His eyes see?

Mary's act was one of spontaneous extravagance. Mary of Bethany revealed in her act of extravagant devotion, that the unconscious sympathy of her life was with Jesus Christ. "She hath done what she could"— to the absolute limit of what a human can do. It was impossible to do more. The only thing that Jesus Christ ever commended was this act of Mary's, and He said: "Wheresoever this gospel shall be preached throughout the whole world, that also which this woman hath done shall be spoken of for a memorial of her," because in the anointing our Lord saw an exact illustration of what He, Himself, was about to do. He put Mary's act alongside His own Cross. God shattered the life of His own Son to save the world. *Are we prepared to pour out our lives for Him?* Our Lord is carried beyond Himself with joy when He sees any of us doing what Mary of Bethany did. *Have I ever produced in the heart of the Lord Jesus what Mary of Bethany produced?* "She hath done what she could"— to the absolute limit. *I have not done what I could until I have done the same.*

OSWALD CHAMBERS

Is the precious ointment poured on the feet of the Master ever wasted? Eternity will answer the question. GOLD CORD

> *The only way to keep a thing is to throw it away!*
> *Seeds which mildew in the garner*
> *Scattered, fill with gold the plain.*
> *To keep your treasure is to die—to lose it is to live—*
> *The angels keep the records in God's countinghouse—so give!*
> PATIENCE STRONG

June 1

∽◯∽

This is the rest wherewith ye may cause the weary to rest;
and this is the refreshing (ISA. 28:12).

*W*hy dost thou worry thyself? What use can thy fretting serve? Thou art on board a vessel which thou couldst not steer even if the great Captain put thee at the helm, of which thou couldst not so much as reef a sail, yet thou worriest as if thou wert captain and helmsman. Oh, be quiet; God is Master!

Dost thou think that all this din and hurly-burly that is abroad betokens that God has left His throne?

No, man, His coursers rush furiously on, and His chariot is the storm; but there is a bit between their jaws, and He holds the reins, and guides them as He wills! Jehovah is Master yet; believe it; peace be unto thee! be not afraid.

C. H. SPURGEON

> *Tonight, my soul, be still and sleep;*
> *The storms are raging on God's deep—*
> *God's deep, not thine; be still and sleep.*
>
> *Tonight, my soul, be still and sleep;*
> *God's hands shall still the tempter's sweep—*
> *God's hands, not thine; be still and sleep.*
>
> *Tonight, my soul, be still and sleep;*
> *God's love is strong while night hours creep—*
> *God's love, not thine; be still and sleep.*
>
> *Tonight, my soul, be still and sleep;*
> *God's heaven will comfort those who weep—*
> *God's heaven, not thine; be still and sleep.*

I entreat you, give no place to despondency. This is a dangerous temptation—a refined, not a gross temptation of the adversary. Melancholy contracts and withers the heart, and renders it unfit to receive the impressions of grace. It magnifies and gives a false coloring of objects, and thus renders your burdens too heavy to bear. God's designs regarding you, and His methods of bringing about these designs, are infinitely wise.

MADAME GUYON

〜❦〜

Pray without ceasing. (1 THESS. 5:17)

*I*s it hypocritical to pray when we don't feel like it?

Perhaps there is no more subtle hindrance to prayer than that of our *moods*. Nearly everybody has to meet that difficulty at times. Even God's prophets were not wholly free from it. Habakkuk felt as if he were facing a blank wall for a long time. What shall we do when moods like this come to *us*? Wait until we *do feel like* praying? It is easy to persuade ourselves that it is hypocrisy to pray when we do not feel like it; but we don't argue that way about other things in life. If you were in a room that had been tightly closed for some time you would, sooner or later, begin to feel very miserable—so miserable, perhaps, that you would not want to make the effort to open the windows, especially if they were difficult to open. But your weakness and listlessness would be proof that you were beginning to need fresh air very desperately—that you would soon be ill without it.

If the soul *perseveres* in a life of prayer, there will come a time when *these seasons of dryness will pass away and the soul will be led out*, as Daniel says, *"into a large place"* (margin "into a *moist* place"). Let nothing discourage you. If the soil is dry, *keep cultivating it*. It is said, that in a dry time this harrowing of the corn is equal to a shower of rain.

When we are listless about prayer *it is the very time when we need most to pray*. The only way we can overcome listlessness in anything is to put more of ourselves, not less, into the task. To pray when you do not feel like praying *is not hypocrisy*—it is faithfulness to the greatest duty of life. Just *tell the Father* that you don't feel like it—ask Him to show you what is making you listless. *He will help us to overcome our moods,* and give us courage to persevere in spite of them.

"When you cannot pray as you would, pray as you can."

If I feel myself disinclined to pray, then is the time when I need to pray more than ever. Possibly when the soul leaps and exults in communion with God it might more safely refrain from prayer than at those seasons when it drags heavily in devotion. CHARLES H. SPURGEON

June 2

❧

For Abraham, when hope was gone, hoped on in faith.
His faith never quailed (ROM. 4:18, 19).

We shall never forget a remark that George Mueller once made to a gentleman who had asked him the best way to have strong faith.

"The *only* way," replied the patriarch of faith, "to learn strong faith is to endure great trials. I have learned my faith by standing firm amid severe testings." This is very true. *The time to trust is when all else fails.*

Dear one, you scarcely realize the value of your present opportunity; if you are passing through great afflictions you are in the very soul of the strongest faith, and if you will only let go, He will teach you in these hours the mightiest hold upon His throne which you can ever know.

"Be not afraid, only believe." And if you are afraid, just look up and say, "What time I am afraid I will trust in thee," and you will yet thank God for the school of sorrow which was to you the school of faith.

A. B. SIMPSON

"Great faith must have great trials."

"God's greatest gifts come through travail. Whether we look into the spiritual or temporal sphere, can we discover anything, any great reform, any beneficent discovery, any soul-awakening revival, which did not come through the toils and tears, the vigils and blood-shedding of men and women whose sufferings were the pangs of its birth? If the temple of God is raised, David must bear sore afflictions; if the gospel of the grace of God is to be disentangled from Jewish tradition, Paul's life must be one long agony."

Take heart, O weary, burdened one, bowed down
Beneath thy cross;
Remember that thy greatest gain may come
Through greatest loss.
Thy life is nobler for a sacrifice,
And more divine.
Acres of bloom are crushed to make a drop
Of perfume fine.

Because of storms that lash the ocean waves,
The waters there

Keep purer than if the heavens o'erhead
Were always fair.
The brightest banner of the skies floats not
At noonday warm;
The rainbow traileth after thunder-clouds,
And after storm.

EVENING

Unload on Him all your cares. (1 PETER 5:7, FRENCH)

Hurling all your care upon him. (GREEK)

Who among us has not occasionally experienced anxiety? And yet the Bible clearly prohibits it, and as clearly provides an unfailing remedy: *"Blessed is the man who trusteth in Jehovah, and whose confidence Jehovah is; for he shall be like a tree . . . which stretcheth forth its roots by the water course, so that it shall not fear when heat cometh, but its leaf shall be verdant; which is not uneasy in the year of drought."*   SPURRELL

Not uneasy! Not uneasy in the year of drought—in a time of spiritual darkness. Not uneasy about spiritual supplies; not uneasy concerning temporal supplies—food or raiment; not uneasy concerning our lip witness—how, or what to say. Then what is there left about which we may be anxious? Nothing. For the Lord went on to say, *"Why take ye thought for the rest?"* And Paul further says, *"Be careful for nothing,"* or, *"In nothing be anxious."* And again, Peter says, *"Do not begin to be anxious."*

Anxiety is therefore prohibited in the Bible. But how is it to be prevented? By hurling all your care or worry upon Him, *because with Him there is care about you.*

Blessed is the man who is not *uneasy!*   APHRA WHITE

June 3

❧

Let us pass over unto the other side (MARK 4:35).

Even when we go forth at Christ's command, we need not expect to escape storms; for these disciples were going forth at Christ's command, yet they encountered the fiercest storm and were in great danger of being overwhelmed, so that they cried out in their distress for Christ's assistance.

Though Christ may delay His coming in our time of distress, it is only that our faith may be tried and strengthened, and that our prayers may be more intense, and that our desires for deliverance may be increased, so that when the deliverance does come we will appreciate it more fully.

Christ gave them a gentle rebuke, saying, "Where is your faith?" Why did you not shout victory in the very face of the storm, and say to the raging winds and rolling waves, "You can do no harm, for Christ, the mighty Savior is on board"?

It is much easier to trust when the sun is shining than when the storm is raging.

We never know how much real faith we have until it is put to the test in some fierce storm; and that is the reason why the Savior is on board.

If you are ever to be strong in the Lord and the power of His might, your strength will be born in some storm.　　**SELECTED**

With Christ in the vessel,
I smile at the storm.

Christ said, "Let us go to the other side"—not to the middle of the lake to be drowned.　　**DAN CRAWFORD**

❧

Though the root thereof wax old in the earth, and the stock thereof die in the ground; yet through the scent of water it will bud, and bring forth boughs like a plant. (JOB 14:8–9)

My root was spread out by the waters, and the dew lay all night upon my branch. My glory was fresh in me, and my bow was renewed in my hand. (JOB 29:19–20)

Once there was an oak tree that clung to a crag on a mountainside. The wind swept its crest, and the snows and rains tore at its soil. Its roots ran along a pathway and were trampled by the feet of men. But the rain and the snows ran down the mountain, and the oak tree was dying of drought. Patiently and persistently its underground tendrils had gone forth in every direction for relief. All its power was put into the quest by which it would save its life. And, by and by, the roots reached the mountain spring. The faithful stream that touched the lips of man and beast ran up the trunk and laved the branches and gave new life to the utmost twig. The tree stood in the same place; it met the same storms; it was trodden by the same hurrying feet. *But it was planted by the rivers of water and its leaf could not wither.* Out into the same old life *you* must go today as ever, but *down underneath you can be nourished by the everlasting streams of God.*

Travelers returning from Palestine report that beneath the streets of Shechem there are rivers flowing. During the daytime it is impossible to hear the murmuring of the waters because of the noise. But when night comes and the clamor dies away, then can be heard the music of the hidden rivers.

Are there not "hidden rivers" flowing under the crowded streets of our twentieth-century life? If we can be assured that there is still the music of deep-flowing waters beneath all the noise and tumult of the working hours, we can walk the way of the conqueror.

Keep your roots deep in the living waters.

June 4

MORNING

❧

The Lord caused the sea to go back . . . all that night (EXOD. 14:21).

In this verse there is a comforting message showing how God works in the dark. The real work of God for the children of Israel was not when they awakened and found that they could get over the Red Sea; but it was *"all that night."*

So there may be a great working in your life when it all seems dark and you cannot see or trace, but yet God is working. Just as truly did He work "all that night," as all the next day. The next day simply manifested what God had done during the night. Is there anyone reading these lines who may have gotten to a place where it seems dark? You believe to see, but you are not seeing. In your life-progress there is not constant victory; the daily, undisturbed communion is not there, and all seems dark.

"The Lord caused the sea to go back . . . all that night." Do not forget that it was *"all that night."* God works all the night, until the light comes. You may not see it, but all that *"night"* in your life, as you believe God, He works.　　　　　　　　　　　　　　　　　　　　C. H. P.

> *"All that night" the Lord was working,*
> *Working in the tempest blast,*
> *Working with the swelling current,*
> *Flooding, flowing, free and fast.*
>
> *"All that night" God's children waited—*
> *Hearts, perhaps in agony—*
> *With the enemy behind them,*
> *And, in front, the cruel sea.*
>
> *"All that night" seemed blacker darkness*
> *Than they ever saw before,*
> *Though the light of God's own presence*
> *Near them was, and sheltered o'er.*
>
> *"All that night" that weary vigil*
> *Passed; the day at last did break,*
> *And they saw that God was working*
> *"All that night" a path to make.*

EVENING

The hand of the LORD was there upon him. (EZEK. 1:3)

*B*ones cannot be quickened into life by manipulation. Only the touch of God can give them life.

Some of us must be taught this by bitter experiences of failure. So writes Dr. A. C. Dixon.

"While I was pastor of the Baptist Church in Chapel Hill, the university town of North Carolina, I was made to realize that, as a preacher, I was a dismal failure. Parents all over the state wrote me and requested that I look after the spiritual welfare of their sons in the university. I prepared sermons with the students in mind, and was glad to see that they showed their appreciation by attending our Sunday services in large numbers. We appointed a week of prayer and preaching with the single purpose of winning them to Christ, and they attended the evening meetings.

"About the middle of the week their interest seemed to turn into opposition; the spirit of mischief possessed them—one night they tried to put out the lights. As I walked through the grove around the university buildings, I sometimes heard my voice coming from behind a tree: a bright student had caught a part of my sermon the night before, and he was giving it in thought and tone for the benefit of his fellow students, who showed their appreciation by applause and laughter. As I walked before an open window I heard my voice in prayer floating out. I felt I was defeated and was seriously considering resigning the pastorate. No one had been saved.

"After a restless night I took my Bible and went into the grove and remained there until three o'clock in the afternoon. As I read I asked God to show me what was the matter, and the Word of God searched me through and through giving me a deep sense of sin and helplessness, such as I had never had before.

"That evening the students listened reverently, and at the close two pews were filled with those who had responded to the invitation. The revival continued day after day until more than seventy of the students had confessed Christ.

"Now the practical question is *what did it?* Certainly not I; I fear it was the *I* that kept God from doing it for a long time. There came to me out of the day's experience a clear-cut distinction between influence and power. Influence is made up of many things: intellect, education, money, social position, personality, organization—all of which ought to be used for Christ. Power is God Himself at work *unhindered by our unbelief and other sins.*

"The word *influence* occurs but once in the Bible, and that in Job where Jehovah speaks to the old patriarch of *the sweet influences of the Pleiades*—a good text for a young minister to preach on in the springtime, but not sufficient in dealing with a group of mocking university students.

"The New Testament word *power* holds the secret, and *the power from on high* was no other than God the Holy Spirit *touching the soul through the living word, and giving it a birth from above.*

"I had been trusting and testing many other good things, only to fail; *the touch of God* did in a minute what my best efforts could not do."

June 5

MORNING

◦⤜∽⤛◦

Make thy petition deep (ISA. 7:11, MARGIN).

Make thy petition deep, O heart of mine,
Thy God can do much more
Than thou canst ask;
Launch out on the Divine,
Draw from His love-filled store.
Trust Him with everything;
Begin today,
And find the joy that comes
When Jesus has His way!
SELECTED

We must keep on *praying* and *waiting* upon the Lord, until the sound of a mighty rain is heard. There is no reason why we should not ask for large things; and without doubt we shall get large things if we ask in faith, and have the courage to wait with patient perseverance upon Him, meantime doing those things which lie within our power to do.

We cannot create the wind or set it in motion, but we can set our sails to catch it when it comes; we cannot make the electricity, but we can stretch the wire along upon which it is to run and do its work; we cannot, in a word, control the Spirit, but we can so place ourselves before the Lord, and so do the things He has bidden us do, that we will come under the influence and power of His mighty breath.   SELECTED

"Cannot the same wonders be done now as of old? Where is the God of Elijah? He is *waiting* for Elijah to call on Him."

The greatest saints who ever lived, whether under the old or new dispensation, are on a level which is quite within our reach. The same forces of the spiritual world which were at their command, and the exertion of which made them such spiritual heroes, are open to us also. If we had the same faith, the same hope, the same love which they exhibited, we would achieve marvels as great as those which they achieved. A word of prayer in our mouths would be as potent to call down the gracious dews and melting fires of God's Spirit, as it was in Elijah's mouth to call down literal rain and fire, if we could only speak the word with that full assurance of faith wherewith he said it.   DR. GOULBURN, DEAN OF NORWICH

EVENING

❧

And God heard their groaning, and God remembered his covenant with Abraham, with Isaac, and with Jacob. (EX. 2:24)

God always hears, and He never forgets. His silence does not mean that He is not listening and is not planning. Probably it means that the best time of deliverance has not come yet, and that He is patiently waiting for the moment to arrive when He may prove His love and His power.

Cromwell said to his soldiers just before a great battle: "Know ye soldiers all, that *God always comes to man's help in the nick of time.*"

Yes, God is always *on time; never behind* and *never ahead.* Happy the man who learns *to wait as he prays,* and never loses patience with God.

MEN WHO PRAYED

There is a set time for putting into the furnace, and a set time for taking out of the furnace.

There is a time for pruning the branches of the vine, and there is a time when the husbandman lays aside the pruning hook.

Let us wait His time; "He that believeth shall not make haste." God's time is the best time. But shall we come out the same as we went in? Ah, no! We "shall come forth as gold." We shall become purer vessels to hold the sweet-smelling incense of praise and prayer. We shall become holy golden vessels for the Master's use in time and in Eternity.

"When a great issue is in the balance and the path is obscure, wait; but with that waiting shirk not the work that lieth before thee, for *in that task may be the solution of thy problem.*"

God will justify you before the universe in His own time.

OTTO STOCKMAYER

June 6

MORNING

〜

Watch unto prayer (1 PETER 4:7).

Go not, my friend, into the dangerous world without prayer. You kneel down at night to pray, drowsiness weighs down your eyelids; a hard day's work is a kind of excuse, and you shorten your prayer, and resign yourself softly to repose. The morning breaks; and it may be you rise late, and so your early devotions are not done, or are done with irregular haste.

No watching unto prayer! Wakefulness once more omitted; and now is that reparable? We solemnly believe not.

There has been that done which cannot be undone. You have given up your prayer, and you will suffer for it.

Temptation is before you, and you are not ready to meet it. There is a guilty feeling on the soul, and you linger at a distance from God. It is no marvel if that day in which you suffer drowsiness to interfere with prayer be a day in which you shrink from duty.

Moments of prayer intruded on by sloth cannot be made up. We may get experience, but we cannot get back the rich freshness and strength which were wrapped up in those moments.

FREDERICK W. ROBERTSON

If Jesus, the strong Son of God, felt it necessary to rise before the breaking of the day to pour out His heart to God in prayer, how much more ought you to pray unto Him who is the Giver of every good and perfect gift, and who has promised all things necessary for our good.

What Jesus gathered into His life from His prayers we can never know; but this we do know, that the prayerless life is a powerless life. A prayerless life may be a noisy life, and fuss around a great deal; but such a life is far removed from Him who, by day and night, prayed to God.

SELECTED

EVENING

He delivers magnificently, and showeth loving-kindness.
(PS. 18:50, FRENCH TRANS.)

Someone who knew what it was to trust God once said: "During the last two years, though I have said little about them, I have had many a crevasse open up before me. The ice has seemed to split asunder, and I have looked down into the blue depths.

"It is a glorious thing to have a big trouble, a great Atlantic billow, that takes you off your feet and sweeps you right out to sea, and lets you sink down into the depths, into old ocean's lowest caverns, till you get to the foundation of the mountains, and there see God, and then come up again to tell what a great God He is, and how graciously He delivers His people."

SELECTED

"He calmeth the storm to a whisper" *(Ps. 107:29, Rotherham).*

Life is to be just hard enough to bring out the heroic! I shall go across battlefields and into twisting storms that I may have an experience of the Father's care, protection and glorious deliverance. *I am to share in the tremendous experiences of the great!*

Only when Christ opened thine ear to the *storm*, did He open thine ear to the *stillness.*

GEORGE MATHESON

Prize your storms!

June 7

❧

Where is God my maker, who giveth songs in the night? (Job 35:10).

Do you have sleepless nights, tossing on the hot pillow, and watching for the first glint of dawn? Ask the divine Spirit to enable you to fix your thoughts on God your Maker, and believe that He can fill those lonely, dreary hours with song.

Is yours the night of bereavement? Is it not often at such a time that God draws near, and assures the mourner that the Lord has need of the departed loved one, and called "the eager, earnest spirit to stand in the bright throng of the invisible, liberated, radiant, active, intent on some high mission"; and as the thought enters, is there not the beginning of a song?

Is yours the night of discouragement and fancied or actual failure? No one understands you, your friends reproach; but your Maker draws nigh, and gives you a song—a song of hope, the song which is harmonious with the strong, deep music of His providence. Be ready to sing the songs that your Maker gives. **SELECTED**

> *What then? Shall we sit idly down and say*
> *The night hath come; it is no longer day?*
> *Yet as the evening twilight fades away,*
> *The sky is filled with stars, invisible to day.*

The strength of the vessel can be demonstrated only by the hurricane, and the power of the gospel can be fully shown only when the Christian is subjected to some fiery trial. If God would make manifest the fact that "He giveth songs in the night," He must first make it night.

WILLIAM TAYLOR

EVENING

❧

God was in Christ, reconciling the world unto himself. (2 COR. 5:19)

There is on record a story of how a tribe of North American Indians who roamed in the neighborhood of Niagara offered, year by year, a young virgin as a sacrifice to the Spirit of the Mighty River.

She was called *the Bride of the Falls.*

The lot fell one year on a beautiful girl who was the only daughter of an old chieftain. The news was carried to him while he was sitting in his tent; but on hearing it the old man went on smoking his pipe, and said nothing of what he felt.

On the day fixed for the sacrifice a white canoe, full of ripe fruits and decked with beautiful flowers, was ready, waiting to receive "the Bride."

At the appointed hour she took her place in the frail bark, which was pushed out into midstream where it would be carried swiftly toward the mighty cataract.

Then, to the amazement of the crowd which had assembled to watch the sacrifice, a second canoe was seen to dart out from the river's bank a little lower down the stream. In it was seated the old chieftain. With swift strokes he paddled toward the canoe in which sat his beloved child. Upon reaching it he gripped it firmly and held it fast. The eyes of both met in one last long look of love; and then, close together, father and daughter were carried by the racing current until they plunged over the thundering cataract and perished side by side.

In their death they were not divided. The father was *in it* with his child!

"God was in Christ, reconciling the world unto himself." He did not have to do this. Nobody forced Him. *The only force behind that sacrifice was the force of His seeking love for His lost world.*   SELECTED

June 8

MORNING

{~~~}

For every child of God overcomes the world:
and the victorious principle which has overcome the world
is our faith (1 JOHN 5:4 WEYMOUTH).

At every turn in the road one can find something that will rob him of his victory and peace of mind, if he permits it. Satan is a long way from having retired from the business of deluding and ruining God's children if he can. At every milestone it is well to look carefully to the thermometer of one's experience, to see whether the temperature is well up.

Sometimes a person can, if he will, actually snatch victory from the very jaws of defeat, if he will resolutely put his faith up at just the right moment.

Faith can change any situation. No matter how dark it is, no matter what the trouble may be, a quick lifting of the heart to God in a moment of real, actual faith in Him, will alter the situation in a moment.

God is still on His throne, and He can turn defeat into victory in a second of time, if we really trust Him.

> *God is mighty! He is able to deliver;*
> *Faith can victor be in every trying hour;*
> *Fear and care and sin and sorrow be defeated*
> *By our faith in God's almighty, conquering power.*

> *Have faith in God, the sun will shine,*
> *Though dark the clouds may be today;*
> *His heart has planned your path and mine,*
> *Have faith in God, have faith alway.*

When one has faith, one does not retire; one stops the enemy where he finds him.

MARSHAL FOCH

EVENING

We glory in tribulations . . . knowing that tribulation worketh patience; And patience, experience; and experience, hope: And hope maketh not ashamed. (ROM. 5:3–5)

A story is told of the great artist Turner, that one day he invited Charles Kingsley to his studio to see a picture of a storm at sea. Kingsley was rapt in admiration. "How did you do it, Turner?" he exclaimed. Turner answered: "I wished to paint a storm at sea; so I went to the coast of Holland, and engaged a fisherman to take me out in his boat in the next storm. The storm was brewing, and I went down to the boat and bade him bind me to its mast. Then he drove the boat out into the teeth of the storm. The storm was so furious that I longed to be down in the bottom of the boat and allow it to blow over me. But I could not: I was bound to the mast. *Not only did I see that storm, and feel it, but it blew itself into me until I became part of the storm. And then I came back and painted the picture.*"

His experience is a parable of life: sometimes cloud and sometimes sunshine; sometimes pleasure, sometimes pain. *Life is a great mixture of happiness and tragic storm. He who comes out of it rich in living, is he who dares to accept it all, face it all, and let it blow its power, mystery and tragedy into the inmost recesses of the soul. A victory so won in this life will then be an eternal possession.*　　CHARLES LEWIS SLATTERY

June 9

MORNING

⤛⤜

Feed on his faithfulness (PS. 37:3 RV).

I once met a poor colored woman, who earned a precarious living by hard daily labor; but who was a joyous triumphant Christian.

"Ah, Nancy," said a gloomy Christian lady to her one day, "it is well enough to be happy now; but I should think the thoughts of your future would sober you. Only suppose, for instance, you should have a spell of sickness, and be unable to work; or suppose your present employers should move away, and no one else should give you anything to do; or suppose—"

"Stop!" cried Nancy, "I never supposes. De Lord is my Shepherd, and I knows I shall not want. And, Honey," she added, to her gloomy friend, "it's all dem *supposes* as is makin' you so mis'able. You'd better give dem all up, and just trust de Lord."

There is one text that will take all the "supposes" out of a believer's life, if it be received and acted on in childlike faith; it is Hebrews 13:5–6: "Be content with such things as ye have: for *he* hath said, I will never leave thee, nor forsake thee. So that we may boldly say, The Lord is my helper, and I will not fear what man shall do unto me."　　H. W. S.

> *There's a stream of trouble across my path;*
> *It is black and deep and wide.*
> *Bitter the hour the future hath*
> *When I cross its swelling tide.*
> *But I smile and sing and say:*
> *"I will hope and trust alway;*
> *I'll bear the sorrow that comes tomorrow,*
> *But I'll borrow none today."*
>
> *Tomorrow's bridge is a dangerous thing;*
> *I dare not cross it now.*

I can see its timbers sway and swing,
And its arches reel and bow.
O heart, you must hope alway;
You must sing and trust and say:
"I'll bear the sorrow that comes tomorrow,
But I'll borrow none today."

The eagle that soars in the upper air does not worry itself as to how it is to cross rivers. SELECTED

EVENING

❧

They shall mount up with wings as eagles. (ISA. 40:31)

Those who wait upon the Lord shall obtain a marvelous addition to their resources: *they shall obtain wings!* They become endowed with power to rise above things. Men who do not soar always have small views of things. Wings are required for breadth of view. The wing-life is characterized by a sense of proportion. To see things aright we must get away from them. An affliction looked at from the lowlands may be stupendous; looked at from the heights, it may appear little or nothing. This "light affliction, which is but for a moment, worketh for us a far more exceeding and eternal weight of glory." What a breadth of view!

And here is another great quotation: "The sufferings of this present time are not worthy to be compared with the glory which shall be revealed in us." This is a bird's-eye view. It sees life as a whole. How mighty the bird from which the picture is taken! "As eagles!" What strength of wing! *Such is to be ours if we wait upon the Lord.* We shall be able to soar above disappointment—no matter how great—and to wing our way into the very presence of God. *Let us live the wing-life!*

The little bird sat on a slender limb,
Upward swinging,
And though wind and rain were rough with him,
Still kept singing.
"O little bird, quick, seek out your nest!"
I could not keep from calling;
"The bleak winds tear your tender breast,
Your tiny feet are falling."
"More need for song
When things go wrong,

> *I was not meant for crying;*
> *No fear for me,"*
> *He piped with glee,*
> *"My wings are made for flying!"*
>
> *My heart had been dark as the stormy sky*
> *In my sorrow,*
> *With the weight of troubles long passed by,*
> *And the morrow.*
> *"O little bird, sing!" I cried once more,*
> *"The sun will soon be shining.*
> *See, there's a rainbow arching o'er*
> *The storm cloud's silver lining."*
> *I, too, will sing*
> *Through everything;*
> *It will teach blessing double;*
> *Nor yet forget.*
> *When rude winds fret,*
> *To fly above my trouble.*
>
> **SELECTED**

Wing-power gives us the gift of soaring and we see how things are related one to another.

Wide soaring gives wide seeing!

June 10

MORNING

❧

And we know that all things work together for good to them that love God (ROM. 8:28).

How wide is this assertion of the apostle Paul! He does not say, "We know that *some* things," or *"most* things," or *"joyous* things," but "ALL things." From the minutest to the most momentous; from the humblest event in daily providence to the great crisis hours in grace.

And all things *"work"*—they *are* working; not all things *have* worked, or *shall* work; but it is a present operation.

At this very moment, when some voice may be saying, "Thy judgments are a great deep," the angels above, who are watching the development of the great plan, are with folded wings exclaiming, "The Lord is righteous in *all* his ways, and holy in *all* his works" (Ps. 145:17).

And then all things *"work together."* It is a beautiful blending. Many different colors, in themselves raw and unsightly, are required in order to weave the harmonious pattern.

Many separate tones and notes of music, even discords and dissonances, are required to make up the harmonious anthem.

Many separate wheels and joints are required to make the piece of machinery. Take a thread separately, or a note separately, or a wheel or a tooth of a wheel separately, and there may be neither use nor beauty discernible.

But *complete* the web, *combine* the notes, *put together* the separate parts of steel and iron, and you see how perfect and symmetrical is the result. Here is the lesson for faith: "What I do thou knowest not now, but thou shalt know hereafter."

MACDUFF

In one thousand trials it is not five hundred of them that work for the believer's good, but nine hundred and ninety-nine of them, *and one beside.*

GEORGE MUELLER

GOD MEANT IT UNTO GOOD (GEN. 50:20)

"God meant it unto good"—O blest assurance,
Falling like sunshine all across life's way,
Touching with Heaven's gold earth's darkest storm clouds,
Bringing fresh peace and comfort day by day.

'Twas not by chance the hands of faithless brethren
Sold Joseph captive to a foreign land;
Nor was it chance which, after years of suffering,
Brought him before the monarch's throne to stand.

One Eye all-seeing saw the need of thousands,
And planned to meet it through that one lone soul;
And through the weary days of prison bondage
Was working towards the great and glorious goal.

As yet the end was hidden from the captive,
The iron entered even to his soul;
His eye could scan the present path of sorrow,
Not yet his gaze might rest upon the whole.

Faith failed not through those long, dark days of waiting,
His trust in God was recompensed at last,

The moment came when God led forth his servant
To succour many, all his sufferings past.

"It was not you but God, that sent me hither,"
Witnessed triumphant faith in after days;
"God meant it unto good," no "second causes"
Mingled their discord with his song of praise.

"God means it unto good" for thee, beloved,
The God of Joseph is the same today;
His love permits afflictions strange and bitter,
His hand is guiding through the unknown way.

Thy Lord, who sees the end from the beginning,
Hath purposes for thee of love untold.
Then place thy hand in His and follow fearless,
Till thou the riches of His grace behold.

There, when thou standest in the Home of Glory,
And all life's path lies open to thy gaze,
Thine eyes shall SEE the hand which now thou trustest,
And magnify His love through endless days.

FREDA HANBURY ALLEN

EVENING

The LORD thy God shall bless thee in all that thou doest.
(DEUT. 15:18)

Art thou suddenly called to occupy a difficult position full of responsibilities? Go forward, counting on *Me!* I am giving thee the position
full of difficulties for the reason that Jehovah thy God will bless thee in all
thy works, and in all the business of thy hands.

This day I place in thy hands a pot of holy oil. Draw from it freely, My
child, that all the circumstances arising along thy pathway, each word that
gives thee pain, each manifestation of thy feebleness, each interruption
trying to thy patience, may be anointed with this oil.

Interruptions are Divine instructions.

The sting will go in the measure in which thou seest *Me* in all things.

*"Set your hearts unto all the words which I testify among you this day . . .
because it is your life"* (Deut. 32:46–47).

> *"I will now turn aside, and see this great sight."*

Our Father is always trying to get us to the place of spiritual discoveries. God is not interested in getting mere information into our souls; He wants us to have a revelation of Himself. God has challenging futures for us, and will go to miracle lengths to get us to pay attention. If God calls me from ease and idleness, it will be that His undergirdings are sufficient for a great service. *"I will turn aside,"* for it is God who calls me.

> As *"my expectation is from him,"* I will listen today.

June 11

MORNING

～

> *The servant of the Lord must . . . be gentle* (2 TIM. 2:24).

When God conquers us and takes all the flint out of our nature, and we get deep visions into the Spirit of Jesus, we then see as never before the great rarity of *gentleness of spirit* in this dark and unheavenly world.

The *graces* of the Spirit do not settle themselves down upon us by chance, and if we do not discern certain states of grace, and choose them, and in our thoughts nourish them, they never become fastened in our nature or behavior.

Every advance step in grace must be preceded by first apprehending it, and then a prayerful resolve to have it.

So few are willing to undergo the suffering out of which thorough gentleness comes. We must die before we are turned into gentleness, and crucifixion involves suffering; it is a real breaking and crushing of self, which wrings the heart and conquers the mind.

There is a good deal of mere mental and logical sanctification nowadays, which is only a religious fiction. It consists of mentally putting one's self on the altar, then mentally saying the altar sanctifies the gift, and then logically concluding therefore one is sanctified; and such a one goes forth with a gay, flippant, theological prattle about the deep things of God.

But the natural heartstrings have not been snapped, and the Adamic flint has not been ground to powder, and the bosom has not throbbed with the only, surging sighs of Gethsemane; and not having the real death marks of Calvary, there cannot be that soft, sweet, gentle, floating, victorious, overflowing, triumphant life that flows like a spring morning from an empty tomb.

G. D. W.

"And great grace was upon them all" (Acts 4:33).

EVENING

∽◦∾

I will awake the dawn. (PS. 57:8, SMITH'S TRANS.)

Take time. Give God time to reveal Himself to you. Give yourself time to be silent and quiet before Him, waiting to receive through the Spirit the assurance of His presence with you, His power working in you. Take time to read His Word as in His presence; that from it you may know what He asks of you and what He promises you. Let the Word create around you, create within you, a holy heavenly light in which your soul will be refreshed and strengthened for the work of daily life.

ANDREW MURRAY

We repeatedly come upon entries in the diary of Dr. Chalmers which express what he called the "morning grace of appropriation."

"Began my first waking moments with confident hold upon Christ as my Savior."

"A day of quietness."

"My faith took hold of the precious promises this morning."

"The morning makes the entire day. To think of morning is to think of a bloom and fragrance which if missed, cannot be overtaken later on in the day. The Lord stands upon the shore in the morning and reveals Himself to the weary, disillusioned men who had toiled all night and taken nothing. *He* ever stands upon life's most dreary and time-worn shores, and as we *gaze* upon Him the shadows flee and *it is morning.*"

I met God in the morning
When the day was at its best,
And His presence came like glory
Of the sunrise in my breast.

All day long the Presence lingered,
All day long He stayed with me,
And we sailed in perfect calmness
O'er a very troubled sea.

Other ships were blown and battered,
Other ships were sore distressed.
But the winds that seemed to drive them,
Brought to us a peace and rest.

Then I thought of other mornings,
With a keen remorse of mind.
When I too, had loosed the moorings
With the Presence left behind.

And I think I know the secret,
Learned from many a troubled way;
You must seek God in the morning
If you want Him through the day.
RALPH CUSHMAN

"The early morning hour has always been a time of visions. What discoveries the saints have made while others slept!"

June 12

MORNING

❦

In everything ye are enriched by him (1 COR. 1:5).

Have you ever seen men and women whom some disaster drove to a great act of prayer, and by and by the disaster was forgotten, but the sweetness of religion remained and warmed their souls?

So have I seen a storm in later spring; and all was black, save where the lightning tore the cloud with thundering rent.

The winds blew and the rains fell, as though heaven had opened its windows. What a devastation there was! Not a spider's web that was out of doors escaped the storm, which tore up even the strong-branched oak.

But ere long the lightning had gone by, the thunder was spent and silent, the rain was over, the western wind came up with its sweet breath, the clouds were chased away, and the retreating storm threw a scarf of rainbows over her fair shoulders and resplendent neck, and looked back and smiled, and so withdrew and passed out of sight.

But for weeks long the fields held up their hands full of ambrosial flowers, and all the summer through the grass was greener, the brooks were fuller, and the trees cast a more umbrageous shade, *because the storm passed by*—though all the rest of the earth had long ago forgotten the storm, its rainbows and its rain. THEODORE PARKER

God may not give us an easy journey to the promised land, but He will give us a safe one. BONAR

It was a storm that occasioned the discovery of the gold mines of India. Hath not a storm driven some to the discovery of the richer mines of the love of God in Christ?

Is it raining, little flower?
Be glad of rain;
Too much sun would wither thee;
'Twill shine again.
The clouds are very black, 'tis true;
But just behind them shines the blue.

Art thou weary, tender heart?
Be glad of pain;
In sorrow sweetest virtues grow,
As flowers in rain.
God watches, and thou wilt have sun,
When clouds their perfect work have done.
LUCY LARCOM

EVENING

❧❧

Is thy God . . . able to deliver thee from the lions? (DAN. 6:20)

Thou servant of the living God,
Whilst lions round thee roar,
Look up and trust and praise His Name,
And all His ways adore;
For even now, in peril dire,
He works to set thee free,
And in a way known but to Him,
Shall thy deliverance be.

Dost wait while lions round thee stand?
Dost wait in gloom, alone,
And looking up above thy head
See but a sealed stone?
Praise in the dark! Yea, praise His Name,
Who trusted thee to see
His mighty power displayed again
For thee, His saints, for thee.

Thou servant of the living God,
Thine but to wait and praise;
The living God, Himself, will work,
To Him thine anthem raise;
Though undelivered thou dost wait,
The God who works for thee,
When His hour strikes, will with a word
Set thee forever free.

M. E. B.

"Believe ye that I am able to do this?"
"Yea, Lord."

Strengthen yourself in the Omnipotence of God. Do not say, "Is God able?" Say, rather, "God is able."

ANDREW MURRAY

"The supernatural always slumbers when faith lies sleeping, or dead."

June 13

MORNING

～≈

My own peace I give to you (JOHN 14:27 WEYMOUTH).

Two painters each painted a picture to illustrate his conception of rest. The first chose for his scene a still, lone lake among the far-off mountains.

The second threw on his canvas a thundering waterfall, with a fragile birch tree bending over the foam; and at the fork of the branch, almost wet with the cataract's spray, sat a robin on its nest.

The first was only *stagnation;* the last was *rest.*

Christ's life outwardly was one of the most troubled lives that ever lived: tempest and tumult, tumult and tempest, the waves breaking over it all the time until the worn body was laid in the grave. But the inner life was a sea of glass. The great calm was always there.

At any moment you might have gone to Him and found rest. And even when the human bloodhounds were dogging Him in the streets of Jerusalem, He turned to His disciples and offered them, as a last legacy, "My peace."

Rest is not a hallowed feeling that comes over us in church; it is the repose of a heart set deep in God.   DRUMMOND

> *My peace I give in times of deepest grief,*
> *Imparting calm and trust and My relief.*
>
> *My peace I give when prayer seems lost, unheard;*
> *Know that My promises are ever in My Word.*
>
> *My peace I give when thou art left alone—*
> *The nightingale at night has sweetest tone.*
>
> *My peace I give in time of utter loss,*
> *The way of glory leads right to the cross.*
>
> *My peace I give when enemies will blame,*
> *Thy fellowship is sweet through cruel shame.*
>
> *My peace I give in agony and sweat,*
> *For mine own brow with bloody drops was wet.*
>
> *My peace I give when nearest friend betrays—*
> *Peace that is merged in love, and for them prays.*
>
> *My peace I give when there's but death for thee—*
> *The gateway is the cross to get to Me.*
>
> L. S. P.

EVENING

Who for the joy that was set before him endured the cross, despising the shame. (HEB. 12:2)

The joy of the spirit is no cheap joy. It has scars on it—radiant scars! It is joy won out of the heart of pain. Those who know it have found one of life's deepest and most transforming secrets; the transmuting of pain into a paean. Sorrow becomes not something to escape; we can make it sing. We can set our tears to music, and no music is so exquisite, so compelling. The Christians learned immediately and at once the truth which the philosopher Royce puts in these words: "Such ills we remove only as we assimilate them, take them up into the plan of our lives, give them meaning, set them in their place in the whole." When their heart-strings were stretched upon some cross of pain and the winds of persecution blew through them, then from this human aeolian harp men heard the very music of God. They did not *bear pain,* they *used* it.

SELECTED

Where the rain does not fall we have deserts. When the soil is not torn up by the plow and the harrow we get no crops.

Joy is a rare plant; it needs much rain for its growth and blossoming.

> *I heard an old farmer talk one day,*
> *Telling his listeners how*
> *In the wide, new country far away*
> *The rainfall follows the plow.*
> *"As fast as they break it up, you see,*
> *And turn the heart to the sun,*
> *As they open the furrow deep and free*
> *And the tillage is begun,*
> *The earth grows mellow, and more and more*
> *It holds and sends to the sky*
> *A moisture it never had before,*
> *When its face was hard and dry.*
> *And so wherever the plowshares run*
> *The clouds run overhead,*
> *And the soil that works and lets in the sun*
> *With water is always fed."*
> *I wonder if that old farmer knew*
> *The half of his simple word,*
> *Or guessed the message that, heavenly true,*
> *Within it was hidden and heard.*
> *It fell on my ear by chance that day,*
> *But the gladness lingers now,*
> *To think it is always God's dear way*
> *That the rainfall follows the plow.*

Endure with faith and courage through the frost, and you will see a glorious spring.

June 14

༄

I have prayed that your own faith may not fail (LUKE 22:32).

Christian, take good care of thy faith, for recollect that *faith is the only means whereby thou canst obtain blessings.* Prayer cannot draw down answers from God's throne except it be the earnest prayer of the man who believes.

Faith is the telegraphic wire which links earth to heaven, on which God's messages of love fly so fast that before we call He answers, and while we are yet speaking He hears us. But if that telegraphic wire of faith be snapped, how can we obtain the promise?

Am I in trouble? I can obtain help for trouble by faith. Am I beaten about by the enemy? My soul on her dear Refuge leans by faith.

But take faith away, then in vain I call to God. There is no other road betwixt my soul and heaven. Blockade the road, and how can I communicate with the great King?

Faith links me with divinity. Faith clothes me with the power of Jehovah. Faith insures every attribute of God in my defense. It helps me to defy the hosts of hell. It makes me march triumphant over the necks of my enemies. But without faith how can I receive anything from the Lord?

Oh, then, Christian, watch well thy faith. "If thou canst believe, all things are possible to him that believeth." C. H. SPURGEON

We boast of being so practical a people that we want to have a surer thing than faith. But did not Paul say that the promise was by FAITH that it might be SURE? (Rom. 4:16). DAN CRAWFORD

Faith honors God; God honors faith.

༄

I have commanded the ravens . . . a widow woman there.
(1 KINGS 17:4, 9)

We must be where God desires. Elijah spoke of himself as always standing before the Lord God of Israel. He could as distinctly stand before God when hiding beside Cherith, or sheltering in the widow's house at

Zarephath, as when he stood erect on Carmel, or listened to the voice of God at Horeb.

If we are where God wants us to be, He will see the supply of our need. It is as easy for Him to feed us by the ravens as by the widow woman. As long as God says *stay here,* or *there,* be sure that He is pledged to provide for you. Though you resemble a lonely sentinel in some distant post of missionary service God will see to you. The ravens are not less amenable to His command than of old: and out of the stores of widow women He is able to supply your need as He did Elijah's at Zarephath.

When God said to Elijah, "Hide thyself by the brook Cherith," a carbon copy of the order was given to the ravens. They brought food morning and evening to *the place of Divine appointment.*

When Jesus said, "Go ye into all the world, and preach the gospel," He placed all the resources of heaven at the disposal of the going group.

When I was ordered toward the front in France, I got permission to remain behind ten days for letters. None came. When I reached my objective, where men were dying without a Chaplain's comfort, I found the last thirty days' post. The commanding officer said:

"In the army, the letters go where the orders read."

In the kingdom of God the blessings and equipment are found only where the orders read. Let us all go and tell the story.

JOSIAH HOPKINS

It is in the path of His appointment that we shall find His Presence.

June 15

MORNING

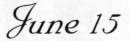

For God hath caused me to be fruitful in the land of my affliction
(GEN. 41:52).

The summer showers are falling. The poet stands by the window watching them. They are beating and buffeting the earth with their fierce downpour. But the poet sees in his imaginings more than the showers which are falling before his eyes. He sees myriads of lovely flowers which shall be soon breaking forth from the watered earth, filling it with matchless beauty and fragrance. And so he sings:

It isn't raining rain for me, it's raining daffodils;
In every dimpling drop I see wild flowers upon the hills.
A cloud of gray engulfs the day, and overwhelms the town;
It isn't raining rain for me: it's raining roses down.

Perchance some one of God's chastened children is even now saying, "O God, it is raining hard for me tonight.

"Testings are raining upon me which seem beyond my power to endure. Disappointments are raining fast, to the utter defeat of all my chosen plans. Bereavements are raining into my life which are making my shrinking heart quiver in its intensity of suffering. The rain of affliction is surely beating down upon my soul these days."

Withal, friend, you are mistaken. It isn't raining rain for you. *It's raining blessing.* For, if you will but believe your Father's Word, under that beating rain are springing up spiritual flowers of such fragrance and beauty as never before grew in that stormless, unchastened life of yours.

You indeed see the rain. But do you see also the flowers? You are pained by the testings. But God sees the sweet flower of faith which is upspringing in your life under those very trials.

You shrink from the suffering. But God sees the tender compassion for other sufferers which is finding birth in your soul.

Your heart winces under the sore bereavement. But God sees the deepening and enriching which that sorrow has brought to you.

It isn't raining afflictions for you. It is raining tenderness, love, compassion, patience, and a thousand other flowers and fruits of the blessed Spirit, which are bringing into your life such a spiritual enrichment as all the fullness of worldly prosperity and ease was never able to beget in your innermost soul. — J. M. MCC.

SONGS ACROSS THE STORM

A harp stood in the moveless air,
Where showers of sunshine washed a thousand fragrant blooms;
A traveler bowed with loads of care
Essayed from morning till the dusk of evening glooms
To thrum sweet sounds from the songless strings;
The pilgrim strives in vain with each unanswering chord,
Until the tempest's thunder sings,
And, moving on the storm, the fingers of the Lord
A wondrous melody awakes;
And though the battling winds their soldier deeds perform,
Their trumpet-sound brave music makes
While God's assuring voice sings love across the storm.

I sought the LORD, and he heard me. (PS. 34:4)

*A*ndrew Murray says: It is one of the terrible marks of the diseased state of the Christian life in these days, *that there are so many that rest content without the distinct experience of answered prayer.* They *pray daily,* but know little of direct, definite *answer to prayer as the rule of their daily life.*

And it is this the Father wills. He seeks daily intercourse with His children in *listening to and granting* their petitions. He wills that I should come to Him day by day with distinct requests. He wills day by day to do for me what I ask.

There may be cases in which the answer is a refusal, but our Father lets His child know when He cannot give him what he requests, and like the Son in Gethsemane, he will withdraw his petition.

Whether the request be according to His will or not, God will by His Word and His Spirit *teach those who are teachable* and who will give Him time. Let us withdraw our requests if they are not according to God's mind, or persevere until the answer comes.

Prayer is appointed to obtain the answer!

It is in prayer and its answer that *the interchange of love between the Father and His child takes place.*

Are your prayers answered?

June 16

MORNING

My expectation is from him (PS. 62:5).

*O*ur too general neglect of looking for answers to what we ask, shows how little we are in earnest in our petitions. A husbandman is not content without the harvest; a marksman will observe whether the ball hits the target; a physician watches the effect of the medicine which he gives; and shall the Christian be careless about the effect of his labor?

Every prayer of the Christian, made in faith, according to the will of

God, for which God has promised, offered up in the name of Jesus Christ, and under the influence of the Spirit, whether for temporal or for spiritual blessings, is, or will be fully answered.

God always answers the general design and intention of His people's prayers, in doing that which, all things considered, is most for His own glory and their spiritual and eternal welfare. As we never find that Jesus Christ rejected a single supplicant who came to Him for mercy, so we believe that no prayer made in His name will be in vain.

The answer to prayer may be approaching, though we discern not its coming. The seed that lies under ground in winter is taking root in order to a spring and harvest, though it appears not above ground, but seems dead and lost. BICKERSTETH

Delayed answers to prayer are not only trials of faith, but they give us opportunities of honoring God by our steadfast confidence in Him under apparent repulses. C. H. SPURGEON

EVENING

O that thou hadst hearkened to my commandments! then had thy peace been as a river. (ISA. 48:18)

Do we not see how God's purposes are thwarted and deferred by human perversity? At the very time when God had determined upon the election and consecration of Aaron to the priesthood, Aaron was spending his time in molding and chiseling the golden calf.

We might have been crowned fifty years ago, but just as the coronation was about to take place we were discovered in the manufacture of an idol. *The Lord was just ready to make kings of us when we made fools of ourselves.* JOSEPH PARKER

> One small life in God's great plan—
> How futile it seems as the ages roll,
> Do what it may or strive how it can
> To alter the sweep of the infinite whole!
> A single stitch in the endless web,
> A drop in the ocean's flow or ebb;
> But the pattern is rent where the stitch is lost,
> Or marred where the tangled threads have crossed:
> And each life that fails of true intent
> Mars the perfect plan that its Master meant.

Remember the awful truth *that I can limit Christ's power in the present*, although I can never alter God Almighty's order for a moment.

SEED THOUGHTS CALENDAR

There is a niche in God's own Temple, it is thine;
And the hand that shapes thee for it, is Divine.

June 17

MORNING

And there was a voice from the firmament that was over their heads, when they stood, and had let down their wings. (EZEK. 1:25).

What is the letting down of the wings? People so often say, "How do you get the voice of the Lord?" Here is the secret. They heard the voice when they stood and let down their wings.

We have seen a bird with fluttering wings; though standing still, its wings are fluttering. But here we are told they heard the voice when they stood and had let down their wings.

Do we not sometimes kneel or sit before the Lord and yet feel conscious of a fluttering of our spirits? Not a real stillness in His presence.

A dear one told me several days ago of a certain thing she prayed about. "But," said she, "I did not wait until the answer came."

She did not get still enough to hear Him speak, but went away and followed her own thought in the matter. And the result proved disastrous and she had to retrace her steps.

Oh, how much energy is wasted! How much time is lost by not letting down the wings of our spirit and getting very quiet before Him! Oh, the calm, the rest, the peace which come as we wait in His presence until we hear from Him!

Then, ah then, we can go like lightning, and turn not as we go but go straight forward whithersoever the Spirit goes (Ezek. 1:1, 20).

Be still! Just now be still!
Something thy soul hath never heard,
Something unknown to any song of bird,
Something unknown to any wind, or wave, or star,
A message from the Fatherland afar,

That with sweet joy the homesick soul shall thrill,
Cometh to thee if thou canst be still.

Be still! Just now be still!
There comes a presence very mild and sweet;
White are the sandals of His noiseless feet.
It is the Comforter whom Jesus sent
To teach thee what the words He uttered meant.
The willing, waiting spirit, He doth fill.
If thou would'st hear His message,
Dear soul, be still!

EVENING

༄

The crooked shall be made straight, and the rough places plain: And
the glory of the LORD shall be revealed,
and all flesh shall see it together. (ISA. 40:4–5)

And what is God's glory? It is the ministration of love. We are not to wait for a union of *opinions;* we are to begin with a union of hearts. *We are to be united, while yet we do not "see together."* You and I may look at the same stars and call them by different names. You are an astronomer, and I am a peasant; to you they are masses of worlds; to me they are candles in the sky set up to light me home.

What matter? Shall we not enjoy the glory though we do not agree about it? *Let us join hands over the message ere we settle the dispute about the messenger.*

Ye who stand upon the shore and wrangle about the number of the waves, there is meantime a work for you to do, *and to do together.* There are shipwrecked voyagers out yonder, crying and calling. They have folded their hands in prayer, and have heard no answer save the echo of their cry. Shall they call in vain? Shall they wait till you have counted the billows that consume them? Shall they stand shivering in the storm while you are disputing the name of the lifeboat? *What matter how we name the lifeboat if only we each believe in it?*

Come out to the wreck, my brothers. Come to the souls who have lost their compass, to lives that have broken their helm, to hearts that have rent their sails. They will not ask *the name of your lifeboat;* even Jacob's angel had no name. You may not see together, *but you shall reveal together*—reveal the glory of the Lord. You shall be the church of united sympathizers.

You shall see together the face of the Master, but you shall touch together the print of the nails. Tomorrow, you shall see Him as He is.

GEORGE MATHESON

When crew and captain understand each other to the core,
It takes a gale and more than a gale to put their ship ashore;
For the one will do what the other commands,
although they are chilled to the bone;
And both together can live through weather
that neither could face alone.

KIPLING

A battleship cannot go into action with a mutiny raging on board.

June 18

MORNING

෴

Wherefore lift up the hands which hang down, and the feeble knees; and make straight paths for your feet, lest that which is lame be turned out of the way; but let it rather be healed (HEB. 12:12–13).

This is God's word of encouragement to us to lift up the hands of faith, and confirm the knees of prayer. Often our faith grows tired, languid, and relaxed, and our prayers lose their force and effectiveness.

The figure used here is a very striking one. The idea seems to be that we become discouraged and so timid that a little obstacle depresses and frightens us, and we are tempted to walk around it, and not face it: to take the easier way.

Perhaps it is some physical trouble that God is ready to heal, but the exertion is hard, or it is easier to secure some human help, or walk around in some other way.

There are many ways of walking around emergencies instead of going straight through them. How often we come up against something that appalls us, and we want to evade the issue with the excuse:

"I am not quite ready for that now." Some sacrifice is to be made, some obedience demanded, some Jericho to be taken, some soul that we have not the courage to claim and carry through, some prayer that is hanging fire, or perhaps some physical trouble that is half-healed and we are walking around it.

God says, "Lift up the hands that hang down." March straight through the flood, and lo, the waters will divide, the Red Sea will open, the Jordan will part, and the Lord will lead you through to victory.

Don't let your feet "be turned out of the way," but let your body "be healed," your faith strengthened. Go right ahead and leave no Jericho behind you unconquered and no place where Satan can say that he was too much for you. This is a profitable lesson and an intensely practical one. How often have we been in that place. Perhaps you are there today.

A. B. SIMPSON

Pay as little attention to discouragement as possible. Plough ahead as a steamer does, rough or smooth—rain or shine. To carry your cargo and make your port is the point.

MALTBIE D. BABCOCK

EVENING

Who maketh the clouds his chariot. (PS. 104:3)

We cannot ride in our own chariots and God's at the same time. God must burn up with the fire of His love *every earthly chariot* that stands in the way of our mounting into His.

Would you mount into God's chariots? Then take each thing that is wrong in your life as one of God's chariots for you. Ask Him daily to *open your eyes,* and you will see His unseen chariots of deliverance.

Whenever we mount into God's chariots we have a translation—not into the heavens above us as Elijah did, but into the heaven *within us;* away from the low, groveling plane of life, up into the heavenly places in Christ Jesus, where we shall ride in triumph over all below. But the chariot that carries the soul over this road is generally some chastening, *that for the present doth not seem joyous but grievous.*

NEVERTHELESS AFTERWARD!

No matter what the source of these chastenings, look upon them as God's chariots sent to carry your soul into the high planes of spiritual achievement and uplifting. You will find, to your glad surprise, that it is God's love that sends the chariots—His chariots in which you may *ride prosperously* over all darkness.

Let us be thankful for every trial that will help to destroy our earthly chariots, and will compel us to take refuge in the chariots of God, which always stand ready and waiting beside us in every trial.

"My soul, wait thou *only* upon God; for my expectation is from him. *He only* is my rock and my salvation: he is my defense; I shall not be moved."

We have to be brought to the place where all other refuges fail, before we can say HE ONLY. We say, He *and* my experience; He *and* my church relationships; He *and* my Christian work. All that comes after the *and* must be taken away from us, or must be proved useless, before we can come to the *He only*. Only then we mount into God's chariots.

If we want to ride with God *upon the heavens,* all earth riding must be brought to an end.

He who rides with God rides above all earthborn clouds!

> *Oh, may no earthborn cloud arise*
> *To hide Thee from Thy servant's eyes.*

No obstacle can hinder the triumphant course of God's chariots!

HANNAH WHITALL SMITH

June 19

MORNING

Bread corn is bruised (ISA. 28:28).

*M*any of us cannot be used to become food for the world's hunger until we are broken in Christ's hands. "Bread corn is bruised." Christ's blessing ofttimes means sorrow, but even sorrow is not too great a price to pay for the privilege of touching other lives with benediction. The sweetest things in this world today have come to us through tears and pain.

J. R. MILLER

God has made me bread for His elect, and if it be needful that the bread must be ground in the teeth of the lion to feed His children, blessed be the name of the Lord.

IGNATIUS

"We must burn out before we can give out. We cease to bless when we cease to bleed."

"Poverty, hardship and misfortune have pressed many a life to moral heroism and spiritual greatness. Difficulty challenges energy and perseverance. It calls into activity the strongest qualities of the soul. It was the weights on father's old clock that kept it going. Many a headwind has been utilized to make port. God has appointed opposition as an incentive to faith and holy activity.

"The most illustrious characters of the Bible were bruised and threshed and ground into bread for the hungry. Abraham's diploma styles him as 'the father of the faithful.' That was because he stood at the head of his class in affliction and obedience.

"Jacob suffered severe threshings and grindings. Joseph was bruised and beaten and had to go through Potiphar's kitchen and Egypt's prison to get to his throne.

"David, hunted like a partridge on the mountain, bruised, weary and footsore, was ground into bread for a kingdom. Paul never could have been bread for Caesar's household if he had not endured the bruising, whippings and stonings. He was ground into fine flour for the royal family."

"Like combat, like victory. If for you He has appointed special trials, be assured that in His heart He has kept for you a special place. A soul sorely bruised is a soul elect."

EVENING

❧

I will be as the dew. (Hos. 14:5)

*H*osea leads us to the source of *the dew-drenched life.* It is from *Him* that this priceless gift comes. Those who spend much time with the Master come forth with the dew of blessing upon their lives.

The dew falls in the still night when all nature is hushed to rest. What is true in nature holds true in spiritual things: in this we have the key reason why so many of God's people are living dewless lives. They are restless, anxious, impatient, fussy, busy, with not time at all to be still before the Lord.

The finer things are being sacrificed for the coarser; the things of value for the worthless.

In Job 38:28 the question is asked, "Who hath begotten the drops of dew?" It is one of God's secrets. It comes quietly, and yet works so mightily. We cannot produce it, but we may receive it and live, moment by moment, in that atmosphere where the Holy Spirit may continually drench us with His presence.

W. MALLIS

But the sensitive dew and the stillness are friends,
In the storm, it is true that it never descends.
Let me fuss not, nor pine, but on God cast my care,
And the dew shall be mine in the quiet of prayer.

Let Him hush the sad riot of temper and will,
Till rested and quiet the cleansed heart is still.
When the atmosphere's so, 'tis attractive to dew,
And the first thing you know 'twill be failing on you.
MAMIE PAYNE FERGUSON

"Thy dew is as the dew of herbs."

God feeds the wildflowers on the lonely mountainside without the help of any man, and they are as fresh and lovely as those that are daily watched over in our gardens. So God can feed His own planted ones without the help of man, by the sweet falling dew on his spirit.
ROBERT MURRAY MCCHEYNE

"Wait before the Master until your whole heart is drenched by Him, and then go forth in the power of a fresh, strong, and fragrant life."

Lord, let Thy Spirit bedew my dry fleece!

June 20

MORNING

❧

Thine ears shall hear a word behind thee, saying,
This is the way, walk ye in it, when ye turn to the right hand,
and when ye turn to the left. (ISA. 30:21).

When we are in doubt or difficulty, when many voices urge this course or the other, when prudence utters one advice and faith another, then let us be still, hushing each intruder, calming ourselves in the sacred hush of God's presence; let us study His Word in the attitude of devout attention; let us lift up our nature into the pure light of His face, eager only to know what God the Lord shall determine—and ere long a very distinct impression will be made, the unmistakable forthtelling of His secret counsel.

It is not wise in the earlier stages of Christian life to depend on this alone, but to wait for the corroboration of circumstances. But those who have had many dealings with God know well the value of secret fellowship with Him, to ascertain His will.

Are you in difficulty about your way? Go to God with your question; get direction from the light of His smile or the cloud of His refusal.

If you will only get alone, where the lights and shadows of earth cannot interfere, where human opinions fail to reach—and if you will dare to wait there silent and expectant, though all around you insist on immediate decision or action—the will of God will be made clear; and you will have a new conception of God, a deeper insight into His nature and heart of love, which shall be for yourself alone—a rapturous experience, to abide your precious perquisite forever, the rich guerdon of those long waiting hours.　　　　　　　　　　　　　　　　　　　　　　　　DAVID

"STAND STILL," my soul, for so thy Lord commands:
E'en when thy way seems blocked, leave it in His wise hands;
His arm is mighty to divide the wave.
"Stand still," my soul, "stand still" and thou shalt see
How God can work the "impossible" for thee,
For with a great deliverance He doth save.

Be not impatient, but in stillness stand,
Even when compassed 'round on every hand,
In ways thy spirit does not comprehend.
God cannot clear thy way till thou art still,

That He may work in thee His blessed will,
And all thy heart and will to Him do bend.
"BE STILL," my soul, for just as thou art still,
Can God reveal Himself to thee; until

Through thee His love and light and life can freely flow;
In stillness God can work through thee and reach
The souls around thee. He then through thee can teach
His lessons, and His power in weakness show.

"BE STILL"—a deeper step in faith and rest.
"Be still and know" thy Father knoweth best
The way to lead His child to that fair land,
A "summer" land, where quiet waters flow;
Where longing souls are satisfied, and "know
Their God," and praise for all that He has planned.

SELECTED

≈≈≈

And the song sang, and the trumpeters sounded: this continued until the burnt offering was finished. (2 CHRON. 29:28, MARGIN)

There is a joy that is *attained* and another joy that is *given*. The first joy needs things to make it joy—congenial circumstances, attentive friends; the second joy joys because it is filled with a bubbling spring of internal and eternal gladness—a gladness because it is *always in God, and God is always in it*. It glows and grows under all circumstances—it sings *because it is a song*.

It *sings after prayer*. "Ask, and ye shall receive, that your joy may be full." This implies that there must have been a need, a place to fill. As we believe and receive, *the song sings!*

It *sings after faith*. "Though now ye see him not, yet believing, ye rejoice with joy unspeakable and full of glory." Nothing seen and nothing sensed, at least not by natural sense—yet *the song sang*, and with a fullness of glory not before known.

It *sings after yielding*. "The meek also shall increase their joy in the LORD." Making room for the Lord is a secret of receiving more of Himself.

It *sings after sorrow*. "Weeping may endure for a night, but singing [margin] cometh in the morning." He, who is *Light*, who gives the morning signal to every feathered songster to tune his song, will also give you a *song that sings*.

It *sings after sacrifice*. "Neither count I my life dear unto myself, so that I might finish my course with joy."

Did you ever find *the song that sang of itself* in the quiet of your closet, when you heard His "Yes" to your prayer for His glory to come on earth? When nothing was seen of His working for you and your loved ones, did you hear the sweet strains of *the song that sang*?

The world awaits you—the singer with the new song!

June 21

It was noised that he was in the house (MARK 2:1).

The polyps which construct the coral reefs, work away under water, never dreaming that they are building the foundation of a new island on which, by-and-by, plants and animals will live and children of God be born and fitted for eternal glory as joint-heirs of Christ.

If your place in God's ranks is a hidden and secluded one, beloved, do not murmur, do not complain, do not seek to get out of God's will, if He has placed you there; for without the polyps, the coral reefs would never be built, and God needs some who are willing to be spiritual polyps, and work away out of sight of men, but sustained by the Holy Ghost and in full view of heaven.

The day will come when Jesus will give the rewards, and He makes no mistakes, although some people may wonder how you came to merit such a reward, as they had never heard of you before. **SELECTED**

> *Just where you stand in the conflict,*
> *There is your place.*
> *Just where you think you are useless,*
> *Hide not your face.*
> *God placed you there for a purpose,*
> *Whate'er it be,*
> *Think He has chosen you for it;*
> *Work loyally.*
> *Gird on your armor! Be faithful*
> *At toil or rest!*
> *Whate'er it be, never doubting*
> *God's way is best.*
> *Out in the fight or on picket,*
> *Stand firm and true;*
> *This is the work which your Master*
> *Gives you to do.*
> **SELECTED**

Safely we may leave the crowded meeting, the inspiring mountaintop, the helpful fellowship of "just men," and betake ourselves to our dim homely Emmaus, or to our dread public Colossae, or even to our far

Macedonia in the mission field, quietly confident that just where He has placed us, in the usual round of life, He ordains that the borderland may be possessed, the victory won.   NORTHCOTE DECK

EVENING

❧

This God is our God. (PS. 48:14)

God is *great* in great things, but *very great* in little things," says Henry Dyer.

A party stood on the Matterhorn admiring the sublimity of the scene, when a gentleman produced a pocket microscope, and having caught a fly placed it under the glass. He reminded us that the legs of the household fly in England are naked, then called attention to the legs of this little fly which were thickly covered with hair; thus showing that the same God who made the lofty Swiss mountain attended to the comfort of His tiniest creatures, even providing socks and mittens for the little fly whose home these mountains were. *This God is OUR GOD!*

A doubting soul beheld a robin's nest in a gigantic elm and heard a still small voice saying, "If God spent a hundred years in creating a tree like that for a bird, He will surely take care of you." God is so interested, that He takes us one by one and arranges for every detail of our life. To Him, *there are no little things.*

"The God of the *infinite* is the God of the *infinitesimal.*"

I saw a human life ablaze with God,
I felt a power Divine
As through an empty vessel of frail clay
I saw God's glory shine.

Then woke I from a dream, and cried aloud:
"My Father, give to me
The blessing of a life consumed by God
That I may live for Thee."

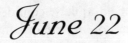

June 22

MORNING

❦

Love covereth (PROV. 10:12).

Be eager in pursuit of this love (1 COR. 13:7–13 WEYMOUTH).

Rehearse your troubles to God only. Not long ago I read in a paper a bit of personal experience from a precious child of God, and it made such an impression upon me that I record it here. She wrote:

"I found myself one midnight wholly sleepless as the surges of a cruel injustice swept over me, and the love which covers seemed to have crept out of my heart. Then I cried to God in an agony for the power to obey His injunction, 'Love covereth.'

"Immediately the Spirit began to work in me the power that brought about the forgetfulness.

"Mentally I dug a grave. Deliberately I threw up the earth until the excavation was deep.

"Sorrowfully I lowered into it the thing which wounded me. Quickly I shoveled in the clods.

"Over the mound I carefully laid the green sods. Then I covered it with white roses and forget-me-nots, and quickly walked away.

"Sweet sleep came. The wound which had been so nearly deadly was healed without a scar, and I know not today what caused my grief."

> *There was a scar on yonder mountain-side,*
> *Gashed out where once the cruel storm had trod;*
> *A barren, desolate chasm, reaching wide*
> *Across the soft green sod.*
>
> *But years crept by beneath the purple pines,*
> *And veiled the scar with grass and moss once more,*
> *And left it fairer now with flowers and vines*
> *Than it had been before.*
>
> *There was a wound once in a gentle heart,*
> *Whence all life's sweetness seemed to ebb and die;*
> *And love's confiding changed to bitter smart,*
> *While slow, sad years went by.*

Yet as they passed, unseen an angel stole
And laid a balm of healing on the pain,
Till love grew purer in the heart made whole,
And peace came back again.

EVENING

∽✇∾

Not I, but Christ. (GAL. 2:20)

Full of the Holy Ghost. (ACTS 11:24)

We would in Thee abide,
In Thee be glorified,
And shine as candles "lighted by the Lord."

For long the wick of my lamp had served my purpose, silently ministering as I read beside it. I felt ashamed that I had not before noticed its unobtrusive ministry. I said to the wick:

"For the service of many months I thank thee."

"What have I done for thee?"

"Hast thou not given light upon my page?"

"Indeed, no; I have no light to give, in proof whereof take me from my bath of oil, and see how quickly I expire. Thou wilt soon turn from me as a piece of smoking tow. It is not I that burns, but *the oil with which my texture is saturated.* It is this that lights thee. I simply mediate between the oil in the cistern and the fire on my edge. This blackened edge slowly decays, but the light continually burns."

"Dost thou not fear becoming exhausted? See how many inches of coil remain! Wilt thou be able to give light till every inch of this is slowly charred and cut away?"

"I have no fear so long as the supply of oil does not fail, if only some kindly hand will remove from time to time the charred margin . . . exposing a fresh edge to the flame. This is my twofold need: *oil and trimming.* Give me these and I shall burn to the end!"

God has called His children to shine as "lights in the world." Let us, then, beware of hiding our light—whether household candle, street lamp, or lighthouse gleam—lest men stumble to their death.

It is at variance with the teaching of the wick to try and accumulate a stock of grace in a sacrament, a convention, or a night of prayer. The wick has no such stores, but is always supplied!

You may seem altogether helpless and inadequate; but a living fountain of oil is prepared to furnish you with inexhaustible supplies: *Not by your might or power, but by His Spirit.* Hour after hour the oil climbs up the wick to the flame!

You Cannot Exhaust God!

Let us not *flinch* when the snuffers are used; they only cut away the black charred debris. He thinks so much of His work that He uses *golden* snuffers! And the Hand that holds the snuffers bears *the nailprint of Calvary!*

F. B. MEYER

June 23

MORNING

When Peter was come down out of the ship, he walked on the water, to go to Jesus. But when he saw the wind boisterous, he was afraid; and beginning to sink, he cried, saying, Lord, save me
(MATT. 14:29, 30).

*P*eter had a little faith in the midst of his doubts, says Bunyan; and so with crying and coming he was brought to Christ.

But here you see that sight was a hindrance; the waves were none of his business when once he had set out; all Peter had any concern with, was the pathway of light that came gleaming across the darkness from where Christ stood. If it was tenfold Egypt beyond that, Peter had no call to look and see.

When the Lord shall call to you over the waters, "Come," step gladly forth. Look not for a moment away from Him.

Not by measuring the waves can you prevail; not by gauging the wind will you grow strong; to scan the danger may be to fall before it; to pause at the difficulties, is to have them break above your head. Lift up your eyes unto the hills, and go forward—there is no other way.

> *Dost thou fear to launch away?*
> *Faith lets go to swim!*
> *Never will He let thee go;*
> *'Tis by trusting thou shalt know*
> *Fellowship with Him.*

Men ought always to pray, and not to faint. (LUKE 18:1)

*T*hat little "ought" is emphatic. It implies obligation as high as heaven. *Jesus* said, "Men ought *always* to pray," and added, "and *not to faint.*"

I confess I do not always *feel* like praying—when, judging by my feelings, there is no listening to my prayer. And then these words have stirred me to pray:

I ought to pray—
I ought always to pray—
I should not grow faint in praying.

Praying is a form of work. The farmer plows his field often when he does not *feel* like it, but he confidently expects a crop for his labors. Now, if prayer is a form of work, and *our labor is not in vain in the Lord,* should we not pray regardless of feelings? Once when I knelt for morning prayers I felt a sort of deadness in my soul, and just then the "accuser of the brethren" became busy reminding me of things that had long since been under the Blood. I cried to God for help, and the blessed Comforter reminded me that my Great High Priest was pleading my case; that I must come boldly to the throne of grace. I did, and the enemy was routed! What a blessed time of communion I had with my Lord! Had I fainted instead of *fighting* I could not have received wages because I had not labored fervently in prayer; I could not have *reaped* because I had not *sown.*   COMMISSIONER BRENGLE

June 24

MORNING

❧❧

Concerning the work of my hands command ye me (ISA. 45:11).

*O*ur Lord spoke in this tone when He said, "Father, I will." Joshua used it when, in the supreme moment of triumph, he lifted up his spear toward the setting sun, and cried, "Sun, stand thou still!"

Elijah used it when he shut the heavens for three years and six months, and again opened them.

Luther used it when, kneeling by the dying Melanchthon, he forbade death to take his prey.

It is a marvelous relationship into which God bids us enter. We are familiar with words like those which follow in this paragraph: "I, even my hands, have stretched out the heavens, and all their host have I commanded." But that God should invite us to command His, this is a change in relationship which is altogether startling!

What a difference there is between this attitude and the hesitating, halting, unbelieving prayers to which we are accustomed, and which by their perpetual repetition lose edge and point!

How often during His earthly life did Jesus put men into a position to command Him! When entering Jericho, He stood still, and said to the blind beggars:

"What will ye that I shall do unto you?" It was as though He said, "I am yours to command."

Can we ever forget how He yielded to the Syrophoenician woman the key to His resources and told her to help herself even as she would?

What mortal mind can realize the full significance of the position to which our God lovingly raises His little children? He seems to say, "All my resources are at your command." *"Whatsoever ye shall ask in my name, that will I do."*

F. B. MEYER

Say to this mountain, "Go,
Be cast into the sea";
And doubt not in thine heart
That it shall be to thee.
It shall be done, doubt not His Word,
Challenge thy mountain in the Lord!

Claim thy redemption right,
Purchased by precious blood;
The Trinity unite
To make it true and good.
It shall be done, obey the Word,
Challenge thy mountain in the Lord!

Self, sickness, sorrow, sin,
The Lord did meet that day
On His beloved One,
And thou art "loosed away."

It has been done, rest on His Word,
Challenge thy mountain in the Lord!

Compass the frowning wall
With silent prayer, then raise—
Before its ramparts fall—
The victor's shout of praise.
It shall be done, faith rests assured,
Challenge thy mountain in the Lord!

The two-leaved gates of brass,
The bars of iron yield,
To let the faithful pass,
Conquerors in every field.
It shall be done, the foe ignored,
Challenge thy mountain in the Lord!

Take then the faith of God,
Free from the taint of doubt;
The miracle-working rod
That casts all reasoning out.
It shall be done, stand on the Word,
Challenge thy mountain in the Lord!

SELECTED

EVENING

*Yet amid all these things we are more than conquerors through him
who has loved us.* (ROM. 8:37 WEYMOUTH)

The best steel is subjected to the alternatives of extreme heat and extreme cold. In a cutlery you will notice that knife blades are heated and beaten, and then heated again and plunged into the coldest water in order to give them the right shape and temper. You will also observe a large heap of rejected blades, rejected because they would not bear the tempering process; when put upon the grindstone little flaws appeared in some that up to that point had seemed perfect; others would not bear the tempering process.

Souls are heated in the furnace of affliction, plunged into the cold waters of tribulation, and ground between the upper and nether stones of adversity and disaster. Some come out ready for the highest services; others are unfit for any but the lowest uses. Would you be of account among the forces which are working out the salvation of the world? *Be still in the Hands of God until He tempers you.*

"Stop now!" says the Knife-blade to the Cutler. "I have been in the fire often enough! Would you burn the life out of me?"

But again it goes into the glowing furnace and is heated to white heat.

"Stop hammering! I have been pounded enough already."

But down comes the sledge.

"Keep me out of this cold water! One moment in the fiery furnace, and the next in ice water. It is enough to kill one!"

But in it goes.

"Keep me off the grindstone! You'll chafe the life out of me!"

But it is made to kiss the stone until the Cutler is satisfied.

Now see! You may bend it double; yet it springs back straight as an arrow. It is as bright as polished silver, hard as a diamond, and will cut like a Damascus blade. *It has been shaped, tempered, and polished; it is worth something.*

Be still, and *let God temper and polish you, and you will be worth something, too. Allow yourself to be prepared for usefulness. He will give you a post of holy renown if you will let Him fit you for it.*

Be still in the furnace fire *while the Holy Ghost molds and polishes your soul.*

R. V. LAWRENCE

June 25

MORNING

❧

Speak unto the children of Israel, that they go forward
(EXOD. 14:15).

Imagine, O child of God, if you can, that triumphal march! The excited children restrained from ejaculations of wonder by the perpetual hush of their parents; the most uncontrollable excitement of the women as they found themselves suddenly saved from a fate worse than death; while the men followed or accompanied them ashamed or confounded that they had ever mistrusted God or murmured against Moses; and as you see those mighty walls of water piled by the outstretched hand of the Eternal, in response to the faith of a single man, learn what God will do for His own.

Dread not any result of implicit obedience to His command; fear not the angry waters which, in their proud insolence, forbid your progress. Above the voice of many waters, the mighty breakers of the sea, "the Lord sitteth King for ever."

A storm is only as the outskirts of His robe, the symptom of His advent, the environment of His presence.

Dare to trust Him; dare to follow Him! And discover that the very forces which barred your progress and threatened your life, at His bidding become the materials of which an avenue is made at liberty.

F. B. MEYER

Have you come to the Red Sea place in your life,
Where, in spite of all you can do,
There is no way out, there is no way back,
There is no other way but through?
Then wait on the Lord with a trust serene
Till the night of your fear is gone;
He will send the wind, He will heap the floods,
When He says to your soul, "Go on."

And His hand will lead you through—clear through—
Ere the watery walls roll down,
No foe can reach you, no wave can touch,
No mightiest sea can drown;
The tossing billows may rear their crests,
Their foam at your feet may break,
But over their bed you shall walk dry shod
In the path that your Lord will make.

In the morning watch, 'neath the lifted cloud,
You shall see but the Lord alone,
When He leads you on from the place of the sea
To a land that you have not known;
And your fears shall pass as your foes have passed;
You shall be no more afraid;
You shall sing His praise in a better place,
A place that His hand has made.

ANNIE JOHNSON FLINT

I told them of the hand of my God which was good upon me.
(NEH. 2:18)

*I*s the work God's work? Has He called you to do it, and equipped you for it? *Be sure on these points.* Take time to consider and pray and find what the will of the Lord is. Then, when the difficulties have been considered and the needs fairly measured, and the clear conviction remains that God calls you to rise and build, then, *put your hand to the plow and never look back.*

Power to endure to the end—patience to outlast all discouragements—zeal that will not die out, and that will enkindle the zeal of others—*all these are given and secured to him who knows that the work and call are from God.*

For every worker and every work in the kingdom of God the principles are the same. The only way to avoid being repelled and discouraged in the work, so as to give it up in irritation, disgust or despair, is to get the work put upon the *right lines* from the very start. These must *begin* in the secret place of the Most High—the Holy of Holies—*alone with God.* They must *proceed* to the Holy Place, for the light and strength contained therein—the guidance and equipment needed. Then, and not till then can they safely *come out,* their success secure and their permanence established, because they are thus truly *"wrought in God."*

HUBERT BROOKE

While the yoke of the Lord Jesus is easy and His burden light, nevertheless the furrow that He calls us to undertake is not always by any means easy plowing. There is no yoke that fits so smoothly and handily as His, but there is no work that requires more steady trudging and persistent faithfulness than His. Three stages of that work are strikingly set forth by Hudson Taylor when he says: "Commonly there are three stages in work for God:

Impossible, Difficult, Done!"

Said General William Booth, *"God loves with a special love the man who has a passion for the impossible."* Are you confronting today the *impossible* in work for God? Praise Him for that, because you are in a way to discover the blessing of finding that *work difficult,* and then to experience the deep joy of finding it *done,* by the same Lord who started you on the furrow.

Am I Thy friend?
And canst Thou count on me,
Lord, to be true to Thee?
Canst Thou depend
On sympathy and help of mine,
In purpose, aim,
Or work of Thine,
And trust me with the honor of Thy name?

June 26

MORNING

For what if some did not believe? Shall their unbelief make the faith of God without effect? (ROM. 3:3).

I think that I can trace every scrap of sorrow in my life to simple unbelief. How could I be anything but quite happy if I believed always that all the past is forgiven, and all the present furnished with power, and all the future bright with hope because of the same abiding facts which do not change with my mood, do not stumble because I totter and stagger at the promise through unbelief, but stand firm and clear with their peaks of pearl cleaving the air of eternity, and the bases of their hills rooted unfathomable in the rock of God. Mont Blanc does not become a phantom or a mist because a climber grows dizzy on its side.

JAMES SMETHAM

Is it any wonder that, when we stagger at any promise of God through unbelief, we do not receive it? Not that faith merits an answer, or in any way earns it, or works it out; but God has made *believing* a condition of receiving, and the Giver has a sovereign right to choose His own terms of gift.

REV. SAMUEL HART

Unbelief says, "How can such and such things be?" It is full of "hows"; but faith has one great answer to the ten thousand "hows," and that answer is—GOD!

C. H. M.

No praying man or woman accomplishes *so much* with *so little* expenditure of time as when he or she is praying.

If there should arise, it has been said—and the words are surely true to the thought of our Lord Jesus Christ in all His teaching on prayer—if there should arise ONE UTTERLY BELIEVING MAN, *the history of the world might be changed.*

Will YOU not be that one in the providence and guidance of God our Father?
A. E. MCADAM

Prayer without faith degenerates into objectless routine, or soulless hypocrisy. Prayer with faith brings omnipotence to back our petitions. Better not pray unless and until your whole being responds to the efficacy of your supplication. When the true prayer is breathed, earth and heaven, the past and the future, say Amen. And Christ prayed such prayers.
P. C. M.

"Nothing lies beyond the reach of prayer except that which lies outside the will of God."

EVENING

Lo, I am with you always, even to the close of the age.
(MATT. 28:20, TRANS.)

Many with lacerated feet have come back to tell the story and to testify that when the very foundations of earth seemed giving way, He remained whom no accident could take away, no chance ever change. This is the power of the Great Companionship.

Stretched on a rack, where they were torturing him piteously, one of the martyrs saw with cleansed and opened eyes, a Young Man by his side—*not yet fifty years old*—who kept wiping the beads of sweat from his brow.

When the fire is hottest, He is there. *"And the form of the fourth is like the Son of God." (Dan. 3:25). "He that is near Me is near the fire."* That is why the heart of the Divine furnace is the place of the soul's deepest peace. There is always ONE beside us when we go through the fire.

When John G. Paton stood beside that lonely grave in the South Sea Islands; when he with his own hands made his wife's coffin, and with his own hands dug her grave, the savages were looking on. They had never seen it in this fashion. That man must fill in the sepulcher, and soon leave it. He says, "If it had not been for Jesus and the Presence that He vouchsafed me there, I would have gone mad and died beside that lonely grave." But John G. Paton found his Master with him through the dire darkness.

Sir Ernest Shackleton and two of his companions spent thirty-six hours among the snow mountains of New Georgia, seeking for a station that meant life or death to them and their waiting crew on Elephant Island. Writing of that journey, he says, *"It seemed to me, often, that we were four, not three."* He refers to the "guiding Presence" that went with them. Then in closing he writes, "A record of our journey would be incomplete without a reference to a subject so near to our hearts."

Paul was not peculiarly privileged when he saw the Living One while en route to Damascus.

Kahlil Gibran, the Syrian, explaining his remarkable modern painting of Jesus, said: "Last night I saw His face again, clearer than I have ever seen it."

Handel, composer of the "Hallelujah Chorus," declared: "I did see God on His throne."

During the terrible stress of war many affirmed positively that they saw "The White Comrade."

Phillips Brooks testified, "He is here. I know Him. He knows me. It is not a figure of speech. It is the realest thing in the world."

> *No distant Lord have I,*
> *Loving afar to be;*
> *Made flesh for me, He cannot rest*
> *Until He rests in me.*
>
> *Brother in joy or pain,*
> *Bone of my bone was He;*
> *Now—intimacy closer still—*
> *He dwells Himself in me.*
>
> *I need not journey far,*
> *This dearest Friend to see;*
> *Companionship is always mine,*
> *He makes His home with me.*
>
> MALTBIE D. BABCOCK

June 27

MORNING

❦

The Lord hath sent strength for thee (PS. 68:28 PBV).

The Lord imparts unto us that primary strength of character which makes everything in life work with intensity and decision. We are "strengthened with might by his Spirit in the inner man." And the strength is continuous; reserves of power come to us which we cannot exhaust.

"As thy days, so shall thy strength be"—strength of will, strength of affection, strength of judgment, strength of ideals and achievement.

"The Lord is my strength" *to go on.* He gives us power to tread the dead level, to walk the long lane that seems never to have a turning, to go through those long reaches of life which afford no pleasant surprise, and which depress the spirits in the sameness of a terrible drudgery.

"The Lord is my strength" *to go up.* He is to me the power by which I can climb the Hill Difficulty and not be afraid.

"The Lord is my strength" *to go down.* It is when we leave the bracing heights, where the wind and the sun have been about us, and when we begin to come down the hill into closer and more sultry spheres, that the heart is apt to grow faint.

I heard a man say the other day concerning his growing physical frailty, "It is the coming down that tires me!"

"The Lord is my strength" *to sit still.* And how difficult is the attainment! Do we not often say to one another, in seasons when we are compelled to be quite, "If only I could do something!"

When the child is ill, and the mother stands by in comparative impotence, how severe is the test! But to do nothing, just to sit still and wait, requires tremendous strength. "The Lord is my strength!" "Our sufficiency is of God."   *FROM* THE SILVER LINING

EVENING

❦

Stormy wind fulfilling his word. (PS. 148:8)

Did you ever go into the woods late in the afternoon on a day of howling wind and driving rain; and did you ever see a drearier spectacle, or hear drearier sounds? The sough of the winds through the almost bare branches, the drip, drip of the rain upon the masses of withered leaves, the air filled with flying leaves fluttering down in the gloom of the forest as into a grave, the delicate colors of trunk and moss all changed and stained and blended by the soaking of the rain: how hard to believe that such dreariness is related in any way to the beauty of the summer forest!

And yet we know that it is that very wind which is rocking the trees and howling so dismally—just that streaming rain and those rotting leaves which will help to clothe the forest trees next year with verdure, and to make the woods sing with joy and pulsate with life. All winds and weathers are favorable to the development of the sturdy, well-rooted tree; even the hurricane which strips it of its leaves and branches, quickens all its vital powers, challenging it to put forth greater strength.

If the tree is cut down in part, the result is a sturdier trunk and a more compact and symmetrical growth. Even if it is toppled over by a storm, its acorns are scattered and become the seeds of the forest. In its ruin it goes back to the soil from which spring other trees.

So you are better and purer and stronger today because of the tears and the sighing and the desolation. You know, and the world knows, that your life is richer, better poised, more trustful, less selfish, more detached from the things of sense—that the whole atmosphere is somehow purer and more vitalizing.

"Stormy wind fulfilling his word," and the soul that hears in their tumult the rustling of Almighty Wings praises God for the storm—the storm that swings free from enervating ease; the flood that casts upon the Eternal Rock.

> *Storms make a strong tree—*
> *Sufferings make a strong saint!*

June 28

MORNING

∽

A door was opened in heaven (REV. 4:1).

You must remember that John was in the Isle of Patmos, a lone, rocky, inhospitable prison, for the Word of God and the testimony of Jesus. And yet to him, under such circumstances, separated from all the loved ones of Ephesus; debarred from the worship of church; condemned to the companionship of uncongenial fellow-captives, were vouchsafed these visions. For him, also a door was opened.

We are reminded of Jacob, exiled from his father's house, who laid himself down in a desert place to sleep, and in his dreams beheld a ladder which united heaven with earth, and at the top stood God.

Not to these only, but to many more, doors have been opened into heaven, when, so far as the world was concerned, it seemed as though their circumstances were altogether unlikely for such revelations.

To prisoners and captives; to constant sufferers, bound by iron chains of pain to sick couches; to lonely pilgrims and wanderers; to women detained from the Lord's house by the demands of home, how often has the door been opened to heaven.

But there are conditions. You must know what it is to be in the Spirit; you must be pure in heart and obedient in faith; you must be willing to count all things but loss for the excellency of the knowledge of Jesus Christ; then when God is all in all to us, when we live, move and have our being in His favor, to us also will the door be opened.

FROM DAILY DEVOTIONAL COMMENTARY

God hath His mountains bleak and bare,
Where He doth bid us rest awhile;
Crags where we breathe a purer air,
Lone peaks that catch the day's first smile.

God hath His deserts broad and brown—
A solitude—a sea of sand,
Where He doth let heaven's curtain down,
Unknit by His Almighty hand.

EVENING

With God nothing shall be impossible. (LUKE 1:37)

Those who have had the joy of climbing the Swiss mountains in springtime will have learned to love the Soldanella, with its delicate little mauve bells. Many years ago there appeared a booklet by Lilias Trotter, "The Glory of the Impossible," with a sketch of this little plant just above the snow. We have never forgotten her exquisite application of the lesson, as she traced the power of this fragile plant to melt its way through the icy covering into the sunshine overhead.

We love to see the impossible done and so does God!

"Canst thou prevail
To pierce the snow?
Thou art so frail,
And icy winds do blow!"
"I will lift up my head
And trusting, onward go."

"Now hard as rock
Frozen and dry,
Thy strength to mock,
What profits it to try?
The snow will bar thy way."
"On God I will rely."

"Thou art so weak,
Tender and fair,
Why not go, seek
A balmier softer air?"
"God chose my lot for me,
And will sustain me there."

"Wilt thou keep on?
Alas! the fight
Is stern from dawn
Til eve." "Tis not by might
The victory is won;
God puts my foes to flight."

And now above
In blaze of day,
Wonder of love,
We see the flower and say,
"Naught is impossible
To him who trusts alway."
JUST TRUSTING, BY J. B. L.

The incense buds of the kiku (chrysanthemum) will open even in the frost.　　　　　　　　　　　　　　　**JAPANESE PROVERB**

June 29

MORNING

❧❧

There we saw the giants (NUM. 13:33).

Yes, they saw the giants, but Caleb and Joshua saw God!
Those who doubt say, *"We be not able to go up."* Those who believe
says, *"Let us go up at once and possess it, for we are well able."*

Giants stand for great difficulties; and giants are stalking everywhere.
They are in our families, in our churches, in our social life, in our own
hearts; and we must overcome them or they will eat us up, as these men
of old said of the giants of Canaan.

The men of faith said, "They are bread for us; we will eat them up."
In other words, "We will be stronger by overcoming them than if there
had been no giants to overcome."

Now the fact is, unless we have the overcoming faith we shall be eaten
up, consumed by the giants in our path. Let us have the spirit of faith that
these men of faith had, and see God, and He will take care of the difficulties.   SELECTED

It is when we are in the way of *duty* that we find *giants*. It was when
Israel was going *forward* that the giants appeared. When they turned back
into the wilderness they found none.

There is a prevalent idea that the power of God in a human life should
lift us above all trials and conflicts. The fact is, the power of God always
brings a conflict and a struggle. One would have thought that on his great
missionary journey to Rome, Paul would have been carried by some
mighty providence above the power of storms and tempests and enemies.
But, on the contrary, it was one long, hard fight with persecuting Jews,
with wild tempests, with venomous vipers and all the powers of earth and
hell, and at last he was saved, as it seemed, by the narrowest margin, and
had to swim ashore at Malta on a piece of wreckage and barely escape a
watery grave.

Was that like a God of infinite power? Yes, just like Him. And so Paul
tells us that when he took the Lord Jesus Christ as the life of his body, a
severe conflict immediately came; indeed, a conflict that never ended, a
pressure that was persistent, but out of which he always emerged victorious through the strength of Jesus Christ.

The language in which he describes this is most graphic. "We are troubled on every side, yet not distressed; perplexed, but not in despair; per-

secuted, but not forsaken; cast down, but not destroyed, always bearing about in the body the dying of the Lord Jesus, that the life also of Jesus might be manifested in our body."

What a ceaseless, strenuous struggle! It is impossible to express in English the forcible language of the original. There are five pictures in succession. In the first, the idea is crowding enemies pressing in from every side, and yet not crushing him because the police of heaven cleared the way just wide enough for him to get through. The literal translation would be, "We are crowded on every side, but not crushed."

The second picture is that of one whose way seems utterly closed and yet he has pressed through; there is light enough to show him the next step. The Revised Version translates it, "Perplexed but not unto despair." Rotherham still more literally renders it, "Without a way, but not without a by-way."

The third figure is that of an enemy in hot pursuit while the Divine Defender still stands by, and he is not left alone. Again we adopt the fine rendering of Rotherham, "Pursued but not abandoned."

The fourth figure is still more vivid and dramatic. The enemy has overtaken him, has struck him, has knocked him down. But it is not a fatal blow; he is able to rise again. It might be translated, "Overthrown but not overcome."

Once more the figure advances, and now it seems to be even death itself, "Always bearing about in the body the dying of the Lord Jesus." But he does not die, for "the life also of Jesus" now comes to his aid and he lives in the life of another until his life work is done.

The reason so many fail in this experience of divine healing is because they expect to have it all without a struggle, and when the conflict comes and the battle wages long, they become discouraged and surrender. God has nothing worth having that is easy. There are no cheap goods in the heavenly market. Our redemption cost all that God had to give, and everything worth having is expensive. Hard places are the very school of faith and character, and if we are to rise over mere human strength and prove the power of life divine in these mortal bodies, it must be through a process of conflict that may well be called the birth travail of a new life. It is the old figure of the bush that burned, but was not consumed, or of the vision in the house of the interpreter of the flame that would not expire, notwithstanding the fact that the demon ceaselessly poured water on it, because in the background stood an angel ever pouring oil and keeping the flame aglow.

No, dear suffering child of God, you cannot fail if only you dare to believe, to stand fast and refuse to be overcome.   *FROM A* TRACT

❧❧

Thy people shall be a freewill offering in the day of thy power . . .
thou shalt have the dew of thy youth. (PS. 110:3, TRANS.)

This is what the term *consecration* properly means. It is the voluntary surrender or self-offering of the heart, by the constraint of love *to be the Lord's.* Its glad expression is "I am my Beloved's."

It must spring, of course, from faith. There must be the full confidence that we are safe in this abandonment; that we are not falling over a precipice, or surrendering ourselves to the hands of a judge, but that we are sinking into the Father's arms and stepping into an infinite inheritance. Oh, *it is an infinite inheritance!* Oh, it is an infinite privilege to be permitted thus to give ourselves up to One who pledges Himself to make us all that we would love to be; nay, all that His infinite wisdom, power, and love will delight to accomplish in us!

It is the clay yielding itself to the porter's hands, that it may be shaped into a vessel of honor, meet for the Master's use.

It is the poor street waif consenting to become the child of a prince, that he may be educated and provided for; that he may be prepared to inherit all the wealth of his guardian.   **DAYS OF HEAVEN UPON EARTH**

He ventured all: the loss of place,
and power, and love of kin—
O bitter loss! O loneliness and pain!
He gained the Christ! Who would not dare
the loss
Such priceless bliss to win?
Christ for today, and each tomorrow—
Christ!
PAUL, BY J. MANNINGTON DEXTER

Make a supreme consecration!

June 30

❧❧

There was silence, and I heard a still voice (JOB 4:16, MARGIN).

A score of years ago, a friend placed in my hand a book called *True Peace*. It was an old medieval message, and it had but one thought—that God was waiting in the depths of my being to talk to me if I would only get still enough to hear His voice.

I thought this would be a very easy matter, and so began to get still. But I had no sooner commenced than a perfect pandemonium of voices reached my ears, a thousand clamoring notes from without and within, until I could hear nothing but their noise and din.

Some were my own voices, my own questions, some my very prayers. Others were suggestions of the tempter and the voices from the world's turmoil.

In every direction I was pulled and pushed and greeted with noisy acclamations and unspeakable unrest. It seemed necessary for me to listen to some of them and to answer some of them; but God said,

"Be still, and know that I am God!" Then came the conflict of thoughts for tomorrow, and its duties and cares; but God said, "Be still."

And as I listened, and slowly learned to obey, and shut my ears to every sound, I found after a while that when the other voices ceased, or I ceased to hear them, there was a still small voice in the depths of my being that began to speak with an inexpressible tenderness, power and comfort.

As I listened, it became to me the voice of prayer, the voice of wisdom, the voice of duty, and I did not need to think so hard, or pray so hard, or trust so hard; but that "still small voice" of the Holy Spirit in my heart was God's prayer in my secret soul, was God's answer to all my questions, was God's life and strength for soul and body, and became the substance of all knowledge, and all prayer and all blessing: for it was the living GOD Himself as my life, as all.

It is thus that our spirit drinks in the life of our risen Lord, and we go forth to life's conflicts and duties like a flower that has drunk in, through the shades of night, the cool and crystal drops of dew. But as *dew never falls on a stormy night,* so the dews of His grace never come to the restless soul.

A. B. SIMPSON

❧❧

*And there was a voice from the firmament . . . when they stood, and
had let down their wings.* (EZEK. 1:25)

*If in God's starry universe there throbbed
No heart but His and mine, I would not plod
With eyes earthbound, hungry of soul, and robbed
Of a sweet sense of nearness to my God.
For mystic notes that issue from His soul
Would wing their shining way in singing showers
Into my waiting heart, when spared the toll
Of intercourse with men that wastes my powers.*

*Alone with God! My soul, invite the art,
As One who climbed the heights alone to pray,
And in the gentle stillness, heart to heart,
Let Heaven's dew transform this house of clay.
Oh, God is everywhere. Yes, God is here!
Only my faith is dim . . . the world too near.*

EDITH ALICE BANG

In the silences I make in the midst of the turmoil of life I have appointments with God. From these silences I come forth with spirit refreshed,
and with a renewed sense of power. I hear a Voice in the silences, and
become increasingly aware that it is the Voice of God.

Oh, how comfortable is a little glimpse of God!

DAVID BRAINERD

July 1

MORNING

❧❧

There shall be a performance (LUKE 1:45).

*My words shall be fulfilled in their season
[their fixed appointed time]* (LUKE 1:20, GREEK VERSION).

There shall be a performance of those things
That loving heart hath waited long to see;
Those words shall be fulfilled to which she clings,
Because her God hath promised faithfully;
And, knowing Him, she ne'er can doubt His Word;
"He speaks and it is done." The mighty Lord!

There shall be a performance of those things,
O burdened heart, rest ever in His care;
In quietness beneath His shadowing wings
Await the answer to thy longing prayer.
When thou hast "cast thy care," the heart then sings,
There shall be a performance of those things.

There shall be a performance of those things,
O tired heart, believe and wait and pray;
At eventide the peaceful vesper rings,
Though cloud and rain and storm have filled the day.
Faith pierces through the mist of doubt that bars
The coming night sometimes, and finds the stars.

There shall be a performance of those things,
O trusting heart, the Lord to thee hath told;
Let Faith and Hope arise, and plume their wings,
And soar towards the sunrise clouds of gold;
The portals of the rosy dawn swing wide,
Revealing joys the darkening night did hide.

BESSIE PORTER

Matthew Henry says: "We must depend upon the performance of the promise, when all the ways leading up to it are shut up. 'For all the promises of God in him are yea [yes], and in him Amen [so be it], unto the glory of God by us' " (2 Cor. 1:20).

EVENING

Having spoiled principalities and powers, he made a show of them openly, triumphing over them in it. (COL. 2:15)

Here Satan is represented as a conquered foe, and even as a degraded and disarmed antagonist. He has been "spoiled." One is reminded of the figure of a scarecrow on a farmer's field where the dead birds are hung up as warnings against other depredators. He cannot harm us although he may alarm us. He is beaten before the battle begins. We enter the fray with the prestige of victors. Let us hold this high place as we meet our adversary. Let us treat him as a defeated enemy. Let us not honor him by our doubts and fears. It is not our valor or our victory. It is *our confidence in Christ, the Victor, that wins.*

"This is the victory that overcometh the world, even our faith." Our triumph has already been won by our Leader, *but we must identify ourselves with His victory. Let us never dare to doubt!*

"And the hostile princes and rulers He shook off from Himself, and *boldly displayed them as His conquests* when by the Cross He triumphed over them" (Col. 2:15 WEYMOUTH).

Says Dr. Weymouth: "Stand your ground in the day of battle, and having fought to the end, remain victors on the field!" "Victors on the field"—I am thrilled by the inspiring word. After every temptation—the temptation which comes to me in sunshine or the temptation that comes to me in the gloom—after every fight, victors on the field, the Lord's banner flying, and the evil one and all his hosts in utter rout, and in full and dire retreat! J. H. JOWETT

Describing the force of the waves which beat on the Eddystone Lighthouse a writer says: "But without a quiver the lighthouse supports those terrible attacks. Yet it bends toward them as if to render homage to the power of its adversaries."

Let us meet the storms of life with the fixedness and plasticity with which the lighthouse overcomes the wild tempest.

Fastened to the Rock of Ages, I shall not be moved.

July 2
MORNING

When thou goest, thy way shall be opened up before thee step by step
(PROV. 4:12, FREE TRANSLATION).

The Lord never builds a bridge of faith except under the feet of the faith-filled traveler. If He builds the bridge a rod ahead, it would not be a bridge of faith. That which is of sight is not of faith.

There is a self-opening gate which is sometimes used in country roads. It stands fast and firm across the road as a traveler approaches it. If he stops before he gets to it, it will not open. But if he will drive right at it, his wagon wheels press the springs below the roadway, and the gate swings back to let him through. He must push right on at the closed gate, or it will continue to be closed.

This illustrates the way to pass every barrier on the road of duty. Whether it is a river, a gate, or a mountain, all the child of Jesus has to do is to go for it. If it is a river, it will dry up when you are near enough to it, and are still pushing on. If it is a mountain, it will be lifted up and cast into a sea when you come squarely up without flinching, to where you thought it was.   HENRY CLAY TRUMBULL

We sit and weep in vain. The voice of the Almighty said, "Up and onward forevermore." Let us move on and step out boldly, though it be into the night, and we can scarcely see the forest, or the alpine pass, which discloses but a few rods of its length from any single point of view. Press on! If necessary, we will find even the pillar of cloud and fire to mark our journey through the wilderness. There are guides and wayside inns along the road. We will find food, clothes and friends at every stage of the journey, and as Rutherford so quaintly says: "However matters go, the worst will be a tired traveler and a joyful and sweet welcome home."

> *I'm going by the upper road, for that*
> *still holds the sun,*
> *I'm climbing through night's pastures where*
> *the starry rivers run:*
> *If you should think to seek me in my*
> *old dark abode,*
> *You'll find this writing on the door,*
> *"He's on the Upper Road."*
> SELECTED

EVENING

When I was hemmed in, Thou hast freed me often. (PS. 4:1, TRANS.)

It is a little thing to trust God as far as we can see Him, as far as the way lies open before us; but to trust Him when we are hedged in on every side and can see no way to escape, this is good and acceptable with God. This is the faith of Abraham, our father.

"Under hopeless circumstances, he hopefully believed."

Abraham Lincoln, during the Civil War, once said: "I have been driven many times to my knees by the overwhelming conviction that I had nowhere else to go. My own wisdom and that of all about me seemed insufficient for the day."

The greatest men, without God, are nothing but dismal failures.

> The devil may wall you 'round
> But he cannot roof you in;
> He may fetter your feet and tie your hands
> And strive to hamper your soul with bands
> As his way has ever been;
> But he cannot hide the face of God
> And the Lord shall be your light,
> And your eyes and your thoughts can rise to the sky,
> Where His clouds and His winds and His birds go by,
> And His stars shine out at night.
>
> The devil may wall you 'round;
> He may rob you of all things dear,
> He may bring his hardest and roughest stone
> And thinks to cage you and keep you alone,
> But he may not press too near;
> For the Lord has planted a hedge inside,
> And has made it strong and tall,
> A hedge of living and growing green;
> And ever it mounts and keeps between
> The trusting soul and the devil's wall.
>
> The devil may wall you 'round,
> But the Lord's hand covers you,
> And His hedge is a thick and thorny hedge,
> And the devil can find no entering wedge
> Nor get his finger through;
> He may circle about you all day long,
> But he cannot work as he would,
> For the will of the Lord restrains his hand,
> And he cannot pass the Lord's command
> And his evil turns to good.
>
> The devil may wall you 'round,
> With his gray stones, row on row,
> But the green of the hedge is fresh and fair,

July 3

MORNING

❧

Doth the plowman plow all day to sow? (ISA. 28:24).

One day in early summer I walked past a beautiful meadow. The grass was as soft and thick and fine as an immense green Oriental rug. In one corner stood a fine old tree, a sanctuary for numberless wild birds; the crisp, sweet air was full of their happy songs. Two cows lay in the shade, the very picture of content.

Down by the roadside the saucy dandelion mingled his gold with the royal purple of the wild violet.

I leaned against the fence for a long time, feasting my hungry eyes, and thinking in my soul that God never made a fairer spot than my lovely meadow.

The next day I passed that way again, and lo! the hand of the despoiler had been there. A plowman and his great plow, now standing idle in the furrow, had in a day wrought a terrible havoc. Instead of the green grass there was turned up to view the ugly, bare, brown earth; instead of the singing birds there were only a few hens industriously scratching for worms. Gone were the dandelion and the pretty violet. I said in my grief, "How could anyone spoil a thing so fair?"

Then my eyes were opened by some unseen hand, and I saw a vision, a vision of a field of ripe corn ready for the harvest. I could see the giant, heavily laden stalks in the autumn sun; I could almost hear the music of the wind as it would sweep across the golden tassels. And before I was aware, the brown earth took on a splendor it had not had the day before.

Oh, that we might always catch the vision of an abundant harvest, when the great Master Plowman comes, as He often does, and furrows through our very souls, uprooting and turning under that which we thought most fair, and leaving for our tortured gaze only the bare and the unbeautiful.   SELECTED

Why should I start at the plough of my Lord, that maketh the deep furrows on my soul? I know He is no idle husbandman, He purposeth a crop.   SAMUEL RUTHERFORD

EVENING

⊷⊶

Your reasonable service. (ROM. 12:1)

*W*hy are we saved? We are saved in order *to be sacrificed*. There is a striking lesson in God's saving certain of the clean beasts and clean fowl at the time of the flood. At God's direction, Noah brought these, as well as other beasts and fowl that were not clean, into the ark of salvation. These clean creatures were favored above those that were lost in the flood. It must have been a wonderful experience to step out from the ark onto dry land again. But what happened then?

"And Noah builded an altar unto the LORD; and took of every clean beast, and of every clean fowl, and offered burnt offerings on the altar" (Gen. 8:20).

Thus it appears *that certain of these creatures were saved in order to be sacrificed after their salvation was complete.* If this surprises us, have we realized that we who believe in Christ are saved for exactly that purpose?

"I beseech you therefore, brethren, by the mercies of God, that ye present your bodies a living sacrifice" *(Rom. 12:1).*

This is *acceptable unto God,* and it is *our reasonable service.*

Noah's sacrifice of the clean animals brought great blessing to the earth, as the record goes on to show us; and the "living sacrifice" of God's children brings great blessing to mankind.

Let us thank God, indeed, that we are saved to be sacrificed.

                                                            SUNDAY SCHOOL TIMES

Laid on Thine altar, O my Lord, Divine,
Accept this day my gift for Jesus' sake.
I have no jewels to adorn Thy shrine,
Nor any world-famed sacrifice to make;
But here I bring within my trembling hand

This will of mine: a thing that seemeth small;
And only Thou dear Lord, canst understand
That when I yield Thee this, I yield Thee all.
It hath been wet with tears and dimmed with sighs,
Clenched in my clasp, till beauty it hath none.

Now from Thy footstool, where it vanquished lies,
The prayer ascendeth: "Let Thy will be done."
Take it, O Father, ere my courage fail,
And blend it so with Thine own will, that e'en
If in some desperate hour my cry prevail,
And Thou giv'st back my gift, it may have been
So changed, so purified, so fair have grown,
So one with Thee, so filled with peace Divine,
I may not know nor feel it as my own,
But gaining back my will may find it Thine.

All I have I am bringing to Thee!

July 4

MORNING

❧

For the vision is yet for an appointed time . . . though it tarry, wait
for it; because it will surely come, it will not tarry (HAB. 2:3).

In the charming little booklet, *Expectation Corner*, Adam Slowman
was led into the Lord's treasure houses, and among many other wonders there revealed to him was the *"Delayed Blessing Office,"* where God
kept certain things, prayed for, until the wise time came to send them.

It takes a long time for some pensioners to learn that *delays are not
denials.* Ah, there are secrets of love and wisdom in the *"Delayed Blessings
Department,"* which are little dreamt of! Men would pluck their mercies
green when the Lord would have them ripe. *"Therefore will the Lord
WAIT, that He may be gracious unto you"* (Isa. 30:18). He is watching
in the hard places and will not allow one trial too many; He will let the
dross be consumed, and then He will come gloriously to your help.

Do not grieve Him by doubting His love. Nay, lift up your head, and
begin to praise Him *even now* for the deliverance which is on the way to

you, and you will be abundantly rewarded for the delay which has tried
your faith.

O Thou of little faith,
God hath not failed thee yet!
When all looks dark and gloomy,
Thou dost so soon forget—

Forget that He has led thee,
And gently cleared thy way;
On clouds has poured His sunshine,
And turned thy night to day.

And if He's helped thee hitherto,
He will not fail thee now;
How it must wound His loving heart
To see thy anxious brow!

Oh! doubt not any longer,
To Him commit thy way,
Whom in the past thou trusted,
And is "just the same today."
SELECTED

EVENING

❧

He shall dwell in the heights: his place of defense shall
be the munitions of rock. . . . Thine eyes . . . shall behold
the land of far distances.
(ISA. 33:16–17, MARGIN)

Up yonder on the rocky cliff in a rough nest of sticks lies an egg. The
eagle's breast-feathers warm it; the sky bends down and invites it;
the abysses of the air beckon it, saying:

All our heights and depths are
for you; come and occupy them.

And all the peaks and the roomy places up under the rafters of the sky,
where the twinkling stars sit sheltered like twittering sparrows, call down
to the pent-up little life, "Come up hither!" and the live germ inside hears
through the thin walls of its prison, and is coaxed out of its shell, and out

of the nest, and off the cliff, and then up and away into the wide ranges
of sunlit air, and down into the deep gulfs that gash mountains apart.

A PILGRIM OF THE INFINITE

I stand upon the mount of God
With sunlight in my soul;
I hear the storms in vales beneath,
I hear the thunders roll.

But I am calm with Thee, my God,
Beneath these glorious skies;
And to the height on which I stand,
No storms, nor clouds, can rise.

Oh, THIS *is life! Oh, this is joy!*
My God, to find Thee so;
Thy face to see, Thy voice to hear,
And all Thy love to know.

HORATIUS BONAR

July 5

MORNING

I will allure her, and bring her into the wilderness.... And I will
give her her vineyards from thence (HOS. 2:14–15).

A strange place to find vineyards—in the wilderness! And can it be
that the riches which a soul needs can be obtained in the wilderness,
which stands for a lonely place, out of which you can seldom find your
way? It would seem so, and not only that, but the "Valley of Achor,"
which means bitterness, is called a door of hope. *And she shall sing there,*
as in the days of her youth!

Yes, God knows our need of the wilderness experience. He knows
where and how to bring out that which is enduring. The soul has been
idolatrous, rebellious; has forgotten God, and with a perfect self-will has
said, "I will follow after my lovers." But she did not overtake them. And,
when she was hopeless and forsaken, God said, "I will allure her, and

bring her into the wilderness, and speak comfortably unto her." What a loving God is ours! *FROM* CRUMBS

We never know where God hides His pools. We see a rock, and we cannot guess it is the home of the spring. We see a flinty place, and we cannot tell it is the hiding place of a fountain. God leads me into the hard places, and then I find I have gone into the dwelling place of eternal springs. SELECTED

EVENING

I will not be afraid of ten thousands of people, that have set themselves against me round about. (PS. 3:6)

*E*vening. Felt much turmoil of spirit, in prospect of having all my plans for the welfare of this great region and this teeming population, knocked on the head by savages tomorrow. But I read that Jesus said: "All power is given unto me in heaven and in earth. Go ye therefore, and teach all nations . . . and, lo, I am with you always, even unto the end of the world"! *It is the word of a Gentleman, of the strictest and most sacred honor.* So there's an end of it! I will not cross furtively tonight as I intended. Should such a man as I flee? Nay, verily, I shall take observations for latitude and longitude tonight, though they may be the last. I feel quite calm now, thank God! FROM THE DIARY OF DAVID LIVINGSTONE

During the terrible days of the Boxer uprising in China, as one report followed another of mission stations destroyed and missionaries massacred, Hudson Taylor sat quietly at his desk singing softly the hymn he loved so dearly:

> *Jesus, I am resting, resting,*
> *In the joy of what Thou art.*

When our confidence is in God we may be superior to circumstances. "If God be for us, who can be against us?" However impossible it may seem to the reasoning of the earthly-minded, it is nevertheless a blessed reality to the trustful child of God, that *"Faith can sing through days of sorrow: 'All, ALL is well!' "*

"Though I was afraid of many things," said John Buchan, *"the thing I feared most mortally was being afraid."*

> *Fierce was the wild billow,*
> *Dark was the night,*

Oars labored heavily;
Foam glimmered white.
Trembled the mariners,
Peril was nigh;
Then said the God of Gods,
"Peace! It is I."

Ridge of the mountain wave,
Lower thy crest.
Wail of the stormy wind,
Be thou at rest.
Peril there none can be;
Sorrow must fly,
Where saith the Light of Life,
"Peace! It is I."

SELECTED

Come into port greatly, or sail with God the seas!

RALPH WALDO EMERSON

July 6

MORNING

Neither know we what to do; but our eyes are upon thee
(2 CHRON. 20:12).

A life was lost in Israel because a pair of human hands were laid unbidden upon the ark of God. They were placed upon it with the best intent, to steady it when trembling and shaking as the oxen drew it along the rough way; but they touched God's work presumptuously, and they fell paralyzed and lifeless. *Much of the life of faith consists in letting things alone.*

If we wholly trust an interest to God, we must keep our hands off it; and He will guard it for us better than we can help Him. "Rest in the Lord, and wait patiently for him: fret not thyself because of him who prospereth in his way, because of the man who bringeth wicked devices to pass."

Things may seem to be going all wrong, but He knows as well as we; and He will arise in the right moment if we are really trusting Him so fully as to let Him work in His own way and time. There is nothing so masterly as inactivity in some things, and there is nothing so hurtful as restless working, for God has undertaken to work His sovereign will.

A. B. SIMPSON

> Being perplexed, I say,
> "Lord, make it right!
> Night is as day to Thee,
> Darkness as light.
> I am afraid to touch
> Things that involve so much;
> My trembling hand may shake,
> My skilless hand may break;
> Thine can make no mistake."
>
> Being in doubt I say,
> "Lord, make it plain;
> Which is the true, safe way?
> Which would be gain?
> I am not wise to know,
> Nor sure of foot to go;
> What is so clear to Thee,
> Lord, make it clear to me!"

It is such a comfort to drop the tangles of life into God's hands and leave them there.

EVENING

For I reckon that the suffering of this present time are not worthy to be compared with the glory which shall be revealed in us.
(ROM. 8:18)

For developing character an imperfect man needs the stimulus and discipline of a *developing* environment, not yet perfected—a world of struggle and resistance: obstacles to be overcome, battles to be won, baffling problems to be solved. He needs not a soft world of ease to lull him to sleep, but a changing environment of action and reaction: cold and heat, summer and winter, sunshine and shadow, light and darkness, pleasure and pain, prosperity and adversity.

As Dr. Hillis said: "He who would ask release from suffering *would take the winter out of the seasons, the glory of the night out of the round of day, the cloud and rainstorms out of the summer; would expel the furrows from the face of Lincoln; would rob Socrates of his dignity and majesty, would make Saint Paul a mere esthetic feeling; would steal the sweetness from maternity; would rob the Divine Sufferer of His sanctity.*"

When the little girl told her music teacher that it hurt her fingers to practice the piano, the teacher answered: *"I know it hurts, but it strengthens them, too."* Then the child packed the philosophy of the ages in her reply: "Teacher, *it seems that everything that strengthens, hurts.*"

God never wastes His children's pain!

God loves much those whom He trusts with sorrow, and designs some precious soul enrichment which comes only through the channel of suffering.

There are things which even God cannot do for us unless He allows us to suffer. *He cannot have the result of the process without the process.*

If you are among "them that love God," *all things are yours!* The stars in their courses fight for you. Every wind that blows can only fill your sails.

God does not test worthless souls!

July 7
MORNING

He hath . . . made me a polished shaft (ISA. 49:2).

There is a very famous "Pebble Beach" at Pescadero, on the California coast. The lone line of white surf comes up with its everlasting roar, and rattles and thunders among the stones on the shore. They are caught in the arms of the pitiless waves, and tossed and rolled, and rubbed together, and ground against the sharp-grained cliffs. Day and night forever the ceaseless attrition goes on—never any rest. And the result?

Tourists from all the world flock thither to gather the round and beautiful stones. They are laid up in cabinets; they ornament the parlor mantels. But go yonder, around the point of the cliff that breaks off the face of the sea; and up in that quiet cove, sheltered from the storms, and lying ever in the sun, you shall find abundance of pebbles that have never been chosen by the traveler.

Why are these left all the years through unsought? For the simple reason that they have escaped all the turmoil and attrition of the waves, and the quiet and peace have left them as they found them, rough and angular and devoid of beauty. *Polish comes through trouble.*

Since God knows what niche we are to fill, let us trust Him to shape us to it. Since He knows what work we are to do, let us trust Him to drill us to the proper preparation.

> *O blows that smite! O hurts that pierce*
> *This shrinking heart of mine!*
> *What are ye but the Master's tools*
> *Forming a work Divine?*

"Nearly all God's jewels are crystallized tears."

EVENING

~∞~

He performeth the thing that is appointed for me. (JOB 23:14)

Let us have confidence in the *purposes of God*. The thought occurs in the writings of Goulburn, Adolph Monod, and others, that the Lord owed that wonderful calmness which marked His life—a calmness which never forsook Him, whether teaching, or traveling, however engaged, however tried—very much to the fact that His Father had a plan for Him; not a plan for a lifetime merely, but a plan for each day; and that He had but to discover what the plan was, and then carry it out; and so, however puzzling and perplexing the maze of duties through which He had to thread His way, nothing ever perplexed or puzzled Him, because, putting His hand in His Father's, *He just walked in the paths prepared for Him.*

Well, now, what if God should have a plan for everyone? What if God should have a plan for *you*? In such a case—surely it is the true case—everything we have to do, everything we have to bear, comes to us as part of a prearranged plan. Things that disturb our work, things that upset our purposes, things that thwart our wishes, interruptions, annoyances—these may all be a part of the plan—God's plan—and should be met accordingly. LIVING WATERS

> *I doubt not through the ages*
> *One Eternal purpose runs.*

There's a throne above the world. There's a Man on the throne. He has a plan for things down here during this time of turmoil and strife. His Spirit is down here to get that plan done. He needs each one of us. He puts His Hand on each Christian life and says, "Separate yourself from all else for the bit I need you to do." His Hand is on *you*. Are you doing it? *Anything else classes as failure.*

THE BENT KNEE TIME, BY S.D. GORDON

July 8
MORNING
~~∞~~

They shall mount up with wings as eagles (ISA. 40:31).

There is a fable about the way the birds got their wings at the beginning. They were first made without wings. Then God made the wings and put them down before the wingless birds and said to them, "Come, take up these burdens and bear them."

The birds had lovely plumage and sweet voices; they could sing, and their feathers gleamed in the sunshine, but they could not soar in the air. They hesitated at first when bidden to take up the burdens that lay at their feet, but soon they obeyed, and taking up the wings in their beaks, laid them on their shoulders to carry them.

For a little while the load seemed heavy and hard to bear, but presently, as they went on carrying the burdens, folding them over their hearts, the wings grew fast to their little bodies, and soon they discovered how to use them, and were lifted by them up into the air—*the weights became wings.*

It is a parable. We are the wingless birds, and our duties and tasks are the pinions God has made to lift us up and carry us heavenward. We look at our burdens and heavy loads, and shrink from them; but as we lift them and bind them about our hearts, they become wings, and on them we rise and soar toward God.

There is no burden which, if we lift it cheerfully and bear it with love in our hearts, will not become a blessing to us. God means our tasks to be our helpers; to refuse to bend our shoulders to receive a load, is to decline a new opportunity for growth. J. R. MILLER

Blessed is any weight, however overwhelming, which God has been so good as to fasten with His own hand upon our shoulders.

F. W. FABER

EVENING

⤜⤝

I was crushed. (2 COR. 1:8, TRANS.)

𝒴ou smell delightfully fragrant," said the Gravel Walk to the bed of Camomile flowers under the window.

"We have been trodden on," replied the Camomiles.

"Does that cause it?" asked the Gravel Walk. "Treading on me produces no sweetness."

"Our natures are different," answered the Camomiles. "Gravel walks become only the harder by being trodden upon; but the effect on our own selves is that, if pressed and bruised when the dew is upon us we give forth the sweet smell you now delight in."

"Very delightful," replied the Gravel Walk.

Trials come alike to the Christian and to the man of the world. The one grows bitter and hardened under the experience, while the other becomes mellow and Christlike. It is because their natures are different.

> *Oh, beautiful rose, please tell me,*
> *For I would like to know,*
> *Why I must crush your petals*
> *That sweet perfume may flow.*
>
> *Oh, life that is clothed in beauty,*
> *Perhaps like that beautiful rose,*
> *You will need to be crushed by suffering*
> *Ere you give out your best; who knows?*
>
> *A life that is crushed by sorrow*
> *Can feel for another's grief,*
> *And send out that sweet perfume of love*
> *That will bring some heart relief.*
>
> *Oh, do not repine at your testing,*
> *When called to pass under the rod,*
> *It is that life might the sweeter be,*
> *And comes from the Hand of God.*
>
> *He knows how much we are needing,*
> *Of sorrow, or suffering, or test,*
> *And only gives to His children*
> *The things that He knoweth are best.*
>
> *Then let us rejoice when He sendeth*

Some sorrow or hardship that tries,
And be glad to be crushed as the rose leaf,
That a sweeter perfume may arise.
FLORA L. OSGOOD

July 9
MORNING

❧

I have chosen thee in the furnace of affliction (ISA. 48:10).

Does not the Word come like a soft shower, assuaging the fury of the flame? Yes, is it not an asbestos armor, against which the heat has no power? Let the affliction come—God has chosen me. Poverty, thou mayest stride in my door; but God is in the house already, and He has *chosen* me. Sickness, thou mayest intrude; but I have a balsam ready—God has *chosen* me. Whatever befall me in this vale of tears, I know that He has *chosen* me.

Fear not, Christian; Jesus is with thee. In all thy fiery trials, His presence is both thy comfort and safety. He will never leave one whom He has chosen for His own. "Fear not, for I am with thee," is His sure word of promise to His chosen ones in "the furnace of affliction."

C. H. SPURGEON

Pain's furnace heat within me quivers,
God's breath upon the flame doth blow;
And all my heart in anguish shivers
And trembles at the fiery glow;
And yet I whisper, "As God will!"
And in the hottest fire hold still.

He comes and lays my heart, all heated,
On the hard anvil, minded so
Into His own fair shape to beat it
With His great hammer, blow on blow;
And yet I whisper, "As God will!"
And at His heaviest blows hold still.

He takes my softened heart and beats it;
The sparks fly off at every blow;

He turns it o'er and o'er and heats it,
And lets it cool, and makes it glow;
And yet I whisper, "As God will!"
And in His mighty hand hold still.

Why should I murmur? for the sorrow
Thus only longer-lived would be;
The end may come, and will tomorrow,
When God has done His work in me;
So I say trusting, "As God will!"
And, trusting to the end, hold still.

JULIUS STURM

The burden of suffering seems a tombstone hung about our necks, while in reality it is only the weight which is necessary to keep down the diver while he is hunting for pearls.   RICHTER

EVENING

My soul thirsteth for thee, my flesh longeth for thee in a dry and thirsty land. (PS. 63:1)

An interesting story is told concerning the northern reindeer. It seems that on those far-off plains, a hundred miles from the sea, at a certain season, in the midst of the Laplander's village a young reindeer will raise his broad muzzle to the north wind, and stare at the limitless distance for the space of a minute or more. He grows restless from that moment, but he is yet alone. The next day a dozen of the herd look up from cropping the moss, snuffing the breeze. Then the Laps nod to one another, and the camp grows daily more unquiet.

At times the whole herd of young deer stand and gaze, as it were, breathing hard through wide nostrils, then jostling each other and stamping the soft ground. They grow unruly and it is hard to harness them into the light sleds. As the days pass the Laps watch them more and more closely, well knowing what will happen sooner or later.

And then, at last, in the northern twilight, the great herd begins to move! The impulse is simultaneous, irresistible; their heads are all turned in one direction. They move slowly at first, still biting here and there at the bunches of rich moss. Presently the slow step becomes a trot, they crowd more closely together, while the Laps hasten to gather up their last unpacked possessions, their cooking utensils and their wooden gods.

The great herd together breaks from a trot to a gallop, from a gallop to a breakneck pace; the distant thunder of their united tread reaches the camp for a few minutes, and then they are gone out of sight and hearing, to drink of the Polar Sea.

The Laps follow after them, dragging painfully their laden sledges in the broad track left by the thousands of galloping beasts; a day's journey, and they are yet far from the sea, and the track is yet broad.

On the second day the path grows narrower, and there are stains of blood to be seen; far on the distant plain before them their sharp eyes distinguish in the direct line a dark, motionless object, another, and yet another. The race has grown more desperate and more wild as the stampede nears the sea. The weaker reindeer have been trampled by their stronger fellows. A thousand sharp hoofs have crushed and cut through hide and flesh and bone. Ever swifter and more terrible in their motion, the ruthless herd has raced onward, careless of the slain, careless of the food, careless of any drink but the sharp, salt water ahead of them. And when the Laplanders reach the shore, their deer are once more quietly grazing, once more tame and docile, once more ready to drag the sled.

Once in its life the reindeer must taste of the sea in one long satisfying draft, and if he is hindered, he perishes! Neither man nor beast dare stand between him and the ocean, in the hundred miles of his arrowlike path!

> *I hear the voice of Jesus say,*
> *"Behold, I freely give*
> *The living water; thirsty one,*
> *Stoop down, and drink, and live!"*
> *I came to Jesus, and I drank*
> *Of that life-giving stream;*
> *My thirst was quenched, my soul revived,*
> *And now I live in Him.*

"Come, O come YE to the Waters!"

July 10

MORNING

❧◦❧

I called him, but he gave me no answer (SONG OF SOL. 5:6).

The Lord, when He hath given great faith, hath been known to try it by long delayings. He has suffered His servants' voices to echo in their ears as from a brazen sky. They have knocked at the golden gate, but it has remained unmovable, as though it were rusted upon its hinges. Like Jeremiah, they have cried, *"Thou hast covered thyself with a cloud, that our prayer should not pass through."* Thus have true saints continued long in patient waiting without reply, not because their prayers were not vehement, nor because they were unaccepted, but because it so pleased Him who is Sovereign, and who gives according to His own pleasure. If it pleases Him to bid our patience exercise itself, shall He not do as He will with His own!

No prayer is lost. Praying breath was never spent in vain. There is no such thing as prayer unanswered or unnoticed by God, and some things that we count refusals or denials are simply delays.　　H. BONAR

Christ sometimes delays His help that He may try our faith and quicken our prayers. The boat may be covered with the waves, and He sleeps on; but He will wake up before it sinks. He sleeps, but He never oversleeps; and there are no "too lates" with Him.

ALEXANDER MACLAREN

Be still, sad soul! lift thou no passionate cry,
But spread the desert of thy being bare
To the full searching of the All-seeing eye;
Wait! and through dark misgiving, black despair,
God will come down in pity, and fill the dry
Dead place with light, and life, and vernal air.
J. C. SHAIRP

❦

And the LORD took me as I followed the flock. (AMOS 7:15)

"Whom have You left behind to carry out the work?" asked the angels. "A little band of men and women who love Me," replied the Lord Jesus.

"But what if they should fail when the trial comes? Will all You have done be defeated?"

"Yes, if they should fail all I have done will be defeated; but *they will not fail!*"

And the angels wondered as they saw the sublime confidence of love which this betokened!

> *"Wilt thou follow Me?"*
> *The Savior asked.*
> *The road looked bright and fair,*
> *And filled with youthful hope and zeal*
> *I answered, "Anywhere."*
>
> *"Wilt thou follow Me?"*
> *Again He asked.*
> *The road looked dim ahead;*
> *But I gave one glance at His glowing face*
> *"To the end, dear Lord," I said.*
>
> *"Wilt thou follow Me?"*
> *I almost blanched,*
> *For the road was rough and new,*
> *But I felt the grip of His steady Hand,*
> *And it thrilled me through and through.*
>
> *"Still followest thou?"*
> *'Twas a tender tone,*
> *And it thrilled my inmost heart.*
> *I answered now, but He drew me close,*
> *And I knew we would never part.*

SELECTED

The way lies through Gethsemane, through the city gate, outside the camp. The way lies alone, and the way lies until there is no trace of a footstep, only the Voice, "Follow Me!" But in the end it leads to "the joy that was set before him" and to the Mount of God.   SELECTED

The hour is desperately dark; your flame is needed.

July 11

MORNING

❧

It came to pass after a while, that the brook dried up, because there had been no rain in the land (1 KINGS 17:7).

Week after week, with unfaltering and steadfast spirit, Elijah watched the dwindling brook; often tempted to stagger through unbelief, but refusing to allow his circumstances to come between himself and God. Unbelief sees God through circumstances, as we sometimes see the sun shorn of his rays through smoky air; but faith puts God between itself and circumstances, and looks at them through Him. And so the dwindling brook became a silver thread; and the silver thread stood presently in pools at the foot of the largest boulders; and the pools shrank. The birds fled; the wild creatures of field and forest came no more to drink; the brook was dry. Only then to his patient and unwavering spirit, "the word of the Lord came saying, Arise, get thee to Zarephath."

Most of us would have gotten anxious and worn with planning long before that. We should have ceased our songs as soon as the streamlet caroled less musically over its rocky bed; and with harps swinging on the willows, we should have paced to and fro upon the withering grass, lost in pensive thought. And probably, long ere the brook was dry, we should have devised some plan, and asking God's blessing on it, would have started off elsewhere.

God often does extricate us, because His mercy endureth forever; but if we had only waited first to see the unfolding of His plans, we should never have found ourselves landed in such an inextricable labyrinth; and we should never have been compelled to retrace our steps with so many tears of shame. *Wait, patiently wait!*   F. B. MEYER

EVENING

❧

He leadeth me beside the waters of quietness. (PS. 23:2, MARGIN)

Is it worthwhile, this ceaseless chase by which so many are affected? Does it pay? And, after all, why this exciting pace which has all too truly become a part of our national program?

Must the sons of men be forever driven like so many beasts of prey? Is there no escape from the feverish haste which persists in manifesting itself in all the walks of life?

It is possible for a Christian to make his active life restful. He may carry the atmosphere of the closet into the street. The Shepherd promises to lead him beside still waters; and those are the deepest waters.

This feverish hurried life which too many of us lead *is not in God's economy, depend upon it.* If we live in this way it is because we push on before the Shepherd instead of letting Him lead us beside still waters.

If we were more docile, we should be more restful.

Only when the soul is brimful of the life of faith does it work in rest. Not until we shall have let our life drop back behind God, *to follow at the rate which He prescribes,* shall we learn what the words mean,

"Thou wilt keep him in perfect peace,
whose mind is stayed on thee."

Our little restless earth, and our little breathless lives will take on dignity and deeper worth if we catch step with the rhythmic movement of the quiet stars.

Most strong men know times of silence. Abraham, alone with God, made the father of a Nation; Moses, in the quietness and stillness of the desert, received God's message at the burning bush. The most of their training was in the school of silence.

It takes time to be spiritual; it doesn't happen!

In the deep jungles of Africa, a traveler was making a long trek. Men had been engaged from a tribe to carry the loads. The first day they marched rapidly and went far. The traveler had high hopes of a speedy journey. But the second morning these jungle tribesmen refused to move. For some strange reason they just sat and rested. On inquiry as to the reason for this strange behavior, the traveler was informed that they had gone too fast the first day, and that *they were now waiting for their souls to catch up with their bodies.*

This whirling rushing life which so many of us live does for us what that first march did for those poor jungle tribesmen. The difference: *they knew* what they needed to restore life's balance; too often *we do not.*

Jesus calls us o'er the tumult
Of our life's wild restless sea.

July 12

MORNING

༄

He hath acquainted himself with my beaten path.
When he hath searched me out, I shall come out shining
(JOB 23:10, FREE TRANSLATION).

"Faith grows amid storms"—just four words, but oh, how full of import to the soul who has been in the storms!

Faith is that God-given faculty which, when exercised, brings the unseen into plan view, and by which the impossible things are made possible. It deals with supernaturals.

But it *"grows amid storms";* that is, where there are disturbances in the spiritual atmosphere. Storms are caused by the conflicts of elements; and the storms of the spiritual world are conflicts with hostile elements.

In such an atmosphere faith finds its most productive soil; in such an element it comes more quickly to full fruition.

The staunchest tree is not found in the shelter of the forest, but out in the open where the winds from every quarter beat upon it, and bend and twist it until it becomes a giant in stature—this is the tree which the mechanic wants his tools made of, and the wagon-maker seeks.

So in the spiritual world, when you see a giant, remember the road you must travel to come up to his side is not along the sunny lane where wild-flowers ever bloom; but a steep, rocky, narrow pathway where the blasts of hell will almost blow you off your feet; where the sharp rocks cut the flesh, where the projecting thorns scratch the brow, and the venomous beasts hiss on every side.

It is a pathway of sorrow and joy, of suffering and healing balm, of tears and smiles, of trials and victories, of conflicts and triumphs, of hardships and perils and buffetings, of persecutions and misunderstandings, of troubles and distress; through all of which we are made more than conquerors through Him who loves us.

"Amid storms." Right in the midst where it is fiercest. You may shrink back from the ordeal of a fierce storm of trial . . . but go in! God is there to meet you in the center of all your trials, and to whisper His secrets which will make you come forth with a shining face and an indomitable faith that all the demons of hell shall never afterwards cause to waver.

E. A. KILBOURNE

I am pressing on . . . forgetting everything which is past.
(PHIL. 3:12–13 WEYMOUTH)

*I*n the very depths of yourself, dig a grave. Let it be like some forgotten spot to which no path leads; and there, in the eternal silence, bury the wrongs that you have suffered. Your heart will feel as if a weight had fallen from it, and a Divine peace come to abide with you.

CHARLES WAGNER

To be misunderstood even by those whom one loves is the cross and bitterness of life. It is the secret of that sad melancholy smile on the lips of great men which so few understand. It is what must have oftenest wrung the heart of the Son of Man.

AMIEL

Blasted rock and broken stone,
Ordinary earth,
Rolled and rammed and trampled on,
Forgotten, nothing worth,
And blamed, but used day after day;
An open road—the king's highway.

Often left outside the door,
Sometimes in the rain,
Always lying on the floor,
And made for mud and stain:
Men wipe their feet, and tread it flat,
And beat it clean—the master's mat.

Thou wast broken, left alone,
Thou wast blamed, and worse,
Thou wast scourged and spat upon,
Thou didst become my curse—
Lord Jesus, as I think of that
I pray, make me Thy road, Thy mat.

GOLD CORD

"The power to help others depends upon the acceptance of a trampled life."

July 13

∽

God . . . calleth those things which be not as though they were
(ROM. 4:17).

What does that mean? Why Abraham did this thing: he dared to believe God. It seemed an impossibility at his age that Abraham should become the father of a child; it looked incredible; and yet God called him a "father of many nations" before there was a sign of a child; and so Abraham called himself "father" because God called him so. That is faith; it is to believe and assert what God says, "Faith steps on seeming void, and finds the rock beneath."

Only say you have what God says you have, and He will make good to you all you believe. Only it must be real faith, all there is in you must go over in that act of faith to God.
FROM CRUMBS

Be willing to live by believing and neither think nor desire to live in any other way. Be willing to see every outward light extinguished, to see the eclipse of every star in the blue heavens, leaving nothing but darkness and perils around, if God will only leave in thy soul the inner radiance, the pure bright lamp which faith has kindled.
THOMAS C. UPHAM

The moment has come when you must get off the perch of distrust, out of the nest of seeming safety, and onto the wings of faith; just such a time as comes to the bird when it must begin to try the air. It may seem as though you must drop to the earth; so it may seem to the fledgling. It, too, may feel very like falling; but it does not fall—its pinions give it support, or, if they fall, the parent bird sweeps under and bears it upon its wings. Even so will God bear you. Only trust Him; "thou shalt be holden up." "Well, but," you say, "am I to cast myself upon nothing?" That is what the bird seems to have to do; but we know the *air is there,* and the air is not so unsubstantial as it seems. And *you* know the *promises of God are there,* and they are not unsubstantial at all. "But it seems an unlikely thing to come about that my poor weak soul should be girded with such strength." Has God said it shall? "That my tempted, yielding nature shall be victor in the strife." Has God said it shall? "That my timorous, trembling heart shall find peace?" Has God said it shall? For, if He has, you surely do not mean to give Him the lie! Hath He spoken, and shall He not do it? If you have gotten a word—"a sure word" of promise—take it implicitly, trust it absolutely. And this sure word you have; nay, you have more—you have Him who speaks the word confidently. "Yea, I say unto you," trust Him. J. B. FIGGIS, M.A.

EVENING

༄

The place whereon thou standest is holy ground. (EX. 3:5)

We cannot depend upon great events, striking circumstances, exalted moments and great occasions to measure our zeal, courage, faith, and love. These are measured by the commonplace, workaday tasks, the homely hidden paths of common life.

Thank God for the new vision, the beautiful idea, the glowing experience of the mountain; but unless we bring it down to the level of life, and teach it to walk with feet, work with hands, and stand the strain of daily life, we have worse than lost it—we have been hurt by it. *The uncommon life is the product of the day lived in the uncommon way.* Conspicuous efficiency in a lowly sphere is the best preparation for a higher one.

The incidents of which Jesus' work was made up are, humanly speaking, very humble and unpretentious. Human details fill the compass of His vast experience and work. He might have stilled a tempest every night. He could have walked upon the sea or flown over it, had the need existed. He could have transfigured Himself before Pilate and the astonished multitude in the Temple. He could have made visible association at noon every day, had He been minded so to do.

The most faithful cannot compare with Jesus in lowliness of manner: He taught only one woman at Jacob's well; He noticed a finger-touch on the hem of His garment, He stooped to take little children up in his arms and bless them; even so small a thing as a cup of cold water, He said, would yield its recompense of a heavenly reward. SELECTED

It may be on a kitchen floor,
Or in a busy shopping store,
Or teaching, nursing, day by day,
Till limb and brain almost give way;
Yet if, just there, by Jesus thou art found,
The place thou standest on is Holy Ground.

M. COLLEY

"*I will make the place of my feet glorious,*" said the Lord. Be it never so rough, be it never so steep, be it never so miry—*the place of His feet is glorious!*

429

Take God on thy route and thou shalt banish wrinkles from thy brow. Gethsemane itself shall not age thee if thou tread by the side of Jesus; for it is not the place of thy travel that makes thee weary—it is the heaviness of thy step.   GEORGE MATHESON

July 14

MORNING

乆

Bind the sacrifice with cords, even unto the horns of the altar
(PS. 118:27).

*I*s not this altar inviting thee? Shall we not ask to be *bound* to it, that we may never be able to start back from our attitude of consecration? There are times when life is full of roseate light, and we choose the cross; at other times, when the sky is gray, we shrink from it. It is well to be *bound*.

Wilt Thou bind us, most blessed Spirit, and enamor us with the cross, and let us never leave it? Bind us with the scarlet cord of redemption, and the gold cord of love, and the silver cord of Advent-hope, so we will not go back from it, or wish for another lot than to be the humble partners with our Lord in His pain and sorrow!

The horns of the altar invite thee. Wilt thou come? Wilt thou dwell ever in a spirit of resigned humility, and give thyself wholly to the Lord?

SELECTED

The story is told of a colored brother who, at a camp meeting, tried to give himself to God. Every night at the altar he consecrated himself; but every night before he left the meeting, the Devil would come to him and convince him that he did not *feel* any different and therefore he was not consecrated.

Again and again he was beaten back by the adversary. Finally, one evening he came to the meeting with an ax and a big stake. After consecrating himself, be drove the stake into the ground just where he had knelt. As he was leaving the building, the Devil came to him as usual and tried to make him believe that it was all a farce.

At once he went back to the stake and, pointing to it, said, "Look here, Mr. Devil, do you see that stake? Well, that's my witness that God has forever accepted me." Immediately the Devil left him, and he had no further doubts on the subject.   *FROM* THE STILL SMALL VOICE

Beloved, if you are tempted to doubt the finality of your consecration, drive a stake down somewhere and let it be your witness before God and even the Devil that you have settled the question forever.

Are you groping for a blessing,
Never getting there?
Listen to a word in season,
Get somewhere,

Are you struggling for salvation
By your anxious prayer?
Stop your struggling, simply trust, and—
Get somewhere.

Does the answer seem to linger
To your earnest prayer?
Turn your praying into praise, and—
Get somewhere.

You will never know His fulness
Till you boldly dare
To commit your all to Him, and—
Get somewhere.
SONGS OF THE SPIRIT

EVENING

The chariots of God are twenty thousand. (PS. 68:17)

Chariots of victory, or deliverance. (HAB. 3:8, VARIORUM)

But Lord, they do not *look* like chariots. They look instead like enemies, sufferings, trials, defeats, misunderstandings, disappointments, unkindnesses; juggernaut cars of misery and wretchedness that are only waiting to roll over us and crush us into the earth.

But they *are* chariots; chariots of triumph in which we may rise to those very heights of victory for which our souls have been longing and praying.

Earthly chariots are subject to the laws of matter and may be hindered or overturned; *God's* chariots are controlled by spiritual forces, *and triumph over all hindering things!*

"Very many" says the text; and although our spiritual eyes may not as yet have been opened to see them, all around us on every side *they must be waiting for us.*

Elisha prayed, and said, LORD, I pray thee, open his eyes, that he may see. And the LORD opened the eyes of the young man; and he saw: and, behold, the mountain was full of horses and chariots. 2 Kings 6:17, emphasis added

Chariots the King of Syria was unable to see; nor could the servant of the prophet see them. But the prophet himself sat calmly in his house without fear—his eyes had been opened to see the invisible. Now, what he asked for his servant was, "LORD . . . *open his eyes, that he may see.*"

Open our eyes that we may see!

I have not a shadow of a doubt that if all our eyes were opened today we would see our home, our places of business, the streets we traverse, filled with the "chariots of God." There is no need for any one of us to walk for lack of a chariot in which to ride: that cross inmate of your household, who has hitherto made life a burden to you, and who had been the juggernaut car to crush your soul into the very dust, may henceforth be a glorious chariot to carry you to the heights of heavenly patience and long-suffering; that misunderstanding, that mortification, that unkindness, that disappointment, that loss, that defeat—these are the chariots waiting to carry you to those places of victory you have so often longed to reach.

Somewhere in the trial His will must be hidden, and you must accept His will whether known or unknown, and so hide yourself in His invisible arms of love. Say, "Thy will be done! Thy will be done!" again and again. Shut out every other thought but the one thought of submission to His will and of trust in His love. Thus will you find yourself *riding with God* in a way you never dreamed could be.

No words can express the glorious places to which that soul shall arrive who travels in the chariots of God! *Would* YOU *ride on the high places of the earth?*

Then get into the chariots that will take you there!

HANNAH WHITALL SMITH

July 15

MORNING

❦

This is the victory that overcometh the world, even our faith
(1 JOHN 5:4).

It is easy to love Him when the blue is in the sky,
When the summer winds are blowing, and we smell the roses nigh;
There is little effort needed to obey His precious will
When it leads through flower-decked valley, or over sun-kissed hill.

It is when the rain is falling, or the mist hangs in the air,
When the road is dark and rugged, and the wind no longer fair,
When the rosy dawn has settled in a shadowland of gray,
That we find it hard to trust Him, and are slower to obey.

It is easy to trust Him when the singing birds have come,
And their canticles are echoed in our heart and in our home;
But 'tis when we miss the music, and the days are dull and drear,
That we need a faith triumphant over every doubt and fear.

And our blessed Lord will give it; what we lack He will supply;
Let us ask in faith believing—on His promises rely;
He will ever be our Leader, whether smooth or rough the way,
And will prove Himself sufficient for the needs of every day.

To trust in spite of the look of being forsaken; to keep crying out into the vast, whence comes no returning voice, and where seems no hearing; to see the machinery of the world pauselessly grinding on as if self-moved, caring for no life, nor shifting a hairbreadth for all entreaty, and yet believe that God is awake and utterly loving; to desire nothing but what comes meant for us from His hand; to wait patiently, ready to die of hunger, fearing only lest faith should fail—such is the victory that overcometh the world, such is faith indeed. GEORGE MACDONALD

❧❧

He shall receive the crown of life . . . promised. (JAMES 1:12)

The greatest helpers of humanity have been its cross-bearers. The leaders of men have suffered in loneliness; the prophets have learned their lessons in the school of pain. The corals in the sheltered lagoon grow rank and useless; those that are broken and crushed by the surf form the living rock and the foundations of continents. Ease has not produced greatness.

Men who have had to struggle with an unfavorable environment, to fight cold, to buffet the storm, to blast the rock or wring a livelihood from a niggardly soil, have won character by their pains.

The bird rises against a strong head wind, not only in spite of the wind, but *because of it.*

The *opposing force* becomes a *lifting force* if faced at the right angle.

The storm may buffet ships and rend the rigging, but it makes strong hands and brave hearts. Oh, fellow-voyager amid the storms and calms of life's wide sea,

"Spread thy sails to catch the favoring breezes of adversity."

If the greatest character of all time, even He who was the very touchstone of destiny, could be made perfect only through suffering, is it not probable that you and I must be also?

The best things all lie beyond some battle plain: you must fight your way across the field to get them!

> *High natures must be thunder-scarred*
> *With many a scarring wrong!*
> *Naught unmarred with struggle hard*
> *Can make the soul's sinews strong.*
> **LOWELL**

Take the hardest thing in your life—the place of difficulty, outward or inward, and expect God to triumph gloriously in that very spot. Just there He can bring your soul into blossom.   **LILIAS TROTTER**

July 16

❧

Because thou hast done this thing, and hast not withheld thy son,
thine only son. . . . I will multiply thy seed as the stars of the heaven;
. . . because thou hast obeyed my voice (GEN. 22:16–18).

*A*nd from that day to this, men have been learning that when, at God's voice, they surrender up to Him the one thing above all else that was dearest to their very hearts, *that* same thing is returned to them by Him a thousand times over. Abraham gives up his one and only son, at God's call, and with this disappear all his hopes for the boy's life and manhood, and for a noble family bearing his name. But the boy is restored, the family becomes as the stars and sands in number, and out of it, in the fullness of time, appears Jesus Christ.

That is just the way God meets every real sacrifice of every child of His. We surrender all and accept poverty; and He sends wealth. We renounce a rich field of service; He sends us a richer one than we had dared to dream of. We give up all our cherished hopes, and die unto self; He sends us the life more abundant, and tingling joy. And the crown of it all is our Jesus Christ. For we can never know the fullness of the sacrifice. The earthly founder of the family of Christ must commence by losing himself and his only son, just as the heavenly Founder of that family did. We cannot be members of that family with the full privileges and joys of membership *upon any other basis.*   C. G. TRUMBULL

We sometimes seem to forget *that what God takes He takes in fire;* and that the only way to the resurrection life and the ascension mount is the way of the garden, the cross, and the grave.

Think not, O soul of man, that Abraham's was a unique and solitary experience. It is simply a specimen and pattern of God's dealings with all souls who are prepared to obey Him at whatever cost. After thou hast patiently endured, thou shalt receive the promise. The moment of supreme sacrifice shall be the moment of supreme and rapturous blessing. God's river, which is full of water, shall burst its banks, and pour upon thee a tide of wealth and grace. There is nothing, indeed, which God will not do for a man who dares to step out upon what seems to be the mist; though as he puts down his foot he finds a rock beneath him.

F. B. MEYER

EVENING

⤜⤚

In the LORD PUT I MY TRUST. (PS. 11:1)

*T*hat is a jubilant bird note, but the bird is singing, not on some fair dewy spring morning, but in a cloudy heaven, and in the very midst of a destructive tempest. A little while ago I listened to a concert of mingled thunder and birdsong. Between the crashing peals of thunder, I heard the clear thrilling note of the lark. The melody seemed to come out of the very heart of the tempest. The environment of this Psalm is stormy. The sun is down. The stars are hid. The waters are out. The roads are broken up. And in the very midst of the darkness and desolation one hears the triumphant cry of the Psalmist, "In the LORD put I my trust." The singer is a soul in difficulty. He is the victim of relentless antagonists. He is pursued by implacable foes. The fight would appear to be going against him. The enemies are overwhelming, and, just at this point of seeming defeat and imminent disaster, there emerges this note of joyful confidence in God. "In the LORD put I my trust." It is a song in the night.

J. H. JOWETT

There is a bird of the thrush family found in the South of Ireland, called "The Storm Thrush," from its peculiar love of storms. In the wildest storms of rain and wind it betakes itself to the very topmost twig of the highest tree and there pours out its beautiful song—its frail perch swaying in the wind.

A beautiful story is told of some little birds whose nest had been ruined. As the poet walked among the trees in his garden after the storm, he found a torn nest laying on the ground. He began to brood sadly over it, pitying the birds whose home had thus been wrecked. But as he stood there and mused he heard a twittering and chattering over his head; looking up he saw the birds *busy building again their ruined nest!*

I heard a bird at break of day
Sing from the autumn trees
A song so musical and calm,
So full of certainties,
No man, I think, could listen long
Except upon his knees.
Yet this was but a simple bird
Alone among dead trees.

Robert Louis Stevenson closes one of his prayers with these words: "Help us with the grace of courage that we be none of us cast down while we sit lamenting over the ruins of our happiness. *Touch us with the fire of Thine altar, that we may be up and doing, to rebuild our city."*

Begin to build anew!

July 17

MORNING

∽

I will be still, and I will behold in my dwelling place (ISA. 18:4 RV).

*A*ssyria was marching against Ethiopia, the people of which are described as tall and smooth. And as the armies advance, God makes no effort to arrest them; it seems as though they will be allowed to work their will. He is still watching them from His dwelling place, the sun still shines on them; but before the harvest, the whole of the proud army of Assyria is smitten as easily as when sprigs are cut off by the pruning hook of the husbandman.

Is not this a marvelous conception of God—being still and watching? His stillness is not acquiescence. His silence is not consent. He is only biding His time, and will arise, in the most opportune moment, and when the designs of the wicked seem on the point of success, to overwhelm them with disaster. As we look out on the evil of the world; as we think of the apparent success of wrongdoing; as we wince beneath the oppression of those that hate us, let us remember these marvelous words about God being still and beholding.

There is another side to this. Jesus beheld His disciples toiling at the oars through the stormy night; and watched though unseen, the successive steps of the anguish of Bethany, when Lazarus slowly passed through the stages of mortal sickness, until he succumbed and was borne to the rocky tomb. But He was only waiting the moment when He could interpose most effectually. Is He *still* to thee? He is not unobservant; He is beholding all things; He has His finger on thy pulse, keenly sensitive to all its fluctuations. He will come to save thee when the precise moment has arrived. **FROM DAILY DEVOTIONAL COMMENTARY**

Whatever His questions or His reticences, we may be absolutely sure of an unperplexed and undismayed Savior.

∼ 437 ∼

O troubled soul, beneath the rod,
Thy Father speaks, be still, be still;
Learn to be silent unto God,
And let Him mould thee to His will.

O praying soul, be still, be still,
He cannot break His plighted Word;
Sink down into His blessed will,
And wait in patience on the Lord.

O waiting soul, be still, be strong,
And though He tarry, trust and wait;
Doubt not, He will not wait too long,
Fear not, He will not come too late.

EVENING

And God made a wind to pass over the earth,
and the waters assuaged. The fountains also of the deep and the
windows of heaven were stopped, and the rain from heaven
was restrained; And the waters returned from off the
earth continually. (GEN. 8:1–3)

All this because God remembered Noah! The forces of heaven and earth were enlisted, reversed, ordered about, solely because God remembered Noah and had plans for him.

God has not forgotten *you*. He will as readily order about the forces of the universe on your account as He did on Noah's. His plans for Noah were also plans for the whole world through Noah. So they are for you. He will use you for the good of the whole world if you will let Him.

SELECTED

We may forget; God does not!

God's time is never wrong,
Never too fast nor too slow;
The planets move to its steady pace
As the centuries come and go.

Stars rise and set by that time,
The punctual comets come back

With never a second's variance,
From the round of their viewless track.

Men space their years by the sun,
And reckon their months by the moon,
Which never arrive too late
And never depart too soon.

Let us set our clocks by God's,
And order our lives by His ways,
And nothing can come and nothing can go
Too soon or too late in our day.
ANNIE JOHNSON FLINT

"There are not dates in His fine leisure."

July 18
MORNING
≈∾∾

The eyes of the Lord run to and fro throughout the whole earth,
to show himself strong in the behalf of them whose heart is
perfect toward him (2 CHRON. 16:9).

God is looking for a man, or woman, whose heart will be always set on Him, and who will trust Him for all He desires to do. God is eager to work more mightily now than He ever has through any soul. The clock of the centuries points to the eleventh hour.

"The world is waiting yet to see what God can do through a consecrated soul." Not the world alone, but God Himself is waiting for one, who will be more fully devoted to Him than any who have ever lived; who will be willing to be nothing that Christ may be all; who will grasp God's own purposes; and taking His humility and His faith, His love and His power, will, without hindering, continue to let God do exploits.

C. H. P.

"There is no limit to what God can do with a man, providing he will not touch the glory."
In an address given to ministers and workers after his ninetieth birth-

day, George Mueller spoke thus of himself: *"I was converted* in November, 1825, but I only came into *the full surrender of the heart* four years later, in July, 1829. The love of money was gone, the love of place was gone, the love of position was gone, the love of worldly pleasures and engagements was gone. God, God alone became my portion. I found my all in Him; I wanted nothing else. And by the grace of God this has remained, and has made me a happy man, an exceedingly happy man, and it led me to care only about the things of God. I ask affectionately, my beloved breathen, have you fully surrendered the heart to God, or is there this thing or that thing with which you are taken up irrespective of God? I read a little of the Scriptures before, but preferred other books; but since that time the revelation He has made of Himself has become unspeakably blessed to me, and I can say from my heart, God is an infinitely lovely Being. Oh, be not satisfied until in your own inmost soul you can say, God is an infinitely lovely Being!" SELECTED

I pray to God this day to make me an extraordinary Christian.

WHITEFIELD

EVENING

Whereby shall I know that I shall inherit it? . . . Take me an heifer. . . . And when the fowls came down . . . Abram drove them away.
(GEN. 15:8–9, 11)

When God promises us a great blessing, and we ask how we may know that we shall have it, the answer is always the same: *By your own sacrifice to Me.* God cannot fulfill His richest promises to any of us until we have offered up to Him, *in utter completeness of surrender, ourselves. Then He can do glorious things for and with our lives.*

And then, also, "the birds of prey" attack a life as never before. The devil does not like to see any life sacrificed to God, *for he knows how mightily God will use that life to defeat the works of darkness.* So the birds of prey come down. We must expect to be attacked and tempted more fiercely and continuously after our life has been *wholly surrendered to God* than we ever were before. MESSAGES FOR THE MORNING WATCH

There is a Chinese legend of a potter who sought for many years to put a certain tint on the vases he made, but all his efforts failed. At last discouraged and in despair he threw himself into his furnace and his body was consumed in the fire; then, when the vases were taken out they bore the exquisite color which he had striven so long to produce.

The legend illustrates that truth that we can do our noblest and best work only at cost of self. The alabaster box must be broken before its odors can flow out.

Christ lifted up and saved the world not by an easy, pleasant, successful life in it; but by suffering and dying for it. And *we* can never bless the world merely by having a good time in it; but only by giving our lives for it.

It takes heart's blood to heal hearts. *Saving of life proves, in the end, the losing of it.*

> *My wild will was captured, yet under the yoke*
> *There was pain and not peace at the press of the load;*
> *Till the glorious burden the last fiber broke,*
> *And I melted like wax in the furnace of God.*
>
> *And now I have flung myself recklessly out,*
> *Like a chip on the stream of His infinite will;*
> *I pass the rough rocks with a smile and a shout,*
> *And just let my God His dear purpose fulfill.*

July 19

MORNING

∽◦∾

The cup which my Father hath given me, shall I not drink it?
(JOHN 18:11)

This was a greater thing to say and do than to calm the seas or raise the dead. Prophets and apostles could work wondrous miracles, but they could not always do and suffer the will of God. To do and suffer God's will is still the highest form of faith, the most sublime Christian achievement. To have the bright aspirations of a young life forever blasted; to bear a daily burden never congenial and to see not relief; to be pinched by poverty when you only desire a competency for the good and comfort of loved ones; to be fettered by some incurable physical disability; to be stripped bare of loved ones until you stand alone to meet the shocks of life—to be able to say in such a school of discipline, "The cup which my Father has given me, shall I not drink it?"—this is faith at its highest and spiritual success at the crowning point. Great faith is exhibited not so much in ability to do as to suffer. **DR. CHARLES PARKHURST**

To have a sympathizing God we must have a suffering Savior, and there is no true fellow-feeling with another save in the heart of him who has been afflicted like him.

We cannot do good to others save at a cost to ourselves, and our afflictions are the price we pay for our ability to sympathize. He who would be a helper, must first be a sufferer. He who would be a savior must somewhere and somehow have been upon a cross; and we cannot have the highest happiness of life in succoring others without tasting the cup which Jesus drank, and submitting to the baptism wherewith He was baptized.

The most comforting of David's psalms were pressed out by suffering; and if Paul had not had his thorn in the flesh we had missed much of the tenderness which quivers in so many of his letters.

The present circumstance, which presses so hard against you (if surrendered to Christ), is the best-shaped tool in the Father's hand to chisel you for eternity. Trust Him, then. Do not push away the instrument lest you lose its work.

> *Strange and difficult indeed*
> *We may find it,*
> *But the blessing that we need*
> *Is behind it.*

The school of suffering graduates rare scholars.

EVENING

For all the promises of God in him are yea, and in him Amen.
(2 COR. 1:20)

Sometimes Christians go for a good while in trouble, not realizing that riches are laid up for them in a familiar promise.

When Christian and Hopeful strayed out of the path upon forbidden ground, and found themselves locked up in Doubting Castle by Giant Despair for their carelessness, there they lay for days, until one night they began to pray. "Now a little before it was day, Good Christian, as one half-amazed, broke out in passionate speech: 'What a fool!' quoth he, 'am I, thus to lie in this horrible dungeon, when I may as well walk at liberty. I have a key in my bosom called PROMISE, that will, I am persuaded, open any lock in Doubting Castle.' Then said Hopeful, 'That's good news good brother; pluck it out of thy bosom and try.' Then Christian pulled it out of his bosom, and began to try the dungeon door, whose bolts gave back, and the door flew open with ease, and Christian and Hopeful came out."   PILGRIM'S PROGRESS, BY JOHN BUNYAN

Often you cannot get at a difficulty so as to deal with it aright and find your way to a happy result. You pray, but have not the liberty in prayer which you desire. A definite promise is what you want. You try one and another of the inspired words, but they do not fit. You try again, and in due season a promise presents itself which seems to have been made for the occasion; it fits exactly as a well-made key fits the lock for which it was prepared. Having found the identical word of the living God you hasten to plead it at the throne of grace, saying, "O Lord, Thou hast promised this good thing unto Thy servant; be pleased to grant it!" The matter is ended: sorrow is turned to joy; prayer is heard.   CHARLES H. SPURGEON

> Faith, mighty faith, the promise sees
> And looks to God alone,
> Laughs at impossibilities,
> And cries, "It shall be done."

Try all your keys! Never despair! God leaves no treasure-house locked against us!

July 20
MORNING

Seeing then that we have a great high priest . . . Jesus, the Son of God, let us hold fast our profession. Let us therefore come boldly unto the throne of grace, that we may obtain mercy, and find grace to help in time of need (HEB. 4:14, 16).

Our great Helper in prayer is the Lord Jesus Christ, our Advocate with the Father, our Great High Priest, whose chief ministry for us these centuries has been intercession and prayer. He it is who takes our imperfect petitions from our hands, cleanses them from their defects, corrects their faults, and then claims their answer from His Father on His own account and through His all-atoning merits and righteousness.

Brother, are you fainting in prayer? Look up. Your blessed Advocate has already claimed your answer, and you would grieve and disappoint Him if you were to give up the conflict in the very moment when victory is on its way to meet you. He has gone in for you into the inner chamber, and already holds up your name upon the palms of His hands; and the messenger, which is to bring you your blessing, is now on his way, and the Spirit is only waiting your trust to whisper in your heart the echo of the answer from the throne, *"It is done."*   A. B. SIMPSON

The Spirit has much to do with acceptable prayer, and His work in prayer is too much neglected. He enlightens the mind to see its wants, softens the heart to feel them, quickens our desires after suitable supplies, gives clear views of God's power, wisdom, and grace to relieve us, and stirs up that confidence in His truth which excludes all wavering. Prayer is, therefore, a wonderful thing. In every acceptable prayer the whole Trinity is concerned.   J. ANGELL JAMES

EVENING

Hitherto have ye asked nothing in my name: ask, and ye shall receive, that your joy may be full. (JOHN 16:24)

Alexander the Great had a famous, but indigent, philosopher in his court. This man adept in science was once particularly straightened in his circumstances. To whom should he apply but to his patron, the conqueror of the world? His request was no sooner made than granted.

Alexander gave him a commission to receive of his treasury whatever he wanted. He immediately demanded in his sovereign's name ten thousand pounds. The treasurer, surprised at so large a demand, refused to comply, but waited upon the king and represented to him the affair, adding withal how unreasonable he thought the petition and how exorbitant the sum. Alexander listened with patience, but as soon as he heard the remonstrance replied, "Let the money be instantly paid. I am delighted with this philosopher's way of thinking; he has done me a singular honor: by the largeness of his request he shows the high idea he has conceived both of my superior wealth and my royal munificence."

Saints have never yet reached the limit to the possibilities of prayer. Whatever has been attained or achieved *has touched but the fringe of the garment of a prayer-hearing God.* We honor the riches both of His power and love *only* by large demands.   A. T. PIERSON

You cannot think of prayer so large that God, in answering it, will not wish that you had made it larger. *Pray not for crutches, but for wings!*

PHILLIPS BROOKS

> *Make thy petition deep.*
> *It is thy God who speaks with love o'erflowing,*
> *Thy God who claims the rapture of bestowing,*
> *Thy God who whispers, all thy weakness knowing,*
> *"Wouldst thou in full reap?*
> *Make thy petition deep."*
>
> *Make thy petition deep.*
> *Now to the fountainhead thy vessel bringing,*
> *Claim all the fullness of its glad upspringing;*
> *At Calvary was proclaimed its boundless measure;*
> *Who spared not then, withholds from thee no treasure;*
> *This word—His token, keep:*
> *Make thy petition deep.*

If Alexander gave like a King, shall not Jehovah give like a God?

July 21

MORNING

Let me prove, I pray thee, but this once with the fleece (JUDG. 6:39).

There are degrees to faith. At one stage of Christian experience we cannot believe unless we have some sign or some great manifestation of feeling. We feel our fleece, like Gideon, and if it is wet we are willing to trust God. This may be true faith, but it is imperfect. It always looks for feeling or some token beside the Word of God. It marks quite an advance in faith when we trust God without feelings. It is blessed to believe without having any emotion.

There is a third stage of faith which even transcends that of Gideon and his fleece. The first phase of faith believes when there are favorable emotions, the second believes when there is the absence of feeling, but this third form of faith believes God and His Word when circumstances, emotions, appearances, people, and human reason all urge to the contrary. Paul exercised this faith in Acts 27:20, 25, "And when neither sun nor stars in many days appeared, and no small tempest lay on us, all hope that we should be saved was then taken away." Notwithstanding all this Paul said, "Wherefore, sirs, be of good cheer; *for I believe God*, that it shall be even as it was told me."

May God give us faith to fully trust His Word though everything else witness the other way. C. H. P.

When is the time to trust?
Is it when all is calm,
When waves the victor's palm,
And life is one glad psalm
Of joy and praise?
Nay! but the time to trust
Is when the waves beat high,
When storm clouds fill the sky,
And prayer is one long cry,
O help and save!

When is the time to trust?
Is it when friends are true?
Is it when comforts woo,
And in all we say and do
We meet but praise?
Nay! but the time to trust
Is when we stand alone,
And summer birds have flown,
And every prop is gone,
All else but God.

What is the time to trust?
Is it some future day,
When you have tried your way,
And learned to trust and pray
By bitter woe?
Nay! but the time to trust
Is in this moment's need,
Poor, broken, bruised reed!
Poor, troubled soul, make speed
To trust thy God.

What is the time to trust?
Is it when hopes beat high,

When sunshine gilds the sky,
And joy and ecstasy
Fill all the heart?
Nay! but the time to trust
Is when our joy is fled,
When sorrow bows the head,
And all is cold and dead,
All else but God.

SELECTED

EVENING

What things soever ye desire . . . ye shall have them. (MARK 11:24)

Oh, the victories of prayer! They are the mountaintops of the Bible. They take us back to the plains of Mamre, to the fords of Peniel, to the prison of Joseph, to the triumphs of Moses, to the victories of Joshua, to the deliverances of David, to the miracles of Elijah and Elisha, to the holy story of the Master's life, to the secret of Pentecost, to the keynote of Paul's unparalleled ministry, to the lives of saints and the deaths of martyrs, to all that is most sacred and sweet in the history of the church and the experience of the children of God.

And when for us the last conflict shall have passed, and the *footstool of prayer shall have given place to the harp of praise,* the scenes of time that shall be gilded with eternal radiance shall be those linked with deepest sorrow and darkest night, over which we have written.

Jehovah Shammah (The Lord was there).
Beyond thy utmost wants,
His power can love and bless;
To trusting souls He loves to grant
More than they can express.

July 22

❦

And therefore will the Lord wait, that he may be gracious unto you
... blessed are all they that wait for him (ISA. 30:18).

We must not only think of our waiting upon God, but also of what is more wonderful still, of God's waiting upon us. The vision of Him waiting on us, will give new impulse and inspiration to our waiting upon Him. It will give us unspeakable confidence that our waiting cannot be in vain. Let us seek even now, at this moment, in the spirit of waiting on God, to find out something of what it means. He has inconceivably glorious purposes concerning every one of His children. And you ask, "How is it, if He waits to be gracious, that even after I come and wait upon Him, He does not give the help I seek, but waits on longer and longer?"

God is a wise husbandman, "who waiteth for the precious fruit of the earth, and hath long patience for it." He cannot gather the fruit till it is ripe. He knows when we are spiritually ready to receive the blessing to our profit and His glory. Waiting in the sunshine of His love is what will ripen the soul for His blessing. Waiting under the cloud of trial, that breaks in showers of blessings, is as needful. Be assured that if God waits longer than you could wish, it is only to make the blessing doubly precious. God waited four thousand years, till the fullness of time, ere He sent His Son. Our times are in His hands; He will avenge His elect speedily; He will make haste for our help, and not delay one hour too long.

ANDREW MURRAY

EVENING

❦

Unto you that fear my name shall the Sun of righteousness arise with
healing in his wings. (MAL. 4:2)

A South American traveler tells of a curious conflict which he once witnessed between a little quadruped and a poisonous reptile of great size. The little creature seemed no match for its antagonist that threatened to destroy it by a blow, as well as its helpless young, but it fearlessly faced its mighty enemy and rushing at him, struck him with a succession of fierce and telling blows, but received at the onset a deep and apparently fatal wound from the poisonous fangs, which flashed for a moment with an angry fire, and then fastened themselves deep into the flesh of the daring little assailant.

For a moment it seemed as if all were over, but the wise little creature immediately retired into the forest, and hastening to the plantain tree eagerly devoured some of its leaves, and then hurried back, seemingly fresh and restored, to renew the fray with vigor and determination. Again and again this strange spectacle was repeated: the serpent, although greatly exhausted, ferociously attacked, and again and again wounded its antagonist to death, as it seemed; but the little creature each time repaired to its simple prescription, and returned to renewed victory. In the course of an hour or two the battle was over—the mammoth reptile lay still and dead and the little victor was unharmed, in the midst of the nest and the helpless little ones.

How often we are wounded by the dragon's sting—wounded, it would seem to death! and if we had to go through some long ceremony to reach the source of life, we must faint and die. But blessed be His Name as near at hand as that which the forest holds in its shade, *there is ever for us a Plant of healing to which we may continually repair* and come back refreshed, invigorated, transfigured—like Him who shone with the brightness of celestial light as He prayed in the mount; who, as He prayed in the garden arose triumphant over the fear of death, strengthened from on high to accomplish the mighty battle of our redemption. A. B. SIMPSON

It is His wings that heal our pains,
And soothe the serpent's poisoned stings;
Close to His bosom we must press
To feel His healing wings.

July 23

MORNING

Giving thanks always for all things unto God (EPH. 5:20).

No matter what the source of evil, if you are in God and surrounded by Him as by an atmosphere, all evil has to pass through Him before it comes to you. Therefore you can thank God for everything that comes, not for the sin of it, but for what God will bring out of it and through it. May God make our lives thanksgiving and perpetual praise, then He will make everything a blessing.

We once saw a man draw some black dots. We looked and could make nothing of them but an irregular assemblage of black dots. Then he drew a few lines, put in a few rests, then a clef at the beginning, and we saw these black dots were musical notes. On sounding them we were singing,

> *Praise God from whom all blessings flow,*
> *Praise Him all creatures here below.*

There are many black dots and black spots in our lives, and we cannot understand *why* they are there or *why* God permitted them to come. But if we let God come into our lives, and adjust the dots in the proper way, and draw the lines He wants, and separate this from that, and put in the rests at the proper places; out of the black dots and spots in our lives He will make a glorious harmony. Let us not hinder Him in this glorious work! C. H. P.

> *Would we know that the major chords were sweet,*
> *If there were no minor key?*
> *Would the painter's work be fair to our eyes,*
> *Without shade on land or sea?*
>
> *Would we know the meaning of happiness,*
> *Would we feel that the day was bright,*
> *If we'd never known what it was to grieve,*
> *Nor gazed on the dark of night?*

Many men owe the grandeur of their lives to their tremendous difficulties. C. H. SPURGEON

When the musician presses the black keys on the great organ, the music is as sweet as when he touches the white ones, but to get the capacity of the instrument he must touch them all. SELECTED

❦

Whatsoever . . . that the Father may be glorified in the Son.
(JOHN 14:13)

Do we pray for His glory?

This is the privilege and possibility for every man who can speak to God *"in His Name."*

In the Lone Star Mission at Ongole, India, a faithful few had held on believingly and courageously year after year. Now the mission was about to be abandoned. The work had apparently failed; money had failed. The only hope now was God.

Dr. Jowett and his wife took with them that famous old Hindu woman, Julia, nearly one hundred years of age, and ascended the hills above Ongole to ask God to save the Lone Star Mission and the lost souls of India. The old Hindu saint mingled her tears with her description of the most important and most thrilling moment of her life—that memorable sunrise meeting on "Prayer Meeting Hill," as she rehearsed the story one night in Nellore, India, to Dr. Cortland Myers.

"*They all prayed, and they all believed!* They talked and then they prayed again! They wrestled before heaven's throne in the face of a heathen world, like Elijah on Carmel. At last the day dawned. Just as the sun rose above the horizon Dr. Jowett arose out of darkness and seemed to see a great light. He lifted his hand heavenward and turned his tearstained face toward the great Heart of Love. He declared that his vision saw the cactus field below transformed into a church and mission buildings!

"*His faith grasped and gripped the great fact!* He claimed the promise and challenged God to answer *a prayer that was entirely for His own glory and the salvation of men!*

"The money came *immediately,* and *clearly from God's hand!*

"The man—God's choice, came *immediately!* Clearly it was of God that Dr. Clough was called to put new life and hope into the almost abandoned mission.

"Today on that very cactus field stands the Christian church with the largest membership of any church on earth—20,000 members! If it had not been divided by necessity there would now be 50,000 members—the greatest miracle of the modern missionary world.

"On that well-nigh abandoned field, Dr. Clough baptized 10,000 persons in one year; 2,222 in one day!

"Prayer Meeting Hill *moved the throne of God,* and made the world to tremble! The battlements of heaven must have been crowded to watch these many workings of a prayer of *His* glory!"

July 24

MORNING

∽≫∾

Then believed they his words; they sang his praise. They soon forgot his works; they waited not for his counsel; but lusted exceedingly in the wilderness, and tempted God in the desert. And he gave them their request; but sent leanness into their soul (PS. 106:12–15).

We read of Moses, that "he endured, as seeing him who is invisible." Exactly the opposite was true of the children of Israel in this record. They endured only when the circumstances were favorable; they were largely governed by the things that appealed to their senses, in place of resting in the invisible and eternal God.

In the present day there are those who live intermittent Christian lives because they have become occupied with the outward, and center in circumstances, in place of centering in God. God wants us more and more to see Him in everything, and to call nothing small if it bears us His message.

Here we read of the children of Israel, *"Then* they believed his words." They did not believe till *after* they saw—when they saw Him work, then they believed. They really doubted God when they came to the Red Sea; but when God opened the way and led them across and they *saw* Pharaoh and his host drowned—"then they believed."

They led an up-and-down life because of this kind of faith; it was a faith that depended upon circumstances. This is not the kind of faith God wants us to have.

The world says "seeing is believing," but God wants us to believe in order to see. The psalmist said, "I had fainted, unless I had *believed to see* the goodness of the Lord in the land of the living."

Do you believe God only when the circumstances are favorable, or do you believe no matter what the circumstances may be? C. H. P.

Faith is to believe what we do not see, and the reward of this faith is to see what we believe. SAINT AUGUSTINE

EVENING

Blessed are they that have not seen, and yet have believed.
(JOHN 20:29)

There are those to whom no visions come, no moments upon the mount suffused with a glory that never was on land or sea. Let not such envy the men of vision. It may be that the vision is given to strengthen a faith that else were weak. It is to the people who can live along the line of what others call the commonplace, and yet trust, that the Master says, "Blessed."

Beware of a life of fitful impulse. Live and act on sustained principle. It is a poor thing—the flash of summer lightning, compared with the steady luster of moon and star.

"The darkest night has stars in it!"

When the low mood comes, open your New Testament. Read it imaginatively: stand on the shore at Capernaum; visit the home at Bethany; sit by Jacob's well and in the Upper Room; look into the eyes of Jesus; listen to His voice; take a walk around by Calvary; remember the crown of thorns; then tell yourself (for it is true), *"All this was for me! The Son of God loved me, and gave Himself for me."* And see if a passion of praise does not send the low mood flying.

"Praise and service are great healers." When life grows sore and wounding, and it is difficult to be brave, *praise God!* Sing something, and you will rally your own heart with the song!

You must learn to swim and hold your head above the water even when the sense of His Presence is not with you to hold up your chin.

GARDEN OF SPICES

Do not depend on *frames* or *feelings*. You cannot always live in the tropics.

What I do thou knowest not now, but thou shalt know hereafter
(JOHN 13:7).

We have only a partial view here of God's dealings, His half-completed, half-developed plan: but all will stand out in fair and graceful proportions in the great finished temple of eternity! Go, in the reign of Israel's greatest king, to the heights of Lebanon. See that noble cedar, the pride of its compeers, an old wrestler with northern blasts! Summer loves to smile upon it, night spangles its feathery foliage with dewdrops, the birds nestle on its branches, the weary pilgrim or wandering shepherd reposes under its shadows from the midday heat or from the furious storm; but all at once it is marked out to fall. The aged denizen of the forest is doomed to succumb to the woodman's stroke!

As we see the ax making its first gash on its gnarled trunk, then the noble limbs stripped of their branches, and at last the "Tree of God," as was its distinctive epithet, coming with a crash to the ground, we exclaim against the wanton destruction, the demolition of this proud pillar in the temple of nature. We are tempted to cry with the prophet, as if inviting the sympathy of every lowlier stem—invoking inanimate things to resent the affront *"Howl, fir tree; for the cedar has fallen!"*

But wait a little. Follow that gigantic trunk as the workmen of Hiram Launch it down the mountainside; thence conveyed in rafts along the blue waters of the Mediterranean; and last of all, behold it set a glorious polished beam in the temple of God. As you see its destination, placed in the very Holy of Holies, in the diadem of the Great King—say, can you grudge that "the crowns of Lebanon" was despoiled, in order that this jewel might have so noble a setting?

That cedar stood as a stately prop in nature's sanctuary, but "the glory of the latter house was greater than the glory of the former!"

How many of our souls are like these cedars of old! God's axes of trial have stripped and bared them. We see no reason for dealings so dark and mysterious, but He has a noble end and object in view; to set them as everlasting pillars and rafters in His heavenly Zion; to make them a "crown of glory in the hand of the Lord, and a royal diadem in the hand of our God."

MACDUFF

I do not ask my cross to understand,
My way to see—
Better in darkness just to feel Thy hand,
And follow Thee.

EVENING

‿◦‿

To whomsoever I shall send thee thou shalt go. (JER. 1:7)

*H*ave you ever read George Eliot's poem called "Stradivarius"? Stradivari was the famous old violin maker whose violins, nearly two centuries old, are almost worth their weight in gold today. Says Stradivari in the poem:

If my hand slacked,
I should rob God—since He is fullest good,
Leaving a blank instead of violins.
He could not make Antonio Stradivari's violins
Without Antonio.

You are God's opportunity in your day. He has waited for ages for a person just like you. If you refuse Him, then God loses His opportunity which He sought through you, and He will never have another for there will never be another person on the earth just like you.

Bring to God your gift, my brother,
He'll not need to call another,
You will do;
He will add His blessing to it,
And the two of you will do it,
God and you.
R. E. NEIGHBOUR

Get taken clear out into the purpose of God and let Him lade you with merchandise for others.

We find scores of people in middle life who are in the unhappy position of doing everyday work which they hate and which does not express the personality, when each one might have done brilliantly in another sphere if he had given a day's prayerful thought to a decision which affected half a century.

July 26

MORNING

For we through the Spirit by faith wait for the hope of righteousness
(GAL. 5:5 RV).

There are times when things look very dark to me—so dark that I have to wait even for hope. It is bad enough to wait *in* hope, to see no glimmer of a prospect and yet refuse to despair; to have nothing but night before the casement and yet to keep; the casement open for possible stars; to have a vacant place in my heart and yet to allow that place to be filled by no inferior presence—that is the grandest patience in the universe. It is Job in the tempest; it is Abraham on the road to Moriah; it is Moses in the desert of Midian; it is the Son of Man in the Garden of Gethsemane.

There is no patience so hard as that which endures, "as seeing him who is invisible"; it is the waiting for hope.

Thou hast made waiting beautiful; Thou hast made patience divine. Thou hast taught us that the Father's will may be received just because it *is* His will. Thou hast revealed to us that a soul may see nothing but sorrow in the cup and yet may refuse to let it go, convinced that the eye of the Father sees further than its own.

Give me this divine power of Thine, the power of Gethsemane. Give me the power to wait for hope itself, to look out from the casement where there are no stars. Give me the power, when the very joy that was set before me is gone, to stand unconquered amid the night, and say, "To the eye of my Father it is perhaps shining still." I shall reach the climax of strength when I have learned to wait for hope. GEORGE MATHESON

Strive to be one of those—so few—who walk the earth with ever-present consciousness—all mornings, middays, star-times—that the unknown which men call heaven is "close behind the visible scene of things."

EVENING

⌘

He breathed on them, and saith unto them,
Receive ye the Holy Ghost. (JOHN 20:22)

I had an opportunity to preach in a little schoolhouse two miles from my first pastorate—an afternoon meeting. After the morning church service the rain was pouring in torrents. It seemed useless to go two miles through such a storm, for who would venture out in such weather? But a young woman had come for me in her buggy, and I went with her rather reluctantly.

There were seven men present; the young woman went home to get out of the rain. My first impression was that it was hardly worthwhile to preach a sermon to so small an audience, but I repented of that and gave them the best I had. The dew of heaven was upon us: we were conscious of God's presence, and two of the seven men, who were not Christians, expressed a desire to be saved.

An old farmer arose and said: "My young brother, God is working in our midst. Will you not preach tonight? The clouds are clearing away and we will go out and tell the people about the meeting." I consented, though it rather upset my plans for the following day. That night about twenty-five persons came, and there were six or seven inquirers and two or three decisions for Christ.

The meetings went on from day to day for two weeks. There were over seventy conversions, and on Sunday morning I baptized forty new members of my church. I could not explain it; no one seemed to be expecting a revival, or praying for it. It seemed like a case of God's sovereignty in giving His *breath-touch* without demanding that anyone should pray for it.

The last day of the meetings solved the mystery. At the close of the service a plainly dressed, gray-haired, motherly woman grasped my hand and said: "This is my home, though I spend most of my time teaching school sixty miles from here. When my niece wrote that you were preaching at three in the afternoon and at seven-thirty in the evening, I dismissed my school a half hour earlier than usual, that I might spend in prayer every minute that you preached. And, sir, *I have come to see what God has been doing. Those you baptized this morning were all my neighbors and friends, and among them my brother, nephew, and niece.*"

Neither my preaching or praying brought that revival. It was the good woman sixty miles away, whose prayers brought the *breath-touch* of God upon dead souls of that community.

Let no day pass without a prayer to God for His *breath-touch* upon the spiritual dry bones of your community.

> Breathe on me, Breath of God
> Till I am wholly Thine,
> Till all this earthly part of me
> Glows with Thy fire Divine.

In Wales during the great revival there was no accounting for the way the Spirit worked. It was all *"a-bend to God."*

July 27
MORNING

Prove me now (MAL. 3:10)

What is God saying here but this: "My child, I still have windows in heaven. They are yet in service. The bolts slide as easily as of old. The hinges have not grown rusty. I would rather fling them open, and pour forth, than keep them shut, and hold back. I opened them for Moses, and the sea parted. I opened them for Joshua, and Jordan rolled back. I opened them for Gideon, and hosts fled. I will open them for you—*if you will only let Me*. On this side of the windows, heaven is the same rich storehouse as of old. The fountains and streams still overflow. The treasure rooms are still bursting with gifts. The lack is not on MY side. It is on yours. I am waiting. *Prove Me* now. Fulfill the conditions, on *your* part. Bring in the tithes. *Give Me a chance.* **SELECTED**

I can never forget my mother's very brief paraphrase of Malachi 3:10. The verse begins, "Bring ye the whole tithe in," and it ends up with "I will pour" the blessing *out* till you'll be embarrassed for space. Her paraphrase was this: "Give all He asks; take all He promises." **S. D. GORDON**

The ability of God is beyond our prayers, beyond our largest prayers! I have been thinking of some of the petitions that have entered into my supplication innumerable times. What have I asked for? I have asked for a cupful, and the ocean remains! I have asked for a sunbeam, and the sun abides! My best asking falls immeasurably short of my Father's giving; it is beyond what we can ask. **J. H. JOWETT**

All the rivers of Thy grace I claim,
Over every promise write my name (Eph. 1:8–19).

EVENING

❧

Thy name shall be called no more Jacob,
but Israel: for as a prince hast thou power with God and with men,
and hast prevailed. (GEN. 32:28)

Napoleon was once reviewing his troops near Paris. The horse on which he sat was restless, and the Emperor having thoughtlessly dropped the reins from his hand in the eagerness of giving a command, the spirited animal bounded away and the rider was in danger of being hurled to the ground. A young private standing in the lines leaped forward and, seizing the bridle, saved his beloved Commander from a fall. The Emperor glancing at him said in his quick abrupt way, "Thank you, Captain." The private looked up with a smile and asked, "Of what regiment, sir?" "Of my guards," answered Napoleon, and instantly galloped to another part of the field.

The young soldier laid down his musket with the remark, "Whoever will may carry that gun; I am done with it," and proceeded at once to join a group of officers who stood conversing at a little distance. One of them, a General, observing his self-possessed approach, angrily said, "What is this insolent fellow doing here?"

"This insolent fellow," answered the young soldier looking the other steadily in the eye, "is a Captain of the Guards." "Why, man," responded the officer, "you are insane; why do you speak thus?" *"He said it,"* replied the soldier, pointing to the Emperor, who was far down the lines. "I beg your pardon, Captain," politely returned the General, "I was not aware of your promotion."

To those looking on he was still a private, dressed in the coarse rough garb of a common soldier; but in the bold assertion of his dignity, he could meet all the jeers of his comrades and all the scoffs of his superiors with the ready reply, "He said it."

He said it! He said it!!

July 28

MORNING

❦

The Lord hath his way in the whirlwind and in the storm
(NAH. 1:3).

I recollect, when a lad, and while attending a classical institute in the vicinity of Mount Pleasant, sitting on an elevation of that mountain, and watching a storm as it came up the valley. The heavens were filled with blackness, and the earth was shaken by the voice of thunder. It seemed as though that fair landscape was utterly changed, and its beauty gone never to return.

But the storm swept on, and passed out of the valley; and if I had sat in the same place on the following day, and said, "Where is that terrible storm, with all its terrible blackness?" the grass would have said, "Part of it is in me," and the daisy would have said, "Part of it is in me," and the fruits and flowers and everything that grows out of the ground would have said, "Part of the storm is incandescent in me."

Have you asked to be made like your Lord? Have you longed for the fruit of the Spirit, and have you prayed for sweetness and gentleness and love? Then fear not the stormy tempest that is at this moment sweeping through your life. A blessing is in the storm, and there will be the rich fruitage in the "afterward."   HENRY WARD BEECHER

The flowers live by the tears that fall
From the sad face of the skies;
And life would have no joys at all,
Were there no watery eyes.
Love thou thy sorrow; grief shall bring
Its own excuse in after years;
The rainbow!—see how fair a thing
God hath built up from tears.
HENRY S. SUTTON

EVENING

❧

Why . . . this waste? (MARK 14:4)

here is nothing that seems more prodigal than the waste of nature. The showers fall and sink into the ground, and seem to be lost. The rain cometh down from heaven and returneth not thither; the rivers run into the sea, and become absorbed in the ocean's brine. All this seems like a waste of precious material; and yet, science has taught us that no force is ever wasted, but simply converted into another form in which it goes on its way with an altered ministry, but an undiminished force.

Someone has represented in a sort of poetic parable a little raindrop trembling in the air, and questioning with the Genius of the sky whether it should fall upon the earth or still linger in the beautiful cloud.

"Why should I be lost and buried in the dirty soil? Why should I disappear in the dark mud, when I may glisten like a diamond or shine like an emerald or ruby in the rainbow's arch?"

"Yes," the Genius agrees, "but, if you fall in the earth you will come forth with a better resurrection in the petal of the flower, in the fragrance of the rose, in the hanging cluster of the vine."

And so, at last, the timid crystal drops one tear of regret, disappears beneath the soil, and is speedily drunk by the parched ground; it has gone out of sight—apparently out of existence. But lo! the root of yonder lily drinks in the moisture; the sap vessels of that damask rose absorb its refreshing draft; the far-reaching rootlet of yonder vine has found that fountain of life—and in a little while that raindrop comes forth in the snowy blossom of the lily, in the rich perfume of the rose, in the purple cluster of the vine, and as it meets once more the Genius of the air it answers back its glad acknowledgment: "Yes, I died, but I have risen, and now I live in a higher ministry, in a larger life, in a better resurrection."

A. B. SIMPSON

Pour out thy love like the rush of a river,
Wasting its waters forever and ever,
Through the burnt sands that reward not the giver:
Silent or songful, thou nearest the sea.
Scatter thy life as the summer's shower pouring;
What if no bird through the pearl rain is soaring?
What if no blossom looks upward adoring?
Look to the life that was lavished for thee!

So the wild wind strews its perfumed caresses:
Evil and thankless the desert it blesses;
Bitter the wave that its soft pinion presses;
Never it ceases to whisper and sing.
What if the hard heart give thorns for thy roses?
What if on rocks thy tired bosom reposes?
Sweeter is music with minor-keyed closes,
Fairest the vines that on ruin will cling.

July 29
MORNING

Hast thou seen the treasures of the hail, which I have reserved against the time of trouble? (JOB 38:22–23).

Our trials are great opportunities. Too often we look on them as great obstacles. It would be a haven of rest and an inspiration of unspeakable power if each of us would henceforth recognize every difficult situation as one of God's chosen ways of proving to us His love and look around for the signals of His glorious manifestations; then, indeed, would every cloud become a rainbow, and every mountain a path of ascension and a scene of transfiguration.

If we will look back upon the past, many of us will find that the very time our heavenly Father has chosen to do the kindest things for us, and given us the richest blessing, has been the time we were strained and shut in on every side. God's jewels are often sent us in rough packages and by dark liveried servants, but within we find the very treasures of the King's palace and the Bridegroom's love. A. B. SIMPSON

Trust Him in the dark, honor Him with unwavering confidence even in the midst of mysterious dispensations, and the recompense of such faith will be like the molting of the eagle's plumes, which was said to give them a new lease of youth and strength. J. R. MACDUFF

If we could see beyond today
As God can see;
If all the clouds should roll away,
The shadows flee;

O'er present griefs we would not fret.
Each sorrow we would soon forget,
For many joys are waiting yet
For you and me.

If we could know beyond today
As God doth know,
Why dearest treasures pass away
And tears must flow;
And why the darkness leads to light,
Why dreary paths will soon grow bright;
Some day life's wrongs will be made right,
Faith tells us so.

"If we could see, if we could know,"
We often say,
But God in love a veil doth throw
Across our way;
We cannot see what lies before,
And so we cling to Him the more,
He leads us till this life is o'er
Trust and obey.

EVINING

EVENING

What! know ye not that your body is the temple of the Holy Ghost
which is in you, which ye have of God, and ye are not your own?
For ye are bought with a price: therefore glorify God in your body,
and in your spirit, which are God's. (1 COR. 6:19–20)

The Christian who truly enters into these two verses has solved some of the deepest problems in life. Those who recognize God's absolute proprietorship of their bodies are not long in doubt as to where they should go, or what they should do. *Consecration is simply a matter of letting God have what He has paid for, or returning stolen property.*

"Ye are bought with a price." It was an infinite price that God paid. It was something more than silver and gold—the precious Blood of His only begotten Son (see 1 Peter 1:18–19). God emphasizes the tremendous cost of redemption as an appeal to the heart of the redeemed. The price He has paid measures His estimate of us. He does not give *a life so dear to Him for a soul that is worth nothing to Him.* He has laid down the gold of His heart—even Jesus Christ. If we would go and stand on Calvary's hill, and consider what it has cost heaven to purchase our salvation, we could not long withhold from Him what He rightfully owns—*the full service of spirit, soul, and body.* Yet how many are satisfied to say, "Jesus is mine," who never go on to say, "I am His." *One who takes this higher ground is bound to be careful what he does with property which belongs to another.*

When the thought of His proprietorship becomes uppermost, then we will simultaneously recognize the fact that being His, we are temples of the Holy Spirit. Conscious of God's ownership, and thoughtful of our Divine Guest—the Holy Spirit—it is only natural that *we should glorify God in our bodies and in our spirits, which are His.* To glorify Him thus, is simply to exhibit the power and character of God in that which is His.

The Christian's greatest joy is found in letting God possess His own property.

July 30

MORNING

~∞~

A cup of cold water only (MATT. 10:42).

What am I to do? I expect to pass through this world but once. Any good work, therefore, any kindness, or any service I can render to any soul of man or animal, let me do it now. Let me not neglect or defer it, for I shall not pass this way again. **AN OLD QUAKER SAYING**

It isn't the thing you do, dear,
It's the thing you leave undone,
Which gives you the bitter heartache
At the setting of the sun;
The tender word unspoken,
The letter you did not write,
The flower you might have sent, dear,
Are your haunting ghosts at night.

The stone you might have lifted
Out of your brother's way,
The bit of heartsome counsel

You were hurried too much to say;
The loving touch of the hand, dear,
The gentle and winsome tone,
That you had no time or thought for,
With troubles enough of your own.

These little acts of kindness,
So easily out of mind,
These chances to be angels,
Which even mortals find—
They come in night and silence,
Each chill reproachful wraith,
When hope is faint and flagging,
And a blight has dropped on faith.

For life is all too short, dear.
And sorrow is all too great,
To suffer our slow compassion
That tarries until too late.
And it's not the thing you do, dear,
It's the thing you leave undone,
Which gives you the bitter heartache,
At the setting of the sun.

ADELAIDE PROCTOR

Give what you have; to someone it may be better than you dare to think.

LONGFELLOW

EVENING

~⁓~

The Lord will be the place of repair of His people.
(JOEL 3:16, TRANS.)

Soldiers may be wounded in battle and sent to the hospital. A hospital isn't a shelf; it is a place of repair.

A soldier on service in the spiritual army is never off his battlefield. He is only removed to another part of the field when a wound interrupts what he meant to do, and sets him doing something else.

Is it not joy, pure joy, that there is no question of *the shelf*? No soldier on service is ever "laid aside"; he is only given another commission to fight among the unseen forces of the field. Never is he shelved as of no further use to his beloved Captain! The soldier must let his Captain say when and for what He needs him most, and he must not cloud his mind with questions. A wise master never wastes his servant's time, nor a commander his soldiers'. So let us settle it once for all and find heart's ease in doing so. *There is no discharge in warfare*—no, not for a single day. We may be called to serve on the visible field, going continually into the invisible both to renew our strength and to fight the kind of battle that can only be fought there. Or, we may be called off the visible altogether for a while and drawn deep into the invisible. That dreary word "laid aside" is never for *us*. *We* are soldiers of the King!   ROSE FROM BRIER

Place of repair: O blessed place of refuge!
How gladly will I come to meet Him there,
To cease awhile from all the joy of service
To find a deeper joy with Him to share.

Place of repair: for tired brain and body!
How much I need that place just out of sight
Where only He can talk, and be beside me,
Until again made strong by His great might.

Place of repair: when trials press upon me
And God permits the unexpected test,
'Tis there I learn some lesson sweet and precious
As simply on His faithfulness I rest.

Place of repair: the place to take my sorrow,
The thing that hurts and would be hard to bear,
But somehow in the secret place I'm finding
That all the hurt is healed since He is there.

Place of repair: to wait for fresh enduement
I silently with Him alone would stay
Until He speaks again, and says, "Go forward
To help some other sheep to find the way."

Place of repair: O trysting-place most hallowed,
The Lord Himself is just that place to me,
His grace, His strength, His glory and His triumph,
Himself alone my all-sufficiency.

July 31

MORNING

∽∾

He . . . guided them by the skillfulness of his hands (Ps. 78:72).

When you are doubtful as to your course, submit your judgment absolutely to the Spirit of God, and ask Him to shut against you every door but the right one. . . . Meanwhile keep on as you are, and consider the absence of indication to be the indication of God's will that you are on His track. . . . As you go down the long corridor, you will find that He has preceded you, and locked many doors which you would fain have entered; but be sure that beyond these there is one which He has left unlocked. Open it and enter, and you will find yourself face-to-face with a bend of the river of opportunity, broader and deeper than anything you had dared to imagine in your sunniest dreams. Launch forth upon it; it conducts to the open sea.

God guides us, often by circumstances. At one moment the way may seem utterly blocked; and then shortly afterward some trivial incident occurs, which might not seem much to others, but which to the keen eye of faith speaks volumes. Sometimes these things are repeated in various ways, in answer to prayer. They are not haphazard results of chance, but the opening up of circumstances in the direction in which we would walk. *And they begin to multiply as we advance toward our goal,* just as the lights do as we near a populous town, when darting through the land by night express.

F. B. MEYER

If you go to Him to be guided, He will guide you; but He will not comfort your distrust or half-trust of Him by showing you the chart of all His purposes concerning you. He will show you only into a way where, if you go cheerfully and trustfully forward, He will show you on still farther.

HORACE BUSHNELL

As moves my fragile bark across the storm-swept sea,
Great waves beat o'er her side, as north wind blows;
Deep in the darkness hid lie threat'ning rocks and shoals;
But all of these, and more, my Pilot knows.
Sometimes when dark the night, and every light gone out,
I wonder to what port my frail ship goes;
Still though the night be long, and restless all my hours,
My distant goal, I'm sure, my Pilot knows.

THOMAS CURTIS CLARK

❧❧

Unto him shall the gathering of the people be. (GEN. 49:10)

*W*hat a scene of unimaginable grandeur that will be, when at last *all nations are gathered to His Feet!* That will include representatives from all the European States, from Iceland in the far North to Greece in the South, and from Portugal in the West to hidden saints of God in Soviet Russia in the East. There will be many from Algeria, Morocco, and the Atlas mountains; from Egypt and the Nile Valley; from the sandy deserts and the mountains of the Sahara; from the great lakes in Central Africa, from the banks of the Niger, the Calabar, the Congo, and the Zambesi rivers; and from the uplands of South Africa. There will be *gathered to Christ* many from Palestine, Transjordan, and Arabia; India will contribute her millions; and even from closed lands like Nepal, Sikkim, and Tibet, *Christ will gather His own.*

From the Islands in the Dutch East Indies they will come—Java, Sumatra, Bali, Celebes, Lombok, Soembawa, Borneo, and the rest, and *will be gathered to the feet of the Redeemer.* From the teeming millions of Central Asia, from China, Japan, Korea, Manchukuo and Mongolia, there will be an immense home-going to the Savior. From the myriad Islands of the Pacific the peoples of Polynesia and Melanesia will *be gathered to the Lord who redeemed them.*

From Australia and New Zealand there will be multitudes who will *join in the glad song of praise.* From every republic of Central, South, and North America, and from the West Indies Islands—Cuba, Haiti, Jamaica, Puerto Rico, and the Lesser Antilles, *they will come.* From the far-off forests and lakes of Canada *there will be a similar home-going.*

Whether the tongues be those of the white race, or of the red, or of the black, *the gathering to Christ* will be overwhelmingly splendid.

From earth's wide bounds, from ocean's farthest coast,
Through gates of pearl streams in the countless host,
Singing to Father, Son, and Holy Ghost, "Hallelujah!"
BIBLE SOCIETY RECORD

I hear ten thousand voices singing
Their praises to the Lord on high;
Far distant shores and hills are ringing
With anthems of their nation's joy:

Praise ye the Lord! for He hath given
To lands in darkness hid, His light,
As morning rays light up the heaven,
His word has chased away our night.

Hark! Hark! a louder sound is booming
O'er heaven and earth, o'er land and sea;
The angel's trump proclaims His coming—
Our day of endless Jubilee.

Hail to Thee, Lord! Thy people praise Thee;
In every land Thy Name we sing;
On heaven's eternal throne upraise Thee,
Take Thou Thy power, Thou glorious King!
HYMNS OF CONSECRATION AND FAITH

August 1

MORNING

❧

Surrender your very selves to God as living men who have risen from the dead (ROM. 6:13 WEYMOUTH KC).

I went one night to hear an address on consecration. No special message came to me from it, but as the speaker kneeled to pray, he dropped this sentence: "O Lord, Thou knowest we can trust the Man that died for us." And that was my message. I rose and walked down the street to the train; and as I walked, I pondered deeply all that consecration might mean to my life and—I was afraid. And then, above the noise and clatter of the street traffic came to me the message: "You can trust the Man that died for you." I got into the train to ride homeward; and as I rode, I thought of the changes, the sacrifices, the disappointments which consecration might mean to me and—I was afraid.

I reached home and sought my room, and there upon my knees I saw my past life. I had been a Christian, an officer in the church, a Sunday school superintendent, but had never definitely yielded my life to God.

Yet as I thought of the darling plans which might be baffled, of the cherished hopes to be surrendered, and the chosen profession which I might have to abandon—I *was afraid.*

I did not see the better things God had for me, so my soul was shrinking back; and then for the last time, with a swift rush of convicting power, came to my innermost heart that searching message:

"My child, you can trust the Man that died for you. If you cannot trust Him whom can you trust?"

That settled it for me, for in a flash I saw the Man who so loved me as to die for me could be absolutely trusted with all the concerns of the life He had saved.

Friend, you can trust the Man that died for you. You can trust Him to baffle no plan which is not best to be foiled, and to carry out every one which is for God's glory and your highest good. You can trust Him to lead you in the path which is the very best in this world for you.

J. H. MCC.

Just as I am, thy love unknown,
Has broken every barrier down,
Now to be Thine, yea, Thine ALONE,
O Lamb of God, I come!

"Life is not salvage to be saved out of the world, but an investment to be used in the world."

EVENING

Tell me, O thou whom my soul loveth . . . where thou makest thy flock to rest at noon? (SONG 1:7)

We have lost the art of *"resting at noon."* Many are slowly succumbing to the strain of life *because they have forgotten how to rest.* The steady stream, the continuous uniformity of life, is what kills.

Rest is not a sedative for the sick, but a tonic for the strong. It spells emancipation, illumination, transformation. It saves us from becoming slaves even of good works.

One of our Cambridge naturalists told me once of an experiment he had made with a pigeon. The bird had been born in a cage and had never been free; one day his owner took the bird out on the porch of the house and flung it into the air. To the naturalist's surprise the bird's capacity for flight was perfect. Round and round it flew as if born in the air; but soon its flight grew excited, panting, and the circles grew smaller, until at last the bird dashed full against its master's breast and fell to the ground.

What did it mean? It meant that, though the bird had inherited the instinct of flight it had not inherited the capacity to stop, and if it had not risked the shock of a sudden halt the little life would have been panted out in the air.

Isn't that a parable of many a modern life: completely endowed with the instinct of action, but without the capacity to stop? Round and round life goes in its weary circle until it is almost dying at full speed. Any shock, even some severe experience, is a mercy if it checks the whirl. Sometimes God stops such a soul abruptly by some sharp blow of trouble, and the soul falls in despair at His Feet, and then He bends over it and says: *"Be still,* my child; be still, and know that I am God!"* until by degrees the despair of trouble is changed into submission and obedience, and the poor, weary, fluttering life is made strong to fly again.

> *When, spurred by tasks unceasing or undone,*
> *You would seek rest afar,*
> *And cannot, though repose be rightly won—*
> *Rest where you are.*
>
> *Neglect the needles; sanctify the rest;*
> *Move without stress or jar;*
> *With quiet of a spirit self-possessed*
> *Rest where you are.*
>
> *Not in event, restriction, or release,*
> *Not in scenes near or far,*
> *But in ourselves are restlessness or peace:*
> *Rest where you are.*
>
> *Where lives the soul lives God; His day, His world,*
> *No phantom mists need mar;*
> *His starry nights are tents of peace unfurled;*
> *Rest where you are.*

Is it so long since we trod the road to our "resting-place," that the path has become a jungle?

August 2

MORNING

❦

I will make all my mountains a way (ISA. 49:11).

God will make obstacles serve His purpose. We all have mountains in our lives. There are people and things that threaten to bar our progress in the divine life. Those heavy claims, that uncongenial occupation, that thorn in the flesh, that daily cross—we think that if only these were removed we might live purer, tenderer, holier lives; and often we pray for their removal.

"Oh, fools, and slow of heart!" These are the very conditions of achievement; they have been put into our lives as the means to the very graces and virtues for which we have been praying so long. Thou hast prayed for patience through long years, but there is something that tries thee beyond endurance; thou hast fled from it, evaded it, accounted it an unsurmountable obstacle to the desired attainment, and supposed that its removal would secure thy immediate deliverance and victory.

Not so! Thou wouldest gain only the cessation of temptations to impatience. But this would not be patience. Patience can be acquired only through just such trials as now seem unbearable.

Go back; submit thyself. Claim to be a partaker in the patience of Jesus. Meet thy trials in Him. There is nothing in life which harasses and annoys that may not become subservient to the highest ends. They are *His* mountains. He puts them there. We know that God will not fail to keep His promise. "God understandeth the way thereof and knoweth the place thereof. For he looketh to the ends of the earth, and seeth under the whole heaven"; and when we come to the foot of the mountains, we shall find the way.   *FROM* **CHRIST IN ISAIAH, BY MEYER**

The meaning of trial is not only to test worthiness, but to increase it; as the oak is not only tested by the storms, but toughened by them.

∽◦∾

They waited for me as for the rain; and they opened their mouth
wide as for the latter rain. (JOB 29:23)

The LORD shall . . . satisfy thy soul in drought . . .
and thou shalt be like a watered garden,
and like a spring of water, whose waters fail not. (ISA. 58:11)

Travelers are enthusiastic over a species of palm tree which grows in South America. They call it *the rain tree*. This tree has the remarkable power of attracting, in a wondrous degree, atmospheric moisture, which it condenses and drops on the earth in refreshing dew. It grows straight up in the parched and arid desert and daily distributes its refreshing showers, with the result that around it an oasis of luxuriant vegetation soon springs up. The floodgates of heaven refuse to open, the fountains cease to flow, the rivers evaporate—all true, but the rain tree getting its moisture from above, renews the garden which it has created about its base, and gives the weary traveler shade and fruit, a new life and a delightful rest!

God would have *us* to be like the rain tree growing alongside the desert highways of the world—sources of new spiritual life. God HIMSELF is our atmosphere, and we carry our atmosphere with us wherever we go.

This atmosphere is proof against all infection, and to breathe it is constant health.

Christ's power was in His separateness. He did not withdraw Himself from the world, but lived in the very midst of it. No man ever came into such close external contact with the devil. Jesus was not a recluse. He was social—mingling with men; yet He kept intact His separateness from the world. He was *Jesus!* Men felt this! This was His power!

In the secret of Christ's power we see the secret of *our* power. If we are to have any power in the world we must become partakers of His holiness; we must be *separated* with Him; and be *kept separated* and set apart to the same great life.

The angel, grateful for each borrowed sense,
Gazed at the sight:
A girl so white,
With slender fingers tense
Upon the table edge (around his head
The smell of new-baked bread)

The while unhurried tones fell low, and clear,
And near.
Alone, yet not alone, yet not alone,
She fell not prone;
But learning a little against the wall,
The while the sun grew late,
She knew . . . she knew . . . she knew—why all
Her life she had been separate.
THE ANNUNCIATION, BY FLORENCE G. MAGEE

"To reveal his Son in me" (Gal. 1:16).

August 3

MORNING

❧

Quit you like men, be strong (1 COR. 16:13).

Do not pray for easy lives! Pray to be stronger men. Do not pray for tasks equal to your powers. Pray for powers equal to your tasks. Then the doing of your work shall be no miracle, but you shall be a miracle.

PHILLIPS BROOKS

We must remember that it is not in any easy or self-indulgent life that Christ will lead us to greatness. The easy life leads not upward, but downward. Heaven always is above us, and we must ever be looking up toward it. There are some people who always avoid things that are costly, that require self-denial, or self-restraint and sacrifice, but toil and hardship show us the only way to nobleness. Greatness comes not by having a mossy path made for you through the meadow, but by being sent to hew out a roadway by your own hands. Are you going to reach the mountain splendors? **SELECTED**

Be strong!
We are not here to play, to dream, to drift;
We have hard work to do, and loads to lift.
Shun not the struggle; face it.
'Tis God's gift.

Be strong!
Say not the days are evil—Who's to blame?
And fold the hands and acquiesce—O shame!
Stand up, speak out, and bravely,
In God's name.

Be strong!
It matters not how deep entrenched the wrong,
How hard the battle goes, the day how long,
Faint not, fight on!
Tomorrow comes the song.

MALTBIE D. BABCOCK

EVING

Christ in you, the hope of glory. (COL. 1:27)

The greatest thing that any of us can do is not to live for Christ but to live Christ. What is holy living? It is Christ-life. It is not to be Christians, but Christ-ones. It is not to try to do or be some great thing but simply to have Him and let Him live His own life in us; abiding in Him and He in us, and letting Him reflect His own graces, His own faith, His own consecration, His own love, His own patience, His own gentleness, His own words in us, while we "show forth the virtues of Him who hath called us out of darkness into His marvelous light." *This is at once the sublimest and the simplest life that it is possible to live.* It is a higher standard than human perfection, and yet it is possible for a poor, sinful, imperfect man to realize it through the perfect Christ who comes to live within us.

God help us so to live, and thus to make real to those around us the simplicity, the beauty, the glory, and the power of the Christ life.

"I cannot tell," said the humble shepherd's wife, "what sermon it was that led me into a life of victory. I cannot even explain the creed or the catechism, but I know that something has changed me entirely. Last summer John and I washed the sheep in yonder stream. I cannot tell you where the water went, but I can show you the clean white fleece of the sheep. And so I may forget the doctrine, but I have its blessed fruit in my heart and life."

Two of us were chatting with Sadhu Sundar Singh in my office one morning. The Sadhu had just arrived in London. We knew little concerning him, and my friend was anxious to find out if he knew the doctrine of that "perfect love" of which Saint John speaks.

"Does he understand?" asked my friend, turning to me.

The Sadhu smiled and quietly said: "When I throw a stone at the fruit tree, the fruit tree throws no stone back, but gives me *fruit*. Is it that?" Then he went on to ask: "Should not we, who love the Lord Jesus, be like sandalwood, which imparts its fragrance to the ax which cuts it?"

SELECTED

August 4

MORNING

And Jesus lifted up his eyes, and said, Father, I thank thee that thou hast heard me (JOHN 11:41).

This is a very strange and unusual order. Lazarus is still in the grave, and the thanksgiving *precedes* the miracle of resurrection. I thought that the thanksgiving would have risen when the great deed had been wrought, and Lazarus was restored to life again. But Jesus gives thanks for what He is about to receive. The gratitude breaks forth *before* the bounty has arrived, in the assurance that it is certainly on the way. The song of victory is sung *before* the battle has been fought. It is the sower who is singing the song of the harvest home. It is thanksgiving before the miracle!

Who thinks of announcing a victory-psalm when the crusaders are just starting out for the field? Where can we hear the grateful song for the answer which has not yet been received? And after all, there is nothing strange or forced, or unreasonable to the Master's order. *Praise* is really the most vital preparatory ministry to the working of the miracles. Miracles are wrought by spiritual power. Spiritual power is always proportioned to our *faith*.

DR. JOWETT

Praise Changes Things

Nothing pleases God in connection with our prayer and our praise, and nothing so blesses the man who prays as the praise which he offers. I got a great blessing once in China in this connection. I had received bad and sad news from home, and deep shadows had covered my soul. I prayed, but the darkness did not vanish. I summoned myself to endure, but the darkness only deepened. Just then I went to an inland station and saw on the wall of the mission home these words: "Try Thanksgiving." I did, and in a moment every shadow was gone, not to return. Yes, the psalmist was right, "It is a good thing to give thanks unto the Lord."

REV. HENRY W. FROST

EVENING

The LORD is good unto them that wait for him, to the soul that seeketh him. It is good that a man should both hope and quietly wait for the salvation of the LORD. (LAM. 3:25–26)

It is easier to work than to wait. It is often more important to wait than to work. *We can trust God to do the needed working while we are waiting;* but if we are not willing to wait, and insist upon working while He would have us be still, we may interfere with the effective and triumphant working that He would do in our behalf. *Our waiting may be the most difficult thing we can do; it may be the severest test that God can give us.*

Oswald Chambers has said truly: "One of the greatest strains in life is the strain of *waiting for God.* God takes the saint like a bow which He stretches; we get to a certain point and say *I cannot stand any more;* but God goes on stretching. He is not aiming at our mark, but at His own, and the patience of the saints is that we hold on until He lets the arrow fly straight to His goal. If we are willing to remember God's call and assurance there need be no strain at all while we are waiting. The "stretched bow" time may be a time of unbroken rest for us as we "rest in the LORD, and wait patiently for him" (Ps. 37:7).

Unless a violin string is stretched until it cries out when the bow is drawn over it, there is no music. A loose violin string with no strain upon it is of no use—it is dead, has no voice. But when stretched till it strains it is brought to the proper tone, and then only is it useful to the music-maker.

A. B. SIMPSON

In God's eternal plan, a month, a year,
Is but an hour of some slow April day,
Holding the germs of what we hope or fear,
To blossom far away.
The Almighty is tedious, but He's sure!

August 5

❧

Is (2 Cor. 12:9).

$\mathcal{I}$t had pleased God to remove my youngest child under circumstances of peculiar trial and pain; and as I had just laid my little one's body in the churchyard, on return home, I felt it my duty to preach to my people on the meaning of trial.

Finding that this text was in the lesson for the following Sabbath, I chose it as my Master's message to them and myself; but on trying to prepare the notes, I found that in honesty I could not say that the words were true; and therefore I knelt down and asked God to let His grace be sufficient for me. While I was thus pleading, I opened my eyes and saw a framed illuminated text, which my mother had given me only a few days before, and which I had told my servant to place upon the wall during my absence at the holiday resort where my little one was taken away from us.

I did not notice the words on returning to my house; but as I looked up and wiped my eyes, the words met my gaze, "My grace *is* sufficient for thee."

The "is" was picked out in bright green while the "My" and the "thee" were painted in another color.

In one moment the message came straight to my soul, as a rebuke for offering such a prayer as, "Lord, let Thy grace be sufficient for me"; for the answer was almost as an audible voice, "How dare you ask that which is?" God cannot make it any more sufficient than He has made it; get up and believe it, and you will find it true, because the Lord says it in the simplest way: "My grace *is* (not shall be or may be) sufficient for thee."

"My," "is," and "thee" were from that moment, I hope, indelibly fixed upon my heart; and I (thank God) have been trying to live in the reality of the message from that day forward to the present time.

The lesson that came to me, and which I seek to convey to others, is, *Never turn God's facts into hopes, or prayers, but simply use them as realities, and you will find them powerful as you believe them.*

PREBENDARY H. W. WEBB PEPLOE

He giveth more grace when the burdens grow greater,
He sendeth more strength when the labors increase;
To added affliction He addeth His mercies,
To multiplied trials His multiplied peace.

When we have exhausted our store of endurance,
When our strength has failed ere the day is half done,
When we reach the end of our hoarded resources
Our Father's full giving is only begun.

His love has no limit, His grace has no measure,
His power no boundary known unto men;
For out of His infinite riches in Jesus
He giveth and giveth and giveth again.
ANNIE JOHNSON FLINT

EVENING

∽

My God with his loving kindness shall come to
meet me at every corner. (PS. 59:10, LIT.)

*I*t matters not how great the scheme if God draws it out; it matters
not how insurmountable the difficulties appear if God undertakes the
responsibility. *If we, His children, when we get into tangled corners even by*
our own folly and sometimes wrongdoing, would only turn to God as a King
and as a Father and cast ourselves upon Him, He would work for us and
lead us out of our troubles safely and in a manner worthy of a King.

This morning, Lord, I pray
Safeguard us through the day,
Especially at corners of the way.
For when the way is straight,

We fear no sudden fate,
But see ahead the evening's open gate.
But few and far between
Are days when all is seen

Of what will come, or yet of what has been.
For unexpected things
Swoop down on sudden wings
And overthrow us with their buffetings.

And so, dear Lord, we pray,
Control and guard this day
Thy children at the corners of their way.
CORNERS, BY M. G. L.

Dr. S. D. Gordon says in his writings: *"It is a good thing for us to be put in a tight corner.* To be pushed and hemmed in on every side until you are forced to stand with your back to the wall, facing a foe at every angle, with barely standing room—*that is good.* For one thing, you find out that *no matter how close the fit of that corner may be, it still can hold another in addition to yourself.* Its very tightness brings you and your Lord into the very closest quarters. And *only at closest touch will you find out what a wondrous Friend He is.*

"Tight corners are famous places for chamber concerts. The acoustics are wonderful. David's exile Psalms have rung out a strangely sweet melody down all the ages, and out through all the world, and into thousands of hearts."

August 6

MORNING

∿

Awake, O north wind; and come, thou south, blow upon my garden, that the spices thereof may flow out! (SONG OF SOL. 4:16).

Look at the meaning of this prayer a moment. Its root is found in the fact that, as delicious odors may lie *latent* in a spice tree, so *graces* may lie unexercised and undeveloped in a Christian's heart. There is many a plant of profession; but from the ground there breathes forth no fragrance of holy affections or of godly deeds. The same winds blow on the thistle bush and on the spice tree, but it is only *one* of them which gives out rich odors.

Sometimes God sends severe blasts of trial upon His children to develop their graces. Just as torches burn most brightly when swung to and fro; just as the juniper plant smells sweetest when flung into the flames; so the richest qualities of a Christian often come out under the north wind of suffering and adversity. Bruised hearts often emit the fragrance that God loveth to smell.

I had a tiny box, a precious box
Of human love—my spikenard of great price;
I kept it close within my heart of hearts
And scarce would lift the lid lest it should waste.
Its perfume on the air. One day a strange

Deep sorrow came with crushing weight, and fell
Upon my costly treasure, sweet and rare
And broke the box to atoms. All my heart
Rose in dismay and sorrow at this waste,
But as I mourned, behold a miracle
Of grace Divine. My human love was changed
To Heaven's own, and poured in healing streams
On other broken hearts, while soft and clear
A voice above me whispered, "Child of Mine,
With comfort wherewith thou art comforted,
From this time forth, go comfort others,
And thou shalt know blest fellowship with Me,
Whose broken heart of love hath healed the world."

EVINING

EVENING

No plan [which comes] from thee can be hindered. (JOB 42:2, LIT.)

We believe in the providence of God, but we do not believe half enough in it. Remember that Omnipotence has servants everywhere, set in their places at every point of the road. In the old days of the post horses, there were always swift horses ready to carry onward the king's mails.

It is wonderful how God has His relays of providential agents; how when He has done with one there is always another ready to take his place. Sometimes you have found one friend fail you—he is just dead and buried. "Ah!" you say, "what shall I do?" Well, well, *God knows how to carry on the purposes of His providence;* He will raise up another. How strikingly punctual providence is! You and I make appointments and miss them by half an hour; but *God never missed an appointment yet!* God never is before His time though *we* often wish He were; but He is never behind—no, *not by one tick of the clock.*

When the children of Israel were to go down out of Egypt, all the Pharaohs in the pyramids, if they had risen to life again, could not have kept them in bondage another half minute. "Thus saith the LORD . . . Let my people go!" It was time, and go they must! All the kings of the earth, and all the princes thereof, are in subjection to the kingdom of God's providence, and He can move them just as He pleases. And now, trembler, wherefore are you afraid? "Fear thou not; for I am with thee." *All the mysterious arrangements of providence work for our good.*

CHARLES H. SPURGEON

August 7

And when they had prayed, the place was shaken where they were assembled together, and they were all filled with the Holy Ghost and they spake the word of God with boldness. And with great power gave the apostles witness of the resurrection (ACTS 4:31, 33).

Christmas Evans tells us in his diary that one Sunday afternoon he was traveling a very lonely road to attend an appointment, and he was convicted of a cold heart. He says, "I tethered my horse and went to a sequestered spot, where I walked to and fro in an agony as I reviewed my life. I waited three hours before God, broken with sorrow, until there broke over me a sweet sense of His forgiving love. I received from God a new baptism of the Holy Ghost. As the sun was westering, I went back to the road, found my horse, mounted it and went to my appointment. On the following day I preached with such new power to a vast concourse of people gathered on the hillside, that a revival broke out that day and spread through all Wales."

The greatest question that can be asked of the "twice born" ones is, *"Have ye received the Holy Ghost since ye believed?"*

This was the password into the early church.

O the Spirit filled life; is it thine, is it thine?
Is thy soul wholly filled with the Spirit Divine?
O thou child of the King, has He fallen on thee?
Does He reign in thy soul, so that all men may see
The dear Savior's blest image reflected in thee?

Has He swept through thy soul like the waves of the sea?
Does the Spirit of God daily rest upon thee?
Does He sweeten thy life, does He keep thee from care?
Does He guide thee and bless thee in answer to prayer?
Is it joy to be led of the Lord anywhere?

Is He near thee each hour, does He stand at thy side?
Does He gird thee with strength, has He come to abide?
Does He give thee to know that all things may be done
Through the grace and the power of the Crucified One?
Does He witness to thee of the glorified Son?

Has He purged thee of dross with the fire from above?
Is He first in thy thoughts, has He all of thy love?
Is His service thy choice, and is sacrifice sweet?
Is the doing His will both thy drink and thy meat?
Dost thou run at His bidding with glad eager feet?

Has He freed thee from self and from all of thy greed?
Dost thou hasten to succor thy brother in need?
As a soldier of Christ dost thou hardness endure?
Is thy hope in the Lord everlasting and sure?
Hast thou patience and meekness, art tender and pure?

O the Spirit filled life may be thine, may be thine,
In thy soul evermore the Shekinah may shine;
It is thine to live with the tempests all stilled,
It is thine with the blessed Holy Ghost to be filled;
It is thine, even thine, for thy Lord has so willed.

EVERNING

EVENING

I Am That I Am. (EX. 3:14)

God is His own equivalent, and God needs nothing but Himself to achieve the great purposes on which He has set His heart.

God gave Moses a blank, and as life went forward for the next forty years, Moses kept filling in the blank with his special need. He *filled in fearlessness* before Pharaoh. He *filled in guidance* across the Red Sea. He *filled in manna* for the whole population. He *filled in water* from the rock. He *filled in guidance* through the wilderness. He *filled in victory* over Amalek. He *filled in clear revelation* at Sinai. And so Moses, for the rest of his life, had little else to do than to go quietly alone, and taking God's blank checkbook, signed by God's name, I AM THAT I AM, write in I *AM guidance; I AM bread.* He presented the check and God honored it.

And whenever you come to live upon God's plan as Moses from that moment did, *you may absolutely trust God.* And when you come down to the hoar-head you will say, *"Not one thing hath failed of all the good things which the LORD your God spake concerning you" (Josh. 23:14).*   A. B. SIMPSON

Joshua had tried God forty years in the brick kilns, forty years in the desert, and thirty years in the Promised Land, and this was his dying testimony.   D. L. MOODY

Whatever life may bring to you,
"God" will ring true to you:
Star in your sky—
Food in your store—
Staff in your hand—
Friend by your side—
Light on your path—
Joy in your heart—
In your ears music—
In your mouth songs.
Yes, rapid as your race may run,
And scorching as may shine your sun,
And bitter as may blow your blast,
And lonely as your lot be cast—
Whatever life may bring to you,
"God" will aye ring true to you.

CHARLES HERBERT

August 8

MORNING

༄‿༄

Thou art my king, O God: Command deliverance [victories, margin] for Jacob (PS. 44:4 RV).

There is no foe to your growth in grace, no enemy in your Christian work which was not included in your Savior's conquests.

You need not be afraid of them. When you touch them, they will flee before you. God has promised to deliver them up before you. Only be strong and very courageous! Fear not, nor be dismayed! The Lord is with you, O mighty men of valor—mighty because you are one with the Mightiest. Claim victory!

Whenever your enemies close in upon you, *claim victory!* Whenever heart and flesh fail, look up and claim VICTORY!

Be sure that you have a share in that triumph which Jesus won, not for Himself alone, but for us all; remember that you were in Him when He won it, and *claim victory!*

Reckon that it is yours, and gather spoil. Neither the Anakim nor fenced cities need daunt or abash you. You are one of the conquering legion. *Claim your share in the Savior's victory.*

FROM JOSHUA, BY MEYER

We are children of the King. In which way do we most honor our divine Sovereign, by failing to claim our rights and even doubting whether they belong to us, or by asserting our privilege as children of the Royal Family and demanding the rights which belong to our heirship?

EVENING

He shall come down like rain upon the mown grass. (PS. 72:6)

How grateful the soft rain must feel to the mown grass, all cut as it is, and, as we imagine it, so sore! But the rain is healing: and so God says He will come to His people, "Like rain upon the mown grass."

There is so much in life that is like the cutting-machine, and the heart becomes sore and needs the healing influences that come from God. No matter what we may call that which is healing to us it is God coming "like rain upon the mown grass." And may it not be with us as with the beautiful lawns we admire: the more cutting and the more rain, the more beautiful we shall be; but *it must not be one, but both.*   SELECTED

The absence of joy does not mean the absence of God.

The pruned vine does not suggest an absent vine-dresser, and even if the vine be bleeding it does not mean that he has gone away.

The mower's scythe had passed o'er summer fields,
The grass lay bleeding 'neath the summer sun;
Strong hands swift stored the harvest's wealthy yields,
And left the fields deserted, one by one.

Their glory gone, their beauty swept away,
Still smarting from the swift, keen cut of death,
Their woe the sharp, short work of one brief day
That dawned with sunshine in its balmy breath.

Methought they pleaded to the gentle sky
That smiled above them, bending o'er their grief,
A voiceless pleading in a tearless cry,
A soundless sob soft sighing for relief.

485

And heaven heard the fervor of their call,
And sent them healing balm at eventide,
Sweet raindrops breathing blessing in their fall,
And weeping gently o'er their wounded pride.

Thus shall He come as rain on new-mown grass,
And withered hopes spring up to grace His path,
New life be born where'er His footsteps pass,
And tender grass spring forth—"God's Aftermath."

FRANCES BROOK

August 9
MORNING

Blessed is the man whose strength is in thee . . . who passing through the valley of Baca, make it a well (PS. 84:5-6).

Comfort does not come to the lighthearted and merry. We must go down into "depths" if we would experience this most precious of God's gifts—comfort, and thus be prepared to be co-workers together with Him.

When night—needful night—gathers over the garden of our souls, when the leaves close up, and the flowers no longer hold any sunlight within their folded petals, there shall never be wanting, even in the thickest darkness, drops of heavenly dew—dew which falls only when the sun has gone.

I have been through the valley of weeping,
The valley of sorrow and pain;
But the "God of all comfort" was with me,
At hand to uphold and sustain.

As the earth needs the clouds and sunshine,
Our souls need both sorrow and joy;
So He places us oft in the furnace,
The dross from the gold to destroy.

When he leads thro' some valley of trouble,
His omnipotent hand we trace;

For the trials and sorrows He sends us,
Are part of His lessons in grace.

Oft we shrink from the purging and pruning,
Forgetting the Husbandman knows
That the deeper the cutting and paring,
The richer the cluster that grows.

Well He knows that affliction is needed;
He has a wise purpose in view,
And in the dark valley He whispers,
"Hereafter Thou'lt know what I do."

As we travel thro' life's shadow'd valley,
Fresh springs of His love ever rise;
And we learn that our sorrows and losses,
Are blessings just sent in disguise.

So we'll follow wherever He leadeth,
Let the path be dreary or bright;
For we've proved that our God can give comfort;
Our God can give songs in the night.

EVINING

EVENING

⁓⦿⁓

His praise shall continually be in my mouth. (PS. 34:1)

I heard a joyous strain—
A lark on a leafless bough
Sat singing in the rain.

I heard him singing early in the morning. It was hardly light! I could not understand that song; it was fairly a lilt of joy. It had been a portentous night for me, full of dreams that did disturb me. Old things that I had hoped to forget, and new things that I had prayed could never come, trooped through my dreams like grinning little bare-faced imps. Certainly I was in no humor to sing. What could possess that fellow out yonder to be telling the whole township how joyous he was? He was perched on the rail fence by the spring run. *He was drenched.* It had rained in the night and evidently he had been poorly housed. I pitied him. What comfort could he have had through that night bathed in the storm? He never thought of comfort. His song was not bought by any such duplicity. It was in his heart. Then I shook myself: *The shame that a lark has finer poise than a man!*

G. A. LEICHLITER

"Nothing can break you as long as you sing."

August 10
MORNING

❧

When he had heard therefore that he was sick,
he abode two days still in the same place where he was
(JOHN 11:6).

In the forefront of this marvelous chapter stands the affirmation, "Jesus loved Martha, and her sister, and Lazarus," as if to teach us that at the very heart and foundation of all God's dealings with us, however dark and mysterious they may be, we must dare to believe in and assert the infinite, unmerited, and unchanging love of God. Love permits pain. The sisters never doubted that He would speed at all hazards and stay their brother from death, but, "When he had heard *therefore* that he was sick, he abode two days still in the same place where he was."

What a startling *"therefore"*! He abstained from going, not because He did not love them, but because He did love them. His love alone kept Him back from hasting at once to the dear and stricken home. Anything less than infinite love must have rushed instantly to the relief of those loved and troubled hearts, to stay their grief and to have the luxury of wiping and stanching their tears and causing sorrow and sighing to flee away. Divine love could alone hold back the impetuosity of the Savior's tenderheartedness until the angel of pain had done her work.

Who can estimate how much we owe to suffering and pain? But for them we should have little scope for many of the chief virtues of the Christian life. Where was faith, without trial to test it; or patience, with nothing to bear; or experience, without tribulation to develop it?

SELECTED

Loved! then the way will not be drear;
For One we know is ever near,
Proving it to our hearts so clear
That we are loved.

Loved when our sky is clouded o'er.
And days of sorrow press us sore;
Still we will trust Him evermore,
For we are loved.

Time, that affects all things below,
Can never change the love He'll show;
The heart of Christ with love will flow,
And we are loved.

EVENING

❧

But what things were gain to me, those I counted loss for Christ.
(PHIL. 3:7)

If God has called you to be really like Christ, He may draw you into a life of crucifixion and humility, and put on you such demands of obedience that He will not allow you to follow other Christians, and in many ways He will seem to let other good people do things which He will not let you do.

Other Christians, who seem very religious and useful, may push themselves, pull wires, and work schemes to carry out their plans, but *you cannot do it;* and if you attempt it you will meet with such failure and rebuke from the Lord as to make you sorely penitent.

Others may boast of themselves, of their work, of their success, of their writing, but *the Holy Spirit will not allow you to do any such thing,* and if you begin it He will lead you into some deep mortification, that will make you despise yourself and all your good works.

Others will be allowed to succeed in making money . . . but it is likely *God will keep you poor,* because He wants you to have something far better than gold, and that is a helpless dependence on Him, that He may have the privilege of supplying your needs day by day out of an unseen treasury.

The Lord will let others be honored and put forward, *and keep you hid away in obscurity* because He wants to produce some choice fragrant fruit for His coming glory.

He will let others be great, *but keep you small.* He will let others do a work for Him, and get the credit for it, *but He will make you work and toil without knowing how much you are doing.*

The Holy Spirit will put a strict watch over you . . . rebuking you for lit-tle words and feelings, or for wasting time.

God is an Infinite Sovereign: *He has a right to do as He pleases with His own.*

Settle it forever, then, that *you are to deal directly with the Lord Jesus—that He is to have the privilege of tying your tongue, chaining your hand, or closing your eyes* in ways that He does not deal with others.

Then, *you will have found the vestibule of heaven.*

"Others may. You cannot!"

August 11
MORNING

❧

Although the fig tree shall not blossom,
neither shall fruit be in the vines; the labor of the olive shall fail,
and the fields shall yield no meat; the flock shall be cut off
from the fold, and there shall be no herd in the stalls:
yet I will rejoice in the Lord, I will joy in the God of my salvation
(HAB. 3:17–18).

Observe, I entreat you, how calamitous a circumstance is here sup-posed, and how heroic a faith is expressed. It is really as if he said, "Though I should be reduced to so great extremity as not to know where to find my necessary food, though I should look around about me on an empty house and a desolate field, and see the marks of the divine scourge where I had once seen the fruits of God's bounty, *yet I will rejoice in the Lord.*"

Methinks these words are worthy of being *written as with a diamond on a rock forever.* Oh, that by divine grace they might be deeply engraven on each of our hearts! Concise as the form of speaking in the text is, it evidently implies or expresses the following particulars: That in the day of his distress he would fly to God; that he would maintain a holy compo-sure of spirit under this dark dispensation, nay, that in the midst of all he would indulge in a sacred joy in God, and a cheerful expectation from Him. Heroic confidence! Illustrious faith! Unconquerable love!

DODDRIDGE

Last night I heard a robin singing in the rain,
And the raindrop's patter made a sweet refrain,
Making all the sweeter the music of the strain.

So, I thought, when trouble comes, as trouble will,
Why should I stop singing? Just beyond the hill
It may be that sunshine floods the green world still.

He who faces the trouble with a heart of cheer
Makes the burden lighter. If there falls a tear,
Sweeter is the cadence in the song we hear.

I have learned your lesson, bird with dappled wing,
Listening to your music with its lilt of spring—
When the storm-cloud darkens, then's the TIME to sing.

EBEN E. REXFORD

EVENING

Now therefore be not grieved, nor angry with yourselves,
that ye sold me hither: for God did send me before you
to preserve life. (GEN. 45:5)

When you are disappointed or vexed or hedged in or thwarted; when you are seemingly abandoned, *remember, son of God, heir of Heaven, that you are being prepared for the higher life.* You need courage, patience, perserverance, and it is in the hard places that they are developed. You need faith, and you will never have it unless you are brought to circumstances in which you are compelled to act by the invisible rather than the visible. You need those Christian graces of which the Bible speaks, and of which the pulpit preaches; and practical life, with its various vicissitudes, is God's school in which you are to acquire these things. Do not be discouraged or cast down.

When you are bestead, remember that God is dealing with you as a good schoolmaster. You will thank Him for His severity by and by.

When God is dealing with you, do not accuse Him. Do not cry out, "Why hast thou forsaken me?" Remember, that to those who are exercised thereby God shows His love and His Fatherhood. Bow yourselves meekly to the chastisements of God, and study not how you can get away from the trouble, but how you can rise above it by being made better by it.

I knew I had been sold,
For circumstance
Dark as a desert pit
And dismal as the slaver's caravan
Surrounded me,
And seemed to crush me down;
I had been sold.

I also had been sent.
The circumstance
Shone with the light Divine,
And through the wrath of men
God put me in His own appointed place.
He set on high
And none could bow me down.
I HAD BEEN SENT.
JOSEPH, BY M. MANNINGTON DEXTER

Had *we* no tests, no great hedged-in experience, *we would never know what a wonderful Deliverer and triumphant Guide we have!*

He never limits us, except to liberate us!

August 12
MORNING
∿

Whereby are given unto us exceeding great and precious promises
(2 PETER 1:4).

When a shipwright builds a vessel, does he build it to keep it upon the stocks? Nay, he builds it for the sea and the storm. When he was making it, he thought of tempests and hurricanes; if he did not, he was a poor shipbuilder.

When God made thee a believer, He meant to try thee; and when He gave thee promises, and bade thee trust them, He gave such promises as are suitable for times of tempest and tossing. Dost thou think that God makes shams like some that have made belts for swimming, which were good to exhibit in a shop, but of no use in the sea?

We have all heard of swords which were useless in war; and even of shoes which were made to sell, but were never meant to walk in. God's shoes are of iron and brass, and you can walk to heaven in them without their ever wearing out; and His lifebelts, you may swim a thousand Atlantics upon them, and there will be no fear of your sinking. His Word of promise is meant to be tried and proved.

There is nothing Christ dislikes more than for His people to make a show-thing of Him, and not to use Him. He loves to be employed by us. Covenant blessings are not meant to be looked at only, but to be appropriated. Even our Lord Jesus is given to us for our present use. Thou dost not make use of Christ as thou oughtest to do.

O man, I beseech you do not treat God's promises as if they were curiosities for a museum; but use them as everyday sources of comfort. Trust the Lord whenever your time of need comes on.

C. H. SPURGEON

> *Go to the deeps of God's promise,*
> *And claim whatsoever ye will;*
> *The blessing of God will not fail thee,*
> *His Word He will surely fulfill.*

How can God say no to something He has promised?

EVENING

❧

See how dear he held him. (JOHN 11:36 WEYMOUTH)

*H*e loved, yet lingered. We are so quick to think that delayed answer to prayer means that the prayer is not going to be answered. Dr. Stuart Holden has said truly: "Many a time we pray and are prone to interpret God's silence as a denial of our petitions; whereas, in truth, He only defers their fulfillment until such time as we ourselves are ready to cooperate to the full in His purposes." Prayer registered in heaven is prayer dealt with, although the vision still tarries.

Faith is trained to its supreme mission under the discipline of patience. The man who can wait God's time, knowing that *He* edits his prayer in wisdom and affection, will always discover that He never comes to man's aid one minute too soon or too late.

God's delay in answering the prayer of our longing heart is the most loving thing God can do. He may be waiting for us to come closer to Him, prostrate ourselves at His feet and abide there in trustful submission,

that His granting of the longed-for answer may mean infinitely greater bless-
ing than if we received it anywhere else than in the dust at His feet.

> *O wait, impatient heart!*
> *As winter waits, her songbirds fed.*
> *And every nestling blossom dead;*
> *Beyond the purple seas they sing!*
> *Beneath soft snows they sleep!*
> *They only sleep. Sweet patience keep*
> *And wait, as winter waits the spring.*

Nothing can hold our ship down when the tide comes in!

The aloe blooms but once in a hundred years; but every hour of all that century is needed to produce the delicate texture and resplendent beauty of the flower.

Faith heard the sound of "the tread of rain," and yet God made Elijah wait!

> *God never hastens, and He never tarries!*

August 13

MORNING

✧

If the clouds be full of rain, they empty themselves upon the earth
(ECCLES. 11:3).

Why, then, do we dread the clouds which now darken our sky? True, for a while they hide the sun, but the sun is not quenched; he will be out again before long. Meanwhile those black clouds are filled with rain; and the blacker they are, the more likely they will yield plentiful showers.

How can we have rain without clouds? Our troubles have always brought us blessings, and they always will. They are the dark chariots of bright grace. These clouds will empty themselves before long, and every tender herb will be gladder for the shower. Our God may drench us with grief, but He will refresh us with mercy. Our Lord's love letters often come to us in black-edged envelopes. His wagons rumble, but they are loaded with benefits. His rod blossoms with sweet flowers and nourishing fruits. Let us not worry about the clouds, but sing because May flowers are brought to us through the April clouds and showers.

O Lord, the clouds are the dust of Thy feet! How near Thou art in the cloudy and dark day! Love beholds Thee, and is glad. Faith sees the clouds emptying themselves and making the little hills rejoice on every side.

C. H. SPURGEON

What seems so dark to thy dim sight
May be a shadow, seen aright
Making some brightness doubly bright.

The flash that struck thy tree—no more
To shelter thee—lets heaven's blue floor
Shine where it never shone before.

The cry wrung from thy spirit's pain
May echo on some far-off plain,
And guide a wanderer home again.

The blue of heaven is larger than the clouds.

EVENING

He is able to save to the uttermost. (HEB. 7:25)

What a magnificent prospect! Does it not take your breath away? It may well do so; but nevertheless it is true, gloriously and eternally true, for it is written in the Word of God. *Grip that fact; grip it with your whole heart; take risks on it; stake your all on it; whisper it to yourself with clenched teeth when you are in the heat of the fight; shout it to the heavens when you see the enemy about to flee; triumph in it; exult in it!*

Faith in this one thing can transfigure your whole life, and lift you to the heights of victory and glory that once seemed to you as far off and remote as the distant snows of some shining mountain summit seem to the traveler when, through a haze of sunshine, he lifts up his eyes to gaze as at some holy thing up in the blue air.

Remember, that *the life of sanctification and spiritual power can never be had cheaply. To bestow it upon us the Lord Jesus paid the price of Calvary.* To receive it we must be at least willing to pay the price of obedience to His simple conditions. Remember, too, *it is the only life worth living.*

READER HARRIS

It costs to have a vision, but it costs too much to remember only the price.

August 14

MORNING

～✦～

Thou couldst have no power at all against me, except it were given thee from above (JOHN 19:11).

Nothing that is not God's will can come into the life of one who trusts and obeys God. This fact is enough to make our life one of ceaseless thanksgiving and joy. For "God's will is the one hopeful, glad, and glorious thing in the world"; and it is working in the omnipotence for us all the time, with nothing to prevent it *if we* are surrendered and believing.

One who was passing through deep waters of affliction wrote to a friend: "Is it not a glorious thing to know that, no difference how unjust a thing may be, or how absolutely it may seem to be from Satan, *by the time it reaches us it is God's will for us,* and will work for good to us? For *all things* work together for good to us who love God. And even of the betrayal, Christ said, *"The cup which my Father gave me, shall I not drink it?"* We live charmed lives if we are living in the center of God's will. All the attacks that Satan, through others' sin, can hurl against us are not only powerless to harm us, but are turned into blessings on the way.

H. W. S.

In the center of the circle
Of the Will of God I stand:
There can come no second causes,
All must come from His dear hand.
All is well! for 'tis my Father
Who my life hath planned.

Shall I pass through waves of sorrow?
Then I know it will be best;
Though I cannot tell the reason,
I can trust, and so am blest.
God is Love, and God is faithful.
So in perfect Peace I rest.

With the shade and with the sunshine,
With the joy and with the pain,
Lord, I trust Thee! both are needed,

Each Thy wayward child to train,
Earthly loss, did we but know it,
Often means our heavenly gain.

I. G. W.

EVENING

‹≈›

If it die . . . much fruit. (JOHN 12:24)

*I*nfinite wisdom takes us in hand, and leads us through deep interior crucifixion to our fine parts, lofty reason, brightest hopes, cherished affections, our pious zeal, our spiritual impetuosity, our narrow culture, our creed and churchism, our success, our spiritual experience, our spiritual comforts.

The crucifixion goes on until we are dead and *detached from all creatures, all saints, all thoughts, all hopes, all plans, all tender heart-yearnings, all preferences; dead to all trouble, all sorrow, all disappointments, all praise or blame, success or failure, comforts and annoyances, climates or nationalities;* dead to all desires but Himself.

There is no field without a seed,
Life raised through death is life indeed.
The smallest, lowliest little flower
A secret is, of mighty power.
To die—it lives—buried to rise—
Abundant life through sacrifice.
Wouldst thou know sacrifice?
It is through loss;
Thou can'st not save but by the Cross.
A corn of wheat except it die,
Can never, never multiply.
The glorious fields of waving gold,
Through death are life a hundredfold.
Thou who for souls dost weep and pray,
Let not hell's legions thee dismay.
This is the way of ways for thee,
The way of certain victory.
THE SOUL WINNER'S SECRET

Let go of the old grain of wheat if you want a harvest.

August 15

MORNING

We must through much tribulation enter into the kingdom of God
(ACTS 14:22).

The best things of life come out of wounding. Wheat is crushed before it becomes bread. Incense must be cast upon the fire before it odors are set free. The ground must be broken with the sharp plough before it is ready to receive the seed. It is the broken heart that pleases God. The sweetest joys in life are the fruits of sorrow. Human nature seems to need suffering to fit it for being a blessing to the world.

> *Beside my cottage door it grows,*
> *The loveliest, daintiest flower that blows,*
> *A sweetbriar rose.*
>
> *At dewy morn or twilight's close,*
> *The rarest perfume from it flows,*
> *This strange wild rose.*
>
> *But when the rain-drops on it beat,*
> *Ah, then, its odors grow more sweet,*
> *About my feet.*
>
> *Ofttimes with loving tenderness,*
> *Its soft green leaves I gently press,*
> *In sweet caress.*
>
> *A still more wondrous fragrance flows*
> *The more my fingers close*
> *And crush the rose.*
>
> *Dear Lord, oh, let my life be so*
> *Its perfume when tempests blow,*
> *The sweeter flow.*
>
> *And should it be Thy blessed will,*
> *With crushing grief my soul to fill,*
> *Press harder still.*
>
> *And while its dying fragrance flows*
> *I'll whisper low, "He loves and knows*
> *His crushed briar rose."*

If you aspire to be a son of consolation; if you would partake of the priestly gift of sympathy; if you would pour something beyond common-place consolation into a tempted heart; if you would pass through the intercourse of daily life with the delicate tact that never inflicts pain; you must be content to pay the price of a costly education—like Him, you must suffer. F. W. ROBERTSON

EVENING

◈

Thinketh no evil. (1 COR. 13:5)

"Let it rest!"

Ah! how many hearts on the brink of anxiety and disquietude, by this simple sentence have been made calm and happy!

Some proceeding has wounded us by its want of tact; *let it rest;* no one will think of it again.

A harsh or unjust sentence irritates us; *let it rest;* whoever may have given vent to it will be pleased to see it forgotten.

A painful scandal is about to estrange us from an old friend; *let it rest,* and thus preserve our charity and peace of mind.

A suspicious look is on the point of cooling our affection; *let it rest;* our look of trust will restore confidence.

Fancy! we, who are so careful to remove the briars from our pathway for fear they should wound, yet take pleasure in collecting and piercing our hearts with thorns that meet us in our daily intercourse with one another! How childish and unreasonable we are! GOLD DUST

The rents made by Time will soon mend if you will let God have His way.

August 16

MORNING

◈

In waiting, I waited, for the Lord (PS. 40:1, MARGIN).

Waiting is much more difficult than walking. Waiting requires patience, and patience is a rare virtue. It is fine to know that God builds hedges around His people—when the hedge is looked at from the viewpoint of protection. But when the hedge is kept around one until it grows so high that he cannot see over the top, and wonders whether he is ever to get out of the little sphere of influence and service in which he is pent up, it is hard for him sometimes to understand why he may not have a larger environment—hard for him to "brighten the corner" where he is. But God has a purpose in all HIS holdups. "The steps of a good man are ordered by the Lord," reads Psalm 37:23.

On the margin of his Bible at his verse George Mueller had a notation, "And the *stops* also." It is a sad mistake for men to break through God's hedges. It is a vital principle of guidance for a Christian never to move out of the place in which he is sure God has placed him, until the Pillar of Cloud moves.   FROM SUNDAY SCHOOL TIMES

When we learn to wait for our Lord's lead in everything, we shall know the strength that finds *its climax in an even, steady walk*. Many of us are lacking in the strength we so covet. But God gives full power for every task He appoints. Waiting, holding oneself true to His lead—this is the secret of strength. And anything that falls out of the line of obedience is a waste of time and strength. Watch for His leading.   S. D. GORDON

Must life be a failure for one compelled to stand still in enforced inaction and see the great throbbing tides of life go by? No; victory is then to be gotten by standing still, by quiet waiting. It is a thousand times harder to do this than it was in the active days to rush on in the columns of stirring life. It requires a grander heroism to stand and wait and not lose heart and not lose hope, to submit to the will of God, to give up work and honors to others, to be quiet, confident and rejoicing, while the happy, busy multitude go on and away. It is the grandest life "having done all, to stand."   J. R. MILLER

EVENING

Be silent unto God and let him mold thee. (PS. 46:10, TRANS.)

Let thy soul walk softly in thee
Like a saint in heaven unshod,
For to be alone with silence
Is to be at home with God.

Quiet hearts are as rare as radium. We need every day to be led by the Divine Shepherd into the green pastures and beside the still waters.

We are losing the art of meditation. Inner preparation is necessary to outer service.

"*Rest pauses*" contribute to the finer music of life. "*He* went out into a mountain to pray." "And as *he* prayed, the fashion of his countenance was altered." Therein we have the example of our Lord.

We have yet to learn the power of silence. Not in the college or academy, but in the silence of the soul, do we learn the greater lessons of life and become rooted in spiritual inwardness.

The geologist says that certain crystals can only come to their perfect form in stillness. *In the undistracted moment men are in touch with God and everlasting things.*

The strenuousness of life and the increasing distractions of the world demand a zone of silence and the Quiet Hour.

And Jesus said to them: "Come away to some lonely spot and get a little rest (for there were many coming and going, and they could get no time even to eat). So they went privately in the boat to a lonely spot" (Mark 6:31–32). Let *us* find the spot every day, and the fellowship of silence. On such moments infinite issues hinge!

In every life
There's a pause that is better than onward rush,
Better than hewing or mightiest doing;
'Tis the standing still at Sovereign will.

There's a hush that is better than ardent speech,
Better than sighing or wilderness crying;
'Tis the being still at Sovereign will.

The pause and the hush sing a double song
In unison low and for all time long.
O human soul, God's working plan
Goes on, nor needs the aid of man!
Stand still, and see!
Be still, and know!

August 17
MORNING

⤜⤛⤝⤞

I believe God, that it shall be even as it was told me (ACTS 27:25).

I went to America some years ago with the captain of a steamer, who was a very devoted Christian. When off the coast of Newfoundland he said to me, "The last time I crossed here, five weeks ago, something happened which revolutionized the whole of my Christian life. We had George Mueller of Bristol on board. I had been on the bridge twenty-four hours and never left it. George Mueller came to me, and said, "Captain, I have come to tell you that I must be in Quebec Saturday afternoon." "It is impossible," I said. "Very well, if your ship cannot take me, God will find some other way. I have never broken an engagement for fifty-seven years. Let us go down into the chatroom and pray."

I looked at that man of God, and thought to myself, what lunatic asylum can that man have come from? I never heard of such a thing as this. "Mr. Mueller," I said, "do you know how dense this fog is?" "No," he replied, "my eye is not on the density of the fog, but on the living God, who controls every circumstance of my life."

He knelt down and prayed one of the most simple prayers, and when he had finished I was going to pray: but he put his hand on my shoulder, and told me *not* to pray. "First, you do not believe He will answer; and second I BELIEVE HE HAS, and there is no need whatever for you to pray about it."

I looked at him, and he said, "Captain, I have known my Lord for fifty-seven years, and there has never been a single day that I have failed to get audience with the King. Get up, Captain and open the door, and you will find the fog gone." I got up, and the fog was indeed gone. On Saturday afternoon George Mueller was in Quebec for his engagement.

SELECTED

If our love were but more simple,
We should take Him at His word;
And our lives would be all sunshine,
In the sweetness of our Lord.

※

I am not eloquent. (EX. 4:10)

Nothing is more dishonoring to God, or more dangerous for us, than a mock humility. When we refuse to occupy a position which the grace of God assigns us, because of our not possessing certain virtues and qualifications, this is not humility, for if we could but satisfy our own consciences in reference to such virtues and qualifications, we should then deem ourselves entitled to assume the position. If, for instance, Moses had possessed such a measure of eloquence as he deemed needful, we may suppose he would have been ready to go. Now the question is, how much eloquence would he have needed to furnish him for his mission? The answer is, without God no amount of human eloquence would have availed; but with God the merest stammerer would have proved an efficient minister. This is a great practical truth.

Unbelief is not humility, but thorough pride. It refuses to believe God because it does not find in self a reason for believing. This is the very height of presumption.   C. H. M.

Move to the fore;
Say not another is fitter than thou.
Shame to thy shrinking! Up! Face thy task now.
Own thyself equal to all a soul may,
Cease thy evading—God needs thee today.
Move to the fore!

God Himself waits, and must wait till thou come;
Men are God's prophets though ages lie dumb.
Halts the Christ Kingdom with conquest so near?
Thou art the cause, thou soul in the rear.
Move to the fore!

Find your purpose and fling your life out into it; and the loftier your purpose is, the more sure you will be to make the world richer with every enrichment of yourself.   PHILLIPS BROOKS

August 18

MORNING

❧

Alone (DEUT. 32:12).

The hill was steep, but cheered along the way
By converse sweet, I mounted on the thought
That so it might be till the height was reached;
But suddenly a narrow winding path
Appeared, and then the Master said, "My child,
Here thou wilt safest walk with Me alone."

I trembled, yet my heart's deep trust replied,
"So be it, Lord." He took my feeble hand
In His, accepting thus my will to yield Him
All, and to find all in Him.
One long, dark moment,
And no friend I saw, save Jesus only.

But oh! so tenderly He led me on
And up, and spoke to me such words of cheer,
Such secret whisperings of His wondrous love,
That soon I told Him all my grief and fear,
And leaned on His strong arm confidingly.

And then I found my footsteps quickened,
And light ineffable, the rugged way
Illumined, such light as only can be seen
In close companionship with God.

A little while, and we shall meet again
The loved and lost; but in the rapturous joy
Of greetings, such as here we cannot know,
And happy song, and heavenly embraces,
And tender recollections rushing back
Of pilgrim life, methinks one memory
More dear and sacred than the rest, shall rise

And we who gather in the golden streets,
Shall oft be stirred to speak with grateful love
Of that dark day when Jesus bade us climb
Some narrow steep, leaning on Him alone.

"There is no high hill but beside some deep valley. There is no birth without a pang."

DAN CRAWFORD

EVENING

～∞～

And the angel of the LORD *went further,*
and stood in a narrow place, where was no way to turn
either to the right hand or to the left. (NUM. 22:26)

A narrow place!" *You know that place; you have been there—you will very likely be there again before long—some of you may be there at this very moment;* for it is not merely a defile away somewhere among the mountains to the east of Moab. It is a life passage in individual experience—a time when there we are brought face to face with some inevitable question. . . . Temptation is such a "narrow place." In the serious crisis of the soul's history, it is alone. *It is a path on which there is room only for itself, and before it there is God. Between these two always the matter has to be settled. Yes, or no, is the hinge on which everything turns. Shall I yield and dishonor God, or shall I resist and triumph in His might? There is no possible compromise; for compromise with sin is itself the most insidious form of sin.* No man can pass through these crises, and be after them what he was before. *He has met God face to face, and he must either be the better or the worse for that experience.* Either, like Jacob at Peniel he can say, "My life is preserved," or like Saul after he had thrown off his allegiance to his God, "Jehovah has departed from me, and is become my enemy."

WILLIAM M. TAYLOR

The harder the place the more He loves to show His power. If you wish to find Him real, come to Him in some great trouble. He has no chance to work until you get in a hard place. He led Israel out of the usual way till He got them to the Red Sea. Then there was room for His power to be manifested. God loves the hard places and the narrow places.

Rejoice if you are in such a place! Even if it is in the very heart of the foe, God is able to deliver you. Let not your faith in Him waver for a moment, and you will find *His omnipotence is all upon your side for every difficulty in which you can be placed.*

"When you get into a tight place," said Harriet Beecher Stowe, "and everything goes against you, till it seems as if you could not hold on a minute longer, never give up then, *for that is just the place and the time that the tide will turn."*

August 19

༄

As sorrowful, yet always rejoicing (2 COR. 6:10).

Sorrow was beautiful, but her beauty was the beauty of the moonlight shining through the leafy branches of the trees in the wood, and making little pools of silver here and there on the soft green moss below.

When Sorrow sang, her notes were like the low sweet call of the nightingale, and in her eyes was the unexpectant gaze of one who has ceased to look for coming gladness. She could weep in tender sympathy with those who weep, but to rejoice with those who rejoice was unknown to her.

Joy was beautiful, too, but his was the radiant beauty of the summer morning. His eyes still held the glad laughter of childhood, and his hair had the glint of the sunshine's kiss. When Joy sang his voice soared upward as the lark's, and his step was the step of a conqueror who has never known defeat. He could rejoice with all who rejoice, but to weep with those who weep was unknown to him.

"But we can never be united," said Sorrow wistfully.

"No, never." And Joy's eyes shadowed as he spoke. "*My* path lies through the sunlit meadows, the sweetest roses bloom for my gathering, and the blackbirds and thrushes await my coming to pour forth their most joyous lays."

"*My* path," said Sorrow, turning slowly away, "leads through the darkening woods; with moonflowers only shall my hands be filled. Yet the sweetest of all earth songs—the love song of the night—shall be mine; farewell, Joy, farewell."

Even as she spoke they became conscious of a form standing beside them; dimly seen, but of a kingly Presence, and a great and holy awe stole over them as they sank on their knees before Him.

"I see Him as the King of Joy," whispered Sorrow, "for on His head are many crowns, and the nailprints in His hands and feet are the scars of a great victory. Before Him all my sorrow is melting away into deathless love and gladness, and I give myself to Him forever."

"Nay, Sorrow," said Joy softly, "but I see Him as the King of Sorrow, and the crown on His head is a crown of thorns, and the nailprints in His hands and feet are the scars of a great agony. I, too, give myself to Him forever, for sorrow with Him must be sweeter than any joy that I have known."

"Then we are *one* in Him," they cried in gladness, "for none but He could unite Joy and Sorrow."

Hand in hand they passed out into the world to follow Him through storm and sunshine, in the bleakness of winter cold and the warmth of summer gladness, "as sorrowful yet always rejoicing."

Should Sorrow lay her hand upon thy shoulder,
And walk with thee in silence on life's way,
While Joy, thy bright companion once, grown colder,
Becomes to thee more distant day by day?
Shrink not from the companionship of Sorrow,
She is the messenger of God to thee;
And thou wilt thank Him in His great tomorrow—
For what thou knowest not now, thou then shalt see;
She is God's angel, clad in weeds of night,
With "whom we walk by faith and not by sight."

EVENING

∽∾∾

Whatsoever thy soul desireth, I will even do it for thee.
(I SAM. 20:4)

It is sometimes difficult to realize that the promises of God *are to be taken at their face value.* Too often they are regarded as a part of the general spiritual instruction of the Word, but not to be appropriated for our own need.

We fail to realize because we do not appropriate!

No matter what may be our requirements—guidance, spiritual refreshing, physical or temporal needs, God has given us *some specific word on which to base our faith.*

Then, since the promises are definite, should not our prayers be definite? Prayerfully *search the Word to find the promise that will fit the case. Prove Him!* Back of the word of the Lord is the person and character of God Himself; *God, who cannot lie.*

God honors the person who trusts Him implicitly.

It is not our worth, but *Christ's,* which has secured for us *immediate access to the Throne,* "For all the promises of God *in him* are yea, and *in him* Amen" (2 Cor. 1:20).

With such a basis and assurance, *why hesitate to claim the things the Lord has provided?* Can you not trust the *One* who made the promise?

Whatever desire the Father permits to live in the heart of one of His saints, *He will grant the fulfillment thereof.*   S. CHADWICK

Prove the immutable promises of God!

August 20
MORNING

And Jacob was left alone; and there wrestled a man with him until the breaking of the day (GEN. 32:24).

God is wrestling with Jacob more than Jacob is wrestling with God. It was the Son of Man, the Angel of the Covenant. It was God in human form pressing down and pressing out the old Jacob life; and ere the morning broke, God had prevailed and Jacob fell with his thigh dislocated. But as he fell, he fell into the arms of God, and there he clung and wrestled, too, until the blessing came; and the new life was born and he arose from the earthly to the heavenly, the human to the divine, the natural to the supernatural. And as he went forth that morning he was a weak and broken man, but God was there instead; and the heavenly voice proclaimed, *"Thy name shall be called no more Jacob, but Israel; for as a prince hast thou power with God and with men, and hast prevailed."*

Beloved, this must ever be a typical scene in every transformed life. There comes a crisis hour to each of us, if God has called us to the highest and best, when all resources fail; when we face either ruin or something higher than we ever dreamed; when we must have infinite help from God and yet, ere we can have it, we must let something go; we must surrender completely; we must cease from our own wisdom, strength, and righteousness, and become crucified with Christ and alive in Him. God knows how to lead us up to this crisis, and He knows how to lead us through.

Is He leading you thus? Is this the meaning of your deep trial, or your difficult surroundings, or that impossible situation, or that trying place through which you cannot go without Him, and yet you have not enough of Him to give you the victory?

Oh, turn to Jacob's God! Cast yourself helplessly at His feet. Die to your strength and wisdom in His loving arms and rise, like Jacob, into His strength and all-sufficiency. There is no way out of your hard and narrow place but at the top. You must get deliverance by rising higher and coming into a new experience with God. Oh, may it bring you into all that is meant by the revelation of the Mighty One of Jacob!—*But God.*

> *At Thy feet I fall,*
> *Yield Thee up my ALL,*
> *To SUFFER, LIVE, OR DIE*
> *For my Lord crucified.*

EVENING

Whosoever will save his life shall lose it. (MARK 8:35)

The laying down of life is not only the foundation of a new life for ourselves, but also the foundation of a new life for others, just as the laying down of our Lord's life has brought forth its abundant harvest all through the years.

It is the laying down of life for the sake of the harvest; it is the grain of wheat falling into the ground to die in order that it may not abide alone.

John Coleridge Patterson's life was equipped with every gift to make it rich and happy in his own land; yet he laid it down to go to his hard and toilsome life in the South Seas. Had he been asked, *"Are you regretful for what you have turned your back upon?"* he would have answered, *"The promise has been fulfilled to me."*

An American Consul General in China once said to Matthew Culbertson, *"You might have been a Major-General if you had stayed at home."* He had been the best man in his class at West Point, but his mother's prayers had borne their fruitage and he became a missionary. He was the man of military genius in Shanghai's time of need. *"No,"* he said, *"I do not regret it. The privilege of preaching the Gospel to four hundred millions of one's fellow creatures is the greatest privilege any man can have on earth."* He had *found* his life!

To be sure, Livingstone lost his life, but he had *found* another—a life which spread through Africa, which abides in Africa, which molded the world's thought of Africa.

Henry Martyn put his hand to the plow with these words, "Now, let me burn out for God!" No "looking back." No relinquishing the handles even for a holiday!

Think of James Gilmore in Mongolia in his uncompanioned life! Mongolia stretches from the Sea of Japan on the east to Turkestan on the west—a distance of three thousand miles; from the southern boundary of Asiatic Russia to the Great Wall of China—nine hundred miles. What a field! But what a plowman! He died in the furrow!

Nineteen hundred years ago our Lord lost His life and His fame. Or *did He?*

Speak, history! Who are life's victors? Unveil thy long annals and say,
Are they those whom the world calls the victors, who won the success of a
day?
Thy martyrs, or Nero? The Spartans, who fell at Thermopylae's tryst,
Or the Persians and Xerxes? His judges, or Socrates? Pilate or Christ?

WILLIAM WETMORE STORY

August 21

MORNING

༄

He brought me forth also into a large place; he delivered me, because he delighted in me (PS. 18:19).

And what is this "large place"? What can it be but God Himself, that infinite Being in whom all other beings and all other streams of life terminate? God is a large place indeed. And it was through humiliation, through abasement, through nothingness that David was brought into it.

MADAME GUYON

"I bare you on eagles' wings, and brought you unto myself" (Exod. 19:4).

Fearing to launch on "full surrender's" tide,
I asked the Lord where would its waters glide
My little bark, "To troubled seas I dread?"
"Unto Myself," He said.

Weeping beside an open grave I stood,
In bitterness of soul I cried to God:
"Where leads this path of sorrow that I tread?"
"Unto Myself," He said.

Striving for souls, I loved the work too well;
Then disappointments came; I could not tell
The reason, till He said, "I am thine all;
Unto Myself I call."

Watching my heroes—those I love the best—
I saw them fail; they could not stand the test,
Even by this the Lord, through tears not few,
Unto Himself me drew.

Unto Himself! Nor earthly tongue can tell
The bliss I find, since in His heart I dwell;
The things that charmed me once seem all as naught;
Unto Himself I'm brought.
SELECTED

EVENING

∽∾

Turn to ashes. (PS. 20:3, MARGIN)

Oh, not for Thee my fading fires,
The ashes of my heart.

May I tell you a tale of the African veld? It concerns the *fire lily.*
A grass fire in a hill country is one of the most wonderful sights in
a wonderful land, surpassing in subtle attraction the grandeur of a veld fire
on the plain with its roaring flames leaping skyward as they lick up the tall
dry grass. Among the mountains where the grass is much shorter you
watch with tireless fascination the long running lines of light on the distant
heights—something like the illumination of a town seen from far away.
With morning the scene is changed. You lift your eyes to greet the mountains you love, and they answer you with blackened faces. A little longer
and these same hills are clothed in springing green, and, from the ashes,
one of the first of the flowers, rises the *fire lily* like a little scarlet flame.

Beauty for ashes! Here are the very words of God incarnate in His
works. The matchless message of Isaiah 61:3 comes with a deeper meaning as we consider the *fire lily.* Its story unfolds the Old Testament
promise in the radiance of New Testament light; for it shows *by what*
means God would make actual in our own experience *the glorious possi-*
bility of resurrection life.

When we surrender our old nature to God that He may carry out the death sentence pronounced upon it, He accepts it in the only way He ever accepted a sacrifice, by turning it to ashes (Ps. 20:3, margin). And where the fire has been there springs from the ashes of the old life the fire lily of the beauty of Christ. As more ground is daily yielded, on the fire-swept hills of our inner life will be wrought the miracle of life out of death, and the bare slopes will burst with blossom. One unburnt hill will mean a jungle growth of grass and weeds; one valley spared will mean less Christfulness. This is the law of God—both natural and spiritual—*No fire, no fire lily; no ashes, no beauty.* This is the secret of the fire lily. *This is the meaning of surrender.*   P. E. SHARP

> *But there were only ashes when He came*
> *Saying, "My daughter, thou hast tried to serve*
> *In thine own way? but now, stretch forth thy hands*
> *That I may lead thee out of self's dark cell*
> *And work My will through thee—*
> *When thou hast ceased to be.*
>
> *I said, "My youth is gone; my strength is gone;*
> *My life—it lies before Thee bare and sere.*
> *For very shame I cannot offer Thee*
> *These ashes that are left me, gray and drear.*
> *Yet, work Thy will in me*
> *And teach me not to be."*
>
> *Then through the ashes of that fading fire*
> *He breathed His breath; and when the ash had fled,*
> *Laid on some smoldering embers a live coal*
> *That was His life, His love, all flaming red.*
> *"Thy will be done to me,*
> *So shall I live in Thee."*
>
> **AUTHOR UNKNOWN**

"Before God gives a blessing He writes a sentence of death on the means leading up to it!"

August 22

MORNING

❧

And the rest, some on boards, some on broken pieces of the ship. And so it came to pass that they escaped all safe to land (ACTS 27:44).

The marvelous story of Paul's voyage to Rome, with its trials and triumphs, is a fine pattern of the lights and shades of the way of faith all through the story of human life. The remarkable feature of it is the hard and narrow places which we find intermingled with God's most extraordinary interpositions and providences.

It is the common idea that the pathway of faith is strewn with flowers, and that when God interposes in the life of His people, He does it on a scale so grand that He lifts us quite out of the plane of difficulties. The actual fact, however, is that the real experience is quite contrary. The story of the Bible is one of alternate trial and triumph in the case of everyone of the cloud of witnesses from Abel down to the latest martyr.

Paul, more than anyone else, was an example of how much a child of God can suffer without being crushed or broken in spirit. On account of his testifying in Damascus, he was hunted down by persecutors and obliged to flee for his life, but we behold no heavenly chariot transporting the holy apostle amid thunderbolts of flame from the reach of his foes, but "through a window in a basket," was he let down over the walls of Damascus and so escaped their hands. In an old clothes basket, like a bundle of laundry, or groceries, the servant of Jesus Christ was dropped from the window and ignominiously fled from the hate of his foes.

Again we find him left for months in the lonely dungeons; we find him telling of his watchings, his fastings, and his desertion by friends, of his brutal and shameful beatings, and here even after God has promised to deliver him, we see him for days left to toss upon a stormy sea, obliged to stand guard over the treacherous seaman, and at last when the deliverance comes, there is no heavenly galley sailing from the skies to take off the noble prisoner; there is no angel form walking along the waters and stilling the raging breakers; there is no supernatural sign of the transcendent miracle that is being wrought; but one is compelled to seize a spar, another a floating plank, another to climb on a fragment of the wreck, another to strike out and swim for his life.

Here is God's pattern for our own lives. Here is a gospel of help for people that have to live in this everyday world with real and ordinary surroundings, and a thousand practical conditions which have to be met in a thoroughly practical way.

God's promises and God's providences do not lift us out of the plane of common sense and commonplace trial, but it is through these very things that faith is perfected, and that God loves to interweave the golden threads of His love along the warp and woof of our everyday experience. **FROM HARD PLACES IN THE WAY OF FAITH**

EVENING

So are ye in mine hand. (JER. 18:6)

Ole Bull, the world's most noted violinist, was ever wandering about. One day he became lost in the interminable forests. In the dark of the night he stumbled against a log hut, the home of a hermit. The old man took him in, fed and warmed him; after the supper they sat in front of a blazing fireplace, and the old hermit picked some crude tunes on his screechy, battered violin. Ole Bull said to the hermit, "Do you think I could play on that?" "I don't think so; it took me years to learn," the old hermit replied. Ole Bull said, "Let me try it."

He took the old marred violin and drew the bow across the strings, and suddenly the hermit's hut was filled with music Divine; and, according to the story, the hermit sobbed like a child.

We are battered instruments; life's strings have been snapped; life's bow has been bent. *Yet, if we will only let Him take us and touch us,* from this old battered, broken, shattered, marred instrument, He will bring forth music fit for the angels.

> *I never knew the old, brown violin,*
> *That was so long in some dark corner thrust,*
> *Its strings broken or loose, its pegs run down,*
> *Could ever be of use again. The dust*
> *Of years lay on its shabby case, until*
> *One day a Master took the instrument,*
> *And with caressing fingers touched the wood,*
> *Adjusted pegs and strings; his mind intent*
> *On making music as he drew his bow.*
> *Then from the violin, long silent, sprang*
> *Once more arpeggios, runs, trills. The wood*
> *Quivered, leapt into life, and joyous sang.*

I now believe that any broken life,
Jangling with discords, unadjusted, tossed
In some far corner, wasted, thrown aside,
Can yet be of some use; need not be lost
From Heaven's orchestra. A Master's Hand
Scarred with old wounds, can mend the broken thing
If yielded to Him wholly; and can make
The dumb life speak again, and joyous sing
In praise of One who gave His life that none
Need perish. And this message, glad, most blest,
I now believe; for placing in His Hand
My life, I find my world is now at rest.
DOROTHY M. BARTER-SNOW

August 23

MORNING

❦

He went out, not knowing whither he went (HEB. 11:8).

It is faith without sight. When we can *see*, it is not faith, but reasoning. In crossing the Atlantic we observed this very principle of faith. We *saw* no path upon the sea, nor sign of the shore. And yet day by day we were marking our path upon the chart as exactly as if there had followed us a great chalk line upon the sea. And when we came within twenty miles of land, we knew where we were as exactly as if we had seen it all three thousand miles ahead.

How had we measured and marked our course? Day by day our captain had taken his instruments and, looking up to the sky, had fixed his course by the sun. He was sailing by the heavenly, not the earthly lights.

So faith looks up and sails on, by God's great Sun, not *seeing* one shoreline or earthly lighthouse or path upon the way. Often its steps seem to lead into utter uncertainty, and even darkness and disaster; but He opens the way, and often makes such midnight hours the very gates of day. Let us go forth this day, not knowing, but trusting.

FROM DAYS OF HEAVEN UPON EARTH

"Too many of us want to see our way through before starting new enter-prises. If we could and did, from whence would come the development of our Christian graces? *Faith, hope and love cannot be plucked from trees, like ripe apples.* After the words 'In the beginning' comes the word *'God.'* The first step turns the key into God's powerhouse, and it is not only true that God helps those who help themselves, but *He also helps those who cannot help themselves.* You can depend upon Him every time."

"Waiting on God brings us to our journey's end quicker than our feet." The opportunity is often lost by deliberation.

EVENING

I . . . brought you unto myself. (EX. 19:4)

How we have wondered at those events which stirred us up and set us loose from ties of home and friends; and how we have marveled at the ruthlessness of those providences which sent us headlong from our assured places into the uncertainties of what seemed empty space around and beneath us. *But now we understand that every experience was in God's love and for the fulfillment of His high purposes toward us. No matter what happened, we soon saw His form and heard His heartening cry; and never did we grow weary but we immediately found that strong wings were beneath us. And oh, the wonder of it! when God brought us home to our rest-ing-place beside Himself!*

HENRY W. FROST

Unto Myself, my dear child, I would bring thee!
Who like Myself thy sure solace can be?
Who can reach down, down so deeply within thee?
Give to thy heart such a full sympathy?

Mournest thou sore that thy loved ones have failed thee?
Failed, sadly failed thy true comfort to be?
"Why did they fail" dost thou ask? Let Me whisper—
"That thou should'st find thy heart's comfort in Me."

Unto Myself! Ah, no not unto others,
Dearest, or sweetest, or fairest, or best;
Only in Me lieth unchanging solace;
Only in Me is thy promise of rest!

Child of My love, to Myself I would bring thee!
Not to some PLACE *of most heavenly bliss:*

Places, like people, may all disappoint thee,
Till thou hast learned to drink higher than this.

Unto Myself, my dear child, I would bring thee!
None like Myself thy full portion can be!
While, in my heart, there is hunger and longing
That I might find choicest treasure in thee.

Unto Myself! To Myself—not My service!
Then to most sweetly and certainly prove
That I can make thee My channel of blessing,
Use thee to shed forth the wealth of My love.

J. DANSON SMITH

August 24

MORNING

❧

I have all, and abound (PHIL. 4:18).

In one of my garden books there is a chapter with a very interesting heading, *"Flowers that Grow in the Gloom."* It deals with those patches in a garden which never catch the sunlight. And my guide tells me the sort of flowers which are not afraid of these dingy corners—may rather like them and flourish in them.

And there are similar things in the world of the spirit. They come out when material circumstances become stern and severe. They grow in the gloom. How can we otherwise explain some of the experiences of the Apostle Paul?

Here he is in captivity at Rome. The supreme mission of his life appears to be broken. But it is just in this besetting dinginess that flowers begin to show their faces in bright and fascinating glory. He may have seen them before, growing in the open road, but never as they now appeared in incomparable strength and beauty. Words of promise opened out their treasures as he had never seen them before.

Among those treasures were such wonderful things as the grace of Christ, the love of Christ, the joy and peace of Christ; and it seemed as though they needed an "encircling gloom" to draw out their secret and their inner glory. At any rate the realm of gloom became the home of revelation, and Paul began to realize as never before the range and wealth of his spiritual inheritance.

Who has not known men and women who, when they arrive at seasons of gloom and solitude, put on strength and hopefulness like a robe? You may imprison such folk where you please; but you shut up their treasure with them. You cannot shut it out. You may make their material lot a desert, but "the wilderness and the solitary place shall be glad, and the desert shall rejoice and blossom as the rose." DR. JOWETT

"Every flower, even the fairest, has its shadow beneath it as it swings in the sunlight."
Where there is much light there is much shade.

EVENING

*Gideon threshed wheat. . . . And the angel of the LORD . . .
said unto him, The LORD is with thee.* (JUDG. 6:11–12)

ﾉﾉ﾿ore courage is required when coming to grips with the common place problems of the ordinary day than is required to face batteries of destruction on a field of military conflict.

It is much easier to follow on the track of the heroic than to remain true to Jesus in drab mean streets. Human nature unaided by God cannot do it.

The follower of Jesus is a laborer—but a laborer together with God. He is a man with a hoe—but one who has his part in the harvest whose reapers are the angels.

> *This is the place where Thou didst bid me stand;*
> *And work and wait;*
> *I thought it was a plot of fertile land,*
> *To tend and cultivate:*
> *Flowers and fruit, I said, are surely there,*
> *In rich earth stored,*
> *And I will make of it a garden fair,*
> *For Thee, my Lord!*
>
> *Lo! it is set where only bleak skies frown,*
> *With rank weeds sown,*
> *And over it the vagrant thistle-down*
> *Like dust is blown;*

Long have I labored, but the barren soil
No crop will yield:
This have I won for all my ceaseless toil—
A bare plowed field!

Nay, even here, where thou didst strive and weep,
Some sunny morn
Others shall come with joyous hearts and reap
The full-eared corn;
Yet is their harvest to thy labor due;
On Me 'twas spent—
Are not the furrows driven straight and true?
Be thou content!
A TILLER OF THE SOIL

August 25
MORNING

❧

Shut up unto the faith (GAL. 3:23).

God, in olden time suffered man to be kept in ward by the law that he might learn the more excellent way of faith. For by the law he would see God's holy standard and by the law he would see his own utter helplessness; then he would be glad to learn God's way of faith.

God still shuts us up to faith. Our natures, our circumstances, trials, disappointments, all serve to shut us up and keep us in ward till we see that the only way out is God's way of faith. Moses tried by self-effort, by personal influence, even by violence, to bring about the deliverance of his people. God had to shut him up forty years in the wilderness before he was prepared for God's work.

Paul and Silas were bidden of God to preach the gospel in Europe. They landed and proceeded to Philippi. They were flogged, they were shut up in prison, their feet were put fast in the stocks. They were shut up to faith. They trusted God. They sang praises to Him in the darkest hour, and God wrought deliverance and salvation.

John was banished to the Isle of Patmos. He was shut up to faith. Had he not been so shut up, he would never have seen such glorious visions of God.

Dear reader, are you in some great trouble? Have you had some great disappointment, have you met some sorrow, some unspeakable loss? Are you in a hard place? Cheer up! You are shut up to faith. Take your trouble the right way. Commit it to God. Praise Him that He maketh "all things work together for good," and that "God worketh for him that waiteth for him." There will be blessings, help, and revelations of God that will come to you that never could otherwise have come; and many besides yourself will receive great light and blessing because you were shut up to faith.   C. H. P.

> Great things are done when men and mountains meet,
> These are not done by jostling in the street.

EVENING

Only believe. (MARK 5:36)

*A*n old woman with an halo of silvered hair—the hot tears flowing down her furrowed cheeks—her worn hands busy over a washboard in a room of poverty—praying—for her son John—John who ran away from home in his teens to become a sailor—John, of whom it was now reported that he had become a very wicked man—*praying, praying always,* that her son might be of service to God.

What a marvelous subject for an artist's brush!

The mother believed in two things, the power of prayer and the reformation of her son. So while she scrubbed she continued to pray. God answered the prayer by working a miracle in the heart of *John Newton.* The black stains of sin were washed white in the blood of the Lamb. *"Though your sins be as scarlet, they shall be as white as snow."*

The washtub prayers were heard as are all prayers when asked in His name. John Newton, the drunken sailor, became John Newton, the sailor-preacher. Among the thousands of men and women he brought to Christ was *Thomas Scott,* cultured, selfish, and self-satisfied. Because of the washtub prayers another miracle was worked and Thomas Scott used both his pen and voice to lead thousands of unbelieving hearts to Christ—among them, a dyspeptic, melancholic young man, *William Cowper* by name.

He, too, was washed by the cleansing Blood and in a moment of inspiration wrote:

> There is a fountain filled with blood
> Drawn from Immanuel's veins,

And sinners, plunged beneath that flood,
Lose all their guilty stains.

And this song has brought countless thousands to the Man who died on Calvary. Among the thousands was *William Wilberforce,* who became a great Christian statesman, and unfastened the shackles from the feet of thousands of British slaves. Among those whom he led to the Lord was *Leigh Richmond,* a clergyman of the Established Church in one of the Channel Islands. He wrote a book, *The Dairyman's Daughter,* which was translated into forty languages and with the intensity of leaping flame burned the love of Christ into the hearts of thousands.

All this resulted because a mother *took God at His Word* and prayed that her son's heart might become as white as the soapsuds in the washtub.

August 26

MORNING

～⚬～

It is not in me (JOB 28:14).

I remember a summer in which I said, "It is the ocean I need," and I went to the ocean; but it seemed to say, *"It is not in me!"* The ocean did not do for me what I thought it would. Then I said, "The mountains will rest me," and I went to the mountains, and when I awoke in the morning there stood the grand mountain that I had wanted so much to see; but it said, *"It is not in me!"* It did not satisfy. Ah! I needed the ocean of His love, and the high mountains of His truth within. It was *wisdom* that the "depths" said they did not contain, and that could not be compared with jewels or gold or precious stones. *Christ is wisdom and our deepest need.* Our restlessness within can only be met by the revelation of His eternal friendship and love for us.   MARGARET BOTTOME

My heart is there!
Where, on eternal hills, my loved one dwells
Among the lilies and asphodels;
Clad in the brightness of the Great White Throne,
Glad in the smile of Him who sits thereon,
The glory gilding all His wealth of hair

And making His immortal face more fair—
THERE IS MY TREASURE and my heart is there.

My heart is there!
With Him who made all earthly life so sweet,
So fit to live, and yet to die so meet;
So mild, so grand, so gentle and so brave,
So ready to forgive, so strong to save.
His fair, pure Spirit makes the Heavens more fair,
And thither rises all my longing prayer—
THERE IS MY TREASURE and my heart is there.

FAVORITE POEM OF THE LATE CHAS. E. COWMAN

You cannot detain the eagle in the forest. You may gather around him a chorus of the choicest birds; you may give him a perch on the goodliest pine; you may charge winged messengers to bring him choicest dainties; but he will spurn them all. Spreading his lofty wings, and with his eye on the alpine cliff, he will soar away to his own ancestral halls amid the munition of rocks and the wild music of tempest and waterfall.

The soul of man, in its eagle soarings, will rest with nothing short of the Rock of Ages. Its ancestral halls are the halls of heaven. Its munitions of rocks are the attributes of God. The sweep of its majestic flight is eternity! "Lord, THOU hast been our dwelling place in all generations."

MACDUFF

"My Home is God Himself"; Christ brought me there.
I laid me down within His mighty arms;
He took me up, and safe from all alarms
He bore me "where no foot but His hath trod,"
Within the holiest at Home with God,
And bade me dwell in Him, rejoicing there.
O Holy Place! O Home divinely fair!
And we, God's little ones, abiding there.

"My Home is God Himself"; it was not so!
A long, long road I traveled night and day,
And sought to find within myself some way,
Aught I could do, or feel to bring me near;
Self effort failed, and I was filled with fear,
And then I found Christ was the only way,
That I must come to Him and in Him stay,
And God had told me so.

And now "my Home is God," and sheltered there,
God meets the trials of my earthly life,
God compasses me round from storm and strife,
God takes the burden of my daily care.
O Wondrous Place! O Home divinely fair!
And I, God's little one, safe hidden there.
Lord, as I dwell in Thee and Thou in me,
So make me dead to everything but Thee;
That as I rest within my Home most fair,
My soul may evermore and only see
My God in everything and everywhere;
My Home is God.

UNKNOWN

EVENING

~∞~

And I will betroth thee unto me for ever. (HOS. 2:19)

"Rise up, My love, My fair one, and come away!" He calls. Away from Egypt's bondage—away . . . *but with Him!* Divinely betrothed!

"My Beloved!" are the words. No other voice would have so aroused her. To *His* voice her heart responds. *Expectation quickens the hearing;* and when we are truly desirous toward Christ, how quickly the accents of His voice are caught!

He said: "Wilt thou go with Me
Where shadows eclipse the light?"
And she answered: "My Lord, I will follow Thee
Far, under the stars at night."
But He said: "No starlight pierces the gloom
Of the valley thy feet must tread;
But it leads thee on to a cross and tomb—"
"But I go with Thee," she said.

"Count the cost; canst thou pay the price—
Be a dumb thing led;
Laid on an altar of sacrifice?"
"Bind me there, my Lord," she said.
"Bind me that I may not fail—
Or hold with Thy wounded hand;

∼ 523 ∼

For I fear the knife and the piercing nail,
And I shrink from the burning brand.
Yet whither Thou goest I will go,
Though the way be lone and dread—"
His voice was tender, and sweet, and low—
"Thou shalt go with Me," He said.

And none knew the anguish sore
Or the night of the way she came;
Alone, alone with the cross she bore,
Alone in her grief and shame.
Brought to the altar of sacrifice,
There as a dumb thing slain:
Was the guerdon more than the bitter price?
Was it worth the loss and pain?

Ask the seed-corn, when the grain
Ripples its ripened gold;
Ask the sower when, after toil and pain,
He garners the hundredfold.
HE said (and His voice was glad and sweet):
"Was it worth the cost, My own?"
And she answered, low at His pierced feet,
"I found at the end of the pathway lone
NOT DEATH, BUT LIFE ON A THRONE!"*

ANNIE CLARKE

"Wilt thou go with this man?"

August 27

MORNING

〜❧〜

And he took him aside from the multitude (MARK 7:33).

Paul not only stood the tests in Christian activity, but in the solitude of captivity. You may stand the strain of the most intense labor, coupled with severe suffering, and yet break down utterly when laid aside from all religious activities; when forced into close confinement in some prison house.

That noble bird, soaring the highest above the clouds and enduring the longest flights, sinks into despair when in a cage where it is forced to beat its helpless wings against its prison bars. You have seen the great eagle languish in its narrow cell with bowed head and drooping wings. What a picture of the sorrow in inactivity.

Paul in prison. That was another side of life. Do you want to see how he takes it? I see him looking out over the top of his prison wall and over the heads of his enemies. I see him write a document and sign his name—not the prisoner of Festus, nor of Caesar; not the victim of the Sanhedrin; but the—"prisoner of the Lord." He saw only the hand of God in it all. To him the prison becomes a palace. Its corridors ring with shouts of triumphant praise and joy.

Restrained from the missionary work he loved so well, he now built a new pulpit—a new witness stand—and from that place of bondage come some of the sweetest and most helpful ministries of Christian liberty. What precious messages of light come from those dark shadows of captivity.

Think of the long train of imprisoned saints who have followed in Paul's wake. For twelve long years Bunyan's lips were silenced in Bedford jail. It was there that he did the greatest and best work of his life. There he wrote the book that has been read next to the Bible. He says, "I was at home in prison and I sat me down and wrote, and wrote, for joy did make me write."

The wonderful dream of that long night has lighted the pathway of millions of weary pilgrims. That sweet-spirited French lady, Madam Guyon, lay long between prison walls. Like some caged birds that sing the sweeter for their confinement, the music of her soul has gone out far beyond the dungeon walls and scattered the desolation of many drooping hearts.

Oh, the heavenly consolation that has poured forth from places of solitude!

S. C. REES

Taken aside by Jesus,
To feel the touch of His hand;
To rest for a while in the shadow
Of the Rock in a weary land.

Taken aside by Jesus,
In the loneliness dark and drear,
Where no other comfort may reach me,
Than His voice to my heart so dear.

Taken aside by Jesus,
To be quite alone with Him,

To hear His wonderful tones of love
'Mid the silence and shadows dim.

Taken aside by Jesus,
Shall I shrink from the desert place;
When I hear as I never heard before,
And see Him "face to face"?

EVENING

〜✠〜

Joseph said unto them . . . Ye thought evil against me;
but God meant it unto good, to bring to pass, as it is this day,
to save much people alive. (GEN. 50:19–20)

It had been a long road for Joseph; it had been a desperately rough road, too. There was the slimy pit, the brothers' treachery, the slave chains, the terrible palace temptation, and the prison cell. But what a different ending this story has: "And Pharoah said unto Joseph, See, I have set thee over all the land of Egypt. . . only in the throne will I *be* greater than thou." And can you not hear Joseph speaking to his brethren: "God meant it unto good . . . to save much people alive."

A whole life committed to God in unswerving loyalty is held as a most sacred trust. The processes used in building a great soul are varied and consume much time. Many a long road seems to have no turning. Frequently "The night is dark and we seem to be far from home," but patience cries out, "Lead Thou me on," "Keep Thou my feet; I do not ask to see the distant scene—one step enough for me." *Faith, courage, and patience are* tremendous qualities in a great life, but *the time element* is the factor which is absolutely necessary to work all these out.

Blessed is that life which is so thoroughly rooted down into the life of God that it can feel and know that, though time moves slowly in long drawn-out tests and trials. God's tides move steadily on in accomplishing His glorious purposes.   QUESTS AND CONQUESTS

O tarry thou His leisure,
Praise when He seems to pause,
Nor think that the Eternal One
Will set His clock by yours;
But wait His time, and trust His date,
It cannot be too soon, or late!

The turn on the long road comes at last!

August 28

MORNING

❧

There he proved them (Exod. 15:25).

I stood once in the test room of a great steel mill. All around me were little partitions and compartments. Steel had been tested to the limit, and marked with figures that showed its breaking point. Some pieces had been twisted until they broke, and the strength of torsion was marked on them. Some had been stretched to the breaking point and their tensile strength indicated. Some had been compressed to the crushing point, and also marked. The master of the steel mill knew just what these pieces of steel would stand under strain. He knew just what they would bear if placed in the great ship, building, or bridge. He knew this because his testing room revealed it.

It is often so with God's children. God does not want us to be like vases of glass or porcelain. He would have us like these toughened pieces of steel, able to bear twisting and crushing to the uttermost without collapse.

He wants us to be, not hothouse plants, but storm-beaten oaks; not sand dunes driven with every gust of wind, but granite rocks withstanding the fiercest storms. To make us such He must needs bring us into His testing room of suffering. Many of us need no other argument than our own experiences to prove that suffering is indeed God's testing room of faith.   J. H. MCC.

It is very easy for us to speak and theorize about faith, but God often casts us into crucibles to try our gold, and to separate it from the dross and alloy. Oh, happy are we if the hurricanes that ripple life's unquiet sea have the effect of making Jesus more precious. Better the storm with Christ than smooth waters without Him.   MACDUFF

What if God could not manage to ripen your life without suffering?

Now Jesus loved Martha, and her sister, and Lazarus. (JOHN 11:5)

Jesus does not want all His loved ones to be of one mold or color. He does not seek uniformity. He will not remove our individuality; He only seeks to glorify it. He loved *"Martha,* and *her sister,* and *Lazarus."*

"Jesus loved Martha." Martha is our biblical example of a practical woman; *"Martha served."* In that place is enshrined her character.

"And her sister." Mary was contemplative, *spending long hours in deep communion with the unseen.* We need the Marys as well as the Marthas— the deep contemplative souls, whose spirits shed a fragrant restfulness over the hard and busy streets. We need the souls who sit at Jesus' feet and listen to His Word, and then interpret the sweet Gospels to a tired and weary world.

"And Lazarus." What do we know about him? Nothing! *Lazarus seems to have been undistinguished and commonplace.* Yet Jesus loved him. What a huge multitude come under the category of "nobodies"! Their names are on the register of births, and on the register of deaths, and the space between is a great obscurity. Thank God for the commonplace people! They turn our houses into homes; they make life restful and sweet. Jesus loves the commonplace. Here then is a great, comforting thought: we are all loved—the brilliant and the commonplace, the dreamy and the practical.

"Jesus loved Martha, and her sister, and Lazarus."　　　J. H. JOWETT

"Does the wildflower bloom less carefully and are the tints less perfect because it rises beside the fallen tree in the thick woods where mankind never enters? Let us not bemoan the fact that we are not great, and that the eyes of the world are not upon us."

Loved! then the way will not be drear,
For One we know is ever near,
Proving it to our hearts so clear
That we are loved.

Loved when we sing the glad new song
To Christ, for whom we've waited long,
With all the happy ransomed throng—
Forever loved.

And he went out carrying his own cross (JOHN 19:17).

There is a poem called "The Changed Cross." It represents a weary one who thought that her cross was surely heavier than those of others whom she saw about her, and she wished that she might choose another instead of her own. She slept, and in her dream she was led to a place where many crosses lay, crosses of different shapes and sizes. There was a little one most beauteous to behold, set in jewels and gold. "Ah, this I can wear with comfort," she said. So she took it up, but her weak form shook beneath it. The jewels and the gold were beautiful, but they were far too heavy for her.

Next she saw a lovely cross with fair flowers entwined around its sculptured form. Surely that was the one for her. She lifted it, but beneath the flowers were piercing thorns which tore her flesh.

At last, as she went on, she came to a plain cross, without jewels, without carvings, with only a few words of love inscribed upon it. This she took up and it proved the best of all, the easiest to be borne. And as she looked upon it, bathed in the radiance that fell from heaven, she recognized her own old cross. She had found it again, and it was the best of all and lightest for her.

God knows best what cross we need to bear. We do not know how heavy other people's crosses we need to bear. We envy someone who is rich; his is a golden cross set with jewels, but we do not know how heavy it is. Here is another whose life seems very lovely. She bears a cross twined with flowers. If we could try all the other crosses that we think lighter than our own, we would at last find that not one of them suited us so well as our own. **FROM GLIMPSES THROUGH LIFE'S WINDOWS**

> *If thou, impatient, dost let slip thy cross,*
> *Thou wilt not find it in this world again;*
> *Nor in another: here and here alone*
> *Is given thee to suffer for God's sake.*
> *In other worlds we may more perfectly*
> *Love Him and serve Him, praise Him,*
> *Grow nearer and nearer to Him with delight.*
> *But then we shall not any more*
> *Be called to suffer, which is our appointment here*

Canst thou not suffer, then, one hour or two?
If He should call thee from thy cross today,
Saying: "It is finished—that hard cross of thine
From which thou prayest for deliverance,"
Thinkest thou not some passion of regret
Would overcome thee? Thou would'st say,
"So soon? Let me go back and suffer yet awhile
More patiently. I have not yet praised God."
Whensoe'er it comes, that summons that we look for,
It will seem soon, too soon. Let us take heed in time
That God may now be glorified in us.
UGO BASSI'S SERMON IN A HOSPITAL

EVENING

Is not this the carpenter? (MARK 6:3)

This is my beloved Son, in whom I am well pleased. (MATT. 3:17)

Yes, yes, a carpenter, same trade as mine!
How it warms my heart as I read that line.
I can stand the hard work, I can stand the poor pay,
For I'll see that Carpenter at no distant day.
MALTBIE D. BABCOCK

It suits our best sense that the One who spoke of "putting the hand to the plow," and "taking the yoke upon us," should have made plows and yokes, Himself, and people do not think His words less heavenly for not smelling of books and lamps. Let us not make the mistake of those Nazarenes: *that Jesus was a carpenter* was to them poor credentials of divinity, but it has been *Divine credentials to the poor* ever since. Let us not be deceived by social ratings and badges of the schools.

Carey was a cobbler, but he had a map of the world on his shop wall, and outdid Alexander the Great in dreaming and doing.

What thoughts were in the mind of Jesus at His workbench? One of them was that the kingdoms of this world should become the kingdoms of God—*at any cost!*   SELECTED

"What is that in thine hand?"

Is it a hoe, a needle, a broom? A pen or a sword? A ledger or a school-book? A typewriter or a telegraph instrument? Is it an anvil or a printer's rule? Is it a carpenter's plane or a plasterer's trowel? Is it a throttle or a helm? Is it a scalpel or a yardstick? Is it a musical instrument or the gift of song?

Whatever it is, give it to God in loving service.

Many a tinker and weaver and stonecutter and hard worker has had open windows and a sky, and a mind with wings!

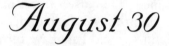

August 30

MORNING

~~~

They that go down to the sea in ships, that do business in great waters; these see the works of the Lord, and his wonders in the deep (PS. 107:23–24).

*H*e is but an apprentice and no master in the art, who has not learned that every wind that blows is fair for heaven. The only thing that helps nobody, is a dead calm. North or south, east or west, it matters not, every wind may help toward that blessed port. Seek one thing only: *keep well out to sea,* and then have no fear of stormy winds. Let our prayer be that of an old Cornishman: "O Lord, send us out to sea—out in the deep water. Here we are so close to the rocks that the first bit of breeze with the Devil, we are all knocked to pieces. Lord, send us out to sea—out in the deep water, where we shall have room enough to get a glorious victory." MARK GUY PEARSE

Remember that we have no more faith at any time than we have in the hour of trial. All that will not bear to be tested is mere carnal confidence. Fair-weather faith is no faith. C. H. SPURGEON

Not disobedient. (ACTS 26:19)

Whither, O Christ? The *vision did not say; nor did Paul ask, but started on the way.* If Paul had asked, and if the Lord had said; if Paul had known the long hard road ahead; if with the heavenly vision Paul had seen stark poverty with cold and hungry mien, black fetid prisons with their chains and stocks, fierce robbers lurking amid tumbled rocks, the raging of the mob, the crashing stones, the aching eyes, hot fever in the bones, perils of mountain passes wild and steep, perils of tempest in the angry deep, the drag of loneliness, the curse of lies, mad bigotry's suspicious peering eyes, the bitter foe, the weakly, blundering friend, the whirling sword of Caesar at the end—would Paul have turned his back with shuddering moan and settled down at Tarsus, had he known? No! and a thousand times the thundering No! *Where Jesus went, there Paul rejoiced to go.* Prisons were palaces where Jesus stayed; with Jesus near, he asked no other aid; the love of Jesus kept him glad and warm, bold before kings and safe in any storm. *Whither, O Christ? The vision did not say. Paul did not care. He started on the way.*   AMOS R. WELLS

"A great *Must* dominated the life of the Son of Man. That *must* will dominate ours if we follow in His footsteps. The Son of Man *must,* and so His followers *must.*"

> *Lord, I would follow, but—*
> *First I would see what means that wondrous call*
> *That peals so sweetly through life's rainbow hall,*
> *That thrills my heart with quivering golden chords,*
> *And fills my soul with joys seraphical.*
>
> *Lord, I would follow, but—*
> *First I would leave things straight before I go—*
> *Collect my dues, and pay the debts I owe:*
> *Lest when I'm gone, and none is here to tend,*
> *Time's ruthless hand my garnering o'erthrow.*
>
> *Lord, I would follow, but—*
> *First I would see the end of this high road*
> *That stretches straight before me fair and broad;*
> *So clear the way I cannot go astray,*
> *It surely leads me equally to God.*

Who answers Christ's insistent call
Must give himself, his life, his all,
Without one backward look.
Who sets his hand upon the plow,
And glances back with anxious brow,
His calling hath mistook;
Christ claims him wholly for His own;
He must be Christ's and Christ's alone.

SELECTED

The Spirit of God does not come with a voice like thunder (that may come ultimately) but as a gentle zephyr, yet it can only be described as an imperative compulsion—*This thing must be done!*

August 31

MORNING

❧

Blessed are they that have not seen, and yet have believed
(JOHN 20:29).

How strong is the snare of the things that are seen, and how necessary for God to keep us in the things that are unseen! If Peter is to walk on the water he must walk; if he is going to swim, he must swim, but he cannot do both. If the bird is going to fly it must keep away from fences and the trees, and trust to its buoyant wings. But if it tries to keep within easy reach of the ground, it will make poor work of flying.

God had to bring Abraham to the end of his own strength, and to let him see that in his own body he could do nothing. He had to consider his own body as good as dead, and then take God for the whole work; and when he looked away from himself, and trusted God alone, then he became fully persuaded that what He had promised, He was able to perform. That is what God is teaching us, and He has to keep away encouraging results until we learn to trust without them, and then He loves to make His Word real in fact as well as faith.   A. B. SIMPSON

I do not ask that He must prove
His Word is true to me,
And that before I can believe

He first must let me see.
It is enough for me to know
'Tis true because He says 'tis so;
On His unchanging Word I'll stand
And trust till I can understand.

E. M. WINTER

EVENING

❧

Thou shalt be above only, and thou shalt not be beneath.
(DEUT. 28:13)

This verse came to me first as a very real message from God in a time of great pressure. We had fourteen guests in the Mission house and were almost without domestic help. I had, perforce, to lay aside correspondence and other duties and give my time and attention to cooking and housework, and was feeling the strain.

Then God's Word spoke to me with power: *"Thou shalt be above only, and thou shalt not be beneath,"* and in a moment I saw there was no need to go under—no need to be overwhelmed by my circumstances. No need to trouble because it seemed as if I could not get through and my ordinary work was getting in arrears—somehow, I could be above it all! *"Above only, and not beneath."* How often I used to say as I went about my kitchen, "I refuse to go down," and how the lesson I learned in those difficult days has been an inspiration ever since. Do you wonder that Deuteronomy 28:13 is one of my favorite verses in the Bible?

I see in it the possibility of a life of constant victory—not up today in heights of blessedness, and down in the depths tomorrow. This is a *steady* life. It is the life that has been established and settled by the God of all grace.

"Above only" is a *position* of victory, too. It is that position which is ours in Christ Jesus. "Quickened us together . . . in heavenly places in Christ Jesus" (Eph. 2:5–6). "Your life is hid with Christ in God" (Col. 3:3).

When we lived in Alexandria, Egypt, we used to see some fierce squalls of wind and rain, which lashed the sea into fury. The great buoys in the harbor would be covered with spray and foam, but when the wind died down again they were still there in their places, unmoved and steady. "Above only" for they had that within them which kept them on the top. And have we not *power* within us, too, which should insure our *triumph*?

Let us absolutely refuse to come down to live and work on a lower level.   **A MISSIONARY'S TESTIMONY**

"Far above all."

September 1

MORNING

❦

I will lay thy stones with fair colors (ISA. 54:11).

The stones from the wall said, "We come from the mountains far away, from the sides of the craggy hills. Fire and water have worked on us for ages, but made us only crags. Human hands have made us into a dwelling where the children of your immortal race are born, and suffer, and rejoice, and find rest and shelter, and learn the lessons set them by our Maker and yours. But we have passed through much to fit us for this. Gunpowder has rent our very heart; pickaxes have cleaved and broken us, it seemed to us often without design or meaning, as we lay misshapen stones in the quarry; but gradually we were cut into blocks, and some of us were chiseled with finer instruments to a sharper edge. But we are complete now, and are in our places, and are of service."

You are in the quarry still, and not complete, and therefore to you, as once to us, much is inexplicable. But you are destined for a higher building, and one day you will be placed in it by hands not human, a living stone in a heavenly temple.

> *In the still air the music lies unheard;*
> *In the rough marble beauty hides unseen;*
> *To make the music and the beauty needs*
> *The master's touch, the sculptor's chisel keen.*
>
> *Great Master, touch us with Thy skillful hands;*
> *Let not the music that is in us die!*
> *Great Sculptor, hew and polish us; nor let,*
> *Hidden and lost, thy form within us lie!*

❧❧

The steps of a good man are ordered by the LORD (PS. 37:23)

We often make a great mistake thinking that God is not guiding us at all, because we cannot see far ahead. But He only undertakes that *the steps* of a good man should be ordered by the Lord; not next year, but tomorrow; not for the next mile, but the next yard: *as you will acknowledge when you review it from the hilltops of Glory.*

"The *stops* of a good man, as well as his *steps,* are ordered by the Lord," says George Müller. Naturally an opened door seems more like guidance to us than a closed one. *Yet God may guide by the latter as definitely as by the former.* His guidance of the children of Israel by the pillar of cloud and of fire is a clear case in point. When the cloud was lifted the Israelites took up their march: it was the guidance of God to move onward. But when the cloud tarried and abode upon the tabernacle, then the people rested in their tents. Both the tarrying and the journeying were guidance from the Lord—the one as much as the other.

I shall never be able to go too fast, if the Lord is in front of me; and I can never go too slowly, if I follow Him always, everywhere.

It is just as dark in advance of God's glorious leading as it is away behind Him.

You may be trying to go faster than He is moving. Wait till He comes up and then the way will no longer lie in darkness. He has left footprints for us to follow. *Make no footprints of thine own!*

> *Not so in haste, my heart!*
> *Have faith in God and wait:*
> *Although He linger long*
> *He never comes too late.*
>
> *Until He cometh, rest,*
> *Nor grudge the hours that roll,*
> *The feet that wait for God*
> *Are soonest at the goal*
>
> *Are soonest at the goal*
> *That is not gained by speed*
> *Then hold thee still, my heart,*
> *For I shall wait His lead.*
>
> **BAYARD TAYLOR**

Let the great Master's steps be thine!

September 2

MORNING

∽∾

Unto you it is given . . . to suffer (PHIL. 1:29).

God keeps a costly school. Many of its lessons are spelled out through tears. Richard Baxter said, "O God, I thank Thee for a bodily discipline of eight and fifty years"; and he is not the only man who has turned a trouble into triumph.

This school of our heavenly Father will soon close for us; the term time is shortening every day. Let us not shrink from a hard lesson or wince under any rod of chastisement. The richer will be the crown, and the sweeter will be heaven, if we endure cheerfully to the end and graduate in glory.   THEODORE L. CUYLER

The finest china in the world is burned at least three times, some of it more than three times. Dresden china is always burned three times. *Why* does it go through that intense fire? Once ought to be enough; twice ought to be enough. No, three times are necessary to burn that china so that the gold and the crimson are brought out more beautifully and then fastened there to stay.

We are fashioned after the same principle in human life. Our trials are burned into us once, twice, thrice; and by God's grace these beautiful colors are there and they are there to stay forever.   CORTLAND MYERS

> *Earth's fairest flowers grow not on sunny plain,*
> *But where some vast upheaval rent in twain*
> *The smiling land. . . .*
> *After the whirlwind's devastating blast,*
> *Father the molten fire and ashen pall,*
> *God's still small voice breathes healing over all.*
> *From riven rocks and fern-clad chasms deep,*
> *Flow living waters as from hearts that weep,*
> *There in the afterglow soft dews distill*
> *And angels tend God's plants when night falls still,*
> *And the Beloved passing by the way*
> *Will gather lilies at the break of day.*
>
> J. H. D.

EVENING

❧

When thou walkest through the fire, thou shalt not be burned.
(ISA. 43:2)

*I*n giving a lecture on flame a scientist once made a most interesting experiment. He wanted to show that in the center of each flame there is a hollow—a place of entire stillness—around which its fire is a mere wall. To prove this he introduced into the midst of the flame a minute and carefully shielded charge of explosive powder. The protection was then carefully removed and no explosion followed. A second time the experiment was tried, and by a slight agitation of the hand the central security was lost and an immediate explosion was the result.

Our safety, then, is only in *stillness of soul.* If we are affrighted and exchange the principle of faith for that of fear, or if we are rebellious and restless, we shall be hurt by the flames and anguish and disappointment will be the result.

Moreover, God will be disappointed in us if we break down. Testing is the proof of His love and confidence, and who can tell what pleasure our steadfastness and stillness give to Him? If He allowed us to go without testing it would not be complimentary to our spiritual experience. Much trial and suffering mean, therefore, that God has confidence in us; that He believes we are strong enough to endure; that we shall be true to Him even when He has left us without outward evidence of His care and seemingly at the mercy of His adversaries. If He increase the trials instead of diminishing them it is an expression of confidence in us up to the present, and a further proof that He is looking to us to glorify Him in yet hotter fires through which He is calling us to pass. *Let us not be afraid! We shall be delivered from the transitory and the outward and drawn into closer fellowship with God Himself!*

O God, make us children of quietness! **AN ANCIENT LITURGY**

September 3

❧

And he saw them toiling in rowing (MARK 6:48).

Straining, driving effort does not accomplish the work God gives man to do. Only God Himself, who always works without strain, and who never overworks, can do the work that He assigns to His children. When they restfully trust Him to do it, it will be well done and completely done. The way to let Him do His work through us is to partake of Christ so fully, by faith, that He more than fills our life.

A man who had learned this secret once said: "I came to Jesus and I drank, and I do not think that I shall ever be thirsty again. I have taken for my motto, *'Not overwork, but overflow';* and already it has made all the difference in my life."

There is no effort in overflow. It is quietly irresistible. It is the normal life of omnipotent and ceaseless accomplishment into which Christ invites us today and always.   *FROM* SUNDAY SCHOOL TIMES

> *Be all at rest, my soul, O blessed secret,*
> *Of the true life that glorifies the Lord:*
> *Not always doth the busiest soul best serve Him,*
> *But he that resteth on His faithful Word.*
> *Be all at rest, let not your heart be rippled,*
> *For tiny wavelets mar the image fair,*
> *Which the still pool reflects of heaven's glory—*
> *And thus the image He would have thee bear.*
>
> *Be all at rest, my soul, for rest is service,*
> *To the still heart God doth His secrets tell;*
> *Thus shalt thou learn to wait, and watch, and labor,*
> *Strengthened to bear, since Christ in thee doth dwell.*
> *For what is service but the life of Jesus,*
> *Lived through a vessel of earth's fragile clay,*
> *Loving and giving and poured forth for others,*
> *A living sacrifice from day to day.*
>
> *Be all at rest, so shalt thou be an answer*
> *To those who question, "Who is God and where?"*
> *For God is rest, and where He dwells is stillness,*
> *And they who dwell in Him, His rest shall share.*

And what shall meet the deep unrest around thee,
But the calm peace of God that filled His breast?
For still a living Voice calls to the weary,
From Him who said, "Come unto Me and rest."
FREDA HANBURY ALLEN

"In resurrection stillness there is resurrection power."

EVENING

~∞~

Employed to sing day and night. (1 CHRON. 9:33, TRANS.)

There is a legend of a man who found the barn where Satan kept his seeds ready to be sown in the human heart, and on finding the seeds of discouragement more numerous than others, learned that those seeds could be made to grow almost anywhere. When Satan was questioned he reluctantly admitted that there was one place in which he could never get them to thrive. "And where is that?" asked the man. Satan replied sadly, *"In the heart of a grateful man."*

The Psalmist realized that *gratitude* plays an essential part in true worship. He sang praises to God at all times; often, in his darkest moments. When in his despair he called on God, his praises soon mingled with his cries of anguish, showing the victory accomplished by his habitual thankfulness.

Sometimes a light surprises
The Christian while he sings.

Is it midnight in your experience? Is it an interminable time since the gold and crimson hope died out in the west—and a seemingly longer interval before the hoped-for dawning of day? *Midnight! Still, dark, and eerie! It is time to pray! and it is time to sing! Strange how prayer and singing open prison doors—but they do!*

Do *you* need doors to be opened? *Try prayer and singing; they go together! They work wonders!*

When the heaven is black with wind, the thunder crackling over our heads, then we may join in the paean of the Storm-spirits to Him whose pageant of power passes over the earth and harms us not in its march.

The choir of small birds, and night crickets, and all happy things, praise Him all the night long.

Not somehow but triumphantly!

September 4

❧

And when you hear the sound of the trumpet,
all the people shall shout with a great shout; and the wall of the city
shall fall down flat, and the people shall ascend up every man
straight before him (JOSH. 6:5).

The shout of steadfast faith is in direct contrast to the moans of wavering faith, and to the wails of discouraged hearts. Among the many "secrets of the Lord," I do not know of any that are more valuable than the secret of this *shout of faith.* The Lord said to Joshua, *"See,* I have given into thine hand Jericho, and the king thereof, and the mighty men of valour." He had not said, "I *will* give," but "I *have* given." It belonged to them already; and now they were called to take possession of it. But the great question was, How? It looked impossible, but the Lord declared His plan.

Now, no one can suppose for a moment that this shout caused the walls to fall. And yet the *secret* of their victory lay in just this shout, for it was the shout of a faith which dared, on the authority of God's Word alone, to claim a promised victory, while as yet there were no signs of this victory being accomplished. And according to their faith God did unto them; so that, when they shouted, He made the walls to fall.

God had declared that He *had given* them the city, and faith reckoned this to be true. And long centuries afterward the Holy Ghost recorded this triumph of faith in Hebrews: "By faith the walls of Jericho fell down, after they were compassed about seven days."

HANNAH WHITALL SMITH

Faith can never reach its consummation,
Till the victor's thankful song we raise:
In the glorious city of salvation,
God has told us all the gates are praise.

He cometh forth like a flower. (JOB 14:2)

The lotus flower (the spiritual symbol of the East) is rooted in the mud. It is quite as much indebted to the mud and water for its beauty as to the air and sunshine in which it blooms.

We must not scorn the study of root culture, nor neglect it in enthusiasm for the beauties of the orchid; for though that exquisite flower is an air plant, it needs to attach itself to a sturdier growth that is rooted in the ground and draws its nourishment from the soil to feed both itself and its parasite. *The tree will outlive many seasons of orchids!*

"Some time ago in the late autumn," says a writer, "I was in the hot-house of one of our florists. We were in the cellar, and in the dimly lighted place one could see arranged in regular file long rows of flowerpots. The florist explained that in these pots had been planted the bulbs for their winter flowers. It was best for them, he said, that they be rooted in the dark." Not in the glaring sunlight, but in the subdued shadows their life-giving roots were putting forth. They would be ready for the open day a little later. Then their gay colors would cheer many hearts; then their sweet perfume would laden the winter air.

Rooted in the shadows to bloom in the light!
Roots, then roses.

September 5

MORNING

※

Blessed are all they that wait for him (ISA. 30:18).

We hear a great deal about waiting on God. There is, however, another side. When we wait *on* God, He is waiting till we are ready; when we wait *for* God, we are waiting till He is ready.

There are some people who say, and many more who believe, that as soon as we meet all the conditions, God will answer our prayers. They say that God lives in an eternal *now;* with Him there is no past nor future; and that if we could fulfill all that He requires in the way of obedience to His will, *immediately* our needs would be supplied, our desires fulfilled, our prayers answered.

There is much truth in this belief, and yet it expresses only one side of the truth. While God *lives* in an eternal *now,* yet He *works* out His purposes in *time.* A petition presented before God is like a seed dropped in the ground. Forces above and beyond our control must work upon it, till the true fruition of the answer is given.   *FROM* THE STILL SMALL VOICE

I longed to walk along an easy road,
And leave behind the dull routine of home,
Thinking in other fields to serve my God;
But Jesus said, "My time has not yet come."

I longed to sow the seed in other soil,
To be unfettered in the work, and free,
To join with other laborers in their toil;
But Jesus said, "'Tis not My choice for thee."

I longed to leave the desert, and be led
To work where souls were sunk in sin and shame,
That I might win them; but the Master said,
"I have not called thee, publish here My name."

I longed to fight the battles of my King,
Lift high His standards in the thickest strife;
But my great Captain bade me wait and sing
Songs of His conquests in my quiet life.

I longed to leave the uncongenial sphere,
Where all alone I seemed to stand and wait,
To feel I had some human helper near,
But Jesus bade me guard one lonely gate.

I longed to leave the round of daily toil,
Where no one seemed to understand or care;
But Jesus said, "I choose for thee this soil,
That thou might'st raise for Me some blossoms rare."

And now I have no longing but to do
At home, or else afar, His blessed will,
To work amid the many or the few;
Thus, "choosing not to choose," my heart is still.

SELECTED

"And Patience was willing to wait."   *FROM* PILGRIM'S PROGRESS

Then the fire of the LORD fell, and consumed the burnt sacrifice, and the wood, and the stones, and the dust, and licked up the water that was in the trench. (1 KINGS 18:38)

*P*rayer is one of the most sacred and precious privileges vouchsafed to mortals. The following is a scene from the life of that mighty *Elijah in prayer,* Charles G. Finney.

The summer of 1853 was unusually hot and dry; pastures were scorched. There seemed likely to be a total crop failure. At the church in Oberlin the great congregation had gathered as usual. Though the sky was clear the burden of Finney's prayer was for rain.

"We do not presume, O Lord, to dictate to Thee what is best for us; yet Thou didst invite us to come to Thee as children to an earthly father and tell Thee all our wants. *We want rain.* Our pastures are dry. The earth is gaping open for rain. The cows are wandering about and lowing in search of water. Even the squirrels are suffering from thirst. Unless Thou givest us rain our cattle will die, and our harvest will come to naught. O Lord, *send us rain, and send it now!* This is an easy thing for Thee to do. *Send it now,* Lord, for Christ's sake."

In a few minutes he had to cease preaching; his voice could not be heard because of the roar and rattle of the rain!   **LIFE OF FINNEY**

> *Life has outgrown*
> *Faith's childish way,*
> *The proud and scoffing*
> *Folk insist;*
> *And so they laugh*
> *At all who say*
> *God's miracles exist.*
>
> *Well, let them laugh!*
> *The trusting heart*
> *Has joys which they*
> *Know naught thereof.*
> *And, daily, miracles are wrought*
> *For us who hold*
> *To faith and love!*

MIRACLES, BY JOHN RICHARD MORELAND

The world wants something that has God in it!

September 6

❦

Thou remainest (HEB. 1:11).

There are always lone hearth fires; so many! And those who sit beside them, with the empty chair, cannot restrain the tears that *will* come. One sits *alone* so much. There *is* some One unseen, just here within reach. But somehow we don't *realize* His presence. Realizing is blessed, but—*rare*. It belongs to the mood, to the feelings. It is dependent on weather conditions and bodily conditions. The rain, the heavy fog outside, the poor sleep, the twinging pain, these make one's mood so much, they seem to blur out the realizing. But there is something a little higher up than realizing. It is yet more blessed. It is independent of these outer conditions, it is something that abides. It is this: *recognizing* that Presence unseen, so wondrous and quieting, so soothing and calming and warming. *Recognize His* presence—the Master's own. He is here, close by; His presence is real. Recognizing will help realizing, too, but it never depends on it. *Aye,* more, immensely more, the truth is presence, not a thing, a fact, a statement. Some *One* is present, a warm-hearted Friend, an all-powerful Lord. And this is the joyful truth for weeping hearts everywhere, whatever be the hand that has drawn the tears; by whatever stream it be that your weeping willow is planted.   S. D. GORDON

> When from my life the old-time joys have vanished,
> Treasures once mind, I may no longer claim,
> This truth may feed my hungry heart, and famished:
> Lord, THOU REMAINEST! THOU art still the same!
>
> When streams have dried, those streams of glad refreshing—
> Friendships so blest, so rich, so free;
> When sun-kissed skies give place to clouds depressing,
> Lord, THOU REMAINEST! Still my heart hath THEE.
>
> When strength hath failed, and feet, now worn and weary,
> On gladsome errands may no longer go,
> Why should I sigh, or let the days be dreary?
> Lord, THOU REMAINEST! Could'st THOU more bestow?
>
> Thus though life's days—whoe'er or what may fail me,
> Friends, friendships, joys, in small or great degree,

Songs may be mine, no sadness need assail me,
Lord, THOU REMAINEST! Still my heart hath THEE.
J. DANSON SMITH

EVENING

❧

Christ in you. (COL. 1:27)

*I*t is a great secret I tell you today, nay, I can give you—if you will take it from *Him,* not from me—a secret which has been to me, oh, so wonderful! Many years ago I came to Him burdened with guilt and fear; I took that simple secret, and it took away my fear and sin. Years passed on, and I found sin overcame me, and my temptations were too strong for me. I came to Him a second time, and He whispered to me, *"Christ in you."* And I have had victory, rest and sweet blessing ever since. . . . I look back with unutterable gratitude to the lonely and sorrowful night, when, mistaken in many things, and imperfect in all, and not knowing but that it would be death in the most literal sense before the morning light, my heart's first full consecration was made, and, with unreserved surrender, I first could say,

Jesus, I my cross have taken,
All to leave and follow Thee:
Destitute, despised, forsaken,
Thou from hence my all shall be.

Never, perhaps, has my heart known such a thrill of joy as when, the following Sunday morning, I gave out these lines, and sang them with all my heart. And, if God has been pleased to use me in any fuller measure, it has been because of that hour. And it will be still, in the measure in which that hour is made the keynote of a consecrated, crucified, and Christ-devoted life. This experience of Christ our Sanctifier, marks a definite and distinct crisis in the history of a soul. We do not grow into it, but we cross a definite line of demarcation, as clear as when the hosts of Joshua crossed the Jordan and were over in the Promised Land, and set up a great heap of stones, so that they never could forget that crisis hour.

A. B. SIMPSON

September 7

∽⤳

God is our refuge and strength, a very present help in trouble
(PS. 46:1).

The question often comes, "Why didn't He help me sooner?" It is not His order. He must first adjust you to the trouble and cause you to learn your lesson from it. His promise is, "I will be with him *in* trouble; I will deliver him and honor him." He must be with you *in* the trouble first all day and all night. Then He will take you out of it. This will not come till you have stopped being restless and fretful about it and become calm and quiet. Then He will say, "It is enough."

God uses trouble to teach His children precious lessons. They are intended to educate us. When their good work is done, a glorious recompense will come to us through them. There is a sweet joy and a real value in them. He does not regard them as difficulties but as opportunities.   **SELECTED**

> *Not always OUT of our troublous times,*
> *And the struggles fierce and grim,*
> *But IN—deeper IN—to our sure rest,*
> *The place of our peace, in Him.*
> **ANNIE JOHNSON FLINT**

We once heard a simple old colored man say something that we have never forgotten: "When God tests you, it is a good time for you to test Him by putting His promises to the proof, and claiming from Him just as much as your trials have rendered necessary."

There are two ways of getting out of a trial. One is to simply try to get rid of the trial, and be thankful when it is over. The other is to recognize the trial as a challenge from God to claim a larger blessing than we have ever had, and to hail it with delight as an opportunity of obtaining a larger measure of divine grace. Thus even the adversary becomes an auxiliary, and the things that seem to be against us turn out to be for the furtherance of our way. Surely, this is to be more than conquerors through Him who loved us.   **A. B. SIMPSON**

◦◦◦

The greatest of these is love. (1 COR. 13:13 RSV)

"I'll master it!" said the ax; and his blows fell heavily on the iron. And every blow made his edge more blunt till he ceased to strike.

"Leave it to me!" said the saw; and with his relentless teeth he worked backward and forward on its surface till his teeth were worn down and broken, and he feel aside.

"Ha, ha!" said the hammer. "I knew you wouldn't succeed! I'll show you the way!" But at the first fierce stroke off flew his head, and the iron remained as before.

"Shall I try?" asked the still, small flame.

They all despised the flame, but he curled gently around the iron and embraced it, and never left it till it melted under his irresistible influence.

Hard indeed is the heart that can resist love.
"And now abideth faith, hope, love . . . the greatest of these is love."

September 8

MORNING

Thou hast enlarged me when I was in distress (PS. 4:1).

This is one of the grandest testimonies ever given by man to the moral government of God. It is not a man's thanksgiving that he has been set free from suffering. It is a thanksgiving that he has been set free through suffering: "Thou hast enlarged me when I was in distress." He declares the sorrows of life to have been themselves the source of life's enlargement.

And have not you and I a thousand times felt this to be true? It is written of Joseph in the dungeon that "the iron entered into his soul." We all feel that what Joseph needed for his soul was just the iron. He had seen only the glitter of the gold. He had been rejoicing in youthful dreams; and dreaming hardens the heart. He who sheds tears over a romance will not be most apt to help reality; real sorrow will be too unpoetic for him. We need the iron to enlarge our nature. The gold is but a vision; the iron is an experience. The chain which unites me to humanity must be an iron chain. That touch of nature which makes the world akin is not joy, but sorrow; gold is partial, but iron is universal.

My soul, if thou wouldst be enlarged into human sympathy, thou must be narrowed into limits of human suffering. Joseph's dungeon is the road to Joseph's throne. Thou canst not lift the iron load of thy brother if the iron hath not entered into thee. It is thy limit that is thine enlargement. It is the shadows of thy life that are the real fulfillment of thy dreams of glory. Murmur not at the shadows; they are better revelations than thy dreams. Say not that the shades of the prison-house have fettered thee; thy fetters are wings—wings of flight into the bosom of humanity. The door of thy prison-house is a door into the heart of the universe. God has enlarged thee by the binding of sorrow's chain.   GEORGE MATHESON

If Joseph had not been Egypt's prisoner, he never would have been Egypt's governor. The iron chain about his feet ushered in the golden chain about his neck.   SELECTED

EVENING

I will not go away from thee. (DEUT. 15:16)

Thy bondman forever. (DEUT. 15:17 RSV, MARGIN)

No man ever makes *Him* supreme and suffers loss; for Jehovah will not be left in any man's debt. When a man holds on, God takes away; when a man lets go, He gives, and that liberally.

> *Make me a captive, Lord,*
> *And then I shall be free.*
> *Force me to render up my sword,*
> *And I shall conqueror be.*
> *I sink in life's alarm*
> *When by myself I stand;*
> *Imprison with Thy mighty arm,*
> *Then strong shall be my hand.*
>
> *My heart is weak and poor,*
> *Until it Master finds;*
> *It has no spring of action sure,*
> *It varies with the wind.*

It cannot freely move
Till Thou hast wrought its chain;
Enslave it with Thy mighty love,
Then deathless I shall reign.

My power is faint and low
Till I have learned to serve:
It wants the needed fire to glow,
It wants the breeze to nerve;
It cannot drive the world
Until itself be driven;
Its flag can only be unfurled
When Thou shalt breathe from heaven.

My will is not my own
Till Thou hast made it Thine;
If it would reach the monarch's throne
It must its crown resign.
It only stands unbent
Amid the clashing strife,
Till on Thy bosom it has leant,
And found in Thee its life.

GEORGE MATHESON

O Master, show me this morning how to yield myself up to Thee completely, and then how to ask of Thee things great enough to be *worthy of a King's giving*. Make me equal in my requests to Thy infinite eagerness to give.

Touch with Thy Pierced Hand the hidden springs that will cause every part of my being to fly wide open to Thee, my Lord and my God!

September 9

MORNING

∞

Not much earth (MATT. 13:5).

Shallow! It would seem from the teaching of this parable that we have something to do with the soil. The fruitful seed fell into "good and honest hearts." I suppose the shallow people are the *soil without much earth*—those who have no real purpose, are moved by a tender appeal, a good sermon, a pathetic melody, and at first it looks as if they would amount to something; but *not much earth*—no depth, no deep, honest purpose, no earnest desire to know duty in order to do it. Let us look after the soil of our hearts.

When a Roman soldier was told by his guide that if he insisted on taking a certain journey it would probably be fatal, he answered, "It is necessary for me to go; it is not necessary for me to live."

This was depth. When we are convicted something like that we shall come to something. The shallow nature lives in its impulses, its impressions, its intuitions, its instincts, and very largely its surroundings. The profound character looks beyond all these, and moves steadily on, sailing past all storms and clouds into the clear sunshine which is always on the other side, and waiting for the afterwards which always brings the reversion of sorrow, seeming defeat and failure.

When God has deepened us, then He can give us His deeper truths, His profoundest secrets, and His mightier trusts. Lord, lead me into the depths of Thy life and save me from a shallow experience!

> *On to broader fields of holy vision;*
> *On to loftier heights of faith and love;*
> *Onward, upward, apprehending wholly,*
> *All for which He calls thee from above.*
> **A. B. SIMPSON**

EVENING

I know WHOM *I have trusted.* (2 TIM. 1:12, TRANS.)

God loves an *uttermost confidence in Himself*—to be *wholly trusted.* This is the sublimest of all the characteristics of a true Christian—the basis of all character.

Is there anything that pleases you more than to be trusted—to have even a little child look up into your face, and put out its hand to meet yours, and come to you confidingly? By so much as God is better than you are, by so much more does He love to be trusted.

There is a Hand stretched out to you; a Hand with a wound in the palm of it. Reach out the hand of your faith to clasp it, and cling to it, for "without faith it is impossible to please God." **HENRY VAN DYKE**

Reach up as far as you can, and God will reach down all the rest of the way.
BISHOP VINCENT

Not what, but WHOM I do believe!
That, in my darkest hour of need,
Hath comfort that no mortal creed
To mortal man may give.
Not what, but WHOM!
For Christ is more than all the creeds,
And His full life of gentle deeds
Shall all the creeds outlive.
Not what I do believe, but WHOM!
WHO walks beside me in the gloom?
WHO shares the burden wearisome?
WHO all the dim way doth illume,
And bids me look beyond the tomb
The larger life to live?
Not what I do believe, BUT WHOM!
Not what,
But WHOM!
JOHN OXENHAM

September 10

MORNING

The Lord will perfect that which concerneth me (PS. 138:8).

There is a divine mystery in suffering, a strange and supernatural power in it, which has never been fathomed by the human reason. There never has been known great saintliness of soul which did not pass through great suffering. When the suffering soul reaches a calm sweet carelessness, when it can inwardly smile at its own suffering, and does not even ask God to deliver it from suffering, then it has wrought its blessed ministry; then patience has its perfect work; then the crucifixion begins to weave itself into a crown.

It is in this state of the perfection of suffering that the Holy Spirit works many marvelous things in our souls. In such a condition, our whole being lies perfectly still under the hand of God; every faculty of the mind and will and heart are at last subdued; a quietness of eternity settles down into the whole being; the tongue grows still, and has but few words to say; it stops asking God questions; it stops crying, "Why hast thou forsaken me?"

The imagination stops building air castles, or running off on foolish lines; the reason is tame and gentle; the choices are annihilated; it has no choice in anything but the purpose of God. The affections are weaned from all creatures and all things; it is so dead that nothing can hurt it, nothing can offend it, nothing can hinder it, nothing can get in its way; for let the circumstances be what they may, it seeks only for God and His will, and it feels assured that God is making everything in the universe, good or bad, past or present, work together for its good.

Oh, the blessedness of being absolutely conquered! of losing our own strength, and wisdom, and plans, and desires, and being where every atom of our nature is like placid Galilee under the omnipotent feet of our Jesus.   **FROM SOUL FOOD**

The great thing is to suffer without being discouraged.   **FENELON**

The heart that serves, and loves, and clings,
Hears everywhere the rush of angel wings.

EVENING

Spread the sail. (ISA. 33:23)

*P*icture a vessel lying becalmed on a glassy sea—not a breath of air stirs a sail. But, presently, the little pennant far up on the masthead begins to stir and lift! There is not a ripple on the water; not the slightest movement of the air on deck, but there is a current stirring *in the upper air!* At once the sails are spread to catch it!

"So in life," says Dr. Miller, "there are higher and lower currents. Too many of us use only the lower sails, and catch only the winds blowing along earthly levels. It would be an unspeakable gain to us all were we to let our life fall under the influence of these upper currents."

Far out to sea, at close of day,
A lonely albatross flew by.
We watched him as he soared away—
A speck against the glowing sky!

Thought I: This lordly feathered one
Is trusting in the faithfulness
Of wind and tide, of star and sun;
And shall I trust the Maker less?

O soul of mine, spread wide thy wings;
Mount up; push out with courage strong!
And—like a bird which, soaring, sings—
Let heaven vibrate with thy song!
SPREAD WIDE THY WINGS, O SOUL OF MINE,
For God will ever faithful be:
His love shall guide thee; winds Divine
Shall waft thee o'er this troubled sea.

Though dangers threaten in the night,
Though tides of death below thee roll,
Though storms attend thy homeward flight,
SPREAD WIDE THY PINIONS, O MY SOUL!
Though shadows veil the verdant shore,
And distant seems the hallowed dawn,
Spread wide thy pinions—evermore
Spread wide thy pinions, and press on.
ROBERT CRUMLY

Spread your sails to catch the upper currents!

September 11

MORNING

❧

And so, after he had patiently endured, he obtained the promise
(HEB. 6:15).

Abraham was long tried, but he was richly rewarded. The Lord tried him by delaying to fulfill His promise. Satan tried him by temptation; men tried him by jealousy, distrust, and opposition; Sarah tried him by her peevishness. But he patiently endured. He did not question God's veracity, nor limit His power, nor doubt His faithfulness, nor grieve His love; but he bowed to divine sovereignty, submitted to infinite wisdom, and was silent under delays, waiting the Lord's time. And so, having patiently endured, he obtained the promise.

God's promises cannot fail of their accomplishment. Patient waiters cannot be disappointed. Believing expectation shall be realized.

Beloved, Abraham's conduct condemns a hasty spirit, reproves a murmuring one, commends a patient one, and encourages quiet submission to God's will and way. Remember, Abraham was tried; he patiently waited; he received the promise, and was satisfied. Imitate his example, and you will share the same blessing.   SELECTED

EVENING

I do not fight with merely human weapons.
No, the weapons with which I war are not weapons of mere flesh and blood, but, in the strength of the Lord, they are mighty enough to raze all strongholds of our foes. I can batter down bulwarks of human reason; I can scale every crag-fortress that towers up bidding defiance to the true knowledge of God. I can make each rebel purpose my prisoner of war and bow it into submission to Messiah. (2 COR. 10:4–5, WAY'S TRANS.)

> *He said not,*
> *"Thou shalt not be*
> *Tempested;*
> *Thou shalt not be*
> *Travailed;*
> *Thou shalt not be*
> *Afflicted":*
> *But he said,*
> *"Thou shalt not be*
> *Overcome!"*

JULIAN OF NORWICK, A.D. 1373

We are not here to be overcome, but we are to rise unvanquished after every knockout blow, *and laugh the laugh of faith—not fear.*

> *Tempested on the sea of life;*
> *Travailed sore, amid earth's strife;*
> *Afflicted often, and sore dismayed;*
> *Look up, faint heart, be not afraid,*
> *Thou shalt not be overcome!*

God's ways are far beyond our ken;
His thoughts are not the thoughts of men;
And He knoweth what is best for you.
Hope on, my friend, He will bear you through.
Thou shalt not be overcome!

Though "The reason why" we cannot see,
Our Father knows—'tis enough that we
But trust His love, when our eyes are dim.
Look up! Hold fast! though the fight is grim.
We shall not be overcome!
MARY E. THOMPSON

September 12

MORNING

∽∾

Who is this that cometh up from the wilderness,
leaning upon her beloved? (SONG OF SOL. 8:5).

Someone gained a good lesson from a southern prayer meeting. A colored brother asked the Lord for various blessings—as you and I do, and thanked the Lord for many already received—as you and I do; but he closed with this unusual petition: "And, O Lord, support us! Yes support us Lord on every leanin' side!" Have you any leaning sides? This humble man's prayer pictures them in a new way and shows the Great Supporter in a new light also. He is always walking by the Christian, ready to extend His mighty arm and steady the weak one on *"every leanin' side."*

Child of My love, lean hard
And let Me feel the pressure of thy care;
I know thy burden, child. I shaped it;
Poised it in Mine Own hand; made no proportion
In its weight to thine unaided strength,
For even as I laid it on, I said,
"I shall be near, and while she leans on Me,
This burden shall be Mine, not hers;

So shall I keep My child within the circling arms
Of My Own love." Here lay it down, nor fear
To impose it on a shoulder which upholds
The government of worlds. Yet closer come:
Thou art not near enough. I would embrace thy care;
So I might feel My child reposing on My breast.
Thou lovest Me? I knew it. Doubt not then;
But loving Me, lean hard.

EVENING

〰

As he was going on his way, there ran one to him . . .
and asked him . . . What shall I do that I may inherit eternal life?
. . . And Jesus looking upon him loved him, and said unto him,
One thing thou lackest: go, sell whatsoever thou hast . . .
and thou shalt have treasure in heaven: come follow me.
But his countenance fell at the saying, and he went away sorrowful:
for he was one that had great possessions.
(Mark 10:17, 21–22, Trans.)

Such was the preparation necessary before this admirable soul could become a disciple of Jesus Christ. To use the language of Dr. Donald Davidson:

"Strip yourself of every possession, cut away every affection, disengage yourself from all *things*, be as if you were a naked soul, alone in the world; be a mere man merely, and then be God's. *'Sell all that thou hast and follow Me!'* Reduce yourself down, if I may say so, till nothing remains but your consciousness of yourself, and then cast the self-consciousness at the feet of God in Christ.

"The only way to Jesus is ALONE. Will you strip yourself and separate yourself and take that lonely road, or will you too 'go away sorrowful'?"

We are not told his name—this "rich young ruler"
Who sought the Lord that day;
We only know that he had great possessions
And that—he went away.

He went away; he kept his earthly treasure
But oh, at what a cost!
Afraid to take the cross and lose his riches—
And God and Heaven were lost.

So for the tinsel bonds that held and drew him
What honor he let slip—
Comrade of John and Paul and friend of Jesus—
What glorious fellowship!

For they who left their all to follow Jesus
Have found a deathless fame,
On his immortal scroll of saints and martyrs
God wrote each shining name.

We should have read his there—the rich young ruler—
If he had stayed that day;
Nameless—though Jesus loved him—ever nameless
Because—he went away.

SELECTED

September 13

MORNING

Come up in the morning . . . and present thyself there to me in the top of the mount (EXOD. 34:2).

The *morning* is the time fixed for my meeting the Lord. The very word *morning* is as a cluster of rich grapes. Let us crush them, and drink the sacred wine. In the morning! Then God means me to be at my best in strength and hope. I have not to climb in my weakness. In the night I have buried yesterday's fatigue, and in the morning take a new lease of energy. Blessed is the day whose morning is sanctified! Successful is the day whose first victory was won in prayer! Holy is the day whose dawn finds thee on the top of the mount!

My Father, I am coming. Nothing on the mean plain shall keep me away from the holy heights. At Thy bidding I come, so Thou wilt meet me. Morning on the mount! It will make me strong and glad all the rest of the day so well begun.

JOSEPH PARKER

Still, still with Thee, when purple morning breaketh,
When the bird waketh, and the shadows flee;
Fairer than morning, lovelier than daylight,
Dawns the sweet consciousness, I am with Thee.

Alone with Thee, amid the mystic shadows,
The solemn hush of nature newly born;
Alone with Thee in breathless adoration,
In the calm dew and freshness of the morn.

As in the dawning o'er the waveless ocean,
The image of the morning-star doth rest,
So in this stillness, Thou beholdest only
Thine image in the waters of my breast.

When sinks the soul, subdued by toil, to slumber,
Its closing eyes look up to Thee in prayer;
Sweet the repose, beneath Thy wings o'er shadowing,
But sweeter still to wake and find Thee there.

HARRIET BEECHER STOWE

My mother's habit was every day, immediately after breakfast, to withdraw for an hour to her own room, and to spend that hour in reading the Bible, in meditation and prayer. From that hour, as from a pure fountain, she drew the strength and sweetness which enabled her to fulfill all her duties, and to remain unruffled by the worries and pettinesses which are so often the trial of narrow neighborhoods. As I think of her life, and all it had to bear, I see the absolute triumph of Christian grace in the lovely ideal of a Christian lady. I never saw her temper disturbed; I never heard her speak one word of anger, of calumny, or of idle gossip; I never observed in her any sign of a single sentiment unbecoming to a soul which had drunk of the river of the water of life, and which had fed upon manna in the barren wilderness.   **FARRAR**

Give God the blossom of the day. Do not put Him off with faded leaves.

EVENING

How precious also are thy thoughts unto me,
O God! how great is the sum of them! (PS. 139:17)

Nothing is more beautiful than our Lord's foresight!

There never was anyone so faithful or considerate or farseeing as Jesus. He had great commendation to give a woman, because she came "beforehand" with her ministry. It was His own manner to anticipate events. He was always thinking ahead of the disciples. When He sent

His disciples to prepare the Passover, there was found an upper room furnished and prepared. He had thought it all out. His plans were not made only for that day. *He was always in advance of time.* When the disciples came back from fishing, Jesus was on the seashore with a fire of coals and fish laid thereon. He thinks of the morning duties before you are astir; He is there before you. He is waiting long before you are awake. His anticipations are all along the way of life before you.

After the Resurrection, the disciples were bewildered, and the way looked black. But the angel said, "Behold, he goeth *before you* into Galilee." He is always ahead, thinking ahead, preparing ahead. Take this text with you into the future, take it into today's experience: "Let not your heart be troubled, neither let it be afraid. . . . I go to prepare a place for you." He is out in the world doing it. *He* will be there *before* you. He will bring you to your appointed place, and you will find *your appointed resources.* You will discover *His insight, His oversight, and His foresight.* You may not always see Him, but you can walk by faith in the dark if you know that He sees you, and you can sing as you journey, even through the night.

JOHN MACBEATH

We mean a lot to Someone;
And 'tis everything to me
That to God His wayward children
Were worth a Calvary.
It's the meaning of my Sunday,
And to Saturday from Monday
It is my hope that one day
My Savior I shall see.
Though the day be dark and dreary,
Here's comfort for the weary—
We mean a lot to Someone
Who died for you and me.

VALUE AND OTHER POEMS

September 14

MORNING

◦⫘◦

Whosoever will come after me, let him deny himself,
and take up his cross, and follow me (MARK 8:34).

The cross which my Lord bids me take up and carry may assume different shapes. I may have to content myself with a lowly and narrow sphere, when I feel that I have capacities for much higher work. I may have to go on cultivating year after year, a field which seems to yield me no harvests whatsoever. I may be bidden to cherish kind and loving thoughts about someone who has wronged me—be bidden speak to him tenderly, and take his part against all who oppose him, and crown him with sympathy and succor. I may have to confess my Master amongst those who do not wish to be reminded of Him and His claims. I may be called to "move among my race, and show a glorious morning face," when my heart is breaking.

There are many crosses, and every one of them is sore and heavy. None of them is likely to be sought out by me of my own accord. But never is Jesus so near me as when I lift my cross, and lay it submissively on my shoulder, and give it the welcome of a patient and unmurmuring spirit.

He draws close, to ripen my wisdom, to deepen my peace, to increase my courage, to augment my power to be of use to others, through the very experience which is so grievous and distressing, and then—as I read on the seal of one of those Scottish Covenanters whom Claverhouse imprisoned on the lonely Bass, with the sea surging and sobbing round— *I grow under the load.*   ALEXANDER SMELLIE

"Use your cross as a crutch to help you on, and not as a stumbling block to cast you down."

You may others from sadness to gladness beguile,
If you carry your cross with a smile.

EVENING

❦

Surely he shall deliver thee from the snare of the fowler.
(PS. 91:3)

The noblest souls are the most tempted. The devil is a sportsman and likes big game. He makes the deadliest assaults on the richer natures, the finest minds, the noblest spirits.   JOHN L. LAWRENCE

Lord!—the fowler lays his net
In Thine evening hour;
When our souls are full of sleep—
Void of full power . . .
Look! The wild fowl sees him not
As he lays it lower!

Creeping round the water's edge
In the dusk of day;
Drops his net, just out of sight,
Weighted lightly!—Stay!
You can see him at his work . . .
Fly to God!—And pray!

Like the wild birds; knowing not
Nets lie underneath!
Gliding near the water's edge—
"Fowler's snare" beneath—
Little feet, caught in the net:
Souls lie, near to death.

But the promise still rings clear:
"He delivers thee,"
From the snare, however great
He will set thee free.
"Pluck my feet out of the net!"
He delivers me.

When Thou dost deliver, Lord,
From the fowler's snare,
Then—the glory is all Thine,
Thou madest us aware,
And though it was stealthy-laid,
We saw it was there!

L. M. WARNER

Those who have the gale of Holy Spirit go forward even in sleep.

BROTHER LAWRENCE

September 15

MORNING

༄

Blow upon my garden that the spices may thereof flow out
(SONG OF SOL. 4:16).

Some of the spices mentioned in this chapter are quite suggestive. The aloe was a bitter spice, and it tells of the sweetness of bitter things, the bitter-sweet, which has its own fine application that only those can understand who have felt it. The myrrh was used to embalm the dead, and it tells of death to something. It is the sweetness which comes to the heart after it has died to its self-will and pride and sin.

Oh, the inexpressible charm that hovers about some Christians simply because they bear upon the chastened countenance and mellow spirit the impress of the cross, the holy evidence of having died to something that was once proud and strong, but is now forever at the feet of Jesus. It is the heavenly charm of a broken spirit and a contrite heart, the music that springs from the minor key, the sweetness that comes from the touch of the frost upon the ripened fruit.

And then the frankincense was a fragrance that came from the touch of the fire. It was the burning powder that rose in clouds of sweetness from the bosom of the flames. It tells of the heart whose sweetness has been called forth, perhaps by the flames of affliction, until the holy place of the soul is filled with clouds of praise and prayer. Beloved, are we giving out the spices, the perfumes, the sweet odors of the heart?

FROM THE LOVE-LIFE OF OUR LORD

A Persian fable says: One day
A wanderer found a lump of clay
So redolent of sweet perfume
Its odors scented all the room.
"What are thou?" was his quick demand,
"Art thou some gem from Samarcand,
Or spikenard in this rude disguise,

Or other costly merchandise?"
"Nay: I am but a lump of clay."

"Then whence this wondrous perfume—say!"
"Friend, if the secret I disclose,
I have been dwelling with the rose."
Sweet parable! and will not those
Who love to dwell with Sharon's rose,
Distill sweet odors all around,
Though low and mean themselves are found?
Dear Lord, abide with us that we
May draw our perfume fresh from Thee.

EVING

EVENING

I count all things but loss for the excellency of the knowledge of
Christ Jesus my Lord. (PHIL. 3:8)

The Swedish Nightingale, Jennie Lind, won great success as an operatic singer, and money poured into her purse. Yet she left the stage while she was singing her best, and never returned to it. She must have missed the money, the fame, and the applause of thousands, but she was content to live in privacy.

Once an English friend found her sitting on the steps of a bathing machine on the sea sands with a Bible on her knee, looking out into the glory of a sunset. They talked, and the conversation drew near to the inevitable question: "Oh, Madame Goldschmidt, how is it that you came to abandon the stage at the very height of your success?"

"When every day," was the quiet answer, "it made me think less of this (laying a finger on the Bible) and nothing at all of that (pointing to the sunset), what else could I do?"

May I not covet the world's greatness! It will cost me the crown of life!

September 16

❧

Hide thyself by the brook Cherith (1 KINGS 17:3).

God's servants must be taught the value of the hidden life. The man who is to take a high place before his fellows must take a low place before his God. We must not be surprised if sometimes our Father says: "There, child, thou hast had enough of this hurry, and publicity, and excitement; get thee hence, and hide thyself by the brook—hide thyself in the Cherith of the sick chamber, or in the Cherith of bereavement, or in some solitude from which the crowds have ebbed away."

Happy is he who can reply, "This Thy will is also mine; I flee unto Thee to hide me. Hide me in the secret of Thy tabernacle, and beneath the covert of Thy wings!"

Every saintly soul that would wield great power with men must win it in some hidden Cherith. The acquisition of spiritual power is impossible, unless we can hide ourselves from men and from ourselves in some deep gorge where we may absorb the power of the eternal God; as vegetation through long ages absorbed these qualities of sunshine, which it now gives back through burning coal.

Bishop Andrews had his Cherith, in which he spent five hours every day in prayer and devotion. John Welsh had it—who thought the day ill spent which did not witness eight or ten hours of closet communion. David Brainerd had it in the woods of North America. Christmas Evans had it in his long and lonely journeys amid the hills of Wales.

Or, passing back to the blessed age from which we date the centuries: Patmos, the seclusion of the Roman prisons, the Arabian desert, the hills and vales of Palestine, are forever memorable as the Cheriths of those who have made our modern world.

Our Lord found His Cherith at Nazareth, and in the wilderness of Judea; amid the olives of Bethany, and the solitude of Gadara. None of us, therefore, can dispense with some Cherith where the sounds of human voices are exchanged for the waters of quietness which are fed from the throne; and where we may taste the sweets and imbibe the power of a life hidden with Christ.

FROM ELIJAH, BY MEYER

❦

Having loved his own . . . he loved them unto the end. (JOHN 13:1)

Sadhu Sundar Singh passed a crowd of people putting out a jungle fire at the foot of the Himalayas. Several men, however, were standing gazing at a tree, the branches of which were already alight.

"What are you looking at?" he asked. They pointed to a nest of young birds in the tree. Above it a bird was flying wildly to and fro in great distress. The men said, "We wish we could save that tree, but the fire prevents us from getting near to it."

A few minutes later the nest caught fire. The Sadhu thought the mother bird would fly away. But no! she flew down, spread her wings over the young ones, and in a few minutes was burned to ashes with them.

> *Such love, such wondrous love,*
> *Such love, such wondrous love,*
> *That God should love a sinner such as I,*
> *How wonderful is love like this!*

Let us have love heated to the point of sacrifice.

September 17

MORNING

❦

It is the Lord: let him do what seemeth him good (1 SAM. 3:18).

See God in everything, and God will calm and color all that thou dost see!" It may be that the circumstances of our sorrows will not be removed, their condition will remain unchanged; but if Christ, as Lord and Master of our life, is brought into our grief and gloom, "HE will compass us about with songs of deliverance." To see HIM, and to be sure that His wisdom cannot err, His power cannot fail, His love can never change; to know that even His direst dealings with us are for our deepest spiritual gain, is to be able to say, in the midst of bereavement, sorrow, pain, and loss, "The Lord gave, and the Lord hath taken away; blessed be the name of the Lord."

Nothing else but *seeing* God *in everything* will make us loving and patient with those who annoy and trouble us. They will be to us then only instruments for accomplishing His tender and wise purposes toward us, and we shall even find ourselves at last inwardly thanking them for the blessing they bring us. Nothing else will completely put an end to all murmuring or rebelling thoughts.   H. W. SMITH

"Give me a new idea," I said,
While musing on a sleepless bed;
"A new idea that'll bring to earth
A balm for souls of priceless worth;
That'll give men thoughts of things above,
And teach them how to serve and love,
That'll banish every selfish thought,
And rid men of the sins they've fought."

The new thought came, just how, I'll tell:
'Twas when on bended knee I fell,
And sought from HIM who knows full well
The way our sorrow to expel.
SEE GOD IN ALL THINGS, great and small,
And give HIM praise whate'er befall,
In life or death, in pain or woe,
See God, and overcome thy foe.

I saw HIM in the morning light,
HE made the day shine clear and bright;
I saw HIM in the noontide hour,
And gained from HIM refreshing shower.
At eventide, when worn and sad,
HE gave me help, and made me glad.
At midnight, when on tossing bed
My weary soul to sleep HE led.

I saw HIM when great losses came,
And found HE loved me just the same.
When heavy loads I had to bear,
I found HE lightened every care.
By sickness, sorrow, sore distress,
HE calmed my mind and gave me rest.
HE's filled my heart with gladsome praise
Since I gave HIM the upward gaze.

'Twas new to me, yet old to some,
This thought that to me has become

A revelation of the way
We all should live throughout the day;
For as each day unfolds its light,
We'll walk by faith and not by sight.
Life will, indeed, a blessing bring,
If we SEE GOD IN EVERYTHING.

A. E. FINN

EVENING

◦∞◦

Even as Christ forgave you, so also do ye. (COL. 3:13)

A custom way out in the African bush which has no equivalent in this part of the world is *"Forgiveness Week."* Fixed in the dry season, when the weather itself is smiling, this is a week when every man and woman pledges himself or herself to forgive any neighbor any wrong, real or fancied, that may be a cause for misunderstanding, coldness, or quarrel between the parties.

It is, of course, a part of our religion that a man should forgive his brother. But among recent converts, and even older brethren, this great tenet is, perhaps naturally, apt to be forgotten or overlooked in the heat and burden of work. *"Forgiveness Week"* brings it forcibly to mind. The week itself terminates with a festival of happiness and rejoicing among the native Christians.

Is it too much to suggest that in this *supposedly more civilized portion of the world* a similar week might be instituted?

Nothing between, Lord—nothing between;
Shine with unclouded ray,
Chasing each mist away,
O'er my whole heart hold sway—
Nothing between.

Let grudges die "like cloudspots in the dawn!"
When God forgives, He forgets!

September 18

⤲⤳

Where there is no vision, the people perish (PROV. 29:18).

Waiting upon God is necessary in order to see Him, to have a vision of Him. The *time element* in vision is essential. Our hearts are like a sensitive photographer's plate; and in order to have God revealed there, we must sit at His feet a long time. The troubled surface of a lake will not reflect an object.

Our lives must be quiet and restful if we would see God. There is power in the sight of some things to affect one's life. A quiet sunset will bring peace to a troubled heart. Thus the vision of God always transforms human life.

Jacob saw God at Jabbok's ford, and became Israel. The vision of God transformed Gideon from a coward into a valiant soldier. The vision of Christ changed Thomas from a doubting follower into a loyal, devout disciple.

But men have had visions of God since Bible times. William Carey saw God, and left his shoemaker's bench and went to India. David Livingstone saw God, and left all to follow Him through the jungles of dark Africa. Scores and hundreds have had visions of God, and are today in the uttermost parts of the earth working for the speedy evangelization of the heathen. — **DR. PARDINGTON**

There is hardly ever a complete silence in the soul. God is whispering to us well-nigh incessantly. Whenever the sounds of the world die out in the soul, or sink low, then we hear the whisperings of God. He is always whispering to us, only we do not hear, because of the noise, hurry, and distraction which life causes as it rushes on. — **F. W. FABER**

> Speak, Lord, in the stillness,
> While I wait on Thee;
> Hushed my heart to listen
> In expectancy.

> Speak, O blessed Master,
> In this quiet hour;
> Let me see Thy face, Lord,
> Feel Thy touch of power.

For the words Thou speakest,
"They are life," indeed;
Living bread from Heaven
Now my spirit feed!

Speak, Thy servant heareth!
Be not silent, Lord;
Waits my soul upon Thee
For the quickening word!

EVENING

Nevertheless, afterward. (HEB. 12:11)

It is not a bit of good struggling for the premature unfolding of the Divine mystery. The revelation awaits our arrival at a certain place in the road, and when *Time* brings us to that place, and we enter into its experiences, we shall find, to our delighted surprise, that it has become luminous.

And so the only thing we need to be concerned about is to be on the King's high road, stepping out in accordance with His most holy will.

"Light is sown for the righteous."

It is the end which justifies all and explains all. It is to the ultimate goal that God's eye is ever turning. At the right moment the shining harvest will appear! What though the seed may seem to perish in the dark cold ground! What will that matter when the blade bursts forth, and the ear unfolds, and the full corn waves over the golden harvest field?

Luther was once in earnest prayer over some matter of great moment, desiring to know the mind of God in it; and it seemed as though he heard God say to him, "I am not to be traced."

If God is not to be traced, He is to be trusted.
"After these things Jesus manifested Himself."

However dark the *nows* may be in your experience, the *afters* of God are worth waiting for!

As we think of God's dealings with His children we are impressed with *His leisureliness*. God's ways may be hidden, but

Wait for God's Afters!

September 19

~∞~

My Father is the husbandman (JOHN 15:1).

It is comforting to think of trouble, in whatever form it may come to us, as a heavenly messenger, bringing us something from God. In its earthly aspect it may seem hurtful, even destructive; but in its spiritual out-working it yields blessing. Many of the richest blessings which have come down to us from the past are the fruit of sorrow or pain. We should never forget that redemption, the world's greatest blessing, is the fruit of the world's greatest sorrow.

In every time of sharp pruning, when the knife is deep and the pain is sore, it is an unspeakable comfort to read, "My Father is the husbandman."

Doctor Vincent tells of being in a great hothouse where luscious clusters of grapes were hanging on every side. The owner said, "When my new gardener came, he said he would have nothing to do with these vines unless he could cut them clean down to the stalk; and he did, and we had no grapes for two years, but this is the result."

There is rich suggestiveness in this interpretation of the pruning process, as we apply it to the Christian life. Pruning *seems* to be destroying the vine, the gardener *appears* to be cutting it all away; but he looks on into the future and knows that the final outcome will be the enrichment of its life and greater abundance of fruit.

There are blessings we can never have unless we are ready to pay the price of pain. There is no way to reach them save through suffering.

DR. MILLER

I walked a mile with Pleasure,
She chattered all the way;
But left me none the wiser
For all she had to say.

I walked a mile with Sorrow,
And ne'er a word said she;
But, oh the things I learned from her
When sorrow walked with me.

EVENING

‿∾∾‿

Them that are quiet in the land. (PS. 35:20)

We are to enter into God's chamber, and hide there, and *be still.* Then God will call us the *"quiet in the land."* Have this stamp upon you. Be quiet outside—you will then be quiet inside. Be quiet in spirit. Beware of soul activities. The dross must be burned out to have the mountain vision. We must get back to *God only,* and cease to see the human instruments. Hide deeper in God. *He* must be *real*—more and more real!

Hide with Christ in God at the Throne;
Be at the Spring of things!

"In quietness and in confidence *shall be* your strength." Set yourself to move everything through God, not man. *Go direct to Him. Every step with God* "in quietness and in confidence" *gives you absolute Victory over everything!*

Keep in step with God.

Get quiet, beloved soul; tell out thy sorrow and complaint to God. Let not the greatest pressure of business divert thee from God. When men rage about thee, go and tell Jesus. Hide thee in His secret place when storms are high.

Get into thy closet, shut thy door, and quiet thyself as a weaned babe. But if thy voice is quiet *to* man, let it never cease to speak loudly and mightily *for* man.

We need to be quiet to get the ear of God!

'Mid all the traffic of the ways,
Turmoils without, within,
Make in my heart a quiet place,
And come and dwell therein!

A little shrine of quietness,
All sacred to Thyself,
Where Thou shalt all my soul possess,
And I may find myself!
JOHN OXENHAM

Pascal said: "One-half of the ills of life come because men are unwilling to sit down quietly for thirty minutes to think through all the possible consequences of their acts."

September 20

MORNING

Said I not unto thee, that, if thou wouldest believe,
thou shouldest see the glory of God?
(JOHN 11:40).

Mary and Martha could not understand what their Lord was doing. Both of them said to Him, *"Lord, if thou hadst been here, my brother had not died."* Back of it all we seem to read their thought: "Lord, we do not understand *why* you have stayed away so long. We do not understand *how* you could let death come to the man whom you loved. We do not understand how you could let sorrow and suffering ravage our lives when your presence might have stayed it all. *Why* did you not come? It is too late now, for already he has been dead four days!"

And to it all Jesus had but one great truth: "You may not understand; but I tell you if you *believe,* you will *see.*"

Abraham could not understand *why* God should ask the sacrifice of the boy; but he trusted. And he *saw* the glory of God in his restoration to his love. Moses could not understand *why* God should keep him forty years in the wilderness, but he trusted; and he *saw* when God called him to lead forth Israel from bondage.

Joseph could not understand the cruelty of his brethren, the false witness of a perfidious woman, and the long years of an unjust imprisonment; but he trusted, and he *saw* at last the glory of God in it all.

Jacob could not understand the strange providence which permitted the same Joseph to be torn from his father's love, but he *saw* the glory of God when he looked into the face of that same Joseph as the viceroy of a great king, and the preserver of his own life and the lives of a great nation.

And so, perhaps in your life. You say, "I do not understand why God let my dear one be taken. I do not understand why affliction has been permitted to smite me. I do not understand the devious paths by which the Lord is leading me. I do not understand why plans and purposes that seemed good to my eyes should be baffled. I do not understand why blessings I so much need are so long delayed."

Friend, you do not *have* to understand all God's ways with you. God does not expect you to understand them. You do not expect your child to understand, only believe. Some day you will see the glory of God in the things which you do not understand.

J. H. MCC.

If we could push ajar the gates of life,
And stand within, and all God's working see,
We might interpret all this doubt and strife,
And for each mystery could find a key.

But not today. Then be content, poor heart;
God's plans, like lilies pure and white, unfold,
We must not tear the close-shut leaves apart—
Time will reveal the calyxes of gold.

And if, through patient toil, we reach the land
Where tired feet, with sandals loosed, may rest,
When we shall clearly know and understand,
I think that we shall say, "God knew best."

EVENING

Shall the thing formed say to him that formed it,
Why hast thou made me thus? (ROM. 9:20)

A piece of wood once bitterly complained because it was being cut and filled with rifts and holes; but he who held the wood and whose knife was cutting into it so remorselessly did not listen to the sore complaining. He was making a flute out of the wood he held, and was too wise to desist when entreated to do so. He said:

"Oh, thou foolish piece of wood, without these rifts and holes thou wouldst be only a mere stick forever—a bit of hard black ebony with no power to make music or to be of any use. These rifts that I am making, which seem to be destroying thee, will change thee into a flute, and thy sweet music then shall charm the souls of men. My cutting thee is the making of thee, for then thou shalt be precious and valuable, and a blessing in the world."

David could never have sung his sweetest songs had he not been sorely afflicted. His afflictions made his life an instrument on which God could breathe the music of His love to charm and soothe the hearts of men.

We are but organs mute till a Master touches the keys—
Verily, vessels of earth into which God poureth the wine;
Harps are we—silent harps that have hung in the willow trees,
Dumb till our heartstrings swell and break with a pulse Divine.

Not till the life is broken is it ready for the Master's use.

September 21

✒︎

I count all things but loss for the excellency of the knowledge of Christ Jesus, my Lord (PHIL. 3:8).

This is the happy season of ripening cornfields, of the merry song of the reapers, of the secured and garnered grain. But let me hearken to the sermon of the field. This is its solemn word to me. You must die in order to live. You must refuse to consult your own ease and well-being. You must be crucified, not only in desires and habits which are sinful, but in many more which appear innocent and right.

If you would save others, you cannot save yourself. If you would bear much fruit, you must be buried in darkness and solitude.

My heart fails me as I listen. But, when Jesus asks it, let me tell myself that it is my high dignity to enter into the fellowship of His sufferings; and thus I am in the best of company. And let me tell myself again that it is all meant to make me a vessel meet for His use. His own Calvary has blossomed into fertility; and so shall mine. Plenty out of pain, life out of death: is it not the law of the kingdom?

FROM IN THE HOUR OF SILENCE

Do we call it dying when the bud bursts into flower?   SELECTED

Finding, following, keeping, struggling,
Is He sure to bless?
Saints, apostles, prophets, martyrs,
Answer, "Yes."

EVENING

✒︎

That ye present your bodies. (ROM. 12:1)

Lend Me *thy body,* our Lord says. For a few brief years, in the body that was prepared for Me I delighted to do My Father's will. By means of that body I came into contact with the children of men—diseased, weary, sin-sick, heavy-laden ones. Those feet carried Me to the homes where sorrow and death had entered; those hands touched leprous bodies, palsied limbs, sightless eyes; those lips told of My Father's remedy for sin,

His love for a prodigal world. In that body I bore the world's sin upon the tree, and through its offering once for all My followers are sanctified.

But I need a body still; *wilt thou not lend Me thine? Millions of hearts are longing,* with an indescribable hunger, *for Me.* On that far-off shore are men, women, and little children sitting in darkness and in the shadow of death—men who have never yet heard of My love. *Wilt thou not lend Me thy body,* that I may cross the ocean and tell them that the light after which they are groping has at last reached them; that the bread for which they have so often hungered is now at their very door?

I want a heart, that I may fill it with Divine compassion; and lips, purged from all uncleanness, wherewith to tell the story that brings hope to the despairing, freedom to the bound, healing to the diseased, and life to the dead. *Wilt thou lend Me thine?*

Wilt thou not lend Me thy body?   J. GREGORY MANTLE

All that we own is Thine alone,
A trust, O Lord, from Thee.

September 22

MORNING

❦

And the Lord said . . . Satan hath desired to have you, that he may sift you as wheat; but I have prayed for thee, that thy faith fail not
(LUKE 22:31–32).

Our faith is the center of the target at which God doth shoot when He tries us; and if any other grace shall escape untried, certainly faith shall not. There is no way of piercing faith to its very marrow like the sticking of the arrow of desertion into it; this finds it out whether it be of immortals or no. Strip it of its armor of conscious enjoyment, and suffer the terrors of the Lord to set themselves in array against it; and that is faith indeed which can escape unhurt from the midst of the attack. Faith must be tried, and seeming desertion is the furnace, heated seven times, into which it might be thrust. Blest the man who can endure the ordeal!

C. H. SPURGEON

Paul said, "I have kept the faith," but he lost his head! They cut that off, but it didn't touch his faith. He rejoiced in three things—this great apostle to the Gentiles; he had "fought a good fight," he had "finished his course," he had "kept the faith." What did all the rest amount to? Saint Paul won the race; he gained the prize, and he has not only the admiration of earth today, but the admiration of heaven. Why do we not act as if it paid to lose all to win Christ? Why are we not loyal to truth as he was? Ah, we haven't his arithmetic. He counted differently from us; we count the things *gain* that he counted *loss*. We must have his faith, and keep it if we would wear the same crown.

EVENING

Himself took our infirmities. (MATT. 8:17)

I think perhaps the greatest of all hindrances in our getting hold of God for our bodies is the lack of *knowing Him,* for after all, in its *deepest essence* Divine healing is not a *thing;* it is not an *experience;* it is not an *"it."* It is the *revelation of Jesus Christ* as a living, almighty *Person,* and then the *union* of this living Christ with your *body,* so that there becomes a tie, a bond, *a living link* by which His life keeps flowing into yours, and because He lives you shall *live* also. This is so very real to me that I groan in spirit for those who do not know Him in this blessed union, and I wonder sometimes why He has let me know Him in this gracious manner. There is not an hour of the day or night that I am not conscious of *Someone* who is closer to me than my heart or my brain. I know that *He is living in me,* and it is the continual inflowing of *the life of Another.* If I had not that I could not live. My old constitutional strength gave out long, long ago, but Someone breathed in me gently, with no violence, no strange thrills, but just His wholesome *life.*   **A. B. SIMPSON**

I remember how once I was taken suddenly and seriously ill alone in my study. I dropped upon my knees and cried to God for help. Instantly all pain left me and I was perfectly well. It seems as if God stood right there, and had put out His hand and touched me. The joy of healing was not so great as the joy of meeting God.   **R. A. TORREY**

She only touched the hem of His garment,
As to His side she stole,
Amid the throng that had gathered around Him
And straightway she was whole.

Oh, touch the hem of His garment,
And thou, too, shall be free;
His healing power this very hour,
Will bring new life to thee.

"Jesus . . . the same yesterday, and today, and for ever."

September 23

MORNING

~~~

He that believeth on me, as the scripture hath said, out of his belly
shall flow rivers of living water (JOHN 7:38).

Some of us are shivering and wondering why the Holy Spirit does not fill us. We have plenty coming in, but we do not give it out. Give out the blessing that you have, start larger plans for service and blessing, and you will soon find that the Holy Ghost is before you, and He will present you with blessings for service, and give you all that He can trust you to give away to others.

There is a beautiful fact in nature which has its spiritual parallels. There is no music so heavenly as an aeolian harp, and the aeolian harp is nothing but a set of musical chords arranged in harmony, and then left to be touched by the unseen fingers of the wandering winds. And as the breath of heaven floats over the chords, it is said that notes almost divine float out upon the air, as if a choir of angels were wandering around and touching the strings.

And so it is possible to keep our hearts so open to the touch of the Holy Spirit that He can play upon them at will, as we quietly wait in the pathway of His service.   **FROM DAYS OF HEAVEN UPON EARTH**

When the apostles received the baptism with the Holy Ghost they did not rent the upper room and stay there to hold holiness meetings, but went everywhere preaching the gospel.   **WILL HUFF**

"If I have eaten my morsel alone,"
The patriarch spoke with scorn;
What would he think of the Church were he shown
Heathendom—huge, forlorn,
Godless, Christless, with soul unfed,

While the Church's ailment is fullness of bread,
Eating her morsel alone?

"Freely ye have received, so give,"
He bade, who hath given us all.
How shall the soul in us longer live
Deaf to their starving call,
For whom the blood of the Lord was shed,
And His body broken to give them bread,
If we eat our morsel alone!
ARCHBISHOP ALEXANDER

"Where is Abel thy brother?" (Gen. 4:9).

EVENING

Job . . . perfect and upright, and one that feared God,
and eschewed evil. (JOB 1:1)

Such was Job's character as given by God. He asked Satan, "Hast thou considered my servant Job, that there is none like him in the earth?" Satan, in reply, says in effect, "Strip him, and he will curse Thee to Thy face." Satan sought Job's fall; God sought his blessing. Satan gets leave from God to strip Job. With malignant energy he sets to work, and in one day he brings the greatest man in all the East into abject poverty and visits him with sore bereavement. Blow after blow of such a crushing nature and with such rapidity falls upon Job, that one marvels at the testimony of the Holy Ghost that: "In all this did not Job sin with his lips." *What a triumph for God! What a defeat for Satan!*

"But these strange ashes, Lord? This nothingness,
This baffling sense of loss?"
"Son, was the anguish of My stripping less
Upon the torturing Cross?

"Was I not brought into the dust of death,
A worm, and no man I;
Yea, turned to ashes by the vehement breath
Of fire, on Calvary?

"O Son beloved, this is thy heart's desire:
This and no other thing

Follows the fall of the consuming fire
On the burnt offering.

"Go on and taste the joy set high afar,
No joy like that for thee;
See how it lights thy way like some great star!
Come now, and follow Me!"
A. W. C.

September 24

MORNING

⤜⤛

After they were come to Mysia, they assayed to go into Bithynia:
but the Spirit suffered them not (ACTS 16:7).

What a strange prohibition! These men were going into Bithynia just to do Christ's work, and the door is shut against them by Christ's own Spirit. I, too, have experienced this in certain moments. I have sometimes found myself interrupted in what seemed to me a career of usefulness. Opposition came and forced me to go back, or sickness came and compelled me to retire into a desert apart.

It was hard at such times to leave my work undone when I believed that work to be the service of the Spirit. But I came to remember that the *Spirit has not only a service of work, but a service of waiting.* I came to see that in the kingdom of Christ there are not only times for action, but times in which to forbear acting. I came to learn that the desert place apart is often the most useful spot in the varied life of man—more rich in harvest than the seasons in which the corn and wine abounded. I have been taught to thank the blessed Spirit that many a darling Bithynia had to be left unvisited by me.

And so, Thou divine Spirit, would I still be led by Thee. Still there come to me disappointed prospects of usefulness. Today the door seems to open into life and work for Thee; tomorrow it closes before me just as I am about to enter.

Teach me to see another door in the very inaction of the hour. Help me to find in the very prohibition thus to serve Thee, a new opening into Thy service. Inspire me with the knowledge that a man may at times be called to do his duty by doing nothing, to work by keeping still, to serve by waiting. When I remember the power of the "still small voice," I shall not murmur that sometimes the Spirit suffers me *not* to go.

GEORGE MATHESON

When I cannot understand my Father's leading.
And it seems to be but hard and cruel fate,
Still I hear that gentle whisper ever pleading,
God is working, God is faithful, ONLY WAIT.

EVENING

⌒∞⌒

Every branch in me that beareth not fruit he taketh away: and every
branch that beareth fruit, he purgeth it,
that it may bring forth more fruit. (JOHN 15:2)

Only a little more cutting." How strange the words sounded; and then I heard the ring of the gardener's ax as he cut away at the lilac bushes. They were very close to the windows and kept out the sunlight and air; more, they obstructed the view. We watched the process and as one bush after another fell, one remarked: "Only a little more cutting and we shall get it. These lilac bushes actually shut out the view of the White Mountains!"

I was glad the gardener did the cutting that day, for so much was brought out by the absence of the bushes and suggested by the exclamations that followed: "How lovely that little tree is! I did not see it before!" "What a beautiful evergreen that is! I never noticed it until now!" Have we not heard similar exclamations after severe cuttings and removals in our lives? Have we not said: "I never loved God so much as I have since He took my little one!" "I never saw the beauty of such and such a Scripture until now!"

Ah, He knows! Only trust Him. We shall see it all in the clear light sometime.

God is a zealous Pruner,
For He knows
Who, falsely tender, spares the knife
But spoils the rose.
THE PRUNER, BY JOHN OXENHAM

Give me the courage to submit to the surgery of Thy Spirit. Give me the bravery to part with what I hold most dear if it separates me from Thee. Through Christ, I pray!

September 25

MORNING

Why go I mourning? (PS. 42:9).

Canst thou answer this, believer? Canst thou find any reason why thou art so often mourning instead of rejoicing? Why yield to gloomy anticipations? Who told thee that the night would never end in day? Who told thee that the winter of thy discontent would proceed from frost to frost, from snow and ice, and hail, to deeper snow, and yet more heavy tempest of despair? Knowest thou not that day follows night, that flood comes after ebb, that spring and summer succeed winter? Hope thou then! Hope thou ever! for God fails thee not. **C. H. SPURGEON**

> *He was better to me than all my hopes;*
> *He was better than all my fears;*
> *He made a bridge of my broken works,*
> *And a rainbow of my tears.*
> *The billows that guarded my sea-girt path,*
> *But carried my Lord on their crest;*
> *When I dwell on the days of my wilderness march*
> *I can lean on His love for the rest.*
>
> *He emptied my hands of my treasured store,*
> *And His covenant love revealed,*
> *There was not a wound in my aching heart,*
> *But the balm of His breath hath healed.*
> *Oh, tender and true was the chastening sore,*
> *In wisdom, that taught and tried,*
> *Till the soul that He sought was trusting in Him,*
> *And nothing on earth beside.*
>
> *He guided my paths that I could not see,*
> *By ways that I have not known;*
> *The crooked was straight, and the rough was plain*
> *As I followed the Lord alone.*

I praise Him still for the pleasant palms,
And the water-springs by the way,
For the glowing pillar of flame by night,
And the sheltering cloud by day.

Never a watch on the dreariest halt,
But some promise of love endears;
I read from the past, that my future shall be
Far better than all my fears.
Like the golden pot, of the wilderness bread,
Laid up with the blossoming rod,
All safe in the ark, with the law of the Lord,
Is the covenant care of my God.

EVENING

My glory was fresh in me. (JOB 29:20)

It was when Job's glory was fresh in him that his "bow was renewed" in his hand. Freshness and glory! And yet, the brilliant music of these words is brought down to *a minor strain* by the little touch "it *was*"— not it *is.*

"All my fresh springs are *in Thee.*"

If our glory is to be fresh in us, it all depends upon what the glory in us *is!* There is only one unfailing source—*Christ Himself!* He is *"in you, the hope of glory,"* if you have admitted Him; and He *is* your glory. Then you may sing, "My glory *is* fresh in me."

Jesus Christ is *always fresh!*

And so is the oil with which He anoints us. "I *shall be* anointed with *fresh oil.*" Fresh oil of joy! Fresh oil of consecration! Fresh oil upon the sacrifice as we offer to God continually *"the fruit of our lips* giving thanks to his name."

My heart is parched by unbelief,
My spirit sere from inward strife;
The heavens above are turned to brass,
Arid and fruitless is my life.

Then falls Thy rain, O Holy One;
Fresh is the earth, and young once more;
Then falls Thy Spirit on my heart;

My life is green; the drought is o'er!
DROUGHT, BY BETTY BRUECHERT

A desert road? when the Christian has ever at his command
Fresh springs! Fresh oil! Fresh glory!

September 26

MORNING

❧

We walk by faith, not by appearance (2 COR. 5:7 RV).

By faith, not appearance; God never wants us to look at our feelings. Self may want us to; and Satan may want us to. But God wants us to face facts, not feelings; the facts of Christ and of His finished and perfect work to us.

When we face these precious facts, and believe them because God says they are facts, God will take care of our feelings.

God never gives feeling to enable us to trust Him; God never gives feeling to encourage us to trust Him; God never gives feeling to show that we have already and utterly trusted Him.

God gives feeling only when He sees that we trust Him apart from all feeling, resting on His own Word, and on His own faithfulness to His promise.

Never until then can the feeling (which is from God) possibly come; and God will give the feeling in such a measure and at such a time as His love sees best for the individual case.

We must choose between facing toward our feelings and facing toward God's facts. Our feelings may be as uncertain as the sea or the shifting sands. God's facts are as certain as the Rock of Ages, even Christ Himself, who is the same yesterday, today, and forever.

When darkness veils His lovely face
I rest on His unchanging grace;
In every high and stormy gale,
My anchor holds within the veil.

❧❧❧

And the famine was sore. . . . They had eaten up the corn which they had. . . . Except we had lingered, surely now we had returned. . . . And they took double money in their hand, and Benjamin; and rose up, and went. (GEN. 43:1–2, 10, 15)

*P*raise God for the famine in our life, that drives us in utter helpless- *ness back to Him!* Praise Him that what we have gets eaten up, and we must turn to Him for more! But how like unto the faltering, fearful family of Israel we act! We could find absolute relief, sufficiency, satisfaction in Jesus Christ; yet we delay, debate, wonder, waste time, and *stay hungry.*

When finally in desperation we are driven to Him we think we must do some great thing to meet His terms, and we try to carry "double money" in all sorts of ways, to make sure of *what He is yearningly waiting to give us.* He *does ask* us for one thing, and one only: and that is the dearest possession of our lives. With Israel's family the dearest possession was Benjamin. When we lay down our dearest possession, then the treasures of the kingdom are flung open to us and lavished into our life.

MESSAGES FOR THE MORNING WATCH

A drying well will often lead the spirit to the river that flows from the throne of God.

September 27

MORNING

❧❧❧

I have found an atonement (JOB 33:24, MARGIN).

*D*ivine healing is just divine life. It is the headship of Christ over the body. It is the life of Christ in the frame. It is the union of our members with the very body of Christ and the inflowing life of Christ in our living members. It is as real as His risen and glorified body. It is as reasonable as the fact that He was raised from the dead and is a living Man with a true body and a rational soul today at God's right hand.

That living Christ belongs to us in all His attributes and powers. We are members of His body, His flesh, and His bones, and if we can only believe and receive it, we may live upon the very life of the Son of God. Lord, help me to know "the Lord for the body and the body for the Lord."   A. B. SIMPSON

"The Lord thy God in the midst of thee is mighty" (Zeph. 3:17). This was the text that first flashed the truth of divine healing into my mind and worn-out body nearly a quarter century ago. It is still the door, wide open more than ever, through which the living Christ passes moment by moment into my redeemed body, filling, energizing, vitalizing it with the presence and power of His own personality, turning my whole being into a "new heaven and new earth." *"The Lord, thy God."* Thy God, my God. Then all that is in God Almighty is mine and in me just as far as I am able and willing to appropriate Him and all that belongs to Him. This God, "Mighty," ALL Mighty God, is our INSIDE God. He is, as Father, Son, and Holy Spirit, in the midst of me, just as really as the sun is in the center of the heavens, or like the great dynamo in the center of the power-house of my threefold being. He is in the midst, at the center of my physical being. He is in the midst of my brain. He is in the midst of my nerve centers.

For twenty-one years it has been not only a living reality to me, but a reality growing deeper and richer, until now at the age of seventy years, I am in every sense a younger, fresher man than I was at thirty. At this present time I am in the strength of God, doing full twice as much work, mental and physical, as I have ever done in the best days of the past, and this observe, with less than half the effort then necessary. My life, physical, mental, and spiritual, is like an artesian well—always full, overflowing. To speak, teach, travel by night and day in all weather and through all the sudden and violent changes of our variable climate, is no more effort to me than it is for the mill-wheel to turn when the stream is full or for the pipe to let the water run through.

> *My body, soul and spirit thus redeemed,*
> *Sanctified and healed I give, O Lord, to Thee,*
> *A consecrated offering Thine ever more to be.*
> *That all my powers with all their might*
> *In Thy sole glory may unite—Hallelujah!*
>   DR. HENRY WILSON

〜◦〜

Will give you . . . as he hath promised. (EX. 12:25)

God is to be trusted for *what He is,* and not for *what He is not.* We may confidently expect Him to act according to His nature, but never contrary to it. To *dream* that God will do this and that because we wish that He would *is not faith, but fanaticism. Faith can only stand upon truth.* We may be sure that God will so act as to honor His own justice, mercy, wisdom, power—in a word, so as to be Himself. Beyond all doubt He will fulfill His promises; and *when faith grasps a promise she is on sure ground.* To believe that God will give us *what He has never promised to give is mere dreaming. Faith without a promise revealed or implied is folly.* Yea, though our trust should cry itself hoarse in prayer, it should be nonetheless a vain dotard if it had no word of God to warrant it. Happily, the promises and unveilings of Scripture are ample for every real emergency; but when unrestrained credence catches at every whim of its own crazy imagination and thinks to see it realized, the disappointment is not to be wondered at.

It is ours to believe the sure things of God's revelation, but we are not to waste a grain of precious reliance upon anything outside of that circle.

CHARLES H. SPURGEON

"Faith does not mean that we are trying to believe something that is not so; *it just means that we are taking God at His Word.*"

> *Faith is a thread*
> *Slender and frail,*
> *Easy to tear;*
> *Yet it can lift*
> *The weight of a soul*
> *Up from despair.*

MATTHEW BILLER

September 28

✧✧✧

In me . . . peace (JOHN 16:33).

There is a vast difference between happiness and blessedness. Paul had imprisonments and pains, sacrifice and suffering up to the very limit; but in the midst of it all, he was blessed. All the beatitudes came into his heart and life *in the midst* of those very conditions.

Paganini, the great violinist, came out before his audience one day and made the discovery just as they ended their applause that there was something wrong with his violin. He looked at it a second and then saw that it was not his famous and valuable one.

He felt paralyzed for a moment, then turned to his audience and told them there had been some mistake and he did not have his own violin. He stepped back behind the curtain thinking that it was still where he had left it, but discovered that someone had stolen his and left that old secondhand one in its place. He remained back of the curtain a moment, then came out before his audience and said:

"Ladies and Gentlemen: I will show you that the music is not in the instrument, but in the soul." And he played as he had never played before; and out of that secondhand instrument, the music poured forth until the audience was enraptured with enthusiasm and the applause almost lifted the ceiling of the building, because the man had revealed to them that music was not in the machine but in his own soul.

It is your mission, tested and tried one, to walk out on the stage of this world and reveal to all earth and heaven that the music is not in conditions, not in the things, not in externals, but the music of life is in your own soul.

> *If peace be in the heart,*
> *The wildest winter storm is full of solemn beauty,*
> *The midnight flash but shows the path of duty,*
> *Each living creature tells some new and joyous story,*
> *The very trees and stones all catch a ray of glory,*
> *If peace be in the heart.*
> **CHARLES FRANCIS RICHARDSON**

❧

Keep thyself pure. (1 TIM. 5:22)

Does the judge know the story of the spotless fur that lines his robes of State? Does the society leader realize the sacrifice which makes possible the lovely ermine wrap which lies so gracefully about her shoulders? Do they know that the little animal whose coat they now wear, as he roamed the forest of Asia was as proud as they—aye, inordinately proud of his beautiful snowy coat? And we do not wonder, for it is the most beautiful fur to be found in all the markets of the world!

Such pride does the little carnivore take in his spotless coat, that nothing is permitted to soil it in the slightest degree. Hunters are well acquainted with this fact and take very unsportsmanlike advantage of this knowledge. No traps are set for him. No, indeed! Instead, they seek out his home—a tree stump, or rocky cleft, and then—be it said to their everlasting shame, they daub filth within and around the entrance. As the dogs are loosed and the chase begins the little animal naturally turns to his one place of refuge. Reaching it, rather than enter such a place of uncleanness, he turns to face the yelping dogs.

Better to be stained by blood than sully his white coat!

Only a white *coat,* little ermine, but how your act condemns *us!* *"Made in the image and likeness of God," with minds and immortal spirits;* and yet, how often in order to obtain something we desire, our character is sacrificed on the altars of worldly pleasure, greed, selfishness!

Everything is lost when purity is gone—purity, which has been called *the soul of character.* Keep thyself pure: *every thought, every word, every deed, even the motive behind the deed—all, ermine-pure.*

I ask this gift of thee—
A life all lily fair,
And fragrant as the garden be
Where seraphs are.

September 29

❦

I will give myself unto prayer (PS. 109:4).

We are often in a *religious hurry* in our devotions. How much *time* do we spend in them daily? Can it not be easily reckoned in minutes? Who ever knew an eminently holy man who did *not* spend much of his time in prayer? Did ever a man exhibit *much* of the *spirit* of prayer, who did not devote much time in his closet?

Whitefield says, "Whole days and weeks have I spent prostrate on the ground, in silent or vocal prayer." "Fall upon your knees and *grow* there," is the language of another, who knew whereof he affirmed.

It has been said that no great work in literature or science was ever wrought by a man who did not love solitude. We may lay it down as an elemental principle of religion, that no large growth in holiness was ever gained by one who did not *take* time to be often, and long, *alone with* God. —FROM THE STILL HOUR

"Come, come," He saith, "O soul oppressed and weary,
Come to the shadows of my desert rest;
Come walk with Me far from life's babbling discords,
And peace shall breathe like music in thy breast."

❦

And they shall be mine . . . in that day when I make up my jewels.
(MAL. 3:17)

Christ died that He might make us a "peculiar people." A great many Christians are afraid that they *will* be peculiar. A few weeks before Enoch was translated his acquaintances would probably have said that he was a little peculiar; they would have told you that when they had a Bridge Party and the whole countryside were invited, you would not find Enoch or one of his family present. He was very peculiar, very.

We are not told that he was a great warrior or a great scientist or a great scholar. In fact, we are not told that he was anything that the world would call great, but he walked with God three hundred and sixty-five years, and he is the brightest star that shone in that dispensation.

If he could walk with God, cannot you and I? He took a long walk one day, and has not come back as yet. The Lord liked his company so well that He said, "Enoch, come up higher."

I suppose that if we asked the men in Elijah's time what kind of a man he was, they would have said, *"He is very peculiar."* The King would have said, "I hate him." Jezebel did not like him; the whole royal court did not like him and a great number of the nominal Christians did not like him; he was too radical.

I am glad that the Lord had seven thousand that had not bowed the knee to Baal; but I would rather have Elijah's little finger than the whole seven thousand. I would not give much for seven thousand Christians in hiding. They will just barely get into heaven; they will not have crowns.

See that *"no man take thy crown."* Be willing to be one of Christ's peculiar people, no matter what men may say of you! D. L. MOODY

September 30

MORNING

∽◦∾

As an eagle stirreth up her nest, fluttereth over her young, spreadeth abroad her wings, taketh them, beareth them on her wings: so the Lord alone did lead him, and there was no strange god with him (DEUT. 32:11, 12).

Our Almighty Parent delights to conduct the tender nestlings of His care to the very edge of the precipice, and even to thrust them off into the steeps of air, that they may learn their possession of unrealized power of flight, to be forever a luxury; and if, in the attempt, they be exposed to unwonted peril, He is prepared to swoop beneath them, and to bear them upward on His mighty pinions. When God brings any of His children into a position of unparalleled difficulty, they may always count upon Him to deliver them. *FROM* THE SONG OF VICTORY

"When God puts a burden upon you He puts His own arm underneath."

There is a little plant, small and stunted, growing under the shade of a broad-spreading oak; and this little plant values the shade which covers it, and greatly does it esteem the quiet rest which its noble friend affords. But a blessing is designed for this little plant.

Once upon a time there comes along the woodman, and with his sharp ax he fells the oak. The plant weeps and cries, "My shelter is departed; every rough wind will blow upon me, and every storm will seek to uproot me!"

"No, no," saith the angel of that flower, "now will the sun get at thee; now will the shower fall on thee in more copious abundance than before; now thy stunted form shall spring up into loveliness, and thy flower, which could never have expanded itself to perfection shall now laugh in the sunshine, and men shall say, "How greatly hath that plant increased! How glorious hath become its beauty, through the removal of that which was its shade and its delight!"

See you not, then, that God may take away your comforts and your privileges, to make you the better Christians? Why the Lord always trains His soldiers, not by letting them lie on feather beds, but by turning them out, and using them to forced marches and hard service. He makes them ford through streams, and swim through rivers, and climb mountains, and walk many a long march with heavy knapsacks of sorrow on their backs. This is the way in which He makes them soldiers—not by dressing them up in fine uniforms, to swagger at the barrack gates, and to be fine gentlemen in the eyes of the loungers in the park. God knows that soldiers are only to be made in battle; they are not to be grown in peaceful times. We may grow the stuff of which soldiers are made; but warriors are really educated by the smell of powder, in the midst of whizzing bullets and roaring cannonades, not in soft and peaceful times. Well, Christian, may not this account for it all? Is not thy Lord bringing out thy graces and making them grow? Is He not developing in you the qualities of the soldier by throwing you into the heat of battle, and should you not use every appliance to come off conqueror?   SPURGEON

EVENING

∽৹৯

Why art thou cast down, O my soul? (PS. 43:5)

The other evening I found myself staggering alone under a load that was heavy enough to crush half a dozen strong men. Out of sheer exhaustion I put it down and had a good look at it. I found that it was all borrowed; part of it belonged to the following day; part of it belonged to the following week—and here was I borrowing it that it might crush me *now!* It is a very stupid, but a very ancient blunder.   F. W. BOREHAM

You and I are to take our trials, our black Fridays, our lone and long nights, and we are to come to Him and say, "Manage these, Thou Wondrous Friend who canst turn the very night into the morning; *manage these for me!*"

Sparrow, He guardeth thee;
Never a flight but thy wings He upholdeth;
Never a night but thy nest He enfoldeth;
Safely He guardeth thee.

Lily, He robeth thee;
Though thou must fade, by the Summer bemoaned,
Thou art arrayed fair as monarch enthroned;
Spotless He robeth thee.

Hear, thou of little faith;
Sparrow and lily are soulless and dying;
Deathless art thou; will He slight thy faint crying?
Trust, thou of little faith!

R. G. W.

October 1

MORNING

❧

It is good for me that I have been afflicted (PS. 119:71).

It is a remarkable circumstance that the most brilliant colors of plants are to be seen on the highest mountains, in spots that are most exposed to the wildest weather. The brightest lichens and mosses, the loveliest gems of wildflowers, abound far up on the bleak, storm-scalped peak.

One of the richest displays of organic coloring I ever beheld was near the summit of Mount Chenebettaz, a hill about 10,000 feet high, immediately above the great Saint Bernard Hospice. The whole face of an extensive rock was covered with a most vivid yellow lichen which shone in the sunshine like the golden battlement of an enchanted castle.

There, in that lofty region, amid the most frowning desolation, exposed to the fiercest tempest of the sky, this lichen exhibited a glory of color such as it never showed in the sheltered valley. I have two specimens of the same lichen before me while I write these lines, one from the great Saint Bernard, and the other from the wall of a Scottish castle, deeply embossed among sycamore trees; and the difference in point of form and coloring between them is most striking.

The specimen nurtured amid the wild storms of the mountain peak is of a lovely primrose hue, and is smooth in texture and complete in outline, while the specimen nurtured amid the soft airs and the delicate showers of the lowland valley is of a dim rusty hue, and is scurfy in texture, and broken in outline.

And is it not so with the Christian who is afflicted, tempest-tossed, and not comforted? Till the storms and vicissitudes of God's providence beat upon him again and again, his character appears marred and clouded; but trials clear away the obscurity, perfect the outlines of his disposition, and give brightness and blessing to his life.

Amidst my list of blessings infinite
Stands this the foremost, that my heart has bled;
For all I bless Thee, most for the severe.
HUGH MACMILLAN

EVENING

Lest I should be exalted above measure . . .
there was given to me a thorn. (2 COR. 12:7)

*F*lowers there are all along life's way; but the thorns are rife also. "*When the thorns of life have pierced us till we bleed,*" where but to heaven shall we look? To whom shall we go but to Him—the Christ who cures? He was crowned with thorns. He alone can transform our testing, torturing thorns into triumphal experiences of grace and glory.

B. MCCALL BARBOUR

Your path is thorny and rough? Tramp it! You will find wherever you set your foot upon a thorn, *Another Foot* has been there before and taken off the sharpness.
THE MORNING MESSAGE

Strange gift indeed!—a thorn to prick,
To pierce into the very quick;
To cause perpetual sense of pain;
Strange gift!—and yet, 'twas given for gain.

Unwelcome, yet it came to stay;
Nor could it e'en be prayed away.
It came to fill its God-planned place,
A life-enriching means of grace.

God's grace-thorns—ah, what forms they take;
What piercing, smarting pain they make!
And yet, each one in love is sent,
And always just for blessing meant.

And so, whate'er thy thorn may be,
From God accept it willingly;
But reckon Christ—His life—the power
To keep, in thy most trying hour.

And sure—thy life will richer grow;
He grace sufficient will bestow;
And in Heav'n's morn thy joy 'twill be
That, by His thorn, He strengthened thee.

J. DANSON SMITH

October 2

MORNING

And he took them, and went aside privately into a desert place
(LUKE 9:10).

In order to grow in grace, we must be much alone. It is not in society that the soul grows most vigorously. In one single quiet hour of prayer it will often make more progress than in days of company with others. It is in the desert that the dew falls freshest and the air is purest.

ANDREW BONAR

Come ye yourselves apart and rest awhile,
Weary, I know it, of the press and throng,
Wipe from your brow the sweat and dust of toil,
And in My quiet strength again be strong.

Come ye aside from all the world holds dear,
For converse which the world has never known,
Alone with Me, and with My Father here,
With Me and with My Father not alone.

Come, tell Me all that ye have said and done,
Your victories and failures, hopes and fears.
I know how hardly souls are wooed and won;
My choicest wreaths are always wet with tears.

Come ye and rest; the journey is too great,
And ye will faint beside the way and sink;
The bread of life is here for you to eat,
And here for you the wine of love to drink.

Then fresh from converse with your Lord return,
And work till daylight softens into even:
The brief hours are not lost in which ye learn
More of your Master and His rest in Heaven.

EVING

EVENING

They shall not be ashamed that wait for me. (ISA. 49:23)

They shall not be ashamed that wait for me." Such is the veritable
record of the living God—a record made good in the experience of
all those who have been enabled, through grace, to exercise a living faith.
We must remember how much is involved in these three words—*"wait*
for me." The waiting must be a real thing. It will not do to *say* we are waiting on God, when in reality, our eye is askance upon some human prop.
We must absolutely be "shut up" to God. We must be brought to *the end*
of self and to *the bottom of circumstance,* in order fully to prove what *God's*
resources are. "My soul, wait thou only upon God."

Thus it was with Jehoshaphat, in that scene recorded in 2 Chronicles 20.
He was wholly wrecked upon God; it was either *God or nothing.* "We have no
might." But what then? "Our eyes are upon thee." This was enough.
Jehoshaphat was in the very best attitude and condition to prove what God
was. To have been possessed of creature strength or creature wisdom would
only have proved a hindrance to him in leaning exclusively upon the arm
and the counsel of the Almighty God.   THINGS NEW AND OLD

When you feel at the end of your tether, remember God is at the other end!

October 3

⤬

*And after the earthquake a fire; and after the fire a sound of
gentle stillness* (1 KINGS 19:12, MARGIN RV).

A soul, who made rapid progress in her understanding of the Lord,
was once asked the secret of her easy advancement. She replied
tersely, *"Mind the checks."* And the reason that many of us do not know
and better understand Him is, we do not give heed to His gentle checks,
His delicate restraints and constraints. His is a still, small voice. A still
voice can hardly be heard. It must be felt; a steady, gentle pressure upon
the heart and mind like the touch of a morning zephyr in one's heart, but
if heeded growing noiselessly clearer to your inner ear. His voice is for the
ear of love, and love is intent upon hearing even faintest whispers. There
comes a time also when love ceases to speak if not responded to, or
believed in. He is love, and if you would know Him and His voice, give
constant ear to His gentle touches. In conversation, when about to utter
some word, give heed to that gentle voice, mind the check and refrain
from speech. When about to pursue some course that seems all clear and
right and there comes quietly to your spirit a suggestion that has in it the
force almost of a conviction, give heed, even if changed plans seem highest folly from standpoint of human wisdom. Learn also to wait on God
for the unfolding of His will. Let God form your plans about everything
in your mind and heart and then let Him execute them. Do not possess
any wisdom of your own. For many times His execution will seem so con-
tradictory to the plan He gave. He will seem to work against Himself.
Simply listen, obey, and trust God even when it seems highest folly so to
do. He will in the end make "all things work together," but so many
times in the first appearance of the outworking of His plans,

> *In His own world He is content
> To play a losing game.*

So if you would know His voice, never consider results or possible
effects. Obey even when He asks you to move in the dark. He Himself
will be gloriously light in you. And there will spring up rapidly in your
heart an acquaintanceship and a fellowship with God which will be overpowering in itself to hold you and Him together, even in severest testings
and under most terrible pressures. **FROM WAY OF FAITH**

*And we know that all things work together for good to them that love
God, to them who are the called according to his purpose.*
(ROM. 8:28)

The poet Cowper was subject to fits of depression. One day he
ordered a cab, and told the driver to take him to London Bridge.
Soon a dense fog settled down upon the city. The cabby wandered about
for two hours, and then admitted he was lost. Cowper asked him if he
thought he could find the way home. The cabby thought that he could,
and in another hour landed him at his door. When Cowper asked what
the fare would be the driver felt that he should not take anything since he
had not gotten his fare to his destination. Cowper insisted, saying, *"Never
mind that, you have saved my life. I was on my way to throw myself off
London Bridge."* He then went into the house and wrote:

> *God moves in a mysterious way*
> *His wonders to perform;*
> *He plants His footsteps on the sea,*
> *And rides upon the storm.*

The plans at the chapel went wrong; the minister was snowed up. The
plans of the boy under the gallery went wrong; the snowstorm shut him
off from the church of his choice. *Those two wrongs together made a
tremendous right, for out of those shattered plans and programs came an
event that has incalculably enriched mankind—Spurgeon's conversion.*

An old Chinese, a very old man named Sai, had only one son and one
horse. Once the horse ran away and Sai was very worried. Only one horse
and lost! Someone said, *"Don't suffer, wait a little."* The horse came back.
Not long after this the only son went out to the field riding the horse.
Returning home he fell from the horse and broke his leg. What a sorrow
had poor Sai then! He could not eat; he could not sleep; he could not
even attend well to the wants of his son. Only one son and crippled! But
someone said, *"More patience, Sai!"* Soon after the accident a war broke
out. All the young men went to the war; none of them returned. *Only
Sai's son, the cripple, stayed at home, and remained to live long to his father's
joy.* CHINESE LEGEND

October 4

MORNING

So the Lord blessed the latter end of Job more than his beginning
(JOB 42:12).

*T*hrough his griefs Job came to his heritage. He was tried that his godliness might be confirmed. Are not my troubles intended to deepen my character and to robe me in graces I had little of before? I come to my glory through eclipses, tears, death. My ripest fruit grows against the roughest wall. Job's afflictions left him with higher conceptions of God and lowlier thoughts of himself. *"Now,"* he cried, *"mine eye seeth thee."*

And if, through pain and loss, I feel God so near in His majesty that I bend low before Him and pray, *"Thy will be done,"* I gain very much. God gave Job glimpses of the future glory. In those wearisome days and nights, he penetrated within the veil, and could say, *"I know that my Redeemer liveth."* Surely the latter end of Job was more blessed than the beginning.   *FROM* IN THE HOUR OF SILENCE

"Trouble never comes to a man unless she brings a nugget of gold in her hand."

Apparent adversity will finally turn out to be the advantage of the right if we are only willing to keep on working and to wait patiently. How steadfastly the great victor souls have kept at their work, dauntless and unafraid! There are blessings which we cannot obtain if we cannot accept and endure suffering. There are joys that can come to us only through sorrow. There are revealings of divine truth which we can get only when earth's lights have gone out. There are harvests which can grow only after the plowshare has done its work.   SELECTED

Out of suffering have emerged the strongest souls; the most massive characters are seamed with scars; martyrs have put on their coronation robes glittering with fire, and through their tears have the sorrowful first seen the gates of heaven.   CHAPIN

I shall know by the gleam and glitter
Of the golden chain you wear,
By your heart's calm strength in loving,
Of the fire you have had to bear.
Beat on, true heart, forever;
Shine bright, strong golden chain;

And bless the cleansing fire
And the furnace of living pain!
ADELAIDE PROCTOR

EVENING

୰

God hath chosen the weak things of the world . . . to bring to nought things that are: That no flesh should glory in his presence.
(1 COR. 1:27–29)

*O*nly a blast of rams' horns and a shout—and God made the walls of proud Jericho crumble to their foundations, and the key of all Canaan was in the hand of Israel! (Josh. 6)

Only two women—one, Deborah, inspired courage in the fainting hearts of Israel's men—the other, Jael, with a hammer and nail laid Israel's master low; thus the end came to twenty years of mighty oppression! (Judg. 4 and 5)

Only an ox goad—but with it six hundred Philistines were slain, and Israel delivered by Shamgar's God! (Judg. 3:31)

Only a trumpet blast, the smash of a lighted pitcher, a shout—but by these, and Gideon, God delivered Israel from the seven-year yoke of the Midianites! (Judg. 6, 7, 8)

Only the jawbone of an ass—yet heaps of Philistines fell before it, because God strengthened the arm that wielded it! (Judg. 15)

Only a sling, and a stone sent with unerring precision and directed by Almighty God—and that day Israel's mighty men were put to shame: the giant Philistine was slain, and God's honor was vindicated! (1 Sam. 17)

Only a few ignorant, yet wholehearted and consecrated men and women; but by the power of God they were to put men in possession of that Eternal Salvation which would transform its possessors into the likeness of the Son Himself, and ultimately land them in Eternal Glory!

If you are one of the base, foolish, weak ciphers of this world, *then the very same power, from the very same Lord, for the very same purpose, will be yours!*   W. T.

Under the control of God ordinary instruments become extraordinary.

October 5

MORNING

〰️

It came to pass . . . that the brook dried up (1 KINGS 17:7).

The education of our faith is incomplete if we have not learned that there is a providence of loss, a ministry of failing and of fading things, a gift of emptiness. The material insecurities of life make for its spiritual establishment. The dwindling stream by which Elijah sat and mused is a true picture of the life of each of us. *"It came to pass . . . that the brook dried up"*—that is the history of our yesterday, and a prophecy of our morrows.

In some way or other we will have to learn the difference between trusting in the gift and trusting in the Giver. The gift may be good for a while, but the Giver is the eternal love.

Cherith was a difficult problem to Elijah until he got to Zarephath, and then it was all as clear as daylight. God's hard words are never His last words. The woe and the waste and the tears of life belong to the interlude and not to the finale.

Had Elijah been led straight to Zarephath he would have missed something that helped to make him a wiser prophet and a better man. He lived by faith at Cherith. And whensoever in your life and mine some spring of earthly and outward resource has dried up, it has been that we might learn that our hope and help are in God who made heaven and earth.

F. B. MEYER

Perchance thou, too, hast camped by such sweet waters,
And quenched with joy thy weary, parched soul's thirst;
To find, as time goes on, thy streamlet alters
From what it was at first.

Hearts that have cheered, or soothed, or blest, or strengthened;
Loves that have lavished so unstintedly;
Joys, treasured joys—have passed, as time hath lengthened,
Into obscurity.

If thus, ah soul, the brook thy heart hath cherished
Doth fail thee now—no more thy thirst assuage—
If its once glad refreshing streams have perished,
Let HIM thy heart engage.

He will not fail, nor mock, nor disappoint thee;
His consolations change not with the years;
With oil of joy He surely will anoint thee,
And wipe away thy tears.
J. DANSON SMITH

EVENING

❦

Not hidden from the Almighty. (JOB 24:1)

Thy Savior is near thee, suffering, lonely, tempted friend!

Thou art not the plaything of wild chance. There is a purpose in thy life which Jesus is working out. Let thy spirit flee for rest to Christ, and to His pierced hand which opens the book of thy life! Rest thee there! Be patient and trustful! All will work out right. Someday thou wilt understand. In the meantime, trust Him "though sun and moon fail, and the stars drop into the dark."

What though the way may be lonely,
And dark the shadows fall;
I know where'er it leadeth,
My Father planned it all.

The sun may shine tomorrow,
The shadows break and flee;
'Twill be the way He chooses,
The Father's plan for me.

He guides my halting footsteps
Along the weary way,
For well He knows the pathway
Will lead to endless day.

A day of light and gladness,
On which no shade will fall,
'Tis this at last awaits me—
My Father planned it all.

I sing through shade and sunshine,
And trust what'er befall;

His way is best—it leads to rest;
My Father planned it all.

"God is working out His purpose."

October 6

MORNING

⤜⤛

He opened not his mouth (ISA. 53:7).

How much grace it requires to bear a misunderstanding rightly, and to receive an unkind judgment in holy sweetness! Nothing tests the Christian character more than to have some evil thing said about him. This is the file that soon proves whether we are electroplate or solid gold. If we could only know the blessings that lie hidden in our trials we would say like David, when Shimei cursed him, "Let him curse; . . . it may be . . . that the Lord will requite me good for his cursing this day."

Some people get easily turned aside from the grandeur of their life-work by pursuing their own grievances and enemies, until their life gets turned into one little petty whirl of warfare. It is like a nest of hornets. You may disperse the hornets, but you will probably get terribly stung, and get nothing for your pains, for even their honey is not worth a search.

God give us more of His Spirit, "who, when he was reviled, reviled not again"; but "committed himself to him that judgeth righteously." "Consider him that endureth such contradiction of sinners against himself."

A. B. SIMPSON

"Before you" He trod all the path of woe,
He took the sharp thrusts with His head bent low.
He knew deepest sorrow and pain and grief,
He knew long endurance without relief,
He took all the bitter from death's deep cup,
He kept not a blood-drop but gave all up.
"Before you" and for you, He won the fight
To bring you to glory and realms of light.

L. S. P.

❦

He that loseth his life for my sake shall find it. (MATT. 10:39)

*I*n my early life I entered into a partnership with a friend in the wholesale ice business. For two seasons in succession our ice was swept away by winter freshets. In the winter of which I speak, things had come to a serious pass and it seemed very necessary that we should have ice. The weather became very cold; the ice formed and grew thicker and thicker until it was fit to gather. Then there came an order for thousands of tons of ice which would lift us entirely from our financial stress.

Not long before this, God had showed me that it was His will that I should commit my business to Him and trust Him with it absolutely. I never dreamed what testing was coming. At midnight there came an ominous sound—that of rain. By noon the storm was raging in all its violence; by afternoon I had come into a great spiritual crisis in my life.

I have learned this: *a matter may be seemingly trivial, but the crisis that turns upon a small matter may be a profound and far-reaching one in our lives.*

By midafternoon of that day I had come face to face with the tremendous fact that *down deep in my heart was a spirit of rebellion against God.* And that rebelliousness seemed to develop in a suggestion to my heart like this: "You gave all to God. This is the way He requites you." Then another voice: "My child, *did you mean it when you said you would trust Me? Would I suffer anything to come into your life which will not work out for good for you?*" And then the other voice: "But it is hard! Why should He take your business when it is clean and honest?"

At the end of two hours (during which waged one of the greatest spiritual battles of my life) by the grace of God I was able to cry out, "Take the business; take the ice; take everything; only give me the supreme blessing of a will absolutely submitted to Thee." *And then came peace!*

By midnight there came another sound—that of wind. By morning the mercury had fallen to zero, and in a few days we were harvesting the finest ice we ever had. He gave back the ice; He blessed the business; and He led me on and out, until He guided me from it entirely into the place He had for me from the beginning—that of a teacher of His Word.

JAMES H. MCCONKEY

Give your life to God, and God will give you back your life!

October 7

❦

Who is among you that feareth Jehovah, that obeyeth the voice of his servant? He that walketh in darkness and hath no light, let him trust in the name of Jehovah and rely upon his God (ISA. 50:10 RV).

*W*hat shall the believer do in times of darkness—the darkness of perplexity and confusion, not of heart but of mind? Times of darkness come to the faithful and believing disciple who is walking obediently in the will of God; seasons when he does not know what to do, nor which way to turn. The sky is overcast with clouds. The clear light of heaven does not shine upon his pathway. One feels as if he were groping his way in darkness.

Beloved, is this you? What shall the believer do in times of darkness? Listen! "Let him trust in the name of the Lord, and rely upon his God."

The first thing to do is do nothing. This is hard for poor human nature to do. In the West there is a saying that runs thus, "When you're rattled, don't rush"; in other words, "When you don't know what to do, don't do it."

When you run into a spiritual fog bank, don't tear ahead; slow down the machinery of your life. If necessary, anchor your bark or let it swing at its moorings. We are to simply trust God. While we trust, God can work. Worry prevents Him from doing anything for us. If the darkness that overshadows us strikes terror to us; if we run hither and yon in a vain effort to find some way of escape out of a dark place of trial, where divine providence has put us, the Lord can do nothing for us.

The peace of God must quiet our minds and rest our hearts. We must put our hand in the hand of God like a little child, and let Him lead us out into the bright sunshine of His love.

He knows the way out of the woods. Let us climb up into His arms, and trust Him to take us out by the shortest and surest road.

DR. PARDINGTON

Remember we are never without a pilot when we know not how to steer.

> *Hold on, my heart, in thy believing—*
> *The steadfast only wins the crown;*
> *He who, when stormy winds are heaving,*

Parts with its anchor, shall go down;
But he who Jesus holds through all,
Shall stand, though Heaven and earth should fall.

Hold out! There comes an end to sorrow;
Hope from the dust shall conquering rise;
The storm foretells a summer's morrow;
The Cross points on to Paradise;
The Father reigneth! cease all doubt;
Hold on, my heart, hold on, hold on.

EVENING

The LORD is my shepherd. (PS. 23:1)

The great Father above is a Shepherd Chief. I am His and with Him. I want not. He throws out to me a rope, and the name of the rope is love, and He draws me to where the grass is green and the water is not dangerous.

Sometimes my heart is very weak, and falls down, but He lifts it up again and draws me into a good road.

Sometime, it may be very soon, it may be longer, it may be a long, long time, He will draw me into a place between mountains. It is dark there, but I'll draw back not. I'll be afraid not, for it is in there between the mountains that the Shepherd Chief will meet me, and the hunger I have felt in my heart all through this life will be satisfied. Sometimes He makes the love rope into a whip, but afterwards He gives me a staff to lean on.

He spreads a table before me with all kinds of food. He puts His hands upon my head, and all the "tired" is gone.

My cup He fills, till it runs over.

What I tell you is true, I lie not. The roads that are "away ahead" will stay with me through this life, and afterwards I will go to live in the "Big Tepee" and sit down with the Shepherd Chief forever.

AN AMERICAN INDIAN'S VERSION OF THE TWENTY-THIRD PSALM

Fear not, little flock, He goeth ahead,
Your Shepherd selecteth the path you must tread;
The water of Marah He'll sweeten for thee,
He drank all the bitter in Gethsemane.

Fear not, little flock, whatever your lot,
He enters all rooms, "The doors being shut";
He never forsakes; He never is gone,
So count on His presence in darkness and dawn.
PAUL RADER

October 8

MORNING

~∞~

Do not begin to be anxious (PHIL. 4:6 PBV).

Not a few Christians live in a state of unbroken anxiety, and others fret and fume terribly. To be perfectly at peace amid the hurly-burly of daily life is a secret worth knowing. What is the use of worrying? It never made anybody strong; never helped anybody to do God's will; never made a way of escape for anyone out of perplexity. Worry spoils lives which would otherwise be useful and beautiful. Restlessness, anxiety, and care are absolutely forbidden by our Lord, who said: "Take no thought," that is, no anxious thought, "saying what shall we eat, or what shall we drink, or wherewithal shall we be clothed?" He does not mean that we are not to take forethought and that our life is to be without plan or method; but that we are not to worry about these things. People know you live in the realm of anxious care by the lines on your face, the tones of your voice, the minor key in your life, and the lack of joy in your spirit. Scale the heights of a life abandoned to God, then you will look down on the clouds beneath your feet. **REV. DARLOW SARGEANT**

It is always weakness to be fretting and worrying, questioning and mistrusting. Can we gain anything by it? Do we not unfit ourselves for action, and unhinge our minds for wise decision? We are sinking by our struggles when we might float by faith.

Oh, for grace to be quiet! Oh, to be still and know that Jehovah is God! The Holy One of Israel must defend and deliver His own. We may be sure that every word of His will stand, though the mountains should depart. He deserves to be confided in. Come, my soul, return unto thy rest, and lean thy head upon the bosom of the Lord Jesus. **SELECTED**

Peace thy inmost soul shall fill Lying still!

EVENING

∽∾

Restore such an one in the spirit of meekness . . .
lest thou also be tempted. (GAL. 6:1)

From the converts in Uganda
Comes to us a story grander,
In the lesson that it teaches,
Than a sermon often preaches.
For they tell what sore temptations
Come to them; what need of patience,
And a need, all else outweighing,
Of a place for private praying.
So each convert chose a corner

Far away from eye of scorner,
In the jungle, where he could
Pray to God in solitude.
And so often went he thither,
That the grass would fade and wither
Where he trod and you could trace
By the paths, each prayer place.

If they hear the evil tiding
That a brother is backsliding,
And that some are even saying,
"He no longer cares for praying,"
Then they say to one another,
Very soft and gently, "Brother,
You'll forgive us now for showing,
On your path the grass is growing."
And the erring one, relenting,
Soon is bitterly repenting:
"Ah, how sad I am at knowing
On my path the grass is growing.
But it shall be so no longer;
Prayer I need to make me stronger;
On my path so oft I'm going,
Soon no grass will there be growing."

GRASS ON THE PRAYER PATH

October 9

MORNING

❧◈❧

Therefore will the Lord wait, that he may be gracious unto you
(ISA. 30:18).

Where showers fall most, there the grass is greenest. I suppose the fogs and mists of Ireland make it "the Emerald Isle"; and whenever you find great fogs of trouble, and mists of sorrow, you always find emerald green hearts; full of the beautiful verdure of the comfort and love of God. O Christian, do not thou be saying, "Where are the swallows gone? They are gone; they are dead." They are not dead; they have skimmed the purple sea, and gone to a far-off land; but they will be back again by and by. Child of God, say not the flowers are dead; say not the winter has killed them, and they are gone. Ah, no! though winter hath coated them with the ermine of its snow; they will put up their heads again, and will be alive very soon. Say not, child of God, that the sun is quenched, because the cloud hath hidden it. Ah, no; he is behind there, brewing summer for thee; for when he cometh out agai, he will have made the clouds fit to drop in April showers, all of them mothers of the sweet May flowers. And oh! above all, when thy God hides His face, say not that He hath forgotten thee. He is but tarrying a little while to make thee love Him better; and when He cometh, thou shalt have joy in the Lord, and shalt rejoice with joy unspeakable. Waiting exercises our grace; waiting tries our faith; therefore, wait on in hope; for though the promise tarry, it can never come too late. C. H. SPURGEON

Oh, every year hath its winter,
And every year hath its rain—
But a day is always coming
When the birds go north again.

When new leaves swell in the forest,
And grass springs green on the plain,
And alders' vein turn crimson—

And the birds go north again.

Oh, every heart hath its sorrow,
And every heart hath its pain—
But a day is always coming
When the birds go north again.

'Tis the sweetest thing to remember,
If courage be on the wane,
When the cold, dark days are over—
Why, the birds go north again.

EVENING

∽◦◦∾

And Abraham built an altar there . . . and took the knife to slay his son. And the angel of the LORD called unto him . . . Lay not thine hand upon the lad. (GEN. 22:9–12)

Our hardest sacrifices are never so hard as we thought they were going to be, *if* we go on with them to the uttermost that God asks. A sacrifice of self to God's will made halfway, *or even nine-tenths, is a grinding, cruel experience.* When it is made the *whole* way, with the altar built and self laid upon the altar, God always *comes with an unexpected blessing that so overwhelms us with love and joy that the hardship of the sacrifice sinks out of sight.* "Now I know that thou fearest God, seeing thou hast not withheld."

Can He say that to *us* today? No one ever knows the full joy of hearing the word from God until the altar has been built, and the knife is laid to the sacrifice. **MESSAGES FOR THE MORNING WATCH**

Is your all on the altar of sacrifice laid?
Your heart, does the Spirit control?
You can only be blest and have peace and sweet rest
As you yield Him your body and soul.

October 10

∾∾∾

Fret not (PS. 37:1).

his to me is a divine command; the same as *"Thou shalt not steal."*
Now let us get to the definition of fretting. One good definition is,
"Made rough on the surface." "Rubbed, or worn away"; and a peevish,
irrational, fault-finding person not only wears himself out, but is very
wearing to others. To fret is to be in a state of vexation, and in this psalm
we are not only told not to fret because of evildoers, but to fret not "in
anywise." It is injurious, and God does not want us to hurt ourselves.

A physician will tell you that a fit of anger is more injurious to the system
than a fever, and a fretful disposition is not conducive to a healthy body; and
you know rules are apt to work both ways, and the next step down from
fretting is crossness, and that amounts to anger. Let us settle this matter, and
be obedient to the command, *"Fret not."*   **MARGARET BOTTOME**

Overheard in an Orchard

Said the Robin to the Sparrow:
"I should really like to know
Why these anxious human beings
Rush about and worry so."

Said the Sparrow to the Robin:
"Friend, I think that it must be
That they have no Heavenly Father
Such as cares for you and me."
ELIZABETH CHENEY

∾∾∾

They held their lives cheap. (REV. 12:11 WEYMOUTH)

he persecution of the Christians during the reign of Marcus Aurelius
was very bitter. The Emperor himself decreed the punishment of forty
of the men who had refused to bow down to his image.

"Strip to the skin!" he commanded. They did so. "Now, go and stand on that frozen lake," he commanded, "until you are prepared to abandon your Nazarene-God!"

And forty naked men marched out into that howling storm on a winter's night. As they took their places on the ice they lifted up their voices and sang:

"Christ, forty wrestlers have come out to wrestle for Thee; to win for Thee the victory; to win from Thee the crown."

After a while, those standing by and watching noticed a disturbance among the men. One man had edged away, broken into a run, entered the temple and prostrated himself before the image of the Emperor.

The Captain of the Guard, who had witnessed the bravery of the men and whose heart had been touched by their teaching, tore off his helmet, threw down his spear, and disrobing himself, took up the cry as he took the place of the man who had weakened. The compensation was not slow in coming, for as the dawn broke there were forty corpses on the ice.

> *Who shall dream of shrinking,*
> *By our Captain led?*

At least a thousand of God's saints served as living torches to illuminate the darkness of Nero's gardens, wrapped in garments steeped in pitch. *"Every finger was a candle."*

> *"Who follows in their train?"*

> *I'm standing, Lord.*
> *There is a mist that blinds my sight.*
> *Steep jagged rocks, front, left, and right,*
> *Lower, dim, gigantic, in the night.*
> *Where is the way?*

> *I'm standing, Lord.*
> *The black rock hems me in behind.*
> *Above my head a moaning wind*
> *Chills and oppresses heart and mind.*
> *I am afraid!*

> *I'm standing, Lord.*
> *The rock is hard beneath my feet.*
> *I nearly slipped, Lord, on the sleet.*
> *So weary, Lord, and where a seat?*
> *Still must I stand?*

> *He answered me, and on His face*
> *A look ineffable of grace,*

Of perfect, understanding love,
Which all my murmuring did remove.

I'm standing, Lord.
Since Thou hast spoken, Lord, I see
Thou hast beset; these rocks are Thee;
And since Thy love encloses me,
I stand and sing!
BETTY STAM, MARTYRED IN CHINA

October 11

MORNING

∞

As dying and behold we live (2 COR. 6:9).

J had a bed of asters last summer, that reached clear across my garden in the country. Oh, how gaily they bloomed. They were planted late. On the sides were yet fresh blossoming flowers, while the tops had gone to seed. Early frosts came, and I found one day that that long line of radiant beauty was seared, and I said, "Ah! the season is too much for them; they have perished"; and I bade them farewell.

I disliked to go and look at the bed, it looked so like a graveyard of flowers. But, four or five weeks ago one of my men called my attention to the fact that along the whole line of that bed there were asters coming up in the greatest abundance; and I looked, and behold, for every plant that I thought the winter had destroyed there were fifty plants that it had planted. What did those frosts and surly winds do?

They caught my flowers, they slew them, they cast them to the ground, they trod with snowy feet upon them, and they said, leaving their work, *"This is the end of you."* And the next spring there were for every root, fifty witnesses to rise up and say, *"By death we live."*

And as it is in the floral tribe, so it is in God's kingdom. By death came everlasting life. By crucifixion and the sepulchre came the throne and the palace of the eternal God. By overthrow came victory.

Do not be afraid to suffer. Do not be afraid to be overthrown.

It is by being cast down and not destroyed; it is by being shaken to pieces, and the pieces torn to shreds, that men become men of might, and that one a host; whereas men that yield to the appearance of things, and go with the world, have their quick blossoming, their momentary prosperity and then their end, which is an end forever.   BEECHER

Measure thy life by loss and not by gain,
Not by the wine drunk, but by the wine poured forth.
For love's strength standeth in love's sacrifice,
And he who suffers most has most to give.

EVENING

Until he come whose right it is. (EZEK. 21:27)

Years ago in Cincinnati Handel's *Messiah* was rendered by perhaps the greatest chorus on earth: Patti, then in her prime, was the leading soprano; Whitney, the bass; Theodore Toedt, the tenor; Carey, the alto; and this quartet was supported by more than four thousand voices.

Just before the "Hallelujah Chorus" a deathlike stillness brooded over that vast assemblage. Suddenly the bass sang, "For He shall reign for ever and ever," the alto lifted it a little higher—"For ever and ever," and the tenor lifted it still higher—"For ever and ever," then Patti broke in as though inspired—"King of Kings, and Lord of Lords." As she broke off, paused, and lifted her eyes, a voice seemed to float down from above as the voice of an Angel flinging out through the great hall the question, "How long shall He reign?"—and the thousand sopranos in unison responded, "For ever and ever." Then the four thousand of the chorus broke forth like the shout of an angelic host, "Hallelujah! Hallelujah! Hallelujah!"

What a day for this poor sin-ruined, storm-torn, heartbroken, groping-in-the-blind world, when He shall take His rightful throne and reign in all hearts and over all lives for ever and ever!

ELMER ELLSWORTH HELMS

Hail, universal Lord!
Messiah—David's Son!
Take Thou the scepter of the world,
And reign supreme, alone!

Oh, it seems to me like a prophecy of the glad day when every knee shall bow, and all the nations of the earth shall confess that Jesus Christ is

Lord, to the glory of God the Father. And from the teeming millions of Asia shall sound the anthem, "King of Kings, and Lord of Lords"; the shout from Europe will give it power; and the deep undertone of Africa's redeemed will lend it volume; and America, and faraway Australia, and the islands of the sea will join the refrain and pour their matchless music into the ear of Christ; and together, from the uttermost parts of the earth, breaking out in triumphant voice, the whole world shall sing, "King of Kings, and Lord of Lords; the Lord God Omnipotent reigneth!"

Come back! Come back! Take the scepter of our lives! Mount the throne of our hearts! All hail the King! My King! *And thine?*

October 12

MORNING

╼◦◦╾

And Joseph's master took him, and put him into the prison. . . .
But the Lord was with Joseph . . . and that which he did, the Lord
made it to prosper (GEN. 39:20, 21, 23).

When God lets us go to prison because we have been serving Him, and goes there with us, prison is about the most blessed place in the world that we could be in. Joseph seems to have known that. He did not sulk and grow discouraged and rebellious because "everything was against him." If he had, the prisonkeeper would never have trusted him so. Joseph does not even seem to have pitied himself.

Let us remember that if *self-pity* is allowed to set in, that is the end of us—until it is cast utterly from us. Joseph just turned over everything in joyous trust to God, and so the keeper of the prison turned over everything to Joseph. Lord Jesus, when the prison doors close in on me, keep me trusting, and keep my joy full and abounding. Prosper Thy work through me in prison: even there, make me free indeed.   SELECTED

A little bird I am,
Shut from the fields of air,
And in my cage I sit and sing
To Him who placed me there;
Well pleased a prisoner to be,
Because, My God, it pleaseth Thee.

My cage confines me round,
Abroad I cannot fly,
But though my wing is closely bound,
My soul is at liberty;
For prison walls cannot control
The flight, the freedom of the soul.

I have learnt to love the darkness of sorrow; there you see the brightness of His face.

MADAME GUYON

EVENING

❦

My meditation of him shall be sweet. (PS. 104:34)

Isaac went into the fields *to meditate. Jacob* lingered on the eastern bank of the brook Jabbok after all his company had passed over; there he wrestled with the angel and prevailed. *Moses,* hidden in the clefts of Horeb, beheld the vanishing glory which marked the way by which Jehovah had gone. *Elijah* sent Ahab down to eat and drink while he himself withdrew to the lonely crest of Carmel. *Daniel* spent weeks in ecstasy of intercession on the banks of Hiddakel, which once had watered Paradise. And *Paul,* no doubt in order that he might have an opportunity for undisturbed meditation and prayer, was minded to go afoot from Troas to Assos.

Have you learned to understand the truths of these great paradoxes: the blessing of a curse, the voice of silence, the companionship of solitude?

I walk down the Valley of Silence,
Down the dim voiceless valley alone,
And I hear not the sound of a footstep
Around me, but God's and my own;
And the hush of my heart is as holy
As the bowers whence angels have flown.

In the hush of the Valley of Silence
I hear all the songs that I sing,
And the notes float down the dim Valley
Till each finds a word for a wing,
That to men, like the dove of the deluge
The message of peace they may bring.

But far on the deep there are billows
That never shall break on the beach;
And I have heard songs in the silence
That never shall float into speech;
And I have had dreams in the Valley
Too lofty for language to reach.

Do you ask me the place of the Valley?
To hearts that are harrowed by care
It lieth afar, between mountains,
And God and His angels are there—
One is the dark mountain of sorrow,
And one the bright mountain of prayer.
THE SONG OF A MYSTIC

October 13

MORNING

֍

In nothing be anxious (PHIL. 4:6).

No anxiety ought to be found in a believer. Great, many, and varied may be our trials, our afflictions, our difficulties, and yet there should be no anxiety under any circumstances, because we have a Father in heaven who is almighty, who loves His children as He loves His only-begotten Son, and whose very joy and delight it is to succor and help them at all times and under all circumstances. We should attend to the Word, "In nothing be anxious, but in everything by prayer and supplication with thanksgiving let your requests be made known unto God."

"In everything," that is not merely when the house is on fire, not merely when the beloved wife and children are on the brink of the grave, but in the smallest matters of life, bring everything before God, the little things, the very little things, what the world calls trifling things—*everything*—living in holy communion with our heavenly Father, and with our precious Lord Jesus all day long. And when we awake at night, by a kind of spiritual instinct again turning to Him, and speaking to Him, bringing our various little matters before Him in the sleepless night, the difficulties

in connection with the family, our trade, our profession. Whatever tries us in any way, speak to the Lord about it.

"By prayer and supplication," taking the place of beggars, with earnestness, with perseverance, going on and waiting, waiting, waiting on God.

"With thanksgiving." We should at all times lay a good foundation with thanksgiving. If everything else were wanting, this is always present, that He has saved us from hell. Then, that He has given us His Holy Word—His Son, His choicest gift—and the Holy Spirit. Therefore we have abundant reason for thanksgiving. O let us aim at this!

"And the peace of God which passeth all understanding, shall keep your hearts and minds in Christ Jesus." And this is so great a blessing, so real a blessing, so precious a blessing, that it must be known *experimentally* to be entered into, for it passeth understanding. O, let us lay these things to heart, and the result will be, if we habitually walk in this spirit, we shall far more abundantly glorify God, than as yet we have done.

FROM GEORGE MUELLER, IN LIFE OF TRUST

Twice or thrice a day, look to see if your heart is not disquieted about something; and if you find that it is, take care forthwith to restore it to calm.   FRANCIS DE SALES

EVENING

～∞～

If ye shall ask . . . I will do. (JOHN 14:14)

Who is it here who offers to do for us *if we will only ask?* It is *God Himself!* It is the mightiest doer in the universe who says, "I will do, if you ask."

Think a moment *who* it is that promises: the God who holds the sea in the hollow of His hand; the God who swings this ponderous globe of earth in its orbit; the God who marshals the stars and guides the planets in their blazing paths with undeviating accuracy; the heaven-creating, devil-conquering, dead-raising God. It is this very God who says: *"If ye ask . . . I will do!"*

Unrivaled wisdom, boundless skill, limitless power, infinite resources are His.

Wouldst thou not rather call forth *Mine omnipotent doing* by thine asking, if to this I have called thee, than even to be busy with thine own doing?   JAMES H. MCCONKEY

"I will do marvels!"

October 14

の

*The angel of the Lord came upon him [Peter] and a light shined in
the prison; and he smote Peter on the side, and raised him up,
saying, Arise up quickly. And his chains fell off* (ACTS 12:7).

*And at midnight Paul and Silas prayed and sang praises unto God.
. . . And suddenly there was a great earthquake, so that the foundations of the prison were shaken; and immediately all the doors were
opened and every one's bands were loosed*
(ACTS 16:25, 26).

This is God's way. In the darkest hours of the night, His tread draws
near across the billows. As the day of execution is breaking, the angel
comes to Peter's cell. When the scaffold for Mordecai is complete, the
royal sleeplessness leads to a reaction in favor of the favored race.

Ah, soul, it may have to come to the worst with thee ere thou art delivered; but thou wilt be delivered! God may keep thee waiting, but He will
ever be mindful of His covenant, and will appear to fulfill His inviolable
Word. **F. B. MEYER**

There's a simplicity about God in working out His plans, yet a
resourcefulness equal to any difficulty, and an unswerving faithfulness to
His trusting child, and an unforgetting steadiness in holding to His purpose. Through a fellow-prisoner, then a dream, He lifts Joseph from a
prison to a premiership. And the length of stay in the prison prevents
dizziness in the premier. It's safe to trust God's methods and to go by His
clock. **S. D. GORDON**

Providence hath a thousand keys to open a thousand sundry doors for
the deliverance of His own, when it is even come to a desperate case. Let
us be faithful; and care for our own part which is to suffer for Him, and
lay Christ's part on Himself, and leave it there. **GEORGE MACDONALD**

Difficulty is the very atmosphere of miracle—it is a miracle in its first
stage. If it is to be a great miracle, the condition is not difficulty but
impossibility.

The clinging hand of His child makes a desperate situation a delight
to Him.

When he had heard therefore that he was sick, he abode two days still in the same place where he was. (JOHN 11:6)

*A*nd so the silence of God was itself an answer. It is not merely said that there was no audible response to the cry from Bethany; it is distinctly stated that the absence of an audible response was itself the answer to the cry—it was *when* the Lord heard that Lazarus was sick that *therefore* He abode two days still in the same place which He was. I have often heard the outward silence. A hundred times have I sent up aspirations whose only answer has seemed to be the echo of my own voice, and I have cried out in the night of my despair, *"Why art Thou so far from helping me?"* But I never thought that the seeming farness was itself the nearness of God—that the very silence was an answer.

It was a very grand answer to the household of Bethany. They had asked *not too much,* but *too little.* They had asked only the life of Lazarus. They were to get the life of Lazarus and a revelation of eternal life as well.

There are some prayers that are followed by a Divine silence *because we are not yet ripe for all we have asked;* there are others which are so followed *because we are ripe for more. We do not always know the full strength of our own capacity; we have to be prepared for receiving greater blessings than we have ever dreamed of.* We come to the door of the sepulcher and beg with tears the dead body of Jesus; we are answered by silence *because we are to get something better—a living Lord.*

My soul, be not afraid of God's silence, it is another form of His voice. God's silence is more than man's speech. God's negative is better than the world's affirmative. Have thy prayers been followed by a calm stillness? Well! Is not that God's voice—a voice that will suffice thee in the meantime till the full disclosure comes? Has He moved not from His place to help thee? Well, but His stillness makes *thee* still, and He has something better than help to give thee.

Wait for Him in the silence, and ere long it shall become vocal; death shall be swallowed up in victory! **GEORGE MATHESON**

All God's dealings are slow!

Think not that God's silence is coldness or indifference. When birds are on the nest preparing to bring forth life, they never sing. *God's stillness is full of brooding. Be not impatient of God!*

When the Lord is to lead a soul to *great faith,* He for a time leaves his prayer unanswered.

October 15

❧

By reason of breakings they purify themselves (JOB 41:25).

God uses most for His glory those people and things which are most perfectly broken. The sacrifices He accepts are broken and contrite hearts. It was the breaking down of Jacob's natural strength at Peniel that got him where God could clothe him with spiritual power. It was breaking the surface of the rock at Horeb, by the stroke of Moses' rod, that let out the cool waters to thirsty people.

It was when the three hundred elect soldiers under Gideon broke their pitchers, a type of breaking themselves, that the hidden lights shone forth to the consternation of their adversaries. It was when the poor widow broke the seal of the little pot of oil, and poured it forth, that God multiplied it to pay her debts and supply means of support.

It was when Esther risked her life and broke through the rigid etiquette of a heathen court, that she obtained favor to rescue her people from death. It was when Jesus took the five loaves and broke them, that the bread was multiplied in the very act of breaking, sufficient to feed five thousand. It was when Mary broke her beautiful alabaster box, rendering it henceforth useless, that the pent-up perfume filled the house. It was when Jesus allowed His precious body to be broken to pieces by thorns and nails and spear, that His inner life was poured out, like a crystal ocean, for thirsty sinners to drink and live.

It is when a beautiful grain of corn is broken up in the earth by DEATH, that its inner heart sprouts forth and bears hundreds of other grains. And thus, on and on, through history, and all biography, and all vegetation, and all spiritual life, God must have BROKEN THINGS.

Those who are broken in wealth, and broken in self-will, and broken in their ambitions, and broken in their beautiful ideals, and broken in worldly reputation, and broken in their affections, and broken ofttimes in health; those who are despised and seem utterly forlorn and helpless, the Holy Ghost is seizing upon, and using for God's glory. "The lame take the prey," Isaiah tells us.

> *O break my heart; but break it as a field*
> *Is by the plough up-broken for the corn;*
> *O break it as the buds, by green leaf sealed,*
> *Are, to unloose the golden blossom, torn;*

Love would I offer unto Love's great Master,
Set free the odor, break the alabaster.

O break my heart; break it victorious God,
That life's eternal well may flash abroad;
O let it break as when the captive trees,
Breaking cold bonds, regain their liberties;
And as thought's sacred grove to life is springing,
Be joys, like birds, their hope, Thy victory singing.
THOMAS TOKE BUNCH

EVENING

We have an assured confidence that whenever we ask anything in accordance with his will, he listens to us: And since we know that he listens to us, then whatever we ask, we know that we have the things which we have asked from him. (1 JOHN 5:14–15 WEYMOUTH)

Prayer can obtain everything: it can open the windows of heaven, and shut the gates of hell; it can put a holy constraint upon God, and detain an angel until he leave a blessing; it can open the treasures of rain, and soften the iron ribs of rocks till they melt into tears and a flowing river; prayer can unclasp the girdles of the north—saying to a mountain of ice, "Be thou removed hence, and cast into the bottom of the sea"; it can arrest the sun in the midst of his course, and send the swift-winged winds upon our errands; and to all these strange tings and secret decrees, add unrevealed transactions which are above the stars.

When Hudson Taylor was asked if he ever prayed *without any consciousness of joy,* he replied: "Often: sometimes I pray on with my heart feeling like wood; often, too, the most wonderful answers have come when prayer has been a real effort of faith without any joy whatever."

I never prayed sincerely and earnestly for anything but it came; at some time—no matter how distant the day—somehow, in some shape, probably the last I should have devised, *it came.* **ADONIRAM JUDSON**

For years I've prayed, and yet I see no change.
The mountain stands exactly where it stood;
The shadows that it casts are just as deep;
The pathway to its summit e'en more steep.
Shall I pray on?

Shall I pray on with ne'er a hopeful sign?
Not only does the mountain still remain,
But, while I watch to see it disappear,
Becomes the more appalling year by year.
Shall I pray on?

I shall pray on. Though distant as it seems
The answer may be almost at my door,
Or just around the corner on its way,
But, whether near or far, yes, I shall pray—
I shall pray on.
EDITH MAPES

If thou wilt keep the incense burning there, His glory thou shalt see—
sometime, somewhere!

October 16

MORNING

❧❧

Let us lay aside every weight, and the sin which doth so easily beset us,
and let us run with patience the race that is set before us
(HEB. 12:1).

There are weights which are not sins themselves, but which become distractions and stumbling blocks in our Christian progress. One of the worst of these is despondency. The heavy heart is indeed a weight that will surely drag us down in our holiness and usefulness.

The failure of Israel to enter the land of promise began in murmuring, or, as the text in Numbers literally puts it, *"as it were murmured."* Just a faint desire to complain and be discontented. This led on until it blossomed and ripened into rebellion and ruin. Let us give ourselves no liberty ever to doubt God or His love and faithfulness to us in everything and forever.

We can set our will against doubt just as we do against any other sin; and as we stand firm and refuse to doubt, the Holy Spirit will come to our aid and give us the faith of God and crown us with victory.

It is very easy to fall into the habit of doubting, fretting, and wondering if God has forsaken us and if, after all, our hopes are to end in failure.

Let us refuse to be discouraged. Let us refuse to be unhappy. Let us "count it all joy" when we cannot feel one emotion of happiness. Let us rejoice by faith, by resolution, by reckoning, and we shall surely find that God will make the reckoning real.　　　SELECTED

The Devil has two master tricks. One is *to get us discouraged;* then for a time at least we can be of no service to others, and so are defeated. The other is to *make us doubt,* thus breaking the faith link by which we are bound to our Father. Look out! Do not be tricked either way.　　G. E. M.

Gladness! I like to cultivate the spirit of gladness! It puts the soul so in tune again, and keeps it in tune, so that Satan is shy of touching it—the chords of the soul become too warm, or too full of heavenly electricity, for his infernal fingers, and he goes off somewhere else! Satan is always very shy of meddling with me when my heart is full of gladness and joy in the Holy Ghost.

My plan is to shun the spirit of *sadness* as I would Satan; but, alas! I am not always successful. Like the Devil himself it meets me on the highway of *usefulness,* looks me so fully in my face, till my poor soul changes color!

Sadness discolors everything; it leaves all objects *charmless;* it involves future prospects in darkness; it deprives the soul of all its aspirations, enchains all its powers, and produces a mental paralysis!

An *old believer* remarked, that *cheerfulness* in religion makes all its services come off with delight; and that we are never carried forward so swiftly in the ways of duty as when borne on the wings of *delight;* adding, that *melancholy* clips such wings; or, to alter the figure, takes off our chariot wheels in duty, and makes them, like those of the Egyptians, drag heavily.

EVENING

༄༅

If . . . God command thee . . . thou shalt be able. (EX. 18:23)

Charles G. Finney once said: "When God commands you to do a thing, it is the highest possible evidence, equal to an oath, that we can do it."

The thing that taxes Almightiness is the very thing that you as a disciple of Jesus Christ ought to believe He would do. Sometimes we must be shipwrecked upon the supernatural; we must be thrown upon God; we must lose the temporal—that we may find the Eternal.

"It is God who worketh." Men work like men and nothing more is

expected of man than what man can do. But God worketh like a God, and with Him nothing is impossible.

There is for us *a source of heightened power.* A most suggestive translation of 1 Samuel 2:1 reads:

> *My heart thrills over the Eternal;*
> *my powers are heightened by my God.*

Amos was just a herdsman from Tekoa, but *his powers were heightened* by his God. It happened to Peter. It happened to Paul. Abraham Lincoln faced the impossible when he set out to uproot the slave trade.

We are all in need of more power, more courage, more wisdom than we actually possess. This *"plus extra"* comes to him whose heart thrills over the Eternal; who daily waits for Divine resources.

"Difficulty" is a relative term. It all depends upon the power you have available. Difficulty diminishes as the power increases; and altogether vanishes when the power rises to Omnipotence. "Our sufficiency is of God." All God's biddings are enablings. *Always provided that we are on the line of God's written Word, in the current of His revealed purpose, there is nothing you may not trust Him for.*

> *As one of a thousand you may just fail;*
> *But as "ONE, PLUS GOD," YOU ARE BOUND TO WIN.*

October 17

MORNING

∽§∽

God forbid that I should glory, save in the cross of our Lord Jesus Christ, by whom the world is crucified unto me, and I unto the world (GAL. 6:14).

They were living to themselves; self with its hopes, and promises and dreams, still had hold of them; but the Lord began to fulfill their prayers. They had asked for contrition, and had surrendered for it to be given them at any cost, and He sent them sorrow; they had asked for purity, and He sent them thrilling anguish; they had asked to be meek, and He had broken their hearts; they had asked to be dead to the world, and He slew all their living hopes; they had asked to be made like unto Him, and He placed them in the furnace, sitting by "as a refiner and purifier of silver," until they should reflect His image; they had asked to lay hold of His cross, and when He had reached it to them it lacerated their hands.

They had asked they knew not what, nor how, but He had taken them at their word, and granted them all their petitions. They were hardly willing to follow Him so far, or to draw so nigh to Him. They had upon them an awe and fear, as Jacob at Bethel, or Eliphaz in the night visions, or as the apostles when they thought that they had seen a spirit, and knew not that it was Jesus. They could almost pray Him to depart from them, or to hide His awfulness. They found it easier to obey than to suffer, to do than to give up, to bear the cross than to hang upon it. But they cannot go back, for they have come too near the unseen cross, and its virtues have pierced too deeply within them. He is fulfilling to them His promise, "And I, if I be lifted up from the earth, will draw all men unto me" (John 12:32).

But now at last their turn has come. Before, they had only heard of the mystery, but now they feel it. He has fastened on them His look of love, as He did on Mary and Peter, and they can but choose to follow.

Little by little, from time to time, by flitting gleams, the mystery of His cross shines out upon them. They behold Him lifted up, they gaze on the glory which rays from the wounds of His holy passion; and as they gaze they advance, and are changed into His likeness, and His name shines out through them, for He dwells in them. They live alone with Him above, in unspeakable fellowship; willing to lack what others own (and what they might have had), and to be unlike all, so that they are only like Him.

Such, are they in all ages, "who follow the Lamb whithersoever he goeth."

Had they chosen for themselves, or their friends chosen for them, they would have chosen otherwise. They would have been brighter here, but less glorious in His kingdom. They would have had Lot's portion, not Abraham's. If they had halted anywhere—if God had taken off His hand and let them stray back—what would they not have lost? What forfeits in the resurrection?

But He stayed them up, even against themselves. Many a time their foot had well nigh slipped; but He in mercy held them up. Now, even in this life, they know that all He did was done well. It was good to suffer here, that they might reign hereafter; to bear the cross below, for they shall wear the crown above; and that not their will but His was done on them and in them.   ANONYMOUS

❦

For he commandeth, and raiseth the stormy wind, which lifteth up the waves thereof. (PS. 107:25)

Stormy wind fulfilling His word. *By the time the wind blows upon us it is His wind for us.* We have nothing to do with what first of all stirred up that wind. It could not ruffle a leaf on the smallest tree in the forest had He not opened the way for it to blow through the fields of air. He commandeth even the winds, and they obey Him. To the winds as to His servants He saith to one, "Go," and it goeth; and to another, "Come," and it cometh; and to another, "Do this," and it doeth it. So, whatever wind blows on us it is His wind for us, *His wind fulfilling His word.*

God's winds do effectual work. *They shake loose from us the things that can be shaken, that those things which cannot be shaken may remain, those eternal things which belong to the Kingdom which cannot be moved.* They have their part to play in stripping us and strengthening us so that we may be the more ready for the uses of Eternal Love. Then can we refuse to welcome them?

Art thou indeed willing for any wind at any time?

GOLD BY MOONLIGHT

Be like the pine on the hilltop,
Alone in the wind for God.

There is a curious comfort in remembering that the Father depends upon His child not to give way. *It is inspiring to be trusted with a hard thing.* You never asked for summer breezes to blow upon your tree. It is enough that you are not alone upon the hill.

And let the storm that does Thy work
Deal with me as it may.

October 18

MORNING

❧

*Know of a surety that thy seed shall be a stranger in a land that is
not theirs; . . . they shall afflict them four hundred years; . . .
and afterward they shall come out with great substance*
(GEN. 15:13–14).

An assured part of God's pledged blessing to us is delay and suffering. A delay in Abram's own lifetime that seemed to put God's pledge beyond fulfillment was followed by seemingly unendurable delay of Abram's descendants. But it was only a delay: they *"came out with great substance."* The pledge was redeemed.

God is going to test me with delays; and with the delays will come suffering, but through it all stands God's pledge: His new covenant with me in Christ, and His inviolable promise of every lesser blessing that I need. The delay and the suffering are part of the promised blessing; let me praise Him for them today; and let me wait on the Lord and be of good courage and He will strengthen my heart. C. G. TRUMBULL

Unanswered yet the prayer your lips have pleaded
In agony of heart these many years?
Does faith begin to fail? Is hope departing?
And think you all in vain those falling tears?
Say not the Father hath not heard your prayer;
You shall have your desire sometime, somewhere.

Unanswered yet? Nay do not say ungranted;
Perhaps your work is not yet wholly done.
The work began when first your prayer was uttered,
And God will finish what He has begun.
If you will keep the incense burning there,
His glory you shall see sometime, somewhere.

Unanswered yet? Faith cannot be unanswered,
Her feet are firmly planted on the Rock;
Amid the wildest storms she stands undaunted,
Nor quails before the loudest thunder shock.
She knows Omnipotence has heard her prayer,
And cries, "It shall be done"—sometime, somewhere.

MISS OPHELIA G. BROWNING

And it came to pass after a while, that the brook dried up.
(1 KINGS 17:7)

God sent Elijah to the brook and it dried up. It did not prove equal to the need of the prophet. It failed; God knew it would; He made it to fail. *"The brook dried up."* This is an aspect of the Divine providence that sorely perplexes our minds and tries our faith. God knows that there are heavenly whispers that men cannot hear till the drought of trouble and perhaps weariness has silenced the babbling brooks of joy. And He is not satisfied until we have learned to depend, *not upon His gifts, but upon Himself.*
PERCY AINSWORTH

> *His camp was pitched where Cherith's stream was flowing—*
> *The man of God! 'Twas God's appointed spot!*
> *When it might fail, he knew not; only knowing*
> *That God cared for his lot.*
>
> *Full many days on Cherith's bank he camped him,*
> *And from its cool refreshing, drew his share;*
> *And foolish fears of failing streams ne'er damped him;*
> *Was he not God's own care?*
>
> *Yet, lo, at length, the prospect strangely altered;*
> *The drought e'en Cherith's fountain had assailed;*
> *Slowly but sure, the flowing waters faltered*
> *Until, at last, they failed!*
>
> *THEN came the word from One whose eye beholding*
> *Saw that the stream, the living stream had dried,*
> *Sending him forth, to find by new unfolding,*
> *None of his needs denied.*
>
> *Perchance thou, too, hath camped by such sweet waters.*
> *And quenched with joy thy weary, parched soul's thirst;*
> *To find, as time goes on, thy streamlet alters*
> *From what it was at first.*
>
> *Hearts that have cheered, or soothed, or blest, or strengthened,*
> *Loves that have lavished so unstintedly,*
> *Joys, treasured joys—have passed, as time hath lengthened,*
> *Into obscurity.*

If thus, ah soul, the brook thy heart hath cherished
Doth fail thee now—no more thy thirst assuage—
If its once glad, refreshing streams have perished,
Let HIM thy heart engage.

He will not fail, nor mock, nor disappoint thee;
His consolations change not with the years;
With oil of joy He surely will anoint thee,
And wipe away thy tears.
J. DANSON SMITH

October 19

MORNING

❧

The ark of the covenant of the Lord went before them
(NUM. 10:33).

God does give us impressions, but not that we should act on them as impressions. If the impression be from God, He will Himself give sufficient evidence to establish it beyond the possibility of a doubt.

How beautiful is the story of Jeremiah, of the impression that came to him respecting the purchase of the field of Anathoth. But Jeremiah did not act upon this impression until after the following day, when his uncle's son came to him and brought him external evidence by making a proposal for the purchase. Then Jeremiah said: *"I knew this was the word of the Lord."*

He waited until God seconded the impression by a providence, and then he acted in full view of the open facts, which could bring conviction unto others as well as to himself. God wants us to act according to His mind. We are not to ignore the Shepherd's personal voice but, like Paul and his companions at Troas, we are to listen to all the voices that speak and "gather" from all the circumstances, as they did, the full mind of the Lord. DR. SIMPSON

"Where God's finger points, there God's hand will make the way."
Do not say in thine heart what thou wilt or wilt not do, but wait upon God until He makes known His way. So long as that way is hidden it is clear that there is no need of action, and that *He accounts Himself responsible for all the results of keeping thee where thou art.* SELECTED

For God through ways we have not known,
Will lead His own.

EVENING

⤞⤝

Except a corn of wheat fall into the ground and die,
it abideth alone. (JOHN 12:24)

A peasant once came to Tauler to confess; but in place of the peasant confessing to Tauler, Tauler confessed to the peasant. The great preacher said, "I am not satisfied." The peasant replied, "Tauler has to die before he can be satisfied."

That great man, who had thousands listening to him, withdrew to a place of quiet and asked God to work out that death in him.

After he had been there for two years, he came out and assembled his congregation. A great multitude came to hear him, for he had been a wonderful preacher. He began to preach, but he broke down and wept. The audience dispersed saying, "What is the matter with Tauler? He can't preach as he once did. He failed today!"

The next time he preached only a little handful came together—those who had caught a glimpse of something—and he preached to them in a brokenhearted way; *but the power of God came down.* God, by the power of the Spirit, *had put John Tauler to death!*   SELECTED

Beloved, are you willing to be crucified with Christ?
Higher than the highest heavens,
Deeper than the deepest sea,
Lord, Thy love at last hath conquered:
Grant me now my supplication,
None of self, and all of Thee.

October 20

〜✦〜

And the peace of God, which transcends all our powers of thought,
will be a garrison to guard your hearts and minds in Christ Jesus
(PHIL. 4:7 WEYMOUTH).

*T*here is what is called the "cushion of the sea." Down beneath the surface that is agitated by storms, and driven about with winds, there is a part of the sea that is never stirred. When we dredge the bottom and bring up the remains of animal and vegetable life we find that they give evidence of not having been disturbed in the least, for hundreds and thousands of years. The peace of God is that eternal calm which, like the cushion of the sea, lies far too deep down to be reached by any external trouble or disturbance; and he who enters into the presence of God, becomes partaker of that undisturbed and undisturbable calm.

DR. A. T. PIERSON

When winds are raging o'er the upper ocean,
And billows wild contend with angry roar,
'Tis said, far down beneath the wild commotion,
That peaceful stillness reigneth evermore.

Far, far beneath, the noise of tempest dieth,
And silver waves chime ever peacefully,
And no rude storm, how fierce soe'er it flieth,
Disturbs the Sabbath of that deeper sea.

So to the heart that knows Thy love, O Purest,
There is a temple sacred evermore,
And all the babble of life's angry voices
Dies in hushed silence at its peaceful door.

Far, far away, the roar of passion dieth,
And loving thoughts rise calm and peacefully,
And no rude storm, how fierce soe'er it flieth,
Disturbs the soul that dwells, O Lord, in Thee.

HARRIET BEECHER STOWE

"The Pilgrim they laid in a large upper chamber, facing the sunrising. The name of the chamber was Peace."

FROM BUNYAN'S **PILGRIM'S PROGRESS**

And they came to the place which God had told him of. (GEN. 22:9)

There the LORD *commanded the blessing.* (PS. 133:3)

> *Up, up the hill, to the whiter than snow-shine,*
> *Help me to climb, and dwell in pardon's light.*
> *I must be pure as Thou, or ever less*
> *Than Thy design of me—therefore incline*
> *My heart to take men's wrongs as Thou tak'st mine.*

Have you come to the *place* God *told you* of? Have you gone through the sacrifice of death? Are you willing to make the moral decision that the thing die out in you which never was in Jesus?

Up to that whiter than snow-shine; up to that place that is as strong and firm as the Throne of God. Do not say, "That pure, white, holy life is never for me!" Let God lift you; let Him take the shrouds away; let Him lift up; up to the hill, *to the whiter than snow-shine.* And when you get to the top what do you find? A great, strong tableland, where your feet are on a rock; your steps enlarged under you; your goings established.

OSWALD CHAMBERS

Jesus offers you "life more abundantly." Grasp the offer! Quit the boggy and dark low ground, and let Him lead you up higher!

MOUNTAIN TOPS WITH JESUS

> *Take the supreme climb!*
> *Jesus lead me up the mountain,*
> *Where the whitest robes are seen,*
> *Where the saints can see the fountain,*
>
> *Where the pure are keeping clean.*
> *Higher up, where light increases,*
> *Rich above all earthly good,*
> *Where the life of sinning ceases,*
> *Where the Spirit comes in floods.*
>
> *Lead me higher, nothing dreading,*
> *In the race to never stop;*
> *In Thy footsteps keep me treading,*
> *Give me grace to reach the top.*
> *Courage, my soul, and let us journey on!*

October 21

∽◦∾

For we know that if our earthly house of this tabernacle were
dissolved, we have a building of God,
an house not made with hands, eternal in the heavens
(2 COR. 5:1).

The owner of the tenement which I have occupied for many years has given notice that he will furnish but little or nothing more for repairs. I am advised to be ready to move.

At first this was not a very welcome notice. The surroundings here are in many respects very pleasant, and were it not for the evidence of decay, I should consider the house good enough. But even a light wind causes it to tremble and totter, and all the braces are not sufficient to make it secure. So I am getting ready to move.

It is strange how quickly one's interest is transferred to the prospective home. I have been consulting maps of the new country and reading descriptions of its inhabitants. One who visited it has returned, and from him I learn that it is beautiful beyond description; language breaks down in attempting to tell of what he heard while there. He says that, in order to make an investment there, he has suffered the loss of all things that he owned here, and even rejoices in what others would call making a sacrifice. Another, whose love to me has been proven by the greatest possible test, is not there. He has sent me several clusters of the most delicious fruits. After tasting them, all food here seems insipid.

Two or three times I have been down by the border of the river that forms the boundary, and have wished myself among the company of those who were singing praises to the King on the other side. Many of my friends have moved there. Before leaving they spoke of my coming later. I have seen the smile upon their faces as they passed out of sight. Often I am asked to make some new investments here, but my answer in every case is, "I am getting ready to move." **SELECTED**

The words often on Jesus' lips in His last days express vividly the idea, "going to the Father." We, too, who are Christ's people, have vision of something beyond the difficulties and disappointments of this life. We are journeying toward fulfillment, completion, expansion of life. We, too, are "going to the Father." Much is dim concerning our home-country, but two things are clear. It is home, "the Father's house." It is the nearer presence of the Lord. We are all wayfarers, but the believer knows it and accepts it. He is a traveler, not a settler. R. C. GILLIE

> *The little birds trust God, for they go singing*
> *From northern woods where autumn winds have blown,*
> *With joyous faith their trackless pathway winging*
> *To summer-lands of song, afar, unknown.*
>
> *Let us go singing, then, and not go sighing:*
> *Since we are sure our times are in His hand,*
> *Why should we weep, and fear, and call it dying?*
> *'Tis only flitting to a Summer-land.*

EVINING

EVENING

Let patience have her perfect work, that ye may be perfect and entire, wanting nothing. (JAMES 1:4)

Look with Edison at his deafness, with Milton at his blindness, with Bunyan at his imprisonment, and see how patience converted these very misfortunes into good fortunes.

Michelangelo went to Rome to carve statues, and found that other artists had taken over all the Carrara marble—all but one crooked and misshapen piece. He sat down before this and studied with infinite patience its very limitations, until he found that by bending the head of a statue here, and lifting its arms there, he could create a masterpiece: thus *The Boy David* was produced.

Let us sit down in front of our very limitations, and with the aid of patience dare to produce, with God's help, *a masterpiece!*

> *"I see the stubborn heights,*
> *The bruising rocks, the straining soul."*
>
> *"I see the goal!"*
>
> *"I see the tearing plow,*
> *The crushing drag, the beating rain."*
>
> *"I see the grain!"*
>
> *"I see compressing walls,*
> *And seething flux, and heats untold."*
>
> *"I see the gold!"*

"I see the cruel blows,
The chisel sharp, the hammer's mace."

"I see My face!"
OUR VIEW AND HIS, BY PHILIP WENDELL CRANNELL

October 22

MORNING

❧

Now Moses kept the flock of Jethro his father-in-law,
the priest of Midian: and he led the flock to the backside of the desert,
and came to the mountain of God, even to Horeb.
And the angel of the Lord appeared unto him in a flame of
fire out of the midst of a bush (EXOD. 3:1–2).

The vision came in the midst of common toil, and that is where the Lord delights to give His revelations. He seeks a man who is on the ordinary road, and the divine fire leaps out at his feet. The mystic ladder can rise from the marketplace to heaven. It can connect the realm of drudgery with the realms of grace.

My Father God, help me to expect Thee on the ordinary road. I do not ask for sensational happenings. Commune with me through ordinary work and duty. Be my Companion when I take the common journey. Let the humble life be transfigured by Thy presence.

Some Christians think they must be always up to mounts of extraordinary joy and revelation; this is not after God's method. Those spiritual visits to high places, and that wonderful intercourse with the unseen world, are *not* in the promises; the daily life of communion *is*. And it is enough. We shall have the exceptional revelation if it be right for us.

There were but three disciples allowed to see the Transfiguration, and those three entered the gloom of Gethsemane. No one can stay on the mount of privilege. There are duties in the valley. Christ found His life-work, not in the glory, but in the valley and was there truly and fully the Messiah. The value of the vision and glory is but their gift of fitness for work and endurance. **SELECTED**

〰

Understanding what the will of the Lord is. (EPH. 5:17)

*I*t may seem a very terrible thing for the soul to yield itself wholly and unreservedly to the will of Christ. "What is going to happen? What about tomorrow? Will He not put a very heavy burden upon me if I yield; if I take the yoke?" Ah, you have not known my Master; you have not looked into His face; you have not realized His infinite love for you. Why, God's will for you means your fullest happiness! Christ's will and your deepest happiness are synonymous terms. How can you doubt that your Lord has planned for you the very best thing?

The admiral that goes out with his fleet under sealed orders does not know what is in the packet; but he goes out prepared to do the will of the Government of his country. And although it seems to you that you take from Christ the sealed packet of His will and know not *what* is in it, yet knowing *who He is* that has *planned your future* you can step out without realizing all that it means, just as you take His promises. *The value of any promise depends upon the promiser; and so it is with His will. Whose* will is it? *Whose* yoke is it? *"My yoke,"* says the gentle, loving Jesus; "Take *my yoke* upon you." To take His yoke is cheerfully to accept His will for us, not only in the present moment, but for the whole future that He has mapped out.

Surrender your will to God. He will never take advantage of you.

EVAN H. HOPKINS

"I dare not promise, Lord," I cried,
"For future years close-sealed.
Surrender is a fearful thing—
I long—but dare not yield."

How clear and swift the answer came:
"I only ask of thee
A present of THYSELF for time
And for eternity."

An easy thing to MAKE A GIFT!
My fears found swift release.
I gave myself to Him, and found
Past understanding, peace.

BERTHA GERNEAUX WOODS

October 23

∾

There hath not failed one word of all his good promise
(1 KINGS 8:56).

Someday we shall understand that God has a reason in every NO which He speaks through the slow movement of life. "Somehow God makes up to us." How often, when His people are worrying and perplexing themselves about their prayers not being answered, is God answering them in a far richer way! Glimpse of this we see occasionally, but the full revelation of it remains for the future.

> *If God says "Yes" to our prayer, dear heart,*
> *And the sunlight is golden, the sky is blue,*
> *While the smooth road beckons to me and you,*
> *And the song-birds warble as on we go,*
> *Pausing to gather the buds at our feet,*
> *Stopping to drink of the streamlets we meet,*
> *Happy, more happy, our journey will grow,*
> *If God says "Yes" to our prayer, dear heart.*
>
> *If God says "No" to our prayer, dear heart,*
> *And the clouds hang heavy and dull and gray;*
> *If the rough rocks hinder and block the way,*
> *While the sharp winds pierce us and sting with cold;*
> *Ah, dear, there is home at the journey's end,*
> *And these are the trials the Father doth send*
> *To draw us as sheep to His Heavenly fold,*
> *If God says "No" to our prayer, dear heart.*

Oh for the faith that does not make haste, but waits patiently for the Lord, waits for the explanation that shall come in the end, at the revelation of Jesus Christ! When did God take anything from a man, without giving him manifold more in return? Suppose that the return had not been made immediately manifest, what then? Is today the limit of God's working time? Has He no provinces beyond this little world? Does the door of the grave open upon nothing but infinite darkness and eternal silence?

Yet, even confining the judgment within the hour of this life, it is true that God never touches the heart with a trial without intending to bring upon it some grander gift, some tenderer benediction. *He has attained to an eminent degree of Christian grace who knows how to wait.*

SELECTED

When the frosts are in the valley,
And the mountain tops are grey,
And the choicest buds are blighted,
And the blossoms die away,
A loving Father whispers,
"This cometh from my hand";
Blessed are ye if ye trust
Where ye cannot understand.

If, after years of toiling,
Your wealth should fly away
And leave your hands all empty,
And your locks are turning grey,
Remember then your Father
Owns all the sea and land;
Blessed are ye if ye trust
Where ye cannot understand.

SELECTED

EVENING

Mending their nets; and he called them. (MATT. 4:21)

Salome! Had you been with me in the boat,
You would not chide and moan because our boys
Have gone with the Beloved from this our home.
Let me, Salome, tell you how it came.
The night was still—the tide was running strong,
Heavy our nets—the strain reached breaking point,
And while 'twas dark we docked, and as we worked
I felt as though new strength and steady joy
Surged through my being, so I sang a Psalm—
As David sang—a song to greet the morn;
And then my heart was filled with quiet calm.

The boat was soon in order, and we turned
To dry and mend our nets. Then Jesus came—
He called the boys, first John, then James, by name,
And they arose and went to follow Him.
I turned and gazed on Jesus standing there—
He seemed to me all clothed in shining light
As He stood in the pathway with the night
Behind Him and the dawn breaking around,
His form so radiant and glad and free.

And when He climbed the hill our sons went too—
James was behind, and John was by His side;
And when they talked, John scarcely seemed our John—
I felt that he had caught a marvelous light.
And all my being seemed to overflow;
I knew that night had passed—the dawn had come,
And then I knew that we must let them go.
ZEBEDEE'S SONS

"So shall his part be that tarrieth by the stuff: they shall part alike" (1 Sam. 30:24).

To some Christ calls: "Leave boat and bay,
And white-haired Zebedee";
To some the call is harder: "Stay
And mend the nets for Me."
SELECTED

October 24

MORNING

~~~

I will make thee a new sharp threshing instrument (ISA. 41:15).

A bar of steel worth five dollars, when wrought into horseshoes, is worth ten dollars. If made into needles, it is worth three hundred and fifty dollars; if into penknife blades, it is worth thirty-two thousand dollars; if into springs for watches it is worth two hundred and fifty thousand dollars. What a drilling the poor bar must undergo to be worth this!

But the more it is manipulated, the more it is hammered, and passed through the fire, and beaten and pounded and polished, the greater the value.

May this parable help us to be silent, still, and long-suffering. Those who suffer most are capable of yielding most; and it is through pain that God is getting the most out of us, for His glory and the blessing of others.

SELECTED

> Oh, give Thy servant patience to be still,
> And bear Thy will;
> Courage to venture wholly on the arm
> That will not harm;
> The wisdom that will never let me stray
> Out of my way;
> The love that, now afflicting, knoweth best
> When I should rest.

Life is very mysterious. Indeed it would be inexplicable unless we believed that God was preparing us for scenes and ministries that lie beyond the veil of sense in the eternal world, where highly-tempered spirits will be required for special service.

"The turning-lathe that has the sharpest knives produces the finest work."

EVENING

Return to thy place, and abide with the king. (2 SAM. 15:19)

There is a little fable which says that a primrose growing by itself in a shady corner of the garden became discontented as it saw the other flowers in their gay beds in the sunshine, and begged to be removed to a more conspicuous place. Its prayer was granted. The gardener transplanted it to a more showy and sunny spot. It was greatly pleased, but there came a change over it immediately. Its blossoms lost much of their beauty, and became pale and sickly. The hot sun caused them to faint and wither. So it prayed again to be taken back to its old place in the shade. The wise gardener knew best where to plant each flower.

So God, the Divine Husbandman, knows where His children will best grow into what He would have them to be. Some require the fierce storms; some will only thrive spiritually in the shadow of worldly adversity; and some come to ripeness more sweetly under the soft and gentle influences of prosperity, whose beauty rough experiences would mar.

Humbolt, the great naturalist and traveler, said that the most wonderful sight he had ever seen was a primrose flourishing on the bosom of a glacier.

The brightest souls which glory ever knew
Were rocked in storms and nursed when tempests blew.

October 25

MORNING

Hitherto have ye asked nothing in my name: ask and ye shall receive, that your joy may be full (JOHN 16:24).

During the Civil War, a man had an only son who enlisted in the armies of the Union. The father was a banker and, although he consented to his son's going, it seemed as if it would break his heart to let him go.

He became deeply interested in the soldier boys, and whenever he saw a uniform, his heart went out as he thought of his own dear boy. He spent his time, neglected his business, gave his money to caring for the soldiers who came home invalid. His friends remonstrated with him, saying he had no right to neglect his business and spend so much thought upon the soldiers, so he fully decided to give it all up.

After he had come to this decision, there stepped into his bank one day a private soldier in a faded, worn uniform, who showed in his face and hands the marks of the hospital.

The poor fellow was fumbling in his pocket to get something or other, when the banker saw him and, perceiving his purpose, said to him:

"My dear fellow, I cannot do anything for you today. I am extremely busy. You will have to go to your headquarters; the officers there will look after you."

Still the poor convalescent stood not seeming to fully understand what was said to him. Still he fumbled in his pockets and, by and by, drew out a scrap of dirty paper, on which there were a few lines written with a pencil, and laid this soiled sheet before the banker. On it he found these words:

"Dear Father: This is one of my comrades who was wounded in the last fight, and has been in the hospital. Please receive him as myself.—Charlie."

In a moment all the resolutions of indifference which this man made, flew away. He took the boy to his palatial home, put him in Charlie's room, gave him Charlie's seat at the table, kept him until food and rest and love had brought him back to health, and then sent him back again to imperil his life for the flag.   SELECTED

"Now shalt thou SEE what I will do" (Exod. 6:1).

EVENING

He that goeth aside to sit quietly in the secret place with the Most High, will find him coming over so close that this man shall be lodging under the very shadow of the Almighty.
(PS. 91:1, FREE TRANS.)

*I*t was my practice to rise at midnight for worship. God came to me at that precise time and awoke me from sleep that I might enjoy HIM. He seemed to pervade my being. My soul became more and more attracted to Himself like the waters of a river which pass into the ocean and after a time become one with it. Oh, unutterable happiness! Who could have thought that one should ever find happiness equal to this!

Hours passed like moments, when I could do nothing else but pray. It was a prayer of rejoicing, of possession, when the taste of GOD was so great, so pure, so unblended that it drew and absorbed the soul into a profound state of confiding and affectionate rest in God, without intellectual effort for I had no sight but of Jesus only.

                                                        MADAME GUYON

A moment in the morning ere the cares of the day begin,
Ere the heart's wide door is open for the world to enter in;
Ah, then, alone with Jesus, in the silence of the morn,
In heavenly sweet communion, let your happy day be born;
In the quietude that blesses with a prelude of repose,
Let your soul be soothed and softened as the dew revives the rose.

Two men were confessing to each other the causes of their failure in the ministry. "I let my hand slip out of God's hand," said one. The other said, "My soul-life raveled at the point where I ceased to pray, because there were things in my life I could not speak to God about." *Prayer is a handclasp with God.*

Take time for prayer if you have to take it by violence. *Take time to behold Him!*

October 26

MORNING

He went up into a mountain apart to pray: and when the evening was come, he was there alone (MATT. 14:23).

The man Christ Jesus felt the need of perfect solitude—*Himself alone*, entirely by Himself, alone with Himself. We know how much intercourse with men draws us away from ourselves and exhausts our powers. The man Christ Jesus knew this, too, and felt the need of being by Himself again, of gathering all His powers, of realizing fully His high destiny, His human weakness, His entire dependence on the Father.

How much more does the child of God need this—*himself alone* with spiritual realities, *himself alone* with God the Father. If ever there were one who could dispense with special seasons for solitude and fellowship, it was our Lord. But He could not do His work or maintain His fellowship in full power, without His quiet time.

Would God that every servant of His understood and practiced this blessed art, and that the church knew how to train its children into some sense of this high and holy privilege, that every believer may and must have his time when he is indeed himself alone with God. Oh, the thought to have God all alone to myself, and to know that God has me all alone to Himself!   **ANDREW MURRAY**

Lamertine speaks in one of his books of a secluded walk in his garden where his mother always spent a certain hour of the day, upon which nobody ever dreamed for a moment of intruding. It was the holy garden of the Lord to her. Poor souls that have no such Beulah land! Seek thy private chamber, Jesus says. It is in the solitude that we catch the mystic notes that issue from the soul of things.

A Meditation

My soul, practice being alone with Christ! It is written that *when they were alone He expounded all things to His disciples.* Do not wonder at the saying; it is true to thine experience. If thou wouldst understand *thyself* send the multitude away. Let them go out one by one till thou art left alone with Jesus. . . . Has thou ever pictured thyself the one remaining creature in the earth, the one remaining creature in all the starry worlds?

In such a universe thine every thought would be "God and I! God and I!" And yet He is as near to thee as that—as near as if in the boundless spaces there throbbed no heart but His and thine. Practice that solitude, O my soul! Practice the expulsion of the crowd! Practice the stillness of thine own heart! Practice the solemn refrain "God and I! God and I!" Let none interpose between thee and thy wrestling angel! Thou shalt be both condemned and pardoned when thou shalt meet Jesus alone!

GEORGE MATHESON

EVENING

Because this widow troubleth me, I will avenge her. (LUKE 18:5)

We should be careful about what we ask from God; but when once we begin to pray for a thing we should never give up praying for it until we receive it, or until God makes it very clear and definite that it is not His will to grant it. R. A. TORREY

It is said of John Bradford that he had a peculiar art in prayer. When asked his secret, he said: "When I know what I want, I always stop on that prayer until I feel that I have pleaded it with God, and until God and I have had dealings with each other upon it. I never go on to another petition until I have gone through the first."

To the same point Mr. Spurgeon said: "Do not try to put two arrows on the string at once—they will both miss. He that would load his gun with two charges cannot expect to be successful. Plead once with God and prevail, and then plead again. Get the first answer and then go after the second. Do not be satisfied with running the colors of your prayers into one another until there is no picture to look at, but just a huge daub—a smear of colors badly laid on."

Far better would it be to know what our real needs are, and then concentrate our earnest supplications upon those definite objects, taking them thoughtfully one at a time.

"Ask what I shall give thee."

October 27

〜

All thy waves and thy billows are gone over me (PS. 42:7).

They are HIS billows, whether they go o'er us,
Hiding His face in smothering spray and foam;
Or smooth and sparkling, spread a path before us,
And to our haven bear us safely home.

They are HIS billows, whether for our succor
He walks across them, stilling all our fears;
Or to our cry there comes no aid nor answer,
And in the lonely silence none is near.

They are HIS billows, whether we are toiling
Through tempest-driven waves that never cease,
While deep to deep with clamor loud is calling;
Or at His word they hush themselves in peace.

They are HIS billows, whether He divides them,
Making us walk dryshod where seas had flowed;
Or lets tumultuous breakers surge about us,
Rushing unchecked across our only road.

They are HIS billows, and He brings us through them;
So He has promised, so His love will do.
Keeping and leading, guiding and upholding,
To His sure harbor, He will bring us through.
ANNIE JOHNSON FLINT

Stand up in the place where the dear Lord has put you, and there do your best. God gives us trial tests. He puts life before us as an antagonist face-to-face. Out of the buffeting of a serious conflict we are expected to grow strong. The tree that grows where tempests toss its boughs and bend its trunk often almost to breaking, is often more firmly rooted than the tree which grows in the sequestered valley where no storm ever brings stress or strain. The same is true of life. The grandest character is grown in hardship. **SELECTED**

❧❧

God spake. (GEN. 46:2)

*A*ny man may hear the voice of God.

When man will listen, God speaks. When God speaks, men are changed. When men are changed, nations are changed.

In the ancient days *God spake,* and the wonderful things which He told Moses on the mountaintop have inspired mankind for centuries.

Down through the years men of God have heard His voice. *God spake* to George Müller, and he became the modern apostle of faith. Hudson Taylor heard Him speak, as he walked by the seashore on a memorable Sabbath morning, and in obedience to that Voice he launched forth into inland China, establishing Mission Stations in every province of that vast country.

God spake to Dr. A. B. Simpson and he stepped aside from a well-beaten path, and like Abraham of old "went forth, not knowing whither he went." Today, *The Christian and Missionary Alliance,* operating in more than twenty Mission Fields of the world, is the result of his obedience and untold numbers have been blessed through his ministry.

Charles Cowman heard the "soft and gentle Voice," when *God spake* saying, "Get thee out of thy country, and from thy kindred, and from thy father's house, unto a land that I will show thee." The result—The Oriental Missionary Society, with hundreds of Mission Stations dotted all over the Orient! And now its activities embrace the wide world.

God is not dumb that He should speak no more.
If thou hast wanderings in the wilderness
And find'st not Sinai, 'tis thy soul is poor:
There towers the mountain of the Voice no less,
Which whoso seeks shall find; but he who bends
Intent on manna still, and mortal ends,
Sees it not, neither hears its thundering lore.
LOWELL

October 28

But God, who is rich in mercy, for his great love wherewith he loved us, even when we were dead in sins, hath quickened us together with Christ . . . and hath raised us up together, and made us sit together in heavenly places in Christ Jesus (EPH. 2:4–6).

This is our rightful place, to be "seated in heavenly places in Christ Jesus," and to "sit still" there. But how few there are who make it their actual experience! How few, indeed, think even that it is possible for them to "sit still" in these "heavenly places" in the everyday life of a world so full of turmoil as this.

We may believe perhaps that to pay a little visit to these heavenly places on Sundays, or now and then in times of spiritual exaltation, may be within the range of possibility; but to be actually "seated" there *every day and all day long* is altogether another matter; and yet it is very plain that it is for Sundays and weekdays as well.

A quiet spirit is of inestimable value in carrying on outward activities; and nothing so hinders the working of the hidden spiritual forces, upon which, after all, our success in everything really depends, as a spirit of unrest and anxiety.

There is immense power in stillness. A great saint once said, "All things come to him who knows how to trust and be silent." The words are pregnant with meaning. A knowledge of this fact would immensely change our ways of working. Instead of restless struggles, we would "sit down" inwardly before the Lord, and would let the divine forces of His Spirit work out in silence the ends to which we aspire. You may not see or feel the operations of this silent force, but be assured it is always working mightily, and will work for you, if you only get your spirit still enough to be carried along by the currents of its power.   **HANNAH WHITALL SMITH**

> There is a point of rest
> At the great center of the cyclone's force,
> A silence at its secret source;
> A little child might slumber undisturbed,
> Without the ruffle of one fair curl,
> In that strange, central calm, amid the mighty whirl.

It is your business to learn to be peaceful and safe in God in every situation.

EVENING

Ye have compassed this mountain long enough: turn . . . northward.
(DEUT. 2:3)

*L*ast summer a party of us lost our way among the lakes of Ontario. A violent storm came up, but we found shelter under a great rock till the storm raged past. Then we resumed our hunt dispiritedly until one said, *"Let us climb this rock; we may spy the trail from the top."* It was a hard climb, but the challenge of the rock restored our courage. As we *conquered the heights* we gained confidence and mastery, and *the hilltop gave us a vision of* our way out.

Get high enough up, you will be above the fog; and while the men down in it are squabbling as to whether there is anything outside the mist, you from your sunny station will see the far-off coasts, and haply catch some whiff of perfume from their shores, or see some glinting of glory upon the shining turrets of "the city that hath foundations."

The soul which hath launched itself forth upon God is in a free place, filled with the fresh air of the hills of God.

Oh, there are heavenly heights to reach
In many a fearful place,
While the poor, timid heir of God
Lies blindly on his face;
Lies languishing for light Divine
That he shall never see
'Till he goes forward at Thy sign,
And trusts himself to Thee.
C. A. FOX

We are continually retreating behind our limitations and saying, "Thus far and no farther can I go." God is ever laying His hand upon us and thrusting us into the open, saying, *"You can be more than you are; you must be more than you are."*

Are the hills of God thine atmosphere?

October 29

He shall sit as a refiner and purifer of silver (MAL. 3:3).

Our Father, who seeks to perfect His saints in holiness, knows the value of the refiner's fire. It is with the most precious metals that the assayer takes the most pains, and subjects them to the hot fire, because such fires melt the metal, and only the molten mass releases its alloy or takes perfectly its new form in the mold. *The old refiner never leaves his crucible, but sits down by it,* lest there should be one excessive degree of heat to mar the metal. But as soon as he skims from the surface the last of the dross, and sees his own face reflected, he puts out the fire.

ARTHUR T. PIERSON

He sat by a fire of seven-fold heat,
As He watched by the precious ore,
And closer He bent with a searching gaze
As He heated it more and more.
He knew He had ore that could stand the test,
And He wanted the finest gold
To mould as a crown for the King to wear,
Set with gems with a price untold.
So He laid our gold in the burning fire,
Tho' we fain would have said Him "Nay,"
And He watched the dross that we had not seen,
And it melted and passed away.
And the gold grew brighter and yet more bright,
But our eyes were so dim with tears,
We saw but the fire—not the Master's hand,
And questioned with anxious fears.
Yet our gold shone out with a richer glow,
As it mirrored a Form above,
That bent o'er the fire, tho' unseen by us,
With a look of ineffable love.
Can we think that it pleases His loving heart
To cause us a moment's pain?
Ah, no! but He saw through the present cross
The bliss of eternal gain.
So He waited there with a watchful eye,

With a love that is strong and sure,
And His gold did not suffer a bit more heat,
Than was needed to make it pure.

EVENING

❦

We will flee upon horses. (ISA. 30:16)

God is never slow from *His* standpoint, but He is from *ours,* because impetuosity and doing things prematurely are universal weaknesses.

God lives and moves in eternity, and every little detail in His working must be like Himself, and have in it the majesty and measured movement, as well as the accuracy and promptness of infinite wisdom. We are to *let God do the swiftness* and *we do the slowness.*

The Holy Spirit tells us to "be swift to hear, slow to speak, slow to wrath," that is, *swift* to *take in from God,* but *slow* to *give out the opinions, the emotions of the creature.*

We miss a great many things from God by not going slow enough with Him. Who would have God change His perfections to accommodate our whims? Have we not had glimpses into God's perfections, insight into wonderful truths, quiet unfoldings of daily opportunities, gentle checks of the Holy Spirit upon our decisions or words, sweet and secret promptings to do certain things?

There is a time for everything in the universe to get ripe—and *to go slow with God is the heavenly pace that gathers up all things at the time they are ripe.*

What they win, who wait for God, is worth waiting for!
Going slow with God is our greatest safety!

October 30

❧≈❧

Let us run with patience (HEB. 12:1).

To *run* with patience is a very difficult thing. Running is apt to suggest the *absence* of patience, the eagerness to reach the goal. We commonly associate patience with lying down. We think of it as the angel that
guards the couch of the invalid. Yet, I do not think the invalid's patience
the hardest to achieve.

There is a patience which I believe to be harder—the patience that
can run. To lie down in the time of grief, to be quiet under the stroke
of adverse fortune, implies a great strength; but I know of something
that implies a strength greater still: It is the power to *work* under a
stroke; to have a great weight at your heart and still to run; to have a
deep anguish in your spirit and still perform the daily task. It is a Christlike thing!

Many of us would nurse our grief without crying if we were *allowed*
to nurse it. The hard thing is that most of us are called to exercise our
patience, not in bed, but in the street. We are called to bury our sorrows
not in lethargic quiescence, but in active service—in the exchange, in the
workshop, in the hour of social intercourse, in the contribution to another's joy. There is no burial of sorrow so difficult as that; it is the *"running
with patience."*

This was *Thy* patience, O Son of man! It was at once a waiting and a
running—a waiting for the goal, and a doing of the lesser work meantime.
I see Thee at Cana turning the water into wine lest the marriage feast
should be clouded. I see Thee in the desert feeding a multitude with
bread just to relieve a temporary want. All, all the time, Thou wert bearing a mighty grief, unshared, unspoken. Men ask for a rainbow in the
cloud; but I would ask *more* from Thee. I would be, in my cloud, myself
a rainbow—a minister to others' joy. My patience will be perfect when it
can *work* in the vineyard.   GEORGE MATHESON

When all our hopes are gone,
'Tis well our hands must keep toiling on
For others' sake:
For strength to bear is found in duty done;
And he is best indeed who learns to make
The joy of others cure his own heartache.

༄

Not yours, but God's. (2 CHRON. 20:15)

*T*here are times when doing nothing is better than doing something. Those are the times when only God can do what is needed. True faith trusts Him then, and Him alone, to do the miracle. Moses and Jehoshaphat knew this secret; they knew the same Lord and the same Divine grace.

As the pursuing Egyptians trapped the helpless Israelites at the Red Sea, Moses said: "Fear ye not, stand still, and see the salvation of the LORD. . . . The LORD shall fight for you, and ye shall hold your peace" (Ex. 14:13–14).

As the Moabites and the Ammonites, a vast multitude, closed in on Judah, King Jehoshaphat said to the helpless people: "Be not afraid nor dismayed by reason of this great multitude; for *the battle is not yours, but God's*. . . . Ye shall not need to fight in this battle: set yourselves, stand ye still, and see the salvation of the LORD." (2 Chron. 20:15, 17, emphasis added).

When God alone can win the victory, faith lets God do it all. It is better to trust than to try.   **SUNDAY SCHOOL TIMES**

"Faith is the Victory that Overcomes."

> *The battle is not yours, but God's;*
> *Therefore why fight?*
> *True faith will cease from struggling,*
> *And rest upon His might:*
> *Each conflict into which you come*
> *Was* WON *on Calvary,*
> *Tis ours to claim what Christ has done,*
> *And "hold" the victory.*

H. E. JESSOP

"Hold thee still." "And this," says Saint Jerome, "is the hardest precept that is given to man: inasmuch as the most difficult precept of action sinks into nothingness when compared with this command to inaction."

October 31

～ふ⌒

Likewise the Spirit also helpeth our infirmities;
for we know not what we should pray for as we ought;
but the Spirit itself maketh intercession for us with groanings
which cannot be uttered. And he that searcheth the hearts knoweth
what is the mind of the Spirit, because he maketh intercession
for the saints according to the will of God (ROM. 8:26–27).

This is the deep mystery of prayer. This is the delicate divine mechanism which words cannot interpret, and which theology cannot explain, but which the humblest believer knows even when he does not understand.

Oh, the burdens that we love to bear and cannot understand! Oh, the inarticulate outreachings of our hearts for things we cannot comprehend! And yet we know they are an echo from the throne and a whisper from the heart of God. It is often a groan rather than a song, a burden rather than a buoyant wing. But it is a blessed burden, and it is a groan whose undertone is praise and unutterable joy. It is "a groaning which cannot be uttered." We could not ourselves express it always, and sometimes we do not understand any more than that God is praying in us, for something that needs His touch and that He understands.

And so we can just pour out the fullness of our heart, the burden of our spirit, the sorrow that crushes us, and know that He hears, He loves, He understands, He receives; and He separates from our prayer all that is imperfect, ignorant and wrong, and presents the rest, with the incense of the great High Priest, before the throne on high; and our prayer is heard, accepted, and answered in His name. **A. B. SIMPSON**

It is not necessary to be always speaking to God or always hearing from God, to have communion with Him; there is an inarticulate fellowship more sweet than words. The little child can sit all day long beside its busy mother and, although few words are spoken on either side, and both are busy, the one at his absorbing play, the other at her engrossing work, yet both are in perfect fellowship. He knows that she is there, and she knows that he is all right. So the saint and the Savior can go on for hours in the silent fellowship of love, and he be busy about the most common things, and yet conscious that every little thing he does is touched with the complexion of His presence, and the sense of His approval and blessing.

And then, when pressed with burdens and trouble too complicated to put into words and too mysterious to tell or understand, how sweet it is to fall back into His blessed arms, and just sob out the sorrow that we cannot speak!

SELECTED

EVENING

And as he lay and slept under a juniper tree, behold, then an angel touched him. (1 KINGS 19:5)

God does not chide His tired child when that weariness is a result of toil for Him: "I know thy toil" (Rev. 2:2)—the Greek is *"labor to weariness."* And what happened? "Behold, then an angel touched him." There is no wilderness without its angels. Though Elijah knew it not, angels guarded him round about in his blackest depression and were actually placing bread and water at his head while he was asking for death.

A man may have to cry in the midst of an apostate community, "I, even I only, am left"; *but he is always companied by legions of holy angels.* But more than that. Who is *this* angel? It is the Angel of the LORD, the *Jehovah Angel;* the One who, centuries later in Gethsemane, had to have an angel to strengthen *Him.* He touched His exhausted child. Blessed exhaustion that can bring such a touch!

As the Psalmist has said (Ps. 127:2), "He giveth to His beloved while they sleep" (RSV, margin). And God does not chide His tired child.

THE DAWN

Dear child, God does not say today, "Be strong";
He knows your strength is spent; He knows how long
The road has been, how weary you have grown,
For He who walked the earthly roads alone,
Each bogging lowland, and each rugged hill,
Can understand, and so He says, "Be still,
And know that I am God." The hour is late,
And you must rest awhile, and you must wait
Until life's empty reservoirs fill up
As slow rain fills an empty upturned cup.
Hold up your cup, dear child, for God to fill.
He only asks today that you be still.

GRACE NOLL CROWELL

November 1

❦

When the cloud tarried . . . then the children of Israel . . .
journeyed not (NUM. 9:19).

This was the supreme test of obedience. It was comparatively easy to strike tents, when the fleecy folds of the cloud were slowly gathering from off the tabernacle, and it floated majestically before the host. Change is always delightful; and there was excitement and interest in the route, the scenery, and the locality of the next halting-place. But, ah, the tarrying.

Then, however uninviting and sultry the location, however trying to flesh and blood, however irksome to the impatient disposition, however perilously exposed to danger—there was no option but to remain encamped.

The psalmist says, *"I waited patiently for the Lord; and he inclined unto me, and heard my cry."* And what He did for the Old Testament saints He will do for believers throughout all ages.

Still God often keeps us waiting. Face to face with threatening foes, in the midst of alarms, encircled by perils, beneath the impending rock. May we not go? Is it not time to strike our tents? Have we not suffered to the point of utter collapse? May we not exchange the glare and heat for green pastures and still waters?

There is no answer. The cloud tarries, and we must remain, though sure of manna, rock-water, shelter, and defense. God never keeps us at post without assuring us of His presence, and sending us daily supplies.

Wait, young man, do not be in a hurry to make a change! Minister, remain at your post! Until the cloud clearly moves, you must tarry. Wait, then, thy Lord's good pleasure! He will be in plenty of time!

FROM DAILY DEVOTIONAL COMMENTARY

An hour of waiting!
Yet there seems such need
To reach that spot sublime!
I long to reach them—but I long far more
To trust HIS time!

"Sit still, my daughter"—
Yet the heathen die,

They perish while I stay!
I long to reach them—but I long far more
To trust HIS way!

'Tis good to get,
'Tis good indeed to give!
Yet is it better still—
O'er breadth, thro' length, down length, up height.
To trust HIS will!

F. M. N.

EVENING

❧

Therefore it is of faith . . . to the end the promise might be sure.
(ROM. 4:16)

The great devotional teacher of the past century, Dr. Andrew Murray, said, *"When you get a promise from God it is worth just as much as fulfillment. A promise brings you into direct contact with God. Honor Him by trusting the promise and obeying Him." Worth just as much as fulfillment.* Do we grasp the truth often? Are we not frequently in the state of *trying* to believe, instead of realizing that these promises bring us into contact with God? *"God's promise is as good as His presence."* To believe and accept the promise of God is not to engage in some mental gymnastics where we reach down into our imaginations and begin a process of auto-suggestion, or produce a notional faith in which we argue with ourselves in an endeavor to believe God. It is absolute confidence in and reliance upon God through His Word.

By a naked faith in a naked promise I do not mean *a bare assent* that God is faithful, and that such a promise in the Book of God *may* be fulfilled in me, but *a bold, hearty, steady venturing* of my soul, body, and spirit upon the truth of the promise with an appropriating act.

FLETCHER

"The faith that will shut the mouths of lions must be more than a pious hope that they will not bite."

November 2

❦

But prayer . . . (ACTS 12:5).

*B*ut prayer is the link that connects us with God. This is the bridge that spans every gulf and bears me over every abyss of danger or of need.

How significant the picture of the apostolic church: Peter in prison, the Jews triumphant, Herod supreme, the arena of martyrdom awaiting the dawning of the morning to drink up the apostle's blood, and everything else against it. *"But prayer was made unto God without ceasing."* And what was the sequel? The prison open, the apostle free, the Jews baffled, the wicked king eaten of worms, a spectacle of hidden retribution, and the Word of God rolling on in greater victory.

Do we know the power of our supernatural weapon? Do we dare to use it with the authority of a faith that commands as well as asks? God baptizes us with holy audacity and divine confidence! He is not wanting great men, but He is wanting men who will dare to prove the greatness of their God. But God! But prayer! A. B. SIMPSON

Beware in your prayer, above everything, of limiting God, not only by unbelief, but by fancying that you know what He can do. Expect unexpected things, *above all* that we ask or think. Each time you intercede, be quiet first and worship God in His glory. Think of what He can do, of how He delights to hear Christ, of your place in Christ; and expect great things. ANDREW MURRAY

Our prayers are God's opportunities.

Are you in sorrow? Prayer can make your affliction sweet and strengthening. Are you in gladness? Prayer can add to your joy a celestial perfume. Are you in extreme danger from outward or inward enemies? Prayer can set at your right hand an angel whose touch could shatter a millstone into smaller dust than the flour it grinds, and whose glance could lay an army low. What will prayer do for you? I answer: All that God can do for you. "Ask what I shall give thee." FARRAR

Wrestling prayer can wonders do,
Bring relief in deepest straits;
Prayer can force a passage through
Iron bars and brazen gates.

Thy way is in the sea, and thy path in the great waters. (PS. 77:19)

God's path is in the sea"—just where you would not expect it to be! So when He leads us out by unexpected ways, off the strong solid land, out upon the changing sea, *then* we may expect to see *His ways.* We are with One who finds a path already tracked out, for it makes us perfectly independent of circumstances.

There is an infinite variety in the paths God makes, and He can make them *anywhere!* Think you not that He, who made the spider able to drop anywhere and to spin its own path as it goes, is not able to spin a path for you through every blank, or perplexity, or depression? God is never lost among our mysteries. He sees the road, "the end from the beginning."

Mystery and uncertainty are only to prepare us for deeper discipline. Had we no stormy sea we should remain weaklings to the end of our days. God takes us out into the deeps; but He knows the track! He knows the haven! and we shall arrive.

And with Jesus
Through the trackless deep move on!
C. A. FOX

"O fathomless abyss of God's rich bounty, of His wisdom, of His knowledge! Who can explore His decisions? Who can track out His paths?" *(Rom. 11:33, Way's trans.).*

November 3

MORNING

On all bare heights shall be their pasture (ISA. 40:9 RV).

Joys and trinkets are easily won, but the greatest things are greatly bought. The topmost place of power is always bought with blood. You may have the pinnacles if you have enough blood to pay. That is the conquest condition of the holy heights everywhere. The story of real heroisms is the story of sacrificial blood. The chief values in life and character are not blown across our way by vagrant winds. Great souls have great sorrows.

Great truths are dearly bought, the common truths,
Such as men give and take from day to day,
Come in the common walk of easy life,
Blown by the careless wind across our way.

Great truths are greatly won, not found by chance,
Nor wafted on the breath of summer dream;
But grasped in the great struggle of the soul,
Hard buffeting with adverse wind and stream.

But in the day of conflict, fear and grief,
When the strong hand of God, put forth in might,
Plows up the subsoil of the stagnant heart,
And brings the imprisoned truth seed to the light.

Wrung from the troubled spirit, in hard hours
Of weakness, solitude, perchance of pain,
Truth springs like harvest from the well-plowed field,
And the soul feels it has not wept in vain.

The capacity for knowing God enlarges as we are brought by Him into circumstances which oblige us to exercise faith; so, when difficulties beset our path, let us thank God that He is taking trouble with us and lean hard upon Him.

EVINING

The life also of Jesus . . . made manifest in our mortal flesh.
(2 COR. 4:11)

We may have two lives. First, our own life inherited from our parents and given us by our Creator. That life has some value, but how soon it fails and feels the forces of disease, decay, and approaching death!

But we may have another life, or rather the Life of Another—*the life also of Jesus.* How much more valuable and transcendent is this life! It has no weakness nor decay nor limitation. Jesus has a physical life as real as ours, and infinitely greater; He is an actual *man* with a glorified body and a human spirit. And that life belongs to us just as much as the precious blood He shed and the spiritual grace He bestows. He has risen and ascended as our living Head and He is ever saying to us, *"Because I live, ye shall live also."*

Why should we limit Him to what we call the spiritual realm? His resurrection body has in it all the vitality and strength that our mortal frame can ever need. Someday He is to raise us from the dead by virtue of that resurrection life. Why should it be thought *a strange thing* if faith may now *foredate its inheritance* and *claim in advance* part of its physical redemption—a little handful of the soil of that better country—just as a seed is to bring forth more glorious fruit?

This was Paul's experience. Why may it not be *ours*? There was a day at Lystra when under a shower of stones Paul's life was ebbing out and he was left for dead outside the city gates. Then it was that *the life also of Jesus* asserted itself, and, calmly rising up in the strength of his Master, he walked back through the streets whose stones were stained by his own blood, and quietly went on his way preaching the Gospel as if nothing had happened.

The secret of this life is to live so close to Jesus that we shall breathe His very breath and ever be in touch with His life and love. So let us live by Him. Healing is in His living body. We *receive* it as we abide in Him. We *keep* it only as we abide in Him. A. B. SIMPSON

There are miraculous possibilities for the one who depends on God.

November 4

MORNING

~∞~

As I was among the captives by the river of Chebar . . .
the heavens were opened and I saw visions of God . . . and the hand
of the Lord was there upon—me—(EZEK. 1:1, 3).

There is no commentator of the Scriptures half so valuable as a captivity. The old psalms have quavered for us with a new pathos as we sat by our "Babel's stream," and have sounded for us with new joy as we found our captivity turned as the streams in the south.

The man who has seen much affliction will not readily part with his copy of the Word of God. Another book may seem to others to be identical with his own; but it is not the same to him, for over his old and tearstained Bible he has written, in characters which are visible to no eyes but his own, the record of his experiences, and ever and anon he comes on Bethel pillars or Elim palms, which are to him the memorials of some critical chapter in his history.

If we are to receive benefit from our captivity we must accept the situation and turn it to the best possible account. Fretting over that from which we have been removed or which has been taken away from us, will not make things better, but it will prevent us from improving those which remain. The bond is only tightened by our stretching it to the uttermost.

The impatient horse which will not quietly endure his halter only strangles himself in his stall. The high-mettled animal that is restive in the yoke only galls his shoulders; and everyone will understand the difference between the restless starling of which Sterne has written, breaking its wings against the bars of the cage, and crying, "I can't get out, I can't get out," and the docile canary that sits upon its perch and sings as if it would outrival the lark soaring to heaven's gate.

No calamity can be to us an unmixed evil if we carry it in direct and fervent prayer to God, for even as one in taking shelter from the rain beneath a tree may find on its branches fruit which he looked not for, so we in fleeing for refuge beneath the shadow of God's wing, will always find more in God than we had seen or known before.

It is thus through our trials and afflictions that God gives us fresh revelations of Himself; and the Jabbok ford leads to Peniel, where, as the result of our wrestling, we "see God face-to-face," and our lives are preserved. Take this to thyself, O captive, and He will give thee "songs in the night," and turn for thee "the shadow of death into the morning."

WILLIAM TAYLOR

"Submission to the divine will is the softest pillow on which to recline."
It filled the room, and it filled my life,

> *With a glory of source unseen;*
> *It made me calm in the midst of strife,*
> *And in winter my heart was green.*
> *And the birds of promise sang on the tree*
> *When the storm was breaking on land and sea.*

EVENING

⮞⮜

Break forth into singing. (ISA. 49:13)

There is a beautiful story which tells of songbirds being brought over the sea. There were thirty-six thousand, mostly canaries. The sea was very calm when the ship first sailed, and the little birds were silent. They kept their little heads under their wings and not a note was heard. But the third day out at sea, the ship struck a furious gale. The passengers were terrified. Children wept. Then a strange thing happened. As the tempest reached its height, the birds began to sing, first one, then another, until the thirty-six thousand were singing as if their little throats would burst.

When the storm rises in its fury, do we then begin to sing? Should not our song break forth in tenfold joy when the tempest begins?

I can hear the songbirds singing their refrain
It is morning in my heart;
And I know that life for me begins again,
It is morning in my heart.

It is morning, it is morning in my heart,
Jesus made the gloomy shadows all depart;
Songs of gladness now I sing,
For since Jesus is my King,
It is morning, it is morning in my heart.

O God, wilt Thou teach us to begin the music of heaven! Grant us grace to have many rehearsals of eternal Hallelujahs! "Bless the LORD, O my soul: and all that is within me, bless his holy name!"

Try singing! Singing in the storm!

November 5

MORNING

❧

Is anything too hard for the Lord? (GEN. 18:14)

*H*ere is God's loving challenge to you and to me today. He wants us to think of the deepest, highest, worthiest desire and longing of our hearts, something which perhaps was our desire for ourselves or for someone dear to us, yet which has been so long unfulfilled that we have looked upon it as only a lost desire, that which might have been but now cannot be, and so have given up hope of seeing it fulfilled in this life.

That thing, if it is in line with what we know to be His expressed will (as a son to Abraham and Sarah was), God intends to *do* for us, even if we know that it is of such utter impossibility that we only laugh at the absurdity of anyone's supposing it could ever now come to pass. *That thing* God intends to do for us, if we will let Him.

"Is anything too hard for the Lord?" Not when we believe in Him enough to go forward and do His will, and let Him do the impossible for us. Even Abraham and Sarah could have blocked God's plan if they had continued to disbelieve.

The only thing too hard for Jehovah is deliberate, continued disbelief in His love and power, and our final rejection of His plans for us. Nothing is too hard for Jehovah to do for them that trust Him.

FROM MESSAGES FOR THE MORNING WATCH

EVENING

⤲⤳

And when Joseph saw Benjamin with them, he said to the steward of his house, Bring the men into the house, and slay, and make ready; for the men shall dine with me at noon. (GEN. 43:16 RSV)

*W*hen their brother, who was to be their savior, saw that they had brought with them the dearest treasure of their family, there went forth the instant word for a king's feast to be prepared for them.

That is all that my Savior is waiting for that He may lavish the fullness of His bounty upon me: my bringing to Him the dearest possession of my life—myself—in unconditional surrender to His mastery, confessing my helplessness and awful need. Then He gives the word that *I may come into His own house and eat at His table the best food of which He Himself partakes.*

The surrender of Benjamin, their dearest possession, was the key to all the treasures of the kingdom—yes, even to the recognition of Joseph by the brothers and Jacob. The surrender of the costliest possession of *my life* is the key to the treasures of the Kingdom for me—yes, even to the full recognition and appropriation of *Christ as my whole and only life.*

Oh, Lord Jesus, show me more that I may give up, that I may have more of Thee! **MESSAGES FOR THE MORNING WATCH**

My friend, beware of me
Lest I should do
The very thing I'd sooner die than do,
In some way crucify the Christ in you.

If you are called to some great sacrifice,
And I should come to you with frightened eyes
And cry, "Take care, take care, be wise, be wise!"

⤲ 664 ⤳

See through my softness then a fiend's attack,
And bid me get me straight behind your back;
To your own conscience and your God be true,
Lest I play Satan to the Christ in you.

And I would humbly ask of you in turn
That if someday in me Love's fires should burn
To whiteness, and a Voice should call
Bidding me leave my little for God's all,
If need be, you would thrust me from your side—
So keep love loyal to the Crucified.

November 6

MORNING

❧

As many as I love I rebuke and chasten (REV. 3:19).

God takes the most eminent and choicest of His servants for the choicest and most eminent afflictions. They who have received most grace from God are able to bear most afflictions from God. Affliction does not hit the saint by chance, but by direction. God does not draw His bow at a venture. Every one of His arrows goes upon a special errand and touches no breast but his against whom it is sent. It is not only the grace, but the glory of a believer when he can stand and take affliction quietly.

JOSEPH CARYL

If all my days were sunny, could I say,
"In His fair land He wipes all tears away"?

If I were never weary, could I keep
Close to my heart, "He gives His loved ones sleep"?

Where no graves mine, might I not come to deem
The Life Eternal but a baseless dream?

My winter, and my tears, and weariness,
Even my graves, may be His way to bless.

I call them ills; yet that can surely be
Nothing but love that shows my Lord to me!

SELECTED

"The most deeply taught Christians are generally those who have been brought into the searching fires of deep soul-anguish. If you have been praying to know more of Christ, do not be surprised if He takes you aside into a desert place, or leads you into a furnace of pain.

"Do not punish me, Lord, by taking my cross from me, but comfort me by submitting me to Thy will, and by making me to love the cross. Give me that by which Thou shalt be best served . . . and let me hold it for the greatest of all Thy mercies, that Thou shouldst glorify Thy name in me, according to Thy will." **A CAPTIVE'S PRAYER**

EVENING

I speak of my severe labors for the Gospel. I am ready even to die in the same cause. If I am required to pour out my life-blood as a libation over the sacrificial offering of your faith, I rejoice myself and I congratulate you all therein. Yea, in like manner I ask you also to rejoice and congratulate me. (PHIL. 2:17–18, TRANS.)

The leading symbol of our Christian faith is not an easy chair, or a featherbed: it is a Cross. If we would be His disciples, let us be prepared to live dangerously; to take up the Cross and carry it into the teeth of opposition.

God is at perfect liberty to waste us if He chooses.

When the fight seems fierce, and you are tempted to be weary and disconsolate, remember that in the interest of His cause your Leader expects you to turn a glad face to the world—*to rejoice and be exceeding glad!*

> *I have shamed Thee; craven-hearted*
> *I have been Thy recreant knight;*
> *Own me yet, O Lord, albeit*
> *Weeping whilst I fight!*
>
> *"Nay," He said, "Wilt thou yet shame Me?*
> *Wilt thou shame thy knightly guise?*
> *I would have my angels wonder*
> *At thy gladsome eyes."*
>
> *Need'st thou pity, knight of Jesus?*
> *Pity for thy glorious hest?*
> *Oh, let God and men and angels*
> *See that thou are blest!*
> SUSO

November 7

❧

But what things were gain to me, those I counted loss for Christ
(PHIL. 3:7).

When they buried the blind preacher, George Matheson, they lined his grave with red roses in memory of his love-life of sacrifice. And it was this man, so beautifully and significantly honored, who wrote,

> *O Love that wilt not let me go,*
> *I rest my weary soul in Thee,*
> *I give Thee back the life I owe,*
> *That in thine ocean depths its flow*
> *May richer, fuller be.*
>
> *O Light that followest all my way,*
> *I yield my flickering torch to Thee*
> *My heart restores its borrowed ray,*
> *That in Thy sunshine's blaze its day*
> *May brighter, fairer be*
>
> *O Joy that seekest me through pain,*
> *I cannot close my heart to Thee,*
> *I trace the rainbow through the rain,*
> *And feel the promise is not vain,*
> *That morn shall tearless be.*
>
> *O Cross that liftest up my head,*
> *I dare not ask to fly from Thee*
> *I lay in dust life's glory dead,*
> *And from the ground there blossoms red,*
> *Life that shall endless be.*

There is a legend of an artist who had found the secret of a wonderful red which no other artist could imitate. The secret of his color died with him. But after his death an old wound was discovered over his heart. This revealed the source of the matchless hue in his pictures. The legend teaches that no great achievement can be made, no lofty attainment reached, nothing of much value to the world done, save at the cost of heart's blood.

❧

Every place that the sole of your foot shall tread upon, that have I given unto you. (JOSH. 1:3)

This blessed inspiring word greeted Israel as they faced the Promised Land. They had the *promise* of it before; *now* they must go forward into it and place their feet upon it. The promise is in the perfect tense and denotes an act just now completed—*"That have I given unto you."*

Our Joshua gives us the same incentive for conquest: *every promise in the New Testament that we put our feet upon is ours!* The upland of spiritual power is yours though Anak may live there! It is yours if you will but go against him and drive him out of his strongholds, in the might of *The Name.*

If we dare to place our foot on anything God has promised *He makes it real to us.* So take Him as the supply for all your need: believe He is yours and never doubt it from this moment.

It may be your need is for spiritual cleansing. His promise covers this: *"Now ye are clean through the word which I have spoken unto you."* If you can believe this you shall be sanctified and kept.

Take the promise that suits your need, and step out on it; not touching it timidly on tiptoe, *but placing your foot flat down upon it.* Do not be afraid it will not hold your weight. *Put your whole need on the Word of the eternal* God for your soul, for your body, for your work, for the dear ones for whom you are praying, for any crisis in your life: *then stand upon it forever!*

All the blessed promises of the Old Book are yours, and *why are you so slack to go up and possess your land?* The size of your inheritance depends upon *how much land you have trodden underfoot, really stood on or walked over.* Between you and your possessions that huge mountain looms up. March up to it and make it yours! Go in this thy might and God will get glory; and you, victory. **A. B. SIMPSON**

Footprints mean possession, but it must be *your own footprints.*

November 8

༈

He took Peter and John and James,
and went up into a mountain to pray.
And as he prayed, the fashion of his
countenance was altered, and his raiment was white
and glistering . . . they saw his glory
(LUKE 9:28–29, 32).

If I have found grace in thy sight, show me now thy way
(EXOD. 33:13).

When Jesus took these three disciples up into that high mountain apart, He brought them into close communion with Himself. They saw no man but Jesus only; and it was good to be there. Heaven is not far from those who tarry on the mount with their Lord.

Who has not in moments of meditation and prayer caught a glimpse of opening gates? Who has not in the secret place of holy communion felt the rush of some white surging wave of emotion—a foretaste of the joy of the blessed?

The Master had times and places for quiet converse with His disciples, once on the peak of Hermon, but oftener on the sacred slopes of Olivet. Every Christian should have his Olivet. Most of us, especially in the cities and towns, live at high pressure. From early morning until bedtime we are exposed to the whirl. Amid all this maelstrom how little chance for quiet thought, for God's Word, for prayer and heart fellowship!

Daniel needed to have an Olivet in his chamber amid Babylon's roar and idolatries. Peter found his on a housetop in Joppa; and Martin Luther found his in the "upper room" at Wittenberg, which is still held sacred.

Dr. Joseph Parker once said: "If we do not get back to visions, peeps into heaven, consciousness of the higher glory and the larger life, we shall lose our religion; our altar will become a bare stone, unblessed by visitant from Heaven." Here is the world's need today—*men who have seen their Lord.*   **FROM THE LOST ART OF MEDITATION**

Come close to Him! He may take you today up into the mountaintop, for where He took Peter with his blundering, and James and John, those sons of thunder who again and again so utterly misunderstood their Master and His mission, there is no reason why He should not take you.

So don't shut yourself out of it and say, "Ah, these wonderful visions and revelations of the Lord are for choice spirits!" They may be for you!

JOHN MCNEILL

EVENING

〜〜

At that day, saith the LORD . . . THOU SHALT CALL ME ISHI [MY HUSBAND]. (HOS. 2:16)

The coming of the Comforter is a holy thing, a solemn act, and must be preceded by an intelligent and solemn covenant between the soul and God. It is the marriage of the soul to the Redeemer, and it is not a "trial marriage." No true marriage is rushed into carelessly. It is carefully considered, and it is based upon complete separation and consecration and the most solemn pledges and vows. So, if the Comforter is come to abide, to be with us and in us evermore, we must come out and be separate for Him, we must consecrate ourselves to Jesus fully and forever, and we must covenant to be the Lord's "for better or for worse," and we must trust Him. The soul that thus truly and solemnly dedicates itself to Him becomes His, and He will come to that soul to abide forever, to be its "shield and exceeding great reward."

Take not back the gift you have voluntarily laid on the altar.

Jesus, Thy life is mine!
Dwell evermore in me;
And let me see
That nothing can untwine
Thy life from mine.

Thy life in me be shown!
Lord, I would henceforth seek
To think and speak
Thy thoughts, Thy words alone,
No more my own.

Thy fullest gift, O Lord,
Now at Thy word I claim,
Through Thy dear Name,
And touch the rapturous chord
Of praise forth-poured.

Jesus, my life is Thine,
And evermore shall be
Hidden in Thee!
For nothing can untwine
Thy life from mine.
FRANCES RIDLEY HAVERGAL

"Thou shalt abide [live] for me many days . . . thou shalt not be for another man: so will I also be for thee" *(Hos. 3:3).*

November 9

MORNING

They that dwell under his shadow shall return; they shall revive as the corn and grow as the vine (HOS. 14:7).

The day closed with heavy showers. The plants in my garden were beaten down before the pelting storm, and I saw one flower that I had admired for its beauty and loved for its fragrance exposed to the pitiless storm. The flower fell, shut up its petals, dropped its head; and I saw that all its glory was gone. "I must wait till next year," I said, "before I see that beautiful thing again."

That night passed, and morning came; the sun shone again, and the morning brought strength to the flower. The light looked at it, and the flower looked at the light. There was contact and communion, and power passed into the flower. It held up its head, opened its petals, regained its glory, and seemed fairer than before. I wonder how it took place—this feeble thing coming into contact with the strong thing, and gaining strength!

I cannot tell how it is that I should be able to receive into my being a power to do and to bear by communion with God, but I know it is a fact.

Are you in peril through some crushing, heavy trial? Seek this communion with Christ, and you will receive strength and be able to conquer. "I will strengthen thee."

Yesterday's Grief

The rain that fell a-yesterday is ruby on the roses,
Silver on the poplar leaf, and gold on willow stem;

The grief that chanced a-yesterday is silence that incloses
Holy loves when time and change shall never trouble them.

The rain that fell a-yesterday makes all the hillsides glisten,
Coral on the laurel and beryl on the grass;
The grief that chanced a-yesterday has taught the soul to listen
For whispers of eternity in all the winds that pass.

O faint-of-heart, storm-beaten, this rain will gleam tomorrow,
Flame within the columbine and jewels on the thorn,
Heaven in the forget-me-not; though sorrow now be sorrow,
Yet sorrow shall be beauty in the magic of the morn.
KATHERINE LEE BATES

EVENING

God also hath set the one [thing] over against the other.
(ECCL. 7:14)

Too often we see life's prose, but not its poetry. Too often we miss the inspiration of the songs. How manifold are our sorrows, but how manifold are His gifts!

Sin is here, but so is boundless grace; the devil is here, but so is Christ; the sword of judgment is crossed by Mercy's scepter.

"Judgment and Mercy," according to a lovely Jewish legend, "were sent forth together after the Fall to minister to the sinning but redeemed race," *and together they still act.* One afflicts, the other heals; where one rends, the other plants a flower; one carves a wrinkle, the other kindles a smile; the rainbow succeeds the storm; the succoring wing covers our naked head from the glittering sword.

Gethsemane had its strengthening Angel!

God everlastingly sets Mercies over against Miseries! His interventions are never mistimed. He never comes at the wrong season. *God has the affairs of the world in His hands.* In your blackest crises the angel presences are doubtless in your neighborhood!

God never strikes the wrong note; never sings the wrong song. If God makes music, the music will prove medicinal. JOSEPH PEARCE

With mercy and with judgment
My web of time He wove.

And aye the dews of sorrow
Were lustered with His love,
I'll bless the Hand that guided,
I'll bless the Heart that planned,
When throned where glory dwelleth,
In Immanuel's land.

Deep waters crossed life's pathway,
The hedge of thorns was sharp;
Now, these lie all behind me—
Oh! For a well-tuned harp!
Oh! to join Hallelujahs
With your triumphant band,
Who sing, where glory dwelleth
In Immanuel's land.

SAMUEL RUTHERFORD

Listen for the Night-songs of God!

November 10

MORNING

∽∾

Under hopeless circumstances he hopefully believed
(ROM. 4:18 WEYMOUTH).

Abraham's faith seemed to be in a thorough correspondence with the power and constant faithfulness of Jehovah. In the outward circumstances in which he was placed, he had not the greatest cause to expect the fulfillment of the promise. Yet he believed the Word of the Lord, and looked forward to the time when his seed should be as the stars of heaven for multitude.

O my soul, thou hast not one single promise only, like Abraham, *but a thousand promises,* and many patterns of faithful believers before thee: it behooves thee, therefore, to rely with confidence upon the Word of God. And though He delayeth His help, and the evil seemeth to grow worse and worse, be not weak, but rather strong, and rejoice, since the most glorious promises of God are generally fulfilled in such a wondrous manner that He steps forth to save us at a time when there is the least appearance of it.

He commonly brings His help in our greatest extremity, that His finger may plainly appear in our deliverance. And this method He chooses that we may not trust upon anything that we see or feel, as we are always apt to do, but only upon His bare Word, which we may depend upon in every state.   C. H. VON BOGATZKY

Remember it is the very time for faith to work when sight ceases. The greater the difficulties, the easier for faith; as long as there remain certain natural prospects, faith does not get on even as easily as where natural prospects fail.   GEORGE MUELLER

EVENING

❧

*Righteousness shall go before him;
and shall set us in the way of his steps.* (PS. 85:13)

How I ascertain the will of God:

I seek at the beginning to get my heart into such a state that it has no will of its own in regard to a given matter.

Nine-tenths of the trouble with people is right here.

Nine-tenths of the difficulties are overcome when our hearts are *ready to do the Lord's will,* whatever it may be. When one is truly in this state it is usually but a little way to the knowledge of what His will is.

Having surrendered my own will, I do not leave the result to feeling or simply impressions. If I do so, I make myself liable to great delusions.

I seek the will of the Spirit of God through, or in connection with *the Word of God.* The Spirit and the Word must be combined. If the Holy Ghost guides us at all, He will do it according to the Scriptures, and never contrary to them.

Next I take into account *providential circumstances.* These often plainly indicate God's will in connection with His Word and Spirit.

I ask God in prayer to reveal His will to me aright.

Thus, through prayer to God, the study of His Word, and reflection, I come to a deliberate judgment, and if my mind is thus at peace, and continues so after two or three more petitions, I proceed accordingly. In *trivial matters,* and in transactions involving *most important issues,* I have found this method *always effective.*   GEORGE MÜLLER

November 11

∽✦∽

He shall come down like rain upon the mown grass
(PS. 72:6).

*A*mos speaks of the king's mowings. Our King has many scythes, and is perpetually mowing His lawns. The musical tinkle of the whetstone on the scythe portends the cutting down of myriads of green blades, daisies, and other flowers. Beautiful as they were in the morning, within an hour or two they lie in long, faded rows.

Thus in human life we make a brave show, before the scythe of pain, the shears of disappointment, the sickle of death.

There is no method of obtaining a velvety lawn but by repeated mowings: And there is no way of developing tenderness, evenness, sympathy, but by the passing of God's scythes. How constantly the Word of God compares man to grass, and His glory to its flower. But when the grass is mown, and all the tender shoots are bleeding, and desolation reigns where flowers were bursting, it is the most acceptable time for showers of rain falling soft and warm.

O soul, thou hast been mown! Time after time the King has come to thee with His sharp scythe. Do not dread the scythe—it is sure to be followed by the shower.
                                                                    F. B. MEYER

When across the heart deep waves of sorrow
Break, as on a dry and barren shore;
When hope glistens with no bright tomorrow,
And the storm seems sweeping evermore;

When the cup of every earthly gladness
Bears no taste of the life-giving stream;
And high hopes, as though to mock our sadness,
Fade and die as in some fitful dream,

Who shall hush the weary spirit's chiding?
Who the aching void within shall fill?
Who shall whisper of a peace abiding,
and each surging billow calmly still?

Only He whose wounded heart was broken
With the bitter cross and thorny crown;

Whose dear love glad words of joy had spoken,
Who His life for us laid meekly down.

Blessed Healer, all our burdens lighten;
Give us peace. Thine own sweet peace, we pray!
Keep us near Thee till the morn shall brighten,
And all the mists and shadows flee away!

EVENING

He was wounded for our transgressions,
he was bruised for our iniquities: the chastisement of our
peace was upon him; and with his stripes we are healed.
(ISA. 53:5)

He is brought as a lamb to the slaughter. (ISA. 53:7)

Yet it pleased the LORD TO BRUISE HIM. (ISA. 53:10)

I came alone to my Calvary,
And the load I bore was too great for me;
The stones were sharp and pierced my feet,
And my temples throbbed with the withering heat.

But my heart was faint with the toil that day,
So I sat down to think of an easy way;
Loomed sharply before me that tortuous trail—
No use to try—I would only fail.

I turned back in sorrow, clothed with defeat,
For my load was too heavy; I would retreat
To easier highways, with scenery more fair—
Yet a moment I lingered watching there.

As I held my gaze on that flinty side,
A man came up to be crucified;
He toiled all the way of that painful road,
And the cross that he bore far surpassed my load:

His brow with thorns was pierced and torn;
His face had a look of pain and was worn;
He stopped for a moment and looked on me—

And I followed in rapture to Calvary!
MY CALVARY, BY MATTHEW BILLER

Haunt the place called Calvary.

November 12
MORNING

❦

These were the potters, and those that dwelt among plants and hedges: there they dwelt with the king for his work
(1 CHRON. 4:23).

Anywhere and everywhere we may dwell "with the king for his work." We may be in a very unlikely and unfavorable place for this; it may be in a literal country life, with little enough to be seen of the "goings" of the King around us; it may be among the hedges of all sorts, hindrances in all directions; it may be furthermore, with our hands full of all manner of pottery for our daily task.

No matter! The King who placed us *"there"* will come and dwell there with us; the hedges are right, or He would soon do away with them. And it does not follow that what seems to hinder our way may not be for its very protection; and as for the pottery, why, that is just exactly what He has seen fit to put into our hands, and therefore it is, for the present, *"His work."*
FRANCES RIDLEY HAVERGAL

> *Go back to thy garden-plot, sweetheart!*
> *Go back till the evening falls,*
> *And bind thy lilies and train thy vines,*
> *Till for thee the Master calls.*
>
> *Go make thy garden fair as thou canst,*
> *Thou workest never alone;*
> *Perhaps he whose plot is next to thine*
> *Will see it and mend his own.*

The colored sunsets and starry heavens, the beautiful mountains and the shining seas, the fragrant woods and painted flowers, are not half so beautiful as a soul that is serving Jesus out of love, in the wear and tear of common, unpoetic life.
FABER

The most saintly spirits are often existing in those who have never distinguished themselves as authors, or let any memorial of themselves to be the theme of the world's talk; but who have led an interior angelic life, having borne their sweet blossoms unseen like the young lily in a sequestered vale on the bank of a limpid stream.   KENELM DIGBY

EVENING

⊱◦⊰

Though it be tried with fire. (1 PETER 1:7)

"What makes this set of china so much more expensive than that?" asked the customer.

"It has more work on it. It has been put through the fire twice. See, in this one the flowers are in a yellow band; in that one they are on the white background. This had to be put *through the fire a second time* to get the design on it."

"Why is the pattern on this vessel so blurred and marred—the design not brought out clearly?"

"That one was *not burned enough*. Had it remained in the furnace longer *the dark background would have become gold*—dazzling gold, and the pattern would have stood out clear and distinct."

Perhaps some of those who seem to have more than their share of suffering and disappointment are, like the costly china, being *doubly tried* in the fire, that they may be more valuable in the Master's service.

The potter never sees his clay take on rich shades of silver, or red, or cream, or brown, or yellow, until after the darkness and the burning of the furnace. These colors come—*after the burning and darkness*. The clay is beautiful—after the burning and darkness. The vase is made possible—after the burning and darkness.

How universal is this law of life! Where did the bravest man and the purest woman you know get their whitened characters? Did they not get them as the clay gets its beauty—after the darkness and the burning of the furnace? Where did Savonarola get his eloquence? In the darkness and burning of the furnace wherein God discovered deep things to him. Where did Stradivari get his violins? Where did Titian get his color? Where did Angelo get his marble? Where did Mozart get his music, and Chatterton his poetry, and Jeremiah his sermons? They got them where the clay gets its glory and its shimmer—in the darkness and the burning of the furnace.   ROBERT G. LEE

Thou who didst fashion man on earth, to be
Strong in Thy strength, and with Thy freedom free,
Complete at last Thy great design in me.

Cost what it may of sorrow and distress,
Of empty hands, of utter loneliness,
I dare not, Lord, be satisfied with less.

So, Lord, reclaim Thy great design in me,
Give or reclaim Thy gifts, but let me be
Strong in Thy strength, and with Thy freedom free.

Let us not rebel at the second breath of the flame if He sends it.

November 13

MORNING

I know him, that he will command his children (GEN. 18:19).

God wants people that He can depend upon. He could say of Abraham, "I know him, that he will command his children . . . that the Lord may bring upon Abraham that which he hath spoken." God can be depended upon; He wants us to be just as decided, as reliable, as stable. This is just what faith means.

God is looking for men on whom He can put the weight of all His love and power and faithful promises. God's engines are strong enough to draw any weight we attach to them. Unfortunately the cable which we fasten to the engine is often too weak to hold the weight of our prayer; therefore God is drilling us, disciplining us to stability and certainty in the life of faith. Let us learn our lessons and stand fast.　　　A. B. SIMPSON

God knows that you can stand that trial; He would not give it to you if you could not. It is His trust in you that explains the trials of life, however bitter they may be. God knows our strength, and He measures it to the last inch; and a trial was never given to any man that was greater than that man's strength, through God, to bear it.

❧❧

Now unto him that is able to keep you from falling, and to present
you faultless before the presence of his glory with exceeding joy.
(JUDE 24)

*T*ake that word *keep* and hold it close to your heart tonight and
tomorrow. It is one of the great and magnificent messages of the
Gospel—"He is able to *keep* you from falling." Put into the word *you* all
the weakness, all the unworthiness, all the sinfulness which belongs to
man since the Fall; yet, He is able to keep *you*. He does not underrate the
disadvantage of its being *you* when *He* bids His messengers say He is "able
to keep you from falling." It would be impossible, utterly impossible,
were it not undertaken by Infinite love. Look out, and up, then. Look *up*
"from the depth"—the vast depth of your weakness, perhaps of your mys-
teriously inherited weakness. Look *out* of your failure under some temptation, inward or outward, inherited so to speak from yourself, from your
own unfaithfulness in the past. Look up, out of your ruined purposes—
unto Himself.

Being what He is, Keeper of Israel, God of the promises, Lord of the
Sacrifice, Prince of life, present Savior, indwelling Power, He is able to
keep *you,* that *your* feet shall not totter. They shall stand "in a large
room"; they shall hold on straight, until at last they enter, step by step—
for it is one step at a time even then—"through the gates into the city."

"He shall never give thy feet to tottering."   H. C. G. MOULE

We may step firmly down upon the temptation which Another has crushed
for us, and we are conquerors in Him.

> *Behind the dim unknown*
> *Standeth God within the shadows*
> *Keeping watch above His own.*

November 14

～∞～

Except a grain of corn fall into the ground and die, it abideth alone: but if it dies it bringeth forth much fruit (JOHN 12:24).

Go to the old burying ground of Northampton, Massachusetts, and look upon the early grave of David Brainerd, beside that of the fair Jerusha Edwards, whom he loved but did not live to wed.

What hopes, what expectations for Christ's cause went down to the grave with the wasted form of that young missionary of whose work nothing now remained but the dear memory, and a few score of swarthy Indian converts! But that majestic old Puritan saint, Jonathan Edwards, who had hoped to call him his son, gathered up the memorials of his life in a little book, and the little book took wings and flew beyond the sea, and alighted on the table of a Cambridge student, Henry Martyn.

Poor Martyn! Why should he throw himself away, with all his scholarship, his genius, his opportunities! What had he accomplished when he turned homeward from "India's coral strand," broken in health, and dragged himself northward as far as that dreary khan at Tocat by the Black Sea, where he crouched under the piled-up saddles, to cool his burning fever against the earth, and there died alone?

To what purpose was this waste? Out of that early grave of Brainerd, and the lonely grave of Martyn far away by the splashing of the Euxine Sea, has sprung the noble army of modern missionaries.

LEONARD WOOLSEY BACON

> Is there some desert, or some boundless sea,
> Where Thou, great God of angels, wilt send me?
> Some oak for me to rend,
> Some sod for me to break,
> Some handful of Thy corn to take
> And scatter far afield,
> Till it in turn shall yield
> Its hundredfold
> Of grains of gold
> To feed the happy children of my God?
>
> Show me the desert, Father, or the sea;
> Is it Thine enterprise? Great God, send me!

And though this body lies where ocean rolls,
Father, count me among all faithful souls.

EVENING

∾

Enoch walked with God. (GEN. 5:22)

A day's walk with God will do more to awaken awe, wonder, and
amazement in your soul than would a century of travel through the
sights of the earth. He chooses for you a way you know not, that you may
be compelled into a thousand intercourses with Him, which will make the
journey ever memorable with glory to Him and blessing to you.

Jesus, these eyes have never seen
That radiant form of Thine;
The veil of sense hangs dark between
Thy blessed face and mine.

I see Thee not, I hear Thee not,
Yet art Thou oft with me;
And earth hath ne'er so dear a spot
As where I meet with Thee.

Like some bright dream that comes unsought
When slumbers o'er me roll,
Thine image ever fills my thought
And charms my ravished soul.

Yet though I have not seen, and still
Must rest in faith alone,
I love Thee, dearest Lord, and will,
Unseen but not unknown.

HYMNS OF CONSECRATION AND FAITH

November 15

✦

Pressed out of measure (2 COR. 1:8).

That the power of Christ may rest upon me (2 COR. 12:9).

God allowed the crisis to close around Jacob on the night when he bowed at Peniel in supplication, to bring him to the place where he could take hold of God as he never would have done; and from that narrow pass of peril, Jacob became enlarged in his faith and knowledge of God, and in the power of a new and victorious life.

God had to compel David, by a long and painful discipline of years, to learn the almighty power and faithfulness of his God, and grow up into the established principles of faith and godliness, which were indispensable for his glorious career as the king of Israel.

Nothing but the extremities in which Paul was constantly placed could ever have taught him, and taught the church through him, the full meaning of the great promise he so learned to claim, "My grace is sufficient for thee."

And nothing but our trials and perils would ever have led some of us to know Him as we do, to trust Him as we have, and to draw from Him the measures of grace which our very extremities made indispensable.

Difficulties and obstacles are God's challenges to faith. When hindrances confront us in the path of duty, we are to recognize them as vessels for faith to fill with the fullness and all-sufficiency of Jesus; and as we go forward, simply and fully trusting Him, we may be tested, we may have to wait and let patience have her perfect work; but we shall surely find at last the stone rolled away, and the Lord waiting to render unto us double for our time of testing. **A. B. SIMPSON**

EVENING

✦

Abide ye here and keep awake with me. (MATT. 26:38, TRANS.)

When He needed God most in the greatest crisis of His life, Jesus sought a garden. Under the olive trees, with the Passover moon shining down upon Him, He prayed in agony for strength to do God's will. Only those who have been through such agony can realize even in part what that bleak hour of renunciation, for the sake of you and me, meant to Christ.

Are we willing that He should suffer Gethsemane and the Cross for us *in vain?*

"I go to pray," He said to the eight,
"Rest here at the gate."
But He spake to the three entreatingly,
"Will you watch with me as I pray
A stone's throw away?
I suffer tonight exceedingly."
The eight slept well at the garden gate
(As tired men will);
The three tossed fitfully within,
(Twice half-roused by His need of them)
But they slept—
Till the black in the East turned gray,
Till their garments were drenched with the
tears of the day:

Slept
Till He called them—each one by his name—
The three within, and the eight at the gate.

The ground was hard where the eight had slept
(As hard as the road the soldiers stepped);
The grass was bent where the three had dreamt,
But red where the Lord had wept.
MIRIAM LEFEVRE CROUSE

"What, could ye not keep awake with me one hour?" *(Matt. 26:40).*

November 16

‿‿∾

They overcame him by the blood of the Lamb . . . and they loved not
their lives unto the death (REV. 12:11).

When James and John came to Christ with their mother, asking Him to give them the best place in the kingdom, He did not refuse their request, but told them it would be given to them if they could do His work, drink His cup, and be baptized with His baptism.

Do we want the competition? The greatest things are always hedged about by the hardest things, and we, too, shall find mountains and forests and chariots of iron. Hardship is the price of coronation. Triumphal arches are not woven out of rose blossoms and silken cords, but of hard blows and bloody scars. The very hardships that you are enduring in your life today are given by the Master for the explicit purpose of enabling you to win your crown.

Do not wait for some ideal situation, some romantic difficulty, some far-away emergency; but rise to meet the actual conditions which the providence of God has placed around you today. Your crown of glory lies embedded in the very heart of these things—those hardships and trials that are pressing you this very hour, week, and month of your life. The hardest things are not those that the world knows of. Down in your secret soul unseen and unknown by any but Jesus, there is a little trial that you would not dare to mention, that is harder for you to bear than martyrdom.

There, beloved, lies your crown. God help you to overcome, and sometime wear it.   SELECTED

It matters not how the battle goes,
The day how long;
Faint not! Fight on!
Tomorrow comes the song.

EVENING

The love of Christ, which passeth knowledge. (EPH. 3:19)

We do not really see the ocean. To do that is beyond our power. Through that vista we glimpse a bit of blue water as though God has painted a picture and framed it with hills and trees. But southward and northward on distance-hidden shores stretches water we have never seen. Bays lie placid by sunlit rocks, and long surges roll in soothing rhythm on smoothly sloping sands. Inlets ripple under tropic moons, and warming currents bear springtime's promise to frozen arctic reefs. Beyond that curved blue line that limits our sight, there rolls an open plain of waters to realms where we have never been, leaving the strands of palmy islands of which we do not know. And this is but the surface! Beneath are miles of depth, fathomless with mysteries beyond the thoughts of men.

God's measureless love is like the ocean. Through the windows of earthly life we catch a gleam. From the valleys of trouble we glimpse it near the shore. On the sands of hope we see it, wave on wave. From the headlands of faith we view a broader tide to the line that blends eternity with time. Our happiest days are islands set in its boundless breadth. Yet, as with the ocean, we have never seen it *all!* Even eternity cannot reveal its greatness to the wondering hosts of heaven, nor all the universe exhaust the fountains whence it flows.

> *We can only see a little of the ocean,*
> *Just a few miles distant from the rocky shore,*
> *But out there—far beyond our eyes' horizon,*
> *There's more—immeasurably more.*
>
> *We can only see a little of God's loving—*
> *A few rich treasures from His mighty store;*
> *But out there—far beyond our eyes' horizon,*
> *There's more—immeasurably more.*

November 17

Hear what the unjust judge saith. And shall not God avenge his own elect which cry day and night unto him, though he bear long with them? I tell you that he will avenge them speedily
(LUKE 18:6–8).

God's seasons are not at your beck. If the first stroke of the flint doth not bring forth the fire, you must strike again. God will hear prayer, but He may not answer it at the time which we in our minds have appointed; He will reveal Himself to our seeking hearts, but not just when and where we have settled in our own expectations. Hence the need of perseverance and importunity in supplication.

In the days of flint and steel and brimstone matches we had to strike and strike again, dozens of times, before we could get a spark to live in the tinder; and we were thankful enough if we succeeded at last.

Shall we not be as persevering and hopeful as to heavenly things? We have more certainty of success in this business than we had with our flint and steel, for we have God's promises at our back.

Never let us despair. God's time for mercy will come; yea, it has come, if our time for believing has arrived. Ask in faith, nothing wavering; but never cease from petitioning because the King delays to reply. Strike the steel again. Make the sparks fly and have your tinder ready; you will get a light before long.　　　　　　　　　　　　　　　　C. H. SPURGEON

I do not believe that there is such a thing in the history of God's kingdom as a right prayer offered in a right spirit that is forever left unanswered.　　　　　　　　　　　　　　　　THEODORE L. CUYLER

LORD, I am oppressed; undertake for me. (ISA. 38:14)

Are you feeling that life for you has become a tangled skein; tangled with problems that seem to be desperately hard to unravel? If so, examine them and see whether it be not true that somewhere in the tangle there is the golden thread of an obvious present duty. Commence with that thread: *what ought you to do next? Now! Never mind tomorrow!*

> *Father, my life is in tangle,*
> *Thread after thread appears*
> *Twisted and broken and knotted,*
> *Viewed through the lapse of years.*
>
> *I cannot straighten them, Father;*
> *Oh, it is very hard;*
> *Somehow or other it seemeth,*
> *All I have done is marred.*
>
> *I did not see they were getting*
> *Into this tangled state;*
> *How it has happened I know not—*
> *Is it too late, too late?*
>
> *Is it? "Ah, no!" Thou dost whisper,*
> *"Out of this life of thine*
> *Yet may come wonderful beauty*
> *Wrought by My Power Divine."*
>
> *Take then, the threads, O my Father,*
> *Let them Thy mind fulfill,*
> *Work out in love a pattern*
> *After Thy holy will!*

CHARLOTTE MURRAY

The case looks utterly hopeless. Hope is dead—yea, buried, and the bones are lying scattered at the grave's mouth. *But the eye fixed on the living God can bring a resurrection*. Hope may yet flourish again. The net of terrible entanglement may be broken *by a Father's hand*, and liberty and life abundant may yet be mine!

> *The Savior can solve every problem,*
> *The tangles of life can undo,*
> *There is nothing too hard for Jesus,*
> *There is nothing that He cannot do.*

OSWALD J. SMITH

November 18

∽∾

Blessed is he, whosoever shall not be offended in me (LUKE 7:23).

$\mathcal{I}$t is sometimes very difficult not to be offended in Jesus Christ. The offenses may be circumstantial. I find myself in a prisonhouse—a narrow sphere, a sick chamber, an unpopular position—when I had hoped for wide opportunities. Yes, but He knows what is best for me. My environment is of His determining. He means it to intensify my faith, to draw me into nearer communion with Himself, to ripen my power. In the dungeon my soul should prosper.

The offense may be mental. I am haunted by perplexities, questions, which I cannot solve. I had hoped that, when I gave myself to Him, my sky would always be clear; but often it is overspread by mist and cloud. Yet let me believe that, if difficulties remain, it is that I may learn to trust Him all the more implicitly—to trust and not be afraid. Yes, and by my intellectual conflicts, I am trained to be a tutor to other storm-driven men.

The offense may be spiritual. I had fancied that within His fold I should never feel the biting winds of temptation; but it is best as it is. His grace is magnified. My own character is matured. His heaven is sweeter at the close of the day. There I shall look back on the turnings and trials of the way, and shall sing the praises of my Guide. So, let come what will come, His will is welcome; and I shall refuse to be offended in my loving Lord.

ALEXANDER SMELLIE

> *Blessed is he whose faith in not offended,*
> *When all around his way*
> *The power of God is working out deliverance*
> *For others day by day;*
>
> *Though in some prison drear his own soul languish,*
> *Till life itself be spent,*
> *Yet still can trust his Father's love and purpose,*
> *And rest therein content.*
>
> *Blessed is he, who through long years of suffering,*
> *But off from active toil,*
> *Still shares by prayer and praise the work of others,*
> *And thus "divides the spoil."*

Blessed are thou, O child of God, who sufferest,
And canst not understand
The reason for thy pain, yet gladly leavest
Thy life in His blest Hand.

Yea, blessed art thou whose faith is "not offended"
By trials unexplained,
By mysteries unsolved, past understanding,
Until the goal is gained.
FREDA HANBURY ALLEN

EVENING

But be of good cheer! (JOHN 16:33)

Jesus said, "Ye shall have tribulation"—not difficulties, but *tribulation*. But "tribulation worketh *patience*."

Millstones are used to grind the corn to powder, and typify the sacredness of the discipline of life.

"No man shall take the nether or the upper millstone to pledge: *for he taketh a man's life to pledge*" (Deut. 24:6, emphasis added).

You have been having a snug time in the granary; then God brings you out and puts you under the millstones, and the first thing that happens is the grinding separation of which our Lord spoke: *"Blessed are ye, when men shall . . . cast out your name as evil, for the Son of man's sake."* Crushed forever is any resemblance to the other crowd.

Hands off! when God is putting His saints through the experience of the millstones. We are apt to want to interfere in the discipline of another saint. *Do not hinder the production of the bread that is to feed the world!*

In the East the women sing as they grind the corn between the millstones. *"The sound of the millstones is music in the ears of God."* It is not music to the worldling, but the saint understands that His Father has a purpose in it all.

Ill-tempered persons, hard circumstances, poverty, willful misunderstandings and estrangements are all millstones. Had Jesus any of these things in His life? Had He not! He had a devil in His company for three years! He was continually thwarted and misunderstood by the Pharisees. And *is the disciple above His Master?*

When these experiences come, *remember that God has His eye on every detail.*

But beware! lest the *tiniest element of self-pity keeps God from putting us anywhere near the millstones.* OSWALD CHAMBERS

November 19

MORNING

∽◦∾

Thou, who hast showed us many and sore troubles, wilt quicken us again (PS. 71:20 RV).

God *shows* us the troubles. Sometimes, as this part of our education is being carried forward, we have to descend into "the lower parts of the earth," pass through subterranean passages, lie buried amongst the dead, but never for a moment is the cord of fellowship and union between God and us strained to breaking; and from the depths God will bring us again.

Never doubt God! Never say that He has forsaken or forgotten. Never think that He is unsympathetic. He will *quicken* again. There is always a smooth piece of every skein, however tangled. The longest day at last rings out the evensong. The winter snow lies long, but it goes at last.

Be steadfast; your labor is not in vain. God turns again, and comforts. And when He does, the heart which had forgotten its psalmody breaks out in jubilant song, as does the psalmist: "I will thank thee, I will harp unto thee, my lips shall sing aloud." SELECTED

> Though the rain may fall and the wind be blowing,
> And cold and chill is the wintry blast;
> Though the cloudy sky is still cloudier growing,
> And the dead leaves tell that the summer has passed;
> My face I hold to the stormy heaven,
> My heart is as calm as the summer sea,
> Glad to receive what my God has given,
> Whate'er it be.
> When I feel the cold, I can say, "He sends it,"
> And His winds blow blessing, I surely know;
> For I've never a want but that He attends it;
> And my heart beats warm, though the winds may blow.

∽∾

If a son shall ask. (LUKE 11:11)

$\mathcal{H}$enry Gibbud was a mission worker in the city of New York. He was a man of great devotion and wonderful power in prayer. On one occasion he had been working all night in the slums of the great city.

Tired and sleepy at the end of his toil, he made his way in the dark of the morning to the Brooklyn ferry dock. He put his hand in his pocket to pay his fare homeward, but to his dismay he discovered that he did not have the three pennies needed. His heart sank in deep discouragement, but he closed his eyes and began to pray. "Lord, I have been toiling all night in Thy service, trying to bring lost men and women to Thee. I am hungry and sleepy and wish to go home, but I do not have even three pennies for my fare. Will You not help me?"

As he closed his simple prayer, he opened his eyes. They fell upon something shining in the dust at his feet. He reached down and picked up the glittering object and found it was a fifty-cent piece. He paid his fare and went on his way rejoicing.

What was the joy that flooded his heart? It was the fulfillment of the precious promise: *"If a son shall ask."*

Have you taken your place in God's presence, not as a stranger, but as a son?

"If a son, then an heir."

Heir of a mighty King, heir to a throne,
Why art thou wandering sad and alone?
Heir to the love of God, heir to His grace,
Rise to thy privilege, claiming thy place.

Heir of a Conqueror, why dost thou fear?
Foes cannot trouble thee when He is near.
Child of the promises, be not oppressed,
Claim what belongs to thee, find sweetest rest.

Heir by inheritance! child of thy God!
Right to thy sonship is found in His Word;
Walk with the noble ones, never alone;
Prince of the Royal Blood, come to thy throne.

Heirs! we are joint-heirs with Jesus our Lord!
Heirs of the Covenant, found in His Word!

Rise to thy privilege, heir to His grace!
Heir to the love of God, rise, claim thy place!
SELECTED

November 20

MORNING

⤳

Blessed is he that waiteth (DAN. 12:12).

It may seem an easy thing to *wait*, but it is one of the postures which a Christian soldier learns not without years of teaching. Marching and quick-marching are much easier to God's warriors than standing still.

There are hours of perplexity when the most willing spirit, anxiously desirous to serve the Lord, knows not what part to take. Then what shall it do? Vex itself by despair? Fly back in cowardice, turn to the right hand in fear, or rush forward in presumption?

No, but simply wait. *Wait in prayer*, however. Call upon God and spread the case before Him; tell Him your difficulty, and plead His promise of aid.

Wait in faith. Express your unstaggering confidence in Him. Believe that if He keeps you tarrying even till midnight, yet He will come at the right time; the vision shall come, and shall not tarry.

Wait in quiet patience. Never murmur against the second cause, as the children of Israel did against Moses. Accept the case as it is, and put it as it stands, simply and with your whole heart, without any self-will, into the hand of your covenant God, saying, "Now, Lord, not my will, but Thine be done. I know not what to do; I am brought to extremities; but I will wait until Thou shalt cleave the floods, or drive back my foes. I will wait, if Thou keep me many a day, for my heart is fixed upon Thee alone, O God, and my spirit waiteth for Thee in full conviction that Thou wilt yet be my joy and my salvation, my refuge and my strong tower."

FROM MORNING BY MORNING

Wait, patiently wait,
God never is late;
Thy budding plans are in Thy Father's holding,
And only wait His grand divine unfolding.

Then wait, wait,
Patiently wait.

Trust, hopefully trust,
That God will adjust
Thy tangled life; and from its dark concealings,
Will bring His will, in all its bright revealings.
Then trust, trust,
Hopefully trust.

Rest, peacefully rest
On thy Saviour's breast;
Breathe in His ear thy sacred high ambition,
And He will bring it forth in blest fruition.
Then rest, rest,
Peacefully rest!

EVENING

*O LORD, I know that the way of man is not in himself:
it is not in man . . . to direct his steps.* (JER. 10:23)

We were at the foot of Mont Blanc in the village of Chamouni. A sad thing had happened the day before. A young physician had determined to reach the heights of Mont Blanc. He accomplished the feat and the little village was illuminated in his honor; on the mountainside a flag was floating that told of his victory.

After they had ascended, and descended as far as the hut, he wanted to be released from his guide; he wanted to be free from the rope, and insisted on going on alone.

The guide remonstrated with him, telling him it was not safe; *but he tired of the rope,* and declared that he would be free. The guide was compelled to yield. The young man had gone only a short distance when his foot slipped on the ice and he could not stop himself from sliding down the icy steeps. The rope was gone, so the guide could not hold him nor pull him back. Out on the shelving ice lay the body of the young physician.

The bells had been rung, the village had been illumined in honor of his success; but alas, in a fatal moment he refused to be guided; *he was tired of the rope.*

Do *you* get tired of the rope? God's providences hold us, restrain us,

and we get tired sometimes. *We need a guide,* and shall *until* the dangerous paths are over. *Never get disengaged from your Guide.* Let your prayer
be "Lead Thou me on," and sometime the bells of heaven will ring that
you are safe at home!

CHARLES H. SPURGEON

Oh, tame me, Lord! rebellious nature calm.
Oh, tame me, Lord!
This heart so tossed and filled with wild alarm;
Oh, tame me, Lord!

These human longings, let them end in Thee,
And let me be Thy bond-slave—
Even me.

THE MARECHAL

November 21

MORNING

❧

Roll on Jehovah thy way (PS. 37:6, MARGIN).

Whatever it is that presses thee, go tell the Father; put the whole matter over into His hand, and so shalt thou be freed from that divid-
ing, perplexing care that the world is full of. When thou art either to do
or suffer anything, when thou art about any purpose or business, go tell
God of it, and acquaint Him with it; yes, *burden Him with it,* and thou
hast done for matter of caring; no more care, but quiet, sweet diligence
in thy duty, and dependence on Him for the carriage of thy matters. Roll
thy cares, and thyself with them, as one burden, all on thy God.

R. LEIGHTON

Build a little fence of trust
Around today;
Fill the space with loving work
And therein stay.
Look not through the sheltering bars
Upon tomorrow;
God will help thee bear what comes
Of joy or sorrow.

MARY BUTTS

We shall find it impossible to commit our way unto the Lord, unless it be a way that He approves. It is only by faith that a man can commit his way unto the Lord; if there be the slightest doubt in the heart that "our way" is not a good one, faith will refuse to have anything to do with it. This committing of our way must be continuous, not a single act. However extraordinary and unexpected may seem to be His guidance, however near the precipice He may take you, you are not to snatch the guiding reins out of His hands. Are we willing to have all our ways submitted to God, for Him to pronounce judgment on them? There is nothing a Christian needs to be more scrutinizing about than about his confirmed habits and views. He is too apt to take for granted the divine approbation of them. Why are some Christians so anxious, so fearful? Evidently because they have not *left their way with the Lord*. They took it to Him, but brought it away with them again. SELECTED

EVENING

❧

I was left alone, and saw this great vision. (DAN. 10:8)

What lonely men were the great prophets of Israel! John the Baptist stood alone from the crowd! Paul had to say, *"all men forsook me."* And, who was ever more alone than the Lord Jesus?

Victory for God is never won by the multitude. The man who dares to go where others hold back will find himself alone, but he will see the glory of God, and enter into the secrets of eternity. GORDON WATT

I go alone
Upon the narrow way that leads
Through shadowed valleys, over rocky heights,
To glorious plains beyond;
And sometimes when the way is very lone
I cry out for companionship, and long
For fellow-travelers on the toilsome path,
Until a Voice of sweetest music whispers,
"My grace sufficient is, no other guide thou needst
But Me." And then the path grows brighter as
I go alone.

My Savior knows
The way I take. Himself has trod
The selfsame road. He knows each stone,

Temptations, pitfalls hid by blossoms fair,
The hour of darkness that my life must share,
The wilderness of sorrow, doubt, and fear,
Renunciation's agony, and every pang
Of loneliness and labor's wear; enough for me
That He has known it all, that now He stays
To strengthen, guide and help me. I am glad
My Savior knows.

Thy will be done
Whether on pleasant paths I walk along,
Or crouch amid the lightnings of the storm,
Whether for me the larks of springtime sing,
Or winter's icy blasts my being sting;
Whatever Thou dost send is best for me,
With joyful heart I take it all from Thee,
Rejoicing in Thy sovereignty, and pray
That Thou wilt lead me on my upward way;
The road grows smoother as I travel on.
Thy will be done.

AMY L. PERSON

The lone wolf travels a lonely path, *but he beats the pack to the kill!*

November 22

MORNING

❧

Believe ye that I am able to do this? (MATT. 9:28).

God deals with impossibilities. It is never too late for Him to do so, when the impossible is brought to Him, in full faith, by the one in whose life and circumstances the impossible must be accomplished if God is to be glorified. If in our own life there have been rebellion, unbelief, sin, and disaster, it is never too late for God to deal triumphantly with these tragic facts if brought to Him in full surrender and trust. It has often been said, and with truth, that Christianity is the only religion that can deal with man's past. God can "restore . . . the years that the locust hath eaten" (Joel 2:25); and unreservedly and believingly into His hands.

Not because of what we are but because of what He is. God forgives and heals and restores. He is "the God of all grace." Let us praise Him and trust Him. FROM SUNDAY SCHOOL TIMES

Nothing is too hard for Jesus
No man can work like Him.

"We have a God who delights in impossibilities." Nothing too hard for Me. ANDREW MURRAY

EVENING

∽✥∾

Lo, all these things worketh God . . . with man.
(JOB 33:29)

*I*n a certain old town was a great cathedral. And in that cathedral was a wondrous stained-glass window. Its fame had gone abroad over the land. From miles around people pilgrimaged to gaze upon the splendor of this masterpiece of art. One day there came a great storm. The violence of the tempest forced in the window, and it crashed to the marble floor, shattered into a hundred pieces. Great was the grief of the people at the catastrophe which had suddenly bereft the town of its proudest work of art. They gathered up the fragments, huddled them in a box, and carried them to the cellar of the church. One day there came along a stranger and craved permission to see the beautiful window. They told him of its fate. He asked what they had done with the fragments; and they took him to the vault and showed him the broken morsels of glass. "Would you mind giving these to me?" said the stranger. "Take them along," was the reply, "they are no longer of any use to us." The visitor carefully lifted the box and carried it away in his arms. Weeks passed by; then one day came an invitation to the custodians of the cathedral. It was from a famous artist, noted for his master-skill in glass-craft. It summoned them to his study to inspect a stained-glass window, the work of his genius. Ushering them into his studio he stood them before a great veil of canvas. At the touch of his hand upon a cord the canvas dropped. And there before their astonished gaze shone a stained-glass window surpassing in beauty all their eyes had ever beheld. As they gazed entranced upon its rich tints, wondrous patterns, and cunning workmanship the artist turned and said: "This window I have wrought from the fragments of your shattered one, and it is now ready to be replaced."

Once more a great window shed its beauteous light into the dim aisles of the old cathedral, but the splendor of the new far surpassed the glory of the old, and the fame of its strange fashioning filled the land.

Do you say that your plans have been crushed? Then know this: Jesus Christ is a matchless life-mender. *Try Him!*　　　JAMES H. MCCONKEY

November 23

MORNING

～❦～

Thou hast shewed thy people hard things (PS. 60:3).

 I have always been glad that the psalmist said to God that some things were *hard*. There is no mistake about it; there are hard things in life. Some beautiful pink flowers were given me this summer, and as I took them I said, "What are they?" And the answer came, "They are rock flowers; they grow and bloom only on rocks where you can see no soil." Then I thought of God's flowers growing in hard places; and I feel, some-how, that He may have a peculiar tenderness for His "rock flowers" that He may not have for His lilies and roses.　　　MARGARET BOTTOME

The tests of life are to make, not break us. Trouble may demolish a man's business but build up his character. The blow at the outward man may be the greatest blessing to the inner man. If God, then, puts or per-mits anything hard in our lives, be sure that the real peril, the real trou-ble, is what we shall lose if we flinch or rebel.　　　MALTBIE D. BABCOCK

Heroes are forged on anvils hot with pain,
And splendid courage comes but with the test.
Some natures ripen and some natures bloom
Only on blood-wet soil, some souls prove great
Only in moments dark with death or doom.

God gets His best soldiers out of the highlands of affliction.

EVENING

✦

These are they which follow the Lamb whithersoever he goeth.
(REV. 14:4)

There are three classes in the Christian life; the men *of the wing*, the men *of the couch*, and the men *of the road*.

The *first* are those who fly before; they are the pioneers of progress; they are in advance of their fellows.

The *second* are those who stand still, or rather lie still; they are the invalids of the human race—they come not to minister, but to be ministered unto.

The *third* are those who follow; they are *the ambulance corps of humanity;* they are the sacrificial souls that come on behind. I think with John that these last are the most beautiful souls of all. They are lovely in their unobtrusiveness; they do not wish to lead, choosing rather to be in the rear; they come forward only when others are driven backward. They want no glory from the battle, no wreath for the victory, no honorable mention among the heroes. They seek the wounded, the dying, the dead; they anoint for life's burial; they bring spices for the crucified; they give the cup of cold water; they wash the soiled feet. They break the fall of Adam; of Magdalene. They take in Saul of Tarsus after he becomes blind. They are attracted by defects; they are lured by every form of helplessness.

> *They come out to meet the shadows:*
> *They go in the track, not of the lark,*
> *but of the nightingale;*
> *They follow the LAMB.*

Give me the trouble without the glitter, O Lord! Let others lead! I am content to follow. Help me to serve Thee in the background! Is it not written *they that tarry at home divide the spoil?* I cannot fight Thy battles, but I can nurse Thy wounded. I cannot repel Thy foes, but I can repair Thy fortress. I cannot conduct Thy marches, but I can succor those who have fainted by the way.

Write my name amongst those *who follow Thee!*

O Captain of my Salvation, *put me with the ambulance corps!*

GEORGE MATHESON

> *What though the hindmost place is thine,*
> *And thou art in the rear?*
> *This need not cause thy heart a pang,*
> *Nor cost thine eye a tear.*

The post of duty is the place
Where oft the Captain shows His face.

All cannot charge or lead the van,
All can be brave and true;
And where the Captain's standards wave
There's work for all to do;
And work from which thou may'st not flee,
Which must be done, and done by thee.

Among the stragglers, faint and few,
Thou dost thy march pursue;
This need not make thy heart to droop,
The weak may yet be true;
Through many a dark and stormy day
The Captain thus holds on His way.

SELECTED

"They shall go hindmost with their standards" (Num. 2:31).

November 24

MORNING

❧

Be still, and know that I am God (PS. 46:10).

Is there any note of music in all the chorus as mighty as the emphatic pause? Is there any word in all the Psalter more eloquent than that one word, Selah (Pause)? Is there anything more thrilling and awful than the hush that comes before the bursting of the tempest and the strange quiet that seems to fall upon all nature before some preternatural phenomenon or convulsion? Is there anything that can touch our hearts as the *power of stillness?*

There is for the heart that will cease from itself, "the peace of God that passeth all understanding," a "quietness and confidence" which is the source of all strength, a sweet peace "which nothing can offend," a deep rest which the world can neither give nor take away. There is in the deepest center of the soul a chamber of peace where God dwells, and where, if we will only enter in and hush every other sound, we can hear His still, small voice.

There is in the swiftest wheel that revolves upon its axis a place in the very center, where there is no movement at all; and so in the busiest life there may be a place where we dwell alone with God, in eternal stillness. There is only one way to know God. "Be still, and know." "God is in His holy temple; let all the earth keep silence before him."   SELECTED

"All-loving Father, sometimes we have walked under starless skies that dripped darkness like drenching rain. We despaired of starshine or moon-light or sunrise. The sullen blackness gloomed above us as if it would last forever. And out of the dark there spoke no soothing voice to mend our broken hearts. We would gladly have welcomed some wild thunderpeal to break the torturing stillness of that over-brooding night.

"But Thy winsome whisper of eternal love spoke more sweetly to our bruised and bleeding souls than any winds that breathe across aeolian harps. It was Thy 'still small voice' that spoke to us. We were listening and we heard. We looked and saw Thy face radiant with the light of love. And when we heard Thy voice and saw Thy face, new life came back to us as life comes back to withered blooms that drink the summer rain."

EVENING

I know the plans which I am planning for you, plans of welfare and not of calamity, to give you a future and a hope.
(JER. 29:11, ROTHERHAM)

The love of God a perfect plan
Is planning now for thee,
It holds "a future and a hope,"
Which yet thou canst not see.

Though for a season, in the dark,
He asks thy perfect trust,
E'en that thou in surrender "lay
Thy treasure in the dust,"

Yet He is planning all the while,
Unerringly He guides
The life of him, who holds His will
More dear than all besides.

Trust were not trust if thou couldst see
The ending of the way,

Nor couldst thou learn His songs by night,
Were life one radiant day.

Amid the shadows here He works
The plan designed above,
"A future and a hope" for thee
In His exceeding love.

"A future"—abiding fruit,
With loving kindness crowned;
"A hope"—which shall thine own transcend,
As Heaven the earth around.

Though veiled as yet, one day thine eyes
Shall see His plan unfold,
And clouds that darkened once the path
Shall shine with Heaven's gold.

Enriched to all eternity
The steadfast soul shall stand,
That, "unoffended," trusted Him
Who all life's pathway planned.

I have an heritage of bliss,
Which yet I may not see;
The Hand that bled to make it mine,
Is keeping it for me.
FREDA HANBURY ALLEN

November 25

MORNING

∽

*Take the arrows. . . . Smite upon the ground. And he smote thrice
and stayed. And the man of God was wroth with him, and said,
Thou shouldest have smitten five or six times* (2 KINGS 13:18–19).

How striking and eloquent the message of these words! Jehoash
thought he had done very well when he duplicated and triplicated
what to him was certainly an extraordinary act of faith. But the Lord and
the prophet were bitterly disappointed *because he had stopped halfway.*

He got something. He got much. He got exactly what he believed for in the final test, but he did not get all that the prophet meant and the Lord wanted to bestow. He missed much of the meaning of the promise and the fullness of the blessing. He got something better than the human, but he did not get God's best.

Beloved, how solemn is the application! How heartsearching the message of God to us! How important that we should learn to pray through! Shall we claim all the fullness of the promise and all the possibilities of believing prayer?   A. B. SIMPSON

"Unto him that is able to do exceeding abundantly above all that we ask or think" (Eph. 3:20).

There is no other such piling up of words in Paul's writings as these, "exceeding abundantly above all," and each word is packed with infinite love and power to "do" for His praying saints. There is one limitation, "according to the power that worketh in us." He will do just as much *for* us as we let Him do *in* us. The power that saved us, washed us with His own blood, filled us with might by His Spirit, kept us in manifold temptations, will work for us, meeting every emergency, every crisis, every circumstance, and every adversary.   THE ALLIANCE

EVENING

∾

Take now thy son . . . whom thou lovest. (GEN. 22:2)

God's command is "Take *now*" not presently. To go to the height God shows can never be done *presently*. It must be done *now*.

"And offer him there for a burnt offering upon one of the mountains which I will tell thee of." The mount of the Lord is the very height of the trial into which God brings His servant. There is no indication of the cost to Abraham; his implicit understanding of God so far outreaches his explicit knowledge that he trusts God utterly and climbs the highest height on which God can ever prove him, and remains unutterably true to Him.

There was not conflict; *that was over.* Abraham's confidence was fixed; he did not consult with flesh and blood—his own or anyone else's; he *instantly* obeyed. The point is, that though all other voices should proclaim differently, obedience to the dictates of the Spirit of God at all costs is to be the attitude of the faithful soul.

Always beware when you want to confer with your own flesh and blood— i.e., your own sympathies, your own insight. When our Lord is bringing us into personal relationship with Himself, it is always the individual relationship He breaks down.

If God has given the command, He will look after everything; your business is to *get up and go!*   OSWALD CHAMBERS

"The Holy Ghost saith, *Today*" (Heb. 3:7, emphasis added).

> *Not of the sunlight,*
> *Not of the moonlight,*
> *Not of the starlight!*
> *O young Mariner,*
> *Down to the haven*
> *Call your companions,*
> *Launch your vessel*
> *and crowd your canvas,*
> *And, ere it vanishes*
> *Over the margin,*
> *After it, follow it,*
> *Follow the Gleam.*
> TENNYSON

November 26

MORNING

〜✺〜

And Caleb said unto her, What wouldest thou? Who answered, Give me a blessing; for thou hast given me a south land; give me also springs of water. And he gave her the upper springs, and the nether springs (JOSH. 15:18–19).

There are both upper and nether springs. They are *springs,* not stagnant pools. There are joys and blessings that flow from above through the hottest summer and the most desert land of sorrow and trial. The lands of Achsah were "south lands," lying under a burning sun and often parched with burning heat. But from the hills came the unfailing springs, that cooled, refreshed and fertilized all the land.

There are springs that flow in the low places of life, in the hard places, in the desert places, in the lone places, in the *common places,* and no matter what may be our situation, we can always find these upper springs.

Abraham found them amid the hills of Canaan. Moses found them among the rocks of Midian. David found them among the ashes of Ziklag when his property was gone, his family captives and his people talked of stoning him, but "David encouraged himself in the Lord."

Isaiah found them in the awful days of Sennacherib's invasion, when the mountains seemed hurled into the midst of the sea, but faith could sing: "There is a river whose streams make glad the city of God. God is in the midst of her: she shall not be moved."

The martyrs found them amid the flames, and reformers amid their foes and conflicts, and we can find them all the year if we have the Comforter in our hearts and have learned to say with David: *"All my springs are in thee."*

How many and how precious these springs, and how much more there is to be possessed of God's own fullness! A. B. SIMPSON

I said: "The desert is so wide!"
I said: "The desert is so bare!
What springs to quench my thirst are there?
Whence shall I from the tempest hide?"

I said: "The desert is so lone!
Nor gentle voice, nor loving face
Will brighten any smallest space."
I paused or ere my moan was done!

I heard a flow of hidden springs;
Before me palms rose green and fair;
The birds were singing; all the air
Did shine and stir with angels' wings!

And One said mildly: "Why, indeed,
Take over-anxious thought for that
The morrow bringeth! See you not
The Father knoweth what you need?"

SELECTED

∾⤫∿

Come apart with me, and rest awhile. (MARK 6:31, TRANS.)

*T*here is one pause in music of which the untrained singer does not know the value—the pause: it is not the cessation of the music; it is a part of it.

Before the tide ebbs or flows there is always a time of poise when it is neither ebbing nor flowing.

In a Christian life that is to be effective, there will always be the *pause* and the *poise*.

The desert has been God's training school for many of His prophets— Abraham, Moses, Elijah, Paul. But not all who come from Arabia are prophets; and God has other schools. Before the years of witness, there were the years of stillness. Every witness with a great message has these years. Let not the saints shrink from the discipline and training! The sightless days will mean a grander vision; the silent years, the sweeter song. If the Lord puts you in the dark, it is but to strengthen your eyes to bear the glory that He is preparing for you; if He bids you be silent, it is but to tune your tongue to His praise. Remember that the *pause* is part of the music.

The great Composer writes the theme
And gives us each a part to play;
To some a sweet and flowing air,
Smooth and unbroken all the way;

They pour their full heart's gladness out
In notes of joy and service blent;
But some He gives long bars of "rests,"
With idle voice and instrument.

He who directs the singing spheres,
The music of the morning stars,
Needs, for His full creation's hymn,
The quiet of the soundless bars.

Be silent unto God, my soul,
If this the score He writes for thee,
And "hold the rest," play no false note
To mar His perfect harmony.

Yet be thou watchful for thy turn,
Strike on the instant, true and clear,

Lest from the grand, melodious whole
Thy note be missing to His ear.
ANNIE JOHNSON FLINT

November 27

MORNING

~~∞~~

For with God nothing shall be impossible (LUKE 1:37).

ar up in the alpine hollows, year by year God works one of His marvels. The snow patches lie there, frozen with ice at their edge from the strife of sunny days and frosty nights; and through that ice-crust come, unscathed, flowers that bloom.

Back in the days of the bygone summer, the little soldanelle plant spread its leaves wide and flat on the ground, to drink in the sun rays, and it kept them stored in the root through the winter. Then spring came, and stirred the pulses even below the snowshroud, and as it sprouted, warmth was given out in such strange measure that it thawed a little dome in the snow above its head.

Higher and higher it grew and always above it rose the bell of air, till the flower-bud formed safely within it: and at last the icy covering of the air-bell gave way and let the blossom through into the sunshine, the crystalline texture of its mauve petals sparkling like snow itself as if it bore the traces of the flight through which it had come.

And the fragile thing rings an echo in our hearts that none of the jewel-like flowers nestled in the warm turf on the slopes below could waken. We love to see the impossible done. And so does God.

Face it out to the end, cast away every shadow of hope on the human side as an absolute hindrance to the divine, heap up all the difficulties together recklessly, and pile as many more on as you can find; you cannot get beyond the blessed climax of impossibility. Let faith swing out to Him. He is the God of the impossible.   SELECTED

༄

Spikenard, very costly. (JOHN 12:3)

ᴸove's reckoning will always be *unusual*. It was by no means the *ordinary* thing to do for the homeless Savior; *that* breaking of the alabaster and *that* lavish anointing were quite out of the *usual way*.

Did Mary's heart beat painfully as she glided in with her hoarded treasure? Did she intuitively hide her purpose from all eyes but His, who read its irrepressible meaning? Perhaps she thought only of Him who was her ALL.

Apparently she obtained her spikenard *for the very purpose* that she might anoint the Lord's body in burial. Possibly it was only an impulse which made her decide to anoint Him *beforehand*. Let us rejoice that she made the Master's heart glad before it was too late.

One tiny violet of encouragement will mean more to those with whom we live today than will acres of orchids when their pulses are stilled in death.

There were *four women* who set out later with their spices, only to find the empty tomb.

The opportunity for anointing had passed.

It is passing today! Not in realms of glory will we be able to share in His sufferings, to help in bearing the Cross. *Here, and here alone* such service may be ours.

O soul of mine, be extravagant in love of Jesus!

There is no fragrance like that of my alabaster box—the box I break for Him!

> *I shall not pass this way again,*
> *But far beyond earth's "where and when,"*
> *May I look back along the road*
> *Where on both sides good seed I sowed.*
>
> *I shall not pass this way again;*
> *May wisdom guide my tongue and pen,*
> *And love be mine, that so I may*
> *Plant roses all along the way.*
>
> *I shall not pass this way again;*
> *Grant me to soothe the hearts of men,*
> *Faithful to friends, true to my God;*
> *A fragrance on the path I trod.*

November 28

Thou makest the outgoings of the morning and evening to rejoice
(PS. 65:8).

Get up early and go to the mountain and watch God make a morning. The dull gray will give way as God pushes the sun toward the horizon, and there will be tints and hues of every shade, that will blend into one perfect light as the full-orbed sun bursts into view. As the King of day moves forth majestically, flooding the earth and every lowly vale, listen to the music of heaven's choir as it sings of the majesty of God and the glory of the morning.

> *In the holy hush of the early dawn*
> *I hear a Voice—*
> *I am with you all the day,*
> *Rejoice! Rejoice!*

The clear, pure light of the morning made me long for the truth in my heart, which alone could make me pure and clear as the morning, tune me up to the concert-pitch of the nature around me. And the wind that blew from the sunrise made me hope in the God who had first breathed into my nostrils the breath of life; that He would at length so fill me with His breath, His mind, His Spirit, that I should think only His thoughts, and live His life, finding therein my own life, only glorified infinitely. What should we poor humans do without our God's nights and mornings?

GEORGE MACDONALD

> *In the early morning hours,*
> *'Twixt the night and day,*
> *While from earth the darkness passes*
> *Silently away;*
>
> *Then 'tis sweet to talk with Jesus*
> *In thy chamber still—*
> *For the coming day and duties*
> *Ask to know His will.*
>
> *Then He'll lead the way before you,*
> *Mountains laying low;*
> *Making desert places blossom,*

Sweet'ning Marah's flow.

Would you know this life of triumph,
Victory all the way?
Then put God in the beginning
Of each coming day.

EVENING

∾⧸⧹∾

Who keepeth His promise forever. (PS. 146:6, TRANS.)

God never forgets His Word. Long ago He promised a Redeemer; and although *He waited four thousand years,* the promise at last was most surely fulfilled.

He promised Abraham a son; and although a quarter of a century of testing intervened, the promise at last came literally true. He promised Abraham the Land of Promise as an inheritance; and although *four hundred years* of trial intervened, at last the land was possessed. *He promised Jeremiah* that after *seventy years* the captives should return from Babylon; and on the very hour, the action answered to the Word. *He promised Daniel* that at a definite time Messiah should appear; and the most extraordinary evidence that we have to offer to the doubting Hebrew today that Jesus is his Messiah, is the literal fulfillment of the prophecy of Daniel.

Just as true are God's promises to the believer. They are all "Yea and Amen" in Christ Jesus. He has guaranteed them. The promises of God form a great checkbook. Every one is endorsed by the Mediator, and His word and honor are pledged to their fulfillment. To make them "Yea and Amen" *you must sign your name* upon the back of the promise and then *personally appropriate it.*

"No one who believes in Him shall be disappointed" *(Rom. 10:11, Way's trans.).*

November 29

〜❧〜

Nevertheless afterward (HEB. 12:11).

There is a legend that tells of a German baron who at his castle on the Rhine, stretched wires from tower to tower, that the winds might convert them into an aeolian harp. And the soft breezes played about the castle, but no music was born.

But one night there arose a great tempest, and hill and castle were smitten by the fury of the mighty winds. The baron went to the threshold to look out upon the terror of the storm, and the aeolian harp was filling the air with strains that rang out even above the clamor of the tempest. It needed the tempest to bring out the music!

And have we not known men whose lives have not given out any entrancing music in the day of a calm prosperity, but who, when the tempest drove against them have astonished their fellows by the power and strength of their music?

> *Rain, rain*
> *Beating against the pane!*
> *How endlessly it pours*
> *Out of doors*
> *From the blackened sky—*
> *I wonder why!*
> *Flowers, flowers,*
>
> *Upspringing after showers,*
> *Blossoming fresh and fair,*
> *Everywhere!*
> *Ah, God has explained*
> *Why it rained!*

You can always count on God to make the "afterward" of difficulties, if rightly overcome, a thousand times richer and fairer than the forward. "No chastening . . . seemeth joyous . . . nevertheless afterward. . . ." What a yield!

❧❧

From this day will I bless you. (HAG. 2:19)

God has certain dates from which He begins to bless us. On the day of consecration (Gen. 22:16–17), the day when our all is surrendered to Him—on that day untold blessing begins.

Have we come to *that date?*

"It was on the 22nd of July, 1690, that happy day," says Madame Guyon, "that my soul was delivered from all its pains. On that day I was restored, as it were, to perfect liberty. I was *no longer depressed,* no longer borne down under the burden of sorrow. I had thought God lost, and lost forever; but I found Him again. And He returned to me with unspeakable magnificence and purity. In a wonderful manner difficult to explain, *all that which had been taken from me was not only restored, but restored with increase and new advantages. In Thee, O my God, I found it all, and more than all!* The peace which I now possessed was all holy, heavenly, inexpressible. What I had possessed some years before, in the period of my spiritual enjoyment, was consolation, peace—the *gifts* of God, but now that I was fully yielded to the will of God, whether that will was consoling or otherwise, I might now be said to possess not merely consolation, but the God of consolation; not merely peace, but the God of peace.

"*One day of this happiness, which consisted in simple rest or harmony with God's will, whatever that will might be, was sufficient to counterbalance years of suffering.* Certainly it was not I, myself, who had fastened my soul to the Cross and, under the operations of a providence just but inexorable, had drained, if I may so express it, the blood of the life of nature to the last drop. I did not understand it then; but I understand it *now.* It was the Lord who did it. *It was God that destroyed me, that He might give me true life.*"

> *Oh, the Spirit-filled life may be thine, may be thine,*
> *In thy soul evermore the Shechinah may shine;*
> *It is thine to live with the tempests all stilled,*
> *It is thine with the blest Holy Ghost to be filled;*
> *It is thine, even thine, for thy Lord has so willed.*

November 30

And seekest thou great things for thyself? seek them not: for, behold, I will bring evil upon all flesh, saith the Lord: but thy life will I give unto thee for a prey in all places whither thou goest (JER. 45:5).

A promise given for hard places, and a promise of safety and life in the midst of tremendous pressure, a life "for a prey." It may well adjust itself to our own times, which are growing harder as we near the end of the age, and the tribulation times.

What is the meaning of "a life for a prey"? It means a life snatched out of the jaws of the destroyer, as David snatched the lamb from the lion. It means not removal from the noise of the battle and the presence of our foes; but it means a table in the midst of our enemies, a shelter from the storm, a fortress amid the foe, a life preserved in the face of continual pressure: Paul's healing when pressed out of measure so that he despaired of life; Paul's divine help when the thorn remained, but the power of Christ rested upon him and the grace of Christ was sufficient. Lord, give me my life for a prey, and in the hardest places help me today to be victorious. *FROM* DAYS OF HEAVEN UPON EARTH

We often pray to be delivered from calamities; we even trust that we shall be; but we do not pray to be made what we should be, in the very presence of the calamities; to live amid them, as long as they last, in the consciousness that we are held and sheltered by the Lord, and can therefore remain in the midst of them, so long as they continue, without any hurt. For forty days and nights, the Savior was kept in the presence of Satan in the wilderness, and that, under circumstances of special trial, His human nature being weakened by want of food and rest. The furnace was heated seven times more than it was wont to be heated, but the three Hebrew children were kept a season amid its flames as calm and composed in the presence of the tyrant's last appliances of torture, as they were in the presence of himself before their time of deliverance came. And the livelong night did Daniel sit among the lions, and when he was taken up out of the den, "no manner of hurt was found upon him, because he believed in his God." They dwelt in the presence of the enemy, because they dwelt in the presence of God.

The battle is the LORD'S! (1 SAM. 17:47)

*H*ow prone we are to lose sight of this, and to imagine, because we see only our little corner in the conflict, that the battle is ours!

If the battle is the Lord's, then the responsibilities for planning belong to Him. Everything connected with the line of attack, the method of defense, must belong to Him. We need not be anxious as to the enemy's subtlety, activity, or power.

"As captain of the host of the LORD *I am now come."*

He has a full view of the enemy's movements, and a perfect knowledge of the enemy's devices. He has anticipated all the enemy's wiles. It is impossible for Him to be deceived, or to be taken by surprise. It is His glory that is at stake; the honor of His name that is being assailed. *He is able to withstand the mightiest foe!*

If the battle is the Lord's the supplies will be all-sufficient. No one knows how much is wanted in the day of battle like that General who has been through many campaigns. *We shall lack nothing to make us victorious warriors.*

The Victory is certain! The Captain on whose side we are has never known defeat. He goes forth conquering and to conquer. The enemy may apparently gain temporary advantage at different points of the battle, but *victory over Christ by Satan is simply impossible!*

But He expects us to *rest* in His wisdom. In the thick of the fight, in the midst of the smoke and din of battle, we may fail to see the wisdom of all God's ways. When we cannot see, it is then that we must *rest in His wisdom.* Let us have confidence in His power, and be obedient to His commands.

> *I will not fear the battle,*
> *If Thou art by my side.*

"Now thanks be to God who leads us on in the train of his triumph" (2 Cor. 2:14, Conybeare & Howson).

Queen Victoria said, "We are not interested in the possibilities of defeat. They do not exist!"

December 1

There remaineth, therefore, a rest to the people of God (HEB. 4:9).

The rest includes victory, "And the Lord gave them rest round about;
. . . the Lord delivered all their enemies into their hand"
(JOSH. 21:44).

He will beautify the meek with victory
(PS. 149:4, ROTHERHAM MARGIN).

An eminent Christian worker tells of his mother who was a very anxious and troubled Christian. he would talk with her by the hour trying to convince her of the sinfulness of fretting, but to no avail. She was like the old lady who once said she had suffered so much, especially from the troubles that never came.

But one morning the mother came down to breakfast wreathed in smiles. He asked her what had happened, and she told him that in the night she had a dream.

She was walking along a highway with a great crowd of people who seemed so tired and burdened. They were nearly all carrying little black bundles, and she noticed that there were numerous repulsive looking beings which she thought were demons dropping these black bundles for the people to pick up and carry.

Like the rest, she too had her needless load, and was weighed down with the Devil's bundles. Looking up, after a while, she saw a Man with a bright and loving face, passing hither and thither through the crowd, and comforting the people.

At last He came near her, and she saw that it was her Savior. She looked up and told Him how tired she was, and He smiled sadly and said:

"My dear child, I did not give you these loads; you have no need of them. They are the Devil's burdens and they are wearing out your life. Just drop them; refuse to touch them with one of your fingers and you will find the path easy and you will be as if borne on eagle's wings."

He touched her hand, and lo, peace and joy thrilled her frame and, flinging down her burden, she was about to throw herself at His feet in joyful thanksgiving, when suddenly she awoke and found that all her cares were gone. From that day to the close of her life she was the most cheerful and happy member of the household.

And the night shall be filled with music,
And the cares that infest the day,
Shall fold their tents like the Arabs,
And as silently steal away.
LONGFELLOW

EVENING

They saw no man, save Jesus only. (MATT. 17:8)

When Samuel Rutherford lay in Aberdeen prison, we are told he used to write at the top of his letters, *"God's Palace, Aberdeen."*

When Madame Guyon was imprisoned in the castle at Vincennes, she said: "It seems as though I were a little bird whom the Lord has placed in a cage, and that I have nothing now to do but sing."

And prisons shall palaces prove
If Jesus abides with me there.

I never had in all my life so great an inlet into the Word of God as now; those Scriptures that I saw nothing in before, are in this place and state [in Bedford Jail] made to shine upon me; Jesus Christ also was never more real and apparent than now; here I have seen and felt Him indeed!

JOHN BUNYAN

The New Testament tells of no regret on the part of those who sacrificed themselves for Christ. The apostles never pathetically recite the story of what they gave up for the Christian ministry. The ancient martyrs sometimes kissed the stake at which they suffered so cruelly.

This is the spirit in which *we* should lose, suffer, and die for Christ's sake.

By thus renouncing all, we gain all. Nothing yields higher interest than loving self-denials for the highest claims.

"I have seen the headlight of a giant engine rushing onward through the darkness, heedless of opposition and fearless of danger. I have seen the lightning at midnight leap athwart a storm-swept sky, splintering chaotic darkness with beams of light until the heavens glittered like midday sun. I knew this was grand, but the grandest thing this side of the light that flows from God Almighty's throne, is the blessed benediction of a human life that spends itself in forgetful service for a brokenhearted world and finds its home at last in the bosom of the everlasting God."

I walk alone, and I am sore afraid;
My way is dark, my path with thorns o'erlaid;
Draw near me, Lord, and take my trembling hand
And make me brave to join Thy pilgrim band.

Thou hast a band which fears not dark nor death,
Which suffers agony at every breath,
Yet sings with joy e'en in the midst of pain,
With whom the greatest loss is greatest gain.

Who would not walk with such a company?
Who would not sing with such an ecstasy?
Did I say lone and fear? May God forgive
And teach me, e'en through sorrow, how to live.

Life is not life which knows no shrinking fears;
Life is not life which sheds no bitter tears;
This is true life when, through dark suffering,
One learns from Christ and men brave conquering.

Then lead me on thou martyr-host of God!
Then lead me on, O Christ, to Thine abode;
There with Thy holy ones I shall find rest
And learn that death, in life, was God's great best.

HENRY W. FROST

December 2

MORNING

Perfect through sufferings (HEB. 2:10).

Steel is iron *plus* fire. Soil is rock, *plus* heat, or glacier crushing. Linen is flax *plus* the bath that cleans, the comb that separates, and the flail that pounds, and the shuttle that weaves. Human character must have a *plus* attached to it. The world does not forget great characters. But great characters are not made of luxuries, they are made by suffering.

I heard of a mother who brought into her home as a companion to her own son, a crippled boy who was also a hunchback. She had warned her boy to be very careful in his relations to him, and not to touch the sensitive part of his life but go right on playing with him as if he were an ordinary boy. She listened to her son as they were playing; and after a few minutes he said to his companion: "Do you know what you have got on your back?" The little hunchback was embarrassed, and he hesitated a moment. The boy said: "It is the box in which your wings are; and some-day God is going to cut it open, and then you will fly away and be an angel."

Someday, God is going to reveal the fact to every Christian, that the very principles they now rebel against, have been the instruments which He used in perfecting their characters and molding them into perfection, polished stones for His great building yonder.   CORTLAND MYERS

Suffering is a wonderful fertilizer to the roots of character. The great object of this life is character. This is the only thing we can carry with us into eternity. . . . To gain the most of it and the best of it is the object of probation.   AUSTIN PHELPS

By the thorn road and no other is the mount of vision won.

EVENING

He is altogether lovely! (SONG 5:16)

What a glorious fact it is that there is one life that can be held up before the eyes of humanity as *a perfect pattern!* There were lips that never spoke unkindness, that never uttered an untruth; there were eyes that never looked aught but love and purity and bliss; there were arms that never closed against wretchedness or penitence; there was a bosom which never throbbed with sin, nor ever was excited by unholy impulse; there was a man free from all undue selfishness, and whose life was spent in going about doing good.

There was One who loved all mankind, and who loved them more than Himself, and who gave Himself to die that they might live; there was One who went into the gates of death, that the gates of death might never hold us in; there was One who lay in the grave, with its dampness, its coldness, its chill, and its horror, and taught humanity how it might ascend above the grave; there was One who, though He walked on earth, had His conversation in heaven, who took away the curtain that hid immortality from view, and presented to us the Father God in all His glory and in all His love.

Such an One is the standard held up in the Church of Christ. The

Church rallies round the Cross and gathers around Jesus; and it is because He is so attractive, and lovely, and glorious, that they are coming from the ends of the earth to see the salvation of God.

BISHOP MATTHEW SIMPSON

Less than Thyself, Oh do not give.
In might Thyself within me live;
Come all Thou hast and art.

Oh, there is nothing so admirable, nothing which seems to us in our best moods so worthy of our seeking, and so rich in its possession as that holiness which is the summit of true perfection; not a holiness which is distant and frigid, but a holiness which makes the eyes more tender in their softened light, and the lips more affluent of genial speech, and the hand more helpful in its ready service; which makes an end in the human heart of its passions and selfishness, its moroseness and its meanness; which lifts man up to God, and brings God down to man; and which, should it become pervasive and universal, would make every soul a miniature heaven, and change our woeful earth into a Paradise regained.

"We . . . beholding . . . the glory of the Lord, are changed into the same image . . . even as by the Spirit of the Lord" (2 Cor. 3:18).

BISHOP NINDE

The honeysuckle blossoms drenched with rain
That lend enchantment to a summer night;
The purple violet hidden from the sight
Beside the border of a country lane;
The jasmine vine, which hangs its golden chain
Within the forest like a twinkling light,
Have flourished for a time and taken flight—
Their ashes have returned to earth again.
But what of one whose life was like a flower
Which scatters gentle perfume everywhere,
Whose face had caught the radiance of the sky
From looking ever upward till that hour
When the Great Gardener stripped the branches bare?
God smells such fragrance from His throne on high.

FRAGRANCE, BY THOMAS KIMBER

December 3

Is it well with thy husband? Is it well with the child? And she answered, It is well (2 KINGS 4:26).

> Be strong, my soul!
> Thy loved ones go
> Within the veil. God's thine, e'en so;
> Be strong.
>
> Be strong, my soul!
> Death looms in view.
> Lo, hear thy God! He'll bear thee through;
> Be strong.

For sixty-two years and five months I had a beloved wife, and now, in my ninety-second year I am left alone. But I turn to the ever-present Jesus, as I walk up and down in my room, and say, "Lord Jesus, I am alone, and yet not alone—Thou art with me, Thou art my Friend. Now, Lord, comfort me, strengthen me, give to Thy poor servant everything Thou seest he needs." And we should not be satisfied till we are brought to this, that we know the Lord Jesus Christ experimentally, habitually to be our Friend: at all times, and under all circumstances, ready to prove Himself to be our Friend.

GEORGE MUELLER

Afflictions cannot injure when blended with submission.

Ice breaks many a branch, and so I see a great many persons bowed down and crushed by their afflictions. But now and then I meet one that sings in affliction, and then I thank God for my own sake as well as his. There is no such sweet singing as a song in the night. You recollect the story of the woman who, when her only child died, in rapture looking up, as with the face of an angel, said, "I give you joy, my darling." That single sentence has gone with me years and years down through my life, quickening and comforting me.

HENRY WARD BEECHER

> E'en for the dead I will not bind my soul to grief;
> Death cannot long divide.
> For is it not as though the rose that climbed my garden wall
> Has blossomed on the other side?
> Death doth hide,

But not divide;
Thou art but on Christ's other side!
Thou art with Christ, and Christ with me;
In Christ united still are we.

EVENING

❧

That they may have life . . . more abundantly. (JOHN 10:10)

What a contrast there is between a barren desert and the luxuriant oasis with its waving palms and its glorious verdure! between gaunt and hungry flocks and the herds that lie down in green pastures and beside the still waters; between the viewless plain and the mountain height with its "land of far distances."

What a difference there is between the aridity of an artificial, irrigated, stinted existence—a desert existence, and a life of abundant rains, crowding vegetation, and harvests that come almost of themselves—*the abundant life!*

The former is like the *shallow stream* where your boat every moment touches bottom or strikes some hidden rock; the latter is where your deep keel never touches ground and you ride *the ocean's wildest swells!*

There are some Christians who always seem to be kept on scant measure. Their spiritual garments are threadbare, their whole bearing that of people who are poverty-stricken and kept on short allowance—hard up, and on the ragged edge of want and bankruptcy. They come through "by the skin of their teeth" and are "saved so as by fire."

There are other souls who *"have life . . . more abundantly."* Their love "beareth all things, believeth all things, hopeth all things, endureth all things," and "never faileth." Their patience has "all long-suffering with joyfulness." Their peace "passeth all understanding." Their joy is "joy unspeakable and full of glory." Their service is so free and glad that duty is a delight. In a word, this life reaches out into the infinite as well as the eternal, sailing on the shoreless and fathomless seas of God and His infinite grace.

Oh, *where* is such a life to be found? How can the desert place be made to bring forth *abundant life?*

"Oh, where is the sea?" the fishes cried,
As they swam the crystal waters through
"We have heard from of old of the ocean tide,
And we long to look on the waters blue.
The wise ones speak of the infinite sea—
Oh, who can tell us if such there be?"

Are we who live in the sea of the infinite to imitate those silly fishes, and ask, *"Where* is the God who is 'not far from everyone of us,' who may be in our inmost hearts by faith, and in whom 'we live, and move, and have our being'? DEAN FARRAR

"Hast thou entered into the fountains of the sea?" *(Job 38:16, Trans.).*
The Psalmist said: "O God, with Thee is the fountain of life." "All my fresh springing fountains are in Thee!"

Gushing Fountains!

December 4

MORNING

He went up into a mountain apart (MATT. 14:23).

One of the blessings of the old-time Sabbath was its calm, its restfulness, its holy peace. There is a strange strength conceived in solitude. Crows go in flocks and wolves in packs, but the lion and the eagle are solitaires.

Strength is not in bluster and noise. Strength is in quietness. The lake must be calm if the heavens are to be reflected on its surface. Our Lord loved the people, but how often we read of His going away from them for a brief season. He tried every little while to withdraw from the crowd. He was always stealing away at evening to the hills. Most of His ministry was carried on in the towns and cities by the seashore, but He loved the hills the best, and oftentimes when night fell He would plunge into their peaceful depths.

The one thing needed above all others today is that we shall go with our Lord, and sit at His feet in the sacred privacy of His blessed presence. Oh, for the lost art of meditation! Oh, for the culture of the secret place! Oh, for the tonic of waiting upon God! SELECTED

It is well to live in the valley sweet,
Where the work of the world is done,
Where the reapers sing in the fields of wheat,
As they toil till the set of sun.
But beyond the meadows, the hills I see

Where the noises of traffic cease,
And I follow a Voice that calleth to me
From the hilltop regions of peace.

Aye, to live is sweet in the valley fair,
And to toil till the set of sun;
But my spirit yearns for the hilltop's air
When the day and its work are done.
For a Presence breathes o'er the silent hills,
And its sweetness is living yet;
The same deep calm all the hillside fills,
As breathed over Olivet.

Every life that would be strong must have its Holy of Holies into which only God enters.

EVENING

Tender-hearted. (EPH. 4:32)

It is much easier to convince a human soul of its natural impurity, than to convince it of its natural hardness and utter destitution of heavenly and Divine tenderness. *The very essence of the Gospel is Divinely imparted tenderness and sweetness of spirit.* Even among intensely religious people, nothing is rarer to find than a continuous and all-pervading spirit of tenderness.

Tenderness of spirit is not the tenderness of mind and manner which results from high culture and a beautiful social training, though these are very valuable in life. No, *it is a supernatural work throughout the whole spiritual being. It is an exquisitely interior fountain of God's own sweetness and tenderness of nature, opened up in the inner spirit to such a degree that it completely inundates the soul, overflowing all the mental faculties and saturating with its sweet waters the manners, expressions, words, and tones of the voice; mellowing the will, softening the judgment, melting the affections, refining the manners, and molding the whole being after the image of Him who was infinitely meek and lowly in heart.*

Tenderness of spirit cannot be borrowed or put on for special occasions; it is emphatically supernatural, and must flow out incessantly from the inner fountains of the life.

Deep tenderness of spirit is the very soul and marrow of the Christ life.

What specific gravity is to the planet, what beauty is to the rainbow, what perfume is to the rose, what marrow is to the bone, what rhythm is to poetry, what the pulse is to the heart, what harmony is to music, what heat is to the human body—all this, and much more, is tenderness of spirit to religion. It is possible to be very religious, and staunch, and persevering in all Christian duties; possible, even, to be sanctified, to be a brave defender and preacher of holiness, to be mathematically orthodox and blameless in outward life, and very zealous in good works, and yet to be greatly lacking in tenderness of spirit—that all-subduing, all-melting love, which is the very cream and quintessence of Heaven, and which incessantly streamed out from the voice and eyes of the blessed Jesus.

I would that I could be
A wound-dresser
Of souls—
Reaching the aching heart,
The tortured mind,
Calming them as the night
Calms tired bodies
When she drops the mantle of sleep
Over the world.
As each cold, glittering star
So might I stand in mine,
But with the warmth of a smile
On my face,
And in my eyes
An image of the Soul Divine.

December 5

MORNING

O Lord, I know that the way of man is not in himself: it is not in man that walketh to direct his steps (JER. 10:23).

Lead me in a plain path (PS. 27:11).

Many people want to direct God, instead of resigning themselves to be directed by Him; to show Him a way, instead of passively following where He leads.
MADAME GUYON

I said: "Let me walk in the field";
God said: "Nay, walk in the town";
I said: "There are no flowers there";
He said: "No flowers, but a crown."

I said: "But the sky is black,
There is nothing but noise and din";
But He wept as He sent me back,
"There is more," He said, "there is sin."

I said: "But the air is thick,
And fogs are veiling the sun";
He answered: "Yet souls are sick,
And souls in the dark undone."

I said: "I shall miss the light,
And friends will miss me, they say";
He answered me, "Choose tonight,
If I am to miss you, or they."

I pleaded for time to be given;
He said: "Is it hard to decide?
It will not seem hard in Heaven
To have followed the steps of your Guide."

I cast one look at the field,
Then set my face to the town;
He said: "My child, do you yield?
Will you leave the flowers for the crown?"

Then into His hand went mine,
And into my heart came He;
And I walk in a light Divine,
The path I had feared to see.

GEORGE MACDONALD

EVENING

Do not be over-anxious about anything. (PHIL. 4:6 WEYMOUTH)

I recall an experience in my own Christian life," wrote James H. McConkey. "My father was dying of a disease *brought on by worriment.* A great physician had been summoned from the city. He was closeted with my father for a long time. Then he came out of the sick chamber soberly shaking his head. There was no hope. My father's earthly race was run. My dear mother asked the great doctor to take me aside for a conference; for I myself was breaking in body, and from the same dread enemy which overthrows so many Christian people—*anxious care.*

"The kind physician took me into another room and we sat down for a heart-to-heart talk. Very searchingly, and with all the skill of an expert, did he draw from me the humiliating fact that I was a prey of worriment and suffering from its dread results. In a few keen, incisive sentences, with no attempt at concealment he told me that I had fallen a victim of the same habit that had been my father's undoing, and that unless I overcame it there was no hope for me even as there was none for him.

"I went upstairs. I threw myself upon my knees in my bedchamber. I cried out in my agony of soul: 'O Christ! He says I must overcome worriment, and Thou alone knowest how I have *tried* to do so. I have fought; I have struggled; I have wept bitter tears. And *I have failed*. Oh, Lord Jesus, unless Thou dost undertake for me now it is all over with me.'

"Then and there I threw myself in utter helplessness upon Christ. Somehow, where before I had been struggling, I now found myself trusting as I had never quite done before. From that time onward Jesus Christ began to give me the beauty of victory for the somber ashes of defeat."

> *It is God's will that I should cast*
> *On Him my care each day;*
> *He also bids me not to cast*
> *My confidence away.*
> *But, Oh! I am so stupid, that*
> *When taken unawares,*
> *I cast away my confidence,*
> *And carry all my cares.*

December 6

∽⁓

Behold, I come quickly: hold that fast which thou hast, that no man take thy crown (REV. 3:11).

George Mueller bears this testimony, "When it pleased God in July, 1829, to reveal to my heart the truth of the personal return of the Lord Jesus, and to show me that I had made a great mistake in looking for the conversion of the world, the effect that it produced upon me was this: From my *inmost soul* I was stirred up to feel compassion for perishing sinners, and for the slumbering world around me lying in the wicked one, and considered, 'Ought I not to do what I can for the Lord Jesus while He tarries, and to rouse a slumbering church?' "

There may be many hard years of hard work before the consummation, but the signs are to me so encouraging that I would not be unbelieving if I saw the wing of the apocalyptic angel spread for its last triumphal flight in this day's sunset; or if tomorrow morning the ocean cables should thrill us with the news that Christ the Lord had alighted on Mount Olivet or Mount Calvary to proclaim universal dominion. O you dead churches wake up! O Christ, descend! Scarred temple, take the crown! Bruised hand, take the sceptre! Wounded foot, step the throne! Thine is the kingdom.   REV. T. DEWITT TALMAGE, D.D.

It may be in the evening,
When the work of the day is done,
And you have time to sit in the twilight,
And watch the sinking sun,
While the long bright day dies slowly
Over the sea,
And the hours grow quiet and holy
With thoughts of Me;
While you hear the village children
Passing along the street—
Among those passing footsteps
May come the sound of My Feet.
Therefore I tell you, Watch!
By the Light of the evening star
When the room is growing dusky
As the clouds afar,

Let the door be on the latch
In your home,
For it may be through the gloaming
I will come.

EVENING

He shall deliver the needy when he crieth. (PS. 72:12)

*B*ending down to us in infinite love God says: "My child, *how needy are you?* What heavy burden is upon *you?* What grievous sorrow is darkening your faith? What fear of future ill is shadowing your pathway? What spiritual thirst do you want slaked? What barrenness of soul enriched? What do you need this hour? For I will deliver the needy."

To miss a need may be to miss a miracle!

You are just the one God is looking for—just the one who is ripe for deliverance—just the special individual to whom His promise is made. The human incompleteness meets the Divine completeness and the want is filled. The deepest yearning in every soul finds in Him the longed-for satisfaction.

Do not be too anxious to be free from needs, unless you want to be free from prayer-power.

We need our needs!

O God, I need Thee!
When morning crowds the night away
And the tasks of waking seize my mind,
I need Thy Poise.

O God, I need Thee!
When clashes come with those
Who walk the way with me,
I need Thy Smile.

O God, I need Thee!
When the path to take before me lies,
I see it—courage flees—
I need Thy Faith.

O God, I need Thee!
When the day's work is done,

Tired, discouraged, wasted;
I need Thy Rest.

December 7

MORNING

～⚮～

Ye shall not see wind, neither shall ye see rain;
yet that valley shall be filled with water, that ye may drink,
both ye, and your cattle, and your beasts.
And this is but a light thing in the sight of the Lord:
He will deliver the Moabites also into your hand
(2 KINGS 3:16–17).

To human thinking it was simply impossible, but nothing is hard for God.

Without a sound or sign, from sources invisible and apparently impossible, the floods came stealing in all night long; and when the morning dawned, those ditches were flooded with the crystal waters, and reflecting the rays of the morning sun from the red hills of Edom.

Our unbelief is always wanting some *outward sign*. The religion of many is largely sensational, and they are not satisfied of its genuineness without manifestations, etc.; but the greatest triumph of faith is to be still and know that He is God.

The great victory of faith is to stand before some impassable Red Sea, and hear the Master say, *"Stand still, and see the salvation of the Lord,"* and *"Go forward!"* As we step out without any sign or sound—not a wave-splash—and wetting our very feet as we take the first step into the waters, still marching on we shall see the sea divide and the pathway open through the very midst of the waters.

If we have seen the miraculous workings of God in some marvelous case of healing or some extraordinary providential deliverance, I am sure the thing that has impressed us most has been the quietness with which it was all done, the absence of everything spectacular and sensational, and the utter sense of nothingness which came to us as we stood in the presence of this mighty God and felt how easy it was for Him to do it all without the faintest effort on His part or the slightest help on ours.

It is not the part of faith to *question*, but to *obey*. The ditches were made, and the water came pouring in from some supernatural source. What a lesson for our faith!

Are you craving a spiritual blessing? Open the trenches, and God will fill them. And this, too, in the most unexpected *places* and in the most unexpected *ways*.

Oh, for that faith that can act by faith and not by sight, and expect God to work although we see no wind or rain. — A. B. SIMPSON

EVENING

~∞~

Of thine own have we given thee. (1 Chron. 29:14)

Who gives himself with his gifts feeds three—
Himself, his hungering neighbor, and Me.
LOWELL

*A*ndrew, I have only five barley loaves left and a couple of fish, but the Master shall have most of it. Here are three loaves, four—but one loaf I should like to keep. You know, Andrew, it is a long way home, but the four loaves and the fishes I will give to Him."

As Andrew explains that the Master would like to have *all*, a struggle goes on in the boy's heart. He looks repeatedly, first at the fifth loaf, then at the Master. "Andrew, take all," he exclaims joyously as the light breaks. "Take all five, and the fishes, too."

What is the fifth loaf that you have not yet surrendered? Let me plead with you to let Him have ALL. — PASTOR DOLMAN

Was it the "widow's mite," or "all her living" that caught our Lord's attention?

It was Martin Luther who wrote: "I have had many things in my hands, and I have lost them all; but whatever I have been able to place in God's hands I still possess."

There is a Divine law in connection with our giving. Christ with a few loaves and fishes, feeds thousands.

Give! as the morning that flows out of heaven;
Give! as the waves when their channel is riven;
Give! as the free air and sunshine are given!
Lavishly, utterly, joyfully give!
Not the waste drops of thy cup overflowing;
Not the faith sparks of thy hearth ever glowing;

Not a pale bud from the June roses blowing:
Give as He gave thee who gave thee to live.
Almost the day of thy giving is over;
Ere from the grass dies the bee-haunted clover
Thou wilt have vanished from friend and from lover:
What shall thy longing avail in the grave?
Give as the heart gives whose fetters are breaking—
Life, love, and hope, all thy dreams and thy waking;
Soon, heaven's river thy soul-fever slaking,
Thou shalt know God and the gift that He gave.
ROSE TERRY COOKE

December 8

MORNING

Put on . . . as the elect of God, . . . kindness (COL. 3:12).

There is a story of an old man who carried a little can of oil with him everywhere he went, and if he passed through a door that squeaked, he poured a little oil on the hinges. If a gate was hard to open, he oiled the latch. And thus he passed through life lubricating all hard places and making it easier for those who came after him.

People called him eccentric, queer, and cranky; but the old man went steadily on refilling his can of oil when it became empty, and oiled the hard places he found.

There are many lives that creak and grate harshly as they live day by day. Nothing goes right with them. They need lubricating with the oil of gladness, gentleness, or thoughtfulness. Have you your own can of oil with you? Be ready with your oil of helpfulness in the early morning to the one nearest you. It may lubricate the whole day for him. The oil of good cheer to the downhearted one—Oh, how much it may mean! The word of courage to the despairing. Speak it.

Our lives touch others but once, perhaps, on the road of life; and then, mayhap, our ways diverge, never to meet again. The oil of kindness has worn the sharp, hard edges off of many a sin-hardened life and left it soft and pliable and ready for the redeeming grace of the Savior.

A word spoken pleasantly is a large spot of sunshine on a sad heart. Therefore, "Give others the sunshine, tell Jesus the rest."

> *We cannot know the grief*
> *That men may borrow;*
> *We cannot see the souls*
> *Storm-swept by sorrow;*
> *But love can shine upon the way*
> *Today, tomorrow;*
> *Let us be kind.*
> *Upon the wheel of pain so many weary lives are broken,*
> *We live in vain who give no tender token.*
> *Let us be kind.*

"Be kindly affectioned one to another with brotherly love" (Rom. 12:10).

EVENING

For a great door and effectual is opened unto me, and there are many adversaries. (1 COR. 16:9)

Another expedition of Englishmen is trying to conquer Mt. Everest, the highest peak in the world.

Bitter cold, raging winds, a rarefied atmosphere, blinding blizzards, engulfing avalanches of snow and rock—all these dangers stand between brave men and the top of that towering mountain.

The last expedition came the nearest to success. A little more than two thousand feet below the peak the main body of the party pitched their highest camp. From that base two men, Mallory and Irvine, equipped with oxygen tanks, attempted a final dash to the top. They hoped to climb to the peak and return in about sixteen hours. They never came back. Of them the official record of the expedition said in simple words, "When last seen, *they were heading toward the summit.*"

> *Press on! Surmount the rocky steeps,*
> *Climb boldly o'er the torrent's arch;*
> *He fails alone who feeble creeps,*
> *He wins who dares the hero's march.*
> *Be thou a hero! Let thy might*
> *Tramp on eternal snows its way*

And through the ebon walls of night
Hew down a passage unto day.
PARK BENJAMIN

The Kingdom of God will be brought in by Christians who, when last seen, *were heading toward the summit;* Christians who, with Paul, can accept the challenge of the "many adversaries" that guard the open door, even though they go down to defeat in their generation.

December 9

MORNING

For this our light and transitory burden of suffering is achieving for us a weight of glory (2 COR. 4:17 WEYMOUTH).

*I*s achieving for us. . . ." The question is repeatedly asked—Why is the life of man drenched with so much blood, and blistered with so many tears? The answer is to be found in the word "achieving"; these things are achieving for us something precious. They are teaching us not only the way to victory, but better still the laws of victory. There is a compensation in every sorrow, and the sorrow is working out the compensation. It is the cry of the dear old hymn:

Nearer my God to Thee, nearer to Thee,
E'en tho' it be a cross that raiseth me.

Joy sometimes needs pain to give it birth. Fanny Crosby could never have written her beautiful hymn, "I shall see Him face-to-face," were it not for the fact that she had never looked upon the green fields nor the evening sunset nor the kindly twinkle in her mother's eye. It was the loss of her own vision that helped her to gain her remarkable spiritual discernment.

It is comforting to know that sorrow tarries only for the night; it takes its leave in the morning. A thunderstorm is very brief when put alongside the long summer day. "Weeping may endure for the night but joy cometh in the morning." **FROM SONGS IN THE NIGHT**

There is a peace that cometh after sorrow,
Of hope surrendered, not of hope fulfilled;

A peace that looketh not upon tomorrow,
But calmly on a tempest that it stilled.

A peace that lives not now in joy's excesses,
Nor in the happy life of love secure;
But in the unerring strength the heart possesses,
Of conflicts won while learning to endure.

A peace there is, in sacrifice secluded,
A life subdued, from will and passion free;
'Tis not the peace that over Eden brooded,
But that which triumphed in Gethsemane.

EVMENING

I am doing a great work, so that I cannot come down. (NEH. 6:3)

One of Satan's favorite employees is the "switchman." He likes nothing better than to sidetrack one of God's express trains, sent on some blessed mission and filled with the fire of a holy purpose.

Something will come up in the pathway of an earnest soul, to attract its attention, and occupy its strength and thought. Sometimes it is a little irritation and provocation. Sometimes it is some petty grievance we stop to pursue or adjust.

Very often, and *before we are aware of it,* we are absorbed in a lot of distracting cares and interests that quite turn us aside from *the great purpose of our life.*

We may not do much harm, but we have missed our connection. We have gotten off the main line.

Let these things alone. Let distractions come and go, but press forward steadily and irresistibly with your God-given task. The eagle flying in the upper air pays but little or no attention to what is going on in the earth below him. As children of God we are to occupy our rightful place, "in the heavenlies," "far above all" these petty things. God would have us to be "eagle saints." *Let us not stoop from our position!*

A. B. SIMPSON

An eagle does not catch flies!

December 10

❧

If I am in distress, it is in the interests of your comfort, which is effective as it nerves you to endure the same sufferings as I suffered myself. Hence my hope for you is well-founded, since I know that as you share the sufferings you share the comfort also (2 COR. 1:6–7).

*A*re there not some in your circle to whom you naturally betake yourself in times of trial and sorrow? They always seem to speak the right word, to give the very counsel you are longing for; you do not realize, however, the cost which they had to pay ere they became so skillful in binding up the gaping wounds and drying tears. But if you were to investigate their past history you would find that they have suffered more than most. They have watched the slow untwisting of some silver cord on which the lamp of life hung. They have seen the golden bowl of joy dashed to their feet, and its contents spilt. They have stood by ebbing tides, and drooping gourds, and noon sunsets; but all this has been necessary to make them the nurses, the physicians, the priests of men. The boxes that come from foreign climes are clumsy enough; but they contain spices which scent the air with the fragrance of the Orient. So suffering is rough and hard to bear; but it hides beneath it discipline, education, possibilities, which not only leave us nobler, but perfect us to help others. Do not fret, or set your teeth, or wait doggedly for the suffering to pass; but get out of it all you can, both for yourself and for your service to your generation, according to the will of God. **SELECTED**

Once I heard a song of sweetness,
As it cleft the morning air,
Sounding in its blest completeness,
Like a tender, pleading prayer;
And I sought to find the singer,
Whence the wondrous song was borne;
And I found a bird, sore wounded,
Pinioned by a cruel thorn.

I have seen a soul in sadness,
While its wings with pain were furl'd,
Giving hope, and cheer and gladness
That should bless a weeping world

And I knew that life of sweetness,
Was of pain and sorrow borne,
And a stricken soul was singing,
With its heart against a thorn.

Ye are told of One who loved you,
Of a Saviour crucified,
Ye are told of nails that pinioned,
And a spear that pierced His side;
Ye are told of cruel scourging,
Of a Saviour bearing scorn,
And He died for your salvation,
With His brow against a thorn.

Ye "are not above the Master."
Will you breathe a sweet refrain?
And His grace will be sufficient,
When your heart is pierced with pain.
Will you live to bless His loved ones,
Tho' your life be bruised and torn,
Like the bird that sang so sweetly,
With its heart against a thorn?

SELECTED

EVENING

For we walk by faith, not by sight. (2 COR. 5:7)

Faith is taking God at His word. Faith is not belief without evidence. It is belief on the very best of evidence—the Word of Him "that cannot lie" (Titus 1:2). Faith is so rational that it asks no other evidence than this all-sufficient evidence. To ask other than the Word of Him who cannot lie is not *rationalism*, but consummate *irrationalism*.

R. A. TORREY

When we can *see*, it is *not faith but reasoning*.

Look at the faith of the master mariner! He looses his cable, he steams away from the land. For days, weeks, or even months, he sees neither sail nor shore; yet on he goes day and night without fear, till one morning he finds himself exactly opposite the desired haven toward which he had been steering.

How had he found his way over the trackless deep? He has trusted in his compass, his nautical almanac, his glass, and the heavenly bodies; and obeying their guidance, without sighting land, he has steered so accurately that he has not changed a point to enter port.

It is a wonderful thing—that sailing or steaming without sight. Spiritually it is a blessed thing to leave altogether the shores of sight and feeling; to say "Good-bye" to inward feelings, cheering providences, signs, tokens, and so forth. It is glorious to be far out on the ocean of Divine love, believing in God, and steering for Heaven straightaway, by the direction of the Word of God.   CHARLES H. SPURGEON

December 11

MORNING

Ye servants of the Lord, which by night stand in the house of the Lord. The Lord that made heaven and earth bless thee out of Zion (PS. 134:1, 3).

Strange time for adoration, you say, to stand in God's house by night, to worship in the depth of sorrow—it is indeed an arduous thing. Yes, and therein lies the blessing; it is the test of perfect faith. If I would know the love of my friend I must see what it can do in the winter. So with divine love. It is easy for me to worship in the summer sunshine when the melodies of life are in the air and the fruits of life are on the tree. But let the song of the bird cease and the fruit of the tree fall, and will my heart still go on to sing? Will I stand in God's house by night? Will I love Him in His own right? Will I watch with Him even one hour in His Gethsemane? Will I help to bear His cross up the dolorous way? Will I stand beside Him in His dying moments with Mary and the beloved disciple? Will I be able with Nicodemus to take up the dead Christ? Then is my worship complete and my blessing glorious. My love has come to Him in His humiliation. My faith has found Him in His lowliness. My heart has recognized His majesty through His mean disguise, and I know at last that I desire not the gift but the Giver. When I can stand in His house by night I have accepted Him for Himself alone.   GEORGE MATHESON

My goal is God Himself, not joy, nor peace,
Nor even blessing, but Himself, my God;

'Tis His to lead me there, not mine, but His—
"At any cost, dear Lord, by any road!"

So faith bounds forward to its goal in God,
And love can trust her Lord to lead her there;
Upheld by Him, my soul is following hard
Till God hath full fulfilled my deepest prayer.

No matter if the way be sometimes dark,
No matter though the cost be ofttimes great,
He knoweth how I best shall reach the mark,
The way that leads to Him must needs be straight.

One thing I know, I cannot say Him nay;
One thing I do, I press towards my Lord;
My God my glory here, from day to day,
And in the glory there my Great Reward.

EVENING

The LORD bindeth up the breach of his people,
and healeth the stroke of their wound.
(ISA. 30:26)

When some friend has proved untrue—betrayed your simple trust; used you for his selfish end, and trampled in the dust the Past, with all its memories, and all its sacred ties, the light is blotted from the sky—for something in you dies.

Bless your false and faithless friend, just smile and pass along—God must be the judge of it: He knows the right and wrong. . . . Life is short—don't waste the hours by brooding on the past; His great laws are good and just; Truth conquers at the last.

Red and deep our wounds may be—but after all the pain—God's own finger touches us, and we are healed again. . . . With faith restored, and trust renewed—we look toward the stars—the world will see the smiles we have—but God will see the scars.　　**SCARS, BY PATIENCE STRONG**

Love grows stronger when assailed;
Love conquers where all else has failed.
Love ever blesses those who curse;
Love gives the better for the worse.

Love unbinds others by its bonds;
Love pours forgiveness from its wounds.

Lord, let me love like Thee!

December 12

❧

The last drops of my sacrifice are falling; my time to go has come. I have fought in the good fight; I have kept the faith (2 TIM. 4:6–7).

As soldiers show their scars and talk of battles when they come at last to spend their old age in the country at home, so shall we in the dear land to which we are hastening, speak of the goodness and faithfulness of God who brought us through all the trials of the way. I would not like to stand in the white-robed host and hear it said, "These are they that came out of great tribulation, *all except one.*"

Would *you* like to be there and see yourself pointed at as the one saint who never knew sorrow? Oh, no! for you would be an alien in the midst of the sacred brotherhood. We will be content to share the battle, for we shall soon wear the crown and wave the palm.   C. H. SPURGEON

"Where were you wounded?" asked the surgeon of a soldier on Lookout Mountain. *"Almost at the top,"* he answered. He forgot even his gaping wound—he only remembered that he had won the heights. So let us go forth to higher endeavors for Christ and never rest till we can shout from the very top, "I have fought a good fight, I have finished my course, I have kept the faith."

Finish thy work, then rest,
Till then rest never;
The rest for thee by God
Is rest forever.

"*God will not look you over for medals, degrees or diplomas, but for scars.*" Of an old hero the minstrel sang—

With his Yemen sword for aid;
Ornament it carried none,
But the notches on the blade.

What nobler decoration of honor can any godly man seek after than his scars of service, his losses for the crown, his reproaches for Christ's sake, his being worn out in his Master's service!

EVENING

He is faithful that promised. (HEB. 10:23)

God's power will keep God's promises! Promises for the soul, promises for the body, promises for others, promises for our work, promises for our business, promises for time and for eternity: *these are all ours!* It is not your weakness that can defeat God's promise, nor your strength that can fulfill the promise: He that spoke the Word will Himself make it good. *It is neither your business nor mine to keep God's promises:* that is His grace.

The signed check is given us. How foolish if we fear to present it! *Never yet has one single check been dishonored!* "He is faithful that promised."

I take; He undertakes!

We may pray much over a promise, and yet never obtain it. *Asking* is not *taking. Beseeching* is not *claiming.*

I clasp the hand of Love Divine,
I claim the gracious promise mine,
And add to His my countersign.
I take, He undertakes.

I simply take Him at His Word;
I praise Him that my prayer is heard
And claim my answer from the Lord.
I take, He undertakes.
A. B. SIMPSON

Remember what you take is all you will ever get.

December 13

∞

I will give thee the treasures of darkness (ISA. 45:3).

*I*n the famous lace shops of Brussels, there are certain rooms devoted to the spinning of the finest and most delicate patterns. These rooms are altogether darkened, save for a light from one very small window, which falls directly upon the pattern. There is only one spinner in the room, and he sits where the narrow stream of light falls upon the threads of his weaving. "Thus," we are told by the guide, "do we secure our choicest products. Lace is always more delicately and beautifully woven when the worker himself is in the dark and only his pattern is in the light."

May it not be the same with us in our weaving? Sometimes it is very dark. We cannot understand what we are doing. We do not see the web we are weaving. We are not able to discover any beauty, any possible good in our experience. Yet if we are faithful and fail not *and faint not*, we shall some day know that the most exquisite work of all our life was done in those days when it was so dark.

If you are in the deep shadows because of some strange, mysterious providence, do not be afraid. Simply go on in faith and love, never doubting. God is watching, and He will bring good and beauty out of all your pain and tears.

J. R. MILLER

> The shuttles of His purpose move
> To carry out His own design;
> Seek not too soon to disapprove
> His work, nor yet assign
> Dark motives, when, with silent tread,
> You view some sombre fold;
> For lo, within each darker thread
> There twines a thread of gold.
>
> Spin cheerfully,
> Not tearfully,
> He knows the way you plod;
> Spin carefully,
> Spin prayerfully,
> But love the thread with God.

FROM THE CANADIAN HOME JOURNAL

❦

The peace of God, which passeth all understanding, shall keep your hearts and minds through Christ Jesus. (PHIL. 4:7)

There are depths in the ocean, I am told, which no tempest ever stirs—beyond the reach of all storms that sweep and agitate the surface of the sea. And there are heights in the blue sky above, to which no cloud ever ascends; where no tempest ever rages; where all is perpetual sunshine; where naught exists to disturb the deep serenity. Even *at the center of the cyclone there is rest.*

Each of these is an emblem of the soul which Jesus visits, to whom He speaks peace, whose fear He dispels, whose lamps of hope He trims.

During the test of a submarine it remained submerged for many hours. When it had returned to the harbor, the commander was asked: "Well, how did the storm affect you last night?" The Commander looked at him in surprise and said: "Storm? We knew nothing of any storm!"

> *Dwell deep. When doubts assail and stealthy shadows creep*
> *Across your sky, and fill you with a sense of doom,*
> *And thunders roar, and lightnings frighten with their glare,*
> *And old foundations seem to crumble 'neath your feet,*
> *Dwell deep and rest your soul amid eternal things.*
> *Upon the surface storms may rage, and billows break*
> *On every beach of life, and fling disaster*
> *Far and wide; but if your soul is dwelling quiet*
> *In the depths, naught can harm you evermore. Therefore*
> *Dwell deep, and rest your head upon the heart of God.*

"When he giveth quietness, who then can make trouble?" (Job 34:29).

December 14

❦

His disciples said unto him, Lord, teach us to pray . . . and he said unto them, When ye pray, say . . . Thy kingdom come (LUKE 11:1–2).

When they said, "Teach us to pray," the Master lifted His eyes and swept the far horizon of God. He gathered up the ultimate dream of the eternal, and, rounding the sum of everything God intends to do in the life of man, He packed it all into these three terse pregnant phrases and said, "When you pray, pray after this manner."

What a contrast between this and much praying we have heard. When we follow the devices of our own hearts, how runs it? "O Lord bless *me*, then my family, my church, my city, my country," and away on the far fringe as we close up, there is a prayer for the extension of His kingdom throughout the wide parish of the world.

The Master begins where we leave off. The world *first*, my personal needs second, is the order of this prayer. Only after my prayer has crossed every continent and every far-flung island of the sea, after it has taken in the last man in the last backward race, after it has covered the entire wish and purpose of God for the world, only then am I taught to ask for a piece of bread for myself.

When Jesus gave His all, Himself for us and to us in the holy extravagance of the cross, is it too much if He asks us to do the same thing? No man or woman amounts to anything in the kingdom, no soul ever touches even the edge of the zone of power, until this lesson is learned that Christ's business is the supreme concern of life and that all personal considerations, however dear or important, are tributary thereto.   DR. FRANCIS

When Robert Moffat, the veteran African missionary and explorer, was asked once to write in a young lady's album, he penned these lines:

> *My album is a savage breast,*
> *Where tempests brood and shadows rest,*
> *Without one ray of light;*
> *To write the name of Jesus there,*
> *And see that savage bow in prayer,*
> *And point to world more bright and fair,*
> *This is my soul's delight.*

"And His Kingdom shall have no frontier" (Luke 1:33, old Moravian version).

The missionary enterprise is not the church's afterthought; it is Christ's forethought.

They shall be abundantly satisfied.

(PS. 36:8)

Ask the eagle that splashes in the glory of the sun if it ever longs for its cage away down among the dim, distant earth scenes. If it ever stops to look at the old cage of former days, it is to sing its doxology of deliverance and soar away to its home near the sun.

The life of the Spirit-filled heart is *the winged life.* The unsurrendered life is the life of the cage. The best that the cage can give is a momentary thrill that soon gives place to a pitiful beating against the bars.

Our precious Savior, by His death on the Cross, proclaims "liberty to the captives," and you may be *set free;* free, not to take refuge on the branches of a nearby tree, but to "rise and walk in heaven's own light, above the world and sin, with heart made pure, and garments white, and Christ enthroned within!"

"They shall be abundantly satisfied." The song in your heart will daily be:

> *Thou, O Christ, art all I want;*
> *More than all in Thee I find.*

Forget the past, throw off your last fear, and leap boldly forward to *complete emancipation!*

> *O Christ, in Thee my soul hath found,*
> *And found in Thee alone,*
> *The peace, the joy I sought so long;*
> *The bliss till now unknown.*
>
> *I sighed for rest and happiness,*
> *I yearned for them, not Thee;*
> *But while I passed my Savior by,*
> *His love laid hold on me.*
>
> *I tried the broken cisterns, Lord,*
> *But ah! the waters failed.*
> *E'en as I stooped to drink they'd fled,*
> *And mocked me as I wailed.*
>
> *Now none but Christ can satisfy,*
> *None other name for me;*
> *There's love, and life, and lasting joy,*
> *Lord Jesus, found in Thee!*

December 15

∽

Trust also in him (PS. 37:5).

The word *trust* is the heart word of faith. It is the Old Testament word, the word given to the early and infant stage of faith. The word faith expresses more the act of the will, the word belief the act of the mind or intellect, but trust is the language of the heart. The other has reference more to a truth believed or a thing expected.

Trust implies more than this, it sees and feels, and leans upon a person, a great, true, living heart of love. So let us "trust also in him," through all the delays, in spite of all the difficulties, in the face of all the denials, notwithstanding all the seemings, even when we cannot understand the way, and know not the issue; still "trust also in him, and he will bring it to pass." The way will open, the right issue will come, the end will be peace, the cloud will be lifted, and the light of eternal noonday shall shine at last.

> *Trust and rest when all around thee*
> *Puts thy faith to sorest test;*
> *Let no fear or foe confound thee,*
> *Wait for God and trust and rest.*

> *Trust and rest with heart abiding,*
> *Like a birdling in its nest,*
> *Underneath His feathers hiding,*
> *Fold thy wings and trust and rest.*

EVENING

∽

If any man will come after me, let him deny himself,
and take up his cross, and follow me. (MATT. 16:24)

In the light of eternity, who are those who shall stand before the throne arrayed in white robes? Are they those who have come out of ease and pleasure, out of untroubled calm and unbroken human relationships? Nay, rather they are those who have come out of great tribulation. Had Milton not been blind, neither he nor we could have seen so clearly, and he could never have written,

My vision Thou hast dimmed,
That I may see Thyself, Thyself alone.

Out of blindness he learned the lesson so needed today by those cut off from an active life, that "They also serve who only stand and wait."

If Tennyson had not lost his friend Hallam, we should never have had his "In Memoriam."

One cannot have a victory without a battle! Character without conflict!
Perfect love without suffering!

As we visit the pearl fisheries, we find that life without pain leaves no pearl; that the life lived in sluggish ease, unwounded, without suffering or long-continued friction, forms no jewel.

As we pass the dwellings of men we find that without suffering *the pearl of great price*, the highest human character, is not formed.

Suffering is linked with joy for those who take it aright. *If you suffer without succeeding, it is that someone else may succeed. If you succeed without suffering, it is because someone else has suffered.*

"Is there no other way, O God,
Except through sorrow, pain and loss,
To stamp Christ's image on my soul?
No other way except the Cross?"

And then a voice stills all my soul,
As stilled the waves on Galilee:
"Canst thou not bear the furnace heat,
If 'mid the flames I walk with thee?

"I bore the Cross, I know its weight,
I drank the cup I hold for thee;
Canst thou not follow where I lead?
I'll give the strength—lean thou on me."

SELECTED

December 16

And there was Anna, a prophetess . . . which departed not from the
temple, but served God with fastings and prayers night and day
(LUKE 2:36–37).

No doubt by praying we learn to pray, and the more we pray the oftener we can pray, and the better we can pray. He who prays in fits and starts is never likely to attain to that effectual, fervent prayer which availeth much.

Great power in prayer is within our reach, but we must go to work to obtain it. Let us never imagine that Abraham could have interceded so successfully for Sodom if he had not been all his lifetime in the practice of communion with God.

Jacob's all-night at Peniel was not the first occasion upon which he had met his God. We may even look upon our Lord's most choice and wonderful prayer with his disciples before His Passion as the flower and fruit of His many nights of devotion, and of His often rising up a great while before day to pray.

If a man dreams that he can become mighty in prayer just as he pleases, he labors under a great mistake. The prayer of Elias which shut up heaven and afterwards opened its floodgates, was one of a long series of mighty prevailings with God. Oh, that Christian men would remember this! Perseverance in prayer is necessary to prevalence in prayer.

Those great intercessors, who are not so often mentioned as they ought to be in connection with confessors and martyrs, were nevertheless the grandest benefactors of the church; but it was only by abiding at the mercy-seat that they attained to be such channels of mercy to men. We must pray to pray, and continue in prayer that our prayers may continue.

C. H. SPURGEON

EVENING

I am come that they might have life,
and that they might have it more abundantly. (JOHN 10:10)

What a breathtaking truth! "I am come." Just another way of saying, *"Before Abraham was, I AM."* All others began to be; our Lord is *pretemporal*, definitely coming out of the eternities for a definite purpose:

"That they might have life." This quality of life which the Biologist from Eternity gives, increases in *quantity* forever—*"Abundantly!"*

The abundant life which Christ offers is the possession alone of those whom He designates "my sheep." It is not an entering into material blessedness. It is a spiritual fullness conditional altogether upon likeness to the Lord, and walking in that obedience toward God wherein He walked. Its first condition is the acceptance of the Cross whereby the world is crucified unto the believer and the believer unto the world. But, as this separation is recognized and accepted, and the life is wholly yielded and kept subject to the will of the Father, the Master's incoming and indwelling meets every longing and every need. Then alone will be understood the meaning of the promise of our text: "I am come that they might have life, and that they might have it more abundantly."

Have *we* come to the fountain of life? Are *we* drinking of its fullness? Are *we* living in His love? This is *the life of our spirit; the health of our body; the secret of our joy!*

May we seek this overflowing life, and become *"channels only,"* with *"all His wondrous power flowing through us"* so that He can use us every day and every hour!   EVAN H. HOPKINS

Come to the everlasting spring and drink freely. It never runs dry!

Though millions their thirst are now slaking,
It never runs dry,
And millions may still come partaking,
It never runs dry!

December 17

MORNING

And the very God of peace sanctify you wholly;
and I pray God your whole spirit and soul and body be preserved
blameless unto the coming of our Lord Jesus Christ. Faithful is he
that calleth you who also will do it (1 THESS. 5:23–24).

Many years since I saw that "without holiness no man shall see the Lord," I began by following after it and inciting all with whom I had intercourse to do the same. Ten years after, God gave me a clearer view than I ever had before of the way to obtain it; namely, by faith in the

Son of God. And immediately I declared to all, "We are saved from sin, we are made holy by faith." This I testified in private, in public and in print, and God confirmed it by a thousand witnesses. I have continued to declare this for above thirty years, and God has continued to confirm my work.   JOHN WESLEY (1771)

"I knew Jesus, and He was very precious to my soul; but I found something in me that would not keep sweet and patient and kind. I did what I could to keep it down, but it was there. I besought Jesus to do something for me, and, when I gave Him my will, He came to my heart, and took out all that would not be sweet, all that would not be kind, all that would not be patient, and then HE shut the door."   GEORGE FOX

My whole heart has not one single grain, this moment, of thirst after approbation. I feel alone with God; He fills the void; I have not one wish, one will, one desire, but in Him; He hath set my feet in a large room. I have wondered and stood amazed that God should make a conquest of all within me by love.   LADY HUNTINGTON

"All at once I felt as though a hand—not feeble, but omnipotent; not of wrath, but of love—was laid on my brow. I felt it not outwardly but inwardly. It seemed to press upon my whole being, and to diffuse all through me a holy, sin-consuming energy. As it passed downward, my heart as well as my head was conscious of the presence of this soul-cleansing energy, under the influence of which I fell to the floor, and in the joyful surprise of the moment, cried out in a loud voice. Still the hand of power wrought without and within; and wherever it moved, it seemed to leave the glorious influence of the Savior's image. For a few minutes the deep ocean of God's love swallowed me up; all its waves and billows rolled over me."   BISHOP HAMLINE

Holiness—as I then wrote down some of my contemplations on it—appeared to me to be of a sweet, calm, pleasant, charming, serene nature, which brought an inexpressible purity, brightness, peacefulness, ravishment to the soul; in other words, that holiness made the soul like a field or garden of God, with all manner of pleasant fruits and flowers, all delightful and undisturbed, enjoying a sweet calm and the gentle vivifying beams of the sun.   JOHNATHAN EDWARDS

Love's resistless current sweeping
All the regions deep within;
Thought and wish and senses keeping
Now, and every instant clean:
Full salvation! Full salvation!
From the guilt and power of sin.

I will restore to you the years that the locust hath eaten. (JOEL 2:25)

How many years we are not told; only this: *"I will restore the years."* Human lives are often laid bare—barren patches produced by our own failures; a wilderness stretching across our life. But what comfort in these words: *"I will RESTORE to you the years that the locust hath eaten."*

Have you been brooding over some sorrow? Has it darkened your life as a swarm of locusts might darken the sun at midday? And have you cried out in your anguish, "The sun will never shine again"? But read the word He has promised:

"I will restore to you the years that the locust hath eaten."

Turn to Him, dear reader—turn to the One whom you may have been inclined to forget when you lived in the larger house. He is waiting; and if He does not see fit to give you back the earthly possession once so highly prized by you, remember this: *in a higher and better way He will restore those years.*

The years that the locust hath eaten sometimes take another form: years spent away from God in pursuit of worldly pleasure and self-gratification! How many have tried this! No wonder the fields are bare! *Can* God restore these years? Did He not restore the years for Naomi?

GOD CAN!

The blue water lily abounds in several of the canals in Alexandria, Egypt, which at certain seasons become dry; and the beds of these canals, which quickly become burnt as hard as bricks by the action of the sun, are then used as carriage roads. When, however, the water is admitted again, the lily resumes its growth with redoubled vigor and splendor.

December 18

MORNING

In all these things we are more than conquerors through him that loved us (ROM. 8:37).

The gospel is so arranged and the gift of God so great that you may take the very enemies that fight you and the forces that are arrayed against you and make them steps up to the very gates of heaven and into the presence of God.

Like the eagle, who sits on a crag and watches the sky as it is filling with blackness, and the forked lightnings are playing up and down, and he is sitting perfectly still, turning one eye and then the other toward the storm. But he never moves until he begins to feel the burst of the breeze and knows that the hurricane has struck him; with a scream, he swings his breast to the storm, and uses the storm to go up to the sky; away he goes, borne upward upon it.

That is what God wants of every one of His children, to be more than conqueror, turning the storm-cloud into a chariot. You know when one army is more then conqueror it is likely to drive the other from the field, to get all the ammunition, the food and supplies, and to take possession of the whole. That is just what our text means. There are spoils to be taken!

Beloved, have you got them? When you went into the terrible valley of suffering did you come out of it with spoils? When that injury struck you and you thought everything was gone, did you so trust in God that you came out richer than you went in? To be more than conqueror is to take the spoils from the enemy and appropriate them to yourself. What he had arranged for your overthrow, take and appropriate for yourself.

When Dr. Moon, of Brighton, England, was stricken with blindness, he said: "Lord, I accept this talent of blindness from Thee. Help me to use it for Thy glory that at Thy coming Thou mayest receive Thine own with usury." Then God enabled him to invent the Moon Alphabet for the blind, by which thousands of blind people were enabled to read the Word of God, and many of them were gloriously saved.   SELECTED

God did not take away Paul's thorn; He did better—He mastered that thorn, and made it Paul's servant. The ministry of *thorns* has often been a greater ministry to man than the ministry of *thrones*.   SELECTED

EVENING

Thou thyself art . . . a light of them which are in darkness.
(ROM. 2:19)

We are kindled that we might kindle others. I would like, if I might have my choice, to burn steadily down, with no guttering waste, and as I do so to communicate God's fire to as many unlit candles as possible, and to burn on steadily until the socket comes in view; then to light in the last flicker, twenty, thirty, or a hundred candles at once, so that as one expires they may begin burning and spreading light which shall shine until Jesus comes.

Let me burn out for Thee, dear Lord,
Burn and wear out for Thee;
Don't let me rust, or my life be
A failure, my God, to Thee.
Use me, and all I have, dear Lord,
And get me so close to Thee
That I feel the throb of the great heart of God,
Until I burn out for Thee.
BESSIE F. HATCHER

December 19

MORNING

It shall turn to you for a testimony (Luke 21:13).

Life is a steep climb, and it does the heart good to have somebody "call back" and cheerily beckon us on up the high hill. We are all climbers together, and we must help one another. This mountain climbing is serious business, but glorious. It takes strength and steady step to find the summits. The outlook widens with the altitude. If anyone among us has found anything worthwhile, we ought to "call back."

If you have gone a little way ahead of me, call back—
'Twill cheer my heart and help my feet along the stony track;
And if, perchance, Faith's light is dim, because the oil is low,
Your call will guide my lagging course as wearily I go.

Call back, and tell me that He went with you into the storm;
Call back, and say He kept you when the forest's roots were torn;
That, when the heavens thunder and the earthquake shook the hill,
He bore you up and held you where the very air was still.

Oh, friend, call back, and tell me for I cannot see your face;
They say it glows with triumph, and your feet bound in the race;

But there are mists between us and my spirit eyes are dim,
And I cannot see the glory, though I long for word of Him.

But if you'll say He heard you when your prayer was but a cry,
And if you'll say He saw you through the night's sin-darkened sky—
If you have gone a little way ahead, oh, friend, call back—
Twill cheer my heart and help my feet along the stony track.
SELECTED

EVENING

∽≫∾

Though he was rich, yet for your sakes he became poor. (2 COR. 8:9)

The poorest man that ever walked the dirt roads of earth! Born in poverty, reared in obscurity, *yet He enriched all mankind!*

For twenty years He worked as a carpenter in that village which bore the scorn of men: "Can there any good thing come out of Nazareth?"

As far as we know He never possessed the value of one penny. In the wilderness without food, by Jacob's well without water, in the crowded city without a home—thus *He lived, and loved, and died!*

The foxes find rest,
And the birds have their nests
In the shade of the forest tree,
But Thy couch was the sod,
O Thou Son of God,
In the desert of Galilee.

He preached without price, and wrought miracles without money. His parish was the world. He sought breakfast from a leafing fig tree. He ate grain as He walked through the field of corn. *Without money,* did I say? He sent Peter to the sea for the fish that they might have money for the tax! He had no cornfields or fisheries, yet He could spread a table for five thousand and have bread and fish to spare! No beautiful carpets to walk on, yet the waters supported Him!

So poor was He that He must needs bear His own cross through the city, till fainting He fell. His value was thirty pieces of silver—the price of a slave, the lowest estimate of human life. But, on God's side, *no lower price than His infinite agony* could have made possible our Redemption! When He died, few men mourned; but a black crepe was hung over the sun. *His crucifixion was the crime of crimes!*

IT WAS NOT MERELY HUMAN BLOOD THAT WAS SPILLED ON CALVARY'S HILL!

He did not have a house where He could go
When it was night—when other men went down
Small streets where children watched with eager eyes,
Each one assured of shelter in the town,
The Christ sought refuge anywhere at all:
A house, an inn, the roadside, or a stall!

He borrowed the boat in which He rode that day,
He talked to throngs along the Eastern lake;
It was a rented room to which He called
The chosen twelve the night He bade them break
The loaf with Him, and He rode, unafraid,
Another's colt in that triumph-parade.

A man from Arimathea had a tomb
Where Christ was placed when nails had done their deed.
Not ever in the crowded days He knew,
Did He have coins to satisfy a need.
They should not matter, these small things I crave.
Make me forget them, Father, and be brave!

THE TRANSIENT, BY HELEN WELSHIMER

December 20

MORNING

❧

Yet I am not alone, because the Father is with me
(JOHN 16:32).

It need not be said that to carry out conviction into action is a costly sacrifice. It may make necessary renunciations and separations which leave one to feel a strange sense both of deprivation and loneliness. But he who will fly, as an eagle does, into the higher levels where cloudless day abides, and live in the sunshine of God, must be content to live a comparatively lonely life.

No bird is so solitary as the eagle. Eagles never fly in flocks; one, or at most two, ever being seen at once. But the life that is lived unto God, however it forfeits human companionships, *knows divine fellowship.*

God seeks eagle-men. No man ever comes into a realization of the best things of God, who does not, upon the Godward side of his life, learn to walk alone with God. We find Abraham alone in Horeb upon the heights, but Lot, dwelling in Sodom. Moses, skilled in all the wisdom of Egypt must go forty years into the desert alone with God. Paul, who was filled with Greek learning and had also sat at the feet of Gamaliel, must go into Arabia and learn the desert life with God. Let God isolate us. I do not mean the isolation of a monastery. In this isolating experience He develops an independence of faith and life so that the soul needs no longer the constant help, prayer, faith or attention of his neighbor. Such assistance and inspiration from the other members are necessary and have their place in the Christian's development, but there comes a time when they act as a direct hindrance to the individual's faith and welfare. God knows how to change the circumstances in order to give us an isolating experience. We yield to God and He takes us through something, and when it is over, those about us, who are no less loved than before, are no longer depended upon. We realize that He has wrought some things in us, and that the wings of our souls have learned to beat the upper air.

We must dare to be alone. Jacob must be left alone if the angel of God is to whisper in his ear the mystic name of Shiloh; Daniel must be left alone if he is to see celestial visions; John must be banished to Patmos if he is deeply to take and firmly to keep "the print of heaven."

He trod the winepress alone. Are we prepared for a "splendid isolation" rather than fail Him?

EVENING

⤭

Behold your God! (ISA. 40:9)

*H*e became the Son of Man that *we* might become the sons of God. Here is a man who was born in an obscure village, child of a peasant woman. He had neither wealth nor influence, neither training nor education; yet in infancy he startled a king; in boyhood He puzzled the doctors. In manhood He walked upon the billows and hushed the sea to sleep. He healed the multitudes without medicine and made no charge for His services. He never wrote a book, *yet all the libraries of the world could not hold the books that could be written about Him.* He never wrote a song, *yet He has furnished the theme of more songs than all songwriters combined.* He never founded a college, *yet all the colleges together cannot boast of as many students as He.*

"He was rich, yet for your sakes he became poor."

How poor? Ask Mary! Ask the Wise Men! He slept in another's manger. He cruised the lake in another's boat. He rode on another man's ass. He was buried in another man's tomb.

While still a young man the tide of popular opinion turned against Him. His friends ran away from Him. One of them denied Him; another betrayed Him and turned Him over to His enemies. He went through the mockery of a trial. He was nailed upon the Cross between two thieves. His executioners gambled for His coat.

Yet, *all the armies that ever marched, all the navies that were ever built, all the parliaments that ever sat, all the kings that ever reigned, put together,* have not affected the life of man as powerfully as has *this one solitary life!*

Great men have come and gone, *yet He lives on!* Death could not destroy Him! The grave could not hold Him!

"Behold, the world is gone after him!" (John 12:19).

"Let us also go" (John 11:16).

"If thou seek him, he will be found of thee" (1 Chron. 28:9).

FIND HIM!

December 21

MORNING

⌒∾◦∾⌒

To him will I give the land that he hath trodden upon . . .
because he hath wholly followed the Lord
(DEUT. 1:36).

Every hard duty that lies in your path, that you would rather not do, that it will cost you pain and struggle or sore effort to do, has a blessing in it. Not to do it, at whatever cost, is to miss the blessing.

Every hard piece of road on which you see the Master's shoeprints and along which He bids you follow Him, surely leads to blessing, which you cannot get if you cannot go over to the steep, thorny path.

Every point of battle to which you come, where you must draw your sword and fight the enemy, has a possible victory which will prove a rich blessing to your life. Every heavy load that you are called to lift hides in itself some strange secret of strength. J. R. MILLER

I cannot do it alone;
The waves run fast and high,
And the fogs close all around,
The light goes out in the sky;
But I know that we two
Shall win in the end,
Jesus and I.

Coward and wayward and weak,
I change with the changing sky;
Today so eager and bright,
Tomorrow too weak to try;
But He never gives in,
So we two shall win,
Jesus and I.

I could not guide it myself,
My boat on life's wild sea;
There's One who sits by my side,
Who pulls and steers with me.
And I know that we two
Shall safe enter port,
Jesus and I.

EVENING

Save thyself. (MATT. 27:40)

Save thyself! These words have a familiar ring in the Master's ears. He had heard them in all their variations throughout the whole period of His public ministry. When a messenger came to Peraea carrying tidings fo the passing of Lazarus, His disciples tried to dissuade Him from going to Bethany, *to save Himself.*

An anxious family waited on Him in Capernaum and begged Him to return to Nazareth *to save Himself.*

Certain Greeks approached Him during the Last Passover and evidently afforded Him an opportunity to slip out of the picture gracefully, *to save Himself.*

In Gethsemane His final decision was made, quite in accord with all of His previous decisions. He would *not* save Himself. Now, agonizing on the cross, He heard the malefactors suggesting that He save Himself—and them. His critics and crucifiers joined the chorus and cried, "Come down from the cross—*save thyself.*"

But He who taught His disciples to deny themselves and to save their lives by losing them had definitely determined to give Himself.

THE UPPER ROOM

When a Roman soldier was told by his guide that if he insisted on taking a certain journey it would probably be fatal, he answered, "It is necessary for me to go; it is not necessary for me to live."

That was depth. When we have convictions like that we shall come to something worthy of our name Christian.

> *More than half beaten, but fearless,*
> *Facing the storm and the night,*
> *Reeling and breathless, but fearless,*
> *Here in the lull of the fight.*
> *I who bow not but before Thee,*
> *God of the fighting clan,*
> *Lifting my fists I implore Thee,*
> *Give me the heart of a man!*
>
> *What though I stand with the winners,*
> *Or perish with those that fall?*
> *Only the cowards are sinners;*
> *Fighting the fight, that is all.*
> *Strong is my foe, who advances,*
> *Snapped is my blade, O Lord;*
> *See their proud banners and lances,*
> *But spare me the stub of a sword!*

December 22

∽∾

Lo, an honor of great darkness fell upon him (GEN. 15:12).

The sun at last went down, and the swift, eastern night cast its heavy veil over the scene. Worn out with the mental conflict, the watchings, and the exertions of the day, Abraham fell into a deep sleep, and in that sleep his soul was oppressed with a dense and dreadful darkness, such as almost stifled him, and lay like a nightmare upon his heart. Do you understand something of the horror of that darkness? When some terrible sorrow which seems so hard to reconcile with perfect love, crushes down upon the soul, wringing from it all its peaceful rest in the pitifulness of God, and launching it on a sea unlit by a ray of hope; when unkindness, and cruelty maltreat the trusting heart, till it begins to doubt whether there be a God overhead who can see and still permit—these know something of the "horror of great darkness." It is thus that human life is made up; brightness and gloom; shadow and sun; long tracks of cloud, succeeded by brilliant glints of light, and amid all divine justice is working out its own schemes, affecting others equally with the individual soul which seems the subject of special discipline. O ye who are filled with the horror of great darkness because of God's dealings with mankind, learn to trust that infallible wisdom, which is co-assessor with immutable justice; and know that He who passed through the horror of the darkness of Calvary, with the cry of forsakenness, is ready to bear you company through the valley of the shadow of death till you see the sun shining upon its farther side. Let us, by our Forerunner, send forward our anchor. Hope, within the veil that parts us from the unseen; where it will grapple in ground and will not yield, but hold until the day dawns, and we follow it into the haven guaranteed to us by God's immutable counsel.

F. B. MEYER

The disciples thought that that angry sea separated them from Jesus. Nay, some of them thought worse than that; they thought that the trouble that had come upon them was a sign that Jesus had forgotten all about them, and did not care for them. Oh, dear friend, that is when troubles have a sting, when the Devil whispers, "God has forgotten you; God has forsaken you"; when your unbelieving heart cries as Gideon cried, "If the Lord be with us, why then is all this befallen us?" The evil has come upon you to bring the Lord nearer to you. The evil has not come upon you to separate you from Jesus, but to make you cling to Him more faithfully, more tenaciously, more simply. F. S. WEBSTER, M.A.

Never should we so abandon ourselves to God as when He seems to have abandoned us. Let us enjoy light and consolation when it is His pleasure to give it to us, but let us not attach ourselves to His gifts, but to Himself; and when He plunges us into the night of *pure faith,* let us still press on through the agonizing darkness.

> *Oh, for faith that brings the triumph*
> *When defeat seems strangely near!*
> *Oh, for faith that brings the triumph*
> *Into victory's ringing cheer—*
> *Faith triumphant; knowing not defeat or fear.*
> HERBERT BOOTH

EVENING

⤜∾⤛

He endured, as seeing him who is invisible. (HEB. 11:27)

The life of Moses was a much-enduring one. He endured the banishment from palatial surroundings and the most brilliant court then in existence; he endured the forfeiture of privilege, and the renunciation of splendid prospects; he endured the flight from Egypt, and the wrath of the king; he endured the lonely exile in Midian, where for years he was buried alive; he endured the long trudge through the wilderness at the head of a slave people, whom he sought to consolidate into a nation; he endured the ill manners and the countless provocations of a froward and perverse generation; he endured the lonely death on Nebo, and the nameless grave that angels dug for him there! And here we have the secret of his wondrous fortitude disclosed to us:

"He endured, as seeing him who is invisible."

He realized the presence of God. He lived in the consciousness, "Thou God seest me." He looked up, and had an habitual regard to the heavenly and eternal. In the upper chambers of his soul there was a window that opened skyward, and commanded a view of things unseen. As an old author puts it, "He had a greater view than Pharaoh in his eye, and this kept him right." Yes, and this will keep any of us right: to live under the sense that God is overlooking us—to walk by faith and not by sight.

"There is nothing," says a great modern preacher, "that enables a man so well to carry on things that are terraqueous and material, as to have in ascendancy every day that part of his nature which dwells with the invisible."

S. LAW WILSON

December 23

MORNING

~~∞~~

The journey is too great for thee (1 KINGS 19:7).

*A*nd what did God do with His tired servant? Gave him something good to eat, and put him to sleep. Elijah had done splendid work, and had run alongside of the chariot in his excitement, and it had been too much for his physical strength, and the reaction had come on, and he was *depressed*. The physical needed to be cared for. What many people want is sleep, and the physical ailment attended to. There are grand men and women who get where Elijah was—under the juniper tree! and it comes very soothingly to such to hear the words of the Master: "The journey is too great for thee, and I am going to refresh you." Let us not confound physical weariness with spiritual weakness.

> *I'm too tired to trust and too tired to pray,*
> *Said one, as the over-taxed strength gave way.*
> *The one conscious thought by my mind possessed,*
> *Is, oh, could I just drop it all and rest.*
>
> *Will God forgive me, do you suppose,*
> *If I go right to sleep as a baby goes,*
> *Without an asking if I may,*
> *Without ever trying to trust and pray?*
>
> *Will God forgive you? why think, dear heart,*
> *When language to you was an unknown art,*
> *Did a mother deny you needed rest,*
> *Or refuse to pillow your head on her breast?*
>
> *Did she let you want when you could not ask?*
> *Did she set her child an unequal task?*
> *Or did she cradle you in her arms,*

And then guard your slumber against alarms?

Ah, how quick was her mother love to see,
The unconscious yearnings of infancy.
When you've grown too tired to trust and pray,
When over-wrought nature has quite given way:

Then just drop it all, and give up to rest,
As you used to do on mother's breast,
He knows all about it—the dear Lord knows,
So just go to sleep as a baby goes;

Without even asking if you may,
God knows when His child is too tired to pray.
He judges not solely by uttered prayer,
He knows when the yearnings of love are there.

He knows you do pray, He knows you do trust,
And He knows, too, the limits of poor weak dust.
Oh, the wonderful sympathy of Christ,
For His chosen ones in that midnight tryst,

When He bade them sleep and take their rest,
While on Him the guilt of the whole world pressed—
You've given your life up to Him to keep,
Then don't be afraid to go right to sleep.

ELLA CONRAD COWHERD

EVENING

What lack I yet? (MATT. 19:20)

When Jesus answered the rich young ruler's question, the young man said: "All these things have I kept . . . what lack I yet?" Then Jesus told him what his lack was and "he went away sorrowful." The interview was over; Jesus asked for *the Master Key* and the young man refused to give it.

Has Jesus the keys to your life? Has He the key to the *Library* of your life, or do you just read what you please? Has He the key to the *Dining room* of your life—do you feed your soul on His Word? Has He the key to the *Recreation* compartment, or do you just go where you please? Have you given Christ the Master Key to *your* life?

We may have *all* of the Holy Ghost, but has He *all* of us? Are there spaces yet to be filled with the Holy Ghost—spaces, places, rooms, and closets in our spiritual house into which He has not *"fully come,"* because we have not yet given up *all* the keys from cellar to attic of our spiritual homestead?

> *The House of the Lord has many chambers,*
> *Large and lofty, or low and small;*
> *And some who turn from the world's broad highways*
> *And find the door to the* ENTRANCE HALL,
> *Are satisfied with its shade and coolness,*
> *To know they have come to the House of a Friend,*
> *And, resting there in the peace and quiet,*
> *They think they have fared to their journey's end.*
>
> *And some are content with the antechamber*
> *That opens out of the entrance hall,*
> *With the winds that blow from the spicy gardens,*
> *The musical splash of the fountain's fall;*
> *They feast on the fruits of the Spirit's giving*
> *And muse on the thought of the joys to come,*
> *And resting there in the peace and quiet,*
> *Are glad that the Lord has brought them home.*
>
> *But those who have heeded His invitation*
> *To come up higher and enter in*
> *To the* UPPER ROOM *of the Master's dwelling,*
> *To stores of treasures their way shall win.*
> *What eye hath seen them? What mind conceived them?*
>
> *What heart hath dreamed of the things concealed,*
> *The joys prepared for the Lord's beloved,*
> *To those who seek them alone revealed?*
> *Clothed with His glory they leave His presence,*
> *Girt with His power they walk abroad*
> *Who find the door to the inner chamber,*
> *The secret place of the Most High God.*
>
> THE INNER CHAMBER,
> BY ANNIE JOHNSON FLINT

December 24

And Isaac went out to meditate in the field at the eventide
(GEN. 24:63).

*W*e should be better Christians if we were more alone; we should do more if we attempted less, and spent more time in retirement, and quiet waiting upon God. The world is too much with us; we are afflicted with the idea that we are doing nothing unless we are fussily running to and fro; we do not believe in "the calm retreat, the silent shade." As a people, we are of a very practical turn of mind; "we believe," as someone has said, "in having all our irons in the fire, and consider the time not spent between the anvil and the fire as lost, or much the same as lost." Yet no time is more profitably spent than that which is set apart for quiet musing, for talking with God, for looking up to heaven. We cannot have too many of these open spaces in life, hours in which the soul is left accessible to any sweet thought or influence it may please God to send.

"Reverie," it has been said, "is the Sunday of the mind." Let us often in these days give our mind a "Sunday," in which it will do no manner of work but simply lie still, and look upward, and spread itself out before the Lord like Gideon's fleece, to be soaked and moistened with the dews of heaven. Let there be intervals when we shall do nothing, think nothing, plan nothing, but just lay ourselves on the green lap of nature and "rest awhile."

Time so spent is not lost time. The fisherman cannot be said to be losing time when he is mending his nets, nor the mower when he takes a few minutes to sharpen his scythe at the top of the ridge. City men cannot do better than follow the example of Isaac, and, as often as they can, get away from the fret and fever of life into fields. Wearied with the heat and din, the noise and bustle, communion with nature is very grateful; it will have a calming, healing influence. A walk through the fields, a saunter by the seashore or across the daisy-sprinkled meadows, will purge your life from the sordidness, and make the heart beat with new joy and hope.

The little cares that fretted me,
I lost them yesterday,
Out in the fields with God.

Christmas Eve

Bells Across the Snow

O Christmas, merry Christmas,
Is it really come again,
With its memories and greetings,
With its joy and with its pain!
There's a minor in the carol
And a shadow in the light,

And a spray of cypress twining
With the holly wreath tonight.
And the hush is never broken
By laughter light and low,
As we listen in the starlight
To the "bells across the snow."

O Christmas, merry Christmas,
'Tis not so very long
Since other voices blended
With the carol and the song!
If we could but hear them singing,
As they are singing now,
If we could but see the radiance
Of the crown on each dear brow,
There would be no sigh to smother,
No hidden tear to flow,
As we listen in the starlight
To the "bells across the snow."

O Christmas, merry Christmas,
This never more can be;
We cannot bring again the days
Of our unshadowed glee,
But Christmas, happy Christmas,
Sweet herald of good will,
With holy songs of glory
Brings holy gladness still.
For peace and hope may brighten,
And patient love may glow,
As we listen in the starlight
To the "bells across the snow."

FRANCES RIDLEY HAVERGAL

❧❧

Buried with him . . . that . . . even so we also should
walk in newness of life. (ROM. 6:4)

No one enters into the experience of entire sanctification without going through a "white funeral," i.e., the burial of the old life. If there has never been this crisis of death, sanctification is nothing more than a vision. There must be a "white funeral," the death that has only one resurrection—a resurrection into the life of Jesus. Nothing can upset this life; it is one with God, for one purpose, to be a witness to Him.

Have I come to my last days really? I have come to them in sentiment, but have I come to them *really?* You cannot go to your funeral in excitement, nor die in excitement. Death means stopping being. Do I agree with God that I stop being the striving earnest kind of Christian I have been? We skirt the cemetery and all the time refuse to go to death. It is not striving to go to death, it is dying—"baptized into his death."

Have I had a "white funeral," or am I sacredly playing with my soul? Is there a place marked in my life as the last day, a place that the memory goes back to with a chastened and extraordinary grateful remembrance—Yes, it was then, that I made an agreement with God. "This is the will of God, even your sanctification." When you realize what the will of God is, you will enter into sanctification as naturally as can be. Are you willing to go through the "white funeral" now?

Do you agree with Him that this is your last day on earth? That moment depends on you.

MY UTMOST FOR HIS HIGHEST, BY OSWALD CHAMBERS

December 25

MORNING

❧❧

His name shall be called Emmanuel. . . . God with us
(MATT. 1:23 RSV).

The Prince of Peace (ISA. 9:6).

There's a song in the air!
There's a star in the sky!

There's a mother's deep prayer,
And a baby's low cry!
And the star rains its fire
With the beautiful song,
For the manger of Bethlehem cradles a King.

A few years ago a striking Christmas card was published, with the title, "If Christ had not come." It was founded upon our Savior's words, "If I had not come." The card represented a clergyman falling into a short sleep in his study on Christmas morning and dreaming of a world into which Jesus had never come.

In his dream he found himself looking through his home, but there were no little stockings in the chimney corner, no Christmas bells or wreaths of holly, and no Christ to comfort, gladden, and save. He walked out on the public street, but there was no church with its spire pointing to heaven. He came back and sat down in his library, but every book about the Savior had disappeared.

A ring at the doorbell, and a messenger asked him to visit a poor dying mother. He hastened with the weeping child and as he reached the home, he sat down and said, "I have something here that will comfort you." He opened his Bible to look for a familiar promise, but it ended at Malachi, and there was no gospel and no promise of hope and salvation, and he could only bow his head and weep with her in bitter despair.

Two days afterward he stood beside her coffin and conducted the funeral service, but there was no message of consolation, no word of a glorious resurrection, no open heaven, but only "dust to dust, ashes to ashes," and one long eternal farewell. He realized at length that "He had not come" and burst into tears and bitter weeping in his sorrowful dream.

Suddenly he woke with a start, and a great shout of joy and praise burst from his lips as he heard his choir singing in his church close by:

O come, all ye faithful, joyful and triumphant,
O come ye, O come ye to Bethlehem;
Come and behold Him, born the King of Angels,
O come let us adore Him, Christ, the Lord.

Let us be glad and rejoice today, because "He *has* come." And let us remember the annunciation of the angel, "Behold I bring you good tidings of great joy, *which shall be to all people,* for unto you is born this day in the city of David a Savior, which is Christ the Lord" (Luke 2:10–11).

He comes to make His blessing flow,
Far as the curse is found.

May our hearts go out to the people in heathen lands who have no blessed Christmas day. "Go your way, eat the fat, drink the sweet, and send portions unto them for whom nothing is prepared" (Neh. 8:10).

GOOD TIDINGS OF GREAT JOY! (LUKE 2:10)

Tidings of glory! all the sky aflame, all Heaven hymning one imperial Name! radiant glimpses of a Throne, a Crown, all splendor focused on one little town! Tidings of joy, good tidings of great joy! Supernal ecstasy without alloy! The death of sorrow and the end of pain, the bliss, bliss, bliss eternally to reign! News of Salvation! Jesus, Savior, Christ, bearer of mercy ample, and unpriced herald of freedom from the chains of sin, come to our hearts, Lord Jesus, enter in! Tidings to all the people, yea, to all! to kings and shepherds, to the great and small, to rich and poor, to ignorant and wise, to each his blessing from the liberal skies! Oh, for the ready eye and quickened ear, the Advent light to see, and song to hear! To every man and woman, girl and boy, in all the world, *GOOD TIDINGS OF GREAT JOY!*   AMOS R. WELLS

HE GAVE US THE BEST THAT HE HAD!

To Bethlehem they went to be enrolled;
And there, in Caesar's census book of old,
His name was written 'mong the sons of men
As Caesar's subject: "Jesus"—followed then
By "Son of Mary, born in David's Town,
Of David's line"—the record thus set down.
In a world's book of life, a place they gave
To "Jesus" who was born a world to save.
They numbered Him with sinful men and poor,
Though He was Son of God, Divine and pure.

A heavenly census book His name alone
Bears, on the title page; for 'tis His own,
That Book of Life; and there, writ clear and plain
Are names of those born in that King's domain;
All who alive forevermore shall be
Are there enrolled for all eternity.
Since He was numbered once with sinful men,

We may be numbered as God's own again.
Though Caesar's book has long since passed away,
The Lamb's blest Book of Life shall stand for aye.
THE CENSUS BOOKS, BY KAY MCCULLOUGH

Was it merely the son of Joseph and Mary who crossed the world's horizon nineteen hundred years ago? Your own heart must answer—

"My Lord and my God!"

December 26

MORNING

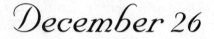

Sit ye here while I go and pray yonder (MATT. 26:36).

It is a hard thing to be kept in the background at a time of crisis. In the Garden of Gethsemane eight of the eleven disciples were left to do nothing. Jesus went to the front to pray; Peter, James, and John went to the middle to watch; the rest sat down in the rear to wait. Methinks that party in the rear must have murmured. They were *in* the garden, but that was all; they had no share in the cultivation of its flowers. It was a time of crisis, a time of storm and stress; and yet they were not suffered to work.

You and I have often felt that experience, that disappointment. There has arisen, mayhap, a great opportunity for Christian service. Some are sent to the front; some are sent to the middle. But *we* are made to lie down in the rear. Perhaps sickness has come; perhaps poverty has come; perhaps obloquy has come; in any case we are hindered and we feel sore. We do not see why we should be excluded from a part in the Christian life. It seems like an unjust thing that, seeing we have been allowed to enter the garden, no path should be assigned to us there.

Be still, my soul, it is not as thou deemest! Thou are *not* excluded from a part of the Christian life. Thinkest thou that the garden of the Lord has only a place for those who walk and for those who stand! Nay, it has a spot consecrated to those who are compelled to *sit*. There are three voices in a verb—active, passive, and neuter. So, too, there are three voices in Christ's verb "to live." There are the active, watching souls, who go to the front, and struggle till the breaking of day. There are the passive, watching souls, who stand in the middle, and report to others the progress of the fight. But there are also the neuter souls—those who can neither fight, nor be spectators of the fight, but have simply to lie down.

When that experience comes to thee, remember, thou are not shunted. Remember it is *Christ* that says, "Sit ye here." *Thy* spot in the garden has *also* been consecrated. It has a special name. It is not "the place of waiting." There are lives that come into this world neither to do great work nor to bear great burdens, but simply to be; they are the neuter verbs. They are the flowers of the garden which have had no active mission. They have wreathed no chaplet; they have graced no table; they have escaped the eye of Peter and James and John. But they have gladdened the sight of *Jesus*. By their mere perfume, by their mere beauty, they have brought Him joy; by the very preservation of their loveliness in the valley they have lifted the Master's heart. Thou needst not murmur shouldst thou be one of these flowers!

SELECTED

EVENING

∿∿

And now shall mine head be lifted up above mine enemies round about me. (PS. 27:6)

There is an old Scottish mansion quite close to where I have a little summer home in the north of Scotland, which has in it a room noted for the sketches and pictures that from time to time have been drawn upon the walls by visiting artists. It is a room to which people came from the ends of the world, and it all began in this way.

That room had been redecorated. Its plaster walls had been repainted. There was an accident in that room with a syphon of soda water which burst and covered the newly decorated plaster wall with stain. The woman of the house was, of course, not unnaturally irritated at such an accident to her newly decorated room, and she was not slow to express her irritation.

There was a great artist staying in the house, no less than Sir Edwin Landseer. He did not say anything to her, but when even the next day her irritation had not altogether abated—for the stain had dried, and it looked even worse then, and was seen to be permanent—he stayed at home when the rest of the party in the house went out on the moors. He took a piece of charcoal, and with a few deft touches and strokes he transformed that disfigurement into a thing of priceless beauty. He made it the background of a waterfall, and he put in the surrounding crags and one or two fir trees, a noble stag.

It is regarded, indeed, that sketch upon the wall, as one of Landseer's most successful sketches of Highland life. The point is this. That which was a disfigurement has become a thing of permanent beauty and pricelessness. . . .

I do not care where you have failed. I do not care if it is in the deepest motive of your being. I do not care how far you have fallen. I do not care how deeply you have disfigured and defaced the image of God—the great Craftsman, the great Master and Lord of us all, can turn your soul from that very failure into a positive endowment for future service.

J. STUART HOLDEN

Let God do it for you!

December 27

MORNING

><><

His soul entered into iron (PS. 105:18).

Turn that about and render it in our language, and it reads thus, *"Iron entered his soul."* Is there not a truth in this? That sorrow and privation, the yoke borne in the youth, the soul's enforced restraint, are all conducive to an iron tenacity and strength of purpose, and endurance or fortitude, which are the indispensable foundation and framework of a noble character.

Do not flinch from suffering; bear it silently, patiently, resignedly; and be sure that it is God's way of infusing iron into your spiritual life. The world wants iron dukes, iron battalions, iron sinews, and thews of steel. *God wants iron saints;* and since there is no way of imparting iron to the moral nature but by letting people suffer, He lets them suffer.

Are the best years of your life slipping away in enforced monotony? Are you beset by opposition, misunderstanding, and scorn, as the thick undergrowth besets the passage of the woodsman pioneer? Then take heart; the time is not wasted; God is only putting you through the iron regimen. The iron crown of suffering precedes the golden crown of glory. And iron is entering into your soul to make it strong and brave.

F. B. MEYER

But you will not mind the roughness nor the sleepness of the way,
Nor the chill, unrested morning, nor the searness of the day;

And you will not take a turning to the left or the right,
But go straight ahead, nor tremble at the coming of the night,
For the road leads home.

EVENING

∽◦∾

In returning and rest shall ye be saved; in quietness and in
confidence shall be your strength. (ISA. 30:15)

*D*esert sweetened." It was only a sign in a wayside fruit stand. But the golden grapefruit that it advertised took on new value! So will any life that follows the formula given by the Master: "Come ye yourselves apart into a desert place, and rest a while." It was in the loneliness of desert reaches that some of the mightiest of the Old Testament prophets received their message: "Thus saith the Lord." In the desert Jesus met and mastered temptation. Out of a three-year desert retreat came Paul to be the greatest missionary of all time!

"Desert sweetened!" A quiet place at the beginning and the close of day. A "little chapel of silence"—"where, though the feet may join the throng, the soul may enter in and pray." Sunshine and silence—synonyms for the desert. May they bring special gifts of calm and courage and confidence—because we have kept our appointment with Christ in these moments of devotion! SELECTED

The road to the Promised Land of spiritual power always leads through desert places where "the still small voice" has a chance to be heard. GLENN RANDALL PHILLIPS

In the secret of His presence how my soul delights to hide!
Oh, how precious are the lessons which I learn at Jesus' side!
Earthly cares can never vex me, neither trials lay me low;
For when Satan comes to tempt me, to the secret place I go.
When my soul is faint and thirsty, 'neath the shadow of His wing
There is cool and pleasant shelter and a fresh and crystal spring;
And my Savior rests beside me, as we hold communion sweet:
If I tried I could not utter what He says when thus we meet.
Only this I know: I tell Him all my doubts, my griefs, and fears.
Oh, how patiently He listens! and my drooping soul He cheers.
Do you think He ne'er reproves me? What a false friend He would be
If He never, never told me of the sins which He must see!
Would you like to know the sweetness of the secret of the Lord?

Go and hide beneath His shadow; this shall then be your reward.
And whene'er you leave the silence of that happy meeting-place,
You must mind and bear the image of the Master in your face.
ELLEN LAKSHMI GOREH

December 28

MORNING

❧

Rejoice in the Lord alway: and again I say, Rejoice (PHIL. 4:4).

Sing a little song of trust,
O my heart!
Sing it just because you must,
As leaves start;
As flowers push their way through dust;
Sing, my heart, because you must.

Wait not for an eager throng—
Bird on bird;
'Tis the solitary song
That is heard.
Every voice at dawn will start,
Be a nightingale, my heart!

Sing across the winter snow,
Pierce the cloud;
Sing when mists are drooping low—
Clear and loud;
But sing sweetest in the dark;
He who slumbers not will hark.

"An' when He hears yo' sing, He bends down wid a smile on His kin' face an' listens mighty keerful, an' He says, 'Sing on, chile, I hears, an' I's comin' down to deliber yo': I'll tote dat load fer yo'; jest lean hawd on Me and de road will get smoother bime by.' "

≋

Thy love to me was wonderful. (2 SAM. 1:26)

Is it too much to hope that when we see our blessed Lord in the glory, when the trials and the toils and the sacrifices are all at an end— Is it too much to desire that He should say something like this to us: *"Thy love to me was wonderful"*? I tell you it will make the toils of the road and all the renunciations and willing sacrifices of life seem as nothing to have some such words of commendation from the lips of our Savior, and to hear Him say to the one who has sought to be faithful at all cost: "Well done. You were never popular on earth, and nobody knew much about you. The life you lived to My glory in the uninspiring sphere of duty seemed to be wasted and its sacrifice to be worthless by those who knew it; *but your love to Me was wonderful!* Men said you made mistakes and were narrowminded and did not catch the spirit of the age. Men thought you were a fanatic and a fool and called you so; men crucified you as they crucified Me, but *your love to Me was wonderful!"*

> *Savior, Thy dying love Thou gavest me,*
> *Nor should I ought withhold,*
> *Dear Lord, from Thee:*
> *In love my soul would bow,*
> *My heart fulfill its vow,*
> *Some offering bring Thee now,*
> *Something for Thee.*
> *"He is altogether lovely."*

December 29

MORNING

≋

Arise . . . for we have seen the land, and behold, it is very good; and are ye still? be not slothful to go, and enter to possess the land . . . for God hath given it into your hands; a place where there is no want of anything that is in the earth (JUDG. 18:9–10).

Arise! Then there is something definite for us to do. Nothing is ours unless we take it. "The children of Joseph, Manasseh and Ephraim, *took their inheritance"* (Josh. 16:4). "The house of Jacob shall *possess their possessions"* (Obad. 17). "The upright shall have good things *in posses-sion.*"

We need to have appropriating faith in regard to God's promises. We must make God's Word our own personal possession. A child was asked once what appropriating faith was, and the answer was, "It is taking a pencil and underscoring all the me's and mine's and my's in the Bible."

Take any word you please that He has spoken and say, "That word is my word." Put your finger on this promise and say, *"It is mine."* How much of the Word has been endorsed and receipted and said, "It is done." How many promises can you subscribe and say, "Fulfilled to me."

"Son, thou art ever with Me, and *all* that I have *is thine."* Don't let your inheritance go by default.

"When faith goes to market it always takes a basket."

EVENING

Behold, there ariseth a little cloud out of the sea, like a man's hand.
(1 KINGS 18:44)

The fields were parched for lack of rain. The foliage of the green bay tree wilted in the sun. The earth was dry like powder, and gray dust covered leaf and blade. There was no freshness anywhere. As far as eye could see nature seemed to have dressed herself in sackcloth and ashes. We have never seen such drought as that which had fallen upon Israel in the days of Elijah the Tishbite. There had been no rain for three and a half years. The fields had not yielded their increase, and little children cried for food.

Elijah was on Mount Carmel praying for rain. "Go," he said to his servant, "and look out toward the sea and tell me if any sign of rain appears." Seven times he went and surveyed the western horizon, where the sky seemed to drop into the glittering Mediterranean. The seventh time he returned and said, "Behold, there ariseth *a little cloud* out of the sea, like a man's hand."

A very little cloud it was, but sufficient to assure Elijah that God was answering prayer and that the day of refreshment had come for all the land of Israel.

It is not always so with men. When we cry to God we are impatient to see God's finished answer all at once. We rise from our knees, and because the heavens do not hang heavily with clouds we are too quick to think that God is withholding His showers of blessing. *But God usually gives us by slow degrees the things we need.*

We grow impatient because we have not the sensibility of soul to detect *the faint beginnings* of God's mercies. The first gray tints that touch the eastern skies are a promise of the coming day. The first flickering ray of light that steals across our soul when we cry to God is the beginning of His answer. The first indefinable feeling of comfort that slips into the distressed soul is *a little cloud* bearing promise of refreshing showers.

"I knelt and prayed," said a young woman, "and it seemed that I saw a light across my way, and *then I was sure* that the thing perplexing me would come out all right." The light that shone for a moment in the heart's secret places was the harbinger of great happiness and blessing.

Broken heart, crying to God for comfort, take courage from moments which come like respites when the weight of sorrow is for a little while lightened! How delicately God deals with us! These are intimations of the peace which in the process of God's providence shall at last come.

Perplexed heart, crying to God for guidance, be assured by the events that seem to turn your life in a particular direction and by the light that every now and then falls on your problems—be assured that *God is beginning* to answer your prayer!

O Guilty heart, crying to God for forgiveness, let your desires for purity, your bitterness of soul, the faint whisperings of Divine love heard only by the spirit's ear—let all of these tell you that God is already hearing and answering. Our skies are dotted with *little clouds, faint beginnings of God's mercies.* They assure the waiting heart of greater clouds just beyond the horizon, laden with His blessings.   COSTEN J. HARRELL

Watch for God's faint beginnings!

December 30

MORNING

*Peter was kept in prison: but prayer [instant and earnest prayer]
was made for him* (ACTS 12:5, MARGIN).

Peter was in prison awaiting his execution. The church had neither human power nor influence to save him. There was no earthly help, but there was help to be obtained by the way of heaven. They gave themselves to fervent, importunate prayer. God sent His angel, who aroused Peter from sleep and led him out through the first and second wards of the prison; and when they came to the iron gate, it opened to them of its own accord, and Peter was free.

There may be some iron gate in your life that has blocked your way. Like a caged bird you have often beaten against the bars, but instead of helping, you have only had to fall back tired, exhausted, and sore at heart. There is a secret for you to learn, and that is *believing* prayer; and when you come to the iron gate, it will open of its own accord. How much wasted energy and sore disappointment will be saved if you will learn to pray as did the church in the upper room! Insurmountable difficulties will disappear; adverse circumstances will prove favorable if you *learn to pray,* not with your own faith but with the faith of God (Mark 11:22, margin). Souls in prison have been waiting for years for the gate to open; loved ones out of Christ, bound by Satan, will be set free when you pray till you defiantly believe God. C. H. P.

Emergencies call for intense prayer. *When the man becomes the prayer* nothing can resist its touch. Elijah on Carmel, bowed down on the ground, with his face between his knees, that was prayer—the man himself. No words are mentioned. Prayer can be too tense for words. The man's whole being was in touch with God, and was set with God against the powers of evil. They couldn't withstand such praying. There's more of this embodied praying needed. FROM THE BENT-KNEE TIME

"Groanings which cannot be uttered are often prayers which cannot be refused." C. H. SPURGEON

EVENING

He . . . sat down under a juniper tree. (1 KINGS 19:4)

This is Elijah! One is startled, perplexed, disappointed. A while ago we saw him on Mount Carmel surrounded by the thronging thousands of Israel, undismayed by the bold audacity of the worshipers of Baal, and confidently appealing to God to vindicate His own honor, and confound Baalim. Here he is, the prey of deep depression, forgetful of the past, giving all up, wanting God to take away his life. God has not once failed him. Not to any extent at all has one single foe prevailed against him. He should not have lost heart, should not have fled, should not have asked God to take away his life; all this was wrong. He should have remembered how God had wonderfully stood by him in the past, and have firmly trusted Him still. Is not his privilege ours also? May not God's people trust Him fully, firmly, and under all circumstances, and at all times? God is not "afar off," neither has He forgotten to be gracious; and that which He has promised He will unfailingly remember, and do. Are we not always in His hands and under His care? Should we ever have a single fear? Why should we be cast down, or disquieted?   J. T. W.

Have faith in God, the sun will shine,
Though dark the cloud may be today!

HAVE FAITH IN GOD!

December 31

MORNING

⤳⤺

Hitherto hath the Lord helped us (1 SAM. 7:12).

The word "hitherto" seems like a hand pointing in the direction of the *past*. Twenty years or seventy, and yet "hitherto hath the Lord helped us!" Through poverty, through wealth, through sickness, through health; at home, abroad, on the land, on the sea; in honor, in dishonor, in perplexity, in joy, in trial, in triumph, in prayer, in temptation—"hitherto hath the Lord helped!"

We delight to look down a long avenue of trees. It is delightful to gaze from one end of the long vista, a sort of verdant temple, with its branching pillars and its arches of leaves. Even so look down the long aisles of your years, at the green boughs of mercy overhead, and the strong pillars of lovingkindness and faithfulness will bear up your joys.

Are there no birds in yonder branches singing? Surely, there must be many, and they sing of mercy received "hitherto."

But the word also points *forward*. For when a man gets up to a certain mark, and writes "hitherto," he is not yet at the end; there are still distances to be traversed. More trials, more joys; more temptations, more triumphs; more prayers, more answers; more toils, more strength; more fights, more victories; and then come sickness, old age, disease, death.

Is it over now? No! there is more yet—awakening in Jesus' likeness, thrones, harps, songs, psalms, white raiment, the face of Jesus, the society of saints, the glory of God, the fullness of eternity, the infinity of bliss. Oh, be of good courage, believer, and with grateful confidence raise thy "Ebenezer," for,

He who hath helped thee hitherto
Will help thee all thy journey through.

When read in heaven's light, how glorious and marvelous a prospect will thy "hitherto" unfold to thy grateful eye.   C. H. SPURGEON

The alpine shepherds have a beautiful custom of ending the day by singing to one another an evening farewell. The air is so crystalline that the song will carry long distances. As the dusk begins to fall, they gather their flocks and begin to lead them down the mountain paths, singing, "Hitherto hath the Lord helped us. Let us praise His name!"

And at last with the sweet courtesy, they sing to one another the friendly farewell: "Goodnight! Goodnight!" The words are taken up by the echoes, and from side to side the song goes reverberating sweetly and softly until the music dies away in the distance.

So let us call out to one another through the darkness, till the gloom becomes vocal with many voices, encouraging the pilgrim host. Let the echoes gather till a very storm of Hallelujahs break in thundering waves around the sapphire throne, and then as the morning breaks we shall find ourselves at the margin of the sea of glass, crying, with the redeemed host, "Blessing and honor and glory be unto him that sitteth on the throne and to the Lamb forever and ever!"

This my song through endless ages,
Jesus led me all the way.
AND AGAIN THEY SAID, HALLELUJAH! (Rev. 19:3 RV).

EVENING

For here have we no continuing city, but we seek one to come.
(HEB. 13:14)

A great world conqueror was leading his victorious army back to Italy—and home. Onward they marched over rivers and plains, and through wooded forests until they reached the foothills of the towering Alps. Here the thinning ranks of the worn and tired soldiers began to falter as they trudged on over the rocky defiles of the mighty mountain passes. As they climbed higher and still higher, the blinding snow and storms well-nigh discouraged the stoutest hearts. Stopping on an eminence where he could overlook all his men and be heard by them, and pointing upward across the mighty barrier, the great general shouted, "Men, beyond those Alps lies Italy!"

Italy! Waving fields, beautiful orchards, sparkling fountains! Mothers and fathers, wives and children, sweethearts! Home! Ah, sweet home!

Fainting hearts revived. Tired muscles found new strength. Onward and upward that brave army pressed against every obstacle—and won! They reached home.

Another scene. All over the world are members of Prince Emmanuel's army. Many have won decisive battles with the enemy, great victories over sin. They have struggled along life's rugged highway, and many have become worn and weary in the conflict. Long have they marched, homeward bound. But now they have reached great mountains of difficulties, strifes, wars, threatened dissolution of all social and moral standards—the mighty Alps on the stream of time. To this vast army their Captain shouts, "Christian soldiers, beyond these mountains of difficulty lies Home!"

Heaven! Waving fields of living green, kingly forests with never-fading foliage, sparkling fountains! The Tree of Life, and the River of Life! Long-lost friends, mothers and fathers, brothers and sisters, husbands, wives, children, loved ones! Thank God, we are nearing our heavenly home!

I've been to the rim of the world, and beyond,
But I'm headin' home tonight.
E. W. PATTEN

HOMING!

ACKNOWLEDGMENTS

❦

The compiler takes pleasure in acknowledging the kindness of authors and publishers who, very generously, have granted permission to use extracts from their copyrighted publications.

Among those to whom such acknowledgements are due are the following: to Fleming H. Revell Company for selections from the books of F. B. Meyer and Andrew Murray; to Dr. C. G. Trumbull for extracts from *Messages for the Morning Watch* and the *Sunday School Times;* to the Christian Alliance Publishing Company for quotations from *Days of Heaven upon Earth* and other publications, also excerpts from sermons and tracts by Dr. A. B. Simpson; and to Miss Annie Johnson Flint for her poems.

Indulgence is begged in case of failure to reach any other author, or holder of copyrighted selections.

ACKNOWLEDGMENTS

❦

The compiler takes pleasure in acknowledging the kindness of authors and publishers who, very generously, have granted permission to use extracts from their copyrighted publications.

Among those to whom such acknowledgments are due are the following: Fleming H. Revell Company for selections from the writings of F. B. Meyer; Dr. C. G. Trumbull for extracts from *Messages for the Morning Watch* and the *Sunday School Times;* Christian Publications, Inc. for quotations from *Days of Heaven upon Earth,* also excerpts from sermons and tracts by Dr. A. B. Simpson; the American Tract Society for selections from John Oxenham's book *Bees in Amber;* the Yale University Press for the poem by Karle Wilson Baker, taken from their anthology *The World's Greatest Religious Poetry;* Mr. Thomas Kimber for several of his poems; Evangelical Publishers, Toronto, Canada, for the use of the poems of Miss Annie Johnson Flint; the Cokesbury Press for extracts from *Walking with God* by Costen J. Harrel; Mr. Matthew Biller for his *My Calvary* and other poems; Mr. J. Danson Smith for his poems.

An earnest endeavor has been made to locate the authors of all copyrighted selections; indulgence is begged where this endeavor has failed. Should we succeed in locating any further copyright owners, acknowledgment will be given.

About the Author

Along with her husband, **Mrs. Charles E. Cowman** served as a pioneering missionary in Japan and China from 1901 to 1917, during which time they helped to found the Oriental Missionary Society. When her husband's poor health forced the couple to return to the United States, Mrs. Cowman turned her attention to caring for him, and nursed him till his death six years later. Out of these experiences and heartbreak came *Streams in the Desert*, one of the bestselling devotionals of all time, selling millions of copies in several languages. Mrs. Cowman later penned six more devotionals—all tremendously popular—including *Traveling Toward Sunrise* and *Words of Comfort and Cheer*. She died in 1960.